An Introduction to Namibian Law
Materials and Cases

SK Amoo

UNAM PRESS
UNIVERSITY OF NAMIBIA

Acknowledgements

An Introduction to Namibian Law **contains extracts reproduced from various publications. In compliance with laws regulating copyright, every care has been taken to establish and acknowledge copyright, and to contact copyright owners and therefore, in the event of any accidental infringement, I tender my apologies. I am grateful to the authors and publishers for their permission, express or tacit, to reproduce from the undermentioned works:**

Curzon, L.B. 1979. *Jurisprudence*. Macdonald & Evans Ltd.
Du Plessis, L.M. 1999. *An Introduction to Law.* Cape Town: Juta & Co Ltd.
Hinz, M.O., S.K. Amoo, D. van Wyk. 2000. *The Constitution at Work: 10 Years of Namibian Nationhood.* Pretoria: University of South Africa.
Ndulo, M. (ed). 1984. *Law in Zambia.* Zambia: East African Publishing House Ltd.
The Legal Assistance Centre. *NAMLEX.* Windhoek.
Faculty of Law. Materials on Introduction to Law. *Legal Theory I.* Rhodes University.
The author

First published in 2008 by Macmillan Education Namibia Publishers (Pty) Ltd,
P.O. Box 22830, Windhoek, Namibia.

Reprinted with permission in 2018 by
University of Namibia Press
www.unam.edu.na/unam-press
unampress@unam.na
Private Bag 13301, Windhoek, Namibia

Cover design: Cherley du Plessis
Printed by: John Meinert Printers, Windhoek

ISBN 978-99916-42-41-3

Distribution
Namibia Book Market: www.namibiabooks.com

CONTENTS

PREFACE

The University of Namibia (UNAM) was established in 1992 and the Faculty of Law was officially inaugurated by the Vice-Chancellor in February 1994. Compared with other universities in the SADC region UNAM is a relatively new institution and as such has been confronted with many challenges one of which is the dearth of publications by local authors.

In the realm of legal systems, Namibia belongs to the Roman-Dutch Law tradition. It is a truism that Namibia's common law is greatly influenced by the South African legal system because of Namibia's historical connections with the South African Judiciary. However, because of the historical connection Namibian legal literature is dominated by writers of South African pedigree. The Faculty of Law at the University of Namibia has been relying on this literature and this state of affairs is not a healthy one, and, needless to say, must be reversed. Hence, it has been the policy of UNAM to encourage members of the academic staff to produce texts that have local content and that reflect the values and ethos of the Namibian people.

Following the attainment of independence and sovereignty, Namibia has an independent Judiciary with a Supreme Court as the highest Court of Appeal and therefore South African precedents only have persuasive effect on the Namibian Courts. The judicial independence endowed on the Namibian Judiciary has led to the development of a home-grown jurisprudence by the superior Courts. The foregoing, notwithstanding the Parliament of Namibia in the exercise of its sovereign legislative functions, has promulgated pieces of legislation to address the needs of the Namibian people and in the process has amended or repealed some pieces of legislation promulgated by the erstwhile colonial regime.

The cumulative impact is that Namibian law has acquired a national character and identity which must be captured and given due recognition in the legal literature of the country. This can be achieved with the publication of autochthonous, legal literature which reflects the current Namibian jurisprudence. This task is a challenge to the Namibian legal fraternity and the academia must take up the gauntlet and spearhead this initiative. The inspiration for the writing of this book is rooted in this realisation and I have been able to accomplish this task with the assistance of the University of Namibia, especially the Research and Publication Committee.

In writing this book I have, firstly, attempted to bridge this gap by providing much needed local content. I have also reproduced cases and other materials, as extracts, in full in order to enable readers to draw their own impressions of the subject matter and also to provoke them into reading more of the original writings of the authors whose works have been reproduced. This also provides that elasticity that allows any person to teach the Introduction to Law course from any jurisprudential perspective.

Secondly, it is comprehensive as it is meant to be utilised by students at all levels of study in the Law Faculty and beyond. Besides the introductory concepts, the book also contains materials that are covered in other law courses such as Jurisprudence, Introduction to Cases, Comparative Law, Constitutional and Administrative Law, Interpretation of Statutes, and Civil and Criminal Procedure. The materials on Jurisprudence and

Introduction to Cases are meant to provoke students to relate theories of law to decisions of the Courts in order to appreciate the use of legal theories in their application to law especially in the penumbral areas of the law.

Thirdly, it provides an in-depth and detailed treatment of concepts and topics covered to a level not normally seen in such introductory texts. While this certainly makes it fairly complex for beginners, with proper guidance the book will provide them with complete answers to many points of both substantive law and procedure.

As I mentioned earlier, I have been able to write this book with the moral and financial support of the University of Namibia. I ,therefore, wish to express my profound gratitude to the Vice Chancellor Prof. L. Hangula, the Chairperson of the Research and Publications Committee Prof. O. Mwandemele, the Research and Publication Office of Ms P. Claassen and Dr O.C. Ruppel in the Faculty of Law at the University of Namibia.

I would like to extend my sincere appreciation to both the internal and external academic reviewers Prof. M.O. Hinz – University of Namibia, Prof. M. Munalula – University of Zambia, Prof. E. Kalula – University of Cape Town, Prof. L. van der Poll – University of Western Cape and Prof. O. Mireku – University of Venda for their constructive criticism and contributions that shaped this book into an accredited academic publication.

I am also indebted to Mr Prince Zongwe, for his assistance in typing the manuscript and the suggestions he made with respect to the choice of materials, and the Judge President Justice Petrus Damaseb for his encouragement to pursue this endeavour.

I dedicate this publication to my family and grandchildren for their moral support, Prof. W.J. Kamba for his inspiration and the staff of the Faculty of Law, University of Namibia, for their pioneering drive in the promotion of legal education and ethics in Namibia.

SK Amoo

CHAPTER 1
JURISPRUDENCE

1.1 The meaning of law

The definition and nature of law have engaged the attention of legal philosophers and jurists since the time of the ancient Greeks and Romans. The two concepts are so closely interrelated with the theories of law that one cannot discuss them without reference to the various theories of law. It must also be mentioned from the outset that because of the complex nature of law, it is difficult to have a definition or a theory that may be universally acceptable. Since many writers may prefer to attempt a definition of law from a certain premise, the definition of law may have to be determined and delimited within the confines of that particular premise or jurisprudence. Taking this into consideration, one has to appreciate the fact that a definition of law will at this stage not be all embracing in the sense that we are not attempting a definition that will incorporate all the precepts of the various theories of law.

However, law may be simply defined as that body of rules and regulations (or norms) that govern and regulate the conduct and behaviour of the individual in the society for the preservation of order in the society. There is a variety of rules that govern human behaviour; some of these are rules of law, morality and etiquette. Legal rules however are binding and it is this binding element of legal rules that differentiates legal rules from all other types of rules. Legal rules or norms prescribe how the individual ought to behave in a given situation; they prescribe certain behaviour they allow and proscribe those they disallow. They are therefore referred to as normative propositions or ought propositions as opposed to factual propositions or statements of predictable facts.

The regulatory nature of law consists of the provision of rights and corresponding obligations which create in the individual the ability to determine and predict his or her behaviour. The law that provides the individual with certain rights and imposes corresponding obligations is classified as the substantive law as opposed to adjective law or procedural law which lays down the procedure to be followed in the enforcement and realisation of the rights provided by the substantive law.

1.2 The nature of law

Our exploration into the nature of law will necessarily involve a discussion of the theories of law, which is known as jurisprudence. The word jurisprudence has many different meanings to many people and disciplines. The term is derived from the Latin word *iurisprudentia* which means knowledge of the law. The word jurisprudence is also used to refer to a course of study in law schools and it deals with the study of the theories propounded by the various jurists on the definition and nature of law.

There are schools of thought or jurisprudence (which simply means a group of jurists or legal philosophers who share the same or similar views on the subject matter) that have attempted to define and explain the nature of law. These schools of thought approach the study of law from three broad perspectives:

(i) religion and/or metaphysics;

(ii) the State; and

(iii) the society.

On account of the complex nature of law, it is not possible to have only one school of jurisprudence. Hence there are various schools of jurisprudence such as the Natural Law School (religion and/or metaphysics); the School of Analytical Positivism (the State); the Historical School and the Sociological School (the society). Jurisprudence as a course of study is a fifth year course but for our present purposes, our treatment of the subject matter of the theories of some of these schools of thought will be introductory.

1.3 Natural law

The jurists of this school contend in a variety of ways that law depends, for its validity, on the satisfaction of some moral, ethical and formal requirements or imperatives outside the law itself. They begin their exposition and analysis of law from the premise that law consists of a hierarchy of norms and that at the top of this hierarchy is the ultimate or imperative norm that all human laws must substantially conform with for their validity. They contend *a fortiori*, that law is not what it is, but what it ought to be, and that there is no separation between law and principles of morality and justice. For the naturalists therefore, the validity of the law is an essential element of law. They have, however, differed in what constitutes the 'ought' or the imperative or ultimate norm.

This school is generally recognised as the oldest school of jurisprudence and throughout its long history of epistemological and philosophical evolution from the days of the ancient Greeks and Romans to modern times, two pervading and consistent themes of natural law are the satisfaction of some external criteria for the validity of law and the reliance on the concept of reason. The basis of this contention is that the basis of law is in nature and that there exist in reality principles of law that bind human beings. These principles of reality exist outside the human being and since the human mind can determine the truth it can also determine the principles of law because man is part of divine intelligence. The search for the content of the 'ought' has resulted in the hypothesis of such criteria as universal principles of morality, eternal law, divine law or the law of God, inalienable rights of man and principles of justice.

Greek and Roman natural law philosophers (classical natural law) postulated that there are certain principles of morality that are universal and immutable and that man by the application of reason or his rational faculties is able to deduce these principles which must dictate the content of law for its evaluation because man is part of divine intelligence. The source of the imperative norms or standards is said to be inherent in the nature of things; namely, the cosmic law. Natural law therefore constitutes the foundation upon which laws are discovered rather than made. During the medieval period there was a strong relationship between the State and the Catholic Church and as a result of this, the writings of most philosophers of law were largely influenced by the Canon Law or Roman Catholic theology as propounded by St Thomas Aquinas and St Augustine. They postulated that there was a hierarchy of laws and at the top of the hierarchy is eternal law or the law of God and that man by the application of reason is able to deduce eternal law. The law of man must be in substantial conformity with eternal law for its validity and that a law that is not in sufficient conformity with the law of God or eternal law, is not valid and therefore can be disregarded or disobeyed. St Thomas Aquinas, for example, states in Qu.95 Art. 2 and Qu.96 Art. 4 of his *Summa Theologica* as follows:

> **Saint Augustine says (1 De Lib. Arbitrio, 5): 'There is no law unless it be just'. So the validity of law depends upon its justice. But in human affairs a thing is said to be just when it accords aright with the rule of reason: and, as we have already seen, the first rule of reason is the natural law. Thus all humanly enacted laws are in accord with reason to the extent that they derive from the natural law. And if a human law is at variance in any particular with the natural law, it is no longer legal, but rather a corruption of law.'**
>
> **Laws framed by men are either just or unjust. If they be just, they have the power of binding in conscience, from the eternal law whence they are derived.**[1]

However, during the Reformation in Europe there was a schism between the State and the Church and this also influenced legal philosophy. Natural law philosophers such as Locke, Rousseau, Montesquieu and Grotius looked at the external criteria for the validity of law in terms of justice, inalienable rights of the individual and principles of morality.

The critics of natural law have argued that natural law writers have failed to define in definite terms the content of these external criteria or morality and that they rely on abstractions, and *a priori* presumptions which are subject to individual interpretations. As stated by Dennis Lloyd:

> **What the positivist rejects is neither valuations nor their effect on human institutions but only the logical or practical possibility of establishing a scale of absolute values which govern mankind universally without a distinction of time or place.**[2]

Finch[3] puts it as follows:

> **The law of nature must contain guiding principles if it is to have any relevance to the laws which human beings make for the regulation of themselves and others. The wide variations in standards of justice and morality which may be observed at different times, among different peoples and even between different individuals,**

[1] Aquinas, T. 1915. *Summa Theologica*. Literally translated by Fathers of the English Dominican Province. London: Burn Oates and Washborune Ltd Publishers of the Holy See.

[2] Freeman, M.D.A. 2001. *Lloyd's Introduction to Jurisprudence*. 7th edition. London: Sweet & Maxwell Ltd.

[3] Finch, J.D. 1974. *Introduction to Legal Theory*. 2nd edition. London: Sweet & Maxwell Ltd.

> **may lead to the search for one predominant guiding standard; but the variations also serve to indicate the difficulty in determining what the natural principles are to be. "*Honeste vivere, alterum non laedere, suum cuique tribuere*" are the precepts of the law, but the guidance which they offer can only be seen in the application of their attendant principles to particular cases.**

In response to these criticisms and in the attempt to give definite dimensions to what constitutes morality, modern writers such as Lon Fuller[4] have defined morality in terms of principles of procedural justice. Fuller refers to these as the inner morality of law and the central theme of his writings is the principle of reciprocity. Fuller contends that there are certain minimum requirements that the legislator must comply with in the process of law-making and that the individual is able to assess the validity of law or legislation by the inclusion or the lack of these principles. These requirements constitute some of the yardsticks the individual can rely on to determine and evaluate his/her obedience or fidelity to the law. He calls these the eight desiderata and herein lies the core of the principle of reciprocity. The eight desiderata are generality of law, promulgation, retroactive laws, clarity of laws, contradictory laws, laws requiring the impossible, constancy of the law through time, congruence between official action and declared rule. We can also see the relationship between these principles and the rule of law. These principles are at times also referred to as the principles of justice[5].

Natural law has its merits and demerits. As alluded to earlier, natural law has been criticised for its reliance on abstractions, *a priori* presumptions, and undefined dimensions on what constitutes the 'ought' and principles of morality. Natural law has also been blamed for the excesses of the French Revolution. Despite these demerits, however, there are certain positive elements that can be attributed to natural law. One can certainly argue for the influence of the writings of natural law philosophers in the Magna Carta, the Bill of Rights of the American Constitution, the Charter of the United Nations and the Bill of Rights in most modern constitutions including

[4] Fuller, L.L. 1940. *The Law in Quest of Itself.* Beacon Press; and Fuller, L.L. 1969. *The Morality of Law.* New Haven: Yale University Press.

[5](a) Generality of law – there must be rules, so that every issue must not be decided on an ad hoc basis.

(b) Promulgation – the laws must be publicised so that it is made available to the affected party. In this way he/she will know the rules he/she is expected to observe.

(c) Retroactive laws – laws must not be effected retroactively. The purpose of law is to direct and govern human beings by rules and therefore to enact a law to have a retrospective effect amounts to perversion of justice. Fuller describes a retroactive law as a monstrosity.

(d) Clarity of laws – laws must be understandable.

(e) Contradictory laws – laws must be logical and consistent.

(f) Laws requiring the impossible – rules should not require conduct which is beyond the powers of the affected party.

(g) Constancy of the law through time – laws should not be changed too often.

(h) Congruence between offical action and declared rule – there must be consistency between rules as announced and their actual administration.

the Namibian Constitution. In contemporary legal systems, natural law can claim to constitute both the source of values that legislators may turn to in the process of law-making and the source of reason which judges may resort to in exercising their discretion to apply the principles of equity and striking a balance between positive law and public policy.

If we relate the theories of this school to the Namibian legal system in general and the judicial system in particular, we discover for example that the Namibian Constitution does not only contain principles and values that have a moral content but also that their jurisprudential basis can be traced to natural law theories. The Namibian courts, especially the High Court and the Supreme Court[6], have used principles of morality and the values of the people of Namibia as the pinnacles of public policy and have therefore given moral interpretations to some of the provisions of the constitution, and thereby giving the authoritative fiat to morality and value judgments as an integral part of the law. In this regard, one can also observe a shift in constitutional and related epistemological paradigm from the decisions of the South African Courts.

1.4 Extracts

Curzon, L.B. (1979) Jurisprudence, Macdonald and Evans

Law and Morality

10. Fundamental problems. Upon what basis ought the law to be founded? To what concepts ought one to appeal in a case of injustice? If both law and morality are concerned with norms (that is, authoritative rules and standards) ought they not to be derived from the same sources? Ought the law to reflect a changing social morality? Ought the courts to be considered as "guardians of public morality"?

(a) In theocratic societies, dominated by the strict observance of religious codes, the law is seen as an extension, or interpretation of some divinely-given or inspired rules. Law and morality are thus closely linked.

(b) In secular societies, that is, in those in which religious beliefs do not directly dominate government and social organization, law and concepts of strict morality tend to diverge. The use of positive law for the upholding of morality has to be justified, not in terms of appeals to holy writ, but in terms of secular, socially-acceptable standards, such as the need to protect particular groups against exploitation.

(c) The old division of crimes into *mala in se* (crimes which are abhorrent and wrong in themselves) and *mala prohibita* (crimes which result from actions prohibited by law, but which do not arouse deep feelings) epitomizes a division in society's attitudes towards "technical breaches of the law" and those offences touching deep-rooted moral attitudes. Compare popular attitudes towards the offences of failing to obtain licences and robbery.

[6] *Namunjepo & Others v Commanding Officer, Windhoek Prison and Another* 1999 NR (SC) 271; 2000 (6) BCLR 671(NmS); *The Chairperson of the Immigration Selection Board v Erna Elizabeth Frank and Elizabeth Khaxas. Ex Parte Attorney General Namibia in Re Corporal Punishment by Organs of State* 1991 (3) SA 76 (NmS); *Kauesa v Minister of Home Affairs* 1996 (4) SA 965; *Minister of Defence v Mwandingi* 1992 (2) SA 355 (NmSC); *S v Acheson* 1991 NR 1 (HC).

(d) Distinctions have been drawn between law and morality as follows: morality is said to be based on a study of the "supreme good" and is generally valid, whereas law is concerned only with particular circumstances; morality emphasizes the role of the individual whereas law is based upon social interactions; morality stresses motive whereas law is concerned with actions; an individual is free to reject the demands of morality whereas the law will not allow him to "contract out" of its demands. Finally, morality emphasizes duty whereas law gives equal piece to duties and rights.

(e) Paton[7] distinguishes law and "positive morality" (that is, the standards adopted by a community): law emanates from the state, positive morality emerges from particular groups; law is often stated in precise terms, positive morality is rarely stated save in wide terms.

(f) Some jurists illustrate the relationship of law and morals by a diagram showing intersecting circles, one labelled "law", the other "morality". In the area of intersection is common ground in which both morality and law condemn actions, such as murder and stealing. Within the area of the "morality" circle that does not overlap with the "law" circle may be found lying, for example. Within the area of the "law" circle that does not overlap with the "moral" circle may be found failure to pay one's direct taxes, for example.

(g) An unusual relationship between law and morality is posited by Olivecrona[8] (see XXII, **13**). He views the rules of law as "independent imperatives" absorbed by the mind, so that they become binding on a person without reference to any authority in "the outer world". "The law is the primary factor. The individual is caught in its grip from the earliest stage in life and his moral ideas are developed under its influence."

11. Law and morality as reflecting and regulating internal and external aspects of man's life. Some jurists have drawn attention to man's inner life and his outward relations with other men as a key factor in understanding law.

(a) Kant[9] (*see* VIII, **5-11**) suggested that morality regulates a man's inner life and guides his motivations. The law regulates his conduct in accordance with required standards.

(b) Del Vecchio[10] (*see* IX, **28**) writes of juridical consideration as "treating an act as part of the external order interacting with the acts of other agents; moral criteria relate to two or more possible actions of the same agent and tend to settle internal strife".

12. The courts as guardians of morality: Shaw v D.P.P. (1962). The concept of the courts of law as possessing an inherent jurisdiction over the community's morals was discussed at length by the House of Lords in *Shaw v D.P.P.* (1962).

(a) The facts were that Shaw was convicted on charges including publishing an obscene libel (a booklet in which prostitutes advertised their services) and conspiring to corrupt public morals. On appeal to the Lords, the question arose as to whether the courts possessed moral jurisdiction.

(b) "When Lord Mansfield ... said (R v Delaval (1763)) that the Court of King's Bench was the *custos morum* (guardian of morals) of the people and had the superintendence of offences *contra bonos mores* (against good behaviour), he was asserting, as I now

[7] Paton, G.W. 1972. *Jurisprudence*. 4th edition. Oxford: Oxford University Press.

[8] Olivecrona, K. 1971. *Law as Fact.* 2nd Edition. London: Stevens and Sons.

[9] Kant, I. 1999. *The Metaphysical Elements of Justice.* 2nd edition. Indianapolis: Hackett Publishing Company, Inc.

[10] Del Vecchio, G. 1914. *The Formal Bases of Law.* Boston: Boston Book Co.

assert, that there is in that court a residual power, where no statute has yet intervened to supersede the common law, to superintend those offences which are prejudicial to the public welfare. Such occasions will be rare, for Parliament has not been slow to legislate when attention has been thoroughly aroused. But gaps remain and always will remain, since no man can foresee every way in which the wickedness of man may disrupt the order of society": *per* Lord Simonds. (Shaw's conviction was upheld.)

(c) "Notoriously there are wide differences in opinion today of how far the law ought to punish immoral acts which are not done in the face of the public. Some think the law already goes too far, some that it does not go far enough. Parliament is the proper place and, I am firmly of opinion, the only proper place, to settle that": *per* Lord Reid.

(d) The decision of the Lords was attacked vigorously. Hart criticised the House of Lords as having fashioned a weapon "for punishing immorality as such". Others criticized the opinion of Lord Simonds as underwriting "moral populism", which, it was argued, often hides mere intolerance, and as an unwarranted interference with the rights of individuals to behave in ways which, although capable of arousing disgust, do not cause harm.

13. The Wolfenden Report 1957. The Report of the Wolfenden Committee, which recommended that homosexual behaviour between consenting adults in private should no longer be a criminal offence, had, prior to the Shaw case, polarized the views of many legal writers. (The history of the offence, the religious prohibition, the social sense of abhorrence and the ferocious penalties should be recalled.) The Report boldly affirmed the Committee's attitude to the relations between law and morality: "Unless a deliberate attempt is made by society acting through the agency of the law to equate this fear of crime with that of sin, there must remain a realm of private morality and immorality which is, in brief and crude terms, not the law's business."

(a) In the subsequent debate, Lord Devlin[11], who opposed the general findings of the Report, argued that the State has a claim to legislate on matters of morals when it has a need to preserve itself.

> **'A recognized morality is as necessary to society's existence as a recognized government ... and although a particular act of immorality may not harm or endanger or corrupt others, this is not conclusive for we must not view conduct in isolation from its effect on the moral code ... it might threaten one of the great moral principles on which society is based .... In this sense the breach is an offence against society as a whole ... this is why the suppression of vice is as much the law's business as the suppression of subversive activities .... Philosophers may philosophise under the shadow of perpetual doubt, but the rulers of society must act on what their society believes to be right. This is the law of survival for man and society.'**

(b) Hart[12] supported the findings of the Report.

> **"To use coercion to maintain the moral *status quo* at any given point in society's history would be artificially to arrest the process which gives social institutions their value .... Other methods of preservation exist, such as argument, exhortation and advice. These are important and we must not be forced to choose between deliberate coercion or indifference .... There must always be social morality worth preserving even at the cost of damaging the values which legal enforcement**

[11] Devlin, P. 1965. *The Enforcement of Morals*. London: Oxford University Press.

[12] Hart, H.L. 1963. *Law, Liberty and Morality*. London: Oxford University Press.

involves. But the question arises whether the values are sufficient to offset the cost in human misery which legal enforcement entails."

14. Inevitable divergence? It may be that concepts of law and morality must diverge and remain distinct in secular societies. It is possible to recognize, perhaps, that although each concept exists separately, morality might provide a yardstick by which the law could be evaluated. It is possible, also, to accept that, although both concepts might be determined by the same sets of historical circumstances and cultural values, their validation requires reference to different types of criteria. On the matter of legal intervention in matters of private morality, there are few who would deny the right of the State to intervene where immoral behaviour threatened survival; the problem, however, is for the State to recognize the point at which the maintenance of the fabric of social cohesion is threatened. It is a problem which arises repeatedly in every dynamic society in which ethical principles, legal values and political ideologies interact.

****

4. Some views of natural law. The following quotations indicate some shades in the wide spectrum of opinion relating to the essence of natural law.

(i) "The unerring law is right reason; not an ordinance made by this or that mortal, a corruptible and perishable law ... but one imperishable and impressed by immortal Nature on the immortal mind": Philo of Alexandria (first century).

(ii) "Natural law which is observed equally in all nations, being established by divine providence, remains for ever settled and immutable; but that law which each state has established for itself is often changed": Justinian (sixth century).

(iii) "The state of Nature has a law of Nature to govern it ... in transgressing the law of Nature the offender declares himself to live by another rule than that of reason and common equity": Hobbes (seventeenth century).

(iv) "Natural law is a divine law, written in the hearts of all men, obliging them to do those things which are necessarily consonant with the rational nature of mankind and to refrain from those things which are repugnant to it": Thomasius (eighteenth century).

(v) "Natural law, resting on a postulate of the rectitude of nature, is necessarily absolute. As an end in itself, it is to be vindicated for its own sake": Lorimer (nineteenth century).

(vi) "Man is made for an end, and therefore there is a law which comes before him, a law which he must apply to himself in order to attain that end which is, demonstrably, none other than God. This law is the natural law": Miltner (twentieth century).

(vii) "Because an act in harmony with the objective order is a morally good act, and because an act at discord with the same order is a morally bad act, it is natural law's informative function to make clear to man the difference between good and evil or right and wrong": Hill (twentieth century).

(viii) "There is, by the very virtue of human nature, an order or disposition which human reason can discover and according to which the human will must act in order to attune itself to the necessary ends of the human being. The unwritten law, or natural law, is nothing more than that": Maritain (twentieth century).

5. Basic characteristics of natural law doctrines. The following characteristic features of natural law seem to be generally accepted by many of its advocates.

(a) The natural law is based on value-judgments, which emanate from some "*absolute source*", for example God's Revealed Word, and they are in accordance with Nature and Reason.

(b) These absolute value judgments reflect the essential nature of the universe and are *immutable and eternally* valid.

(c) They can be *grasped and understood* by the proper employment of human reason.

(d) When they are perceived *they must overrule all positive law* (that is, man-made law). Indeed, the positive law is truly "law" only if it conforms to the natural law.

(e) Law is a *fundamental requirement of man's life* in society.

6. Fruitless speculation? The search for absolutes in law has been condemned by some legal philosophers as inevitably fruitless. Immutable truth, it has been argued, is a mere chimera; its pursuit is of no value. Some positivist lawyers condemn the concept of natural law because it is derived from unproved and unprovable assumptions. On the other hand, some jurists emphasized the importance of continuous speculation in the theory of values; legislation may be a pragmatic affair, but its value content, it is argued, ought to be a matter for concern at all times. It would seem to be no mere accident that, in the twentieth century, which has seen legal systems used for evil ends, there has been a revival of interest in "the higher law" which might justify disobedience to unjust, man-made law (*see*, for example, the arguments of Radbruch[13]). Wortley[14] suggests that natural law concepts may be of great importance in three cases:

(a) as a source of values to which legislators may turn for modification of the law;

(b) as a source of "reason" to which a judge may turn in the exercise of his discretion to apply equity;

(c) as a source of theories of international law.

NOTE: Perelman[15] enumerates three functions of natural law: supplementary function (when it may be necessary to close the "gaps" in positive law); function of control or regulation (as where a judge compares a positive rule with the model of natural law); creative, metajudicial function (as where there is a call for an alteration to the law).

Development of natural law doctrine by the Greeks

7. Order in the universe: the theories of Heraclitus. Concepts of "harmony" and a "natural law" are found in much writing on natural law. It was the theorizing of Heraclitus (540-480 B.C.) that gave to the Greeks a picture of Nature as a patterned, rhythmical, interrelated order of things. It was possible to reconcile the characteristic features of Nature – identity, difference and change. Opposites were, in reality, identical; different things were

[13] Radbruch, G. 1946. "*The Philosophy of Law*" in Chroust A.H. The Philosophical Review Vol. 53 No. 1 (Jan. 1944) pp. 23-45.

[14] Atkinson, W.B. 1967. *Jurisprudence*. New York: Oceana Publications.

[15] Perelman, C. 1973. "Natural law" in *Dictionary of the History of Ideas. Studies of Selected Pivotal Ideas.* Wiener, P.P. (ed.) New York: Charles Scribner.

also one and the same thing; change was fundamental to the universe ("all things are in flux"), but change could be viewed as a becoming, a process. Destiny, order and reason are fundamental. It was in the ground prepared by this all-embracing theory that concepts of a universal, natural law took root and flourished.

8. The Sophists. The Sophists, who flourished in the fifth and fourth centuries B.C., drew important distinctions between "nature" and "the law".

(a) "Nature" was primary, fundamental and lasting; "law" was secondary, derivative and impermanent.

(b) "Nature" suggested that which was invariably wise: "law" reflected expediency and often appeared not to be based on those unchangeable principles such as justice.

(c) "Nature" had created men equal: "law" had imposed inequality.

(d) "Law", nevertheless, bound men, no matter whether it was good or bad.

(e) The higher "laws of nature" could be considered as norms: human beings ought to obey them, but were free to ignore them.

9. Socrates and Plato. Socrates (470-399 B.C.) and Plato (428-348 B.C.) argued for the existence of unchangeable principles of morality. These principles could be discovered by powers of reason and the application of "insight", so that law becomes the very embodiment of correct reasoning. Natural (divine) law requires obedience to the positive law and authority. Justice is a reflection of society's and man's harmonious, balanced existence; in its positive form, however, it is no more than a "pale shadow" of "real justice". But "only such law can be considered right as aims like a good bowman always at that which has something eternally beautiful and which neglects everything, be it wealth or something else of the kind, which is devoid of virtue".

10. Aristotle. Friedmann[16] enumerates the features of Aristotle's contribution to legal theory as: formulation of the essential problems of justice; formulation of the difference between abstract justice and equity; elucidation of the distinction between legal and natural justice (that is, "positive" and "natural" law). Aristotle (384-322 B.C.) emphasized the following points in his writings.

(a) Man's ultimate aim should be the attainment of a "state of goodness" and the political state is created by nature as a means to this end.

(b) A community's laws should assist in the attainment of the good life. The lawgiver assists the citizen to become "good" by habituating him, through law, to knowledge of the good. Law derives its validity from habit upon which obedience is founded.

(c) Law is just if it allows persons to develop their capacities within society. Laws of that kind will result only from the exercise of man's reason. Law can be determined only in relation to "the just".

(d) There is a perfect, immutable law reflecting human nature; it is universal in mankind.

11. The Stoics. The Stoic School, which was founded in the fourth century B.C., and which is represented by the writings of Zeno (c. 320-250 B.C.), was concerned with the fostering of a tranquil, inner life characterized by personal integrity and a highly-disciplined mode of conduct.

(a) The Stoics believed that the universe was governed by a "rational mind".

[16] Friedmann, W. 1953. *Legal Theory*. 3rd edition. London: Stevens & Sons.

(b) The rationality of the universe was reflected in all men and their power of reason made possible a "natural life" based on "reasonable living".

(c) Man's reason allows him to differentiate right from wrong and law is based on man's concepts of right and rectitude.

(d) Nature's law can be identified with the "higher morality".

(e) Basic law is the ruler of all divine and human things.

Natural law and the Romans

12. Cicero. The Roman lawyer and statesman, Cicero (106-43 B.C.), was affected by the philosophy of the Greeks, in particular the theories of Socrates and the Stoics. He propagated in his teachings the concept of "a true law" which conformed to "right reason", which "agreed with nature", which was diffused among mankind and which was immutable and eternal. Laws must be derived from this "true law".

(a) It was not allowable, according to Cicero, to alter the natural law, to derogate from it, to repeal it.

(b) "We cannot be released from this law, nor is any person required to explain or interpret it."

(c) This law is not "one at Rome and another at Athens"; nor is it "one law today and another hereafter". It is the same law, everlasting and unchangeable. It binds all nations at all times.

(d) "Law is highest reason imbedded in nature which commands what should be done, and forbids the contrary."

(e) "We are born for justice, and law is not based on opinion but on man's very nature[17]."

13. Natural law and the jus gentium. Developments in Roman law resulted in a close approximation of the *jus gentium* (the "law of people") to concepts of *jus naturale* which had been adapted from Greek legal theory.

(a) *Jus gentium* was considered as of universal application. Some jurists believe that the term was originally applied to the legal relationships between Roman citizens and foreigners living within Roman jurisdiction. (Note the rejection of this suggestion by Schultz[18]).

(b) "*Jus naturale* is what nature has taught all living things": *The Institutes*. It was derived from rules of universal application emerging from the common nature of all peoples. (Thus, Paul, the jurist, speaks of leases as "suggested by nature itself and found in the law of all nations").

(c) *Jus naturale* came to be considered as an ideal to which the law should seek to conform.

(d) *Jus gentium* and *jus naturale* were considered to be based on reason so that, in time, there was a large measure of theoretical approximation. "All peoples that are ruled by

---

[17] Cicero, (52 B.C.). *De Legibus* (1) *in Cicero the Philosopher; Twelve Papers* (1990) Powell, J.G.F. (ed.) Oxford Clarendon Press. (2) also *in Cicero: Dere Publica, De Legibus.* Cambridge: Mass Harvard University Press.

[18] Schultz, F. 1946. *History of Roman Legal Science*. New York: Oxford University Press.

laws and customs observe partly law peculiar to themselves and partly law common to all mankind. That which any people has established for itself is called *jus civile* .... But that law which natural reason establishes among all mankind is observed equally by all peoples, and is for that reason called *jus gentium*": Gaius.

****

Natural law in the Middle Ages

1. The position of the church at this time. It is important to understand the position of the Christian church in Europe during the periods in which the early Fathers and Aquinas were writing on the subject of natural law.

(a) Among the early Fathers of the Christian church were Ambrose (339-97) and Augustine (384-430). Augustine, born in North Africa, was a citizen of the later Roman Empire. He wrote during a period in which Rome had been sacked by the Visigoths and Roman civilization in Africa was ending with the seizure of Hippo by the armies of the Vandals. It was an era of continuous turmoil.

(b) Aquinas (1226-74) lived during a period in which the authority of the Roman Catholic Church was growing swiftly. But lawlessness was rife and the doctrines of Catholicism, some of which stressed the importance of justice, were being propagated in a Europe organised on the basis of feudal hierarchy and not yet split into national states. Two important, connected principles of political thought of this era, which impinged on legal doctrine, should be noted. It should be emphasised that they were derived from the unchallengeable authority of the Scriptures.

(i) *Unity.* The principle of Unity (based on the concept of one God) was reflected in "one church and one law".

(ii) *Supremacy of the law.* Law was a part of the "unity of the world"; it could not be altered basically and human rulers were subject to it.

AUGUSTINE, ISIDORE AND THE DECRETUM GRATIANUM

3. Augustine and the Fall of Man. Augustine believed that the absolute ideal of a "law of nature" had been evident during mankind's "golden age" which had preceded the Fall of Man. That age had been characterized by a state of innocence and justice. Men had lived in equality and freedom under the guidance of rules of reason. As a result of the Fall, man had been ruined. The "absolute law of nature" could no longer be realized.

4. The worldly law. Following mankind's fall from its state of nature, novel means had to be devised, on the basis of reason, to deal with the new situation. As a result, human law, property and government institutions had appeared.

(a) Essentially, these new institutions were, according to Augustine, rooted in sin; they had appeared only as a result of Man's fall.

(b) Their functions could, nevertheless, be justified.

(c) Positive law (that is, man-made law) had to strive so as to fulfil the commands of the eternal law. It permits much that God's law forbids; it does not necessarily make men good.

(d) The task of the state was to keep peace among mankind and this necessitated defence of the church and the upholding of *lex temporalis* (man's law).

(e) In its role as guardian or *lex aeterna* (God's eternal law) the church had to exercise total sovereignty over the state.

(f) If worldly law were in conflict with the eternal, natural law, its provisions were to be ignored; if worldly law were unjust it could not be "law".

5. St. Isidore of Seville: an echo of Augustine. Isidore, the last of the Western Latin Fathers of the Church (560-636), repeated Augustine's teachings on law. Governments had come into existence because of the corruption and Fall of mankind. But only those rulers who acted in a spirit of justice ought to command respect. Of natural law he wrote[19]:

> **"Natural law is common to all peoples in that it is possessed by an instinct of nature not by any human agreement, as marriage, the begetting and rearing of children, the common possession of all things, the universal freedom of all ... the restoring of property contracted or lent ... for this or whatever is like this, could never constitute an injustice but must be considered in accord with natural equity."**

6. The Decretum Gratianmum. A collection of texts relating to church discipline and regulations, published in 1140 by the Benedictine monk Gratian, and upon which the teaching of canon law was based for many centuries, indicated a shift in the attitude of the church to natural law.

(a) The law of nature was now considered as the *Law of God*. It was, therefore, immutable.

(b) It prevailed unquestionably over man-made law, which was subsumed under the concept of "custom".

(c) To be recognized as valid law, a custom (that is, a human law, written or unwritten) had to conform to the "golden rule" of the Gospel ("...all things whatsoever ye would that men should do to you, do you even so to them": *Matthew, vii, 12*).

(d) The Catholic Church alone was the true interpreter and teacher of the natural law.

St. Thomas Aquinas

7. The significance of Aquinas. Aquinas occupies a very important place in the history of the Catholic Church and in the development of doctrines of natural law. He studied the works of Aristotle under Albertus Magnus, and was able to produce in his writings a synthesis of the teachings of the Christian Fathers, Aristotelian logic and Roman law. His writings on natural law (recorded largely in the *Summa Theologica*, Part II, c. 1266) have dominated the thinking of Catholic jurists. The contemporary interest in his legal writings, seen in the emergence of the neo-Thomist school, testifies to the *Summa Theologica* as an example of *philosophica perennis* in our day. It should be noted that the Encyclical of Leo XIII, *Aeterni Patris* (1879), provided for Thomism (the philosophical system based on the writings of Aquinas) as a basis for the training of priests and the university education of the laity.

8. What is law? Aquinas defines law[20] as "an ordinance of reason for the common good made by him who has the care of the community and promulgated".

[19] Isidore of Seville. 630. *Etymologiae*. Lindsay, W.M. (ed.) Oxford: University Press.

[20] Aquinas, T. 1915. *Summa Theologica*. Literally translated by Fathers of the English Dominican Province. London: Burn Oates and Washborune Ltd Publishers of the Holy See.

(a) "Law is a rule and measure of acts, whereby man is induced to act or is restrained from acting ... Now the rule and measure of human acts is the reason, which is the first principle of human acts ... Consequently it follows that law is something pertaining to reason."

(b) "The law must needs regard properly the relationship to universal happiness."

(c) "The natural law is nothing else than the rational creature's participation in the eternal law ... Human law falls short of the eternal law."

(d) "The first direction of our acts to their end must needs be in virtue of the natural law."

9. Lex aeterna. Eternal law is God's "rational guidance of created things". All things are, therefore, ruled by this law, but although unreasoning creatures must obey the eternal law, man, who has free will, has the capacity of disobedience. God alone knows the eternal law in its totality; those blessed persons who see God in His Essence may perceive it in its truth.

10. Lex naturalis. Because of man's possession of God-given reason, he may have a share in divine reason itself and derive from it "a natural inclination to such actions and ends as are fitting". *Lex naturalis* is, therefore, the result of man's participation in the cosmic law.

(a) The general precepts of the natural law, which emerge from man's exercise of his reason, include the fundamental principle that good ("that which all things seek after...") is to be done and evil is to be avoided.

(b) There is in man an inclination to good "in accordance with the nature which he has in common with all substances", inasmuch as every substance seeks the preservation of its own being, according to its nature. "By reason of this inclination, whatever is a means of preserving human life and warding off its obstacles belongs to the natural law."

(c) There is in man an inclination to things that pertain to him more specifically according to the nature he has in common with other animals; hence those things which nature has taught to animals – sexual intercourse, education of offspring, etc. – belong to the natural law.

(d) There is in man an inclination to good, according to the nature of his reason. Thus he has a natural inclination to know the truth about God and to live in society. Whatever pertains to this inclination, for example to shun ignorance, belongs to the natural law.

(e) "To the natural law belongs those things to which a man is inclined naturally: and among these it is proper to man to act according to reason."

11. Lex humana. Human law involves the particular application of the natural law. The *jus gentium*, for example, is derived directly from natural law by human reason; the *jus civile* is derived from "particular determination", by applying natural law to the particular circumstances of states and, hence, it may vary from state to state. In conforming to reason, human law would conform to the law of God.

12. Lex divina. Divine law is God's law as revealed in the Scriptures. It is not identical with natural law; but it is not contrary to it. It provides rules for the conduct of man's life.

13. The "groups of principles". Aquinas wrote of three groups of principles of natural law.

(a) *The supreme group* demanded the love of God and of one's neighbour, the doing of good and the avoiding of evil.

(b) *The second group*, based on the first, could be found in the Ten Commandments.

(c) *The third group* was constituted by rules of justice resulting from the application of the principles in *(a)* and *(b)* to particular situations.

14. The immutability of natural law. The law of nature was, according to Aquinas, generally immutable. This principle applied to primary bases of law; it was permitted, however, to subtract from secondary bases where very exceptional circumstances existed.

15. Just and unjust laws. Aquinas acknowledged that "laws framed by man are either just or unjust".

(a) If they are just they have the power of binding in conscience. Such laws are characterized by their being "ordained to the common good" and their laying burdens on subjects "according to an equality of proportion and with a view to the common good."

(b) Laws may be *unjust* in two ways: *first*, by being contrary to human good, either in respect of their end or in respect of their form, as when they impose unequal burdens on the community or in respect of their author, as when he makes a law that goes beyond the power committed to him; *second*, by being opposed to the Divine good, such as the laws of tyrants inducing to idolatry.

(c) The first type of unjust law does not bind in conscience, "except perhaps in order to avoid scandal or disturbance, for which cause a man should even yield his right".

(d) The second type of unjust law "must nowise be observed".

16. Importance of the Thomist view of law. The principles of law evolved by Aquinas resulted from a deliberate attempt to create a unified system which considered the needs of thirteenth-century society in the light of revealed truth as embodied in the aims of the Catholic Church. That system combined a variety of philosophical principles and was rooted in Greek thought; the past was brought to the service of the present; the authority of the Catholic Church was upheld and strengthened. Natural law was seen as a source of general principles rather than detailed rules. Above all, the importance of the system is its *elevation of reason*. God's law was "the reason of divine wisdom"; Christianity was reason; God's purpose could be interpreted in part by the use of man's reason; human institutions were best founded where built on reason. It should be noted that Aquinas' identification of reason and natural law became, in later years, the basis of attacks on the doctrine of a natural law inspired by theological doctrines.

Will, reason and natural law

17. Duns Scotus. The principles formulated by Aquinas did not go unchallenged. John Duns Scotus (1265-1308), a Franciscan, reacted against Aquinas' elevation of the importance of powers of reason. He taught that some matters were beyond the reach of philosophical investigation. In relation to natural law, he argued as follows:

(a) Reason was not, as Aquinas had taught, superior to will. Man's freedom implies that his will is independent of his reason. It is man's will, not his reason, that guides intellectual insight.

(b) God's will is love. Hence the single principle of natural law is to love God.

(c) Other principles of human behaviour are matters for decision within man-made law.

(d) Natural law may not always reflect God's eternal law with precision.

18. William of Occam. William of Occam (1290-1349) argued that philosophical speculation should be confined to the observable; inferences should be drawn rigorously from the observable only. The law was to be identified with God's will, that is, the essential nature of all things, and, by analogy, human laws are valid because those in authority had willed it to be so. Rules of conduct of a universal nature could be derived from exercise of the reason. Natural equity might provide some rules outside those of the positive law. Other rules could be deduced from general natural law principles; their modification by man-made law was permissible.

****

Natural law in the sixteenth to eighteenth centuries

2. Natural law following the Reformation. In 1517 Luther had issued his protest against the sale of indulgences by the Catholic Church and there followed, inexorably, the series of events known as "the Reformation", based on a desire to "purify" the Church and to remove abuses in its institutions. It resulted in the shattering of the unity of Christendom, the rejection of Papal authority by many Christians and the establishment of Protestant churches. It coincided with the growth of separate nation-states. In the sphere of law the following effects are of importance.

(a) Christian natural law was replaced in part by a philosophical, secular natural law.

(b) The new doctrines of natural law moved beyond the mere formulation of first principles to the working out of detailed rules.

(c) The "natural rights" of mankind were increasingly stressed.

Grotius

6. Rationalism and natural law. Grotius, a Dutch statesman and jurist, separated natural law from its narrow theological basis. The universe was for him dominated by a rational law of nature[21]. The natural law – immutable (so that God himself could not change it) and intelligible – was "a dictate of right reason which points out that an act, according as it is or is not in conformity with rational nature, has in it a quality of moral baseness or moral necessity".

(a) The laws of nature would exist even if it were to be conceded "that there is no God, or that the affairs of men are of no concern to him". The natural law is founded, therefore, on *reason* alone.

(b) The law of nature follows from man's essential nature.

(c) There are two methods of proving whether something is in accordance with the law of nature.

(i) "*Proof a priori* consists in demonstrating the necessary agreement or disagreement of anything with a rational or social nature."

[21] Grotius, H. 1652. *De jure belli pacis*. Translated by Kelsey, F.M. Oxford: Clarendon Press.

(ii) "*Proof a posteriori* consists in concluding if not with absolute assurance, at least with every probability, that is according to the law of nature which is believed to be such among all nations, or among all those that are more advanced in civilization."

7. Man in society. Grotius believed that man was distinguished from animals by his *appetites societalis*, a "domestic instinct" which led him to desire "peaceful organized society ... with those of his own kind". Whatever conformed to this instinct was "right and just"; what was in opposition to it was "wrong and unjust".

(a) Grotius defined the State as "a complete association of free men, joined together for the enjoyment of rights and for their common interest."

(b) By a "social contract", people within a State had chosen the type of government best suited for them. Having transferred their right to govern to a ruler, they could no longer claim a right to control him.

(c) Natural law binds the sovereign through his conscience.

(d) If men are to live in a peaceful community they must accept obedience to certain rules, for example, the keeping of promises.

8. International society. Grotius, who laid the foundations of modern international law, believed that, just as man desired to live in peace with his neighbours, so nations must will to live in peace with one another. The jus gentium should be founded on the precept of keeping promises.

NOTE: For a recent reference to Grotius in the context of "the acts of sovereignty exercised by a usurper", ***see*** *the statement of Lord Reid in* ***Madzimbamuto v Lardner-Burke*** *(1969) (question of the government of Rhodesia and its recognition as a lawful government).*

Hobbes

9. The superiority of natural law challenged. Hobbes, the English philosopher and political theoretician, moved the emphasis from natural law as a dominant feature of some order exterior to man to the concept of man's natural rights, based on his essential nature. Civil law, not natural law, was seen as all-important. Natural law was, for Hobbes, "the dictate of right reason conversant about those things which are either to be done or omitted for the constant preservation of life". The natural law had, for Hobbes, no metaphysical basis and no inherent superiority.

10. Bellum omnium contra mores. Hobbes writes[22] of a state of nature in which all men are equal, but there is a continuing state of war "of every man against every man". No rules exist; there is a fundamental right to self-preservation and it is this natural right (rather than natural law) that is important. In this state of conflict "there is no place for industry...no arts, no letters, no society; and which is worst of all, continual fear and danger of violent death. And the life of man, solitary, poor, nasty, brutish and short."

(a) In these circumstances the laws of nature have to be obeyed. The first "law" is to make an end to these conditions, "to seek peace and pursue it". The second "law" is that a man should accept the measure of liberty against other men he would allow to them against himself. A third "law" is that agreements entered into must be kept.

[22] Hobbes, T. 1651. *Leviathan*. Oxford: Blackwell.

(b) Men make a covenant, a "social contract", among themselves under which they submit unconditionally to a sovereign (a monarch, or Parliament, for example). The sovereign becomes the sole judge of what is good for his subjects and they submit to his arbitration. He cannot be deposed; he is not a party to the covenant and is responsible only to God.

(c) The sovereign ought to act according to natural law. He cannot act "unjustly" because his actions are "authorized" as a result of the covenant and are constituted by the exercise of power on behalf of his subjects who cannot act unjustly towards themselves.

(d) A subject's rights to defend his own life cannot be overruled by any command of the sovereign.

(e) "The obligation of subjects to the sovereign is understood to last as long, and no longer, than the power lasteth, by which he is able to protect them."

11. The civil law. The sovereign imposes his will through "civil laws" and his commands determine "right" and "wrong". The civil laws are those laws "that men are bound to observe because they are members not of this or that commonwealth in particular, but of a commonwealth".

(a) "The law of nature is a part of the civil law in all commonwealths. Reciprocally also the civil law is a part of the dictates of nature".

(b) Obedience to the civil law is demanded as a rule of nature.

(c) The sovereign is not bound by the civil law, which is a decision of his will; indeed, he may disregard or change it.

(d) Natural law is binding only when the commonwealth has been constituted under the civil law.

Locke

14. Government as a trust for the benefit of man. Hobbes had advocated a type of absolutism; in contrast, Locke, who had experienced the practice of absolutism under the Stuarts, urged that the power of the state "can never be supposed to extend further than the common good"[23]. Political power involved "the right of making laws ... and of employing the force of the community in the execution of such laws and in the defence of the commonwealth from foreign injury and all this only for the public good".

(a) Locke believed that originally man lived in a state of nature. It was not, as Hobbes thought, a state in which mutual violence was dominant; it was a "state of liberty, not of licence". In that state of nature, governed by laws of nature, man realized that, since all were equal, none should be harmed. But that state involved a lack of security where each man was a judge in his own cause.

(b) So as to end the insecurity, men entered into a "social contract". It comprised a *pactum unionis*, whereby men agree "to unite in one political society" and a *pactum subjectionis*, whereby the majority gives power to a government which will protect the individual.

(c) The contract does not involve total subjection to the government (in contrast with Hobbes' theory). "The law of nature" stands for Locke as "an eternal rule made to all men, legislators as well as others".

[23] Locke, J. 1690. *Treatise on Civil Government in Two Treatises on Government.* 1698. Laslett, P. (ed.) London: Cambridge University Press.

(d) Where the legislature forgets its trust, it can be replaced.

15. Limits of the power of the state. The legislature, although supreme, is limited in its powers.

(a) It cannot rule in a purely arbitrary way. "it is a power that hath no other end but preservation, and therefore can never have a right to destroy, enslave or designedly to impoverish the subjects."

(b) It cannot transfer the power of making laws to any other persons.

(c) It cannot deprive a man of his property without his consent.

(d) It is bound "to dispense justice and decide the rights of the subject by promulgating standing laws".

NOTE: Locke proposed a threefold "division of powers" within the state – a legislative power (to create rules); an executive power (to enforce the rules); a federative power (to control the state's external relations).

16. Natural law according to Locke. For Locke, natural law was superior to positive law; it was immutable and bound all within the state. It was under the natural law that men should enjoy their inborn rights to "life, liberty and estate". Man's natural rights were to be protected by the "social contract". The most fundamental aspects of this natural law related to the preservation of the commonwealth and its individual members; preservation of life was one of man's inalienable rights.

17. Rules and reason. Locke argued that the moral rules which should bind the subjects within a state could be discovered by arguments based on reason. "From self-evident proposition, by necessary consequences, as uncontestable as those in mathematics, the measures of right and wrong might be made out."

Wolff, Montesquieu and Rousseau

18. Wolff: rationalism and the law. Wolff, a German philosopher and mathematician, advocated a doctrine of innate moral and intellectual principles. The power of reason could be used to attain and explain truths incapable of attainment by the senses alone. All phenomena, including the law, had adequate, knowable reasons for their occurrence[24].

(a) Rational, natural law could be explained by duty. Law exists on the basis of moral obligation which precedes it and in which it has taken root.

(b) Because there are innate human duties, there exist innate human rights and they are the same for all men (who are, therefore "equal") because they are the very consequences of human nature.

(c) Although men are, by nature, free, they can perform their duty of self-perfection – the fundamental natural law – only under conditions of security and peace to be provided by a benevolent ruler who is not bound to them by any obligation.

(d) Greater liberty results from obedience to the natural law and, therefore, to the ruler.

[24] Wolff, C. 1740. *Jus Naturae.* Loemker, L. (ed.) Dordrecht: Kluwer Academic Publishers.

19. Montesquieu: the spirit of the laws. Montesquieu, a French political philosopher, wrote of laws as "the necessary relations arising from the nature of things"[25]. Law in general was no more than human reason; it was oriented to justice and should be judged by it. Further, the essence of justice was not to be found exclusively within the positive law; the "just" and the "unjust" were concepts which preceded the creation of positive law.

(a) Natural laws pre-dated the establishment of society and, in general, were superior to the laws of religion and the state.

(b) The law and justice of a particular people, argued Montesquieu, are not unchangeable; they are determined by variables such as environment.

(c) The maintenance of people's liberty – the true purpose of political association – demanded the prevention of the accumulation of power in a few hands. Hence there should be a separation of powers (legislative, executive and judicial) and balances and checks were essential.

(d) The form in which the laws should be promulgated is important. Their style should be simple, avoiding rhetoric and hypothesis; they ought not to be argumentative; they ought not to shock reason or feelings of justice; they should not be subtle and should not take into account the simple reasoning of the average man.

20. Rousseau: the general will and law. Rousseau, a French philosopher, took as an axiom the statement that although man is born free, "everywhere he is in chains"[26]. He sought to explain not how this had come about, but how the situation could be made legitimate; his hypothesis suggests that there was a time when men lived in freedom, equality and happiness, but that these qualities of living had vanished as civilisation advanced. Men, in their search to regain happiness had to discover a mode of social organisation that would guarantee their rights to freedom and equality.

(a) The state is born from, and has its justification in, its guarantees of freedom and equality.

(b) In forming the "social contract", men do not surrender their natural rights to a single ruler; they surrender them to society as a whole and society then confirms these natural rights in the form of civil liberties. The basis of natural rights is morality.

(c) Each person in the state is subject not to any other single person but to the "general will", that is the will is absolute and inalienable. Obedience to it is demanded from all within the community.

(d) The basis of society and its laws was popular sovereignty (not, be it noted, "parliamentary sovereignty" which, for Rousseau, did not necessarily mean freedom). Government and law may be overthrown by the general will in the exercise of its discretion.

(e) "To obey the self-prescribed law is liberty". Legal norms bind only when they emanate from the voluntary participation in law-making of those who will be bound by those norms. Natural law creates not individual rights; it confers on the people as a whole an absolute and inalienable authority. The people's general will is more than the mere sum of individual wills; it is transcendent, "always constant, unalterable and pure".

[25] Montesquieu, C. 1750. *Spirit of the Laws.* Cambridge: Cambridge University Press.

[26] Rousseau, J.J. 1762. *The Social Contract.* London: Penguin.

1.5 The school of analytical positivism

This school of thought grew as a reaction to the *a priori* method of thinking of the natural law jurists[27]. Consequently, the analytical positivist approach and methodology to the study and analysis of law are diametrically different from the natural law approach. They use the empirical methodology and therefore seek to analyse law as a fact by investigating the structure of laws. The analytical positivists logically contend that law is what it is and not what it ought to be and that there is a separation between law and morality. Hence the term positive law. Positive law in this context means the law that is actually found, *positum*, as opposed to what it ought to be. This school of jurisprudence is associated with writers such as John Austin and H.L.A Hart but for our purposes we shall refer to the writings of John Austin.

The purpose of Austin's work in jurisprudence was to study law as a set of rules existing separately and in their own right without reference to any external standards such as, for example, moral principles. The validity of law was to be measured in terms of its own structure. In order to achieve this purpose Austin started his analysis of law with two notions. The first is that of a command. The command is given by a sovereign who wields power and is capable of inflicting pain in case the command is disregarded. The command is given to a people who are in the habit of obedience to this sovereign who is a determinate person. Law then is defined as a set of commands set by a determinate sovereign to the members of an independent political society who are in the habit of obedience[28]. Austin's command theory can be said to regard law as a classification of legal propositions or imperatives which are either set directly by the sovereign or by persons or institutions whose authority to do so is derived from the sovereign. Austin also claims that no positive law emanating from the sovereign can be legally unjust.

Austin's command theory has been criticised on several grounds. It has been pointed out, for example, that law cannot be separated from principles of morality and that his command theory is too simplistic a model to describe, accurately, the legal systems of modern constitutions. Namibia, for example, is a constitutional democracy and operates under a written constitution with a Bill of Rights some of the provisions of which are entrenched and cannot be repealed or amended by legislative intervention. Legislative sovereignty is limited by the constitution and the Judiciary has the power to review legislation that is inconsistent with the constitution, especially the Bill of Rights.

Some critics[29] have also blamed the South African judges during the apartheid era for their over-reliance on analytical positivism or parliamentary sovereignty as the justification for their judgments in support of the *status quo* and giving judicial legitimacy to the apartheid laws that grossly violated the rights of a sector of the South African society.

---

[27] Dias, R.W.M. 1970. *Jurisprudence*. London: Butterworths.

[28] Austin, J. 1995. *The Province of Jurisprudence Determined*. Lecture VI. Cambridge: Cambridge University Press.

[29] Dugard, J. 1971. "The Judicial Process, Positivism and Civil Liberty". *South African Law Journal*, Vol 88. Cape Town: Juta.

1.6 Extracts

Curzon, L.B. (1979) Jurisprudence, Macdonald and Evans

2. Some explanations of the terms. The terms "metaphysics" and "empiricism" appear frequently in discussion of legal positivism. These must be explained and noted carefully.

(a) *Metaphysics*. Metaphysics involves a search for "first principles" by investigating "the essential and absolute nature of reality as a whole". Transcendent metaphysics is based on the belief that what really exists lies beyond the realm and reach of our ordinary experience. *Immanent metaphysics* sees reality as consisting exclusively of the objects of our experience.

(b) *Empiricism*. Empiricism is a doctrine opposed to the concepts of "transcending experience", innate ideas and *a priori* structures of the mind. It holds that all knowledge of fact must be validated in sense experienced or be inferred from those propositions derived clearly from sense data.

3. Positivism: its various meanings. The term "positivism" bears a variety of meanings in legal literature and it is important to take into account the context in which it is used. The phrase *jus positivum* is derived from the "laying down" of a law. (Abelard (1079-1142) wrote of "positive law" as that instituted by men "for their honour or use" or based on unwritten authority or custom. The phrase has been used generally to refer to law laid down ("posited") by men. ("Divine positive law" is that said to have been given to mankind by God.) The term has been used to indicate, for example:

(a) the theory that a law is the command of a sovereign or other recognized authority;

(b) the argument that there is no obvious or necessary link between law and morals;

(c) the contention that rational arguments cannot be used to support or deny moral judgments.

4. Philosophical positivism. The term refers to a doctrine holding that our knowledge of matters of fact is derived solely from the data of experience, so that metaphysical "transcending knowledge", i.e. that which is not based on experience, is to be abjured as of no value.

5. Logical positivism. This doctrine, which stems largely from the writings of Carnap and Wittgenstein, involves a total rejection of statements that are not based on tested and verified experience of the senses. Metaphysical assertions are, therefore, valueless. Ethical imperatives are considered worthless since they are based on norms that cannot be tested empirically. Meaning is ultimately established solely in terms of experience. This doctrine has affected some jurists, such as Hart[30], who stress the importance of understanding the mode in which statements about law are couched.

6. Legal positivism. The phrase is widely used to refer to that mode of jurisprudential analysis involving a scientific study of the body of rules, termed "laws", without reference to extraneous matters such as social context, political and psychological background, etc.

[30] Hart, H.L. 1961. *Definition and Theory in Jurisprudence*. Oxford: Clarendon Press.

"Is" And "Ought"

7. The problem. Consider the use of the word "ought" in the following sentences. "If I release the stone I am holding, it *ought* to fall to the ground." "You *ought* not to tell lies." "Those who steal *ought* to be punished." "*Ought* I to do this rather than that?" The term "ought" can possess different meanings: it may refer, for example, to what is likely to happen as a *physical probability*; or it may connote a "*moral ought*". Is it possible to deduce "*ought*" from "is"? Can one, without fallacy, infer a "normative" statement from a merely "factual statement" if normative rules reflect no more than subjective opinions, they cannot be deduced from physical reality – so the argument runs.

8. The problem in jurisprudence. If we are unable to demonstrate what ought to be merely by inferring from existing fact, we cannot rationally assert the necessity of a rule of moral behaviour as a basis of law. If it is not possible to show the truth or falsity of "what ought to be", is there any value to be derived from a search for the moral verities said to be at the basis of the law? Is the concept of utilitarianism (*see* X, **3**) as a basis of law any more than an assertion of what *ought* to be? Positivists note and accept the very wide gap between "is" and "ought"; their general reaction is, first, to reject the veracity claimed for those metaphysical theories basing positive law on so-called "immutable moral principles" and, second, to concentrate their attention, as legal analysts, on a study of the rules constituting the law *as it is*. (But this is not to imply, however, that positivist jurists are uninterested in problems of social morality: *see* **23** *on p.25.*)

****

The transition to legal positivism

16. The philosophical context. The teachings of Hume and Comte prepared the stage for the appearance of rigorous modes of thought applied to jurisprudence. The law, hitherto the object of metaphysical speculation and considered by some jurists in its context of man's moral aspirations and God's purpose, was to be analysed solely on the basis of the data of experience. "Is" would be separated totally from "ought". The methods of the natural science would be transferred to the study of the social sciences, including the law.

17. The methodology of legal positivism. The positivist approach to legal science necessitates the *investigation of the structure* of laws so as to reveal their foundation; the classification of the *functions* of a legal system; the *identification* and *analysis* of fundamental legal *concepts*. Legal positivism seeks to answer questions such as: What is the law? What are its sources? What are its functions in society? What is meant by "possession", "ownership", "duty" and similar legal concepts?

(a) The positivist approach attempts to exclude value considerations from a study of the law.

(b) It confines its enquiries to an analysis of the legal system as it is.

(c) It separates positive law from social policy and ethics.

(d) It sees only the positive law as "law".

(e) It tends to equate positive law with the juridical norms laid down by the state.

(f) It searches for common elements within different legal systems.

(g) It is exemplified by the analytical positivism of Austin (see (XII) and Kelsen's "pure theory" of law (see XIII).

Criticisms of legal positivism

18. Based on a false theoretical foundation. It has been argued that the doctrine of positivism is false. Hume was mistaken in his theory of knowledge and the legal positivists reply that the falsity of the Humean analysis has not been demonstrated and that Hume provided a basis upon which the natural and social sciences have constructed acceptable laws explaining the behaviour of the phenomena of our world.

19. A mere search for facts. The approach of legal positivists has been condemned as no more than a search for facts, in itself a barren task without any underlying, unifying purpose. The positivists, in reply, stress that their search for facts is guided by the motive of *classifying* and *interpreting* those facts so that general concepts may emerge. An understanding of the concept of "property", for example, involves a search for facts relating to that concept as embodied in legal systems. Without a basis of facts, they argue, there can be no valid analysis of legal concepts.

20. Legal data are often ambiguous. The positivists, it has been suggested, work in an area rarely free from ambiguity and doubt. Thus, the concept of "duty" is very ambiguous and uncertain. Ideas of what is meant by "rights" and "property" may differ from system to system so that no certain principles can emerge from a positivist analysis of "facts" only. The positivist reply acknowledges the uncertainty of the subject area, but insists, nevertheless, that the search for similarities among legal systems is necessary if generalization is to be pursued and utilized.

21. The context of the law should not be excluded from its proper study. Law, it is argued, *does* exist within a social setting; it *is* the product of history; it *is* intertwined with man's needs and desires; it *does* reflect social and religious mores. "Law is a product of human effort, and we risk absurdity if we try to describe it in disregard of what those who brought it into being were trying to do": Fuller[31]. What, then, is the value of analyzing the law out of its context as though its surrounding features had no effect on it? The positivists reply that they are aware of the context of the law and that they do recognize the effect on legal doctrines of man's history and his religious aspirations, for example. But those matters belong, they argue, to the realm of investigation of the historian and the theologian. The laws themselves and their underlying ideas, removed from their social setting, should form the sole study of the jurist. Freed from their context, fundamental examination becomes possible.

22. "Ought" in the law should not be ignored. The positivists are criticized for ignoring the reality of absolute morality which often binds and guides communities. No investigation of the law should fail to take into account the real nature of society's belief in what "ought to be". Positivists reply by accepting the powerful nature of beliefs in "ought" within society. They will not deny that morality exists; they draw attention, however, to its relative nature as exemplified by changing laws. The fact that in English law adultery is not a crime, that incest became a criminal offence only in 1908, that suicide is no longer a crime and that homosexual conduct is not always a criminal offence, exemplifies the positivist teaching that morality is rarely absolute in terms of the law and that investigation of the "ought" is not always profitable.

[31] Fuller, L.L. 1976. *Anatomy of the Law.* New York: Greenwood Publishing Group.

23. The positivist approach leads to the downgrading of concepts of justice. Because the positivists call for a division of law and morality, of law and ideas of "right" or justice, some claim that this can lead to the acceptance of evil. If justice is relative, then justice is unimportant. Positivists reply that they do not advocate the acceptance of evil or injustice any more than economists, separating "is" from "ought" in their study of the labour market, can be said to "accept" the evils of unemployment. The positivist jurist separates "is" and "ought" in his investigations; he does not thereby reject the importance of justice. Positivists have played an important role in the history of social and political improvement. See, for example, Mill's powerful advocacy of liberty and Bentham's role in social reform. (Nor is it true to suggest by implication that the non-positivists are invariably linked with the struggle for justice and liberty. See, for example, Del Vecchio's apologia for Italian Fascism, and the utilization of some natural law theory in support of the corporate state.)

The contribution of legal positivism to jurisprudence

24. Autonomy of law stressed. The positivists have emphasized that law can be studied to advantage as a subject in *its own right*. Its link with society, ethics etc., are not to be ignored; but they are to be put aside if the essential features of the law are to be discerned, classified and analysed.

25. Emphasis on rational investigations. Positivism calls for the utilization of the methodology of the social sciences – investigation, induction and deduction – in the study of law. The techniques of logical thought and empirical investigation that have proved fruitful in many branches of endeavour can be applied to studies of those man-made rules known collectively as "law".

26. A methodology capable of wide application. The historical, anthropological and sociological schools of jurisprudence have provided data for the analytical legal positivist. In turn, the positivist outlook – in particular, the concentration of legal investigation upon what is – has provided a useful *style of analysis* for jurists studying the historical role of law and the anthropological nature of rules among social groups. The concept of the legal order as a "social, empirical fact" provides avenues of investigation for a variety of jurisprudential approaches.

Austin's analytical positivism

2. The essence of Austin's thought. Austin was, basically, a utilitarian (see X). For him, "the proper purpose or end of a sovereign political government is the greatest possible advancement of human happiness"[32]. He made a radical separation of jurisprudence from morals and he based his approach on Bentham's "expository" method (*see* X, **10**).

(a) Law, according to Austin, was the command of the sovereign (*see* **12** *p.28*); hence the term applied to his work – the "*imperative theory of law*".

(b) His method of analytical jurisprudence involved a strictly formal analysis of specific, existing legal institutions. He allowed no place in his method for the consideration of ethical elements.

3. Austin's concept of jurisprudence. (Note his division of jurisprudence into "particular" and "general" categories: *see* II, **13-14**). Jurisprudence was concerned solely with "positive

[32] Austin, J. 1869. *Lectures on Jurisprudence or the Philosophy of Positive Law.* London: John Murray.

laws or with laws strictly so called, as considered without regard to their goodness or badness". *General jurisprudence* involved an exposition of principles common to many systems of law; *particular jurisprudence* related to national systems. (It should be noted that Austin based his own work almost entirely on an enquiry into English law, with some investigation of Roman law, so that, in spite of his professed adherence to a "general jurisprudence", he seems to have relied on an exposition of "particular jurisprudence".)

Austin's concept of law

4. Basis of the concept. "A law, in the most general and comprehensive acceptation in which the term, in its literal meaning, is employed, may be said to be a rule laid down for the guidance of an intelligent being by an intelligent being having power over him." Laws may be "improperly so called" or "properly so called", see Fig. 1 for a break-down.

Fig. 1 Diagrammatic representation of the Austinian classification of law

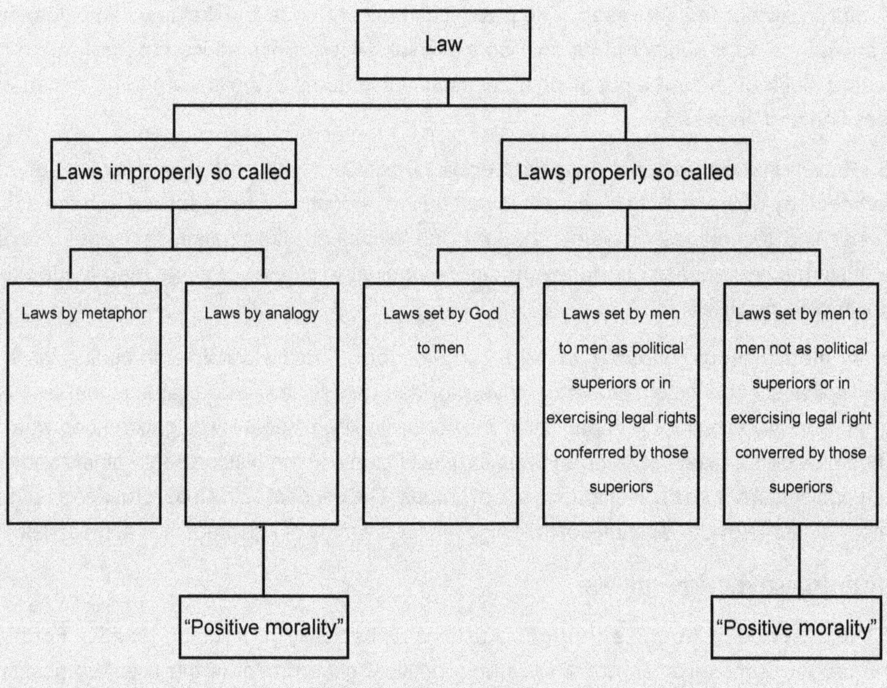

5. Laws improperly so called. These may be divided into two groups.

(a) *Laws by analogy*, that is, "rules set out and enforced by mere opinion", such as the law of honour and the law set by fashion. These laws were aspects of "positive morality" – positive, since they are disjoined from God's law (and are man-made), and related to morality because they must be distinguished from positive law.

(b) *Laws by metaphor*, that is, those resting on slender analogy, describing natural laws, such as those describing the determination of movement of inanimate bodies.

6. Laws properly so called. These are "general commands" and may be divided into the *laws of God* (*see* **7** *p.27*) and *laws set by men to men* (*see* **8** *p.27*).

(a) "General commands" are given to the community, not to individuals, and they call for acts of forbearances *of a class.* (In contrast, "particular commands" determine only specific acts.) They are, by their nature, continuing commands.

(b) "Every positive law is set by a given sovereign to a person or persons in a state of subjection to its author".

(c) "If you express or intimate a wish that I shall do or forebear from some act, and if you will visit me with an evil in case I comply not with your wish, the expression or intimation of your wish is a command. A command is distinguished from other significations of desire not by the style in which the desire is signified, but by the power and the purpose of the party commanding to inflict an evil or pain in case the desire be disregarded."

(d) "Being liable to evil from you if I comply not with a wish which you signify, I am *bound* or *obliged* by your command or I lie under a *duty* to obey it ... Command and duty are, therefore, correlative terms: the meaning denoted by each being implied or supposed by the other."

(e) "The evil which will probably be increased in case a command be disobeyed or (to use an equivalent expression) in case a duty be broken, is frequently called a *sanction*, or an *enforcement of obedience*." (Sanctions are, therefore, based on motivation by fear of "evil".)

7. Laws of God. These "laws properly so called" are "set by God to his human creatures".

8. Laws set by men to men. These fall into two categories:

(a) Laws set by men as political superiors or exercising legal rights conferred by those superiors. They comprise "positive law" or "law" in its strict, simple sense. *The aggregate of these laws is the appropriate matter of jurisprudence*, according to Austin.

(b) Laws set by men, but *not* as political superiors or in exercising legal rights conferred by those superiors. (Together with "laws by analogy" – *see* **5**(a) *p.26* – they are aspects of "positive morality".) Example: rules relating to membership of a private club.

Comments on the Austinian concept of law

9. Law as "a command". The theory of law as a command of a sovereign has been criticized on a variety of grounds, some of which are stated below.

(a) Is law valid *merely* because it is the command of a sovereign? Law may owe its validity, according to some jurists, to the fact that, for example, it expresses feelings of "natural justice" or it embodies a people's wishes. Acceptability by a community is considered by some theorists to be the basis of the validity of a legal system (so that a revolutionary regime may derive the validity of its legal rules from acceptability by the majority).

(b) Does the term "command" provide an appropriate description of *all* laws? What of the law of succession (relating, for example, to testamentary succession)? Is the law of contract based entirely on "command"? How significant for *all* law is the concept of the "sanction"?

(c) Must law be seen solely in terms of "a sovereign"? Some anthropologists suggest that law of a kind has existed in communities lacking a "sovereign" or a state apparatus. Law, they stress, should be seen in terms of its *function*, not its form alone.

(d) Much law results from the decisions of the courts. In what sense may judge-made law be said to emanate from the "commands of a sovereign"? Are judges merely "delegates" of the state?

(e) In what sense may declaratory and repealing statutes be regarded as "sovereign commands"?

10. Fundamental nature of law. Further criticisms of the Austinian concept of law are based on a rejection of the fundamental positivist approach (*see* XI, **27-28**). Is law no more than "an aggregation of rules and command"? What of the unwritten, but potent, standards such as "good faith", and principles interwoven with formal rules in a legal system, which cannot be expressed in the technical vocabulary of legal rules? Is law to be explained solely by a formal analysis of the state?

The Austinian doctrine of sovereignty

11. Sovereignty as a general concept. The term "sovereignty" may be used in jurisprudence to refer to a state's internal or external attributes.

(a) In international law a state's external sovereignty reflects its autonomy or independence. External sovereignty is *positive* in that it suggests the exercise of power in pursuance of objectives such as the maintenance of status and power. It is *negative* in that it involves the absence of subordination to any foreign power.

(b) Internal sovereignty involves the positive exercise of ultimate authority over persons and groups within a state's territory. Bodin (*see* **VII, 3**) spoke of it as "the highest power over citizens and subjects, unrestrained by laws".

12. Obedience to the sovereign power. The exercise of sovereignty demands obedience. Whether the sovereign power be embodied in an absolute monarch, a Parliament or a Supreme Soviet, obedience in varying degrees is demanded from subjects. Some jurists have posed the problem of the precise nature of the obedience demanded by a sovereign as compared with the obedience to the exercise of brute force by, say, an armed bandit. What is the specific, fundamental difference between obeying a call to "Stand and deliver!" and paying "lawfully-levied" taxes? It is suggested that a fundamental distinction is to be found in the legitimacy (based on statute) with which the acts of the sovereign power are invested, so that subjects feel a moral duty to obey, and in the permanence of the sovereign power. (It should be noted, however, that in the final analysis the power of the sovereign may rest in large measure on his ability to employ force – police and army.)

13. Checks on sovereignty. Untrammelled, absolute authority is very rarely found in practice. The theory of sovereignty suggests an omnipotent body; in reality there are limitations to the exercise of power. Dicey[33] states that the actual exercise of authority by a sovereign is bounded and controlled by two limiting factors.

(a) *External limit.* "The possibility or certainty that [a sovereign's] subjects, or a large number of them, will disobey or resist his laws." ("The Sultan could not abolish Mahommedanism.")

(b) *Internal limit.* This arises "from the nature of the sovereign power itself." The moral and religious feelings of the times mould and determine the sovereign's character. A sovereign legislature is determined in its activities by whatever forces determine the face of society and its feelings.

[33] Dicey, A.V. 1982. *An Introduction to the Study of the Law of the Constitution.* Indianapolis: Liberty Classics.

14. Sovereignty according to Austin. Austin distinguishes sovereignty from other types of superiority.

(a) "The bulk of the given society are in the *habit* of obedience or submission to a *determinate* and common superior: let that common superior be a certain individual person, or a certain body or aggregate of individual persons."

(b) "That certain individual or that certain body of individuals is *not* in the habit of obedience to a determinate human superior."

(c) "If a determinate human superior, not in the habit of obedience to a like superior, receive habitual obedience from the bulk of a given society, that determinate superior is sovereign in that society, and the society (including the superior) is a society political and independent". Essentially, therefore, the Austinian "base of sovereignty" is the very fact of obedience; this involves a relation of sovereignty and subjection.

(d) Habitual obedience must be rendered by a number of persons "which cannot be fixed with precision, but which may be called considerable, or not extremely minute".

15. Illimitability of the sovereign power. *See* **13** on *p.28*. "The power of a monarch properly so called or the power of a sovereign number in its collegiate and sovereign capacity is incapable of *legal* limitation." When, therefore, the act of a sovereign is referred to as "unconstitutional", it means that the act has conflicted with "Constitutional law", which is no more than "positive morality" (*see* **5** *p.26*), because the sovereign power cannot be limited by laws relating to its composition.

16. Indivisibility of the sovereign power. Since obedience to more than one sovereign power at any one time is not possible, the sovereign power within a community cannot be divided, according to Austin. In the United States, for example, where a number of federal states exercise power, Austin saw the locus of sovereign power in the individuals and bodies empowered to amend the written constitution.

17. "No law, no sovereign; no sovereign, no law." Austin's view of law as a sovereign command makes the presence of law within a community dependent on the existence of a sovereign power. Where there is no such power (as in a community torn by continuing violence and by refusal to obey rules), there is, effectively, no law.

18. E.E.C. and sovereignty. An interesting problem arises in relation to Britain and membership of the E.E.C., in the light of Austin's concept of sovereignty.

(a) Britain has been a member of E.E.C. since 1st January 1973. Under the European Communities Act 1972, s. 2(1):

> **"All such rights, powers, liabilities, obligations and restrictions from time to time created or arising by or under the Treaties, and all such remedies and procedures from time to time provided for by or under the Treaties, as in accordance with the Treaties are without further enactment to be given legal effect or used in the United Kingdom shall be recognized and available in law, and be enforced, allowed and followed accordingly."**

(b) E.E.C. law appears in English law in the form of the Treaties, regulations, directives and decisions.

(c) English courts *must* take judicial notice of decisions of the European Court of Justice on questions relating to the meaning of the Treaties: European Communities Act 1972, s. 3(2). Further:

"When we come to matters with a European element the Treaty is like an incoming tide. It flows into the estuaries and up the rivers. It cannot be held back ... In the task of interpreting the Treaty the English judges are no longer the final authority ... The Supreme tribunal for interpreting the Treaty is the European Court of Justice, at Luxembourg": ***per*** **Lord Denning in** *H.P. Bulmer, Ltd v J. Bollinger S.A.* **(1974).**

(d) Does this state of affairs constitute limitations on the sovereignty of the British government? (Britain can withdraw from the Treaty, can (and *does*) ignore some E.E.C. decisions.) Has Parliament surrendered some of its sovereignty (in the Austinian sense) to E.E.C. institutions of which it may not be in full control? Given Austin's concept of sovereignty as based on indivisibility, is Britain's Parliament now sovereign in name only?

Comments on the Austinian doctrine of sovereignty

19. Criticisms. Among the criticisms of Austin's analysis of sovereignty are the following.

(a) Did Austin confuse sovereignty *de facto* and *de jure*? Thus, in Britain the Crown is the *de facto* sovereign to whom subjects owe allegiance. Parliament is the *de jure* sovereign invested with sole powers of law-making. Austin, basing his analysis on English practice, may have had in mind the *de jure* sovereign only.

(b) Is the concept of "one sovereign only" essential? Could a state not function effectively if there were within it two or more law-making bodies?

(c) The concept of "illimitability" has no validity in relation to the sovereign body in Parliamentary democracy.

(d) The concept of "indivisibility" creates problems in analyzing the relation of a country to its colonies, or in considering a federal State. *See Re Mwenya* (1960).

(e) The locus of sovereignty during the period of dissolution of Parliament creates a problem for supporters of Austin's concepts. Further, if, as Austin states, the sovereign body is Crown, Lords and Electorate (who decide the composition of the Commons) how can the Electorate be considered as "subjects"?

(f) Some laws may be in existence before a sovereign assumes power; they remain, nevertheless, as laws although they have not resulted from his "commands".

(g) Customary laws are often valid although they emerge independently and not through the sovereign's commands.

(h) Is habitual obedience a requirement of law? Many laws dealing with trivial matters may be ignored by large numbers of a sovereign's subjects, but they remain, nevertheless, part of the state's law.

20. Lack of historical perspective. Austin has been criticized for the exclusion from his enquiry of all save Roman and English law. It has been suggested that, as a result, his theories are mere abstractions with no roots in historical fact. Maine, for example (*See* XVIII, **3-12**), points out[34] that the maxim "no law, no sovereign" is not true in relation to some early Asiatic states and that "no sovereign, no law" had no application to early regimes in Tibet, for example. Much of early law, Maine claims, resulted from religion and custom, not from a political sovereign.

[34] Maine, H.S. 1996. *Ancient Law.* Bristol: Thoemmes Press.

Austin on justice

21. "Just" and "unjust". Positive laws, stated Austin, might be thought of as unjust if considered in comparison with the laws of God. Nevertheless, disobedience to a positive law may be unjust with reference to that law, but just with reference to another law of superior authority. The terms "just" and "unjust" imply a standard and a deviation from it. Disregard of an existing law cannot be justified *legally*.

22. Disobedience. "If human commands conflict with the Divine law, we ought to disobey the command which is enforced by the less powerful sanction." Hence, disregard of an existing law can be justified *morally*.

Austin's analytical jurisprudence today

23. Criticisms. It has been said that Austin is often read today for the sole purpose of criticizing the fundamentals of his teaching. His scheme, simple and internally consistent, continues to be attacked on a number of grounds (*see*, for example, **19-20** *on p.30*). His concentration on form and his ignoring of matters such as ethics, morality, and social systems are said to have vitiated the power of his theories. Further, Allen refers to a suggestion[35] that the emergence of the totalitarian states has elevated Austin's doctrine "to its apotheosis".

24. The characteristic jurisprudence of England? Allen comments that in spite of the unsparing attacks on Austinian doctrine, its vitality remains unexhausted; he speaks of it as "the characteristic jurisprudence of England".

(a) It remains a record of one of the first attempts to analyse systematically the basic forms of a developed legal system.

(b) It provides a useful example of the application of analytical modes of investigation, freed from considerations of morals and ethics, to the problem of the nature of law. Kocourek[36] refers to "the omission of [some types of jurisprudential thought] to isolate from the great mass of available legal material the enduring elements which recur endlessly in concrete legal phenomena, and to analyse and arrange these elements into an abstract system or classification".

(c) Manning[37] suggests that Austin's method helps to provide a "clear if static picture" of how law stands at any time. Its value, therefore, for historical and sociological jurisprudence should be high.

(d) Austin's doctrine continues to affect the thinking of jurists. For example, Holland defined law, in Austinian terms, as "a general rule of external human action enforced by a sovereign political authority". Markby described law as a general body of rules addressed by the rulers of a political society to members of that society and which are generally obeyed.

****

[35] Allen, C.K. 1964. *Law in the Making.* Oxford: Oxford University Press.

[36] Kocourek, A. 1930. *An Introduction to the Science of Law.* Boston: Little, Brown and Company.

[37] Manning, C.A. 1933. "Austin Today" in *Modern Theories of Law.* Lennings, L. (ed). London: Oxford University Press.

Mail and Guardian

February 21. 27, 1997

Serjeant AT THE BAR

Law can't always be moral

New Chief Justice Ismail Mahomed's concern about the moral fibre of the nation doesn't mean the law will concern itself only with morality.

Judge Ismail Mahomed went to Bloemfontein last week to start work as the new Chief Justice. He gave a short interview to SABC television, in which he took the opportunity to voice serious concern about the erosion of the moral fibre of this nation and about corruption. The judiciary, he said, must act to restore morality, albeit not merely by the imposition of harsh prison sentences.

These words are welcome because for far too long our courts lagged behind the democratic world in infusing our law with morality, but equally, the public ought not to conclude from this short statement that henceforth law will concern itself only with morality.

It cannot do that, because it is a system of rules that is concerned with many more interests than just morality. Indeed, sometimes the interests protected by law diverge quite sharply from morality.

This is shown in our law of contract which, in part, is moral, and in part merely sound commercial common sense.

The rule that holds a person to the promise that he or she makes (to sell or lease property, for instance) is clearly a moral precept. It is immoral to break bargains and promises, and the law prohibits this.

But the rule that holds a person to the letter of the written contract he or she signed, regardless of whether it was read or understood or how onerous the terms are, is not a moral rule and can often have harsh consequences that benefit rich and powerful institutions at the expense of poor or even indigent individuals.

Judges are generally not naïve, and most will confess privately that they know many people do not read the fine print of their insurance contracts, their leases, their hire-purchase agreements and even their antenuptial contracts. Yet daily they enforce such enforcements.

The reason for this is the requirement of a modern commercial society, which is what we are. Contracts and other instruments often have consequences for other parties. They can be passed around and traded. Without a rigid adherence to what is written, the Chinese whispers would soon exaggerate some rights and deflate others to the prejudice of traders down the line and third parties. No one would be really certain of the terms of the contracts and instruments they dealt with.

This would make trade and commerce very difficult and, to return to the earlier examples, insurance companies would become reluctant to insure persons and property (drastically raise their premiums when they did), retailers reluctant to develop commercial properties for renting out. All this is deleterious to society, hence the strength of a legal rule that owes nothing to morality.

Our criminal law also derives from hybrid influences. Its rules not only seek morality, but also to shape the kind of society most people want. Laws against theft and murder are entirely consistent with the religious and cultural heritage of virtually every single person in this land; but the laws requiring drivers to stop at stop streets, bottlestore owners to be validly licensed and individuals not to drop sweet papers in the park, owe nothing to morality but stem from a general desire for municipal orderliness. They just make life easier for everyone.

Thus, law exists not just to enforce the general moral values of the populace; it must also order society and promote commerce. These are complex functions, and while the modern trend is to allow morality more and more to temper the harsher effects of the other ends, South Africa (in common with all other democracies) has not yet reached the stage where there is a simple equation between law and moral values.

1.7 The pure theory of law

Hans Kelsen developed his pure theory of law from these premises that a theory of law must deal with law as it is and not as it ought to be. In this sense he can be regarded as a positivist. Kelsen[38] asserts that laws are 'ought' statements that is, statements of obligation contrasted with "is" statements which are statements of fact purporting to describe what exists. Secondly, he insisted that a theory of law must be distinguished from the law itself. In this regard he departs from the theories of analytical positivists such as Austin and Hart who look at law in terms of its structure or the law itself. For Kelsen the law consists of a mass of heterogeneous rules and the function of a theory of law is to relate them in a logical pattern and to organise the field into a single, ordered unity. Thirdly, a theory of law should be uniform, i.e. it should be applicable at all times and in all places. Fourthly, he also postulated that a theory of law must be free from politics, ethics, sociology, history, etc. It must in other words be 'pure'. Finally, jurisprudence to Kelsen is a knowledge of 'norms' and a norm is simply a proposition in hypothetical form; if X happens then Y should happen. For example in the Law of Contract if X accepts Y's firm offer that complies with all the elements of a valid offer, a contract has been created. These propositions deal with what ought to happen given a basic fact. Legal propositions, according to Kelsen, therefore deal with what ought to be and jurisprudence consists of the examination of the nature and organisation of such normative propositions. (Please note that the ought proposition here is different from the concept of 'ought' as postulated in the theories of natural law.)

From the above propositions Kelsen asserts that law as a normative order is conceived of as a system of norms that regulates the behaviour of men. A norm referring to the behaviour of a human being derives its validity from the validity of another norm. A norm which represents the reason for the validity is figuratively spoken of as a higher norm in relation to a lower norm. The search for the reason of a norm's validity cannot go on indefinitely; it must end with a norm which, as the last and highest, is presupposed. Such a presupposed highest norm is referred to

[38] Dias, R.W.M. 1970. *Jurisprudence*. London: Butterworths.

as the basic norm or the *Grundnorm*. All norms whose validity can be traced back to one and the same basic norm constitute a system of norms, a normative order. The basic norm or the *Grundnorm* is the common source for the validity of all norms that belong to the same order – it is the basis of their validity. For Kelsen, therefore, a legal system describes a network or interconnection of legal norms derived from a basic norm or the *Grundnorm* whose validity is presupposed.

Kelsen in his hypothesis of the legal order argues that the validity of each individual rule depends on the effectiveness of the legal order as a whole and that a legal order has to be by and large effective. At the level of the *Grundnorm*, Kelsen argues that the question of its validity is meaningless because, as stated earlier, its validity is presupposed but that it is of utmost importance that the *Grundnorm* should secure for itself a minimum of effectiveness[39] i.e. that a certain number of persons are willing to abide by it. Kelsen's critics argue that if the validity of a particular *Grundnorm* depends on the continued effectiveness of the legal order as a whole, then the adoption of a particular *Grundnorm* will involve an enquiry into political and sociological factors. Therefore the study of jurisprudence should include the study of the environment which includes moral factors.

1.8 Extracts

Curzon, L.B. (1979) Jurisprudence, Macdonald and Evans

2. The essence of Kelsen's theory. According to Kelsen, every legal activity must be traced back to an authoritative standard – *a norm* – which gives *validity* to the behaviour embodied in that activity.

> **"The law, or the legal order, is a system of *legal norms*. The first question we have to answer, therefore, is this: What constitutes the unity in the diversity of legal norms? Why does a particular legal norm belong to a particular legal order? A multiplicity of norms constitutes a unity, a system, an order, when validity can be traced back to its final source in a single norm": Kelsen[40].**

3. Kelsen's approach to law. Kelsen's theory is a theory of positive law, concerned exclusively with the accurate definition of the subject matter; it propounds an answer to the question, what is the law? It does not attempt to answer the question: what ought the law to be? "It is a science and not a politics of law."

(a) Kelsen aims at a *structural analysis* of the positive law.

(b) The *analysis* is intended to be *free* from *all* ethical or political judgments concerning values.

(c) The *analysis* is said to be *positive* because it is concerned solely with *the law as* it is; it pays no attention to ideology, morals, etc.

(d) The *analysis* is said to be *realistic* because it removes from the study of the law those illusions concerning its nature which have made its past study unproductive.

---

[39] Kelsen, H. 1945. *General Theory of Law and State*. Cambridge: Harvard University Press.

[40] Kelsen, H. 1945. *op.cit.*

(e) The *analysis* is said to be *pure* because the resultant theory is free from those elements (e.g. values) that have adulterated methods of study of law.

(f) The *methodology* required for the formulation and exposition of the pure theory is *value-free*, uncommitted to ideology and systematic.

Norms and the law

5. What is a "norm"? For Kelsen, the important feature of a study of law is not an analysis of the facts of human behaviour, but an *elucidation of norms, i.e. the rules and regulations stating expected standards of behaviour.*

(a) A norm is an "ought" statement, setting out what, under certain circumstances, ought to be, or ought to happen, e.g. that a human being ought to behave in a specific way.

(b) "'Norm' is the meaning of an act by which a certain behaviour is commanded, permitted or authorized."

6. Examples of norms. Consider the following circumstances arising out of the working of legal systems.

(a) John Smith, chairman of Lowprice Retail Stores Ltd, pays to the court £400, a fine imposed on conviction for an offence under the Trade Descriptions Act 1968; the court receives the payment. Receipt of that fine is authorized under statute, following conviction; that conviction received its authority from the judgment of a court which acted in pursuance of its authorized powers to determine the case brought against John Smith. The case originated in the 1968 statute which was "authorized" by the Crown in Parliament. Here may be seen a unified system of norms, each giving validity to the other.

(b) Vladimir Ivanovich Antonov, citizen of the Soviet Union, is taken to a corrective-labour colony, having been sentenced as a "dangerous recidivist". The order for his confinement has been signed by the principal judge of the Supreme Court. That order is authorized under a regulation which is utilized following Antonov's conviction. That conviction is authorized under a law of 1958 (Criminal Code, article 21), which derives its authority from a decree of the Supreme Soviet of the U.S.S.R. (1959, No. 1). Here is a series of connected activities, each one deduced and applied on the basis of norms.

7. The hierarchy of norms. It will be observed that in the circumstances outlined in 6(a) and (b) above there is, in each case, a *hierarchy of norms*.

(a) In every legal system there may be seen, according to Kelsen, evidence of a hierarchy of norms in which each proposition depends for its *validity* on another proposition standing behind it from which it derives its quality as a "legal act". The term "validity" refers to the fact that a norm *ought* to be observed, obeyed and applied.

(b) The legal order is not to be seen as a system of co-ordinated norms of equal level; it is rather, a hierarchy of *different levels* of legal norms, a hierarchy of "oughts".

(c) The norms become more concrete, less abstract, as one descends the levels within the hierarchy, so that the final norm (Smith's obligation to pay the fine, resulting in his handing payment to an official of the court, or Antonov's obligation to serve his sentence, resulting in his arrival at the labour colony), which is the *sanction*, is no more than the ultimate "concretization" of the hierarchy of norms.

(d) Thus, the court passing sentence on John Smith (*see* **6**(a) *above*) is "concretizing" the "general norms" by which the case is controlled (as embodied in the 1968 Act). The court's decision constitutes an "individual norm" relating to John Smith.

8. Sanctions. Kelsen views sanctions (*see* **7**(c) *p.35*) as the *final stages in hierarchies of norms.* Law is "a coercive order of human behaviour", according to Kelsen; coercive acts are attached by society to behaviour contrary to that which is desired. An illegal act will attract sanctions, such as deprivation of freedom; those sanctions result directly from *norms* defining how people "ought" to behave.

The basic norm (Grundnorm)

9. The peak of the hierarchy. Consider the examples at **6**(a) and (b) *p.35*. The norms were traced upwards through the hierarchy. They stopped at an action (enactment) of the Crown in Parliament and an action (decree) of the Supreme Soviet. Upon what norm does the action of Parliament rest? How does the decree of the Supreme Soviet acquire its authority? Kelsen answers *there is a basic norm (Grundnorm)* from which, ultimately, a system is able to impute the quality of legal validity to certain forms of human behaviour.

10. Essence of the Grundnorm. The basic norm (Grundnorm) could be, in 6(a) and (b) *p.35*, acceptance of, and obedience to, the unwritten concept of the supremacy of the will of the Crown in Parliament, or the post-1917 revolutionary decrees establishing the legal system of the Soviet Union.

(a) Kelsen speaks of the basic norm as "the norm the validity of which cannot be derived from a higher one".

(b) In the case of a legal system based on a "constitution", one may discover an older constitution and reach, ultimately, the first, historical constitution. It is the validity of this first constitution that provides the "final postulate" upon which the norms of the existing legal, constitutional order are based.

(c) For legal purposes, therefore, the analyst of a legal system cannot go behind the *Grundnorm.*

(d) A *Grundnorm* can be discovered in every type of legal order.

(e) A system of law cannot be established on a foundation of conflicting basic norms.

11. Choosing the basic norm. The legal analyst, in his task of discovering the basic norm (the "initial hypothesis") of a system becomes aware of the difficulty in selecting what is the basis of a complex system embodying many types of norm. "There must be a certain parallelism between what is and what shall be": Lauterpacht[41].

(a) Where there has been, for example, a fundamental breach of an old order, there would be little value in seeking for an "initial hypothesis" among the rules of the old system. The *Grundnorm* for the legal order within the present People's Republic of Bulgaria could not be discovered by an examination of the royal prerogative of King Boris III.

(b) Kelsen believed that the principle of legitimacy, in the case of a norm, is restricted by the "principle of effectiveness", that is, the norm has to be accepted, by and large, within the community. In the case of the *Grundnorm* there ought to be evident a "minimum of support". Universal, total, obedience is not essential; but there must be within the community *a sufficiency of adherence to the essence of the basic norm*

[41] Lauterpacht, H. 1933. "Kelsen's Pure Science of Law" in *Modern Theories of Law.* London: Oxford University Press.

allowing it to be effective in practice. The *Grundnorm* is not general; a basic norm establishing autocratic rule may give way to a new, basic norm of a constitution giving power to an elected assembly.

12. Exclusion of other disciplines from the concept of norms. No discipline such as ethics, sociology, history or psychology, is allowed by Kelsen to affect his discussion of the concept of hierarchy of norms. This is not to say that Kelsen rejects these disciplines as invalid; it is to emphasise that his method involves the formulation of a "pure" theory, requiring the isolation of data from the interpretation of law on the basis of subjective values and ideologies. His concept of law excludes all moral connotations. Metaphysical speculation and the assumptions and methodology of the sociologist and psychologist are unnecessary, he claims, for an accurate determination of what is the law.

****

Natural law and justice

15. Natural law rejected. Kelsen attacks and rejects the concept of natural law. He sees it as based on claims to immutability and absolute validity resting on God, Nature, and Reason. These claims clothe with an objective character that which is no more than normative. (He raises, too, an objection to the manner in which natural law has been used as a façade to support or criticize the scheme of property relationships embodied in the law.)

16. Justice. For Kelsen, "justice" as a concept is no more than the expression of an irrational ideal; it represents an individual's value preferences and no more. As a concept, it may be related to the motivation of men, but it is not subject to cognition. It is not possible to answer scientifically the question: what is justice? One can say no more than that it is "just" for a general rule to be applied and obeyed where, because of the content of that rule, circumstances demand its application. In this sense, justice is seen in "the maintenance of a positive order by conscientious application" of the appropriate general rules[42].

Kelsen and Austin

17. The "pure" theory and the "imperative" theory. There are some important similarities between the approach of Kelsen and that of Austin (*see* XII). For example, both attempt to separate their investigations from morals, ethics, etc. Both employ a formal, rigid analysis. Both are concerned with the positive law. Both see the essence of law in terms of an "ultimate" concept. Both pay attention to the structure and functions of the state.

18. Differences in theories. There are differences between the two theories. For example, Austin pays no attention to the normative aspect of legal rules and regulations. Further, Austin's criterion of the value of human activities is "utility"; Kelsen views moral values as basically irrational. The attitude to sanctions differs: Austin sees them as based on fear (*see* XII, **6**(e) *p.27*); Kelsen views them as no more than the final "concretization" of legal norms (*see* **7** *p.35*). Austin accepts distinctions between sovereign (i.e. state) and the legal order; Kelsen sees the state as no more than the legal order personified.

[42] Kelsen, H. 1957. *What is Justice? Justice, Law and Politics in the Mirror of Science*. Berkeley: University of California Press.

Criticisms of the "Pure Theory"

19. Its arid nature. The pure theory has been attacked as a mere "mental exercise". Laski said of it[43]: "Granted its postulates I believe the pure theory to be unanswerable, but ...its substance is an exercise in logic, not in life." It has been dismissed as totally remote from the real world of the law and from the complexities of legal institutions. As a result, it is argued, its highly formal nature renders it useless as a guide to the application of legal doctrine and the solution of important practical problems.

20. Its rejection of the substance of law. Law in a community includes principles, procedures, practices and doctrines, many of which cannot be traced to an "initial hypothesis". Kelsen, it is argued, has missed the *substance* of the law in his rejection of the facts constituting the legal order in practice. Feelings of justice embodied, for example, in the exercise of judicial discretion, the important history of parliamentary attitudes to the removal of evil by legislative measures, the philosophical positions from which changes in the law have been advocated and the ethical premises underlying many arguments for legal reform, demand recognition and evaluation in any analysis which purports to be a study of what is law.

21. The inadequacy of the concept of the basic norm. It is not always easy – some would say it is often impossible – to find the basic norm of a legal order. The very search may be affected by the investigator's personal value judgments so that the essence of the theory is negated. Further, one is left with a basic norm beyond which one "cannot look". Lloyd points out[44] that this reminds one of the myth of the world carried by an animal, the rules not allowing one to ask, however, what supports that animal. Kelsen's "ultimate" leaves questions unanswered. Nor is the test of "minimum support" (*see* **11**(b) *p.36*) always meaningful, since proof of that minimum would require an investigation into those surrounding facts (political and social) that are unacceptable in terms of the "pure" nature of the theory.

22. The acceptance of power as the creator of norms. Kelsen has been criticized (*see*, for example, Friedrich[45]) as accepting too readily the creation of norms by the exercise of power. This says Friedrich, involves a turning away from the philosophy of law, from the search for truth and justice and a failure to examine and criticize the activities involved in the exercise of power.

23. The attraction of the pure theory. Kelsen's theory continues to attract interest and support from many jurists. Its critical force endures; in particular, its emphasis on a methodology of investigation free from ideology ("politics masquerading as jurisprudence") makes an appeal to those who wish to study the legal order as an organized, systematic structure. The search for the "initial hypothesis" and its dependent norms helps those jurists who are interested in the essence of legal reality and who require, therefore, a "clear" field of enquiry.

---

[43] Laski, H.J. 1941. *A Grammar of Politics.* London: George Allen and Unwin.

[44] Lloyd, D. 1964. *The Idea of Law.* London: Penguin.

[45] Friedrich, C.J. 1963. *The Philosophy of Law in Historical Perspective.* Chicago: University of Chicago Press.

1.9 The historical school

We have seen two different approaches to the analysis of law; one approach looks at law in terms of its conformity with some criteria outside the law itself- not what the law is but what it ought to be. The other approach looks at law in terms of its structure or the factual existence of the law. That is the law as it is.

The historical school approaches the concept of law from a premise which looks at law in terms of its relationship with and satisfaction of some standards outside the law itself, but the difference, however, lies in what constitutes the 'ought'. The historical school hypothesizes that the law must consist of the historical experience and culture of a society. This can be achieved if enquiries are made about the evolution and history of the society with the view to elucidating the position today.

The historical school is at times classified with the social utilitarians, which is a term loosely used to denote the jurists who analyse law in terms of the philosophical, historical and sociological background of the society. This school is associated with the writings of J. Köhler and Frederick Karl von Savigny (1779-1861). Köhler was brought up in the historical school but he later broke away from the school to give it a broader basis.

Joseph Köhler[46] regarded law as the product of the civilization of a people. The civilization of a people consists of a complex mixture of physical, psychological and socio-economic conditions and interactions which are constantly in conflict with each other. These conditions are not static and are relative to every society. It is the function of law to reconcile these forces for the progress of the entire society as opposed to the individual's interests. These interests, known as the 'jural postulates' constitute the criteria for measuring the validity and justness of law.

As mentioned earlier, Köhler gave his analysis of law a broader basis and therefore he is classified more as a social utilitarian than a jurist from the historical school. Savigny is perhaps the jurist mostly associated with the theories of the historical school. Savigny taught that there was an organic connection between law and a people's nature and character as developed through history; the nature of any particular legal system was a reflection of the spirit of the people who evolved it. Consequently, law must reflect the ethos of the society. He postulated that law is the expression of a 'people's spirit' or what he referred to as the *volksgeist* and that law is to be identified with a people's 'folksoul' and its feelings of justice and right. It follows from Savigny's exposition of law that law must be evaluated against some external criteria for its validity. Law must be defined in terms of its validity.

Some of the criticisms of this theory are that the theory minimizes the influence which individuals of alien race have exercised upon legal development; law can be used as a tool of social change and existing ideas; where there is in existence different species of divergent laws, which laws will be selected to represent the will of the people and who the authoritative source to make such pronouncement is.

[46] Stone, J. 1965. *Human Law and Human Justice.* London: Stevens & Sons and Pound, R. 1923. *Interpretations of Legal History.* New York: The Macmillan Company.

1.10 Extracts

Curzon, L.B. (1979) Jurisprudence, Macdonald and Evans

3. Essence of the historical approach. The historical school of jurisprudence is built on the belief that the study of existing law requires an understanding of its historical roots and growth. To what extent has today's law been moulded by its historical development? To what degree do contemporary legal doctrines and institutions bear the mark of past centuries? Is it possible to discern long-term trends in legal history? These and similar problems can be solved, it is suggested, only by examining and interpreting the history of the law. One jurist has described law as "frozen history", in so far as its study – and, indeed, its practice – involves reference to records, reports and other historical documents of the past. The historical approach to jurisprudence may be considered, therefore, to derive from the very nature of law and the legal process.

SAVIGNY: BACKGROUND AND FUNDAMENTALS OF HIS TEACHINGS

4. Background: significance of the French Revolution, 1789. The era in which Savigny wrote was dominated, in Europe, by the French Revolution which had destroyed the feudal order in France. The "law of nature", that is, "reason", would henceforth guide the "general will" of members of society and positive law would express that will. Interpretation of the law by judges was to be forbidden and enacted law would solve all legal questions. The Civil Code would express the legislative will and would enshrine a legal system derived from pure reason.

5. Savigny's attitude to the Revolution. Savigny (1779-1861), a German nobleman, who had studied Roman law, shared with many other European writers a deep hostility to the excesses of the French Revolution and its fundamental philosophical, political and legal doctrines. This hostility brought a reaction against "rationalism", against the natural law (*le droit*) said to express supreme, universal reason applied to a consideration of the very nature of things, and against the rejection of tradition. In Germany, in which historical jurisprudence originated, anti-revolutionary doctrines, which stressed the importance of authority and tradition and which drew attention to the creativity of a people's customs and folklore, became popular. Savigny's abhorrence of revolution found expression in his propagation of a nationalistic, near-mystical doctrine of the origins of law based on the "common consciousness of the people"[47].

7. The fundamentals of Savigny's teaching. Savigny taught that there was an organic connection between law and a people's nature and character as developed through history. *The true "living law" is customary law*; it does not emerge from the arbitrary will of a law-giver, but from "internal, silently-operating forces" within the community. Law is rooted in a people's history; the roots are fed by the consciousness, the faith and the customs of "the people".

8. Savigny's attitude to codification of the law. The publication of Savigny's views was the direct result of his reaction to proposals by a German professor, Thibaut, that German law be codified on the basis of the Roman law and the *Code Napoléon* (*see* XXVIII, **7**).

[47] Savigny, F.C. 1814. *Von Bruf unserer Zeit für Gesetgebug und Rechtswissenschaft* (English translation by Hayward, A. 1975. *Of the Vocation of Our Age for Legislation and Jurisprudence).* New York: Argo.

Savigny opposed codification vigorously. Reform of the law, he argued, ought not to be embarked upon without a deep study of history. Germany had not the appropriate "calling" for the construction of an adequate code; indeed, its jurists lacked the necessary legal vocabulary. A code would "imprison" the development of the law and would merely fix it in an unsatisfactory state. Savigny's opposition was generalized into the theoretical principles underlying his concept of law as flowing from "the spirit of the people".

THE SPIRIT OF THE PEOPLE: THE ORIGIN OF LAW

9. The doctrine in outline. Savigny's principles may be summarized as follows.

(a) All law is originally formed by custom and popular feeling, "that is, by silently operating forces".

(b) Law is a special product of a people's genius. Like language, it evolves gradually and embodies a people's characteristics. It flourishes with the growth of a people; it dies away when a people loses its individuality.

(c) Laws have no universal validity; they apply solely to the nations in which they were created.

(d) Law is not static; it is subject to the same movement and development as every other expression of life of the people.

(e) Law comes from no law-giver, but from a people's instinctive sense of "the right"; hence, because true law is "found and not made", legislation lacks the vital significance of custom.

(f) Law is, therefore, the expression of a "people's spirit". (Savigny's pupil, Puchta popularized the use of the term *Volksgeist.*) Law is to be identified with a people's "folksoul" and its feelings of justice and right.

10. What is "a people"? Savigny gave no formal definition of the concept of "a people" – a fundamental part of his teachings. He tended to see "a people" where spiritual communion of individuals living together culminated in the growth of a common language and common traditions.

11. Custom and law. *See* **9**(a) above. The people's common consciousness is made manifest, is externalized, in custom. The common usages which constitute a people's customs are nurtured by the people's spirit; they alone form the true, "living law". "All law is originally formed in the manner in which in ordinary, but not quite correct, language, customary law is said to have been formed – that it is first developed by custom and popular faith..."

12. Legislation is subsidiary in importance to custom. *See* **9**(e) above. The living law does not flow from the command of a sovereign; it grows organically in the people's spirit. Hence, legislation must be of less importance than custom. Further, legislation will be effective only if it is attuned to the spirit of the people; otherwise it is doomed to failure. Savigny was not opposed to legislation as such; he emphasized that it ought to be employed only where the advanced political status of a people necessitated changes in the formal law, or where doubts within the community had to be resolved by a declaratory statute.

13. The role of jurists and lawyers. The workings of the *Volksgeist* cannot formulate the detailed procedures and rules of the law and its institutions. Savigny believed that a stage was reached in the development of a people where its common consciousness could not take the direct form of regulations, codes, etc. In this advanced stage, jurists and lawyers, who have acquired a specialized knowledge of legal technicalities, become important. Their task is to create the technical rules of the law; in this they are guided by the spirit of the people and they act as trustees of the people. They have, therefore, a dual role: on the one hand they are technical specialists; on the other hand they are representatives of the people's consciousness.

CRITICISM OF THE DOCTRINE

14. A highly-subjective interpretation of historical development. Savigny has been criticized for the personal, selective view of history from which he derived his doctrines. He commits, it has been said, the besetting sin of many historians, namely the writing of history with unwarranted emphasis given to conditions uppermost in the writer's own times. The hostility to the French Revolution prevalent within Germany and Savigny's personal anti-revolutionary feelings have been seen as factors colouring his views of general historical development, as explaining his reverence for "the past" and as underlying his antagonism towards reform.

15. The Volksgeist as a mere fiction. Many critics have failed to find any proof of (indeed, any means of proving) the existence of "the people's spirit". It has been characterized as a mere cloak for reactionary, narrowly-nationalistic views. Savigny, it has been argued, has done no more than personify some aspects of national development. His concept of a "people" is too vague for use in jurisprudential study; his doctrine of the "communal consciousness" is merely a metaphorical structure built upon the existence of communal views and is no more "real" than Rousseau's "general will" of the community (*see* VII, 20 *p.23*).

(a) It is often difficult, sometimes impossible, to ascertain public opinion, which may be said to correspond to Savigny's "communal conscience". A community, close-knit and having a common heritage may be divided fervently on matters of law. Consider for example, the attitude of citizens of the United Kingdom to capital punishment or to the legal implications of membership of the E.E.C. Note, for example, the attitude of "the British people" towards the controversial Industrial Relations Act 1971. Was "the spirit of the people" made manifest in that Act, or in the later statute which repealed it? What of the large number of members of "the people" who act deliberately in defiance of its laws? What of the numerous statutes comprehended by only a very small section of "the people"?

(b) The concept of law as growing in the conscience of the people as a direct response to its nationhood and common culture is not always deduced easily from historical experience, which includes many examples of laws transplanted with success in different nations and cultures. *See*, for example, the reception of Roman law in several countries in Europe, the utilization of the French Code in Egypt and the transfer of Roman-Dutch law to Ceylon.

(c) The role of "the people" in the creation of law may have been exaggerated by Savigny. Law has often resulted from the imposition of an alien conqueror's will. Brute force of arms, not the inner workings of the people's consciousness, has fashioned some law for many peoples. The advocacy of scholars, the decisions of judges, have also played an important role in the development of a nation's law. Some law – trade union legislation, for example – has resulted from active, conscious political struggle of groups within a community.

16. The misinterpretation of the importance of legislation. *See* **9**(e) *p.41* Savigny is criticized for having misinterpreted the balance of custom and legislation. Custom is often of no national significance, having a local nature only (*see* XXV, **6**). In some cultures it has been an alien transplant, and in no sense "the externalization of the people's will". Some customs, mercantile custom, for example, may affect only small sections of a community. Hence, the significance of custom can be over-stressed. Legislation is often the result of deliberate "social engineering", that is, attempts to lead the community in directions considered advantageous to the nation as a whole. The welfare and consumer legislation of recent years provides an example of law-making which cannot be said accurately to be "subordinate" to the "custom of the people". Fuller draws attention to Savigny's failure to realise that custom may become unresponsive to new conditions and, when this occurs, it needs to be supplemented by formal legislation[48].

17. The paradox of Savigny's stance on "law for the German people". In spite of Savigny's insistence on placing the roots of law in a people's nationhood, he advocated a system of refined *Roman* law for the *German* people. There is little reason to suppose that the reception of Roman law in Germany emanated in any way whatsoever from the desires of "the German people"; indeed, the overwhelming mass of the people would have been totally ignorant of it. Rather was that reception the result, primarily, of the work of a very small group of jurists and other scholars in a community in which illiteracy and ignorance of the law were almost universal. The suggestion that legislation based upon the principles of the Roman law coincided with a law previously existing in the "folk-spirit" of Germany is not easily supported by historical evidence.

Positive features of Savigny's teaching

18. Law as a reflection of social attitudes. Savigny drew attention to the general attitudes and values of a people as reflected in its customs and the "living law". Some legal historians have claimed to see in the legislation of the German National Socialist regime of the 1930s a "correct expression" of the general values of the German *Volksgeist* of that period. Similarly, the "welfare legislation" of Parliament in the immediate post-war period of the later 1940s has been interpreted as a direct reflection of changed attitudes of the British people towards matters of communal responsibility. Savigny's emphasis on the *roots of law* is of great importance. Law rarely springs fully-developed from the heads of legislators: Nazi law reflected values which had been growing within Germany for many years; British welfare doctrines had been discussed and advocated for a long period prior to implicit approval by the Crown in Parliament. Savigny's teaching that legislation which is not rooted in a people's aspirations is "doomed to failure" is a reminder that, in the long run, popular values do prevail in some societies and do colour legislation.

19. The importance of social pressures. Even if the concept of the *Volksgeist* be rejected as mere nationalistic hyperbole, it serves to draw attention to the importance of social pressures resulting in changes to the formal law within a community. Within a democracy, in which the legislature responds to important expressions of public concern, the pressures of communal anxieties may result directly in new laws. The success of pressures for the reform

[48] Fuller, L.L. 1976. *Anatomy of the Law.* New York: Greenwood Publishing Group.

of divorce legislation and for the removal of legal disadvantages attaching to illegitimacy, communal concern for the protection of children (*see*, for example, the Protection of Children Act 1978, enacted in spite of initial reluctance expressed by the Government), exemplify the creative role of community consciousness. The exaggerations and mystical trappings of the doctrine of the *Volksgeist* ought not to blind one to the undeniable force of social pressures within some kinds of society.

1.11 The sociological school

The sociological school belongs to the social utilitarians who, as we have already seen, look at the definition and function of law in terms of its instrumental function in society. The social utilitarians hypothesize that the purpose of any law is to secure social interests and where individual and social interests conflict, social interest must prevail. Social advantage and interests should be the underlying principles and objectives of any policy, and individual or class interests can be served by law only to the extent that they coincide with social interests or to the extent that social interests are secured by them. Roscoe Pound, who is probably the most quoted exponent of the sociological school uses the concept of the interest of the society as a point of departure for his theory of law. For Pound[49] the function of law is the adjustment of relations and interests and the ordering of social conduct by judicial process with the least waste. These interests could be public or individual. He defined these interests as "a demand or desire or expectation which human beings either individually or in groups or associations or relations seek to satisfy, of which, therefore, the adjustment of human relations and ordering of human behaviour through the force of a politically organised society must take account"[50]. Pound maintained that it was the business of the legal order to model these interests or jural postulates. Pound stipulated that there is no eternal law but an eternal goal which the law must strive to achieve. The eternal goal is a perfection which is a product of the balance of interests which are dominant in the society. Any legitimate and just law is therefore one which reflects this goal and strives to achieve it. One can see therefore that this school also looks at law in terms of its validity i.e. its instrumental function, which is measured by reference to external criteria. One criticism against Pound is that he does not state what interests or absolute postulates the law must promote at a given time. And neither does he tell us who the valid source of socio-economic values and goals is.

1.12 Extracts

Curzon, L.B. (1979) Jurisprudence, Macdonald and Evans

2. Sociological jurisprudence and the sociology of law. Some writers (e.g. Pound and Lloyd) distinguish carefully between "sociological jurisprudence" and "the sociology of law".

(a) *Sociological jurisprudence*. Pound refers to this as a study of the peculiar characteristics of the legal order, i.e. an aspect of jurisprudence proper. Lloyd writes of it as a branch

---

[49] Pound, R. 1959. *Interpretation of Legal History*. New York: Macmillan.

[50] Pound, R. 1959. *Jurisprudence*. Vol. 111. St Paul Minnesota: West Publishing Co.

of the normative sciences, having the objective of making the law more effective in action, and based on subjective values. Some other writers use the term to refer to the Sociological School of Jurisprudence, that is, those jurists who see in a study of society a means whereby the science of law might be made more precise.

(b) *Sociology of law*. Pound refers to this study as "sociology proper", based on a concept of law as one of the means of social control. Lloyd writes of it as essentially a descriptive science employing empirical techniques. It is concerned with an examination of why the law sets about its tasks in the way it does. It views law as the product of a social system and as a means of controlling and changing that system.

NOTE: The term "legal sociology" has been used in some texts to refer to a specific study of situations in which the rules of law operate, and of behaviour resulting from the operation of those rules.

Pound

11. Essence of his teaching. Pound, an American jurist and Dean of the Harvard Law School, was one of the most influential writers on sociological jurisprudence. He was influenced strongly by the pragmatism of William James (1842-1910), who had taught that "the essence of good is simply to satisfy demand". Pound thought of law as a social institution created to satisfy human, social wants "by giving effect to as much as we may with the least sacrifice, so far as such wants may be satisfied or such claims given effect by an ordering of human conduct through politically organized society". The essence of the legal order was the securing and protection of a variety of interests and this necessitated the modification of traditional and inherited legal codes to existing social conditions[51].

12. The task of sociological jurisprudence. Pound enumerated the sources of legal rules as: usage; religion; moral and philosophical ideas; adjudication; scientific discussion; legislation. It was the task of sociological jurisprudence, which was an important source of ideas, to assist in ensuring that social facts were noted and analysed in the formulation, interpretation and use of laws. This necessitated:

(a) a study of the social effects of legal precepts, doctrines and institutions;

(b) sociological investigation as a preparation for legislation;

(c) a study of methods of making legal precepts effective in practice;

(d) a deep study of judicial method;

(e) a sociological study of legal history;

(f) recognition of the importance of just and reasonable solutions of individual cases;

(g) the setting up, in English-speaking countries, of Ministries of Justice;

(h) recognition of the end of juristic study as the achieving of the purposes of the law.

13. Legal development. Pound enumerated four stages in legal evolution (each characterised by different attitudes to the allocation of liability).

(a) In the *first stage*, in which society was dominated by private war and reprisals, there developed "composition for the desire to be avenged".

[51] Pound, R. 1959. *op.cit.*

(b) In the *second stage*, "strict law" involving formal, inflexible rules, aimed at certainty and uniformity were developed.

(c) In the *third stage*, the stage of equity and "good conscience", reason, rather than adherence to the strict letter of the law, was relied on.

(d) In the *fourth stage*, a marriage of stages (b) and (c) (equality and security) dominate legal concepts.

(e) Pound, in his later writings, envisaged a *fifth stage*, exemplified by law in the 1920s, characterised by "socialisation of the law", in which public interests would predominate.

14. "Social engineering". Jurisprudence, according to Pound[52], was a "science of social engineering" concerned with the ordering of human relations. The legal process could be interpreted as a type of "social control". Legal history could be seen as the record of the recognition and satisfaction of human wants through social control, so that social interests might be secured. This necessitates investigating the relation of law to administration and the limits of effective legal action. Further, judges, jurists and law-makers need to be informed of the social facts involved in legislation. The classification, definition, securing and protection of interests (*see* **15-19** below) were essential to successful social engineering.

15. Interests. Pound defines an interest as "a demand or desire or expectation which human beings either individually or in groups or associations or relations, seek to satisfy, of which, therefore, the adjustment of human relations and ordering of human behaviour through the force of a politically organised society must take account". The recognition and definition of interests demand: an inventory and classification of interests; decision on the selection of interests to be legally recognised; study of the means of delimiting and securing of recognised interests. It is the *balancing of interests* (individual, public and social) which is the main problem for jurists and legislators.

16. Individual interests. These are "interests of personality or interests in domestic relations or interests of substance". They involve claims and demands related to an individual's life, thus:

(a) *Personality*. This involves those interests pertaining to an individual's physical and spiritual existence, e.g. physical security, health, freedom from coercion and deception, free choice of location, freedom of belief and opinion.

(b) *Domestic relations*. This involves the interests of parents and children and the protection of marriage.

(c) *Substance*. This concerns interests of property, freedom of contract and association, i.e. those claims or demands "asserted by individuals in title of the individual economic existence."

17. Public interests. These relate to claims viewed from the field of necessities of public life. They are:

(a) *Interests of the state considered as a "juristic person"*, i.e. its integrity, freedom of action, security, etc.

(b) *Interests of the state as guardian of social interests* (*see* **18** *p.47*).

[52] Pound, R. 1922. *Introduction to the Philosophy of the Law*. New Haven: Yale University Press.

18. Social interests. These important interests are claims or desires of the social group constituting the community; they are as follows:

(a) *General security*, including claims to peace and order against those actions likely to threaten the very existence of society.

(b) *Security of social institutions* (domestic, religious, political and economic).

(c) *General morals*, i.e. security of social life against acts offensive to general moral sentiments.

(d) *Conservation of social resources.*

(e) *General progress* – the "self-assertion of the social group toward higher and more complete development of human powers", including, for example, free speech and cultural progress.

(f) *Individual life* – the most important interest of all, involving the claim or demand of each individual to live a human life according to society's standards.

19. The securing of interests. The law attempts to satisfy, to reconcile, harmonise and adjust overlapping or conflicting claims and demands. It attempts to give effect to "the greatest total of interests or to the interests that weigh most in our civilisation, with the least sacrifice of the scheme of interests as a whole". Interests must be balanced and weighed on the same plane. Pound provides no standards for the evaluation and weighing of interests. Balancing necessitated the use of the following forms of the law:

(a) *Rules*, i.e. "precepts attaching a definite, detailed legal consequence to a definite, detailed statements of facts".

(b) *Principles*, i.e. "authoritative starting points for legal reasoning employed continually and legitimately where cases are not covered or are not fully or obviously covered by rules in 'the narrower sense'."

(c) *Conceptions*, i.e. "authoritative categories to which...cases or situations are referred, in consequence of which a series of rules, principles and standards become applicable". (They are chiefly the work of law teachers and law writers, according to Pound.)

(d) *Standards*, i.e. "the general limits of permissible conduct to be applied according to the circumstances of each case".

20. Pound's jural postulates. Pound suggested, in 1919, the following postulates as underlying civilised society in that era.

(a) Men should be able to assume that others will commit no intentional aggressions upon them.

(c) Men should be able to assume that they may control for beneficial purposes what they have discovered, created and acquired.

(d) Men should be able to assume that those engaged in a course of conduct will act with due care so as not to create unreasonable risk of injury to others.

21. Pound and justice. Justice, according to Pound, was to be seen in administration related to authoritative precepts or norms, ascertainable in advance of a dispute, by which all are assured of receiving like treatment. It involves "impersonal, equal, certain administration" and precepts of general application.

22. The contribution of sociological jurisprudence. The work of the pioneers of the sociological school prepared the way for a more informed attitude towards the setting within which the law operates and towards its functions within society.

(a) Sociological jurisprudence has drawn attention to the need for an *overall analysis* of the relations of law and society.

(b) It has focused attention on the *changing nature* of the law as it reflects variations in the standards of groups and other associations.

(c) It has emphasised the importance in law of *values* held by social groups.

(d) It has drawn attention to the *social ends* of legislation and to the functions of law as a means to those ends.

(e) It has emphasised the *importance of the individual* within the legislative framework.

(f) It has indicated the significance of the *systematic nature of the law*, that is, its internal constituent forms and principles and their effects upon, and reaction to, other parts of the total social environment.

1.13 Modern realism

The term modern realism refers to the American and Scandinavian scholars who started a movement aimed at looking at a theory of law from the premise of the 'real' forces or the actual actors involved in the legal process and the end product of the law. The exponents of this approach to the question of law are referred to as the realists. There are the American and Scandinavian Realists. However, for our purposes, we shall look at the theories of the American Realists.

The American Realist movement is a combination of the analytical positivist and sociological approaches[53]. It is positivist in the sense that it first considers the law as it is. It is sociological in the sense that they admit that the law as it stands is a product of many factors and therefore are interested in inquiring into the effects of social conditions on law as well as the effect of law on society. And most importantly they stress the point that a study of law should involve factual studies of the behaviour of lawyers. They also emphasise that to understand what law is, one should be able to predict how judges decide cases. This school therefore examines the creative function of judges and enquires into the subliminal and external factors that influence the decisions of judges. They argue that law comprises the decisions of judges which are the product of ascertainable factors including their personalities, their social environment, the economic conditions in which they have been brought up, business interests, political leanings, etc. This is referred to in some quarters as the 'inarticulate major premise' of decisions of judges.

One of the pioneers of this movement in the US was Mr Justice Holmes (1841-1935). He wrote that if one wishes to know what law is, one should view it through the eyes of a bad man, who is only concerned with what will happen to him if he does certain things or what the courts are likely to do[54]. Another pioneer of the movement

[53] Dias, R.W.M. 1970. *Op. cit.*

[54] Dias, R.W.M. 1970. *Op.cit.*

was Gray (1839-1915), who drew a basic distinction between law and sources of law. The former is what the judges decide. Everything else including statutes are sources of law until interpreted by a court. Another writer associated with the American Realists is Karl N. Llewellyn.

1.14 Extracts

Curzon, L.B. (1979) Jurisprudence, Macdonald and Evans

2. The effect of American legal experience on her jurists. No writer on law is isolated from the general problems of the society in which he lives and works. The influence of the social, political and legal environment on American jurists such as Pound, Homes and Frank emerges clearly in their analysis of jurisprudential problems. Llewellyn and Schubert, who are discussed below, reflect in their writings some of the vast changes which have occurred in American society. Concern for the stability of legal institutions and an awareness of the profound significance of new technology for methods of investigation are apparent in the theories discussed in this chapter. Twining[55] mentions the following problems deriving from American legal experience as having affected the thinking of many of her jurists; the adapting of common law to American circumstances; the adapting of the formulas of the Constitution of 1787 to changed conditions; the preserving of the common law in a country with a number of separate jurisdictions; the simplifying of sources of law; the modernizing of the formal law. Twining sees the American realist movement as the vanguard of those jurists calling for a "dynamic jurisprudence".

3. Essence of his approach to legal problems. The following points should be noted as an indication of the attitude to law of Llewellyn, an American professor of law.

(a) "There is no school of realists." There is a great doctrinal diversity among the realists, so that the so-called "Realist Movement" was said by Llewellyn to be, in fact, "a ferment".

(b) Llewellyn considered the members of the Realist Movement as sharing certain points of view; these are set out in XX, **5**. Of great importance is his attitude to the Realist examination of "is" and "ought". "The argument is simply that no judgment of what ought to be done in the future with respect to any part of the law can be intelligently made without knowing objectively, as far as possible, what that part of the law is now doing .... This means an insistence on informed evaluations instead of armchair speculations."

(c) "See it fresh. See it as it works. Come back and make sure; these are the essence. They go to *method*. That method is eternal ... it is *not a philosophy*, but it is a *technology*, and that is why it is eternal."

(d) Firm relations between the study of law and other social sciences are essential.

4. What is law? "This doing of something about disputes, this doing of it reasonably, is the business of law. And the people who have the doing in charge, whether they be judges or sheriffs or clerks or jailers or lawyers, are officials of the law. What these officials do about disputes is, to my mind, the law itself"[56].

[55] Twining, E. 1973. *Llewellyn and the Realist Movement*. London: Weidenfeld and Nicolson.

[56] Llewellyn, K.N. 1930. *The Bramble Bush*. New York: Oceana.

(a) In his later writings, Llewellyn apparently rejected this earlier view as no more than a "partial statement of the truth".

(b) This rejection was accompanied by a statement emphasizing the importance in the American legal system of *standards* aimed consciously at the shaping and control of official conduct so as to minimize arbitrariness[57].

5. The problem of rules. Llewellyn emphasized that rules were not as important as some legal theorists had assumed them to be. It was *how a rule* worked that determined its significance; a rule of law conceived merely as a formula of words was "emptiness". *Rules are, therefore, what they do.* "There is less possibility of accurate prediction of what courts will do than the traditional rules would lead us to suppose." But this is not to say that rules are, in themselves, of no value in a legal system; indeed, Llewellyn was the author of a uniform commercial code adopted in several American states. It is important to study rules in action.

1.15 The purpose of law

Our initial definition of law is that law regulates the behaviour of the individual in the society. The law prohibits certain conduct of behaviour and allows other types of behaviour. In this sense it creates rights and corresponding obligations and thereby balances conflicting interests in the society and maintains the equilibrium in the society. The purpose of the law may be said to be the preservation of peace and order in the society. Human society comprises individuals with diverse interests and desires and if society allowed individuals to pursue their ambitions and desires unbridled and without reference to any rules, there would be total chaos in the society. The whole society will cease to function.

Lord Justice Denning once said, "the law as I see it has two great objectives; to preserve order and do justice". The law therefore is made to serve a purpose in the society, i.e. the law has a teleological function in the society. The various theories of the law that are stated above also indicate the purpose of law in the society. Natural law teaches us that the law must be used to promote the moral values of the society and promote justice. Analytical positivism stipulates that once the law has been ordained by an authoritative source it must be obeyed. The sociological school hypothesises the instrumental function of the law and we learn from the historical school that the law must reflect the history and ethos of the society. All these principles are accommodated by various provisions in the Namibian Constitution.

One of the central themes of *Jurisprudence* is justice. As pointed out by Lord Justice Denning one of the objectives of law is the promotion of justice. But what is justice? The concept of justice is just as complex and difficult as law itself. One way of looking at the concept is by reference to the theories of law. The oldest school of jurisprudence, natural law, stipulates that there is no separation between law and justice. But we have also seen that their definition of justice ranges from principles of morality, eternal law, inalienable rights, the procedural principles of justice and

[57] Llewellyn, K.N. 1960. *The Common Law Tradition: Deciding Appeals*. Boston: Little, Brown and Company.

the principle of reciprocity, etc. The sociological school emphasises the balancing of conflicting interests in the society, which approximates to distributive justice.

As much as we concede that the concept of justice is complex and therefore has a multi-faceted approach to its definition, one concept that can hardly be disputed is that the law is made for the people and therefore a law that is not just will not be obeyed by the people. The concept of justice is therefore also related to the concept of the individual's obligation to the law.

1.16 Review questions

The details of some of the theories of *Jurisprudence* are contained in the extracts provided in this chapter. You are required to read these extracts and the cases and attempt to relate the legal theories to the legal system of Namibia in order to ascertain how legal theories assist you to understand the cases and the relevance of jurisprudence in the judicial and legal systems.

1. With reference to at least one case discuss the relationship between natural law and the concept of public policy.
2. Discuss the nature and function of law as propounded by the exponents of natural law and debate the merits and demerits of their approach to the study of law. Credit will be given for the citation of relevant cases and references to the provisions of the Namibian Constitution.
3. Discuss the concept of law in the theories of natural law.
4. Discuss Lon Fuller's contribution to the theories of natural law.
5. Discuss the nature and function of law as propounded by John Austin and debate whether Austin's model accurately describes the Namibian legal system.
6. With reference to the Namibian legal system discuss the extent to which the 'is' can be separated from the 'ought'.
7. "The existence of law is one thing, its merits or demerits is another. Whether it be or be not is one enquiry, whether it be or be not conformable to an assumed standard, is a different enquiry. A law which actually exists is a law though we happen to dislike it or though it varies from the text, by which we regulate our approbation and disapprobation". John Austin: *The Province of Jurisprudence Determined*.

   Critically discuss the above statement with reference to any relevant theories of law and any other relevant literature, including the Namibian Constitution.
8. Compare and contrast the theories of law of the historical and sociological schools.
9. The Minister of Lands Resettlement and Rehabilitation intends on implementing a land reform policy which includes compulsory acquisition of private property in Namibia. The Minister wants to justify the validity of this policy on jurisprudential grounds.

   Advise the Minister with reference to any theories of law you have studied.

10. "However it may be defined it is a study relating to law, and although the term *law* may seem to the uninitiated a simple one, analysis reveals that there are many uses of this word. Hence, one of the first tasks of jurisprudence is to attempt to throw light on the nature of law. At first sight it would seem to be the most logical procedure first to define law and then to discuss the scope of jurisprudence. But there are various ways of approaching the problem, and each school of jurisprudence tends to set up its own definition." Paton: *Jurisprudence*

    Discuss the above statement with reference to the theories of **two** schools of jurisprudence indicating the merits and demerits of the theories.

11. Discuss how the various theories of law treat the concept of a valid and just law.

CHAPTER 2
SOURCES OF LAW

2.1 Introduction

One of the primary objectives of legal training is the inculcation, in the law student, of the ability to analyse facts, to locate the relevant law and to apply the law. When a client consults a legal practitioner for legal advice or representation, he simply states his problem in the form of representation of facts. It is the responsibility of the legal practitioner to analyse the issues that emanate from the facts and search for the law. The legal practitioner is presumed to have appreciable knowledge of the law. But a wise lawyer does not bask in this complacency. The wise lawyer will do further research and explore the extent to which the law applies to his client's case. This process involves, *inter alia*, analysis of the case, distinction between his client's case and the case he is seeking to rely on as authority, including his own evaluation of the law to enable him to argue his case before the court.

A student of law still pursuing the law degree does not have the standing to represent a client. This however does not make his task very different from that of the practitioner. As mentioned earlier, one of the objectives of the training is the creation of analytical skills and the ability to locate the relevant law. One technique employed for the realisation of this objective is the assignment; students are presented with a hypothetical problem and are required to do their own research and write a legal opinion on the matter. In this sense, therefore, there is not much difference between the task of the student and that of the practitioner. Perhaps the only difference is that the student will be dealing with hypothetical facts whereas the practitioner will be dealing with actual facts. But the basic skills needed to solve the problem are the same regardless of whether you are a student or a practitioner. You will be required to analyse the hypothetical facts, locate the relevant law and give a legal opinion on the problem. In this profession one important point that must be borne in mind is that whatever legal opinion or proposition you make must be based on a principle of law or must be supported by an authority, which means that you must cite the source of that law. The source of that legal principle could be the constitution, a statute, case law, custom, juristic writing or a convention.

Different writers use the term 'sources of law' in different senses but the term shall here be used to refer to the location of the law and the basis of the individual's fidelity to law. In the former sense we shall refer to the primary and secondary sources of law and in the latter sense we shall look at the relationships between sources of law and the individual's fidelity to law.

Primary sources are the original sources that spring from some legal authority or fountain-head and they include constitutions, statutes and case law. Secondary sources of law, on the other hand, include the commentaries upon these primary sources by juristic writers. The writings of these jurists can be found in books, articles and treaties but there is no formal hierarchy of authority given to the writings of jurists. The weight or importance of these sources depends on the respect in which the writer is held.

The term sources of law can also be used to refer to the basis or the reasons for its binding effect on the individual. In this sense the source of the law is regarded as the basis of the individual's fidelity to law. The question of the individual's fidelity to law is the subject matter of *Jurisprudence,* but an introductory exploration of the subject matter as a source of law shall be made.

One concept of the source of law is that law is rooted in God and that the law of God can be equated to some higher moral law, or the imperative norm, which is the fountain-head of all human laws. All human laws must be in sufficient conformity with this higher law, and the individual must obey this man-made law because it is rooted in God. *Ipso facto*, the individual has the right to disobey any law, which violates this higher law. Some modern writers have redefined this concept by introducing the concept of reciprocity to the extent that the individual's fidelity to law is not confined to the positive law's conformity to some undefined concept of morality but to some defined postulates which the lawmaker must comply with in the process of legislation. These postulates are known as principles of justice.

Other writers are of the opinion that the source of law lies in a supreme established authority that has the power to make law and to enforce it when it is violated. The individual's fidelity to law is determined in terms of the existence of this supreme established authority and its ability to enforce the law. This authority may be simply referred to as the State through its Legislature, courts and the law enforcement agents. According to this school of thought, the State is the source of law.

There is another theory that looks at law in terms of the functions it plays in society. According to the writers of this school, the binding effect of law is derived from its instrumentality or its functional role in the society. The validity of the law therefore is rooted in its instrumentality, which is derived from society. Hence the source of the law or its validity is rooted in the society.

Another dimension of this argument is that the source of the law for most societies is the people in the societies. The sovereignty of the State and the power of government are ultimately derived from the people, the governed. A government cannot ignore the wishes of the people all the time. The most visible source of law remains the State, but behind the State there must lie further support for the law.

There is another view that the courts or the judges can be regarded as the source of law for, according to these philosophers, the law is what the judges determine it to be. This implies that judges in the exercise of their judicial functions have law-making powers; this phenomenon is also referred to as judicial activism. Judge-made laws are known as judicial precedent or case law and they constitute the core of the common law.

From the above exposition on what constitutes sources of law, we can see that the concept of the source of law is a complex one, ranging from formal sources like the constitution to informal and/or intangible sources like the will of the people.

2.2 The sources of law in Namibia

2.2.1 The Constitution

The Namibian Independence Constitution came into force on the eve of independence as the supreme law of the land and therefore the ultimate source of law in Namibia[58]. All other laws in Namibia trace their legitimacy and source from the Constitution. In order to prevent the creation of a legal vacuum Article 140 of the Constitution, logically, provides that all laws that were in force immediately before the date of independence shall remain in force until repealed or amended by Act of Parliament or until they are declared unconstitutional by a competent court.

By virtue of the above provision therefore, the sources of the laws of Namibia comprise the laws that were in force in Namibia on the eve of independence and after independence. These comprise the laws passed by the German Imperial Government during the German colonial administration, those imposed by the South African regime and the laws in force after independence. These may be classified as follows:

1) Roman-Dutch law and elements of English common law;
2) Legislation consisting of German, South African, English, South West African and Namibian law;
3) Case law;
4) Customary law;
5) International Law; and
6) Juristic writings, old and new.

2.2.1.1 Features of the Namibian Constitution

The Namibian Constitution is a product of a struggle for sovereignty and human rights and this is reflected in the first provision which states that Namibia is a sovereign, secular, democratic and unitary State founded upon the principles of democracy, the rule of law and justice for all[59]. It creates, *inter alia,* the three organs of State; namely the Executive, the Judiciary and the Legislature. It also establishes the various service commissions, and defines State responsibility to obligations, succession to treaties and the status of international law. The Constitution contains a Bill of Rights of fundamental human rights and freedoms, including administrative justice, which are protected and entrenched under general protection and entrenchment provisions[60]. The Constitution does not precisely define the difference between rights and freedoms but it may be argued that the difference lies in the extent of permissive derogation. Whereas some of the rights are absolute and therefore cannot be derogated from,

---

[58] Article 1(6) of the Namibian Constitution provides that 'This Constitution shall be the Supreme Law of Namibia.'

[59] Article (1) (1) ibid.

[60] See Articles 5 and 131 ibid.

not even when a state of emergency has been declared under the provisions of Article 26, specific provisions of the Constitution allow for derogation from the freedoms on specific grounds such as those under the provisions of Articles 21(2) and 22 of the Constitution. In the case of *Kauesa v Minister of Home Affairs and Others*[61], for example, the court had to rule on the constitutionality of regulation 58 (32) of the Police Regulations deemed to have been made under the (Namibia) Police Act 19 of 1990 which prohibited a member of the Namibian Police from commenting unfavourably in public on the administration of the Namibian Police or any other government department and rendered such conduct an offence. Mr Kauesa, the appellant, was a serving warrant officer in the Namibian Police and had appeared on an NBC television panel discussion on the topic of affirmative action in the context of the restructuring of the Namibian Police and the Public Service. He had stated *inter alia* that white officers in the command structure of the police force were determined to undermine the government's policy of reconciliation, facilitated corruption, abused their power and had collaborated with "traitors and terrorists" by supplying police weapons to them. The Namibian Police started disciplinary proceedings against Mr Kauesa because of his remarks. He applied to the Full Bench of the High Court for an order declaring the regulation unconstitutional. The application was dismissed by the High Court whereupon he appealed to the Supreme Court against the whole judgment.

The central issue to be determined was whether regulation 58(32) constituted a permissible restriction on the right to freedom of speech of a serving member of the Namibian Police Force. Article 21(1)(a) of the Namibian Constitution provides that "all persons shall have the right to freedom of speech and expression". A limitation on such right could only be permissible if it fell within the terms of Article 21(2) which provides that: "The fundamental freedoms ...shall be exercised subject to the law of Namibia, in so far as such law imposes reasonable restrictions on the exercise of such rights and freedoms ... which are necessary in a democratic society and are required in the interest of the sovereignty and integrity of Namibia, national security, public order, decency or morality, or in relation to contempt of court, defamation or incitement to an offence".

It was contended on behalf of the appellant that regulation 58(32) imposed an impermissible restriction on the freedom of speech. To proscribe all unfavourable comment "in public upon the administration of the force on any other government department" by a serving member of the police force was not a reasonable restraint on the exercise of the right of speech. It was not necessary in a democratic society and was not required in the interests of sovereignty and integrity, national security, decency or morality.

In his judgment, Dumbutshena A.J.A, stated:

"(T)he sub-regulation (32) casts too wide a net in its attempt to prevent police officers from commenting unfavourably in public on the administration of the force or any government department in order for the force to maintain discipline. .... But

[61] *Kauesa v Minister of Home Affairs and Others* 1995 NR 175 (SC); (4) SA 965 (Nms). See also *Fantasy Enterprise CC t/a Hustler The Shop v The Minister of Home Affairs and Another* 1998 NR 96 (HC); *Nasilowski and Others v The Minister of Justice and Others* 1998 NR 97 (HC).

Namibia is a democracy in which police officers have as much a right to freedom of speech and expression as the citizenry".

The court further held that the limitation in this case was not rationally connected with its objective and Regulation 58(32) was arbitrary and unfair. It failed to specify the ascertainable extent of the limitation it imposed on the right as required by Article 22 of the Namibian Constitution. It proscribed all unfavourable comment, thereby casting the net too wide. True and fair comment was treated in the same manner as false comment. It failed to strike a balance between the need to promote discipline and efficiency in the police force and the serving policeman's interests as a citizen in commenting upon matters of public concern. Its infringement of the right to freedom of speech was not restricted to what was reasonably necessary to achieve its purpose. The court accordingly upheld the appeal and declared regulation 58 (32) to be invalid and without force and effect.

An underlying principle of the Constitution implicit from the preamble and Article 1 is the doctrine of constitutionalism[62], which simply means government according to law rather than according to the whims and caprices of individuals in government is enforced. It is the antithesis of arbitrariness. It aims at preventing over-concentration of power in one individual or one organ of State and abuse of power. In the context of the Namibian political order, there are mechanisms in the Constitution that are meant to impose checks and balances and restraint on the exercise of powers of government and achieve the objectives of constitutionalism.

The executive power of the Republic of Namibia is vested in the President and the Cabinet and the exercise of this power is subject to the Constitution and any other relevant law[63]. The primary constitutional constraint on executive power is the obligation imposed on the President to consult the Cabinet, which is quite legitimate given the fact that the repository of executive power is both the President and the Cabinet. The other constraints on executive power include judicial review of any executive action which abolishes or abridges the fundamental rights and freedoms conferred under the Bill of Rights[64] and the accountability of the Executive to the Legislature through the provision of Article 32(2) of the Constitution which enjoins both the President and the Cabinet to attend Parliament each year during the consideration of the official budget and also imposes a constitutional obligation on the President to address Parliament on the state of the nation, the future policies, the policies of the previous year and to avail himself/herself for questions. Executive power is further controlled by the subjection of the exercise of administrative discretion to the observance of and compliance with the principles of natural justice and other requirements under the generality of the provisions of Article 18[65].

The legislative power is vested in the National Assembly with power to pass laws with the assent of the President subject, where applicable, to the powers and functions

[62] See Chapter 8.

[63] Articles 27 (2) and (3) of the Namibian Constitution.

[64] Article 25 (1) ibid.

[65] See Chapter 8 for details.

of the National Council. The Namibian Legislature is described as bicameral because it consists of two chambers; namely the National Assembly and the National Council. However, to the extent that the recommendations of the National Council are not binding on the National Assembly, it may be concluded that the powers and functions vested in the National Council are advisory.

The legislative process itself has inherent mechanisms relating to the requisite majorities needed for the passage and amendment of bills, acts and the Constitution that are meant as constraints on legislative powers. For the passage of any bill or resolution a simple majority of votes cast in the National Assembly shall be sufficient[66]. For the amendment of the Constitution, however, the requirements are more stringent and vary depending on the nature of the article meant to be amended. With regard to the amendment of the provisions of the Bill of Rights, no repeal or amendment shall be permissible if such repeal or amendment diminishes or detracts from the fundamental rights and freedoms of the Bill of Rights and no such purported repeal or amendment shall be valid or have any force of law[67]. To this extent therefore the provisions of the Bill of Rights can be said to be entrenched. In the case of the amendment of the other provisions of the Constitution, Article 132 provides as follows:

(2) The majorities required in Parliament for the repeal and/or amendment of any of the provisions of this Constitution shall be:
  (a) two-thirds of all the members of the National Assembly and;
  (b) two-thirds of all members of the National Council.

(3) (a) Notwithstanding the provisions of sub-Article (2) hereof, if a bill proposing a repeal and/or amendment of any of the provisions of this Constitution secures a majority of two-thirds of all the members of the National Assembly, but fails to secure a majority of two-thirds of all the members of the National Council, the President may by Proclamation make the bill containing the proposed repeals and/or amendments the subject of a national referendum.

(b) If upon the holding of such a referendum the bill containing the proposed repeals and/or amendments is approved by a two/thirds majority of all the votes cast in the referendum, the bill shall be deemed to have been passed in accordance with the provisions of this Constitution, and the President shall deal with it in terms of Article 56 hereof.

Article 56 deals with the requirement of the presidential assent to the bill for it to acquire the status of an act of Parliament. Another aspect of the constraint exercised by the Executive over the Legislature is the right of veto granted to the President to withhold his or her assent to a bill approved by the National Assembly if in the President's opinion such bill would upon adoption conflict with the provisions of the Constitution.

Other defined control measures over legislative functions are to be found in some of the powers and the functions granted to the other two organs of State. Article 5

[66] Article 67 of the Namibian Constitution.

[67] Article 131 ibid.

enjoins all three organs of State to respect and uphold the fundamental rights and freedoms enshrined in the Bill of Rights and gives express jurisdiction to the courts to enforce them. The jurisdiction of the courts to enforce compliance and respect of the Bill of Rights is complemented with the specific jurisdiction under the provisions of Article 25 to declare any enactment by Parliament invalid, provided that a competent court, instead of declaring such law invalid, shall have the power and the discretion in an appropriate case to allow Parliament within a specified period to correct any defect in the impugned law. Apart from the judicial constraints on legislative authority, there is another form of constraint on legislative authority, that may be described as a political constraint, emanating from the will and the right of the electorate to choose their representatives for the Legislature. This right subjects legislative authority to the political scrutiny of the electorate and makes the Legislature accountable to the electorate, the ultimate source of political and legislative authority.

The third organ of State, the Judiciary, is created by Article 78 of the Constitution and it consists of the Supreme Court for Namibia, the High Court and the Lower Courts. As an organ of a State that is committed to the promotion of human rights and democracy, the Judiciary plays an important role in this regard. The independence of the Judiciary has been recognised in all democracies as a *sine qua non* for the promotion of a culture of democracy and human rights. Consequently the Constitution under Articles 78(2) and (3) guarantees that independence and provides that the Courts shall be independent and subject only to the Constitution and the law and further that no member of the Cabinet or the Legislature or any other person shall interfere with judges or judicial officers in the exercise of their judicial functions, and all organs of the State shall accord such assistance as the courts may require to protect their independence, dignity and effectiveness, subject to the terms of this Constitution or any other law.

This judicial independence is therefore by no means unfettered: the courts are indeed subject to the Constitution and the law. Judicial officers are accountable to the Judicial Service Commission in the performance of their judicial functions and are subject to the rules relating to professional ethics, discipline and dismissal as stipulated in the Constitution and other law.

2.2.1.2 Administrative justice

Principles of administrative justice, that are commonly recognised in many jurisdictions as common law principles constituting as it were constraints on administrative discretion and granting the courts the jurisdiction of judicial review of such discretionary powers, in the Namibian Constitution form part of the Bill of Rights. Under the provisions of Article 18, administrative bodies and officials are enjoined to act fairly and reasonably in the exercise of their discretionary powers[68]. In the context of the rule of law, the principles of administrative justice granted under the Bill of Rights further buttress the doctrine of separation of powers in Namibia as it puts constitutional constraints on executive powers in so far as the exercise of administrative discretion is concerned.

[68] See Chapter 8 for more details on the provisions of Article 18 Supra.

2.3 Roman-Dutch Law: the origins and historical development of the law of Namibia

2.3.1 The introduction of Roman-Dutch Law into Namibia

The introduction of Roman-Dutch Law into Namibia is closely interrelated with the political and historical development of Namibia. After the occupation of the territory by South African troops in 1915, German law remained in force except for such laws as were found necessary to be repealed under martial law. At the end of the First World War, South West Africa was placed under the League of Nations Mandate system as 'C' mandate. The King of Great Britain accepted and delegated the mandate to the government of the Union of South Africa to exercise it under the supervision of the League of Nations. Article 2 of the mandate agreement gave the mandatory all powers of administration and legislation over the mandated territory as an integral portion of the Union and authorised the mandatory to apply the laws of the Union to the territory. Following the imposition of South African Administration on South West Africa, after the granting of the League of Nations Mandate over the territory to South Africa, one obvious historical fact was the extension of the application of South African legal system to the territory. One basic characteristic of the South African legal system is the element of Roman-Dutch law constituting, as it were, the nucleus of South African law, and hence the common law of South Africa. In so far as South West Africa was concerned, Roman-Dutch law was formally introduced as the common law of the territory by Proclamation 21 of 1919, (S.W.A. Gazette, No. 25 of 1919) which provided *inter alia* that Roman-Dutch law was to be applied in the territory 'as existing and applied in the Province of the Cape of Good Hope' and the proclamation remained the legal basis for the application of the common law of the Cape as a source of law of South West Africa until the promulgation of the Namibian Constitution. Article 66(1) stipulates that the common law of Namibia in force on the date of independence shall remain valid to the extent to which such common law does not conflict with the Constitution. It must also be added that since 1959 after amalgamation of the Judiciary of the territory into that of South Africa, which was effected by the Supreme Court Act No. 59 of 1959 resulting in the High Court of South West Africa being made a division of the Supreme Court of South Africa, the courts of the territory were bound by the decisions of the Supreme Court of South Africa. Therefore, the Roman-Dutch law that was developed by the South African courts as the common law of South Africa was binding on Namibian courts.

As a consequence of English colonial administration over the Cape of Good Hope, English common law was introduced into the Cape. By virtue of the application of Proclamation 21 of 1919 English law that applied in the province of the Cape of Good Hope applied in South West Africa or Namibia.

The historical development and the adoption of Roman-Dutch Law as the common law of South Africa can be traced under three identifiable periods:

1. 1652-1795 – when the Cape of Good Hope was administered by the Dutch East India Company on behalf of the seven provinces of the Netherlands;

2. 1795-1910 – when South Africa was placed under British rule; and
3. 1910 – after the creation of the Union of South Africa.

1652 - 1795

In 1652, when Jan van Riebeeck formally took possession of the Cape of Good Hope, for the Dutch Republic, Roman-Dutch law came to South Africa. Holland was the wealthiest and most powerful province and therefore exercised the predominant influence in the affairs of the Dutch East India Company. The law of Holland, comprising Roman-Dutch law and certain statutes, was introduced by van Riebeeck as the law of the Cape. The effective date was 7 April 1652. In fact, South African courts have held that Dutch statutes actually promulgated in the Cape after 1652 became part of Cape law.

1795 - 1910

The Cape was annexed by the British in 1795 and remained under British rule until 1910 when the Union of South Africa was created. The British era was interrupted briefly from 1803 to January 1806 when the Cape came under the Batavian Republic. The British Government could have replaced the law at the Cape with English law if it wished but it decided to retain Roman-Dutch law which was subsequently developed into a mature legal system.

However, there was a general movement towards English law. Professional legal training was fashioned on English lines. Many of the Cape judges and advocates were English trained. They were therefore familiar with English legal literature and cases and referred to detailed English reports aided by the growing improvement of the textbooks on English law. The Privy Council, like in all the British colonies and dominions, was the final court of appeal. Furthermore, English civil and criminal procedure was introduced and the law of evidence was adopted in its entirety. English commercial and company law took over and new legislation was modelled on English legislation. Specific statutes in the areas of negotiable instruments, companies and insolvency were all based on English law. English became the official language.

As more and more territories came under the British influence, beyond the Cape, Roman-Dutch law was introduced. The law of the Cape at a particular date became the law of Rhodesia, Lesotho, Botswana and Swaziland. As the Republics of Transvaal, Orange Free State and Natal were established, Roman-Dutch law was similarly extended.

The Act of Union of 1910 which brought together the four provinces of the Cape, Natal, Transvaal and Orange Free State consolidated the position of Roman-Dutch Law. It created a Supreme Court with a Court of Appeal – the Appellate Division – with Provisional and Local Divisions. It also became the Appellate Division for Rhodesia. There were still appeals to the Privy Council although these were later abolished.

2.3.2 The common law

2.3.2.1 What is the common law[69]

The dictates of Proclamation 21 of 1919 were to the effect that Roman-Dutch law was to be applied in the territory of South West Africa as the common law. But what is the common law? As used in different contexts or by different people, the term, "common law" is remarkably flexible and correspondingly ambiguous. So are most of the lesser constituent terms associated with it, such as "*stare decisis*" and 'binding' or 'persuasive' precedent. These terms can and do encompass a wide range of possible meanings. Thus, it is entirely possible for societies with equal claim to common law status to manifest widely different judicial attitudes that reflect altogether different approaches to the law.

There are several different definitions of the common law. The term may refer, for instance, to a historic and geographic concept, that is to the totality of the law of England and its former colonies. It sometimes is taken simply to mean any of various substantive and procedural rules and concepts. But it involves more areas than these: it involves also the methodology of the law, with the approaches to problem solving and adjudication that have come to be identified with the common law as a system, and more especially of the courts, on the manner in which they reach decisions and the derivation and articulation of legal rules and principles by judges. It is said that the common law differs from other legal systems in this, its judicial methodology. In this context, then, what is the personality of the common law?

In the common law, the rules of today are to a high degree derived from proceeding decisions of courts in similar past cases. If a judge or any other person wants to determine the answer to a legal question he reviews past judicial decisions and analogises from them to the facts of the current case. Hence this common law methodology of derivation of legal rules is known as reasoning by analogy[70]. The common law is typified by this reference to the collective judicial wisdom of the past as the primary source of rules applicable to the problems of the present. This is also referred to as the doctrine of judicial precedent.

There is, of course, nothing unique about the reverence for the past thus displayed. In all walks of life, people tend, almost automatically, to mould their patterns of behaviour on those followed by others. We justify the rightness of our actions on the grounds simply that others are doing or have done likewise[71]. This tendency is pervasive in the law. It is reflected in the processes of the civil law jurisdictions, where there is more reliance on case (and textual) precedent than is often recognised by common lawyers[72]. It is perhaps also the most significant ingredient of most of the customary law systems of Africa, where acceptable principles of behaviour are often frankly based purely on the standards practised by past generations.

[69] Church, W.L. 1984. "The Common Law and Zambia" in *Law in Zambia.* Nairobi: East African Publishing House.

[70] Cross, R. 1977. *Precedent in English Law.* Oxford: Clarendon Press.

[71] Frank, J. 1959. *Courts of Trial.* Princeton: Princeton Press.

[72] Amos, M. and Walton, F. 1967. *Introduction to French Law.* Oxford: Claredon Press.

What is unique about the common law is the way in which the customs of the past are carried over from past cases into the legal rules of the present. In no other major legal system is there such emphasis on the opinions of the courts themselves as the major source of law. Rather, in most other systems the courts have to share their law-making and interpretive powers more with political institutions and scholarly opinion. They tend to look elsewhere than other judicial opinions to ascertain what law must be applied to a particular case.

Although it is accurate to describe the central method of the common law as a reliance by courts on their own past cases as the primary source of the law, an important problem concerning control over the court arises when judges themselves are allowed to determine the law without constant reference to non-judicial sources of authority. This method potentially embodies the delegation of a very high degree of political and social power to the Judiciary, a power viewed jealously by other centres of authority and often with some suspicion by the rest of the population. In order to meet this concern, the authority of judges, even in common law jurisdiction, is usually stated to be severely constrained: they can look to other past cases for their answers, but they must stay within the confines of these cases unless the Legislature changes the rules involved. That is, they must follow the past cases fairly rigorously and are not allowed to deviate much from them on their own. Their role is said to be only to discover the law of today from past cases and custom, not to create a new law based upon their own personal views. Accordingly, a court may be bound to follow an applicable decision of an equal or superior court in the same jurisdiction, and it must acknowledge as a minimum that it is very much persuaded by such decisions as well as by applicable decisions from sister jurisdictions.

This is the theory, at least, of the method of the common law. It is therefore not difficult to depict it in the broad. Its simplicity is deceptive, however. When one notes that the courts ascertain the law for a case by applying rather rigorously the result of previous cases, he has stated only the barest outline of what really happens in the actual cases. The reality of the common law method is much more subtle, and can be much more flexible in the hands of individual judges.

To begin with, no two cases are completely similar – there are always factual differences between them. Equally, no two cases are absolutely different – there are always factual similarities common to each. Cases are like snow flakes; they are always a bit alike but never congruent. Thus a refined review of the common law method reveals that it cannot be merely the location and application of "an analogous" precedent case. It involves instead a selection from a nearly infinite multitude of relatively analogous past cases. The critical points in the process – just what it is that renders one case analogous to another and what degree of factual similarity is required before one case can be considered influential in the resolution of the other – have always defied precise, abstract description.

It is generally agreed that the process involves a grouping of facts into categories or classes in accordance with their relevance to a particular legal theory deemed applicable to both cases, so that some facts can be retained as significant and others dismissed as inconsequential. Then a comparison can be made of the pertinent facts without regard to the others, so the cases can be equated despite dissimilarities respecting these other facts. But agreement has never been reached respecting the method of choice for the particular legal theory deemed applicable.

In order to discover a legal theory for a case that will give coherence to its facts, recourse traditionally has been had to the issues of the case, the court's holding on these issues and the court's reasoning to support these holdings, the *ratio decidendi,* as it is called. However, this process of verbal refinement has not brought clarity to the method of analogising cases: there is no certain way to perceive a correct statement of the issues, holdings or reasoning of a case. Instead there are as many different perceptions of the legal posture of a case. The process is more complex than it may be portrayed in this verbal refinement. Sometimes, too rarely, a case decision will be so lucidly explained by the judge who wrote it that there will be little room for doubt about his perception of its legal posture although there may still be doubt about the influence of other perceptions of its essence. More often the decision will be silent or ambivalent in its exposition of what the court saw as the significant issues and its holdings and reasoning, and it will be up to other judges and lawyers to supply a comprehensive explanation of the place of the case in the law[73].

Most common law scholars agree that the most important, most influential part of a case is the holding of the court, whether this be ascertained directly by the court's express statements or by implication or interpretation offered later and by others in aid of an unclear case opinion. But even if agreement on this point is assumed, clarity still has not been brought to common law methodology, for there are an almost infinite number of possible holdings in every case. In the first place it is entirely possible for a case, particularly an important or complicated case, to yield plausible holdings based on quite unrelated legal issues.

Faced with the ambiguity of *stare decisis* as a method of deriving legal rules and concerned about the artificiality of most attempts at analogising cases on their facts, some observers have urged that the 'real holding' of a case ought not to be restricted closely either to the facts or the court's reasoning. Rather, it is suggested, each case should be perceived as a single instance of a balancing of significant public policies, so that the holding of each case is that one or a group of these policies is more important than the others present. This approach to case analysis has the merit of forcing practical meaning into the law. However, it hardly helps to simplify the original dilemma of the unavoidable ambiguity and resultant flexibility inherent in *stare decisis*, for it is not possible to formulate hard, precise rules of law out of building blocks acknowledged to reflect the fundamental attitudes and beliefs of a society. If the essence of a case is thus to be but a mirror image of basic public policy choices, then the common law method of case precedent must be doomed to the same eternal doubt and vacillation that surrounds such policies. To ignore the policies is to depart from reality and deny rational purpose in the law. Yet to account for them in the process of applying *stare decisis* is to preclude precision or stability in all areas of current legal importance.

[73] Oliphan, H. 1928. A Return to Stare Decisis' 14 American Bar Journal; excerpted in Auerbach, C.A. et al., *The Legal Process San Francisco.* p.48.

Nor is the complexity of the common law method exhausted by showing that it involves more subtlety than a simplified matching of cases on the basis of relative factual similarity or even a comparison and application of case holdings or judicial reasoning or policy hierarchies derived from past decisions. There are at least two other complicating factors. Firstly, there is the problem of contradiction among precedent cases. Secondly, there is the dilemma posed by the usual rule that even if a case is applicable, it is only persuasive not binding on a later court.

In any jurisdiction that has a large number of previously decided cases on record, there will regularly occur instances where review of precedent reveals some contradictions. The inconsistency may be direct in that opposite versions of the same principle may be articulated in cases seemingly similar on the facts. Such obvious contradiction is rare in a jurisdiction with a monolithic judicial structure, but it does occur everywhere. More pervasive and harder to cope with is the inconsistency that occurs when different principles appear to merge from factually unconnected cases. One could, for example, distil a principle of the absolute sanctity of contractual commitments from a whole series of "frustration-of-purpose" cases and principle calling for responsibility notwithstanding contractual limitation from a series of manufacture's liability cases. Which principle should then be applied? Say in a case involving a badly one-sided lease contract? As applied to this new problem the past cases are seen as conflicting, even though they previously appeared not to relate to one another at all[74]. For nearly every rule of law, for every principle derived from past cases, a skilful lawyer should be able to come up with at least a partial antidote, one with fully acceptable credentials of its own in precedent. Confronted with the choice thus inevitably posed, how should a court select among the various precedents available? And faced with this opportunity of choice by the court, how can the lawyer or scholar predict the status of the law on a difficult question?

The problem becomes greater still when it is recognised, as it is openly in most common law jurisdictions, that past precedent is not actually binding on current courts, but is only "persuasive." Of course, no case is unavoidably binding in any jurisdiction, if a court feels strongly enough about it, for by the "limiting it to its facts" device, all cases can be distinguished. But in most jurisdictions today a court does not need to engage in the dissatisfying, arcane process of making narrow factual distinctions. It may merely decline to follow a past case or even expressly overrule it. One can never be certain in advance that an apparently solid precedent from the past will continue to control the future.

Here again the complexity of the method depends on closer analysis. It is not only that a past case may be ignored completely or openly rejected. There are degrees of persuasiveness; there is a whole range of possible reactions to a previous case. This is particularly so because of the degree of flexibility in the interpretation of past holdings described above. A court might feel positively persuaded by a holding in a previous case that emerged directly, rigorously from the facts of the case, while it might be much less impressed with a more generalised, abstracted principle derived from the same case.

[74] See *Hynes v New York Central R.Co.*, 1921. 131 HE 898, and the comments on it by Justice Cord 020. 1924. *The Growth of the Law.* Yale: New Haven p.99.

Similarly, a court will tend not to be very impressed with a legal principle articulated in an earlier case but not necessarily derived from the facts of that case. Such judicial statements will be labelled *obiter dicta* and may be considered not binding, or even very persuasive. However, in practice the line between *obiter dicta* and a legitimate holding of a case is too often blurred and artificial. The more a legal rule is abstracted from the strict factual foundation permitted by the case, the more like *obiter dicta* that rule becomes, and accordingly the less weight it is likely to receive later. Although it is easy enough to state the process of using a past case as applicable precedent as a function of shifting, relative degrees of its persuasiveness, this only increases the doubt about the actual meaning and significance of any single case.

What then is "the method" of the common law? There is no one precise, correct answer to the query. The system is far too complicated to permit that. All the common law jurisdictions subscribe to the dogma of *stare decisis*. All agree that the legal principles of today are derived inductively from case precedents of the past. But within this framework there is a broad range of possible methods which could actually be used. These vary with the degree to which rigorous factual similarity is required before a past case is allowed status as a precedent at all. It varies as well with the flexibility permitted in determining the holding or *ratio decidendi* of a precedent case, with the degree of conflict perceived between precedent cases, and with the degree to which precedent cases are perceived as persuasive in later ones. Thus, the concept of *stare decisis* in the common law is inherently ambiguous. As a set of rules for dealing with precedent, it reveals no single method at all but a whole range of possible uses of past cases.

For this reason, it is not possible to obtain with any precision a true picture of the common law method at work in any jurisdiction merely by reiterating the standard generalised definitions. These are far too soft, too vague. For anything like an accurate portrayal to be obtained, the history and personality of the courts under inquiry should also be studied. Liberally construed, the common law permits judges almost untrammelled authority to reach any decision they please, requiring only that they rationalise the result in the familiar jargon of precedent. Narrowly construed, it imposes very rigorous constraints on the capacity of current judges to deviate from the literal holdings of past decisions, regardless of their own policy preferences. In order to appreciate which of these or of the many possible common law methods in between is actually practised within a jurisdiction or society, recourse must be had to the cases themselves, to study the attitudes of the courts. In order to predict what method will be used in the future, it is further necessary to know something about the personalities of the judges involved. Abstract models just do not serve adequately to describe the methods of the common law in any of the jurisdictions where the system operates.

The degree to which common law methodology varies from place to place is well demonstrated by the very different nature of the derivation of the law in separate common law jurisdictions. For example, legal methodology in England is widely conceded to be much different than it is in America. The two systems, of course, had a common historical origin and both are clearly common law systems, but the status and practice of *stare decisis* in each is not at all similar. In England, it seems fair to say,[75] adherence to past judicial precedent is quite rigorous. For many years the highest court, the House of Lords, held itself absolutely bound by its previous decisions, on the famous reasoning of Lord Halsbury: "There may be a current of opinion in the profession that such a judgment was erroneous; but what is that occasional interference with what is perhaps abstract justice as compared with the inconvenience – the disastrous inconvenience of having each question subject to being reargued and the dealings of mankind rendered doubtful"[76]. Other appellate courts, including the Court of Appeal, Civil Division, (and to a lesser degree, the Criminal division) have reflected a similar reluctance ever to deviate from their own past decisions[77].

The degree of adherence to strict *stare decisis* by the English courts cannot be measured only by their unwillingness to overrule their own prior cases. It is reflected more pervasively in their reluctance to distinguish prior cases factually, or to find conflict in the precedent available, or to perceive and exploit ambiguity in the reasoning offered by a court in prior cases. A court could call itself bound by its prior decisions but then rarely locate any decision found to be applicable and controlling. The English courts have not done this. The method generally followed, at least for about the last century, has been affirmatively to seek out precedent and apply it, and if no cases are found squarely in point, to apply the nearest ones available. Thus, in England the common law method has developed into a system of rigorous *stare decisis* with relatively little room left to judges to read into the law their own notions of public needs and substantive policies. The law of today is narrowly confined to the results of past decisions, extended forward slowly and only within prescribed limits. New inputs of policy are not left to the courts. They are the province of other branches of government.

This is not to say that the development of English methodology has always been inexorably orthodox, or that there has never been any deviation from a purely abstract, mechanical application of *stare decisis*. English jurists and scholars have long been as aware as anybody else of the ultimate flexibility potentially conceived by a liberal approach to *stare decisis*. There has in recent years been vigorous, renewed interest in the nature of case precedent. The House of Lords has finally repudiated its refusal ever to overrule its former decisions. Today there are signs that "a compromise is being gradually worked out between a slavish subjection to precedent on the one hand and a capricious disregard of consistency on the other hand. There seems to be less reluctance than formerly in superior courts either to overrule previous, and sometimes old, precedents, or else to sterilise them by the semi-fictions of 'distinguishing' them on tenuous grounds of fact or law or by recourse to the doctrine of *incuria*."[78] Thus, the doctrine of precendent in English law remains open to continuing challenge and it appears that cases will be followed less

[75] Wasserstrom, R.A. 1961. *The Judical Decision*. Stanford: Stanford University Press.

[76] *London Streets Tramway Company v London Country Council*. 1898. A.C. 375.

[77] See Young v Bristol Aeroplane Co. 1944. K.B. 718.

[78] Allen, C.K. 1969. *Law in the Making*. Oxford: Clarendon Press.

strictly in the future than previously. Never-the-less the doctrine maintains much of its orthodox force in England. There is still relatively little policy discretion accorded to individual courts and judges. A reading of today's English cases reveals that in the overwhelming majority of them the decision is explained primarily on the application of that precedent located by the judges which is nearest not so much in its policy implications as in its orthodox substantive and factual context.

The status of *stare decisis* is considerably different in American law. (There are of course many differences as well among the many different American jurisdictions.) Precedent is still cited with great regularity by all the courts, but there is also a substantial element of the judges' notions of public policy present in many cases, particularly those deemed by the courts to be important cases. Relative to their English counterparts, American judges are very much more explicitly concerned with the practical consequences of a decision and whether these will accord with policy needs than with the logical consistency between a case and past precedent.

There are many reasons, both historical and practical, for the divergence of American legal methodology from its English parent. In part, an early distrust of precedent may have been precipitated precisely because most of the cases available came from England, a source in emotional disfavour after the independence war. In part also, American attitudes towards past cases have been conditioned by the rapidity and magnitude of change and the drive for economic and social development that characterised the new country. In addition to the factors of history, the structural arrangement of America's court system also has had a clear impact on perceptions of *stare decisis.* Because of its federalism, the United States does not have a monolithic court structure. In all the traditional areas of substantive common law there have been as many courts of last resorts as there are States, all of these State Court cases are published – there are tens of thousands of volumes of them. This means that whenever a matter is first broached in one State, there is likely to be a wealth of potentially applicable precedent from other States precedent which is in no sense binding on the first State's courts and which is more often than not in a state of disarray with several States adopting various positions on any given legal issue. The rules usually prescribed for following the doctrine of *stare decisis* do not work very well where most of the decisions available are not binding and may be in hopeless conflict with one another. It is not a very persuasive argument – though it is tried often enough – to offer a judge that he should follow a particular rule just because, say, fifteen out of twenty-five other States have followed it, while ten have chosen a different result.

Strict reference to past cases satisfies neither national philosophy nor the demands of the federal-state judicial system in America. The result is that the doctrine of precedent there is considerably more relaxed than in England. None of the courts considers itself bound by its own cases. At least with respect to the United States Supreme Court, it is frankly conceded that the result in any given case depends on the public policy of the judge far more than on any past decisions and that the legal philosophy of the court varies according to the personality of the justices on it at the moment. Even when precedent is cited it sometimes seems to be more as a rationalization of a policy result independently conceived than as the real reason for the decision in a case. There is thus considerable scepticism over the real role of *stare decisis*. Precedent is not irrelevant – far from it. Some courts, particularly several of the State courts that have developed a tradition of judicial caution will rely on the recitation of precedent as the source of all their legal conclusions fully as much as any English bench, and nearly all the courts, state and federal, rely heavily on precedent in routine, well settled areas of the law.

However, in cases of social importance or where relatively novel issues are raised, many American courts tend explicitly to consider explanations for their conclusions that are not based on precedent decisions. More precisely, they examine in depth the public policies deemed applicable to such cases, and often justify the legal result reached in terms of policy. Lawyers arguing before the courts in such cases accordingly attempt to show both that the result they contend for is technically permissible under the current state of the law, that is, that precedent supports it and that it is desirable from the viewpoint of public policy. The law as a result is "more plastic, more malleable, the moulds less definitively cast, the bounds of right and wrong less pre-ordained and constant, than most of us without the aid of some such analysis, have been accustomed to believe."[79] To be sure, there is in America, as in England, a considerable variation among courts and judges over the methods each uses to reach decisions. On the whole, however, the courts there are much more inclined to decide on the basis of policy than the English courts. America remains a common law jurisdiction and it follows a doctrine of case precedent. But that doctrine is not the same one adhered to in England. The terminology used in both places is often comparable, the method of the law is not. In comparison of the method of the law in these two societies, the great flexibility possible within the framework of 'common law methodology' stands revealed: the range of possible choice is very considerable indeed.

2.3.2.2 Justifications for the common law method

Judges and other commentators have ascribed a number of benefits to the doctrine of precedent in the common law. The lists offered usually include at least some of the following advantages, each of which will be discussed separately below: (a) adherence to *stare decisis* promotes legal certainty; (b) it serves as a desirable check on the power and perhaps the prejudices of judges; (c) it assures equality for all before the law; (d) it increases the efficiency of justice; (e) it serves as a vehicle for preserving the accumulated wisdom of the past; and (f) it is logically, even aesthetically pleasing. None of these claimed attributes are above controversy or without their detractors, but there does seem, on balance, to be merit in each of the claims.

2.3.2.3 Certainty

Certainty – or perhaps better predictability – is assumed as a desirable goal for any legal system[80]. There are several reasons for the near unanimity on this point.

[79] Cardozo, B.N. 1921. *The Nature of Judicial Process*. Yale: New Haven.

[80] Daniëls, E. 1964. *Common Law in West Africa*. London: Butterworths.

Firstly, and most importantly, a legal system which does not attain predictability cannot hope to accomplish the goal of affecting the behaviour of those to whom it applies. No system has ever been completely successful in reaching this goal, and none ever will be, but all systems strive in this direction. If the law, however, is to influence behaviour, those involved must be able to predict the legal consequences of their conduct. To the degree that law is capricious and unpredictable, the people will per force be unable to mould their actions in accordance with its design. Irrational and ignorant men may act without regard to legal constraints and rewards in any event, but others will seek to maximize their position under the law – if only they know with fair certainty what the law is. Thus, in order to reach these people, the law must be comprehensible and predictable enough to be understood. In this way, the law is said to help generate a stable, ordered society, providing the only really viable environment for cooperation, initiative and progress[81].

Another justification for the need for certainty in the law concerns the factor of reliance on the part of those who try to conform their behaviour to the law's mandates. When the law changes, unless such change itself has been predictable, those who have relied on its continuity may find themselves actually disadvantaged by their very faithfulness. This is hardly defensible; it is certainly self-defeating for any system of law seeking respect from the people it governs. The strength of the point is particularly felt in the area of criminal law, where it is widely reflected in the principle that no man should be convicted for a crime which is not clearly defined in the law. It is applicable as well, though, to civil law generally and explains the revulsion to *ex post facto* laws and retroactive case decisions departing from past precedent.

A final justification sometimes offered in support of legal predictability is based purely on deterministic grounds[82]. Regardless of the moral rectitude of the position, it is said, it is in fact a need common to nearly everyone to have a high measure of security in his or her surroundings. Laws that are ambiguous and unpredictable are not subject to our understanding and can only contribute to insecurity. As we all share an aversion to the unknown, a legal system which does not strive for, and at least partially achieves certainty runs counter to the basic wants of the human personality and cannot be counted as a meritorious system. It is accordingly written in our nature that every legal system will strive for predictability (and in fact, all do) and that one critical measure of the success of any system must be the extent to which legal certainty is realised in practice.

While there is general agreement on the universal need for predictability in the law, however, there is considerable controversy over the degree to which this can be attained under the doctrine of *stare decisis*, even as rigorously applied. In the first place, a system committed to *stare decisis* affords no basis for reaching a predictable conclusion in any case which is novel and for which there is no precedent squarely applicable. One might answer to this point that in such an instance the system can merely adopt another methodology than the obviously inappropriate doctrine of precedent, and that in any event, after the passage of centuries, the common

[81] Trubeck, D.M. 1972. "Max Weber on Law and the Rise of Capitalism." Wisconsin Law Review 720.

[82] See Wasserstrom, R.A. (supra).

law had developed precedent cases for nearly every conceivable contingency, so that the problem may rarely occur. The problem is not so easily dispensed with, however. Unfortunately the momentum of the common law commitment to *stare decisis* seems inevitably to carry over into all cases, novel or standard, so that even where there really is no precedent directly applicable, a selection is nonetheless made from various near analogies. As a practical matter is often almost impossible to predict which analogy will be selected – human logic refuses to conform to universal standards in such cases. Hence *stare decisis* does in truth often fail to help reduce legal uncertainty in novel cases. Nor is it sufficient to suggest that by now novel cases are rare. This position ignores the truism that the uniqueness of a case is merely a matter of degree – all cases are different in at least some respect from the past. The question in every instance is how great their difference is, and the doctrine of *stare decisis* has never been able to develop a precise, predictable guide to determine how great this must be in order to permit use of a precedent case in a current case. Although the doctrine imparts sufficient legal certainty to work well in areas where the law is simple and well settled, particularly in cases before the lower courts where appeal is unlikely, it fails to achieve the goal of predictability in the very cases which are of the greatest current social concern.

The consequences of this are especially noticeable in a jurisdiction such as the United States where as noted above, there are so many "persuasive" cases now in the reports that no one can possibly digest more than a tiny fraction of them and anyone with a little imagination and diligence should with luck find at least one to support his position, whatever that may be. The problem is made still more serious because of the failure of the doctrine of precedent ever to define precisely just what a holding of a prior case really is or how broadly or narrowly that holding should be construed in order to be regarded as binding or persuasive.

The result of this is that in a common law jurisdiction only fools pretend to know the law with certainty from their own memory. Wise lawyers and judges always look up the answer to a legal question in the library before they venture their opinion; and that opinion, at least in any case of importance or difficulty is expressed only in terms of possibilities or probabilities, never as a concrete, certain answer. Even for the legal experts, the common law fails to yield a high measure of predictability in such cases. For the rest of the population, especially that part of it that cannot afford to hire expertise to explain the law, predictability is largely illusory. The average person has only the vaguest of the rules of law; and he is considerably less knowledgeable about rules derived from cases than those derived from statutes and other sources.

This is not to suggest as some very strongly have, that *stare decisis* actively promotes uncertainty. To oblige a court to look backwards to a known source of law, that is to previous cases, in order to formulate its opinion in a present case does impose some at least impartially discernible limits on the rules that the court will come up with. Particularly in relatively routine cases, *stare decisis* does afford a fair measure of legal predictability, as any practising lawyer knows. What is suggested, however, is that a rigid adherence to *stare decisis* does not assure nearly the degree of certainty sometimes claimed for it. In important cases and in cases involving significant new circumstances, it imparts very little predictability indeed, and any advantages of certainty it might attain in many easier cases rarely filters down to non-lawyers anyway.

2.3.2.4 Restraint on judicial power

Second only to its claimed connection with predictability, the common law doctrine of precedent is defended as a desirable control on the powers, and sometimes the biases of individual judges. This position has been criticized on the grounds that all the doctrine does is to perpetuate the powers and biases of former judges, but even this much does act as a constraint on the caprice of contemporary courts and does compel the courts to articulate formal and objective grounds for their decisions. If a judge did not need to demonstrate some consistency between his decisions and those of other judges beyond his control, all manner of excess and abuse of power would be possible, and justice too often would not seem to be done. Compliance with precedent does correct these evils, regardless whether the precedent itself once was tainted.

A more serious criticism of the position is that it overstates the degree of constraint imposed on the courts. Because of the nature of the doctrine of precedent, as noted above, it may be possible for a court to justify any of several different, even contradictory decisions in a case; on the basis of *stare decisis*. To the extent that this is so, the doctrine does not operate as a very effective control over judges. This point, again, is particularly telling where important or novel cases are involved because in such instances *stare decisis* fails to yield precisely predictable results.

Perhaps the most serious criticism of *stare decisis* as a measure of controlling judges is the suggestion that in some instances it may actually facilitate arbitrary decisions. This is because the doctrine permits a court to defend a judgment solely in terms of past precedent – no other justification or explanation need be offered. Since precedent, in skilful hands can be used to support so many different conclusions, this means that a court can submit an opinion which artfully conceals the real reason behind it (or the fact that there are no reasons behind it). Citation of precedent may only be a rationalisation, not the actual basis of a decision, but there will be no way to detect this and no sure way to attack the decision as 'incorrect' given the flexibility of precedent. Thus the doctrine may provide sophisticated camouflage to obscure an exercise of uncontrolled judicial power and present it in respectable form. Where *stare decisis* is not recognised as a completely satisfactory basis for judicial decisions, it is necessary for the courts to augment their citation of the past with what must appear to be an objective analysis of the needs of society in the present. Where this is required, the result is probably a greater, not lesser degree of control over judicial powers. It involves an open admission that the courts do have the power to consider public policy as they see it in their decisions. But they have this power anyway in good measure, and this at least forces them to expose for public review their perception of public needs. If the explanation thus offered for the public needs fails to persuade others of their validity or standing in the hierarchy of policy goals, there are ample mechanisms available for bringing the courts back into line.

Some form of control over the arbitrary exercise of power by judges is clearly necessary if what nearly all regard as the aims of justice are to be secured and if an appearance of fairness is to be maintained. The doctrine of precedent provides a measure of such formal control, particularly in routine cases. As with respect to its role in achieving legal certainty however, the doctrine's part in providing effective constraints in other cases is less clear. *Stare decisis* adds little to and it may even detract from the practical control over judges that would exist if courts felt compelled to justify their decisions on grounds of public policy as well as on grounds of prior cases.

2.3.2.5 Equality

Another justification for the doctrine of precedent is that it helps to achieve equality of treatment for all litigants. If there were no obligation on the part of the courts to conform their decisions to those reached in other cases, there would be no guarantee that the same facts and issues would not be found to yield different results for different parties. It is generally conceded that this would be intolerable, both because it would violate one of the common laws and democracy's fundamental postulates and more practically, because it would undermine respect for the law and thus reduce its effectiveness. It is sometimes argued that this is insufficient cause for sustaining the force of iniquitous, badly considered precedents. It might further be charged that the doctrine of precedent is not a very effective device for ensuring equal treatment before the law because, as noted, a determined judge in a non-routine case may reach precisely the result he pleases while still nominally satisfying the requirements of *stare decisis*. Nevertheless the doctrine does have some usefulness in promoting equality and thus in enhancing respect for the law. There are many cases in which the losing part will better accept the decision if he appreciates he lost mostly because others similarly situated have lost in the past. At least he will understand that he has not been singled out, either arbitrarily or accidentally for adverse treatment, and for many this is a comforting realisation.

2.3.2.6 Efficiency

It is also argued that adherence to *stare decisis* serves as an efficient method of streamlining litigation and developing orderly, rational progress in the law. At first blush, this strikes some as a point of minor significance, but on fuller reflection it contains important connotations. One aspect of the argument is that lawyers and judges tend to favour *stare decisis* because it preserves their unique and exalted status in society. *Stare decisis* enshrines the myriad rules and decisions of the past and conduces to a highly sophisticated, refined methodology. Neither the rules, nor still less the mysteries of the processes involved are ever likely to be understood by those not initiated through an artificially complex and comprehensive education in the law. Hence, the profession is able to secure for itself a nice monopoly as unavoidable middlemen in the settlement of disputes, even to justify legislation disqualifying others from paid involvement to the grudging envy of other trade unions[83]. The observation is, it is to be hoped, overly cynical and it is more an explanation of an historical cause of the doctrine of precedent than a reason for justifying its continuance. However, it does help to make plausible the tenacity which characterises many lawyers' devotion to the doctrine, even where the precedent involved may have derived from a wholly different society in a time long past.

Stare decisis, however, has a much more subtle and important role than this to play in the contribution to efficiency in the law. When perceived in the light of the full degree of judicial flexibility it tolerates, it is seen to play a critical part in the smooth development and growth of law. This is because the doctrine is uniquely able to allocate and utilise the widely varying talents of different individual judges.

A rather high proportion of judges, as with lawyers, generally, lacks either the time or the inclination, or both, to analyse every issue in every case in its full depth in order to reach a decision that maximally balances the infinitely competing policy considerations always present. This is after all, a forbidding challenge, one undertaken lightly only by the impetuous. Once entered, the realm of public policy surrounds the conscientious servant of truth with frustrating, shifting complexibility, assuring that at best he will have to be content with reconciling, contending forces and beliefs into a compromised working solution whose only claim to respect will be that it takes account of as many factors as objectively as possible. The challenge is especially hard in a society, which, like most common law countries, frowns on the easy answers provided by ideological orthodoxy.

It is far easier to look up the answer in precedent than it is to try to reason out all the variables anew. A judge, who has to decide several cases a day, even several a week, really has no choice in the matter: no man has the ability to reason out cases and problems in-depth so quickly. Under the doctrine of precedent, a judge does not have to reason out each case if he does not want to or is unable to for lack of time. He can simply locate a previous case on approximately the same subject – or better still, he can ask the lawyers involved to present him with several cases they think are analogous – and then simply apply it without further ado. A reading of the case reports in any common law jurisdiction reveals that this is precisely what occurs in the overwhelming majority of the cases. It enables judges to reach a perfectly respectable decision with a minimum of time and effort. In these cases precedent is used not to obscure analysis based on other factors; it is used as a substitute for such analysis. This use of precedent is especially noticeable, and efficient, in the lower courts, where caseloads are very heavy but usually consist of a recurrence of relatively simple legal issues, easily disposed of by quick reference to precedent. It is thus perhaps no accident that the strength of *stare decisis* is greatly increased with respect to lower courts; they are clearly "bound" by higher court decisions.

Such use of the doctrine of *stare decisis* would be merely trite and ultimately indefensible if this were all the judicial input ever contemplated by the common law method. However, the flexibility of the method also permits a much different role for judges who are so inclined. A judge who, having analysed a problem thoroughly on

[83] See Frank, J. 1959. Courts on Trial (supra).

the basis of his own ideas, finds himself faced with solutions seemingly offered by past precedent that to him are disagreeable has several choices open to him. He can merely select precedent that supports his position, even though there may be other and opposite cases that seem closer. He can openly overrule or criticise precedent he regards as adverse to justice. He can also base all or part of his decision on policy in lieu of precedent. Any of these options will satisfy his perceived policy demands. More significantly though, his decision will then itself become part of "past precedent" available for use in the future. To the extent that his decision has departed from other such precedent, it will be an unsettling element in the operation of *stare decisis*. This will automatically introduce still more flexibility, more room for future manoeuvre in the legal area concerned. It will serve notice on all judges and lawyers who become involved in that area that there is at least one critic, who is entitled to respect by the legal system, that feels that the older precedent can be improved upon.

Any judge who does deviate from the apparent source of precedent, and especially one who challenges it openly, can thus focus the attention of the law on what seems to him to be areas in need of change; this area of law can then return to quiescence until some other future critic re-opens it to further policy scrutiny. If a critical judge's reasons are not persuasive in the context of the policy perceptions of other judges, and of society as a whole, his decision will remain isolated, dwindling in importance as it becomes obscured by time.

Common law methodology can thus incorporate strong, wilful judges, who demand that their notions of justice receive consideration, as well as more passive judges, who tend to follow the past rather than to initiate and impose changes. In times of social stress, when judicial strength is likely to be a critical need, judges will be apt to look especially searchingly at fundamental policies and to agitate for substantial changes in the law; in more placid times the same method may yield only minor adjustments and incremental changes in the law. In this way the methodology can utilise the abilities of both kinds of judges and accommodate itself to different degrees of social upheaval, with marvellous efficiency. It allows the majority of judges to reach simple decisions quickly and consistently. At the same time it permits those with the time capacity and confidence to suggest changes and improvements for the betterment of all, providing a smooth mechanism for institutionalising prophetic innovations and for adroitly ignoring those that are out of step with the march of time.

This ability to utilise the ideas and personalities of all or at least nearly all judges is one of the greatest strengths of the common law. It depends on the one hand on a foundation rooted in *stare decisis*, for without this no way is left for the majority of judges to legitimise their decisions. It also depends however, on a recognition that despite the formal doctrines of precedent, law exists to achieve social, economic and political purposes, and to serve those purposes effectively, to achieve justice, there must be an opportunity to open past and existing rules to continued challenge and review. The doctrine of *stare decisis* permits a very efficient allocation of judicial talent and energy. Pursued too rigorously, it leads to sterility; but coupled with an opportunity for constructive criticism and change, it conduces to an effective yet progressive system of law.

2.3.2.7 Preservation of past wisdom

Another virtue claimed for the method of the common law is that it most effectively preserves the accumulated social wisdom of past generations for application to current problems. This of course, represents the very essence of the justification for relying on past precedents in any legal system; but the common law method is said to be unique in its ability to build on lessons of the past. This is because of the way the common law utilises the insights and practical experience of judges, and not the macro-constructs of academic or ideological theorists, to provide suggestions for current problem resolution. Moreover, because the judges can express their opinions only in actual cases, where the specific social consequences of one judgment or another and the attitudes and beliefs of society are hard to ignore, their decisions should reasonably and faithfully reflect the customs and practices of society as a whole. As compared with other systems, the common law makes use of inputs of far more legal experts in the form of many individual judges called upon to contribute to the development of the law and affords for more decision-making power to widely dispersed and ideologically, politically and geographically decentralised institutions peculiarly responsive to local feelings and opinions. The result is that what comes out in a common law case opinion is not a social theory, divorced from the practical constraints of the day and the aspirations of the people. The process is deliberately conditioned to embody both of these ingredients and thus to ensure that the maximum value will be extracted from the experience of the times, to be accumulated into an ever growing, ever more broadly based legal system.

This process of building on the experience of the past need not be expressly articulated by the judges. In a case of first impression, the court may favour one side for stated or unstated policy reasons. As other courts consider the same kind of problem they also may simply announce a decision, based mostly on a largely unconscious application of current attitudes and policies. Then, as the amount and authority of precedent grows on an issue, future courts will be constrained to reach a like decision, based not only on their own opinion but on their deference to the unexpressed reasoning of the prior decisions.

It may be argued that this process proceeds perfectly well without any need for conscious expression of policy goals at any point along its line of progression, that the strength of precedent lies more in the results of past cases and their number than on the persuasiveness of their policy reasoning. Some even claim that this is the genius of the common law, this ability to give coherent voice to policy aspirations left largely unarticulated by decisions past. It should indeed be recognised that this is one of the strengths of the common law, that it does enable present jurists to distill the best from past experience without a requirement of rigorous rationalisation or conformity to abstraction, so that the law can build on experience as well as theories. At the same time, however, it must also be emphasised that more often progress of the law will be enhanced if the policy foundations for case decisions are explicitly articulated, so that they can be challenged, reconsidered and then re-applied to future cases. The common law relies much on the unspoken wisdom of prior experience. The law is more difficult to develop, but it reflects the social aspirations of society far more faithfully if the policy basis of judicial decisions is more often frankly set forth. Particularly in cases of legal moment and social importance, the growth of the law demands full open discussion of the critical policy issues involved.

2.3.2.8 Logical consistency

A final justification for *stare decisis* that sometimes is offered is that it helps impart logical order into a legal system. Rigid adherence to precedent enables relatively exact, "correct" answers to be given for legal questions at least for the questions that have arisen before. A good part of the value of such consistency, of course, lies in the certainty and legal predictability it engenders, as noted above. But there are some observers who find positive value in the very existence of a logical system even as considered purely in the abstract and without any particular reference to more practical benefits that may also be involved. Such a defence of the doctrine of precedent, based as it is wholly upon considerations of form, almost of aesthetic appreciation, has drawn the fire of critics who look more for substance in their search for the best method of case adjudication. However, it should be recognised that an attraction for mere formal unity and consistency is itself a practical value for most people, including jurists. It may be an irrational goal, in so far it is unrelated to pragmatic ends, but it is never-the-less a desired attribute of the law in the eyes of most lawyers. Hence, it is probably a mistake to discount the significance of the drive towards logical consistency in the law. For many judges it is a major, even the primary, reason behind the decision given in a case and even if at bottom, ironically, it may not itself be logically defensible as a goal of the law. At the same time it is well to recall that mere legal consistency, remorsely pursued, leads to stagnation. If it is short-sighted to ignore the importance of abstract logic in the law, it is at least as dangerous to ignore the other practical policy needs that face every legal system, most of which turn out to be incompatible with formal consistency. Placed in perspective the latter is but one of many factors that should define the application of the doctrine of *stare decisis*, and a not very critical one at that.

2.4 Extracts

Du Plessis, L. M.

An introduction to law (1999)

South African law in historical and comparative perspective

Introduction

It is often claimed that South African law is Roman-Dutch law. What this really means is that the law in force in South Africa (and applied by the courts, for example) has as its basis *Roman-Dutch common law*.

Literally "common" law means: "the law common to a particular geographical region and/or group of people". This term is usually used to refer to the law of a whole country or a large region as opposed to the narrower, area-specific laws (and customs) of, for example, a local community or a smaller group. The concept of "Roman-Dutch law" has many meanings which include, among others, the law of the province of Holland (in the Netherlands) during roughly the eighteenth and nineteenth centuries. According to some writers[84] (and the South African Appeal Court[85]) it is this law of *the province of Holland* (in a narrow, almost literal sense) which, as the law of the original colonial settlers, has (since the arrival of Jan van Riebeeck at the Cape) formed the basis of contemporary South African law. In terms of this view, the laws of the other Dutch provinces of this period do not carry the same weight in South Africa as those of Holland.

Other writers, however, claim that it is the law of the whole of the Netherlands or even a European *ius commune* based on Roman law which was "exported" to South Africa[86]. In this view, the law of the province of Holland is a common law linked to a narrower region and group of people and is to be distinguished from the *ius commune* (which also literally means "common law") of the greater Netherlands or indeed the whole of Western Europe. In any event, writers both inside and outside of Holland continually consulted one another. Many of the best known Roman-Dutch (or "old") writers whose works are frequently referred to by the South African courts as "Roman-Dutch authorities" were in fact from areas outside of Holland – for example, Utrecht, Groningen, Friesland and the Southern Netherlands (or present-day Belgium). Even French, German and Spanish writers are sometimes quoted as "common law authorities".

Of the two approaches described above, the latter, broader view seems the more correct and is subscribed to by most modern legal historians in South Africa.

Whether Roman-Dutch law is understood in a narrow or a broad sense, however, about one thing there is unanimity: *that it is based on Roman law*. The historical roots of South African law thus lie in the legal system of the ancient Roman Empire. Whereas the ancient Greeks are famous particularly for their contributions to philosophy, it is the legal culture of Rome – probably the greatest heritage of the Romans – that is shared to a greater or lesser extent by many modern (especially Western Europe) which means that the history of the South African legal system is thus inseparable from the history of law in Europe.

It is actually not entirely correct to speak of a South African common law in the literal sense of the word, seeing that the "official" law of the whole of South Africa has already been uniform for a very long time and it is thus not usually necessary to distinguish (South African) common law from other narrower, regional and group-orientated legal forms. The term "common law" has, however, become accepted in South African legal terminology to refer primarily to Roman-Dutch law as it was originally transferred to South Africa and adapted and extended through the years in the case-law (that is: the law laid down by the courts[87]), but also through custom. "Common law" refers more specifically to this ("original") historical law as clearly distinguished from (and even in opposition to) other forms of law

[84] Van Zyl and Van der Vyver. 1982. *Inleiding tot die Regswetenskap*. 2nd edition. Durban: Butterworths.

[85] In *Du Plessis v Strauss*. 1988. 2 SA 105 (A) and *Bank of Lisbon and South Africa Ltd v De Ornelas* 1988 3 SA 580 (A).

[86] Van Zyl. 1979. *Geskiedenis van die Romeins-Hollandse Reg*. Durban: Butterworths. and Visser "Daedalus in the Supreme Court – the Common Law Today" 1986 *THRHR*.

[87] See **Chapter 6.3.3**.

currently in force in South Africa, especially *statute law* (that is to say the law laid down by contemporary or relatively recent official legislators)[88].

The law which developed casuistically (that is to say "case by case") in the courts of England is also known as "common law", and forms the basis of contemporary Anglo-American law. *Common law* in this sense, however, refers neither to Roman-Dutch common law in South Africa nor to the historical *ius commune* of Western Europe. Whereas the latter two systems are based on Roman law, English *common law* was comparatively little influenced by Roman law. In addition to *common law,* the *law of equity* is also an important source of English law.

The fact that South African common law is not English common law does of course not mean that South African law was not influenced by English law; in fact it is actually remarkable that English law did not replace Roman-Dutch law entirely as the common law of South Africa after the last British occupation of the Cape (in 1806) and the expansion of Britain's colonial power in South Africa. All this needs to be understood in the light of a particular course of historical events.

In this chapter the history of (particularly "official") South African law is reviewed briefly. First its Roman origins will be looked at and then the fate of Roman law (along with traditional, local legal systems) in Europe will be traced in order to place the origin and development of Roman-Dutch law in perspective. After that the course of Roman-Dutch law in South Africa will be considered as well as the extent of the influence of English law.

Finally, there is a brief account of the development of a distinctively South African law and legal culture, the relationship between official South African law and the more regionally and group-orientated (traditional) legal systems as well as the distinctive nature of South Africa law in comparison with other legal systems in the world.

The historical overview of the law in this chapter concentrates on the *external history* of South African common law (and the South African legal system that developed from it); in other words the focus is primarily on historical facts and events of legal interest. Because South African law depends to such a large extent on a common law developed in the course of history, jurists often have to research the historical origin, growth and development of particular legal rules and legal notions in order to grasp them fully and correctly in their contemporary context. A scientific (or scholarly) method known as *the historical method* is adopted for this purpose. This method focuses on more than just external historical events of legal significance; it also takes account of the *content* or the *internal* historical growth of the law and particular legal notions. The external history of the law, however, forms the framework within which its (more specialized) internal history takes shape. It is thus sufficient for a historical *introduction* to South African law to content itself with but a version of the external history of law.

2. Roman Legal History

2.1 A short history of the Roman Empire

The legal history of a society to a large extent reflects developments within that society – especially at a socio-political level. This is why the establishment and development of

[88] See also **Chapter 6.3** and especially 6.3.1.

Roman law (on Roman soil, so to speak) may best be understood against the background of the establishment, growth and decline of the Roman Empire.

2.1.1 The Monarchy (753-509 BC)

The city of Rome is situated a few kilometres from the mouth of the Tiber River on the west coast of the Italian peninsula. According to tradition[89] it was established by Romulus of *Alba Longa* in the year 753 BC.

Originally the Roman people were ruled by a king or *rex*. The first four kings were Romans but after that they came from among the Etruscans, a powerful tribe which lived to the north of Rome. The Etruscan kings, however, abused their power and in 509 BC the last of them, Tarquinus Superbus, was expelled from Rome and the Etruscans themselves defeated in the battles that followed. After this, the idea of a sole ruler was unacceptable to the Romans.

2.1.2 The Republic (509-27 BC)

Rome was now a republic, ruled by the *senatus*, a council of elder statesmen. Executive power was in the hands of the *consules*, of which there always had to be two. Theoretically power in the last resort was vested in the *comita centuriata*, an assembly of the higher class or patricians.

The early Republic was characterized by a class struggle between the patricians and the lower class, the plebeians. This struggle ended only in 287 BC[90], when the plebeians' assembly also acquired legislative powers. The plebeians had earlier acquired other concessions such as a codification of the law[91] and the appointment of *tribunes* who had to attend to their interests.

After the Romans defeated the Etruscans, they gradually incorporated the territories of the other tribes around them and by 275 BC they were the masters of the whole of the Italian peninsula. After this they gradually extended their power over Sicily, Greece, North Africa and Spain. The two battles against Carthage[92], an empire situated in present-day Tunisia in North Africa, were particularly long and bloody. By the year 246 BC Hannibal, the legendary Carthaginian commander, had occupied Northern Italy and inflicted a crushing defeat on the Romans at Cannae.

After the Carthaginians were finally defeated, the last two centuries of the Republic were characterized by unrest and civil war. Cities were over-populated and most agricultural land was in the hands of wealthy landowners. In 133 and 123 BC two *tribunes*, the Gracchi brothers, attempted (among other things) to redistribute land in Italy. But both of them were killed by conservative opponents in the political unrest that followed. Yet the Gracchi brothers had made the people more politically conscious than ever before. Leaders realized increasingly that they could acquire political influence with the help of popular support.

[89] Recorded in the *Aeneid* of Virgil, an epic written in the time of Emperor Augustus.

[90] With the *Lex Hortensia*.

[91] See 2.2.2.

[92] 264-241 BC and 218-201 BC.

In 90-88 BC Roman subjects in Italy rebelled. The war which followed[93] was ended only once virtually all the inhabitants of the Italian peninsula were given citizenship. Shortly after this, in 88 BC, a civil war broke out. While the consul, Sulla, was in the East fighting against the Greek king, Mithridates, a faction (*populares*) under Marius took over control of Rome. On his return in 83 BC Sulla had to fight to regain power.

After this the writing was on the wall for the Republic. Ambitious people acquired influence by calling upon popular support and recruiting followers while at the same time being engaged as generals in the expansion of the empire.

In 60 BC three of these leaders, Julius Caesar, Crassus and Pompey, formed the first triumvirate (an informal three-man partnership) when they could not agree who should hold sole power. Crassus was killed in 53 BC during a campaign against the Parthians and Pompey took over power in Rome while Caesar was engaged in a campaign in Gaul. Another civil war broke out once Caesar returned to Italy and crossed the Rubicon River; he then drove Pompey out of Italy.

But Caesar, now the undisputed sole ruler, was murdered in 44 BC by members of the senate. His opponents exploited the Romans' fear of a sole ruler and formed a conspiracy against him.

After Caesar's murder there was once again civil war. This was ended in 43 BC when a second triumvirate was formed by Marcus Antonius (Caesar's former adjutant), Octavius (Caesar's grandnephew) and Lepidus (a figure of less importance). By 33 BC Octavius had managed to get rid of Lepidus and challenged Antonius. Antonius's armies were defeated in 31 BC at Actium and Octavius become the sole ruler.

2.1.3 The Principate (27 BC – 284 AD)

By 27 BC Octavius appeared to have restored the old Constitution of the Republic but was in fact now the sole ruler over the empire. In particular he created the impression that he was actually controlling the empire in collaboration with the senate, which he supposedly "restored to honour". He changed his title to *Imperator Caesar Augustus,* the title by which he would be known from then on. He and his successors would play the role of *princeps* or "first citizen" but they were in fact sole rulers. From this time on the Roman Empire was known as the Principate.

The early Principate was characterized by peace and prosperity – the so-called *Pax Romana*. The Empire continued to expand and cultural activities in particular flourished. Succession, however, was a problem and in 69 AD there was once again civil war when no fewer than three people became emperors and were then murdered. The great historian Tacitus noted that people began to realise that emperors could also be made in places other than Rome!

Order was, however, restored and the next emperor of importance was Hadrian (117-138 AD). During his rule the Roman Empire was at its greatest and peace widespread. The Empire did not, however, expand any further and from this point the story of Rome becomes that of an empire whose borders shrank continuously, mainly because of the aggression of the Germanic tribes from the northern reaches of the European continent.

[93] The so-called *Bellum Socii*.

The (apparent) collaboration between the emperor and the senate, referred to as the diarchy, also began to cause more and more problems. The years 235-284 AD were once again characterized by anarchy as battles raged between rival claimants to the throne. In 284 AD, however, Diocletian came into power and abandoned all pretence as to the nature of his authority. From now on the emperor was an absolute ruler or *dominus*.

2.1.4 The Dominate (284 AD and beyond)

From the beginning of the period known as the Dominate the Empire was characterized by decline in the political, economic and social fields. In the west particularly the Germanic tribes, the so-called barbarians, gradually began to conquer Roman territories. The Empire's centre of gravity shifted to the east and Constantine (285-337 AD), the first Christian emperor, built Constantinople as an alternative capital city in what is today Turkey.

In 395 AD the Empire was divided into two parts for administrative purposes, with each empire having its own emperor. The barbarians (Goths, Franks, Teutons and others) began to conquer the western provinces of the Empire. In 476 AD the last emperor of the Western Empire, Romulus Augustulus, was deposed by Odoacer, thus bringing to an end the Western Roman Empire.

The Eastern Roman Empire survived until 1453 AD when Constantinople was conquered by the Turks. An important figure here is Justinian, who was Emperor from 527 to 565 AD. It is largely due to him that Roman law was preserved for humanity.

2.2 Roman law

2.2.1 Introduction

Ancient Roman law, called *ius civile*, initially took the form of unwritten customary law[94]. In other words, it was based on the customs of the ancestors (or *mores maiorum*). From these there developed laws which had to meet the needs of an ever growing Roman Empire.

Originally the administration of justice was in the hands of the patricians and dispensed by the high priest. The law was rigid and formalistic. The validity of legal acts depended on whether certain prescribed formalities (that is, external formal actions) were adhered to. The Romans were not quite sure themselves where some of the formalities came from (or what their point was). It was of little or no interest what it was that parties envisaged by legal acts or what their actual intentions were. There was also no question of a theoretical or principled approach to the law[95].

2.2.2 The Twelve Tables

The first important development occurred in 450 BC when the plebeians rebelled because they were not adequately informed about the law or legal procedures. After a military strike

[94] For the meaning of "customary law", see also **Chapter 6.3.2** (and Chapter 2 *infra)*.

[95] Some would call this kind of law "primitive". Modern studies in ethnological jurisprudence, concentrating mainly on the legal systems of *small-scale societies*, have, however, revealed that not all so-called "primitive law" is rigid and formalistic. The term "primitive" has thus become ambiguous, and will therefore rather be avoided in the following discussion. See also 6.5.

(*secessio plebis*), a commission was appointed to write down the law so that all could know what their position was. The product was the Twelve Tables. The original compilation has been lost but reconstructions based on later writings have survived.

The purpose of the Twelve Tables was not to replace the *ius civile* but only to explain some of its important aspects to the plebeians. They thus dealt primarily with practical aspects of immediate concern.

2.2.3 Further development of the law

As the law of a simple, rural society, the *ius civile* could in the course of time no longer make provision for the complex problems created by the expansion of the Empire and the concomitant growth in prosperity. However, legal development in a society which is institutionally speaking in the first stages of its development is problematic. Traditional law (the *ius civile* in the case of the Romans) was regarded as inviolable. Legislation, it was believed, could thus help to clarify and interpret the existing law, but dare not alter it. It was only in the time of the Emperor Hadrian (117-138 AD) that it became generally accepted that law could also be created by means of legislation.

In the Republic legislation was originally introduced by the *comitia centuriata* and later, after the class struggle, also by the *concilium plebis*, the assembly of plebeians. In the early Principate enactments were laid down by the senate, but later this process was replaced by the decisions of the emperor, the *Constitutions principis*. Up to the time of the middle-Principate, however, legislation was largely restricted to dealing with social crises and purely political matters.

In most non-complex societies legal development normally occurs primarily in the field of the law of procedure. As problems arise in practice so they are dealt with on an *ad hoc* (or casuistic) basis in order to bring about equitable solutions. The result is that in the course of time a set of rules is built up which does not have a fundamental principle as point of departure but a large number of actual, practical cases. A prospective litigant thus has access to the court only if an action has been allowed in the past on the basis of an allegation similar to the one on which the litigant wishes to base his present action. A subsequent development is normally that the person in charge of the process is given the power to allow new actions on the basis of new allegations.

Roman law also developed according to this pattern and a study of its evolution is thus in effect a study of Roman court procedures and the law of procedure. In the approximately thousand years of its development Roman law in fact never really became a system based on legal principles. This is why the availability of an action was always the point of departure in the resolution of legal problems. In modern law, on the other hand, the point of departure is that any person who can show that his or her subjective rights have been violated or threatened is entitled to approach the court for relief[96]. The principles of Roman law underlying modern legal systems were thus abstracted from Roman texts at a much later stage.

[96] See **Chapter 4.3.5**.

2.2.4 The role of the praetor

The central office in the Roman law of procedure was that of the *praetor*, instituted in 367 BC. He was originally bound to allow only those actions authorized by the *ius civile*, but in about 149 BC a new formulary procedure was accepted whereby he could create new actions. He could also, in the interests of justice, create new defences and in this way amend the *ius civile*. This meant that suddenly all legal development was entrusted to the *praetor*. Yet this power was exercised with the conservatism characteristic of the Romans. The *praetor* annually published in his *edictum* (or process programme) the new actions created by him and the succeeding *praetor* normally took over where his predecessor left off. In this way the *ius civile* grew.

2.2.5 The jurists of the classical period

The abovementioned process of legal development meant that the advice of jurists was of great interest. The office of *praetor* was in effect a political one. At that stage neither the *praetor* nor the judges were people with legal training. The *iurisprudentes* thus had to assist the development of the law by way of advice. These jurists played a very important role in the period from about the beginning of the Principate up to 250 AD. This so-called classical period was thus the golden age of Roman law, which was closely linked to the *Pax Romana* of the Principate. The quality of training was high, Greek influences were strong and jurisprudence was the appropriate choice of career for academically inclined people. It was also the ideal way to start a political career. The jurists worked without remuneration and gave primarily legal advice. In the courts themselves, however, cases were argued by *oratores*, who were people with a lower status.

For various reasons this period is regarded as the *classical* period. In the first place, there were the beginnings of a move towards abstract thinking[97], the creation of definitions and the deduction of principles. In the second place, the classical jurists gave a great deal of attention to the precise and elegant use of language. Their pure and economical use of language would impress other jurists for centuries and also resulted in some of their statements surviving in the form of legal maxims in later times[98].

The classical jurists were also prolific writers. The codification of the praetorian edict which took place during the Principate on the one hand facilitated writing by jurists but on the other hand also made it essential. This was because the *praetor's* role as law-maker soon conflicted with instructions that the praetorian edict be codified. After it had been codified it could be amended only by the emperor himself. This ended law-making by the *praetor* but it also made it much easier to write about the law, which had now taken on a fixed form, and to expand on it by way of interpretation. It is claimed that more than 2 000 books were written by the classical jurists and the courts attached a great deal of value to their opinions.

The most important classical jurists were Gaius, Aemilius Papinianus (Papinian), Julius Paulus, Domitius Ulpianus (Ulpian), Herrenius Modestinus and Salvus Julianus. (The first five are also known as "the Five Great Ones".) Gaius wrote a manual for students, the *Institutiones*. It was lost for centuries and parts were rediscovered only in 1816 and 1933.

[97] For the meaning of "abstract thinking" see **Chapter 1.2.1**.

[98] This reminds one of Ulpian's famous pronouncement quoted fully in **Chapter 4.4.1**.

The only other original classical legal works which have survived are a book by Paulus (the *Sententiae Pauli*) and an adaptation of a work by Ulpian.

2.2.6 The period of decline

The decline which the Roman Empire experienced since the beginning of the Dominate also left its mark on the law. Academic standards dropped and jurists increasingly experienced problems in applying the writings of the classical jurists. Private attempts were made in 294 and 334 AD[99] to codify the law but they were not particularly successful. In 426 AD a law was issued[100] which placed the opinions of the classical writers in order of priority. This was done without attempting to establish the merits of a particular writer's arguments on certain individual issues. In 438 AD a number of imperial enactments were compiled into an official collection[101].

2.2.7 The legislative work of Justinian

In 527 AD, that is to say half a century after the fall of the Western Roman Empire, Justinian became Emperor of the Eastern Empire. He wanted to restore the Roman Empire and also Roman law to its position of glory. Almost immediately after coming to power he gave instructions that the sources of Roman law be collected and adapted to keep pace with the demands of the time. At that stage the sources consisted of the *leges*, that is a variety of imperial *Constitutions*, and the *ius*, that is the writings of the classical jurists.

A commission under the chairmanship of Tribonian began in 528 AD to collect and organize the *leges*. The completed work was authorized the following year by Justinian. It was known as the *Codex Iustinianus*.

The next task was to collect the jurists' law. The commission completed this gigantic task in only three years. The final product, called the *Digesta* or *Pandectae*, consisted of 50 volumes containing excerpts from the works of about 39 jurists, 33 of whom were from the classical period. Excerpts from the works of Paulus and Ulpian make up about half of the *Digesta*. Even though the excerpts appear under the names of the various jurists, it is important to note that the quotations are not in their original forms. The commission altered the writers' formulations to adapt them to the law of the time. Such alterations would later be known as *interpolations*.

It was originally intended that the *Digesta* should also be able to serve as a manual for students but it was too comprehensive. A new work, the *Institutiones*, was thus compiled. It was based largely on Gaius's Institutes and consisted of 4 volumes.

During the compilation of the *Digesta* the law was amended to such an extent that the first *Codex* became obsolete. A second one was compiled and it is this *Codex* which today still forms part of the Justinian collection. Justinian's entire collection was given legal force on 29 December 534 and replaced all previous laws in the Eastern Empire.

Justinian ruled the Eastern Roman Empire until his death in 565 AD and in the final years of his rule he issued a large number of additional imperial decrees which are known as

[99] The *Codex Gregorianus* and *Hermogenianus* respectively.

[100] The *Lex Citandi* of Theodosius II.

[101] The *Codex Theodosianus.*

Novellae. These decrees were never officially collected but there are three well known private collections, namely the *Epitome Juliani*, the *Authenticum* and a Greek collection. The three parts of the Justinian compilation along with the *Novellae* have been known as the *Corpus Iuris Civilis* since the sixteenth century.

2.2.8 The ius gentium

Apart from its rigidity and formalism, the original Roman *ius civile* was also exclusive, and only Roman citizens (*cives Romani*) had access to it. The expansion of the empire meant that many Roman subjects were not citizens. Citizenship was gradually extended but there was nevertheless still a need for a legal system for foreigners (or *peregri*).

In 242 BC the office of *praetor peregrinus* was created to deal with adjudication among foreigners. The law created as a result of the rulings of this government official was known as the *ius gentium* ("the law of the nations"). The *praetor peregrinus* could not concern himself too much with formalities in his court – there was just simply too great a diversity of *peregrini* from too large a variety of nations involved in legal disputes. He was thus inclined to accept that which was common to all the nations and to reject the rest. Consequently the *ius gentium* differs greatly from the *ius civile*. The *ius gentium* is more flexible and there is more emphasis on general guidelines. *Bona fides*, that is to say a litigant's disposition of good faith, was a more important criterion, for example, than compliance with formal procedures in trying a case.

In his Institutes Gaius wrote that the principles of the *ius gentium* came into being through natural reason among all nations and are followed by all peoples, and that the Romans follow partly their own legal system and partly this legal system common to all people. This description is repeated in Justinian's Institutes with the addition that *naturalia iura* (created by divine providence and obeyed by all nations) is eternal and unchanging. This view, shaped under Greek influence, was to play an important role in the history of law in Europe centuries later.

3. Roman law in the west after the fall of the empire in 476 AD

3.1 Germanic law

Very little is known about the early tribal laws of the Teutonic tribes which gained control over the Western Roman Empire. Julius Caesar gives some details in his accounts of his campaigns in Gaul as does the historian Tacitus. German law was apparently not written down; legal acts (such as concluding contracts) were concluded in a symbolic form before an assembly of the people and they were accompanied by the utterance of legal maxims.

Very soon after these tribes established themselves on the territory of the Western Roman Empire they began to record their tribal laws. An example of this was the *Lex Salica* of the fifth century, which contained the law of the Salian Franks, the tribe which formed the core of the empire of the Franks. In the sixth century the Ribuarian Franks based a part of their tribal law, the *Lex Riburia*, on Salic law. These written down tribal laws were later called the *leges barbarorum* to distinguish them from the *leges Romanorum* which the Germanic rulers compiled specifically for their Roman subjects (and about which more will be said in the next section).

The Longobardian laws, or the *Edicta Longobardorum*, were undoubtedly among the most important creative legal works produced by the Germanic invaders in Italy. They were promulgated in 643 AD by King Rothari and supplemented by the later Longobardian kings. This Longobardian law (which was studied at the famous law school at Pavia) was observed next to Roman law until the thirteenth century.

3.2 The personality principle and the survival of Roman law

The occupying tribes, especially since the time of the Frankish Empire, applied the *personality principle*, in terms of which someone lived according to the law of his tribe regardless of what (other) tribe's territory he was in. There is no agreement on the origin of this principle[102], but it undoubtedly contributed largely to the survival of Roman law in the West.

The Germanic rulers did not only permit their Roman subjects to live according to their own laws, but they also created codifications of Roman law (the *leges Romanes*) even before Justinian began doing this for the Eastern Roman Empire.

The first of these codes was the *Lex Romana Visighotorum* (also called the *Breviarum Alarici*), which Emperor Alaric II of the Visigoths promulgated for his Roman subjects in 506 AD. It consists, among other things, of excerpts from the *Codex Theodosianus*, the Institutes of Gaius and books of Paulus and Papinian. It also included an interpretation to adapt it to the demands of the time.

This code was replaced by a new Visigothic code in 654 AD after the distinction between Goths and Roman subjects eventually fell away as a result of intermarriage. But it was still used after that date in Lombardy and the south of France. It was regarded with great respect as a legal work during the Middle Ages and was one of the channels through which Roman law passed into Western Europe before its later reception. Another example of a *lex Romanorum* was the *Lex Romana Burgondionum*, which later lost its validity after the Franks conquered the Burgundian Empire.

3.3 The feudal system and the rise of regional and city laws

As a result of intermarriage the various tribes began to lose their own identities. The feudal system also meant that people increasingly regarded themselves as inhabitants of a particular region rather than as members of a particular tribe or subjects of a particular ruler. These and other factors contributed to the personality principle gradually being replaced by the territoriality principle. According to this principle the same legal rules applied to all those who were living in a particular region at a given time regardless of whether they were inhabitants of that region or foreigners. Law thus became regionally binding rather than personality bound.

The rise of the feudal system may be ascribed to the weakness of central governments in pre-medieval Europe which could not protect small landowners or landless people from enemies or invaders. These people promised their services and loyalty to the great landowners (feudal lords) in exchange for land to cultivate and protection from harm. The great landowners thus controlled an area with a number of loyal followers on it. This led inevitably to political disintegration.

[102] De Wet. 1988. *Die Ou Skrywers in Perpektief.* Durban: Butterworths.

Regional laws arose for the inhabitants of such feudal estates; by about 1000 AD these were primarily customary laws. The content of these regional legal systems was largely determined by the earlier history of the various regions. In the north of France, for example, such systems were strongly orientated towards Germanic law while in the south they were more Roman in character. In about 1230 AD one set of these regional laws, that of the Saxons, was set down in writing. This codification is known as the *Sachsenspiegel* and had a great influence in the area known today as Germany. In the north of Italy the Longobardian influence was dominant while in middle-Italy it was the Roman influence. Because of the growth in trade, cities also became very powerful and developed their own customary law, known as city laws.

3.4 Canon law

Apart from the various regional and urban laws referred to in the previous section, the Roman Catholic Church also had its own legal system. The church, with its seat in Rome, lived according to Roman law (*ecclesia vivit secundum legem Romanum*). Works such as the *Lex Romana Canonice Compta* dating from the ninth century, for example, were based on the Institutes and the *Codex* of Justinian.

The church was originally allowed to adhere to Roman law in terms of the personality principle, especially in the Germanic region. As the church grew and its organizational needs increased accordingly, Roman law was supplemented by resolutions of the church councils, papal decrees and ecclesiastical customary law. In this way canon law eventually developed into an independent legal system. Canon law was not applied only in strictly ecclesiastical matters but also to issues which would today be controlled by civil law, such as marriages, wills and executors.

As has been indicated, the feudal system brought about a considerable fragmentation of legal systems. The church, on the other hand, was a unified organization which lived according to the same legal rules (of canon law) in different regions and cities, which is why canon law had a unifying influence.

Canon law was arranged systematically and recorded in the twelfth century by Gratian, a monk from Bologna. The *Decretum Gratiani* (originally known as the *Concordia Discordantium Canonum* – "the reconciliation of conflicting ecclesiastical laws") was widely respected and was used as a manual for students at law schools such as Bologna and Orleans.

In short, the church was in an ideal position to preserve Roman law and in fact played a key role in this respect during the Middle Ages. The church was also responsible for the preservation of Roman legal texts.

Yet the culture of the medieval church also had other effects which eventually affected South African law. The famous Roman Catholic theologian and philosopher, Thomas Aquinas (1225-1274), exerted a great influence on the thinking and writings of the Spanish moral philosophers of the sixteenth century. These philosophers in turn influenced in many respects the thinking of Hugo de Groot, one of the (old) Roman-Dutch writers whose writings have great authority in South Africa even today[103].

[103] See also **Chapter 5.5.2**.

4. THE REVIVAL OF ROMAN LAW IN THE ELEVENTH CENTURY AND ITS RECEPTION IN NORTHERN EUROPE

4.1 The Middle Ages

The history of medieval law in the West extends from the rise of the Eastern Roman Empire and the fall of the Western Roman Empire in 476 AD to the late fifteenth century, by which time the Eastern Roman Empire had also fallen and the cultural and intellectual revival known as the Renaissance had begun. The reformation of the church, the Great Reception of the Roman law, the rise of the idea of nation states and the Europeans' exploration of the surface of the earth all date from the period of cultural and intellectual ferment at the time of and directly after the Renaissance.

Although Roman law had survived in the Middle Ages in the regional legal systems of certain territories and in the church, it did begin to recede into the background. The academic study of Roman law especially left much to be desired. Second-hand sources such as the *Brevarium Alarci* were mostly used in practice, and even though the *Institutiones, Codex* and *Novellae* were sometimes consulted, the most important part of the Justinian code, the *Digesta*, fell into oblivion. Before Roman law could once again take its rightful place in the legal systems of late medieval Europe, it had to become the object of academic study. Precisely this occurred at the end of the eleventh century when Roman law in its Justinian form became the focal point of legal academic interest.

4.2 The Glossators

At this time in Bologna in Northern Italy a law school was established which concentrated particularly on the *Digesta*. The founder was Irnerius (who died in about 1130), a scholar about whom not much is known. After him came the so-called *quattor doctores*, Bulgarus, Martinus, Jacobus and Hugo. During their time there were thousands of law students in Bologna. Irnerus and his followers used the methods of the Longobardian jurists at the law school at Pavia.

This method involved writing explanatory notes, called *glossae*, in the margins of the texts of Roman law. There were probably two reasons why this method was used. Firstly, the scholars who began studying the *Digesta* had a linguistic interest in it. Secondly, the glossators still regarded Justinian law as the existing law of their time and therefore to a large extent respected the emperor's prohibition of a free interpretation of and commentary on his work.

A gloss was originally a note between the lines or in the margin explaining a difficult word or phrase, but it soon developed into a complete exposition and explanation of the relevant principle. Texts were compared and there were attempts to reconcilc conflicting statements. Later the glossators also wrote summaries, treatises and discussions on disputed issues, but the glosses are their most important heritage. They were collected under the name *Glossa Ordinaria* by Accursius, who was born in 1182 AD. These glosses were reprinted with issues of the *Corpus Iuris Civilis* up until the seventeenth century.

The glossators laid a basis for the academic study of law upon which later schools could build, and they exercised a great influence throughout Europe because of their many students.

The authority of the glosses was also soon accepted in the law courts of the time. Yet the glossators are open to the criticism that they totally ignored the law of their own time and considered the *Corpus Iuris Civilis* as the only source of law. From a historical perspective, however, it is precisely this approach of theirs which meant that a purer form of Roman law was eventually received in Europe.

4.3 The Ultramontani

Roman law was well established in the systems of customary law in the south of France. It is therefore not surprising that the work of the glossators was highly regarded there and several schools were founded at places like Orleans, Toulouse and Montpellier, amongst others. The Italians referred to the jurists of these schools as the *Ultramontani*: the people on the other side of the mountain. The French differed from the glossators in the sense that they did not follow the glosses so slavishly and they made a more serious effort to adapt the law to the practical demands of their time.

4.4 The post-glossators or commentators

The scholars who became famous after the glossators are called the commentators. Their chief characteristic is that they copied the glosses of their predecessors slavishly and adopted one of their methods, the writing of commentaries. Their main weaknesses were an exaggerated concern with authority and the so-called *communis opinio*. Many of their works were thus no more than a rewriting and re-arrangement of the opinions of earlier writers.

They did, however, make a contribution in adapting Roman law to the needs of their time. In this process they integrated Roman law with the statutes of the cities, Germanic and medieval customary law and canon law.

The most famous of the commentators was Bartolus de Saxoferrato (1313-1357). From 1343 up to his death he was professor of law at Perugia. He was particularly practically minded and acquired immortal fame as an exponent of Roman law. For the commentators after him his opinions carried the most weight, even apart from their merits in any specific instance. In time the Bartolists came up with their own motto regarding the great master: *nemo jurista nisi bartolisa* – "no one is a jurist who is not a Bartolist"!

In later centuries Bartolus's method of making Roman law serviceable in practice was called the *Mos Italicus* to distinguish it from the French or humanist method, the *Mos Gallicus*.

Apart from their exaggerated emphasis on authority which has already been mentioned, other points of criticism against the commentators are the fragmentary nature of their work, their long-windedness and their sometimes poor use of Latin. Their great merit lies in the creation of a common law by fusing Roman, Germanic and canon law. Furthermore, they played a leading role in the emergence of fields of study such as Criminal Law and Commercial Law and Bartolus himself laid the basis for what would later become known as Conflict of Laws or Private International Law.

4.5 The humanists

Early in the sixteenth century a new cultural and intellectual orientation, humanism, took root in Europe. The humanists reached back to the purest possible forms of classical Greek and Roman culture in an attempt to overcome (what they regarded as) the unacceptable rigidity and the inferiority of medieval culture. In the field of law, for example, the humanists opposed the Bartolists' over-dependence on the authority of the great masters as well as their exaggerated emphasis on the value of a *communis opinio*. According to the humanists there should have been a greater reliance on the original sources of classical Roman law, that is to say the writings of the classical jurists. Their motto was thus *petere fonts* – "back to the sources".

They studied primarily the best source available, namely the *Corpus Iuris Civilis*, with a view to reconstructing (original) classical law. As opposed to the medieval scholars, they also wanted to study Roman law as a complete system and not piecemeal or as fragments.

The most famous members of this school were Jacobus Cujacius (1522-1590) and Hugo Donellus (1527-1591). Cujacius had an extensive knowledge of the Roman texts and made a gigantic contribution towards the reconstruction of classical law. Donellus's great contribution was towards the systematic organization of the law. The humanists were also the precursors of the later searchers for interpolations, that is the altered quotations from the classical writers in the *Digesta*.

The humanists did not take account of the actual practice of their day and completely disregarded the achievements of the medieval writers. They drew for the first time a clear distinction between Roman law as a field of study and as existing law. Donellus and some of his followers, however, are sometimes called the "Bartolist faction" because they did to some extent require that the law should be studied in such a way that practical demands were taken into account. A later follower of the faction was the famous French jurist, Joseph Pothier (1699-1772), who wrote in a humanistic vein about Roman law but took the practical needs of his time into account. His works are still regularly quoted in South African courts.

4.6 The Great Reception

This label is given to the process whereby Roman law was incorporated into the legal systems of the German regions, particularly between 1400 AD. *Reception* refers to the fairly large-scale adoption of the principles of one legal system into another. It has to be distinguished from *infiltration* which is a more gradual adoption or "seepage" of such principles.

Up to about 1400 AD the law of the Germanic tribes in what is today Germany, Austria, Belgium and the Netherlands was customary law supplemented by legislation issued by the respective Germanic emperors. As Christianity spread, the church, with its own legal system, penetrated these regions and this paved the way for Roman law. The revival of the academic study of Roman law was carried from Italy to these areas and the subject was taught at the newly established universities. The uniformity of Roman law was an attractive alternative to the legal fragmentation so characteristic of the various systems of customary law.

4.7 The Usus Modernus Pandectarum

This term was created in the later seventeenth century by Samuel Stryk (1640-1710). It described Roman law as received in Northern Europe from 1500 onwards, adapted to contemporary circumstance and developed by jurists. It was emphasized that Roman law had not been received in its entirety and that a great deal of Germanic law had been retained in the ultimate product of the Great Reception. The basis for this way of thinking was laid by Herman Conring (1606-1681), who demonstrated convincingly that Roman law acquired legal force in Germany by its acceptance into customary law rather than through legislative acts. From then on care was taken to avoid excessive "Romanising" of German legal science.

4.8 The school of natural law (and legal positivism)

The basic idea of natural law and adherence to theories of natural law have been present in philosophy, history of law and in jurisprudence from the earliest times. Briefly the idea amounts to the acceptance of the existence of not only positive legal systems (as products of the human capacity to create structures), but also of a "deeper" (or "higher") legal order. This second order was originally seen as part of an eternal world-order (a natural order or, in the Christian tradition, God's order of creation) but since the sixteenth century it has been regarded as the product of human reason. Natural law is valid universally and *per se* (by itself), that is to say without the intervention of a human legislator, and accommodates a system of values against which time – and place-bound (positive) legal systems and norms can be (and should be) measured. An important characteristic of natural law thinking is that it does not separate legal and moral issues from one another. But there is not unanimity among natural law thinkers about its precise meaning or its relation to positive law.

The basis of natural law as a concept was laid by the Greek philosophers, who compared the natural order with the social order of their day. They exercised great influence on Roman thinkers and jurists, especially the classical jurists. Because of the dominant role of the church and Christianity during the Middle Ages, the idea of natural law was to a large extent deduced from the order God created for the universe. After the Renaissance the intellectual authority of human reason gradually replaced that of divine (or any other "external") law as the basis for natural law.

This new foundation for natural law was laid by Hugo de Groot (Grotius)(1583-1645)[104] in his book *De Jure Belli ac Pacis*. According to him natural law may be deduced from the sound mind or reason (*ratio recta*) of the human being and the needs of society. Natural law is a criterion against which any historical law, including Roman law, can be tested. He did, however, also declare that many Roman legal principles were also principles of natural law.

Not all the scholars of natural law were as accommodating towards Roman law. The German, Christian Thomasius (1655-1728), for example, regarded Germanic law as the true natural law. He also taught in German rather than in Latin.

Natural law scholars played a great role in the eighteenth-century movement which advocated legal codification, that is to say the authoritative recording of the law of a state in such a way that the new statute or code would replace all former legal rules and become the final authoritative source of law in that State. To them the next logical step was recording the natural law concepts which were converted into detailed rules. It was in fact at the insistence of natural law scholars that several states in Europe undertook codification.

[104] See also **Chapter 5.5.2**.

Since about halfway through the nineteenth century there has been a strong reaction against the idea of natural law. This reaction took shape in a movement known as *legal positivism*. But one cannot talk about a positivist school, as legal positivism is expressed in several theoretical approaches to law (among them the approach of the Pandectists, who will be considered shortly in 4.9 below).

Legal positivists do not want to speculate about things like higher or deeper law. For them the law consists of given facts which one can trace to formal sources of law (such as legislation or historical sources). Some legal positivists also emphasise the fact that the law can be deduced empirically (that is to say by sensory perception and experience) from certain social phenomena or principles.

The systematic organization of legal rules and concepts is of greater importance for legal positivists than whether legal rules or legal systems are just. For them issues such as the latter are too speculative and uncertain to occupy jurists. To put this in another way: legal positivists make a clear distinction between the law and morality. According to them the jurist's primary task is to study (and apply) the law as it is (the *lex lata*) and not the law as it should – or ought to – be (the *lex ferenda*)[105].

4.9 The historical school (Pandectists)

This label is given to a group of German jurists who came to prominence at the end of the eighteenth century and who made German legal science very famous in the nineteenth century.

This school was opposed particularly to the school of natural law which maintained that law is the product of reason and may be grasped and formulated apart from its historical growth. In the Pandectists' view law developed gradually in the *Volksgeist* or consciousness of a people. For them the most important source of law is law which has grown historically in the midst of specific social circumstances, that is customary law. Legislation is simply a means of formally affirming the already existing law of a people. The strong opposition of the historical school to codification resulted in Germany accepting a code only about a century after France.

The fame of this school (and the basis of its other name), however, lies in the peculiar fact that its exponents focused their studies not so much on (local) law as it had developed in the course of time, but on the *Digesta* as expounded by the glossators. Their interest was in legal dogmatics and they deduced from the Roman law of Justinian as logical and watertight a system of general legal principles as possible. The product of all this was a system of legal concepts and also many theories which still find favour today, but it also sometimes led to extensive theorizing which had no bearing on practice.

The most famous member of this school (and also the most fervent opponent of codification) was Friedrich Karl von Savigny (1779-1861). He wrote a famous book on legal history, *Geschichte des Romischen Rechts im Mittelatter*. The contribution of the historical school in the field of dogmatics was summarized by Bernhard Windscheid (1817-1892) in his *Lehrbuch des Pandektenrechts*. The influence of Windscheid and his book were to a large extent responsible for the element of Roman law in the German Civil Code which came into operation on 1 January 1900.

[105] For the influence of legal positivism in South Africa see **Chapter 6.4.4**.

5. THE LEGAL HISTORY OF THE NETHERLANDS

5.1 A brief political overview

When the Roman Empire was at its greatest, it included parts of the present-day Netherlands. Roman influence there, however, was not sufficiently permanent or enduring enough to have had a particularly lasting effect. At the time of the fall of the Western Roman Empire in 476 AD, Germanic tribes (Franks in particular) had already been in control of those regions for some time.

Christmas Day in the year 800 saw the beginning of the Carolingian dynasty when Pope Leo III crowned Charles the Great (Charlemagne), the leader of the Franks, as Emperor of the so-called "Holy Roman Empire". In 843 AD the empire was divided among Charlemagne's three grandsons and the Netherlands became part of Lothar 1's empire. Lothar's territory was situated between two others: The West Frankish kingdom (modern France) and the East Frankish kingdom (modern Germany). By 1000 AD, however, the middle kingdom had been finally divided between the Western and Eastern kingdoms. After this there was a great deal of feudal fragmentation and the region consisted of a number of small feudal states, most of whom still showed loyalty to the Holy Roman Empire in name, but wars between them were frequent.

In the fourteenth century the Burgundian dynasty of Eastern France arose as a power-group and campaigned for a new neutral kingdom between France and Germany. They succeeded in getting large parts of the Netherlands under their control.

As a consequence of marriages between the various royal houses, the areas conquered by the Burgundians eventually ended up under the rule of Charles V, the Emperor of the Holy Roman Empire, who at that time still ruled Spain and its colonies as well as certain parts of Germany. In 1555 Charles V renounced his claims to the Netherlands in favour of his son, Philip II, but in 1581 a number of provinces withdrew their allegiance to Philip II as ruler. After years of hostilities Spain in 1609 finally recognised the independence of the United Provinces of the Netherlands (consisting of Holland, Utrecht, Zeeland, Gelderland, Groningen, Friesland and Overijssel), which also became independent from the German kingdom in 1648. The *Republiek der Vereenigde Nederlanden* (Republic of the United Netherlands) survived until 1975.

5.2 The legal system of the early Netherlands

Roman rule in the Netherlands was not long enough to exercise any influence in the sphere of the law. The later Germanic tribes also lived according to the personality principle here and their tribal laws too were replaced by regional and city laws in the course of time. Examples of recorded regional laws were the *Somme rural* (about 1830) and the *Landrecht Overijssel* of 1559. There was also an adaptation of the *Sachsenspiegel* made in the fourteenth century in Holland.

During the fifteenth century courts of law developed from the original government councils; of particular interest are the Court of Holland, the Great Council of Mechlin and the High Council of Holland, Zeeland and West Friesland. By 1473 the Great Council of Mechlin was the highest court of appeal for the regions of the Netherlands, but contact with Mechlin (in present-day Belgium) was permanently broken because of the rebellion against Philip II. The High Council of Holland, Zeeland and West Friesland eventually became the highest court.

From the time of the Burgundians legislation was issued in the form of edicts and placaaten. One well known example is the Perpetual Edict of Charles V of 1540 which is still of interest in modern South African private law. During the Republic provincial proclamations were issued and one of these, the Political Ordinance of Holland of 1580, still plays an important role in our law of husband and wife and law of succession.

5.3 The reception of Roman law

As explained before, after its revival Roman law penetrated Europe and became the *ius commune* of the European continent. The process began early and initially took place very slowly. For example, the *Somme rural*, referred to above, already showed strong signs of Roman influence.

The factors assisting reception were the same here as in the other countries. The church initially served as precursor, because canon law and Roman law went hand in hand. The idea that the Holy Roman Empire was a continuation of the original Roman Empire played a role although there are differences of opinion about this today[106].

Students who went to study in Italy after the revival must naturally have brought back Roman law influences with them. The southern part of the Netherlands was in contact with France which was strongly Romanised. As will be seen, the south was also initially the centre of the reception.

Universities played a great role. The University of Louvain (in modern Belgium) was established in 1425 and Roman law was offered as a subject. Jurists who were trained here eventually had seats in the Great Councils of Holland and Mechlin. The availability of the Roman sources of law, as well as their uniformity in comparison with the diversity of local systems of customary law and legislation, must naturally have made Roman law attractive in practice.

The law which was received was Roman law as expounded by the glossators and commentators. At that stage there was already talk of a European common law (a *ius commune*) based on Roman law, and it was thus not unusual for Dutch writers to quote French or other foreign writers.

5.4 The initial reception in the south

The centre of legal studies in the south was the University of Louvain where Roman and canon law were taught. Louvain is very near Mechlin and the University thus began to exert an influence on the Great Council of Mechlin.

Three members in particular of the so-called school of Louvain deserve to be mentioned. Philipus Wielant (1442-1520) became famous as a historian and a jurist and had a seat on the Great Council of Mechlin. His two most important works are *De Pracktycke Crimile* and *De Pracktycke Civile*. Several of his works were extensively plagiarized by some of his followers, particularly Joost Damhouder.

[106] De Wet Ou Skrywers 111 Supra.

Nicholas Everhardus (1462-1532) is important because he was one of the founders of the humanist movement. He was president of the Court of Holland and then of the Great Council of Mechlin and in these capacities exercised a great influence on the reception of Roman law. His most important works are his *Topica*, a manual for students, and *Responsa sive Consilia*, a compilation of opinions.

Joost Damhouder (1507-1581), as already mentioned, was guilty of extensive plagiarism of his predecessor's works. But as a jurist he had his own merits and exercised a great influence on legal practice in Europe. His works, *Praxis Rerum Criminalium* and *Praxis Rerum Civilium*, were translated into German, Dutch and French soon after they appeared and were widely used in courts.

5.5 The Northern Netherlands

Although the reception began in the south, the focus moved to the north from the end of the sixteenth century. For example, the famous University of Leiden was established in 1575. The fact that contact with the south was broken off because of the rebellion against Philip II possibly played a large role in the independent flourishing of legal science in the north. In the following two centuries the Dutch jurists in the north totally overshadowed their southern predecessors.

There were quite a large number of Dutch jurists in the north and they are not all of equal significance for South African law. Below are some particulars about a few of those jurists whose authority is still taken into account in our courts; they are listed in chronological order according to their dates of birth. Some of them came from provinces other than Holland. Although Holland is of primary importance for us in South Africa, this does not mean that the courts do not attach importance to writers from the other provinces. As mentioned before[107], the concept "Roman-Dutch law" can be understood broadly to incorporate the law of the whole of the seventeenth – and eighteenth – century Netherlands (and even the European *ius commune* of that time).

5.5.1 Johan van den Sande (1568-1638)

Johan van den Sande (or Jan van Sande, in short) is a good example of a writer on common law who writes about the law of one of the Dutch provinces apart from Holland (namely Friesland), but who is still significant for the study of Roman-Dutch law.

He studied at the Universities of Wittenberg and Leiden and at the age of thirty became professor at Franeker (Friesland). He later became a member of the Court of Friesland. His *Decisiones Curiae Frisicae* is a treatise on the law in force in Friesland illustrated with decisions of the Frisian court. He quoted from a wide variety of European writers (medieval, humanist, French, Spanish, Italian, German and of course other Dutch writers) – proof of the fact that there was a very close link between the law of the Netherlands and the European *ius commune*.

5.5.2 Hugo de Groot (Grotius) (1583-1645)

Hugo de Groot, born in Delft, was one of the greatest jurists the world has ever known. He made enormous contributions in the field of private law, legal philosophy and international

[107] See **Chapter 1**.

law. From a South African point of view his contribution in the first area is of greatest significance but it was particularly in the other two fields that he became world famous.

Grotius first studied at Leiden and then at Orleans, where he was awarded a doctor's degree. At the age of sixteen he was already an advocate at the Hague. After this he held a number of public offices and at one stage was legal adviser to the VOC.

He later became involved in one of the many religious controversies of his time and sided with the faction known as the Arminians. The monarchy, however, supported another group, the Gomarists, and De Groot soon found himself in the position of an opponent of the monarchy. He was arrested in 1618, accused of high treason and sentenced to life imprisonment. While he was serving his sentence in a castle at Loevenstein, he escaped in 1621 by hiding in a book trunk and fled to Paris.

De Groot's attempts to return to Holland were not successful and he eventually became the Swedish ambassador in Paris. He visited Sweden in 1645 but was shipwrecked on his return journey. He was saved but died later at Rostock from pneumonia which he contracted as a result of the disaster.

While he was in prison he wrote his famous *Inleidinge tot de Hollandsche Rechtsgeleertheyd* which was published in 1631. It was the first work on Roman-Dutch law as an independent system, in other words on Roman law in received form. The term "Roman-Dutch law", however, was not used by De Groot.

For the following two centuries the *Inleidinge* formed the basis of treatises and lectures on Roman-Dutch law and thus takes a central position in our legal literature. Today's standard edition is based on a 1636 edition of the work which was found in 1948 in Lund, Sweden. It has notes in De Groot's own handwriting.

The *Inleidinge* was translated into English by AFS Maasdorp (in 1878) and RW Lee (in 1926). In its Dutch form it was one of the statute-books of the Zuid-Afrikaanse Republiek.

Because the work was written in prison, De Groot did not have access to sufficient sources. A point of criticism against the work is thus its inadequate source references. De Groot, a pioneer in the field of natural law, also sometimes in this work held up natural law principles as current law. Important supplementary material was added to the work by, among others, Simon Groenewegen and Willem Schorer.

While he was in Paris De Groot wrote the work which made him world famous. It is called *De Jure Belli ac Pacis* ("the law of war and peace") and was the first treatise on international law. He based international law on the principles of natural law derived from the human being's own *ratio recta*. The idea that positive law can be tested against natural law comes to the fore very strongly and after this jurists would do the same with the principles of Dutch private law. The book is also important for a student of private law because De Groot elaborates on the general legal principles which he discussed in the *Inleidinge*.

5.5.3 Arnoldus Vinnius (1588-1657)

Vinnius was a student and later professor at the University of Leiden. His style is strongly humanist and he focused his attention on the "original" Roman sources of law[108]. One of his works which was issued many times and used for centuries in law schools was his

[108] See **Chapter 4.5**.

commentary on the Institutes of Justinian (entitled *In Quattor Libros Institutionum Imperialium Commentarius Academicus et Forensis*). He also prepared a student edition of the Institutes which contains many explanatory notes (and is thus known as the *Notae* for short).

Vinnius's humanist approach to law, however, differed from that of the French founders of humanism in that he also took into account (and wrote about) the indigenous Dutch law of his time (and referred to medieval writers and other later writers whose works were applied in practice).

5.5.4 Antonius Mathaeus II (1601-1654)

Antonius Matthaeus II, professor at Harderwijk and later Utrecht, was a member of a family of outstanding jurists. His father, Antonius Matthaeus I (1564-1637), for example, was professor of law at Marburg and Groningen, and his brother, Antonius Matthaeus III (1635-1710) was professor of jurisprudence at the Universities of Utrecht and Leiden.

His best known work, *De Criminibus, ad Libros XLVII et XLVIII Digestorum Commentarius*, deals with criminal law and made him famous throughout Europe. This work has recently (in 1987) been translated into English by ML Hewett and BC Stoop. Matthaeus also wrote on private law.

5.5.5 Christian Rodenburg (1608-1668)

Christian Rodenburg was a judge in the Court of Utrecht and held several important public offices. He is remembered particularly for his book on the law of husband and wife, *Tractatus de Iure Conjugum*. He did not restrict his discussion only to the law of Utrecht but also dealt with relevant legal principles as they were applied in various Dutch provinces.

5.5.6 Simon Groenewegen (1613-1652)

Simon van Groenewegen van de Made, secretary of Delft, is generally regarded as the most important writer on Roman-Dutch law, next to Grotius and Johannes Voet. He wrote notes on Grotius's *Inleidinge* and in this way filled the many gaps resulting from De Groot having to write his work in prison and not having access to legal literature. He also sometimes criticises De Groot's views.

Groenewegen's own great work is the *Tractatus de Legibus Abrogatis et Inusitatis in Hollandia Vicinisque Regionibus*. In the six-part commentary on the *Corpus Iuris Civilis* he worked systematically through Roman law indicating which parts were still valid in his day and thus enforceable and which parts had become obsolete. This work (also available in English) is thus an excellent source of knowledge about Roman-Dutch law at the beginning of the seventeenth century.

Groenewegen also quoted freely from medieval writers and later European writers. He showed a particular preference for De Groot for whom he had the highest regard. In those instances where Groenewegen differs from De Groot, it is usually safest to give preference to Groenewegen's view.

5.5.7 Paulus Voet (1619-1667)

Paulus Voet, a professor of law at Utrecht, is known primarily as the father of the famous Johannes Voet. He never reached quite the same heights as his son.

Yet he made noteworthy contributions to legal science in works such as those on international and commercial law as well as with a commentary on the Institutes of Justinian.

5.5.8 Simon van Leeuwen (1626-1682)

Van Leeuwen, probably the most prolific of the Roman-Dutch writers, was an advocate, city secretary and assistant registrar at the High Council of The Hague. He was the first Dutch jurist to use the term "Roman-Dutch law".

In his most famous work, the five-part *Het Roomsch-Hollandsch Recht,* he describes the law in force in his day. This work was primarily intended as a handbook for legal practitioners in the courts of Holland and West Friesland. In an 1859 supplement to the Constitution of the Zuid-Afrikaanse Republiek it was declared to be an authoritative source of law for this old Boer republic[109]. Sir JG Kotze translated *Het Roomsch-Hollandsch Recht* into English in 1881 (under the title *Simon van Leeuwen's Commentaries on Roman-Dutch Law*) and made it available in South Africa among particularly English-speaking judges and jurists. Van Leeuwen's later *Censura Forensis Theoretica-Practica* once again focused on the development and application of Roman-Dutch law in the Netherlands.

Van Leeuwen is regarded by many people as a superficial writer – someone who wrote popular works mainly for a public which had no legal background. There are, for example, many contradictions between his *Het Roomsch-Hollandsch Recht* and his *Censura Forensis.* A man by the name of Cornelis Wilhelm Decker, an advocate from Amsterdam, edited the first work and added notes to it. Without Decker's notes it would probably have been a much poorer reference work.

Van Leeuwen wrote many other works – among them a history of the Netherlands.

5.5.9 Ulrichus Huber (1636-1694)

Huber was a Frisian who became professor at the University of Franeker. He turned down two offers of a chair at Leiden. Not only is he among the best known of the old writers, but in his own time he was also famous for his *Praelectiones Juris Civilis*, lectures on Roman law as embodied in the Institutes and the *Digesta* of Justinian. The German jurist, Christian Thomasius, provided notes to sections of this work.

But his *Heedendaagse Rechtsgeleertheyt*, a comprehensive exposition of the law of the Netherlands, is his most important work on Roman-Dutch law. Apart from sporadic references to other Dutch and European writers, Huber also based his exposition on references to decisions of the Court of Friesland, in which he himself was a judge for a time. After Ulrichus's death, his son, Zacharias Huber (1669-1732), who was also a professor of law at Franeker, published further editions of Ulrichus's *Heedendaagse Rechtsgeleertheyt* as well as his *Decisiones Friscae* (a collection of judgments passed by the court of Friesland). The former work was translated into English in 1939 by Mr Justice Percival Gane under the title *Huber's Jurisprudence of my Time*.

5.5.10 Johannes Voet (1647- 1713)

Along with Hugo de Groot, he is the most important Dutch jurist as far as South African law is concerned. He is the writer quoted most often by our courts and he overshadowed

[109] See **Chapter 6.2**.

his father to such an extent that he is the one referred to simply as Voet. It is not known where he acquired his legal degree but it was probably in Orleans, France. He was then an advocate at Utrecht for a few months until he decided that he would prefer to concentrate on academic work. He eventually became professor at the Universities of Herbon (in Germany), Utrecht and Leiden.

Voet's *magnum opus* is undoubtedly the *Commentarius ad Pandectas*, a comprehensive commentary on the *Digesta* of Justinian as well as a description of the Dutch law of his time. He worked on this for eighteen years and even in shortened, translated form it still consists of seven volumes. It was published for the first time in 1698 and there were several later editions published throughout Europe. From 1793 it was usually published along with a supplement (*Supplementum*) by Johannes van der Linden and one of these editions was translated into English in 1955 by Mr Justice Percival Gane under the title *The Selective Voet*. As the name indicates, it was not a complete translation as certain sections regarded as obsolete were left out.

Like the glossators and the commentators, Voet's method was to present the various titles of the *Digesta* with Roman law as the point of departure but with the addition of the law of his own time. Although he was very strongly under humanist influence, he adopted a middle course by not ignoring the contributions of the medieval jurists. His Latin was good although very difficult and there are also signs of the influences of natural law.

A further characteristic of his book is that it is incredibly thorough. There is hardly a topic which he does not deal with in detail. The field covered by Voet was much wider than that covered by De Groot. Whereas De Groot wrote about the law of the province of Holland, Voet's point of departure was the European *ius commune*. This is why the book was so well received in the rest of Europe, especially in France. His work is thus a good guide for researchers on the legal literature of his time.

Points of criticism against the work are the long sentences and sometimes weak paragraphing. There are also sometimes conflicting views within the work and it is always advisable to judge passages from Voet in context. To this end, Van der Linden's *Supplementum*[110] is of great help. The Appellate Division sometimes finds it necessary to translate the original text itself, which is an indication that the jurist has to be careful not to rely only on translated texts. As a writer Voet did not manifest the same kind of originality than De Groot did.

Two of Voet's other well-known works are his *Compendium Iuris* (which was used primarily as a textbook for students, although it was not originally intended as such) and his *De Iure Militari* (which deals with military law).

5.5.11 Cornelis van Bynkershoek (1673-1743)

Van Bynkershoek was a legal practitioner rather than an academic. He originally studied theology but dissension among the professors of theology resulted in his abandoning the subject and training as a jurist. He was a member of the High Council of Holland, Zeeland and West Friesland for almost forty years and later became its president. He was one of the most outstanding judges ever to serve on that council, in spite of misgivings about his appointment as a Zeelander in a court which had a majority of Hollanders as members.

[110] See **Chapter 5.5.15**.

Van Bynkershoek was a versatile jurist and his writings attest to this. He wrote works on Roman law, on international law and the private law in force in his day. In South Africa, however, he is known mainly as the author of the *Observationes Tumultuariae*, a collection of judgments of the High Council (*Hooge Raad*). This work has a very interesting history. Van Bynkershoek drew up this collection for his own use and left it in his will to his son-in-law, Willem Pauw (1712-1787), who was later a member and president of the High Council himself. But he prohibited the publication of the work.

Pauw added to the collection and left it to his grandson, repeating the prohibition on publication. The *Observationes* thus fell into oblivion but was discovered in 1914 in an auctioneer's store by Prof EM Meijers of the University of Leiden. The reasons for prohibiting publication (careless style and the undesirability of making public *in camera* discussions by judges of the High Council) had fallen away by this time and a start was made with publishing the *Observationes*. The last volume of Van Bynkershoek's more than 3 000 *observationes* was published only in 1962. After that Pauw's *Observationes Tumultuariae Novae* was also published in three volumes (the last one appearing in 1972). This added about 2 000 *observationes* to those of Van Bynkershoek so it is clear that these two collections of judgments give a very reliable image of the Roman-Dutch law in force in the time of Van Bynkershoek and Pauw.

5.5.12 Willem Schorer (1717-1780)

Not much is known about Schorer's life but he is remembered today mainly for the Latin notes he wrote on De Groot's *Inleidinge.* These notes were translated into Dutch by JE Austen. Along with a man called Hendrik de Wijn (1740-1831) he also answered thirty legal questions on the *Inleidinge* which were published by a number of jurists from The Hague. Schorer was not very happy about this as he was not aware that his answers were going to be published. He claimed that he would have formulated them better if he had known of the prospective publication.

Schorer was also involved in a stormy debate with Julius Vitringa (1735-1810), a young jurist, on teaching law and on the administration of justice.

5.5.13 Franciscus Lievens Kerstemann (1728-1792)

Kerstemann is known as an adventurer and Don Juan rather than as a jurist. He was a soldier, advocate and astrologer. His money-making schemes even landed him in jail on occasion! He also tried to make money by writing superficial and popular books on law.

A well known legal work which he edited was the *Hollandsch Rechtsgeleert Woordenboek*. This work was another one of his money-making schemes and was compiled by Kerstemann and a number of collaborators on a subscription basis. But before the work was completed Kerstemann disappeared and the *Woordenboek* had to be completed by others. The end product was so defective that the publishers had to add a supplement, probably written by the Amsterdam notary, LW Kramp (c. 1716-1778). This supplement is almost twice as long as the main work! The *Woordenboek* is still quoted today but the entries are of varying quality.

5.5.14 Dionysius van der Keessel (1738-1816)

Van der Keessel was probably the most outstanding Dutch jurist of the eighteenth century.

He was professor of law at Groningen and Leiden. His best known published work is *Theses Selectae Juris Hollandici et Zeelandici* which was already translated into English by 1855 by CA Lorenz. This work contains a selection of subjects from the law in force in his time which are discussed in terms of De Groot's *Inleidinge*. The *theses* (statements) were meant as an aid to his students at the lectures he gave on De Groot's work. The lectures themselves were published by Mijers under the title *Praelectiones Juris Hodierni* (also known as the *Dictata*). The latter work was translated into Afrikaans by a number of professors at the University of Pretoria. Van der Keessel's lectures on Books 47 and 48 of the *Digesta* have also been translated into English. The considerable number of English and Afrikaans translations of Van der Keessel's works means that he is one of the most accessible of the old writers for South African legal practice.

5.5.15 Johannes van der Linden (1756-1835)

Van der Linden, who was an advocate and later a judge, was a very prolific writer particularly on subjects of interest for the legal practice of his time. His many works on the law of procedure are not of much interest today but is *Rechtsgeleerd Practical en Koopmans Handboek* is still well known. This book is a concise and elementary introduction to law and legal procedures primarily for students and businessmen without an in-depth knowledge of the law. (Incidentally, it was declared to be a "statute book of the state" in an 1859 supplement to the Constitution of the Zuid-Afrikaanse Republiek.[111]) The greatest significance of this work is that it was the last treatise on Roman-Dutch law as it was applied just before codification and the importation of French law into the Netherlands. These processes are described in the next section. Van der Linden himself was formally involved in the codification in an official capacity, among other things, as secretary of a commission which had to draw up an initial draft for a civil code.

Van der Linden also wrote a *Supplementum* to Voet's *Commentarius ad Pandectas* which is still used regularly today, and his *Verzameling van Merkwaardige Gewijsden der Gerechtshoven in Holland* also deserves to be mentioned.

2.5 Customary law

2.5.1 Customary law as a source of law

As Max Gluckman[112] and other writers of the jurisprudence and legal systems of traditional African societies have acknowledged, before the advent of colonialism African communities had their own laws and legal systems regulating the behaviour of individuals in the society. These laws covered areas such as civil and criminal liability, marriage, inheritance and succession and land tenure systems and have been conveniently described in contemporary legal literature as customary law or indigenous law. Since it is the aggregate of laws of a particular tribal community, customary law is plural and diverse and it is unwritten as its primary source is oral

[111] See **Chapter 6**. 2.

[112] Gluckman, M. 1967. "Judicial Process Among the Barotse". In: Bohannan, P. (ed.). *Law and Warfare: Studies in the Anthropology of Conflict*. New York: The Natural History Press.

tradition. It must, however, be mentioned that much of legal and anthropological literature has been written on the customary law of particular African societies. There has also been the attempt to codify African customary law. It has been argued, however, that codification will lead to fossilisation of customary law. One of the consequences of the unwritten nature of customary law has been its ascertainment and proof in court, both in terms of procedure and the substantive law. In terms of the former, most legal systems employed the method of assessors and the appointment of traditional chiefs or authorities as presiding justices.

In terms of the admissibility of the substantive customary law the matter was even more complex. Research does not indicate a uniform standard of recognition. For example in the South African case of *Van Breda v Jacobs*[113] the Appellate Division laid down four requirements for the recognition of customary, namely; (1) the custom must be reasonable; (2) the custom must have existed for a long time; (3) the custom must be generally recognised and observed by the community; and, (4) the content of the customary rule must be clear and certain. In other jurisdictions because of the juxtaposition of the received law emanating from the legal systems of the metropolitan countries alongside the customary law of the indigenous African communities, different standards of recognition were applied. This juxtaposition subjected the application of customary law to various tests of recognition. Faced with the problem of accommodation, the colonial administration accorded limited recognition to customary law by subsuming it under the received law and by subjecting it to the all too familiar repugnancy clause test of equity, good conscience and morality. For example, under the provisions of the Native Courts Ordinance, Cap 158, section 14(1)(a) and section 12(1)(a) of the Local Courts Act 1966 of Zambia, the Zambian courts could apply customary law but only so far as such law was 'not repugnant to natural justice or incompatible with the provisions of any written law'. In the case of Tanganyika, Article 24 of the Tanganyika Order in Council, 1920, provided as follows:

> 24. In all cases, civil and criminal, to which natives are parties, every court, (a) shall be guided by native law so far as it is applicable and is not repugnant to justice and morality or inconsistent with any Order in Council or Ordinance or any regulation or rule made under and Order in Council or Ordinance....

The problem that the courts of most African jurisdictions that had these 'repugnancy preconditions' faced was the standard to employ to interpret those preconditions to rule on the admissibility and enforcement of a particular customary law. In the Northern Rhodesian (Zambian) case of *R v Matengula*[114], the court was faced with a defence to murder based on a claim that the defendants had attacked the victim as a part of "pointing out" tradition. The court cited the repugnancy provisions of the statutes and held this tradition unacceptable as "against justice as we people in England see it". Most jurisdictions, including Namibia, have since replaced the repugnancy provisions with the constitutionality provision that renders a particular

[113] 1921 A.D. 330.

[114] 1951 LRNR 148 at 151.

customary law unenforceable on grounds of its inconsistency with the constitution or a provision of a statute[115].

2.5.2 Customary law as a source of law in Namibia

Namibia or South West Africa, like in all other African countries that experienced the imposition of colonial administration and legal systems, had in existence a legal system and judicial structures prior to the advent of colonialism[116]. Customary law was applied by the traditional authorities who presided over the traditional judicial structures known as the Chiefs' Courts and despite the invaluable services that were rendered by these courts, they existed for a long time without any statutory recognition. In 1942, the administration gave these courts, particularly those in the northern areas a degree of statutory authority, including limited criminal matters in prescribed matters[117].

Customary law in South West Africa was also applied by other branches of the judicial structures established by the colonial administration. By virtue of the Native Administration Proclamation 15 of 1928, the South African Administration officially recognised the application of customary law in South West Africa, Namibia. Section 28(1) of the Proclamation gave the administrator the jurisdiction to constitute courts of native commissioners for the hearing of all civil causes and matters between 'natives' only. The commissioners of the courts had the discretion to apply customary law. Section 9 of Proclamation 15 of 1928 provided as follows:

> **(1) Notwithstanding the provisions of any other law, it shall be in the discretion of the courts of native commissioners in all suits or proceedings between natives involving questions of customs followed by natives, to decide such questions according to the native law applying to such customs except in so far as it shall have been repealed or modified: Provided that such native law shall not be opposed to the principles of public policy or natural justice: Provided further that it shall not be lawful for any court to declare that the custom of** *ovitunya* **or** *okuonda* **or other similar custom is repugnant to such principles.**

In addition to the above, Proclamation R348 of 1967, (entitled Civil and Criminal Jurisdiction – Chiefs, Headmen, Chiefs' Deputies and Headmen's Deputies, Territory of South West Africa), was promulgated to become the first legislation to set out rules for the administration of justice by customary courts. Section 2 (1)(a) and (b) allow for the authorisation of chiefs, headmen and their deputies.

> **to hear and determine civil claims arising out of native law and custom brought before...(them) by natives against natives resident within the area of jurisdiction.**

---

[115] In the case of Namibia the repugnancy provision appears to have been repealed in 1985, following the abolition of the native commissioners courts by The Native Administration Proclamation Amendment Act, 27 of 1985. See Hinz, M.O. 2003. *Customary Law in Namibia: Development and Perspective*. Windhoek: CASS.

[116] See Hahn, C.H.L., Vedder, H. and Fourie, L. 1928. *The Native Tribes of South West Africa*. New York: Barnes and Noble. Hinz, Manfred O. Supra.

[117] See Duggal, N.K. (ed.). 1981. *Toward a New Legal System for Independent Namibia.* Lusaka: United Nations Institute for Namibia. p.18: Hinz, M.O. ibid.

This jurisdiction, however, does not include the consideration of "any question of nullity, divorce or separation arising out of a marriage."[118] The status of customary law courts and the application of customary law in Namibia remained under such nebulous condition until the promulgation of the Namibian Independence Constitution under which customary law has been recognised as one of the sources of law in Namibia. In its recognition of customary law as a source of law[119] the Constitution places customary law on the same footing as the common law. In the South African case of *S v Makwanyane and Mchunu*[120], Sachs, J. re-echoes these provisions in these words:

> **indigenous law, like common law, shall be recognized and applied by the courts, subject to the fundamental rights contained in the Constitution and to legislation dealing specifically therewith. .... The court can no longer continue to ignore the legal institutions and values of a very large part of the population.**

The constitutional provision that recognises the application of customary law in Namibia, just as in the case of South Africa, however, imposes the precondition that admissibility of such customary law must not be "in conflict with this Constitution or any other statutory law"[121]. For example, in the case of *S v Sipula*[122]*,* which *inter alia,* discussed the issue of the application of corporal punishment by a traditional court, Justice O'Linn, in an *obiter* stated:

> **The native law and custom providing for corporal punishment was not expressly declared unconstitutional by the aforesaid decision of the Supreme Court.**
>
> **It can be argued that articles 140(1) and 25(1)(b) of the Namibian Constitution envisage and require an express and pertinent order from a competent court to declare a specific law or a specific part of it, unconstitutional.**
>
> **I will, however, assume, without deciding, for the purpose of this judgment, that it will suffice if the judgment, by necessary implication, declares such law or specified part thereof, unconstitutional.**

The constitutionality of a principle of law under the common law *inter alia* was discussed in the case of *Myburgh v Commercial Bank of Namibia*[123] where the court held that the recognition of a particular principle of law under common law must be determined by the basic test as to whether or not it has 'fallen foul' of the constitution or any statutory law. This holding was given with respect to the recognition of common

[118] For the development of the native courts in Namibia see generally, Hinz, M.O. 2003. *Customary law in Namibia: Development and Perspective*. Windhoek: CASS.

[119] Article 66(1) of the Constitution states that both the customary law and the common law of Namibia in force on the date of independence shall remain valid to the extent to which such customary or common law does not conflict with this Constitution or any other statutory law.

[120] 1995 SA (3) 391 CC.

[121] Article 66 (1).

[122] 1994 NR 41 (HC).

[123] 1999 NR 287.

law but the same argument will apply with respect to the admissibility of customary law in the context of Article 66(1) of the Namibian Constitution.

The constitutional recognition of the status of customary law as a source of law in Namibia assumes its application by the existing judicial structures, which until 2003, did not specifically address the status of the traditional courts and traditional authorities whose jurisdiction had been officially recognised by Proclamation 15 of 1928. However, because of the racist tenor of the Proclamation, the jurisdiction and existence of these courts were quite inconsistent with the letter and spirit of the Independence Constitution. By and large, the traditional courts were, in practice, regarded as being outside the mainstream of the Namibian judicial system, as the Constitution is silent on the status of the traditional courts. For instance in the case of *S v Haulondjamba*[124], the accused was found guilty in the magistrates court of attempted rape and sentenced to a fine of N$1000,00 or 12 months imprisonment. The same court then made a sentence imposed by a tribal court a part of the sentence by adding "two heads of cattle or N$800.00 to be paid to the complainant". The High Court, however, found it irregular for a decision of a tribal court to be confirmed and incorporated in the sentence of a Magistrates' Court, the reason being that tribal judgments stand on their own. This vacuum or uncertainty has been addressed by the enactment of the Community Courts Act 10 of 2003, which gives the traditional authorities the necessary statutory recognition and jurisdiction over the application of customary and places the community courts in the mainstream of the judicial structures of Namibia[125].

2.6 Legislation

2.6.1 The legislative sources of Namibian law

The legislative sources of Namibian law range from legislation applied by the German colonial administration to current legislation enacted by the Legislature of the sovereign State of Namibia. The German legislation applicable to the territory during the years of occupation comprised such imperial statutes as had been made applicable by an Act of Imperial Government to the protectorate. These enactments include the Civil Code of 1900, the German Criminal Code and Acts especially passed by the Imperial Government for the government of the territory. In addition to these enactments, which traced their sources from the German Imperial Government, the local Landesrat since 1913 also had the legislative power over the territory. Ordinances passed by the Landesrat became the legislative source of Namibian law. However, it must be added that most of these pieces of legislation have been repealed. With the promulgation of Proclamation 21, the laws that applied in the Province of the Cape of Good Hope were superimposed over the German Imperial enactments.

Another component of the legislative source of Namibian law was the legislation introduced by South Africa. In 1925, the South African Parliament was given full power of legislation over Namibia. Consequently, some South African statutes were

[124] 1993 NR 103 (HC).

[125] See **Chapter 4**.

extended to Namibia by proclamation. It must also be added that legislative authority over the territory was not vested in the South African Union government alone. The local legislature, which comprised the Legislative Assembly of South West Africa and the Administrator-General of South West Africa, had residuary legislative functions subject to the superior legislative functions vested in the Union Parliament. The former exercised its legislative functions in the form of ordinances whereas the latter was in the form of proclamations. The head of the Union of South Africa also had the power to legislate for the territory by proclamations, (section 38(1) of the South West Africa Constitution Act 39 of 1968 as amended by section 1 of the South West Africa Constitution Amendment Act 95 of 1977 and the case of *Binga v Administrator-General, South West Africa, and Others*[126]) but after 1978 South African legislation did not automatically apply to Namibia. This only applied to the extent that it had been declared so by proclamation by the Administrator-General of South West Africa – Namibia. After the promulgation of the Namibian Constitution, however, full legislative power was vested in the National assembly 'with the power to pass laws with the assent of the President'[127]. Current legislative functions therefore vest in the National Assembly but the legislative sources of Namibian law have more components than the enactments passed by the National Assembly of Namibia.

Mention should also be made of the fact that pieces of legislation that were introduced into South West Africa before independence were not purely and authentically of South African origin. There were quite a number of English statutes that applied to Namibia especially after the passing of Proclamation 21 of 1919.

In certain jurisdictions such as South Africa, the constitution is classified as a legislative source of law because of the method of its adoption or promulgation. In Namibia, however, because of the different method of its adoption it is doubtful whether it can be classified as a piece of parliamentary legislation.

Legislation as a source of law also includes subordinate or subsidiary legislation but such subsidiary or subordinate legislation must not be in conflict with either the constitution or enabling legislation.

2.7 Extracts

LEGAL ASSISTANCE CENTRE

NAMLEX: Index to the Laws of Namibia (1997)

Transfer Proclamations

During the years 1977 to 1980, the administration of some South African statutes was transferred from South African government departments to the Administrator-General of South West Africa.

[126] *Binga v Administrator-General, South West Africa, and Others* 1984 (3) SA 949.

[127] Article 44 of the Namibian Constitution provides that 'The legislative power of Namibia shall be vested in the National Assembly with the power to pass Laws with the assent of the President as provided in this Constitution subject, where applicable, to the powers and functions of the National Council as set out in this Constitution'.

Although a few of these transfers were made by Proclamations of the State President of South Africa, most were effected by "Transfer Proclamations" promulgated by the Administrator-General. Each of these Transfer Proclamations applied to all South African statutes administered by a specific South African government department. Exceptions to the general transfer of powers from the department in question were listed in the Transfer Proclamations".

All of the Transfer Proclamations are listed for convenience in the index, in a category entitled "Transfer Proclamations".

The Procedure for Effecting Transfers

Most of the individual Transfer Proclamations refer to the "General Proclamation", which is the Executive Powers Transfer (General Provisions) Proclamation, 1977 (AG. 7/1977, as amended). This General Proclamation sets forth the mechanisms of the transfer of powers.

Section 3(1) of the General Proclamation was the core of the administrative transfer. It stated that any reference to the "Minister", the "Minister of Finance", the "State President", "Parliament" or the "Government of the Republic" should be construed as a reference to the Administrator-General, while a reference to the "State" should be construed as *including* a reference to the Administrator-General. A reference to the "Republic" was to be construed as a reference to the territory of South West Africa, and a reference to the "*Government Gazette"* of the Republic was to be construed as a reference to the "*Official Gazette*" of the territory of South West Africa.

If a statute was completely exempted from the operation of section 3(1) of the General Proclamation, then the administration of the statute was not transferred to South West Africa.

Transfer proclamations which did not actually refer to the General Proclamation followed a similar pattern.

The effect of transfer proclamations on amendments and repeals

If the administration of a statute was transferred to South West Africa by the General Proclamation, section 3(5) of the General Proclamation (as inserted by AG. 10/1978 and amended by AG. 20/1982) had the effect of "freezing" the statute as it stood at the date of transfer.

Section 3(5) as amended states:

No Act of the Parliament of the Republic –

(a) which repeals or amends any law –

(i) passed by Parliament and which applies in the Republic as well as in the territory; and

(ii) of which any or all the provisions are administered by or under the authority of the Administrator-General or the Council of Ministers in terms of a transfer proclamation or any other law; and

(b) which is passed after the commencement of such transfer proclamation or other law shall, notwithstanding any provision of a law referred to in paragraph (a) or any other

> law passed after the commencement referred to in paragraph (b) that the law referred to in paragraph (a) or any amendment thereof applies in the territory, apply in the territory, unless it is expressly declared therein or in any other law that it shall apply in the territory.

The effect was that blanket provisions pre-dating the transfer – such as the frequently – used formula "This Act, and any amendment thereof, shall also apply in the territory of South West Africa" -- no longer operated to make South African amendments to the Act automatically applicable to South West Africa. Amendments to the statute in South Africa subsequent to the date of the relevant transfer proclamation were applicable to South West Africa *only* if the amending act, or some other law passed subsequent to the date of transfer, expressly made the amendments applicable to South West Africa.

The same rule applied to repeals. If a statute which had been transferred to South West Africa was repealed in South Africa, the repeal was not applicable to South West Africa unless the repealing act expressly stated that it also applied to South West Africa.

The effect of transfer proclamations on rules and regulations

The same principle applied to rules and regulations issued under a statute which had been transferred to South West Africa.

Section 3(4) of the General Proclamation states:

> **Any proclamation, regulation or rule which is issued or made after the commencement of any transfer proclamation by, or on the authority or with the approval of, the State President or the Minister under a law which at such commencement applies both in the territory and in the Republic, and which is published in the Government Gazette of the Republic, shall, notwithstanding the provisions of subsection (1), apply in the territory if such proclamation, regulation or rule or the notice by which it is so published, contains a statement that it was or is issued or made with the consent of the Administrator-General, and applies also in the territory: Provided that for the purposes of the application of such proclamation, regulation or rule in the territory, the provisions of subsection (1) [the section which interpreted terminology in the relevant laws so as to effect the transfer] shall apply.**

The effect was that rules and regulations issued under South African laws applicable to South West Africa after the date of transfer did not apply to South West Africa unless this was explicitly stated. If subsequent rules and regulations were made applicable to South West Africa through this procedure, then their administration was transferred to South West Africa in the same way as that of the enabling act.

Additional information

Transfers are currently relevant only where statutes which originated in South West Africa are still applicable in independent Namibia. Transfers of individual statutes are discussed in more detail under the NAMLEX entry for each such statute.

2.8 International law as a source of law in Namibia

Article 144 of the Namibian Constitution provides as follows:

> Unless otherwise provided by this Constitution or Act of Parliament, the general rules of public international law and international agreements binding upon Namibia under this Constitution shall form part of the law of Namibia.

International law may be defined as that body of law that is composed for its greater part of the principles and rules of conduct which States feel themselves bound to observe, and therefore do commonly observe in their relations with each other and which includes also:

a) the rules of law relating to the functioning of international institutions or organisations, their relations with each other, and their relations with states and individuals; and
b) certain rules of law relating to individuals and non-state entities so far as the rights or duties of such individuals and non-state entities are the concern of the international community[128].

From the above definition it may be said that international law is primarily a system regulating the rights and duties of states *inter se* and the main object of international law has been to produce an ordered rather than just system of international relations. Some writers, notably Austin, Hobbes and Hart have raised fundamental theoretical questions relating to the legal character of international law. They have argued that international law is not true law but a code of rules of conduct of moral force only. Their argument is premised on the fact that there is no effective machinery for enforcing the rules of international law. Their observance, the argument goes, in the ultimate analysis, seems to depend on international comity or fear of retaliation. In fact, Austin categorises international law as "positive international morality" only analogous to the rules binding a club or society. However, there is another school of thought that opposes this position and postulates that international law is true law and not merely a moral code. As stated by Sir Frederick Pollock:

> ***"If international law were only a kind of morality, the framers of State papers concerning foreign policy would throw all their strength on moral argument. But, as a matter of fact, this is not what they do. They appeal not to the general feeling of moral rightness, but to precedents, to treaties, and to opinions of specialists. They assume the existence among statesmen and publicists of a series of legal as distinguished from moral obligations in the affairs of nations".***[129]

Despite this theoretical controversy over the true nature of international law, the fact remains that the conduct of international relations today and human rights jurisprudence are greatly determined by international law. The political and constitutional history of Namibia is today, debatably, the best example of the relevance and importance of international law in regulating the relations of States.

---

[128] Shearer, I.A. 1994. *Starke's International Law.* 11th edition. London: Butterworths.

[129] Pollock, F. 1890. *Oxford Lectures and other Lectures.* London: Macmillan Company.

Sir Frederick Pollok's statement above alludes to the sources of international law. Article 38(1) of the Statute of the International Court of Justice is generally regarded as setting out the sources of international law. In terms of that Article, the sources of international law are:

(1) international treaties and conventions;
(2) international custom, as evidence of a general practice accepted as law;
(3) the general principles of law recognised by civilized nations; and
(4) as subsidiary means for the determination of rules of law, judicial decisions and the teachings of the most highly qualified publicists of the various countries.

Namibia has ratified and/or acceded to a considerable number of international conventions and treaties including regional and continental conventions and treaties[130].

2.9 Juristic writings as a source of law in Namibia

Juristic writings are the writings and teachings of eminent publicists and in the context of the sources of law in Namibia, these include the writings of publicists whose works have impacted particularly on the development of Roman-Dutch law. Among these are eminent Dutch jurists of the seventeenth and eighteenth centuries such as Hugo de Groot (Grotius) (1583-1645), Paulus Voet (1619-1667), Simon Van Leeuwen (1626-1682), Johannes Voet (1647-1713), Cornelis Van Bynkershoek (1673-1743), Dionysius Van der Keeseel (1738-1816) and Johannes Van Linden (1756-1835) whose works are generally recognised as authoritative sources of the rules of Roman-Dutch law. The works of modern writers are generally recognised as persuasive and the weight of recognition varies depending on the standing of a particular writer in the academia, in legal practice and most importantly in the Judiciary.

2.10 Review questions

1. Define the source of law and discuss in detail one of the sources of law in Namibia.
2. Discuss legislation as a source of law in Namibia.
3. South African law has been described as a hybrid or mixed system. Discuss the extent to which this description applies to Namibian law.
4. Discuss the common law methodology of *stare decisis* debating its advantages and disadvantages.
5. Discuss **either** the constitution **or** customary law as a source of law in Namibia.
6. How would you classify the Namibian legal system? Does this classification serve any useful purpose?

[130] See footnote 133.

7. To what extent, if at all, have the writings of jurists contributed to Namibian law?
8. To what extent and by what means was the praetor able to influence the development of Roman law?
9. Discuss the origins and place of Roman-Dutch law in the legal system of Namibia.
10. Assess the contribution of juristic writings as a source of law in South Africa and Namibia.
11. Discuss judicial precedent as a source of law.
12. Discuss some of the main features of the Namibian Constitution.
13. Debate the extent to which international law can be regarded as a source of law in Namibia.

CHAPTER 3
CLASSIFICATION OF LAWS

3.1 Introduction

Law can be divided into various branches or classifications. Students of law must know the various branches of the law to be able to identify the category that a legal problem falls into to be able to solve a particular legal problem. It also serves as an indication to the student of the various areas of the law he or she will be dealing with during the course of their studies in the law school. There are many ways[131] of classifying laws but the orthodox classification is to classify the law into two main branches, public law and private law with the respective laws falling under the general pedigree. Laws can also be classified as substantive and procedural (adjectival) laws.

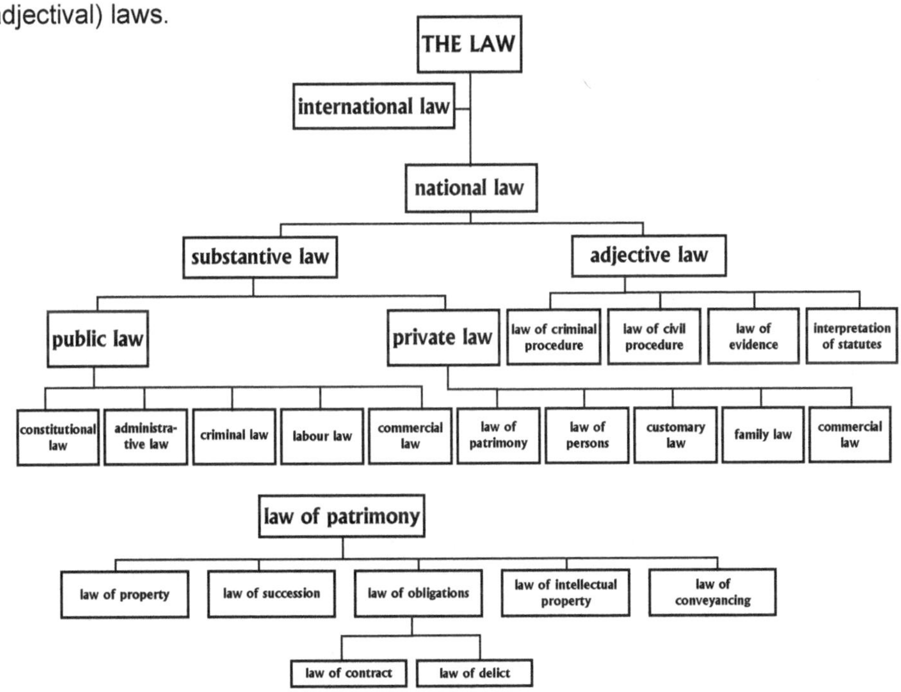

We shall proceed with the classification of law with the diagram as our reference point.

[131] Hosten, W.J.; Edwards, A.B.; Bosman, F. & Church, J. 1997. *Introduction to South African Law and Legal Theory*. 2nd edition. Durban: Butterworths. and Du Plessis, L.M. 1999. *An Introduction to Law*. Kenwyn: Juta & Co.

3.2 International Law

International law is that branch of the law that primarily deals with the relations between States. It consists of a system of rules that govern the conduct of States in their relations with each other and the functioning of international institutions or organisations, their relations with each other and their relations with States. The traditional concept is that international law is primarily concerned with the rights and duties and interests of States and therefore that only States can be considered as subjects of international law. This concept is no longer tenable in the context of contemporary international relations because with current emphasis on human rights and humanitarian law, the modern scope of international law puts as much emphasis on the rights and obligations of the individual. Therefore international law today is not only about the rules relating to the relations of States but also individuals and non-state entities.

3.3 National Law

National law may be simply defined as the sum total of the laws of a particular jurisdiction or State. It is also referred to as municipal or domestic law as opposed to international law and it is broadly divided into substantive law and adjective or procedural law.

3.3.1 Substantive and adjectival or procedural rules of law

Substantive law consists of the rules of law which actually create rights and obligations. They set out the nature and extent of these rights and obligations and how they are constituted. They constitute the main portion of the rules that are enforced by courts. The adjectival or procedural rules are supplementary to the substantive rules of law. Procedural rules set out the manner and method that the substantive rule may be enforced. They thus set out the nature of the proceedings to be taken in a given litigation.

3.3.1.1 Public law and private law

In general, the distinction between public and private law lies in the nature of the juridical relationship between the parties. In the sphere of public law, at least one of the parties exercises State authority or State power, and the relationship between the parties is accordingly one of inequality: it is a vertical relationship. On the other hand, neither party to a private law relationship may resort to State authority; the relationship is therefore one of equality. It is a horizontal relationship. The law is divided into public and private law in order to distinguish between those laws which regulate rights and obligations when one party is the State as opposed to those laws regulating rights and obligations when both parties are private persons. In other words, public law deals with matters relating to the public or national interests such as welfare, health, housing, whereas private law deals with matters that relate to the interests of private individuals such as the enforcement of contracts. The State comprises three organs (the Executive, the Legislature and the Judiciary) and acts through its agents. In law, individuals include artificial legal entities, such as companies, which have rights and obligations like individual persons.

3.3.1.2 Constitutional law

Constitutional law has two major aspects: the first aspect concerns the government's interaction with itself and the second aspect concerns the government's interaction with its subjects. Thus, constitutional law primarily relates to the government of the State and its subjects. As indicated earlier, the State is divided into three arms or organs: the Executive, the Legislature and the Judiciary. A constitution defines the State, its organisation and operation. The Namibian Constitution Act 1 of 1990 defines and distributes the functions of the government and its different organs; it defines its structures, and formulates the State's fundamental policy. For example, the Constitution provides for the procedures for the appointment and removal of judges in the High Court and the Supreme Court. Constitutional law in Namibia includes topics such as the historical development of the Namibian Constitution, the 1982 Constitutional Principles on which it is founded, the international legal context in which it was drafted and implemented, the former constitutional dispensation which mainly consisted of the sovereignty of the Parliament, the principles of interpreting a justiciable supreme constitution, the doctrine of separation of powers and the closely connected doctrine of checks and balances, the independence of the Judiciary, constitutionalism, the rule of law and democracy. Most importantly, the Bill of Rights in the Constitution has so radically revolutionalised the field of constitutional law that a critical examination of the provisions of the Bill of Rights always features in this division of the law.

3.3.1.3 Administrative law

Administrative law is part of public law and deals with the regulation of State institutions, their relationships with one another and with individuals. Article 18 of the Namibian Constitution guarantees the right to administrative justice. Article 18 is thus the constitutional basis of Administrative law in Namibia. Administrative legality is a central concept in Administrative law. It enjoins administrative bodies and administrative officials to comply with constitutional, statutory and common law requirements before performing or making any administrative act or decision. For instance, if the Immigration Selection Board, an administrative organ, performs an act for a purpose other than the one stipulated in the Immigration Control Act (the empowering Act of Parliament), this will amount to an abuse of power for an ulterior or unauthorised purpose. Furthermore, if Selma, an administrative official, exercises her discretion (i.e. power to choose between various courses of action) without following the wording of, or the procedures set out in the empowering Act, or if she acts unreasonably, unfairly or with a corrupt motive, she will be said to have acted *ultra vires* (i.e. outside the powers conferred upon her) or to have failed to properly apply her mind to the matter. Augusto, the person aggrieved by such act or decision is by virtue of Articles 18 and 25(2) entitled to seek redress before a competent Court or Tribunal. The High Court of Namibia has the inherent jurisdiction to review administrative action and may remedy invalid administrative acts by setting aside or correcting it by interdict, a declaratory order, awarding damages to the aggrieved party or by granting a relief provided for in any relevant statute.

3.3.1.4 Criminal law

A crime is a wrong against the State or the society unlike a delict, which is a wrong against another private individual. That is why a person who is accused of a crime is prosecuted by the State and not sued by the victim. In Namibia, the general principles of criminal law come from the common law. For any conduct to be prohibited as a crime, it must: (i) be defined and punished as such (principle of legality); consist of a voluntary human act; (ii) comply with the definition of the crime in question; (iv) be unlawful; (v) be committed with a blameworthy state of mind (intention or *mens rea*); and, (vi) have been caused by the accused person. While the decision to define and punish a certain conduct as criminal may sometimes be based on policy considerations, the defences against such criminal accusation involves a wide range of stereotyped arguments (insanity, intoxication, mistake of fact or law, compulsion, consent or necessity) and depends on the nature and type of the crime (crime against person, property or state; or specific intent crime or crimes based on strict liability).

3.3.1.5 Labour Law

Labour law is that branch of law which regulates the employment relationship between an employer and an employee or between employers' organisations and trade unions. Under common law, if an employer hires a person to work for him, they sign a contract known as 'contract of employment'. This contract of employment becomes the governing law of their employment relationship. The law presumes that the parties to such a contract are equal and therefore the law respects their voluntary relationship. The position of the law was that since such contracts created inter-personal relationships the State should not intervene. However, as time went by, it was realised that the financial position of the employer puts him or her in a more powerful position. Therefore the parties are not equal and consequently the State finds it necessary to intervene by way of introducing laws which regulate the employment relationship.

Before independence, the Namibian labour law was characterised by apartheid laws which were introduced by the South African regime. During the colonial period, black workers were subjected to various exploitative labour laws, whereby black workers provided their labour to produce goods and services in return for only food or little salary. Black workers were unfairly dismissed from employment and their living conditions were inhuman. They were packed like sardines in small rooms. In general, the basic conditions of employment were very poor because the apartheid laws did not provide protection against unfair labour practices against the black workers. Black workers were not allowed to form trade unions unless these unions operated within apartheid laws.

After independence, the Namibian Constitution and the Namibian Labour Act 6 of 1992 introduced a significant change in the employment relationship between employers and employees. There is also now a new Labour Act 11 of 2007.

The Labour Act 6 of 1992 lays down the basic conditions of employment and these conditions of employment include among others:

- the maximum working hours per week;
- night working hours;
- annual leave for workers;
- sick leave; and
- maternity leave days.

Disciplinary actions and termination of employment of employees are regulated by the Act so that a worker may no longer be dismissed from employment without valid reasons and without following lawful procedures.

Disputes which may arise at work between employer and employees are resolved in a certain manner. First, the dispute is reported to the Labour Commissioner who will try to facilitate the parties to resolve the dispute amicably before it is referred to the District Labour Court. This is the court which deals with disputes arising from employment relationship.

The dispute may first be referred to a conciliation board and if it is not resolved there, then it may be referred to an arbitrator. The District Labour Court or the Labour Court would be the last resort.

The Act also stipulates the lawful procedures to establish trade unions and employers' organisations. The law requires that trade unions and employers' organisations must be registered with the office of the Labour Commissioner in order for them to be recognised and thereby acquire rights and obligations under the Labour Act.

The Act also deals with collective agreements whereby employees' representatives negotiate with the employer management on issues relating to basic conditions of employment. After such negotiations, an agreement is reached, and this agreement is known as a "collective agreement".

The Act further provides that employers must ensure that workers work in a healthy and safe environment. The law places a duty on the employer to ensure that the workplace is safe and the health of the workers is guaranteed. In this respect, safety committees are established to ensure compliance.

3.3.1.6 Commercial law

Commercial law may be seen as an umbrella term that encompasses a large number of contract-based legal relationships. The study of commercial law therefore demands solid foundations in the law of contract (see p.120). However, in its strict sense, commercial law may be regarded as covering four types of contract almost omnipresent in commercial life, namely the contract of purchase and sale, the contract of letting and hiring, the contract of agency, and the contract of service. The contract of service is an entry point to the vast complex of legal rules regulating both commercial transactions and labour relations. Hence the presence of commercial law in both the public and private spheres of law. Commercial law attributes rights, obligations and liabilities to the different parties to the specified contracts. It is also concerned with the creation, operation and termination of these contracts.

3.3.1.7 The law of patrimony

The law relating to patrimony regulates or organises the origin, content, transfer and termination of patrimonial rights and duties and makes provision for the protection of these rights and enforcing the concomitant duties by means of the civil process. The law relating to patrimony is further sub-divided according to particular kinds of subjective patrimonial rights and duties with which it is concerned. These sub-divisions are: (1) property law or the law of things; (2) the law of intellectual property or incorporeal things; and (3) the law of obligations.

3.3.1.8 Law of persons

The law of persons defines the legal subject and his or her legal subjectivity; it gives him or her a certain status and determines which factors influence that status. In other words, it is the sub-division of private law which regulates the creation and termination of legal subjectivity and the status of persons.

Company law and the law of insolvency are areas of commercial law which developed from the law of persons. Company law is a specialised law of persons and, in particular, *personae*. It regulates the legal subjectivity and status of companies as *personae*. Insolvency or bankruptcy is a factor which influences the status of a person and the legal rules regulating this are also studied as a unit in the law of insolvency.

3.3.1.9 Customary law

Customary law or indigenous law, as it is sometimes called, is the body of rules originating from customary practices that regulate the affairs of the majority of Namibians in rural and urban areas and on commercial farms. It regulates the diverse Namibian personal status laws, especially in areas such as the laws of marriage, divorce, inheritance and land tenure. Article 66 of the Constitution recognises the validity of customary law within certain qualified boundaries and Article 19 recognises every Namibian's right to culture. On the strength of these Articles, customary law is protected from undesirable statutory encroachments and is given the same status as common law.

3.3.1.10 Family law

Family law consists of private law provisions regulating family relationships and it has three sub-divisions:

(a) The law of husband and wife:
The law of husband and wife regulates marriage – its conclusion, its consequences and its dissolution.

(b) Matrimonial property law:
Matrimonial property law (or the law of patrimonial relationship between husband and wife) regulates the patrimonial or "material" or proprietary consequences of concluding and dissolving a marriage.

(c) The law of wardship/curatorship:
The law of wardship or curatorship regulates the relationship between child and parent or between a minor child and a guardian. The legal rules regarding the supervision of mentally unsound people are also sometimes included under this heading.

3.3.1.11 Law of property

The law of property deals with the sum total of the various norms which regulate the legal relationships between persons and things or between legal subjects and legal objects. It harmonises the competing interests of individuals and guarantees individual property rights. In this context, property refers to both movable and immovable assets of a person or a legal subject. It includes both corporeal and incorporeal things that may constitute the patrimony or the estate of a legal subject.

The law of property explains the initial concepts of things and rights: the acquisition of these rights, the limitations imposed on these rights and the remedies. The sources of property law in Namibia consist of the Namibian Constitution, statutes, Roman-Dutch common law, case law, customary law and its usages and since some of these sources contain local laws, the content of property law in Namibia, has acquired other dimensions which make it different from the South African law. Property Law in Namibia therefore includes the land tenure systems of Namibia, land reform and resettlement, communal land tenure as amended by the Communal Land Reform Act 5 of 2002.

3.3.1.12 Law of succession

The law of succession regulates the management of a legal subject's estate (or patrimony) after the individual's death and is therefore a sub-division of the law relating to patrimony which overlaps with other sub-divisions of the law relating to patrimony for certain purposes. The law of succession also lays down the requirements for making, as well as the form of, a valid will. The law relating to the administration of estates developed as a specialised field from the law of succession.

3.3.1.13 Law of intellectual property

The law of intellectual property is that sub-division of the law relating to patrimony which has to do with rights to intellectual property and their concomitant duties. This area of the law, which deals, largely, with questions of patent rights, copyright and trademarks, took shape mainly as a sub-division of commercial law.

3.3.1.14 Law of conveyancing

The law of conveyancing in Namibia consists, basically, of the provisions of the Deeds Registries Act 47 of 1937 and the relevant common law. However, there are some specific relevant local statutes that govern some aspects of conveyancing which need be mentioned to indicate the local content of the law.

3.3.1.15 Law of obligations

The law of obligations is that sub-division of the law relating to patrimony which deals with personal rights and their concomitant obligations. The two most important sources of personal rights are contract and delict.

3.3.1.16 Law of contract

The law of contract is that sub-division of the law of obligations which is concerned with personal rights *ex contractu* (and their concomitant obligations). It also contains provisions regarding the conclusion, enforcement and termination of contracts. Sometimes the law of contract is regarded as a sub-division of commercial law because the conclusion of contracts plays such an important role in commerce, as contracts form the basis of most commercial transactions and relationships. Furthermore, specialised fields such as insurance law (as a sub-division of commercial law) are actually applied contract law. In other words, insurance is based on a contract concluded between the insurer and the insured.

3.3.1.17 Law of delict

Unlike a crime, a delict is a wrong against an individual. More specifically, a delict refers to the unlawful act of a person, done intentionally or negligently, which causes harm to another. Admittedly, the law of delict rests on three pillars: patrimonial damage, non-patrimonial injury to personality rights, and injury to physical-mental integrity. These three forms of injury are enforced by three distinct actions. Apart from this generalising approach to delict, there are specific forms of delicts such as unlawful competition, defamation and manufacturer's product liability which have developed their own specific rules. The law of delict is the other leg of the law of obligations and it is a remarkable instance of restorative justice.

3.3.2 Adjective law

Adjective law refers to the aggregate of divisions of law whose main object is the expression of substantive rules in practical terms. Simply put, adjective law deals with the procedures, the processes and the rules allowing for the application of substantive law in real situations. Adjective law comprises the law of evidence, the law of criminal procedure, civil procedure and the interpretation of statutes.

3.3.2.1 Law of evidence

The law of evidence forms part of adjective law in the sense that it lays down the procedure for presentation of both oral and documentary evidence in both civil and criminal proceedings in court. It deals with the relevancy and admissibility of evidence; the probative value of evidence; *viva voce* evidence by witnesses and cross-examination of witnesses.

3.3.2.2 Law of criminal procedure[132]

3.3.2.2.1 Course of the process: Scheme

The diagram on p.122 outlines the phases of and steps taken in the course of the process of criminal procedure. The process is described below.

3.3.2.2.2 Introduction

The law of criminal procedure deals with the processes whereby the principles and rules of criminal law find practical application. The criminal procedure is set in motion the moment a person is arrested. After arrest, the arrested person may be charged (he is formally accused of the commission of a crime), detained or released on bail. The accused person will then have to plead to the charges. If he pleads not guilty, he will be given adequate time and facilities to prepare his defence. During the trial, the accused may remain silent or decide to adduce evidence, call witnesses or cross-examine or challenge the evidence of witnesses called against him. If at the end of the trial, the presiding officer is convinced that the accused's guilt has been proved beyond reasonable doubt, the accused will be convicted and sentenced. Otherwise, he will be acquitted. In the event of a conviction, the accused still has the right to appeal against the judgment.

Criminal proceedings are ordinarily initiated by the State or the police[133] where, through its own intelligence, information has been obtained about the actual or potential commission of an offence or where a complaint has been made by a member of the public. Criminal proceedings involve investigation, search, arrest and detention, interrogation, prosecution and punishment. In isolation, these areas stand inconsistent with the Bill of Rights of the Namibian Constitution since they constitute potential violations of the rights of the individual. The Bill of Rights include such rights as the protection of the individual against arbitrary arrest or detention; the right to a fair trial; the right to privacy; protection of children's rights; the right to property. In the context of criminal procedure they are essentially a confirmation of the legal position but where the laws of criminal procedure are in conflict with the guaranteed rights, that law of procedure must be changed.

---

[132] For further reading, see Kleyn, D. & Viljoen, F. 2002. *Beginner's Guide for Law Students.* 3rd edition. Lansdowne: Juta Law.

[133] Article 115 of the Namibian Constitution and section 13 of the Police Act 19 of 1990 as amended by section 6 of the Police Amendment Act 3 of 1999.

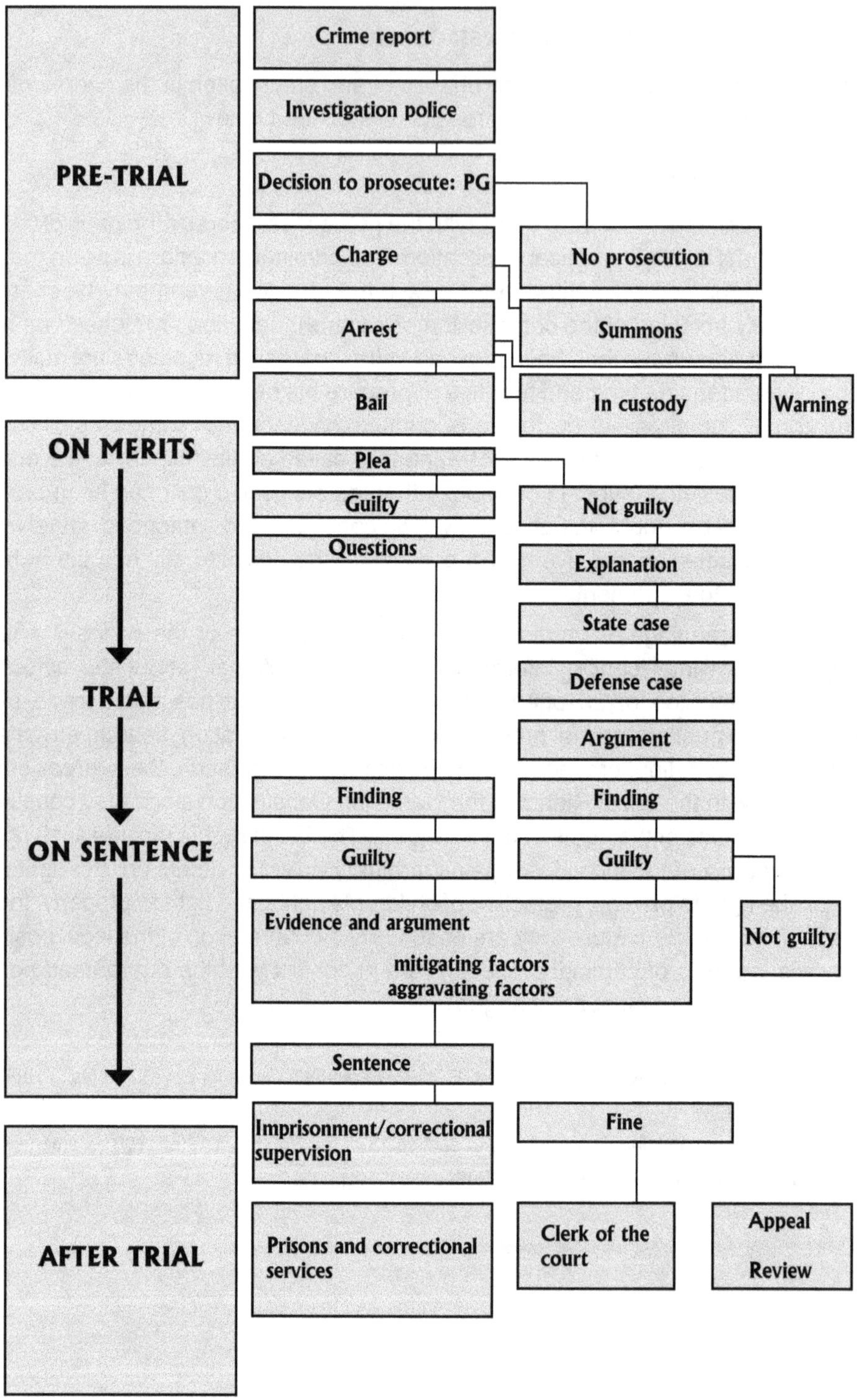
PRE-TRIAL
Crime report
Investigation police
Decision to prosecute: PG
No prosecution
Charge
Summons
Arrest
In custody
Warning
Bail
ON MERITS
TRIAL
ON SENTENCE
Plea
Guilty
Not guilty
Questions
Explanation
State case
Defense case
Argument
Finding
Finding
Guilty
Guilty
Not guilty
Evidence and argument
mitigating factors
aggravating factors
Sentence
Imprisonment/correctional supervision
Fine
AFTER TRIAL
Prisons and correctional services
Clerk of the court
Appeal
Review

The sources of criminal procedure include provisions of the Constitution, relevant international conventions[134], the Criminal Procedure Act 51 of 1977, the Police Act 19 of 1990 and its Regulations as well as the common law.

3.3.2.2.3 Pre-trial

Before a person appears in court, certain steps have to be followed to ensure his or her presence in court.

3.3.2.2.3(a) Report

As stated earlier, criminal investigations may be instituted either at the instance of a member of the public or by the State, i.e. the police. A member of the public may report a crime to the police or sometimes the victim of a crime will lay a charge, for example, the victim of an assault, rape or domestic violence. However, some crimes do not have identifiable victims who are directly affected, for example tax evasion, unlawful dealing in uncut diamonds and certain traffic offences committed after midnight. In such cases, there are no direct victims and the general practice in most jurisdictions is the utilisation by the police of informants or agents.

3.3.2.2.3(b) Investigation: Police and searches

Investigation by the police involves the processes of formally recording the complaints, laying a charge and conducting searches if necessary. After a complaint has been made, the investigating officer opens a docket (a file) and gathers information. He or she will

[134] Namibia has acceded to or ratified the following relevant conventions: African Charter on Human and Peoples' Rights; (1) OAU Document CAB/LEG 24.9/49 (1990) entered into force Nov. 29, 1999; Convention Against Torture and Other Cruel and Inhuman or Degrading Treatment or Punishment; (2) G.A. res. 39/46 [Annexure 39 UN GAOR Supp. (No. 51) at 197. UN Document A139/51 (1984)] entered into force June 26, 1987; Convention Governing the Specific Aspects of Refugee Problems in Africa: (3) 1001 U.N.T.S. 45 entered into force June 20, 1974; Convention on the Elimination of all Forms of Discrimination Against Women; (4) G.A. res. 34/180, 34 UN GAOR Supp. (No. 46) at 193. UN Document A131 entered into force September 3, 1981; Convention on the Prevention and Punishment of the Crime of Genocide; (5) 78 U.N. T.S. 277 entered into force January 12, 1951; Convention of the Rights of the Child; (6) G-A. res. 44/25 annex. 44, UN GAOR Supp. (No. 49) at 167. UN Document A144/49 (1989) entered into force September 2, 1990; Convention relating to the Status of Refugees (1951); 189 U.N.T.S., 150 entered into force April 22, 1954; the Protocol (1967); (8) 606 U.N.T.S. 267 entered into force October 4, 1967; International Convention on the Suppression and Punishment of the Crime of Apartheid; (9) G.A. res. 3068 (XXVIII), UN 28 GAOR Supp. (No. 30) at 75. UN Document A 190/30 (1974); 1015 U.N.T.S. 243 entered into force July 18, 1976; International Covenant on Civil and Political Rights, (10) G.A. res. 2200A (XXI), UN 21 GAOR Supp. (No. 16) at 52. UN Document A 163/16 (1966); 999 U.N.T.S. 171 entered into force March 23, 1976; First Optional Protocol; (11) G.A. res. 2200A (XXI), UN 21 GAOR Supp. (No. 16) at 59. UN Document A 163/16 (1966); 999 U.N.T.S. 302 entered into force March 23, 1976; International Covenant on Civil and Political Rights – Second Optional Protocol; (12) G.A. res. 44/128, Annex. 44, UN GAOR Supp. (No. 49) at 207. UN Document A 144/49 (1989) entered into force July 11, 1991; International Covenant on Economic, Social and Cultural Rights; (13) G.A. res. 44/25, Annex. 44, UN GAOR Supp. (No. 49) at 167. UN Document A 144/49 (1989) entered into force September 2, 1990.

take sworn statements made by eye-witnesses or the complainant and place these in the docket. Sometimes the police will search for clues at the scene of the crime. In some cases it may be necessary to involve specialists (experts). A blood sample of a motorist suspected of driving under the influence of alcohol can, for example, be sent for analysis. The expert's finding is placed in the docket in the form of an affidavit.

It is sometimes necessary to search a suspect's person or property for clues to solve a crime or to prove the case. The personality rights of the suspect and other inhabitants of the property may be affected, for example their privacy may be violated when constables barge into a house at midnight. For this reason, Section 19 of the Criminal Procedure Act 56 of 1977 curtails the powers of the police. Usually such a search may only be done after a search warrant has been issued by a judge or magistrate. There are some exceptions, giving a greater measure of discretion to the police. If the police are of the opinion that such a warrant will be granted, but a delay in obtaining one will defeat the whole object of such a warrant, they may continue their search without one. If their conduct does not comply with statutory requirements, they can be prosecuted or compensation can be claimed from them.

The power to search persons or their homes is paramount for successful discharge of the functions of the members of the Police Force as laid down in the Police Act 19 of 1990. This power, however, may violate the individual's constitutional right to privacy.

Article 13 of the Namibian Constitution provides as follows:

> "(1) No persons shall be subject to interference with the privacy of their homes, correspondence or communications save as in accordance with law and as is necessary in a democratic society in the interests of national security, public safety or the economic well-being of the country, for the protection of health or morals, for the prevention of disorder or crime or for the protection of the rights or freedoms of others.
>
> (2) Searches of the person or the homes of individuals shall only be justified:
>
> (a) where these are authorised by a competent judicial officer; (b) in cases where delay in obtaining such judicial authority carries with it the danger of prejudicing the objects of the search or the public interest, and such procedures as are prescribed by Act of Parliament to preclude abuse are properly satisfied".

The essence of Article 13 is that interference with the privacy of the individual may only be lawful and will not be deemed to be a violation of the individual's right if it is authorised by law and the proper procedures are followed. For this reason, the Constitution stipulates that searches are lawful if they are authorised by a competent judicial officer i.e. by a search warrant. Section 14 of the Police Act 19 of 1990 as amended by Section 7 of the Police Amendment Act 3 of 1999 provides, however, that where it is reasonably necessary for executing any of the functions under Section 13, a member of the Force can search, without warrant, any person, premises, place, vehicle and so on, if the delay in obtaining a warrant would defeat the object of search. A member of the police has the power to seize anything which in his or her opinion has a bearing on the purpose of the search, but it shall not be lawful for a police official during the search to seize an item subject to legal privilege.

Under sections 20 and 21 of the Criminal Procedure Act 51 of 1977, if the police suspect that an article was used in the commission of an offence or that it may be used as evidence in that respect then they may seize such article under search warrant. But as already stated, if the delay in obtaining the search warrant may defeat the object of search, then it would be lawful to conduct the search without such a warrant. This rule is also provided for by Section 22 of the Criminal Procedure Act 51 of 1977.

3.3.2.2.3(c) Arrest and detention

As stated earlier, the Bill of Rights includes such rights as protection of the right to life; protection of liberty; respect of human dignity; protection of the individual against arbitrary arrest. These provisions are entrenched and as stipulated under Article 131 of the Constitution, the rights cannot be repealed or amended by Parliament if such repeal or amendment diminishes or detracts from the fundamental rights and freedoms contained and defined in Chapter 3. In the context of arrest and detention, therefore, whether in the realm of the enabling legislation or the powers given to the police to carry out their mandate, legitimacy thereof can only be claimed either directly from the Constitution or an enabling or subsidiary enactment that traces generic validity eventually to the basic law or the Constitution itself, the *Grundnorm,* as it were. A cursory analysis of some of the fundamental rights will indicate that these rights are to a certain degree not absolute and that some limitations or derogations that are reasonable and necessary in a democratic society and are required in the interest of the sovereignty and integrity of the nation, national security, public decency or morality are imposed or allowed by the Constitution itself. In this context, therefore, the provisions of Articles 7 and 11 are worth mentioning.

Article 7, for example, provides for the right to protection and liberty as follows:

> No persons shall be deprived of personal liberty except according to procedures established by law.

This provision grants the individual the right to liberty, i.e. freedom of movement, and the protection of that right. The second part of Article 7, however, suggests some limitations imposed on that right, namely that the individual is capable of being subjected to lawful arrest and detention, in which case, his right to liberty is limited.

The procedures contemplated under Article 7 are found under Article 11, the Police Act 19 of 1990, the Criminal Procedure Act 5 of 1977, the law of evidence, the Namibian Police Regulations, the common law and any other relevant law. In this sense, therefore, it is necessary to discuss Articles 7 and 11 together since the latter provides the procedures pertaining to arrest and detention.

The right of arrest and detention is essential for members of the police force to effectively perform their statutory functions. It is inconceivable how the Police would be able to function without the power of arrest and detention. However, since an arrest or a detention, *prima facie*, is a deprivation of the individual's fundamental right to personal liberty as provided for under Article 7, the power to arrest and detain a suspect may only be lawful if authorised by the Constitution and relevant legislation.

The first aspect of the protection of this right, under Article 11(1) is that any unlawful arrest or any arrest not authorised by law is arbitrary and therefore unconstitutional. Article 11(2) stipulates that a person who is being arrested and detained should be informed immediately of the grounds of the arrest in a language that the arrested person understands. This does not require that the detained person must be informed in his or her native language.

Article 11(2), furthermore states that a person lawfully arrested under the authority of any law may be detained for questioning pending trial. But detention longer than 48 hours can only be authorised by a magistrate. Article 11(3) requires that an accused be brought before a magistrate within a period of 48 hours, or if this is not reasonably possible, as soon as possible thereafter. Further detention without sanction of a magistrate or a judicial officer is prohibited. It must therefore be emphasised that non-compliance with the rules will render such arrest or detention unlawful and therefore if any person arrested or detained in such unlawful manner escapes, such person cannot be charged with escaping from lawful arrest or lawful custody.

The 48-hour rule is not applicable to illegal immigrants held in custody under any law dealing with illegal immigrant, but persons so detained may not be deported from Namibia unless deportation is authorised by a tribunal empowered by law to give such authority.

Under subarticle 5, no persons who have been arrested and held in custody as illegal immigrants shall be denied the right to confidentially consult legal practitioners of their choice, and there shall be no interference with this right except such as is in accordance with the law and is necessary in a democratic society in the interest of national security or for public safety.

Articles 7 and 11 may be derogated from under certain circumstances, such as in times of emergency authorised by Article 26. However, Article 24(2) provides certain safeguards for persons so detained: they have to be informed in writing as soon as reasonably practicable and not later than 5 days after the detention in detail of the grounds for detention in a language that they understand. Not later than 14 days of detention notification has to be given in the Gazette of the detention and particulars under which law the detention is authorised need to be given. Within one month of their detention an Advisory Board established in terms of Article 26(5)(c) has to review the detention. If it is satisfied that it is not reasonably necessary for the purpose of the emergency to continue the detention of a person, the Advisory Board may order the release of the person. The Board has to review the detention at intervals of not more than 3 months. The detained person shall be afforded the opportunity to make representations as may be desirable or expedient, having regard to the public interest and the interests of the detained person, and the right to access to a lawyer or the court is guaranteed.

Apart from the provisions of the Constitution, the other provisions relating to arrest and detention may be found in the Criminal Procedure Act 51 of 1977, and the Police

Standing Regulations made in pursuance of the Criminal Procedure Act 51 of 1977. Section 39 of the Criminal Procedure Act 51 of 1977 stipulates that an arrest may be effected with or without warrant and reiterates the rule that such a person should be informed of the cause of the arrest before or immediately after the arrest and in case of an arrest effected by virtue of a warrant, the arrested person should be given a copy of the warrant. Section 40 gives a list of situations where arrests may be effected without a warrant.

3.3.2.2.3(d) Bail

Bail has been described as "a contract in terms of which an accused who is being held in custody is set at liberty upon his payment of, or his furnishing of a guarantee to pay, a fixed sum of money and, further, upon his or her express or implied undertaking to comply with the general conditions and specific conditions relating to his release. The State, on the other hand, undertakes to respect the liberty of the accused and where a court by granting of bail has deliberately given official recognition to an accused's right to liberty, the State may only succeed in having bail cancelled if it places 'convincing facts' in support of such cancellation before the court"[135].

The mechanism of bail may be seen in the context of the balance between the interest of the society and the interest of justice. As stated by Mahomed J. in the case of the *State v Acheson*[136].

> **An accused cannot be kept in detention pending his trial as a form of anticipatory punishment. The presumption of the law is that he is innocent until his guilt has been established in Court. The Court will therefore ordinarily grant bail to an accused person unless this is likely to prejudice the ends of justice.**

As a general rule, the discretion whether or not bail should be granted belongs to the courts, but under Section 59 of the Criminal Procedure Act 51 of 1977, under certain limited circumstances, bail may be granted by the police before the first court appearance of an accused. This is normally referred to as 'police bail'. Under Section 59(1)(a) of the Criminal Procedure Act 51 of 1977, an accused person who is in custody in respect of any offence, other than an offence referred to in Part II or Part III of Schedule 2, may be released on bail in respect of such offence by any police official of or above the rank of non-commissioned officer, if the accused deposits at the police station the sum of money determined by such police official. The police official who has the power to determine police bail is required under the Act to consult with the investigating officer[137]. The police official concerned must, at the time of releasing the accused on bail, complete and hand to the accused a recognisance on which a receipt shall be given for the sum of money deposited as bail and on which the offence in respect of which the bail is granted and the place, date and time of the trial of the accused are entered[138]. Immediately after this the police official must

135 Du Toit et al. 1999. *Commenatry on the Criminal Procedure Act.* Cape Town: Juta.

136 1991 (2) SA 805 (Nm) at 822A-B.

137 Section 59 (a) of the Criminal Procedure Act 51 of 1977.

138 Section 59 (1) (b) ibid.

forward a duplicate original of such recognisance to the clerk of the court which has the jurisdiction[139].

3.3.2.2.3(e) Bail granted by the prosecution

Unlike in Namibia, the current South African bail jurisprudence has a provision for prosecutorial bail. Section 59A(1) of the Criminal Procedure Act 51 of 1977 provides that a prosecutor, or a prosecutor authorised thereto in writing by the attorney-general concerned, may in respect of the offences referred to in Schedule 7 and in consultation with the police official charged with the investigation, authorise the release of an accused on bail. This is known as 'prosecutorial bail'. Section 59A (3) provides that the effect of prosecutorial bail is that the person who is in custody shall be released from custody:

> **(a) upon payment of, or the furnishing of a guarantee to pay, the sum of money determined for his or her bail at his or her place of detention contemplated in section 50(1)(a);**
>
> **(b) subject to reasonable conditions imposed by the attorney-general or prosecutor concerned; or**
>
> **(c) payment of such sum of money or the furnishing of such guarantee to pay and the imposition of such conditions.**

In terms of section 59A (1) and 59A (3), a prosecutor may – after consultation with the Prosecutor-General, issue directives. An accused who is released on prosecutorial bail must appear on the first court day at the court and at the time determined by the prosecution; and the release of the accused shall endure until he or she appears before the court on the first day – Section 59A (4). Prosecutorial bail proceedings must be recorded in full, including the conditions imposed – Section 59A (6) as read with Section 64. In terms of Section 59A (7) prosecutorial bail shall be regarded as bail granted by a court in terms of Section 60. However, as pointed out earlier prosecutorial bail only lasts until the accused's appearance on the first day. At this first court appearance judicial intervention or approval is required. Section 59A (5) provides that at the first appearance in court of a person released on prosecutorial bail, the court:

> **(a) may extend the bail on the same conditions or amend such conditions or add further conditions as contemplated in section 62; or**
>
> **(b) shall, if the court does not deem it appropriate to exercise the powers contemplated in paragraph (a), consider the bail application and, in considering such application, the court has the jurisdiction relating to the powers, functions and duties in respect of bail proceedings in terms of section 60.**

3.3.2.2.3(f) Bail after first appearance of accused in lower court

In terms of section 60(1) an accused who is in custody in respect of any offence may at his first appearance in a lower court or at any stage after such appearance, apply to such court or, if the proceedings against the accused are pending in a superior court, to that court, to be released on bail in respect of such offence, and any such court

[139] Section 59 (1) ibid.

may, subject to the provisions of section 61, release the accused on bail in respect of such offence on condition that the accused deposits with the clerk of the court or, as the case may be, the registrar of the court, or with a member of the prisons service at the prison where the accused is in custody, the sum of money determined by the court in question.

The court may, on good cause shown, permit an accused to furnish a guarantee, with or without sureties, that he will pay and forfeit to the State the sum of money determined under subsection (1), or increased or reduced under section 63(1), in circumstances under which such sum, if it has been deposited, would be forfeited to the State.

However, the Prosecutor-General may prevent the granting of bail in certain circumstances:

(1) if an accused who is in custody in respect of any offence referred to in Part III of Schedule 2 applies under section 60 to be released on bail in respect of such offence, and the Prosecutor-General, either by written notice or in person, informs the court before which the accused applies for bail that information is available to him –
   (a) which, in his opinion, cannot be disclosed without prejudice to the public interest or the administration of justice; and
   (b) which, in his opinion, shows that the release of the accused on bail is likely to affect the administration of justice adversely or to constitute a threat to the safety of the public or the maintenance of the public order, and that he on the ground of the likelihood of such adverse effect or of such threat objects to the granting of bail to the accused, the court shall refuse the application of bail.

(2) Any telegraphic notification purporting to be a copy of a written notice under subsection (1), shall for all purposes be *prima facie* proof of the contents of such notification.

(3) If no evidence is within ninety days of his arrest led against an accused referred to in subsection (1), he may, on notice in writing to the Prosecutor-General, apply to the court before which the charge in respect of which bail was refused is pending, to be released on bail, and such court may, in its discretion, release the accused on bail, whereupon any provision of this Act dealing with bail granted under section 60 shall apply with reference to bail so granted.

(4) (a) Where an accused under subsection (1) applies to be released on bail and the prosecutor informs the court before which the accused applies for bail that the matter or bail has been or will be referred to the Prosecutor-General, the court shall postpone the determination of the application pending the decision of the Prosecutor-General.
   (b) if the Prosecutor-General does not within fourteen days of the date on which the application is postponed under subsection (1) inform the court as provided by subsection (1) and object to the granting of bail on any ground contemplated by that subsection, the court shall determine the application.

(5) The Prosecutor-General may at any time after an application for bail has been refused under subsection (1), withdraw his objection to the granting of bail, whereupon the court may proceed to deal with the application under section 60.

3.3.2.2.3(g) Appeal by an accused to High Court against a lower court's decision concerning bail

An accused who considers himself aggrieved by the refusal by a lower court to admit him to bail or by the imposition by such court of a condition of bail, including a condition relating to the amount of bail money and including an amendment or supplementation of a condition of bail, may appeal against such refusal or the imposition of such condition to the High Court or to any judge of that court if the court is not sitting – Section 65(1)(a). The appeal may be heard by a single judge – Section 65(1)(b). The High Court shall have jurisdiction to hear an appeal in terms of Section 65(1)(a) if the area of jurisdiction of the lower court in question or any part hereof falls within the area of jurisdiction of such local division – Section 65(1)(c). Leave to appeal against the refusal of a lower court to grant bail, in cases where the trial is still pending, is not required. When the accused has already been convicted and sentenced, leave to appeal in such circumstances would be necessary[140].

The accused must serve a copy of the notice of appeal on the Prosecutor-General and on the magistrate or the regional magistrate, as the case may be[141].The notice of appeal must set out the specific grounds upon which the appeal is lodged[142]. The magistrate or regional magistrate concerned must forthwith furnish the reasons for his or her decision to the court or judge, as the case may be[143].

An appeal shall not lie in respect of new facts which arise or are discovered after the decision against which the appeal is brought, unless such new facts are first placed before the magistrate or regional magistrate against whose decision the appeal is brought and such magistrate or regional magistrate gives a decision against the accused on such new facts[144].

The court or judge hearing the appeal shall not set aside the decision against which the appeal is brought unless such court or judge is satisfied that the decision was wrong, in which event the court or judge shall give the decision which in its opinion the lower court should have given[145]. In *Porthen*[146] it was said that section 65(4) of the Act 'should be construed in a manner which does not unduly restrict the ambit of an appeal Court's competence to decide that the lower court's decision to refuse bail was 'wrong'.

[140] *S v Siwela* 1999 (2) SACR 685 (W). See also *S v Mohammed* 1999 (2) SACR 507(C); *S v Maseko* 2000 (1) SACR 251 (EC); *S v Potgieter* 2000 (1) SACR 578 (W).

[141] See *Shefer v Director of Public Prosecutions,* Transvaal [2004] 2 All SA 88 (T) at [25].

[142] See *S v Ho* 1979 (3) SA 734 (W) at 738B-C.

[143] Section 65(3) of the Criminal Procedure Act 51 of 1977.

[144] Section 65(2). Ibid; *S v Yanta* 2000 (1) SACR 237 (TkH).

[145] Section 65(4) ibid; *S v Barber* 1979 (4) SA 278 (D); *S v De Abreu* 1980 (4) SA 94 (W) at 96H-97A.

[146] 2004 (2) SACR 242 (C) at [17].

A further appeal against an order of the High Court sustaining a magistrate's refusal of bail is possible[147]. But this may be done only with leave of the High Court concerned and, if such leave is refused, with the leave of the Supreme Court of Appeal. There is a right of appeal without prior leave to the Supreme Court of Appeal against the refusal of bail by the High Court as court of first instance[148].

Bail appeals are *prima facie* urgent[149]. But the urgency of a bail appeal does not entitle a party to ignore the procedures prescribed by Section 65[150].

3.3.2.2.3(h) Appeal by a prosecutor against the decision of court to release accused on bail

A prosecutor may appeal to the High Court against the decision of a lower court to release an accused on bail or against the imposition of a condition of bail[151].

A prosecutor may also appeal to the Supreme Court of Appeal against the decision of the High Court to release an accused on bail[152]. In both instances, the court hearing the appeal may order that the State should pay the accused concerned the whole or any part of the costs which the accused may have incurred in opposing the appeal. In the event of a successful appeal against release on bail the court which heard the appeal shall issue a warrant for the arrest of the accused[153]. It should be noted that this provision does not currently apply in Namibia.

3.3.2.2.4 Trial

The decision to try the suspect will be determined by the nature of the information that the police have in the docket. A prosecution is instituted if a *prima facie* case is made out against the accused. The test is whether a reasonable person will, at first glance, form the opinion that there is sufficient evidence to prove the case against the accused. A charge sheet (or indictment in the High Court) is drafted. This sets out the particulars of the alleged offence with which the accused is charged, which include the alleged unlawful act or omission and where and when it was committed.

If the police (i.e. the investigating officer) is satisfied that the information in the docket is sufficient to prove a *prima facie* case against the suspect, he or she may hand it to the Prosecutor-General (PG previously known as the Attorney-General (AG)), who has the discretion to decide whether a prosecution may be instituted. The PG's power to prosecute is delegated to public prosecutors in the lower courts and state advocates in the higher courts. If the PG or prosecutor refuses to prosecute because the case was not investigated fully, the suspect stands to be discharged but not acquitted. A discharge does not constitute a bar to subsequent prosecution. The

[147] See generally *S v Mohammed* 1977 (2) SA 531 (A).

[148] See *S v Botha* 2002 (1) SACR 222 (SCA).

[149] *Prokureur-Generaal, Vrystaat v Ramokhosi* 1997 (1) SACR 127 (0).

[150] See *Shefer v Director of Public Prosecutions* [2004] 2 All SA 88 (T) at [24].

[151] Section 65A(1)(a) of the Criminal Procedure Act 51 of 1977.

[152] Section 65A(2)(a). ibid.

[153] Section 65A(3). ibid.

police may continue with their investigation and, if more comprehensive information is obtained, the docket may be submitted again. If the PG refuses to prosecute, a complainant may also institute a private prosecution. This is exceptional and requires a monetary deposit. However, if after the plea, the prosecution does not have sufficient evidence against the accused, then, as a general rule, he or she stands acquitted since this constitutes a bar to subsequent prosecution. This principle is known as *autrefois acquit*. There are exceptions to this general rule. In some jurisdictions, for example in England, the Criminal Justice Act 2003 allows for retrial in a limited range of offences where there is new and compelling evidence that the acquitted person is guilty of the offence and a retrial is in the interest of justice.

Before the trial itself there are pre-trial procedures that may determine the outcome of the trial. Pre-trial procedures are crucial as they involve the right of the individual to legal representation when confession statements are taken, preparation of cases for expeditious hearings, etc. It is therefore the right of the police to inform suspects of these rights.

Article 12 of the Namibian Constitution provides for fair trial as follows:

(1)(a) In the determination of their civil rights and obligations or any criminal charges against them, all persons shall be entitled to a fair and public hearing by an independent, impartial and competent Court or Tribunal established by law: provided that such Court or Tribunal may exclude the press and/or the public from all or any part of the trial for reasons of morals, the public order or national security, as is necessary in a democratic society.

(b) A trial referred to in Sub-Article (a) hereof shall take place within a reasonable time, failing which the accused shall be released.

(c) Judgments in criminal cases shall be given in public, except where the interest of juvenile persons or morals otherwise require.

(d) All persons charged with an offence shall be presumed innocent until proven guilty according to law, after having had opportunity of calling witnesses and cross-examining those called against them.

(e) All persons shall be afforded adequate time and facilities for the preparation and presentation of their defence, before the commencement of and during their trial, and shall be entitled to be defended by a legal practitioner of their choice.

(f) No persons shall be compelled to give testimony against themselves or their spouses, who shall include partners in a marriage by customary law, and no Court shall admit in evidence against such person's testimony which has been obtained from such persons in violation of Article 8(2)(b) hereof.

(2) No persons shall be liable to be tried, convicted or punished again for any criminal offence for which they have already been convicted or acquitted according to law: provided that nothing in this Sub-Article shall be construed as changing the provisions of the common law defences of "previous acquittal" and "previous conviction".

(3) No persons shall be tried or convicted for any criminal offence or on account of any act or omission which did not constitute a criminal offence at the time when it was committed, nor shall a penalty be imposed exceeding that which was applicable at the time when the offence was committed.

Under the Namibian legal system and administration of justice, the Supreme Court of Namibia has added another dimension to the right to fair trial; the right of accused persons to legal representation to be provided by the State. Under the laws of Namibia, during trials, it is the responsibility of the presiding officer to ensure compliance with this right but it is submitted that, as stated earlier, this should equally be the responsibility of the police. In the case of *S v Kau and Others,*[154] the Supreme Court of Namibia ruled that the failure to inform appellants of their rights to legal representation is an irregularity.

As regards the duty of the State to provide free legal aid, it should first be noted that Article 95 of the Constitution of the Republic of Namibia generally provides for the promotion of the welfare of the people. Article 95(h) specifically provides for a 'legal system' seeking to promote justice on the basis of equal opportunity by providing free legal aid in defined cases with due regard to the resources of the State. The binding effect of the provisions of Article 95 of the Constitution was one of the issues that had to be determined by the Supreme Court of Namibia in the case of *Government of the Republic of Namibia and Others v Mwilima & all other Accused in the Caprivi Treason Trial*[155]. The Supreme Court ruled that in so-far-as the services impinged on the fundamental rights of the individual as enshrined under Chapter 3 of the Constitution, the government was under a constitutional obligation to provide such services and the Judiciary had the obligation to enforce and protect the fundamental rights of the individual as enshrined in the Constitution.

The trial takes place in the court itself and consists of two stages: the trial on merits and the trial on sentence. The former deals with the determination of the guilt or innocence of the accused person, and the latter deals with the question of an appropriate sentence in the event of the conviction of the accused person. Trial on merit begins with the plea.

3.3.2.2.4(a) Plea

When the State has investigated a case thoroughly and is satisfied that a case can be established against the suspect, and steps have been taken to ensure the presence of the accused at the trial, the charges against the accused will be formulated and the trial will commence. The status of the court before which an accused person may be brought will depend on the nature and seriousness of the case. Irrespective of the court that will have jurisdiction over the case, certain procedures have to be followed before the trial actually commences. The accused must be brought before a Magistrates' Court and be required to plead to the charges or that a preparatory examination be held.

[154] 1995 NR 1 (SC).

[155] 2002 NR 235 (SC).

In terms of Section 106(1)(a) and (b) of the Criminal Procedure Act 51 of 1977, when an accused pleads guilty to a charge he or she may plead that he or she is guilty of the offence charged or of any offence of which he or she may be convicted on the charge; or that he or she is not guilty. Where an accused pleads guilty, in terms of Sections 121(1) read together with Section 112(1)(b), the magistrate is required to question him or her in order to ascertain whether he or she admits the allegations in the charge. If the magistrate is satisfied that the accused admits the allegations, he or she stops the proceedings pending the decision of the Prosecutor-General. In terms of Sections 121(2)(a) and (3) the Prosecutor-General may decide to arraign the accused for sentence before a superior court or any other court having jurisdiction, including the court in which the proceedings were stopped. If the magistrate is not satisfied that the accused admits the allegations in the charge sheet, he or she must, in terms of Section 121(2)(b), record in what respect he or she is not so satisfied, enter a plea of not guilty and deal with the matter in terms of Section 122(1). The magistrate shall advise the accused of the decision of the Prosecutor–General. If the decision is that the accused be arraigned for sentence, then:

(1) in the Magistrates' Court concerned, the court must dispose of the case and the proceedings continue as though no interruption occurred; or

(2) in a regional or the superior court, the magistrate or the judge must adjourn the case for sentence by such court – Section 121(4). This court may convict the accused on his plea of guilty of the offence concerned and impose any competent sentence – Section 121(5)(b). If the accused satisfies the court that the plea of guilty or admission was incorrectly recorded, or if the court is not satisfied that the accused is guilty or has no valid defence to the charge, it records a plea of not guilty and proceeds with the trial as if it is a summary trial in that court.

Where an accused pleads not guilty, Section 122(1) provides that the court must act in terms of Section 115: the magistrate asks the accused whether he or she wishes to make a statement indicating the basis of his or her defence. Where the accused does not make a statement, or does so and it is not clear from the statement to what extent he or she denies or admits the issues raised by the plea, the court may question him or her in order to establish which allegations in the charge the accused disputes. When Section 115 has been complied with, the magistrate must stop the proceedings and adjourn the case pending the decision of the Prosecutor-General. The Prosecutor-General may:

(1) arraign the accused on any charge at a summary trial before a superior court or any other court having jurisdiction (including the Magistrates' Court in which the proceedings were adjourned); or,

(2) institute a preparatory examination against the accused.

The Prosecutor-General advises the magistrate concerned of his decision and the court notifies the accused accordingly.

During the trial the prosecution opens its case by calling witnesses in examination in chief. These witnesses will then be cross-examined by the defence and thereafter be re-examined by the prosecution. At the end of the case for the State, if the State has failed to establish a *prima facie* case against the accused the accused will be discharged, but if *a prima facie* has been established the accused will be put on his defence. In this case the procedure described earlier applies. If the State succeeds in establishing the guilt of the accused beyond a reasonable doubt then the court must impose an appropriate sentence, which may be a fine, incarceration or both, or a suspended sentence. If the State fails to discharge its burden, the accused must be acquitted.

3.3.2.2.4(b) Sentencing

Article 6 of the Namibian Constitution, which deals with the protection of life, provides as follows:

> The right to life shall be respected and protected. No law may prescribe death as a competent sentence. No Court or Tribunal shall have the power to impose a sentence of death upon any person. No executions shall take place in Namibia.

This right is absolute and no exceptions are made. It imposes on the State the responsibility of protecting the lives of its citizens. As provided for by the Banjul Charter this right to life includes the obligation on States to take reasonable steps to prevent situations that could result in the violation of the right.

The right to life is the most important of all human rights. It precedes all other rights in the Constitution. Without life it would not be possible to exercise and enjoy the other rights. But the right to life does not only refer to the right to existence, it also includes the right to dignity. It is a right to be treated as a human being with dignity. It is as a result of this right that capital punishment, or the death penalty, is unconstitutional and unacceptable in Namibia as a punishment. It is also as a result of this right that if a member of the police force shoots and kills a suspect in the process of effecting an arrest, such a member may be liable to prosecution for a *prima facie* case of murder or culpable homicide if unreasonable force was used.

Article 8 of the Namibian Constitution is also of relevance and it provides as follows:

> (1) The dignity of all persons shall be inviolable.
>
> (2)(a) In any judicial proceedings or in other proceedings before any organ of the State, and during the enforcement of a penalty, respect for human dignity shall be guaranteed.
>
> (b) No persons shall be subject to torture or to cruel, inhuman or degrading treatment or punishment.

This is a right that may need to be read in conjunction with other rights, such as the right to equality, as discrimination also violates dignity. The Supreme Court of Namibia has described the right to dignity, along with the right to life, as the most important human rights.

The right to dignity and the prohibition against cruel, inhuman or degrading punishment are inextricably linked, but the former, the right to dignity, means much more than the prohibition of torture or cruel, inhuman or degrading treatment or punishment.

The question whether corporal punishment is a violation of Article 8, more specifically Article 8(2)(b), was decided in *Ex parte Attorney-General, Namibia: In re Corporal Punishment by Organs of State*[156]. Looking at Article 8(2)(b), the court held that the words "no person shall be subject to torture or to cruel, inhuman or degrading treatment or punishment" shall be read separately creating seven different conditions: torture, cruel treatment and punishment, inhuman treatment and punishment and degrading treatment and punishment. The court further held that no derogation from the rights in Article 8 is permitted, and the State's obligation is absolute. This means therefore that any Act of Parliament or a practice authorised by any organ of the State which falls within the seven areas will be deemed inhuman and therefore unconstitutional.

The court further found that corporal punishment upon adults and juveniles, inflicted by an organ of the State in consequence of a sentence directed by a judicial or quasi-judicial authority in Namibia is indeed a form of "inhuman or degrading" punishment and in conflict with Article 8.

The same was held to be the case in respect of corporal punishment at schools pursuant to the provisions of the relevant Code issued by the Ministry of Education, Culture and Sport.

3.3.2.2.5 Appeal and review

A convicted person has the right of appeal against both conviction and sentence or both. He or she may lodge the appeal with a higher court in the judicial hierarchy, with or without leave of the court below. If there is evidence of irregularity in the procedure, the case can also be reviewed by a higher court. Appeal or review is not a second trial and therefore the court will generally not allow new evidence to be introduced. It is therefore said that the proceedings are conducted on record.

3.3.2.3 Law of civil procedure

Civil procedure sets out the remedies available to aggrieved parties when their rights or interests derived from the private law sphere have been transgressed[157]. Civil procedure forms part of the process of public ordering whereby the private rights of citizens are enforced by the State through the court system. The rules of civil procedure are thus concerned with the manner in which an interested party may bring his case before the appropriate court of an authoritative decision which is enforced by the sanction of the State. In a matter which involves a dispute, the first question to be determined is whether the aggrieved party has a right and if

[156] See footnote 6.

[157] Hosten, W.J.; Edwards, A.B.; Bosman, F. & Church, J. 1997. *Introduction to South African Law and Legal Theory*. 2nd edition. Durban: Butterworths.

so, whether that right has been infringed. If a right has been so infringed it follows that the injured party does have a remedy in accordance with the maxim *ubi ius ibi remedius*, that is, where there is a right there is a remedy. Having established that a right does exist, the interested party then has to identify the court which is competent to grant the remedy, or has jurisdiction over the case.

The question of jurisdiction is an issue preliminary to commencement proceedings and the selection of a competent court in turn influences the nature and conduct of the proceedings for the rules involving the selection of procedure differ depending on the court before which the proceedings are brought. (For jurisdiction of courts in general, see Chapter 4.)

3.3.2.3.1 Types of civil proceedings[158]

There are three types of civil procedures that may be followed in the High Court and Magistrates' Courts: provisional sentence proceedings, action proceedings and application or motion proceedings.

3.3.2.3.2 Choice of proceedings in the High Court

3.3.2.3.2(a) Provisional sentence

Where the plaintiff wishes to sue on the basis of a liquid document, it is appropriate to institute provisional-sentence proceedings, since this will usually be the cheapest and quickest method of obtaining judgment. Provisional sentence may be sought only where the plaintiff sues on the basis of a liquid document in his favour.

A liquid document is a written document, signed by the debtor (or the debtor's agent), in which the debtor has unconditionally acknowledged his or her indebtedness to the plaintiff in a fixed and definite amount of money. The acknowledgement of the indebtedness must be unconditional, and the amount of the debt must appear from the document itself, although the obligation to make payment may be dependent on the fulfilment of a simple condition or event extraneous to the document. In the latter instance, it will be sufficient for the plaintiff to allege in the provisional-sentence summons that the condition has been met or that the event has occurred. If this is disputed by the defendant in an answering affidavit, then the plaintiff will have to discharge the onus of establishing compliance with the condition or the event by means of evidence in a replying affidavit.

Rule 8 of the Rules of the High Court of Namibia provides as follows:

> (1) Where by law any person may be summoned to answer a claim made for provisional sentence, proceedings shall be instituted by way of a summons as near as may be in accordance with Form 3 of the First Schedule, calling upon such person to pay the amount claimed or failing such payment to appear personally or by counsel upon a day named in such summons not being less than 15 days after the service upon him or her of such summons, to admit or deny his or her liability:

[158] See generally Dendy, M. "Step-by-Step: Choice of Procedure in Civil Litigation". *De Rebus*. May 2003.

3.3.2.3.2(b) Action and application (motion) proceedings

In all cases other than those in which the plaintiff sues on the basis of a liquid document, the practitioner who initiates High Court proceedings on behalf of a client will have to choose between procedure by way of trial action and procedure on application.

In action proceedings the parties to the proceedings are called the plaintiff and the defendant (including the attorney or counsel appearing for any such party) and the proceedings commence by the issuing of summons. Action proceedings are employed where the parties disagree about the facts of the case. Both the plaintiff and the defendant are given the opportunity to lead evidence in court and to cross-examine the witnesses of the other party.

In motion proceedings the parties (including the attorney or counsel appearing for any such party) are called the applicant and the respondent and the proceedings commence with the issuing of a notice of motion plus affidavit. Motion proceedings are employed where the parties fundamentally agree about the facts of the case. At the hearing of an application, no *viva voce* evidence is presented before the court.

The determination of whether or not a litigant proceeds by way of application (motion) or action proceedings depends on a variety of considerations and are regulated by the rules laid down in the famous case of *Room Hire Co. (Pty) Ltd v Jeppe Street Mansions (Pty) Ltd*[159] and which may be summarised as follows:

- Application proceedings are cheaper and also speedier than action proceedings, but may only be used in very limited circumstances.
- In cases in which, by statute, motion proceedings are specifically authorised or directed, or in which trial actions are by statute rendered compulsory. In such cases, the type of procedure laid down in the statute must be followed. For example Section 346 of the Companies Act 61 of 1973 provides for winding up to take place pursuant to an application to court. Proceedings for the winding-up of a company are therefore motion proceedings.
- In cases involving illiquid (unliquidated) claims for damages. (An illiquid claim for damages is one which the amount claimed has not been agreed upon between the parties prior to institution of action and is, in addition, not capable of speedy and prompt ascertainment.) In this case, procedure by way of trial action is compulsory.
- In cases in which urgent relief is sought. Here a litigant who wishes to institute proceedings must do so by launching an urgent application, since no mechanism exists in trial-action proceedings for the granting of urgent relief to the plaintiff. (A party who seeks relief which is normally obtainable only by way of trial-action may not, however, circumvent the trial-action procedure merely on the basis that relief is required as a matter of urgency. What will happen in such cases is that the court hearing an urgent application will be prepared to grant no more than *interim* relief to operate until such time as a trial action aimed at securing permanent relief has been disposed of. The plaintiff will then have to launch an urgent application as well as

[159] 1949 (3) SA 1155 (T) at 1161-119\63.

a trail action. If a trial action has not been instituted by the time when the court considers the urgent application, the court will direct the applicant to institute action within a time specified by the court, failing which the interim relief granted on an urgent basis will lapse.)

- In cases in which no relief is sought against any other person. Here, the procedure to be followed will always take the form of motion proceedings – more specifically, an *ex parte* application. There will then be no respondent before the court, and the only party will be the applicant (or perhaps two or more co-applicants). Examples would be an application for admission as an attorney or an advocate, or an application by a married couple for authorisation by the court to execute and register postnuptially a notorial contract having the effect of an antenuptial contract in terms of Section 88 of the Deeds Registries Act 47 of 1937.
- In cases where it is not specifically prohibited, or which fall outside the above categories, in which a choice between procedure by way of trial action and motion proceedings is available, and where no real dispute on material questions of fact exists, or is likely to arise in the litigation between the parties. If a material dispute of fact exists, then the party instituting the litigation should proceed by way of trial action.
- Where, if a dispute does exist, it can nevertheless be determined without having recourse to verbal evidence.
- In addition to the above, motion proceedings are prohibited where provisional sentence is sought.

In the case of *Room Hire Co (Pty) Ltd v Jeppe Street Mansions (Pty) Ltd*[160] the court stated the general position as follows:

> **"I propose to set out, first, as I understand it, the general position in regard to the permissibility of motion proceedings as opposed to trial action. Two types of proceedings may be mentioned, as falling outside the scope of this enquiry.**
>
> **There are certain types of proceedings (e.g. in connection with insolvency) in which by statute motion proceedings are specially authorized or directed; in these the matter must be decided upon affidavit.**
>
> **There are the other and certain classes of cases (the instances given by Dowling J are matrimonial causes and illiquid claims for damages) in which motion proceedings are not permissible at all. But between these two extremes there is an area in which (as I see the position) according to recognized practice a choice between motion proceedings and trial action is given according to *whether there is or is not an absence of a real dispute between the parties on any material question of fact.*" (emphasis added)**

The court in the same case specified three ways in which a material dispute of fact may arise in application proceedings:

- The respondent may deny material allegations made by the applicant and/ or the deponents on the applicant's behalf and produce evidence by the deponents to the contrary;

[160] 1949 (3) SA 1155 (T) at 1161.

- The respondent may plead new allegations (not canvassed in the founding affidavit of the applicant) in confession and avoidance of the claim of the applicant, and those allegations may be disputed by the applicant;
- The respondent may concede that he or she has no knowledge of material facts averred by the applicant but may deny them, putting the applicant to the proof of them, and himself or herself giving evidence to show that the applicant and/or the applicant's deponents is/are untruthful or otherwise unreliable, and that certain facts (*facta probantia*) on which the applicant relies in order to prove the main facts (*facta probanda*) are untrue.

Where a dispute of fact arises in the affidavits of motion or application proceedings which cannot be settled without hearing oral evidence, the court may:

(a) dismiss the application;

(b) order that oral evidence be heard on certain specified issues;

(c) order the parties to trial; or,

(d) decide the issue on the respondent's facts.

3.3.2.3.3 Choice of proceedings in Magistrates' Courts

3.3.2.3.3(a) Provisional sentence proceedings

In Magistrates' Courts, provisional sentence proceedings will be appropriate in the same circumstances as in the High Courts, i.e. when the plaintiff wishes to sue on the basis of a liquid document. In South Africa, both uniform r (8)(1) and Magistrates' Court r (14A)(1) provide for the institution of proceedings by way of a provisional sentence.

Rule 14(A)(1) of the South African Magistrates' Courts Rules of Court provides as follows:

> Where by law any person may be summoned to answer a claim made for provisional sentence, proceedings shall be instituted by way of a summons as near as may be in accordance with Form 2 A of Annexure 1, calling upon such person to pay the amount claimed or failing such payment to appear personally or by a practitioner upon a day named in such summons not being less than 10 days after the service upon him of such summons, to admit or deny liability.

The position in Namibia, is however different. Rule 8 of the Rules of the High Court of Namibia makes a provision for provisional sentence but there is no equivalent provision in the Magistrates' Court rules for the institution of proceedings by way of a provisional sentence.

3.3.2.3.3(b) Action and application (motion) proceedings

In cases other than those in which provisional sentence proceedings are appropriate, a practitioner has a choice between proceedings by way of trial action and on application or motion when the litigation is commenced in a Magistrates' Court. The rules in the *Room Hire* case do not govern the choice between the two types of procedure in action proceedings in Magistrates' Courts. This is governed by the Magistrates' Court Act 32 of 1944[161], the Magistrates' Court rules and by other applicable legislation. In the case of *In re Pennington Health Committee*[162] the determination of choice of proceedings was stated as follows:

> **(T)he Legislature drew a clear distinction between actions and applications. Procedure by way of application is recognized, but the intention appears to have been to confer jurisdiction generally in actions (in the narrow sense) while authorizing application proceedings only in specific cases.**

3.3.2.3.4 Action proceedings (both High Court and Magistrates' Court)

The rules of procedure described hereunder relating to action proceedings, apart from a few differences, apply to proceedings in both the High Court and Magistrates' Courts.

3.3.2.3.4(a) Summons[163]

Plaintiff starts the proceedings with the issuing and serving of the summons which informs the defendant to enter an appearance to defend the action within a stated time after service (which shall not be less than 3 days, plus one additional day for each 30 kilometres, distance of the place of service from the court-house, but which shall not exceed 15 days in all) to answer the claim of the plaintiff and warning the defendant of the consequences of failure to do so[164]. In the case of proceedings commenced in the High Court, in terms of rule 17(1)(a) if the defendant disputes the claim and wishes to defend he or she shall within the stated time give notice of intention to defend and thereafter if the summons is a combined summons within 20 days after giving such notice, deliver a plea (with or without a claim in reconvention), an exception or an application to strike out.

(2)The summons shall be signed by the clerk of the court and shall bear the date of issue by him.

The summons is a form that instructs the Sheriff or his or her deputy to inform the defendant of the claim against him or her and the steps that the defendant may take in response to the claim.

The plaintiff usually makes use of

- a simple summons (See Form 1) or
- a combined summons (See Form 2),

A simple summons is a "written judicial demand" in which the cause of action or the substance of the claim is set out briefly. A simple summons is used where the plaintiff's claim is for the payment of a debt or a liquidated demand, (as explained

[161] Act 32 of 1944 as amended by Magistrates' Court Amendment Act 9, 1997.

[162] 1980 (4) SA 243 (N) at 247H.

[163] See generally rule 5 of the Rules of Magistrates' Court of Namibia and Rule 17 of the Rules of the High Court of Namibia.

[164] Rule 5(1) amended by GN R. 1115 of 1974 substituted by GN R.2222 of 1978.

earlier, one which is of such a nature that the ascertainment of the amount is merely a matter of calculation). A combined summons is used where the claim is not for a debt or a liquidated demand. It is called a combined summons because "Particulars of claim" is annexed to the summons. In the High Court it is necessary to have either a combined summons to which the particulars of claim is attached or a simple summons which, after appearance to defend has been entered, is followed by a declaration.

In terms of rule 8(1) of the Rules of the High Court of Namibia, a provisional sentence summons (See Form 3) is available to plaintiffs who have sufficient documentary proof of their claims. The proof required is known as a liquid document. A liquid document is an acknowledgement of debt over a signature, e.g. a cheque. If such a document is produced, a presumption of indebtedness arises and unless the contrary is proved, it will be sufficient to justify a finding in favour of the plaintiff. The nature of such a judgment is provisional and the plaintiff must give security in case he or she has to return what he or she received in terms of the judgment. There is no equivalent provision in respect of the Magistrates' Courts.

3.3.2.3.4(b) Notice of intention to defend

The summons calls upon the defendant to do something with the claim that was instituted against him. If the defendant wishes to defend the claim, he or she has to file a *notice of intention to defend* within a certain time limit. In actions against the State or a servant of the State in his official capacity, appearance to defend may be entered at any time within 20 days after service of the summons in the case of the High Court and 21 days in the case of the Magistrates' Courts[165]. This notice does not set out any defence, but only informs the plaintiff of the defendant's intention to defend the claim against him or her.

Where a notice of intention to defend is filed in reply to a simple summons issued by the Registrar of the High Court the plaintiff has to deliver a declaration which is similar to a particulars of claim. The declaration sets out the nature of the claim and the relief that the plaintiff seeks. A declaration does, however, also include conclusions of law which the plaintiff can deduce from the facts contained in the declaration[166].

3.3.2.3.4(c) Plea

The rules with regard to a defendant's plea in the Magistrates' Courts are substantially similar to those in the High Court.

After delivery of the notice of intention to defend in the instance of a combined summons, or the receipt of the declaration in the instance of a simple summons, the defendant has to reply to the claim of the plaintiff within a certain time limit. In terms of rule 19(4) of the Rules of Magistrates' Court Rules (and rule 22(2) of the Rules of

[165] Rule 19 (2) of the Rules of the High Court of Namibia and 13 (2) of the Rules of the Magistrates'Court of Namibia.

[166] Rule 20 (1) of the Rules of the High Court of Namibia. Note that the provision for the delivery of the declaration applies only to the High Court and not the Magistrates Court.

the High Court of Namibia) the defendant in his or her plea, is required to admit or deny the allegations made in the particulars of claim/declaration and to set out the basis of his or her defence.

3.3.2.3.4(d) Replication/reply

After receipt of the plea of the defendant, the plaintiff can reply to the plea by means of a replication, in the case of proceedings in the High Court, and a reply in the case of the Magistrates' Court[167].

3.3.2.3.4(e) Claims in reconvention

A defendant who has a claim against a plaintiff may link his or her claim to the action of the plaintiff. In such an instance the defendant will, together with his or her plea, deliver his or her claim in reconvention. The defendant will, for purposes of this claim, be called the plaintiff-in-reconvention and the plaintiff will be called the defendant-in-reconvention. The procedure is the same as for claims in convention. Where the plaintiff and the defendant have claims against each other it makes more sense to have both cases heard at the same time rather than to have separate trials where the same people are involved. The claims that they have against each other can arise out of the same transaction or a different transaction. Hearing both cases at the same time prevents one party from getting a judgment against another party where the latter has a claim that could wipe out the first claim.

Rule 24(1) of the Rules of the High Court of Namibia provides as follows:

> a defendant who counterclaims shall, together with his or her plea, deliver a claim in reconvention setting out the material facts thereof in accordance with rules 18 and 20 unless the plaintiff agrees, or if he or she refuses, the court allows it to be delivered at a later stage, and the claim in reconvention shall be set out either in a separate document or in a portion of the document containing the plea but headed 'Claim in Reconvention'.

Rule 20(3) of the Rules of the Magistrates' Court of Namibia has provisions relating to the right of a defendant to set up by claim in reconvention any right or claim of any amount which he may allege against the plaintiff, whether liquid or illiquid, whether liquidated or unliquidated, whether or not it arises out of or is connected with the subject-matter of the claim in convention and such claim (if within the jurisdiction of the court) shall have the same effect as a cross-action, so as to enable the court to pronounce a final judgment in the same action both on the claim in convention and on the claim in reconvention.

In the case of the Magistrates' Court, under the provisions of rule 20(4) it is permissible for a defendant to deliver a claim in reconvention which exceeds the jurisdiction of the Magistrates' Courts and to seek a stay of the action under Section 47 of the Act.

[167] See rule 21 of the Rules of the Magistrates' Court of Namibia and rule 25 of the Rule of the High Court of Namibia.

3.3.2.3.4(f) Judgment by default[168]

If the defendant fails to deliver his or her notice of intention to defend, the plaintiff may set the matter down for judgment by default. If default judgment is granted to the plaintiff it means that the defendant has to satisfy the claim of the plaintiff. If the defendant has a good reason for not filing his or her notice of intention to defend, he or she may apply to the court to set aside the default judgment.

If the plaintiff fails to deliver the declaration (in the instance of a simple summons) on time, the defendant must notify the plaintiff to do so within three days. If the plaintiff then fails to deliver the declaration, he or she is in default and is not allowed to deliver the declaration. The defendant may then either apply for absolution from the instance (see p.146) or apply for judgment.

3.3.2.3.4(g) Special pleas

A defendant can "answer" to the claim of the plaintiff set out in the declaration or particulars of claim by means of a special plea that must be included in the plea of the defendant. Examples of defences raised by means of a special plea are:

- that the court does not have jurisdiction to hear the case;
- that the claim is prescribed; or,
- *res iudicata* – that the case had been dealt with before in a court of law.

3.3.2.3.4(h) Exceptions/striking out

Instead of replying to a particular pleading on the merits, a party may except to the pleading on one of the following grounds:

- that the pleading is vague and embarrassing. A pleading is vague and embarrassing if it contains contradictory allegations, or fails to indicate to the opposing party what case he or she will have to meet. Where an exception is raised on this ground, the other party is afforded the opportunity to remove the cause of complaint;
- that the pleading discloses no cause of action or defence.

Exceptions amount to legal objections, e.g. one would state that although the words were spoken they were not defamatory. Exceptions constitute separate issues and are therefore adjudicated upon separately before the trial starts. If an exception is upheld the court may instruct the other party to amend its pleadings or it may dismiss the case. No new facts may be alleged in the exception.

3.3.2.3.4(i) Summary judgment

If a claim is based on a liquid document or for a liquidated amount in money the summary judgment procedure enables a plaintiff to obtain judgment without having to go to trial, even though the defendant delivered a notice of intention to defend. Application for summary judgment is usually employed to dispose of a defence which has no substance.

[168] See generally rule 12 of the Magistrates' Court Rules of Namibia and rule 31 (2) (a) of the Rules of the High Court of Namibia.

3.3.2.3.4(j) Litis contestatio

The closing of the pleadings is known as *litis contestatio*. After *litis contestatio* the parties are no longer allowed to exchange further pleadings. The plaintiff (who is *dominus litis*) must now place the case on the court roll (i.e. set a date for trial).

3.3.2.3.5 Trial stage (second stage)

3.3.2.3.5(a) Discovery of documents and conference hearing

During the pleading stage the parties must file all pleadings they exchange with the Registrar (in the case of the High Court) or clerk of the court (in the Magistrates' Court). These pleadings are kept together in a file. When the case is heard this file is handed to the presiding officer who hears the case. The pleadings set out the different facts as relied upon by the different parties. After the closing of the pleadings, the plaintiff, the defendant and the presiding officer know which facts are disputed, which facts are admitted and what the limits of the action are. The parties may decide on the evidence that they want to lead at the trial. Before a case goes to trial parties must discover (disclose) all the documents that they intend to use at the trial. The opposing party is entitled to inspect the documents before trial. If a document is not listed in the discovery of a party the document cannot be used at the trial. Similarly, plans, diagrams, photographs and summaries of experts' opinions must be made available to the opposing side.

This procedure is provided for by rule 23 of the Rules of the Magistrates' Court and rule 35 of the Rules of the High Court of Namibia. In the instance of a High Court case, rule 37 provides for a compulsory pre-trial conference or conference hearing in which the parties must attempt to limit their dispute.

In civil proceedings the burden of proof is on the plaintiff and therefore as a general rule, the plaintiff must start the proceedings in court and must establish his or her case on a balance of probabilities, which is a lower standard than beyond reasonable doubt, which is required in criminal proceedings. The plaintiff calls his or her witnesses. The witnesses take the oath, give evidence in chief, are cross-examined and re-examined. After all the evidence of the plaintiff has been heard, the plaintiff closes his or her case.

After the presentation of the case of the plaintiff, the defendant is afforded the same opportunity. The defendant calls his or her witnesses, proceeds with examination in chief, where after cross-examination by the plaintiff and re-examination by the defendant follow. After all the evidence of the defendant has been presented, he or she closes his or her case.

3.3.2.3.5(b) Absolution from the instance

At the close of the case for the plaintiff, in certain cases where the defendant has cause to believe that the plaintiff has not been able to establish the facts in support of his case, the defendant may apply for absolution from the instance[169]. If the court

[169] Rule 40 (6) (7) of the Rules of the High Court of Namibia.

grants absolution, the case ends and it is as if the proceedings have never been instituted. The plaintiff may however institute fresh proceedings on the same grounds again if he or she manages to gather more substantial and better evidence.

3.3.2.3.5(c) Argument

After the presentation of evidence by the parties before the court, both parties are given the opportunity to address the court on the facts and on the applicable law. The plaintiff delivers argument first (assuming that he or she carries the burden of proof), followed by the argument of the defendant. The plaintiff may reply to the argument of the defendant.

3.3.2.3.5(d) Judgment

After hearing the arguments of the plaintiff and the defendant, the court delivers judgment. The court may also give judgment at a later stage and the case may be postponed until the day on which the judgment is delivered. In its judgment the court considers all the evidence presented before it, and applies the law to the facts. The court may find in favour of the plaintiff or the defendant and will make an order according to its finding. Usually the court also makes an order regarding costs.

3.3.2.3.6 Execution (third stage – if applicable)

The party who has received judgment in his or her favour is known as the judgment creditor and the party who has to perform in terms of the court order is known as the judgment debtor. If the judgment debtor complies with the court order voluntarily the case is settled. If the judgment debtor fails to comply with the order, the order must be enforced. The judgment creditor then applies for execution of the court order. In terms of the execution order, the sheriff may attach assets of the judgment debtor which may be sold in execution to satisfy the judgment debt[170].

3.3.2.3.6(a) Appeal

If either of the parties to proceedings before the High Court is of the opinion that the presiding officer has erred in his or her finding as to the facts of the case or in the application of the law to the case, he or she can apply for leave to appeal from the court that delivered the judgement. Permission to appeal will be granted when there is a reasonable prospect of success on appeal, the amount involved is not trifling and the matter is of substantial importance to one or both of the parties concerned. In the event of a matter being heard in the Magistrates' Court the parties have an automatic right of appeal to the High Court, unless there is an agreement to the contrary.

When considering an appeal on the decision of facts, an appeal court will not lightly interfere with such a decision. The trial judge or magistrate has advantages that the appeal court lacks. The trial judge (or magistrate) sees and hears the witnesses, experiences the atmosphere of the trial and can observe the demeanour, appearance and personality of the witnesses. An appeal court will only interfere if it is convinced that the factual findings were wrong and there has been misdirection by the trial judge.

[170] See generally rules 39, 40, 41, 42 and 43 of the Rules of the Magistrates' Court of Namibia and Rules 45 and 46 of the Rules of the High Court of Namibia.

3.3.2.3.6(b) Review

Review is a process by which proceedings in the court *a quo* (the lower court or the court below) are brought before the High Court on the ground of grave irregularities occurring during the proceedings. These grounds include:

- that the court did not have jurisdiction;
- bias, malice, corruption on the part of the presiding officer;
- gross irregularities in the procedure; and,
- the admission of inadmissible evidence or incompetent evidence or the rejection of the admissible and competent evidence.

If the review proceedings are successful the court will set aside the decision. The court then has a choice to remit the matter to the court *a quo* or to substitute a correct decision.

3.3.2.3.7 Motion proceedings (application proceedings) (both High Court and Magistrates' Court)

It was stated earlier that the rules with regard to the choice of proceedings stated in the *Room Hire* case apply to the proceedings instituted in the High Court and that the provisions of both the Magistrates' Court Act 32 of 1944 and the Rules of the Magistrates' Court of Namibia determine the choice of proceedings in the Magistrates' Courts.

With regard to motion or application proceedings, the parties are applicant and respondent and the procedure by way of application in the Magistrates' Courts is limited to those cases specifically laid down and authorised by the Act and rules which include *inter alia* application for orders to set aside automatic rent interdict; to attach property in security of rent; to appoint assessor; for transfer of action or proceedings to another Magistrates' Court; for rescission of judgment; for stay of action under Section 47 for summary judgment, etc.

An application is instituted by means of a notice of motion and supporting affidavit(s), setting out the facts and including the prayers of the applicant. There are two types of notices of motion that may be employed.

3.3.2.3.7(a) Ex parte applications (See Form 4)

Where an applicant asks the court for an order that will not prejudicially affect anyone else, an *ex parte* application is made. No notice is given to another party. The notice of motion is only addressed to the Registrar of the Court or the clerk of the court. It sets out the nature of the order sought by the applicant and an instance where an *ex parte* application is made is when a person applies to be admitted as an attorney or an advocate.

Other instances where an *ex parte* application will be used:

- where the relief sought is merely a preliminary step in the proceedings or,
- where others may be affected by the order, but where giving them notice will cause delay or defeat the purpose of the proceedings.

Where other parties may be affected by the order, the court will grant a *rule nisi*, subject to a return date. A *rule nisi* is a provisional order by a court ordering a person whose interests are likely to be affected to appear as respondent before the court on a particular date, called the return day, and give reasons why the *rule nisi* should not become final.

3.3.2.3.7(b) Applications where notice is given to the respondent (See Form 5)

Where the rights of another party will be affected by the order sought by the applicant, the applicant has to give notice to the other party of the application. The notice of motion and the founding affidavit are issued by the Registrar or clerk of the court, filed in the court file and served on the respondent. If the respondent wishes to oppose the application he or she must give notice of his or her intention to oppose the application and file answering affidavits. The applicant can reply to the answering affidavit by filing a replying affidavit.

The case is then placed on the court roll for the hearing. The legal representatives of the parties appear in court on the agreed date and time. The presiding officer is in possession of all the affidavits of the parties and has time to prepare for the hearing. The legal representative of the applicant asks the court to grant the application on the papers before it and presents argument to court to convince the presiding officer that the application should be granted. The legal representative of the respondent, in turn, argues that the application should not be granted.

As a general principle one uses the *ex parte* application where there is no real dispute. However, if it turns out that there is a real dispute of fact in the case, the presiding officer may order that oral evidence be presented.

After hearing the arguments of the legal representatives the court delivers its judgment, granting or dismissing the application. If the court grants the application it makes an order with which the respondent has to comply. The execution procedures apply where the respondent does not comply voluntarily.

3.3.2.3.8

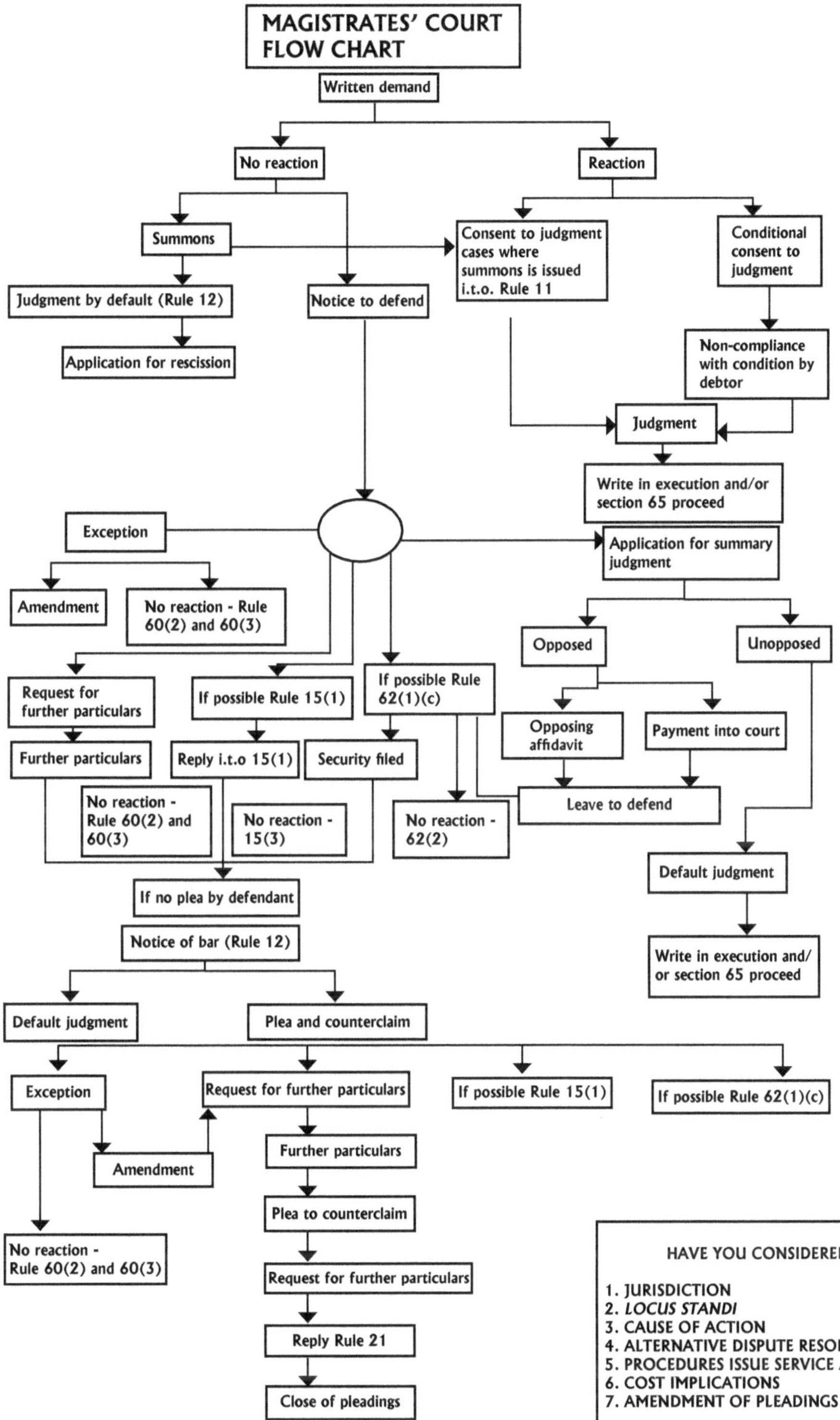

HAVE YOU CONSIDERED

1. JURISDICTION
2. *LOCUS STANDI*
3. CAUSE OF ACTION
4. ALTERNATIVE DISPUTE RESOLUTION
5. PROCEDURES ISSUE SERVICE AND FILE
6. COST IMPLICATIONS
7. AMENDMENT OF PLEADINGS

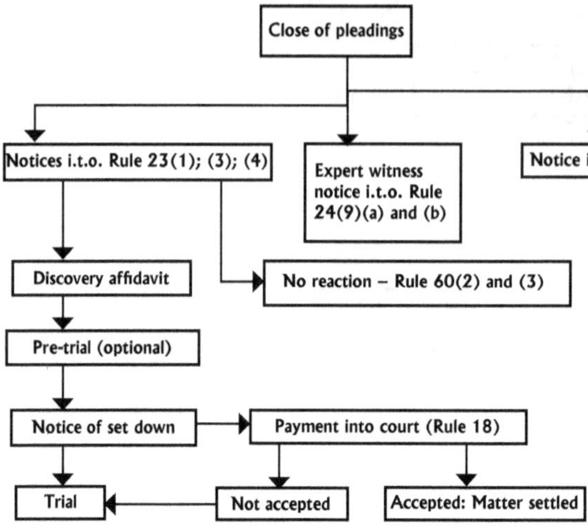

N.B. PREPARATION FOR TRIAL

- Plan effectively and timeously
- Some steps are obligatory
- Others depend on:
  - ❖ Nature of the matter
  - ❖ Circumstances of the case

  e.g. what is in dispute
- Cost implications
- Possible settlement
- Interpreters
- Legal and procedural aspects

N.B. proper consultations and study of discovered documents

- Pleadings: need for amendment

FORM 1

SIMPLE SUMMONS

IN THE HIGH COURT OF NAMIBIA

CASE NO:________

In the matter between:

Siphiwe Manda **Plaintiff**

and

James Boesak **Defendant**

To the Sheriff or his deputy:

INFORM:

James Boesak (hereinafter called the Defendant), an adult male businessman of Old Grüner Kranz 45 Bell St Southern Industria, Windhoek

that

Siphiwe Manda (hereinafter called the Plaintiff), an adult female businesswoman of 3 Carl List Haus Fidel Castro St, Windhoek

Hereby institutes action against the defendant in which action the Plaintiff(s) claims:

Payment of the amount of N$300 000.00 (three hundred thousand Namibian dollars) for goods supplied and delivered on 6 JULY 2003.

INFORM the Defendant further that if Defendant disputes the claim and wishes to defend the action, the Defendant shall: -

(i) Within 10 days of service upon the Defendant(s) of this Summons, file with the Registrar of this Court, notice of Defendant's intention to defend and serve a copy thereof on the Attorneys of the Plaintiff, which notice shall give an address (not being a post office or poste restante) referred to in Rule 13(3)b for the service upon the Defendant(s) of all notices and documents in the action.

(ii) Thereafter and within twenty days after filing and serving notice of intention to defend as aforesaid, file with the Registrar and serve upon the Plaintiff a Plea, Exception, Notice to strike out, with or without a Counterclaim.

INFORM the Defendant further that if the Defendant fails to file and serve notice as aforesaid, Judgment as claimed may be given against the Defendant without further notice to the Defendant, or if having filed and served such notice, the Defendant fails/fail to plead, except, make application to strike out or counterclaim, Judgment may be given against the Defendant.

AND immediately thereafter serve on the Defendant a copy of this Summons and return the same to the Registrar with whatsoever you have done thereupon.

DATED at WINDHOEK on this 20th day of March 2004.

____

Registrar of the High Court

____

Plaintiff's attorney

B. Tjatjara Attorneys – Mr Tjatjara

Address: 5 Nelson Mandela Ave, Klein Windhoek
WINDHOEK
6140
Ref: N123/2004

FORM 2

COMBINED SUMMONS

IN THE HIGH COURT OF NAMIBIA

CASE NO:________

In the matter between:

Sally Hakweenda (born Schröeder) **Plaintiff**

and

Peter Hakweenda **Defendant**

To the Sheriff or his deputy:

INFORM:

Peter Haweenda (hereinafter called the Defendant), an adult male plumber of 34 Eugene Marais St, Windhoek

that

Sally Hakweenda (hereinafter called the Plaintiff), an adult female teacher of 34 Eugene Marais St, Windhoek

Hereby institutes action against the defendant in which action the plaintiff claims the relief and on the grounds set out in the particulars annexed hereto.

INFORM the Defendant further that if Defendant disputes the claim and wishes to defend the action, the Defendant shall: -

(i) Within 10 days of service upon the Defendant(s) of this Summons, file with the Registrar of this Court, notice of Defendant's intention to defend and serve a copy thereof on the Attorneys of the Plaintiff, which notice shall give an address (not being a post office or poste restante) referred to in Rule 13(3)b for the service upon the Defendant(s) of all notices and documents in the action.

(ii) Thereafter and within twenty days after filing and serving notice of intention to defend as aforesaid, file with the Registrar and serve upon the Plaintiff a Plea, Exception, Notice to strike out, with or without a Counterclaim.

INFORM the Defendant further that if the Defendant fails to file and serve notice as aforesaid, Judgment as claimed may be given against the Defendant without further notice to the Defendant, or if having filed and served such notice, the Defendant fails/ fail to plead, except, make application to strike out or counterclaim, Judgment may be given against the Defendant.

AND immediately thereafter serve on the Defendant a copy of this Summons and return the same to the Registrar with whatsoever you have done thereupon.

DATED at WINDHOEK on this 5th day of March 2004.

____

Registrar of the High Court

FORM 2

COMBINED SUMMONS

ANNEXURE

PARTICULARS OF PLAINTIFF'S CLAIM

1. The plaintiff is SALLY HAKWEENDA (born SCHRÖEDER), an adult female teacher of 34 Eugene Marais Street, Windhoek.

2. The defendant is PETER HAKWEENDA, an adult male plumber of 34 Eugene Marais Street, Windhoek.

3. The parties are domiciled within the area of jurisdiction of the Honourable Court.

4. On the 10 February 1991 and at Windhoek, the parties were married to each other in community of property and the marriage still subsits.

5. One minor child was born from the marriage between the parties, namely Sean (male), aged 7 years.

6. By reason of the facts hereinafter set forth, the marriage relationship of the parties has reached such a state of disintegration that there is no reasonable prospect of the restoration of a normal marriage relationship between the parties:
   a. During the subsistence of the marriage, the defendant indicated on numerous occasions that he had lost interest in the plaintiff and the continuation of their marriage.
   b. During the subsistence of the marriage, the defendant started an extra-marital relationship with one Cindy Geraldo which is still going on.
   c. In that the defendant fails to support the plaintiff and the minor child adequately.
   d. Plaintiff has lost all love, respect and affection for the defendant and is not interested in the continuation of the marriage.

7. In the premises there has been an irretrievable breakdown of the marriage;

WHEREFORE Plaintiff claims:

a. A decree of divorce
b. Custody of the minor child, subject to reasonable access of the defendant to the minor child
c. An order directing the defendant to pay maintenance in respect of the minor child in the amount of N$1 500.00 per month until the child becomes self-supporting

d. Division of the joint estate
e. Further and/or alternative relief
f. Costs of suit

DATED at WINDHOEK ON THIS 5th day of MARCH 2004.

____

B. Mbulu
Plaintiff's Attorney

Address: 5 Nelson Mandela Ave, Klein Windhoek
WINDHOEK
6140
Ref: N123/2004

____

V. Kandoni
Plaintiff's Advocate

FORM 3

PROVISIONAL SENTENCE SUMMONS

IN THE HIGH COURT OF NAMIBIA

CASE NO:________

In the matter between:

Plaintiff

and

Defendant

To the Sheriff or his deputy:

INFORM A..B................................(sex) .... (occupation), of .... (residence or place of business) and hereinafter called the defendant:

(i) that he is hereby called upon immediately to pay to C .... D...........................(sex)...........................(occupation)....................... ......(residence or place of business)................................(hereinafter called the plaintiff) an amount of ....together with interest thereon at the rate of ....% per annum as from....................claimed by plaintiff.............. ....(here set out the cause of action)............................and a copy of which document is annexed hereto;

(ii) that failing such payment, he is hereby called to appear before this Court personally or by an advocate at .... on .... the .... day of .... 20... at ....o'clock in the forenoon (or as soon thereafter as the matter can be heard) to admit or deny his liability for the said claim, and to state why the mortgaged property should not be declared executable.

(iii) that if he denies liability for the same, he shall not later than noon on ....the .... day of ....20..... file an affidavit with the Registrar of this Court, and serve a copy thereof on plaintiff's attorney, and in particular states whether he admits or denies his signature to the said .... or whether he admits or denies the signature or authority of his agent.

AND INFORM the said defendant further that in the event of his not paying the amount and interest above-mentioned to the plaintiff immediately and if he (the said defendant) further fails to file and affidavit as aforesaid and to appear before this Court at the time above stated, provisional sentence may forthwith be granted against him with costs, and the mortgaged property may be declared executable, but that against payment of the said amount, interest and costs, he will be entitled to demand security for the restitution thereof if the said sentence should thereafter be reversed.

AND serve a copy of this summons and of the said .... on the said defendant and then return this summons to the Registrar with your return of what you have done thereon.

DATED at .... this .... day of .... 20.......

Registrar of the High Court

Plaintiff's Attorney
Address fort service:

....

....

....

FORM 4

EX PARTE APPLICATION

IN THE HIGH COURT OF NAMIBIA

CASE NO:________

In the ex parte application of

VELIKOSHI, SUSAN **APPLICANT**

For her admission as Attorney of this Honourable Court

NOTICE OF MOTION

PLEASE TAKE NOTICE that an application will be made on .... 2003 to the above-mentioned Honourable Court at .... or as soon thereafter as Counsel for the Applicant may be heard, on behalf of the Applicant for an order in the following terms: -

1. That the Applicant be admitted and enrolled as an attorney of the above Honourable Court and that the Registrar of the above Honourable Court be ordered to enter the Applicant's name on the roll on the attorneys of this Honourable Court;

2. That further and/or alternative relief, as the Honourable Court deems fit, be granted to the Applicant.

PLEASE TAKE FURTHER NOTICE that the Affidavits of the Applicant, SUSAN VELIKOSHI, attached hereto, will be used in support of this application.

To the Sheriff or his deputy:

KINDLY PLACE THIS MATTER ON THE ROLL FOR HEARING ACCORDINGLY

DATED at .... on this .... day of .... 2003.

____

J. Tjatjara

Attorney for the Applicant
Admitted in terms of section 4(2)
of Act 62 of 1995
Tjatjara Attorneys
28 Rendsburger St Lafrenz Ind.
Windhoek

To: The Registrar
High Court
Windhoek

And

To: The Secretary
Law Society of Namibia

Copy received on the

....

____

Secretary

Law Society of Namibia

FORM 4

EX PARTE APPLICATION

IN THE HIGH COURT OF NAMIBIA

CASE NO:________

In the ex parte application of

VELIKOSHI, SUSAN **APPLICANT**

For her admission as Legal Practitioner of this Honourable Court

---

AFFIDAVIT

I, the undersigned

SUSAN VELIKOSHI

Do hereby make oath and state that: -

1.

I am the Applicant in the above matter. The facts contained herein are to the best of my knowledge both true and correct and fall within my personal knowledge unless stated otherwise.

2.

I am a single female, living at 25 Rebother Rd 60 Luther St Pionierspark, Windhoek. I am domiciled within the area of jurisdiction of this Honourable Court.

3.

I was born on 4 MARCH 1975 in Windhoek and at present I am 28 years old. I am a Namibian citizen from birth. In confirmation of the above-mentioned, I respectfully refer the Honourable Court to a copy of my Identity Document containing particulars of my birth, attached hereto and marked Addendum "A". The original document will be available for inspection by this Honourable Court when this application is heard.

4.

In completion of my school career, I passed the matriculation exam, and I specifically passed the examinations in English and Afrikaans on higher grade. In confirmation of this, I respectfully refer the Honourable Court to a copy of my Senior Certificate, attached hereto and marked Addendum "B". The original certificate will be available for inspection by this Honourable Court when this application is heard.

5.

I respectfully submit that I am duly qualified in accordance with Section 5 of the Legal Practitioners Act 15 of 1995, in that: -

5.1 In December 1995 and 1997 I respectively met the requirements of the degrees Baccalaureus Juris and Baccalaureus Legum at the University of Namibia, as is confirmed by the copies of the degree certificates attached hereto and respectively marked as Addenda "C", "D". These degrees were conferred on 4 March 1996 and 4 March 1998 respectively. The original degree certificates will be available for inspection by this Honourable Court when this application is heard. I followed the course of studies for the mentioned degrees over a minimum period of 5 years.

6.

On 4 January 2000 in Windhoek I concluded a written contract of service with Ms Alice Lukusa, a Legal Practitioner of the High Court of Namibia.

A copy of the said contract of service is attached hereto and marked as Addendum "E". In the contract I undertook to work as a candidate Legal Practitioner for one year. The above-mentioned Alice Lukusa worked as a Legal Practitioner, from 4 January 2000 to 3 January 2002 of my contract of service, as Deputy Director of the University of Namibia Legal Aid Clinic, 41 Red Cross St Katutura.

7.

I served the aforesaid Alice Lukusa duly and faithfully as a candidate Legal Practitioner from 4 January 2000 to 3 January 2002. The mentioned service was uninterrupted for a period of 24 months, as will be evident from the affidavit of Alice Lukusa, attached hereto and marked as Addendum "F".

8.

I served the whole of the period of service, as stipulated in my contract of service, in the office of the University of Namibia Legal Aid Clinic, under the direct and personal supervision of the aforesaid Alice Lukusa.

9.

The original contract of service was registered with the Secretary of the Law Society of Namibia, within one month of the date of signature thereof. It was registered under number 148/99 on 3 February 2000. In confirmation of the above-mentioned, I respectfully refer this Honourable Court to a copy of a letter from the Law Society of Namibia, attached hereto and marked Addendum "G".

10.

I respectfully submit that the provisions of Section 4 (1) of the Legal Practitioners, Act 15 of 1995, have been met therein that I, throughout my period of service under the aforementioned contract of service: -

10.1 Did not have any pecuniary interest in the practice and service of a Legal Practitioner;

10.2 Did not occupy any other position or engage in any other business, except that of candidate Legal Practitioner under contract of service;

10.3 Was not absent from service for a period of/or period that exceeds 30 work days in total;

10.4 Attended and completed the practical legal training course, as presented at the Justice Training Centre at the University of Namibia, satisfactorily. In confirmation of the aforementioned, I attach a copy of the Attendance Report of the Law Society of Namibia, marked as Addendum "I". The original report will be available for inspection by this Honourable Court when this application is heard;

10.5 Have never before been admitted as a Legal Practitioner of the Honourable Court and my name has not previously been on the roll of advocates and I have not appeared in that capacity before.

11.

In accordance with the Rules of the High Court of Namibia, a copy of this application, together with copies of the affidavits, certificates and documents, will be served on the Secretary of the Law Society of Namibia, on a date that precedes the date of application by more than one month.

12.

My estate has never been sequestrated before and is not at the point of being sequestrated.

13.

I do not have a criminal record and no civil actions or applications or administrative steps have ever been instituted against me.

14.

I desire to be admitted as a Legal Practitioner of this Honourable Court. I respectfully submit that I meet the requirements of the Legal Practitioners Act, as set out above. I respectfully submit that I am fit and proper to be admitted as a Legal Practitioner of this Honourable Court. I am not aware of any reasons prohibiting my admission as Legal

Practitioner. Consequently, I respectfully request the Honourable Court to grant the order as set out in Notice of Motion.

____

SUSAN VELIKOSHI

I certify that the Deponent acknowledges that he or she knows and understands the contents of this affidavit and that it is the truth. This affidavit was signed and sworn to before me at .... on this .... day of .... 2003.

____

COMMISSIONER OF OATHS

FORM 5

NOTICE OF MOTION & FOUNDING AFFIDAVIT

IN THE HIGH COURT OF NAMIBIA

In the matter between: CASE NUMBER: 457/2004

Nomvula Mbayo **APPLICANT**

and

Enver Nuughweda **RESPONDENT**

NOTICE OF MOTION

TAKE NOTICE THAT Nomvula Mbayo (hereinafter called the applicant) intends to make application to this Court for an order that:

1. The estate of the Respondent is provisionally sequestrated and the assets be placed in the hands of the Master of the High Court.

2. The costs of this application be costs of the sequestration.

3. Such alternative relief as the Honourable Court deems fit.

TAKE NOTICE FURTHER THAT the applicant has appointed Hakweenda Attorneys, 54 Smit Street, Pionierspark, Windhoek as the address at which she will accept notice and service of all process in these proceedings.

TAKE NOTICE FURTHER THAT if you intend opposing the application you are required (a) to notify applicant's attorney in writing on or before the 26 October 2004 (b) and within fourteen days of the service of this notice upon you, to file your answering affidavits, if any; and further that you are required to appoint in such notification an address referred to in rule 6(5)(b) at which you will accept notice and service of all documents in these proceedings.

If no such notice of intention to oppose be given, the application will be made on 25 November 2005 at 10 am.

DATED at WINDHOEK this 20th day of October 2004.

____

Applicant's Attorney

Hakweenda Attorneys
54 Smit Street
Pionierspark
Ref: T22t/Hakweenda

TO: THE REGISTRAR OF THE HIGH COURT
Smit Street
WINDHOEK

AND TO: THE MASTER OF THE HIGH COURT
Bathurst Street
WINDHOEK

AND TO: THE RESPONDENT (per Sheriff)
Enver Nuughweda
25 Milne Street
WINDHOEK

FORM 5

NOTICE OF MOTION & FOUNDING AFFIDAVIT

IN THE HIGH COURT OF NAMIBIA

In the matter between: CASE NUMBER: 457/2004

Nomvula Mbayo **APPLICANT**

and

Enver Nuughweda **RESPONDENT**

AFFIDAVIT

I, the undersigned,

NOMVULA MBAYO

do hereby make oath and say:

1.

I am the applicant in this matter and the facts contained herein are within my personal knowledge. I am a major female presently residing at 50 Coetzee Street, WINDHOEK.

2.

The respondent is Enver Nuughweda a major male born on 24 November 1977 with identity number 771124 1923 090 of 25 Milne Street, WINDHOEK.

3.

The respondent is domiciled within the jurisdiction of the above Honourable Court.

4.

The respondent is lawfully indebted to me in the amount of N$125 000.00 being monies lent and advanced to him, for which amount I obtained judgment from this Honourable Court on 10 October 2003. The judgment remains wholly unsatisfied. I, therefore have a liquidated claim against the respondent in excess of N$100.00. I annex a copy of the judgment marked "A".

5.

I humbly submit that the respondent is factually insolvent.

6.

I hold no security for my claim.

7.

7.1 The respondent is the registered owner of immovable property being 10 Brown Street, SUIDERHOF, which he holds under Deed of Transfer No. C234/01. The property is subject to a mortgage bond in the amount of N$180 000.00 in favour of First National Bank which bond was registered on 23 March 2000.

7.2 The property referred to in 7.1 has been attached by several creditors of the respondent and a sale in execution is to be held on 10 November 2004.

8.

It is respectfully submitted that there is reason to believe that it will be to the advantage of creditors if the estate of the respondent is sequestrated for *inter alia* the following reasons:

8.1 If the sale of the property as advertised proceeds a substantial benefit will accrue to some creditors and all the other creditors will likewise be prejudiced.

8.2 The sale of 10 Brown Street, SUIDERHOF will result in much lower proceeds and this is to the detriment of the creditors.

8.3 The appointment of a trustee will ensure that the property of the respondent can be realized for the true value and to the advantage of the creditors as a group. The trustee will also have the power to take charge of the insolvent's estate, investigate all the circumstances surrounding the respondent's financial difficulties and his actions regarding his estate with the view of reporting to the creditors and taking action accordingly.

9.

As required by section 9(4A)(a)(i) of the Insolvency Act 24 of 1936 I have by registered post furnished copies of the application to every registered trade union that, as far as could reasonably be ascertained, represents any of the debtor's employees. I attach hereto a document as annexure "B" as prescribed by section 9(4A)(b) of the Insolvency Act 24 of 1936 as proof that the application has been furnished to the trade unions.

10.

As required by section 9(4A)(a)(ii) of the Insolvency Act 24 of 1936 I have by registered post furnished copies of the application to the employees of the debtor. I attach hereto a document as annexure "C" as prescribed by section 4(4A)(b) of the Insolvency Act 24 of 1936 as proof that the application has been furnished to the employees.

11.

As required by section 9(4A)(a)(iii) of the Insolvency Act 24 of 1936 I have by registered post furnished a copy of the application to the Namibian Revenue Service. I attach hereto a document as annexure "D" as prescribed by section 9(4A)(b) of the Insolvency 24 of 1936 as proof that the application has been furnished to the Namibian Revenue Service.

12.

I have furnished a copy of the application to the debtor as required by section 9(4A)(a)(iv) of the Insolvency Act 24 of 1936. The application was served on the debtor. See the document attached as annexure "E" as proof.

13.

I have furnished security with the Master of the High Court as required by section 9(3)(b) of the Insolvency Act 24 of 1936. A certificate by the Master of the High Court to this effect is annexed hereto marked annexure "F" to which the Honourable Court is respectfully referred.

14.

I shall, furthermore, see to it that a copy of this application is served timeously on the Master of the High Court, with the view to obtaining his report in terms of section 9(4) of the Insolvency Act 24 of 1936.

15.

Therefore the Honourable Court is respectfully requested to issue an order in accordance with the prayers contained in the Notice of Motion.

____

Nomvula Mbayo

I certify that the deponent acknowledged that she knew and understood the contents of the above declaration, did not have any objection to taking the prescribed oath and considered it to be binding on her conscience. I thereafter administered the oath causing her to utter the following words: "I swear that the contents of this declaration are true, so help me God", and thereafter the deponent in my presence signed the declaration on this ....day of .... 20....... on which date and at which place I also signed this certificate.

____

Commissioner of Oaths
[Stamp of Commissioner]

FORM 6

NOTICE OF MOTION & FOUNDING AFFIDAVIT

IN THE HIGH COURT OF NAMIBIA

In the matter between: CASE NUMBER: 1762/97

Nikiwe Kiama **APPLICANT**

and

Council of the Municipality of Windhoek **RESPONDENT**

NOTICE OF MOTION

TAKE NOTICE that the Applicant intends to apply to this Court on 20 November 1997 at 10h00 or as soon thereafter as Counsel may be heard for the following relief:

1. an order directing that this matter be heard as a matter of urgency and that the failure of the Applicant to comply with the provisions of Rule 6(12) of the Rules of Court be condoned;

2. an order declaring that the Respondent's decision to suspend the payment of arrear pensions is unconstitutional and invalid;

3. an order compelling the Respondent to pay the Applicant her old age pension with effect from 23 May 1996, and to do so within 14 days of the date of this order;

4. an order compelling the Respondent to continue to pay the Applicant an old age pension for as long as she qualifies for one in terms of the law;

5. an order for costs;

6. an order for alternative relief.

TAKE NOTICE FURTHER that the affidavit of NIKIWE KIAMA, together with annexures thereto, will be used in support hereof.

TAKE NOTICE FURTHER that the Applicant has appointed the Legal Resources Centre of 116 Adler Street, Windhoek, as the address at which she will accept notice and service of all process in these proceedings.

TAKE NOTICE FURTHER that if the Respondent intends opposing this application, she is required:

(a) to notify the Applicant's Legal Practitioners in writing, by not later than Monday 3 November 1997, of her intention to oppose;

(b) to file answering affidavits, if any, by not later than Monday 10 November 1997;

and

(c) to appoint in her notice of opposition an address, within eight kilometres of the office of the Registrar, at which she will accept notice and service of all documents in these proceedings.

To the Sheriff or his deputy:

KINDLY PLACE THE MATTER ON THE ROLL

DATED at WINDHOEK on this 28th day of October 1997.

LEGAL RESOURCES CENTRE

Applicant's Attorneys
116 Adler Street
WINDHOEK
Telephone: 0461 29230
Telefax: 0461 23933
(Ref: Mr Clive Plasket)

TO: The Registrar of the above Court
Adler Street
WINDHOEK

AND TO: The Council of the Municipality of Windhoek

C/o The State Attorney
Procurator House
1 Robert Mugabe Ave
WINDHOEK

FORM 7

CERTIFICATE OF URGENCY

IN THE HIGH COURT OF NAMIBIA

In the matter between: CASE NUMBER:

Nikiwe Kiama **APPLICANT**

and

Council of the Municipality of Windhoek **RESPONDENT**

CERTIFICATE OF URGENCY

I, THE UNDERSIGNED,

CLIVE PLASKET

Hereby certify that:

1. I am an attorney of the High Court of Namibia practising as such and admitted in terms of Section 4(2) of the Rights of Appearance in Court Act 62 of 1995.
2. I have read the papers filed in this application and am of the view that the relief sought is sufficiently urgent to justify departure from the ordinary time limits set out in the rules of the High Court.

I am of the view that the Applicant is justified in invoking Rule 6(12) as she will not be afforded substantial redress at a hearing in due course.

DATED at WINDHOEK this 20th day of October 2004.

LEGAL RESOURCES CENTRE

Applicant's Attorneys
116 Adler Street
WINDHOEK
Attorney admitted in terms of
Section 4(2) of the Rights of
Appearance in Court Act 62 of 1995

APPLICANT'S ATTORNEY

Hakweenda Attorneys
54 Smit Street
Pionierspark
Ref: T22t/Hakweenda

TO: THE REGISTRAR OF THE HIGH COURT
Smit Street
WINDHOEK

AND TO: THE MASTER OF THE HIGH COURT
Bathurst Street
WINDHOEK

AND TO: THE RESPONDENT (per Sheriff)
Enver Nuughweda
25 Milne Street
WINDHOEK

3.3.3 Interpretation of statutes[171]

In a study of the interpretation of statutes one investigates the rules, presumptions and procedures which must be followed in the interpretation, comprehension and application of legislation. This is actually a subdivision of an even broader field, namely the science of juridical interpretation, or *legal hermeneutics*. The interpretation of contracts, wills, court decisions, old authorities, and so on are all thus part of legal hermeneutics. In Namibia, however, only the narrower field of interpretation of statutes developed historically into an independent study, and other hermeneutic problems are dealt with in more traditional disciplines (such as the law of contract or the law of succession).

3.4 Review questions

1. You are consulted by Angula. He tells you that he was involved in a car accident last week and that he suffered damage to his car to the amount of N$15 000.00. Neither Angula nor the driver of the other car was insured and Angula wants to recover his damages from the other party. Angula says that he has heard of a quick and easy way to obtain judgment in civil matters, namely motion proceedings. Are motion proceedings suitable in this particular case? Explain the difference between action and motion proceedings to Angula and advise him on how to proceed in this matter.

---

[171] See Chapter 7.

2. Write a note in which you set out and explain the different pleas that an accused person may enter in a criminal matter.
3. Differentiate and explain the burden of proof in civil and criminal cases.
4. Write a note in which you explain the concept of bail and its significance in criminal matters.
5. List and explain the factors a court will consider when imposing sentence on a convicted person.
6. You are acting on behalf of the plaintiff, Sue, who has issued summons against Pam for money due to her for goods that she sold and delivered to Pam. Sue tells you that Pam has no valid defence against the claim. You however receive a Notice of Intention to Defend. What step(s) will you take in response to this? Explain briefly.
7. Write a note on the criminal and civil jurisdiction of Magistrates' Courts.
8. What may a court order in instances where a dispute of fact arises in the affidavits of motion proceedings?
9. Explain the difference between proceedings in terms of Section 112(1)(a) and Section 112(1)(b) of the Criminal Procedure Act 51 of 1977.
10. List and explain the different pleas that may be entered by an accused in a criminal trial.
11. Write a note in which you set out and explain the different sentences that may be imposed by a court in a criminal matter.
12. List the two types of motion proceedings and explain the circumstances under which each will be employed.
13. Mr Clean and Mr Corn Man enter into a contract for the sale of the latter's Mercedes Benz antique motor car for N$20 000.00 (twenty thousand Namibian dollars). A term of the said agreement stipulates the payment of an initial deposit of the N$10 000.00 and the final payment to be made upon delivery of the motor car, which must be effected fourteen days after the deposit. Mr Clean paid the initial deposit four weeks ago but Mr Corn Man has as not yet delivered the car.

    Mr Clean wants to institute a legal action against Mr Corn Man.

    (a) What court has jurisdiction over the case? Give reasons for your answer.
    (b) Explain whether you would institute motion proceedings or action proceedings.
    (c) What course of action would you institute if during the proceedings in court you learn that Mr Corn Man wants to leave the country and is in the process of selling the car to another person who has offered a higher price? Give reasons for your answer.

CHAPTER 4

THE STRUCTURE OF THE NAMIBIAN JUDICIAL SYSTEM

4.1 Introduction

Prior to the attainment of nationhood and the promulgation of the Namibian Independence Constitution, which creates an independent Judiciary and a Supreme Court of a sovereign nation; the courts of Namibia were an extension of the judicial system of South Africa. Following the imposition of South African administration over South West Africa, after the granting of the League of Nations Mandate over the territory to South Africa, one obvious historical fact was the assumption of legislative powers over the territory by South Africa and the resulting extension of the South African legal system. The Administration of Justice Proclamation 21 of 1919 established the High Court of South West Africa. The Appellate Division Act No. 12 of 1920 granted the appellate division of the Supreme Court of South Africa jurisdiction over decisions of the High Court of South West Africa to hear appeals from the judgments and orders from the court. By virtue of the provisions of the Supreme Court Act No. 59 of 1959, the Judiciary of South West Africa was amalgamated into that of South Africa resulting in the High Court of South West Africa being constituted as the South West Africa Provincial Division of the Supreme Court of South Africa. Logically, this meant the maintenance of the jurisdiction of the Appellate Division of the Supreme Court of South Africa over the decisions of the South West Africa Provincial Division of the Supreme Court of South Africa to hear and finally determine matters brought before it on appeal from the South West Africa Division or any other provincial or local division.

With the promulgation of the Namibian Independence Constitution in 1990, the Supreme Court of Namibia became the highest court of appeal for Namibia[172]. It must also be added that by Proclamation 21 of 1919, which *inter alia* provided that Roman-Dutch law was to be applied in the territory 'as existing and applied in the Province of the Cape of Good Hope', Roman-Dutch law became the common law of the territory. The overall impact of all these proclamations on the judicial and legal systems of South West Africa was that the decisions of the Supreme Court of South Africa and the Roman-Dutch law that were developed by the South African Courts, until independence, became binding on the courts of Namibia. This position was affirmed by Article 66(1) of the Namibian Constitution which provides that both the customary law and the common law of Namibia in force on the date of independence shall remain valid to the extent to which such customary law or common law does not conflict with this Constitution or any other law.

[172] See also Hosten, W.J.; Edwards, A.B.; Bosman, F. and Church, J. 1997. *op.cit.*

4.2 Establishment

The establishment of the Judiciary, as one of the main organs of State, is provided for by the Constitution but there are other pieces of legislation that deal with the jurisdiction of the courts and other related matters. Article 78(1)(2) and (3) of the Namibian Constitution provide for the establishment of the Judiciary and its independence as follows;

> (1) The judicial power shall be vested in the Courts of Namibia, which shall consist of:
>
> (a) a Supreme Court of Namibia;
>
> (b) a High Court of Namibia; and,
>
> (c) Lower Courts of Namibia.
>
> (2) The Courts shall be independent and subject only to this Constitution and the law.
>
> (3) No member of the Cabinet or the Legislature or any other person shall interfere with judges or judicial officers in the exercise of their judicial functions, and all organs of State shall accord such assistance as the courts may require to protect their independence, dignity and effectiveness, subject to the terms of this Constitution or any other law.

There are existing legal and extra-legal measures designed to protect and maintain the independence of the Judiciary. The Namibian Constitution under Article 21(a) provides for and protects freedom of speech and expression, subject to the restrictions under paragraph (2)[173]. Contempt of court proceedings are part of the laws of Namibia and are particularly mentioned under paragraph (2) of Article 21 of the Namibian Constitution. All persons in Namibia have the constitutional right to express their opinions on the judgments and decisions of the courts. Such opinions or criticisms, however, should not be made when the matter is *sub judice,* which literally means in course of trial or that the matter has not been finally disposed of by the court. Furthermore, such criticisms should not be scurrilous, *male fide,* or calculated to intimidate or influence the Courts in their performance of their judicial functions. Such measures calculated to interfere with the independence of the Judiciary are subject to contempt of court proceedings[174].

The extra-legal measures meant to protect and maintain the independence, impartiality and dignity of the Judiciary include their conditions of service, i.e.

[173] Article 21 (2) of the Constitution provides as follows; The fundamental freedoms referred to in Sub Article (1) hereof shall be exercised subject to the law of Namibia, insofaras such law imposes reasonable restrictions on the exercise of the rights and freedoms conferred by the said Sub Article, which are necessary in a democratic society and are required in the interests of the sovereignty and integrity of Namibia, national security, public order, decency or morality, or in relation to contempt of court, defamation or incitement to an offence.

[174] See also *S v Heita* 1992 3 SA 785 (NmHC), and *Alfonso Ngoma v Minister of Home Affairs* High Court Case No. A. 206/2000.

remuneration, security of tenure, pension and the manner of appointment. The manner of appointment is relevant to the maintenance of the independence of the Judiciary for if appointments are driven and motivated by political patronage, independence and impartiality of the Judiciary will be greatly compromised.

4.3 The Supreme Court

4.3.1 Composition

The Supreme Court shall consist of a Chief Justice and such additional judges as the President, acting on the recommendation of the Judicial Service Commission, may determine[175] and shall be presided over by the Chief Justice[176]. It must be mentioned that no judge may sit as a judge of the court over a case the decision of which he or she was a party to in a lower court. All appointments of judges to both the Supreme Court and the High Court shall be made by the President on the recommendation of the Judicial Service Commission[177]. In *S v Zemburuka*[178] the Court ruled that the appointments of acting judges should be subjected to the same procedure. All judges so appointed shall hold office until the age of sixty-five but the President shall be entitled to extend the retiring age of any judge until seventy[179]. Before the expiry of the tenure of a judge, he or she may be removed from office only by the President acting on the recommendation of the Judicial Service Commission on the ground of mental incapacity or for gross misconduct[180].

4.3.2 Jurisdiction[181]

4.3.2.1 Appellate jurisdiction of the Supreme Court

The general jurisdiction of the Supreme Court is provided for by the Constitution[182]. It vests in the Supreme Court the inherent jurisdiction which vested in the Supreme Court of South West Africa immediately prior to the date of independence including the power to regulate its own procedures and to make court rules for that purpose[183]. The Supreme Court is primarily a court of appeal and its appellate jurisdiction covers appeals emanating from the High Court, including appeals which involve interpretation, implementation and upholding of the Constitution and the fundamental rights and freedoms guaranteed thereunder[184]. It is the highest court of appeal in

[175] Article 79 (1) of the Namibian Constitution.

[176] Article 79 (2) ibid.

[177] Article 82 (1) of the Namibian Constitution.

[178] 2003 NR 200.

[179] Article 82(4) of the Namibian Constitution.

[180] Article 84 (l) and (2) ibid.

[181] Article 78 (4) ibid.

[182] Article 78 (4) ibid.

[183] Article 78 (4) ibid.

[184] Article 79 (2) ibid.

Namibia and its decisions are final[185]. It must be added, however, that in the exercise of the prerogative of mercy, the President is empowered to pardon or reprieve offenders, either unconditionally or subject to such conditions as the President may deem fit[186]. The Court is not bound by any judgment, ruling or order of any court which exercised jurisdiction in Namibia prior to or after independence[187].

The Constitution further vests in Parliament the power to make legislation providing for the appellate jurisdiction of the Supreme Court[188]. Under the relevant provisions of the Supreme Court Act 15 of 1990, the Supreme Court is vested with unlimited[189] appellate jurisdiction over appeals from any judgment or order of the High Court and any party to any such proceedings before the High Court shall if dissatisfied with any such judgment or order, have a right of appeal to the Supreme Court[190]. In the exercise of the appellate jurisdiction the Supreme Court has the power to receive further evidence, either orally or by deposition before a person appointed by the court. Or it may remit the case to the court of first instance, or to the court whose judgment is the subject of the appeal, for further hearing, with such instructions relating to the taking of further evidence or any other matter as the Supreme Court may deem necessary, and to confirm, amend or set aside the judgment or order which is the subject of the appeal and to give any judgment or make any other order which the circumstances may require[191]. Records indicate that the Supreme Court's jurisdiction to amend or set aside judgment or order of a lower court is used sparingly and on very compelling grounds.

As a general rule, in determining civil appeals from a decision of the High Court, an appeal should take the form of a rehearing of the record, but not a retrial. However, if it appears to the court that there was insufficient evidence before the trial judge, a retrial will be ordered.

4.3.2.2 Jurisdiction of the Supreme Court as Court of first instance

The Supreme Court has original jurisdiction over matters referred to it for decision by the Attorney-General under the Constitution, and with such other matters as may be authorised by Act of Parliament[192]. It can therefore, be concluded in this sense, that the Supreme Court does have original jurisdiction over constitutional

[185] Section 17 (1) of the Supreme Court Act, 15 of 1990.

[186] Article 32 (3) (d) of the Namibian Constitution.

[187] Section 17 (2) of the Supreme Court Act, 15 of 1990.

[188] Article 79 (4) of the Namibian Constitution.

[189] Section 14 (2) (a) of the Supreme Court Act, 15 of 1990 Section 14 (2) states that the right of appeal to the Supreme Court (a) shall not be limited by reason only of the value of the matter in dispute or the amount claimed or awarded in the suit or by reason only of the fact that the matter in dispute is incapable of being valued in money; and (b) shall be subject to the provisions of any law which specifically limits it or specifically grants, limits or excludes such right of appeal, or which prescribes the procedures which have to be followed in the exercise of that right.

[190] Section 14 (1) ibid.

[191] Section 19 (a) (b) of the Supreme Court Act, 15 of 1990.

[192] Article 79 (2) of the Namibian Constitution.

matters but that this original jurisdiction is not exclusive to the Supreme Court because the High Court is also vested with original jurisdiction over constitutional matters[193]. Unlike, for example, in the case of the judicial structure in South Africa where there is a Constitutional Court, the Namibian Constitution does not create a separate Constitutional Court *per se* but the Supreme Court can constitute itself into a Constitutional Court in cases mentioned earlier. By virtue of the provisions relating to the original jurisdiction of the Supreme Court under the Supreme Court Act 15 of 1990[194], whenever any matter is referred to the Supreme Court by the Attorney-General for a decision, the Attorney-General shall be entitled to approach the Supreme Court directly without, first instituting any proceedings in any other court, on application to it, to hear and determine the matter in question[195].

In the exercise of its original jurisdiction, as stated above, the Supreme Court shall have the power to receive evidence either orally or on affidavit or by deposition before a person appointed by the court, or to direct that the matter be heard by the High Court, and grant or refuse the application or to confirm, amend or set aside the proceedings which are the subject of the hearing, and to give any judgment or make any order which in its opinion are in the circumstances of each case just or expedient. The Court is also vested with the jurisdiction to grant or refuse the application or to confirm amend or set aside the proceedings which are the subject of the hearing as the case may be and to give any judgment or make any order which the circumstances may require[196].

4.3.3 Review Jurisdiction of the Supreme Court

The Supreme Court also has review jurisdiction over the proceedings of the High Court or any lower court, or any administrative tribunal or authority established or instituted by or under any law[197]. The Supreme Court may exercise this jurisdiction *mero motu* (from the court's own accord) whenever it comes to the notice of the court or any judge of that court that an irregularity has occurred in any proceedings, notwithstanding that such proceedings are not subject to an appeal or other proceedings before the Supreme Court. This review jurisdiction, however, does not confer upon any person any right to institute any such review proceedings in the Supreme Court as a court of first instance[198].

4.3.4 Sessions of the Supreme Court

The Supreme Court shall hold not less than three sessions during each calendar year and the seat of the court is in Windhoek.

[193] See footnote 195.

[194] Section 15 of the Supreme Court Act 15 of 1990.

[195] Section 15 (1) of the Supreme Court Act, 15 of 1990. See also *Ex Parte Attorney-General, Namibia: In re Corporal Punishment by Organs of State* 1991 NR 178 (SC); 1991 (3) SA 76 and *Ex Parte Attorney-General, Namibia: In Re Constitutional Relationship between the Attorney-General and Prosecutor-General* 1995 (8) BCLR 1070 (NmS).

[196] Section 20 (a) (b) of the Supreme Court Act 15 of 1990.

[197] Section 16 (1) ibid.

[198] Section 16 (2) ibid.

4.3.5 Binding nature of decisions of the Supreme Court

A decision of the Supreme Court shall be binding on all other courts of Namibia and all persons in Namibia unless it is reversed by the Supreme Court itself, or is contradicted by an Act of Parliament lawfully enacted[199], in conformity with the principles of legislative sovereignty.

4.4 The High Court

4.4.1 Composition

The High Court shall consist of the Judge-President and such additional judges as the President, acting on the recommendation of the Judicial Service Commission may determine[200]. The Constitution is silent on the qualifications for appointment as judges and acting judges of High Court but the High Court Act[201] has detailed provisions relating to the qualifications.

Section 8 of the Act provides for the retirement of judges of the High Court as follows:

> (1) Any judge of the High Court holding office in a permanent capacity-
>
> (a) shall retire from office on attaining the age of 65 years;
>
> (b) may retire from office if he has attained the office of 65 years and has completed at least eight years pensionable service as defined by any law relating to the pensions of judges;
>
> (c) may at any time with the approval of the President retire from office if he or she becomes afflicted with a permanent infirmity of mind or body disabling him or her from the proper discharge of his or her duties of office or if any other reason exists which the President deems sufficient.

The constitution of the High Court is provided by section 10 of the Act as follows:

> (1) (a) Subject to the provisions of this Act or any other law, the High Court shall, when sitting as a court of first instance for the hearing of any civil matter, be constituted before a single judge: Provided that the Judge President or, in his or her absence, the senior available judge may, at any time direct that any matter be heard by a full court.
>
> (b) A single judge may at any time discontinue the hearing of any matter being heard before him or her and refer it for hearing to the full court.
>
> (2) Any appeal from a lower court may be heard by one or more judges of the High Court, as the Judge-President may direct.

As a general rule, the judgment of the majority of the judges of the full court shall be the judgment of the court, but where the judgments of a majority of the judges of any

[199] Article 81 of the Namibian Constitution.

[200] Article 80 (1) ibid.

[201] Section 3 of the High Court Act 16 of 1990.

such court are not in agreement, the hearing shall be adjourned and commenced *de novo* before a new court constituted in such manner as the Judge-President or, in his or her absence, the senior available judge may determine[202].

If at any stage during the hearing of any matter by a full court or by a court consisting of two or more judges, any judge of such court dies or retires or becomes otherwise incapable of acting or is absent, the hearing shall, if the remaining judges constitute a majority of the judges before whom it was commenced, proceed before such remaining judges, and if such remaining judges do not constitute such a majority, or if only one judge remains, the hearing shall be commenced *de novo*, unless all the parties to the proceedings agree unconditionally in writing to accept the decision of the majority of such remaining judges or of such one remaining judge, as the case may be, as the decision of the court[203].

4.4.2 Jurisdiction

The High Court is a superior court of record and its jurisdiction is provided for by both the Constitution and the High Court Act. The Constitution vests the High Court with both original and appellate jurisdiction[204] and all proceedings in the High Court shall be carried on in open court[205] provided that the Court may exclude the press and/or the public from all or any part of the trial for reasons of morals, the public order or national security[206]. It is situated permanently in Windhoek and used to go on circuit to Gobabis, Grootfontein, Oshakati, Swakopmund, etc.[207]. The jurisdiction of the High Court is provided for by Section 16 of the High Court Act as follows:

> **The High Court shall have jurisdiction over all persons residing or being in and in relation to all causes arising and all offences triable within Namibia and all other matters of which it may according to law take cognizance, and shall, in addition to any powers of jurisdiction which may be vested in it by law, have power:**
>
> **(a) to hear and determine appeals from all lower courts in Namibia;**
> **(b) to review the proceedings of all such courts;**
> **(c) to hear appeals from the judgments of single judges of the High Court;**
> **(d) in its discretion, and at the instance of any interested person, to enquire into and determine any existing, future or contingent right or obligation, notwithstanding that such person cannot claim any relief consequential upon the determination[208].**

[202] Section 14 (1) of the High Court Act, 16 of 1990.

[203] Section 14 (2) ibid.

[204] Article 80 (2) of the Namibian Constitution.

[205] Section 13 of the High Court Act 16 of 1990.

[206] Article 12 (1) (a) of the Namibian Constitution.

[207] Section 4 of the High Court Act 16 of 1990 provides that the seat of the High Court shall be in Windhoek, but if the Judge President deems it to be necessary or expedient in the interests of the administration of justice, he or she may authorise the holding of its sitting elsewhere in Namibia.

[208] Section 16 ibid.

As stated under the jurisdiction of the Supreme Court, the Supreme Court has the jurisdiction to hear appeals from a judgment or order of the High Court. However, in some cases, these appeals need not go directly to the Supreme Court. Section 18(1) of the High Court Act provides that an appeal from a judgment or order of the High Court in any civil proceedings or against any judgment or order of the High Court given on appeal shall be heard by the Supreme Court.

Section 18(2) provides as follows:

> **An appeal from any judgment or order of the High Court in any civil proceedings shall lie:**
>
> **(a) in the case of a single judge sitting as a court of first instance:**
> **(i) to the full court[209], as of right, and no leave to appeal shall be required; or[210]**
> **(ii) directly to the Supreme Court:**
> **(aa) if all parties to the proceedings concerned agree thereto in writing; or**
> **(bb) in the event of no such agreement, leave to appeal has been granted by the court which has given the judgment or has made the order; or**
> **(cc) in the event of such leave to appeal being refused, leave to appeal being granted by the Supreme Court;**
>
> **(b) in the case of a full Court or two or more judges, sitting as a court of first instance, to the Supreme Court, as of right, and no leave so to appeal shall be required;**
>
> **(c) in the case of a full Court, or one or more judges sitting as a court of appeal, to the Supreme Court if leave to appeal has been granted by the Court which has given the judgment or has made the order or, in the event of such leave to appeal being refused, leave to appeal being granted by the Supreme Court.**

Under the provisions of sections 32(b) and 33(2) of the Legal Practitioners Act No. 15 of 1995, the Court has the power to discipline legal practitioners who have been found guilty of unprofessional or dishonourable or unworthy conduct. In such cases, the Court has the power to reprimand such legal practitioner or to impose a fine of not more than N$10 000.00 and make a restitution order[211].

4.4.2.1 Original jurisdiction

Under its original jurisdiction the court shall have the power to hear and adjudicate upon all civil disputes and criminal prosecutions, including cases which involve the interpretation, implementation and upholding of the Constitution and the fundamental rights and freedoms guaranteed under the Constitution[212], including the power to overrule legislation where legislation is inconsistent with or *ultra vires,* either the

[209] A full court is defined in the Act as a court consisting of more than two judges – Section 1.

[210] It is doubtful whether full bench appeals have not been removed from practice.

[211] Sections 37(a) (b) of the Legal Practioners Act 15 of 1995.

[212] Article 80 (2) of the Namibian Constitution.

Constitution or enabling legislation[213]. The inherent jurisdiction to overrule applies also in the case of subsidiary legislation where it is uncertain, unreasonable or contains an improper delegation. As a general rule the inherent jurisdiction of the superior courts means that they may do anything that the law does not forbid, in contradistinction to the lower courts, such as Magistrates' Courts, which are creatures of statute in that they cannot claim any authority which cannot be found within the four corners of the Magistrates' Courts Act[214]. With regard to the Court's original jurisdiction over cases involving the fundamental rights of the individual, special mention must be made of the provisions of Article 18 and Rule 53 of the High Court Rules that vest in the Court the jurisdiction to review administrative action. The importance of this lies in the development of the law relating to administrative justice by the Namibian Courts[215].

When the High Court sits as a court of first instance for the hearing of any civil matter, it shall be constituted before a single judge but the Judge-President or, in his or her absence, the senior available judge may, at any time direct that any matter be heard by a full court[216]. However, with criminal appeals from a lower court, the High Court shall be constituted in the manner prescribed in the applicable law relating to procedure in criminal matters[217].

4.4.2.2 Appellate jurisdiction

The High Court derives its appellate jurisdiction to hear and adjudicate upon appeals from lower courts primarily from the constitution[218]. There are other provisions in the High Court Act that also deal with the appellate jurisdiction of the court. The High Court as a court of appeal may be constituted by one or more judges[219] but the Judge-President or in his or her absence the senior judge available has the discretion to direct that a matter be heard by a larger number of judges[220]. The powers of High Court on hearing of appeals are provided by section 19 as follows:

> (1) The High Court shall have power:
>
> (a) on the hearing of an appeal to receive further evidence, either orally or by deposition before a person appointed by the court, or to remit the case to the

[213] Article 25 (1) (a) ibid; *Fantasy Enterprise CC and t/a Hustler Shop v The Minster of Home Affairs, and others*. (High Court of Namibia Case No. A 159/96. See also the cases of *Kauesa v Minister of Home Affairs* 1995 (1) BCLR 1540 (NmS) and *Ex Parte Attorney General, Namibia: In re Corporal Punishment by Organs of State* 1991 (3) SA 76 (NmS); *Namunjepo and Others v Commanding Officer, Windhoek Prison and Amother* 2000 (6) BCLR 671 (NMs); *Muller v The President of the Republic of Namibia and Another* 2000 (6) BCLR 655 (NmS).

[214] Hosten, W.J.; Edwards, A.B.; Bosman, F. & Church, J. (1997). *op.cit.*

[215] See *The Chairperson of the Immigration Selection Board v Erna Elizabeth Frank and Elizabeth Khaxas* Case No. SA 8/99; *The Government of the Republic of Namibia v Ngeve Raphael Sikunda,* Case No. SA 5/2001.

[216] Section 10 (1) (a) of the High Court Act 16 of 1990.

[217] Section 10 (4) ibid.

[218] Article 80 (2) of the Namibian Constitution.

[219] Section 10 (2) of the High Court Act 16 of 1990.

[220] Section 10 (3) ibid.

court of first instance or the court whose judgment is the subject of the appeal, for further hearing, with such instructions relating to the taking of further evidence or any other matter as the High Court may deem necessary;

(b) to confirm, amend or set aside the judgment or order which is the subject of the appeal and to give any judgment or make any order which the circumstances may require.

4.4.2.3 Review jurisdiction

The High Court has review or supervisory jurisdiction over all proceedings of inferior courts. Under this jurisdiction the High Court has the power to call for and review the record of any proceedings determined by an inferior court, and if necessary, to revise any judgment or order contained in any such record. As indicated hereunder, the High Court may also either on its own motion, or on application from an interested party, transfer any proceedings pending before any inferior court to another inferior court of competent jurisdiction or to itself, for trial and determination to ensure that the proceedings are determined expeditiously, conveniently, fairly and authoritatively.

The grounds of review of the proceedings of lower courts are stated under Section 20 of the High Court Act as follows:

(a) absence of jurisdiction on the part of the court;

(b) interest in the cause, bias, malice or corruption on the part of the presiding judicial officer;

(c) gross irregularity in the proceedings;

(d) the admission of inadmissible or incompetent evidence or the rejection of admissible or competent evidence.

After review of the proceedings, the court has the power to confirm, alter or set aside the conviction and/sentence.

4.5 The Labour Court

4.5.1 Establishment

The Labour Court belongs to the Superior Courts of Namibia and is established under Section 15 of the Labour Act No. 6 of 1992. The Act establishes two types of Labour Court, namely the Labour Court[221] and the District Labour Court[222] for each district in respect of which a Magistrates' Court is established. In terms of the judicial hierarchy of Namibia therefore, the District Labour Court belongs to the lower courts.

4.5.2 Composition

The Labour Court shall consist of a judge or acting judge of the High Court of Namibia designated by the Judge President for such purpose for the period of the hearing of,

[221] Section 15 (1) (a) of the Labour Court Act No. 6 of 1992.

[222] Section 15 (1) (b) ibid.

or for, such cases as may be determined by the Judge President[223]. The President of the Labour Court may on his or her own motion or on the request of any party to the proceedings in the Labour Court appoint two or more assessors to advise the court on any matter to be adjudicated upon by the court in the proceedings in question[224]. As in the case of the Labour Court, the District Labour Court may also sit with two assessors[225].

The District Labour Court shall consist of a magistrate, designated by the Minister of Justice or any officer in the Ministry of Justice designated by the Minister[226].

4.5.3 Jurisdiction

4.5.3.1 Jurisdiction and powers of Labour Court

Section 18 (1) of the Act provides for the jurisdiction of the Labour Court as follows:

(1) The Labour Court shall have exclusive jurisdiction:

(a) to hear and determine:

(i) any appeal from any district labour court;

(ii) any appeal noted in terms of section 54(4), 68(7), 70(6), 95(4), 100(2) or 114(6);

(b) to consider and give a decision on:

(i) any application made to the Labour Court in accordance with the provisions of this part in terms of any provisions of this Act;

(ii) any application to review and set aside or correct any decision taken by the Minister or the Permanent Secretary, the Commissioner, any inspector or any officer involved in the administration of the provisions of this Act;

(c) to review the proceedings of any district labour court brought under review on the grounds *mutatis mutandis* referred to in section 20 of the High Court Act, 1990 (Act 16 of 1990);

(d) to grant in any application referred to in paragraph (b) or (c) any urgent interim relief until a final order has been made in terms of the said paragraph (b) or (c);

(e) to issue any declaratory order in relation to the application or interpretation of any provision of this Act, or any law on the employment of any person in the service of the State or any term or condition of any collective agreement, any wage order or any contract of employment;

(f) to make any order which it is authorized to make under any provision of this Act or which the circumstances may require in order to give effect to the objects of this Act;

(g) generally to deal with all matters necessary or incidental to its functions under this Act, including any labour matter, whether or not governed by the provisions of this Act, any other law or the common law.

---

[223] Section 16 (1) ibid.

[224] Section 16 (2) (a)(b) ibid.

[225] Section 17 (2) (a) ibid.

[226] Section (17) (1) ibid.

(2) A party to any proceedings before the Labour Court may appear in person or be represented by a legal practitioner admitted to practise as an advocate in terms of the Admission of Advocates Act, 1964 (Act 74 of 1964), or as an attorney in terms of the Attorneys Act, 1979 (Act 53 of 1979).

(3) Subject to the provisions of this section and sections 16 and 22, the Labour Court shall, in the exercise or performance of its powers and functions, have all the powers of the High Court of Namibia under the High Court Act, 1990 (Act 16 of 1990), as if its proceedings were proceedings conducted in, and any order made by it were an order of, the said High Court of Namibia.

4.5.3.2 Jurisdiction and powers of District Labour Courts

Section 19 of the Act provides for the powers of the District Labour Courts as follows:

(1) A district labour court shall have jurisdiction:

(a) to hear all complaints lodged with such district labour court by an employee or employer (hereinafter referred to as the complainant) against an employer or employee (hereinafter referred to as the respondent) for an alleged contravention of, or alleged failure to comply with, any provision of this Act or any term and condition of a contract employment or a collective agreement;
(b) to make any order against, or in respect of, the respondent or the complainant, as the case may be, which it is empowered to make under any such provision of this Act.

(2)(a)A district labour court may on the request of the respondent and with the consent of the complainant, or on its own motion, if it is of the opinion that the subject matter of the complaint relates to a dispute of interests, refer the complaint to the Commissioner.

(b) A complaint referred to the Commissioner in terms of paragraph (a) shall be deemed to be a dispute reported to the Commissioner in terms of section 74.
(c) If a complaint is referred to the Commissioner in terms of paragraph (a) the complainant shall, within a period of 14 days as from the date on which the complaint has so been referred or such longer period as the Commissioner may on good cause shown allow, comply with the provisions of subsection (2) of section 74.

(3) Any complainant, if he or she so desires may be represented in a district labour court by a person who shall be designated by the Permanent Secretary generally or in every particular case for such purpose, and any such complainant and any respondent may appear in person in such district labour court or be represented by his or her own legal practitioner admitted to practise as an advocate in terms of the Admission of Advocates Act, 1964 (Act 74 of 1964), or as an attorney in terms of the Attorneys Act, 1979 (Act 53 of 1979), or by any person duty authorized by such complainant or respondent, as the case may be.

(4) **Subject to the provisions of this section and sections 17 and 22, a district labour court shall, in the exercise or performance of its powers and functions, have all the powers of a Magistrates' Court under the Magistrates' Courts Act No. 32 of 1944, as if its proceedings were proceedings conducted in, and any order made by it were a judgment of, a Magistrates' Court.**

4.5.4 Appeals against judgment or orders of Labour Court or District Labour Court

Any party to any proceedings before the Labour Court may appeal, with the leave of the Labour Court or, if such leave is refused, with the leave of the Supreme Court of Namibia granted on application by way of petition to the Chief Justice, to a full court of the High Court of Namibia, on any question of law against any decision or order of the Labour Court or any judgment or order of the Labour Court given on appeal from a judgment or order from a District Labour Court, as if such judgment or order were a judgment or order of the High Court of Namibia[227].

Similarly, any person to any proceedings before any District Court may appeal to the Labour Court against any judgment or order given by such District Labour Court, as if such judgment or order were a judgment or order of a Magistrates' Court[228].

4.6 The Lower Courts

4.6.1 Establishment

The lower courts are established under Article 78(1) of the Namibian Constitution. Currently, the lower courts in Namibia comprise the Magistrates' Courts and the Community Courts which are specifically established by the Magistrates' Courts Act 32 of 1944 and the Community Courts Act 10 of 2003 respectively. The District Labour Court discussed above is also classified as a lower court.

4.6.2(a) The Magistrates' Court

4.6.2.1 Composition

The Magistrates' Courts in Namibia may be classified into regional, district, subdistrict divisions[229] and periodical courts[230]. The Magistrates' Courts are courts of record[231] and their proceedings in both criminal cases and trial of all defended civil

[227] Section 21 (1) (a) of the Labour Court Act No. 6 of 1992.

[228] Section 21 (1) (b) ibid.

[229] Section 2 (a)-(f) of Magistrates' Court Act 32 of 1944.

[230] Section 2(j) ibid. The periodical courts are meant to serve the more remote areas of the country and as the name suggests they are only held at intervals when the volume of work in the area requires a court sitting.

[231] A court of record is a court whose acts and judicial proceedings are written on parchment or in books for a perpetual memorial which serves as the authentic and official evidence of the proceedings of the court.

actions shall be carried on in open court[232]. The courts are presided over by judicial officers[233] and advocates or attornies of any division of the Supreme Court may appear in any proceeding in any court[234]. The Act also permits articled clerks to appear instead and on behalf of the attorney to whom he or she has been articled[235].

Under the provisions Section 19 of the Legal Practitioners Act No. 15 of 1995, a candidate legal practitioner to whom a certificate has been issued by the Justice Training Centre certifying that such candidate legal practitioner has completed a period of six months training under a course of postgraduate training shall have the right of audience:

(a) in any Lower Court in any matter; and

(b) in Chambers in any High Court proceedings,

but not after expiration of a period of two years after his or her registration as a candidate legal practitioner by the Board.

4.6.2(b) Jurisdiction

4.6.2.1 Civil Jurisdiction

All Magistrates' Courts have equal civil jurisdiction, except the Regional Magistrates' Courts which have only criminal jurisdiction.

4.6.2.1(a) Territorial jurisdiction

The territorial jurisdiction of a Magistrates' Court shall be the district, subdistrict or area for which such court is established and a court established for a district shall have no jurisdiction in a subdistrict[236]. Similar provisions apply to the jurisdiction of the periodical courts except that their territorial jurisdiction is subject to the provision that the court of a district within which the said area or any part thereof is situate shall retain concurrent jurisdiction with the periodical court within such portions of such area as shall be situate within such district[237].

4.6.2.1(b) Jurisdiction in respect of persons

Under the provisions of Section 28(1) of the Magistrates' Court Act 32 of 1944 a Magistrates' Court shall have jurisdiction over the following persons:

(a) any person who resides, carries on business or is employed within the district;

(b) any partnership which has business premises situated or any member whereof resides within the district;

[232] Section 5 of the Magistrates' Court Act.

[233] Section 8 ibid.

[234] Section 20 *ibid.*

[235] Section 21 *ibid.*

[236] Section 26 (1) and (2) of the Magistrates Court Act 32 of 1944.

[237] Section 27 (a) ibid.

(c) any person whatever, in respect of any proceedings incidental to any action or proceeding instituted in the court by such person himself;

(d) any person, whether or not he resides, carries on business or is employed within the district, if the cause of action arose wholly within the district;

(e) any party to interpleader proceedings, if: -

(i) the execution creditor and every claimant to the subject matter of the proceedings reside, carry on business, or are employed within the district; or

(ii) the subject-matter of the proceedings has been attached by process of the court; or

(iii)such proceedings are taken under sub-section (2) of section sixty-nine and the person therein referred to as the "third party" resides, carries on business, or is employed within the district: or

(iv) all the parties consent to the jurisdiction of the court.

(f) any defendant (whether in convention or reconvention) who appears and takes no objection to the jurisdiction of the court;

(g) any person who owns immovable property within the district in actions in respect of such property or in respect of mortgage bonds thereon.

The Magistrates' Courts have civil jurisdiction over matters in which the State is a party[238].

4.6.2.1(c) Jurisdiction in respect of causes of action

In respect of causes of action, the Magistrates' Court shall have in:

(a) actions in which is claimed the delivery or transfer of any property, movable or immovable, not exceeding N$25 000.00 in value;

(b) actions of ejectment against the occupier of any premises or land within the district: Provided that, where the right of occupation of any such premises or land is in dispute between the parties, such right does not exceed N$25 000.00 in clear value to the occupier;

(c) actions for the determination of a right of way, notwithstanding the provisions of Section 46;

(d) actions on or arising out of a liquid document or a mortgage bond, where the claim does not exceed N$100 000.00;

(e) actions on or arising out of any credit agreement as defined in Section 1 of the Credit Agreement Act, 1980 (Act 75 of 1980), where the claim or the value of the matter in dispute does not exceed N$100 000.00;

(f) actions other than those already mentioned in this subsection, where the claim or the value of the matter in dispute does not exceed N$25 000.00;

(2) In subsection 1 'action' includes a claim in reconvention[239].

---

[238] Section 28 (2) of the Magistrates' Court Act 32 of 1944.

[239] Section 29 (ibid) as amended by Section1 of the Magistrates' Court Amendment Act No. 9 of 1997.

4.6.2.1(d) Administration orders

Under Section 74 of the Act, where a judgment has been obtained for the payment of money and the judgment debtor is unable to pay the amount forthwith, or where a debtor is unable to liquidate his liabilities and does not have sufficient assets capable of attachment to satisfy such liabilities or a judgment which has been obtained against him, the court may upon the application of the judgment debtor or the debtor make an order on such terms with regard to security, preservation or disposal of assets, realisation of movables subject to hypothecate or otherwise as it thinks fit, providing for the administration of his estate, and for the payment of his debts by instalments or otherwise.

4.6.2.1(e) Granting of protection orders under the Combating of Domestic Violence Act[240]

Under Section 4(1) of the Combating of Domestic Violence Act 4 of 2003, any person in a domestic relationship may apply to a Magistrates' Court, excluding a regional court, for a protection order.

Section 5(1) of the Act provides as follows:

> **A court of a district where the:**
>
> **(a) complainant permanently or temporary resides, is employed or carries on business;**
>
> **(b) respondent resides, is employed or carries on business; or**
>
> **(c) cause of action arose, has jurisdiction to grant a Protection Order under this Act.**

4.6.2.1(f) The granting of Maintenance Order under the Maintenance Act[241]

Every Magistrates' Court, other than a Regional Magistrates' Court is within its area of jurisdiction a Maintenance Court[242] and as such has the jurisdiction to make the following orders:

(a) in the case where no maintenance order is in force, to make a maintenance order against the person who has been proved to be legally liable to maintain a beneficiary;

(b) in the case where a maintenance order is in force;
   (i) substitute that maintenance order by another maintenance order; or
   (ii) discharge such maintenance order; or
   (iii) suspend such maintenance order on such conditions which the maintenance court determines;

(c) make no maintenance order[243].

---

[240] Act No. 4 of 2003.

[241] Act No. 9 of 2003

[242] Section 6 of the Maintenance Act 9 of 2003

[243] Section 17(1), Act No. 9 of 2003

4.6.2.1 (g) Matters beyond the jurisdiction of Magistrates' Courts

The Magistrates' Courts shall not have jurisdiction in the following:

(1) in matters in which the dissolution of a marriage or separation from bed and board or of goods of married persons is sought[244];

(2)(a) in matters in which the validity or interpretation of a will or other testamentary document is in question;

(2)(b) in which the status of a person in respect of mental capacity is sought to be affected;

(3) in a matter in which is sought specific performance without an alternative of payment of damages, except in-

- (i) the rendering of an account in respect of which the claim does not exceed N$25 000.00;
- (ii) the delivery or transfer of property, movable or immovable, not exceeding N$25 000.00 in value; and
- (iii) the delivery or transfer of property, movable or immovable, exceeding N$25 000.00 in value where the consent of the parties has been obtained in terms of Section 45[245].

4.6.2.1 (h) Removal of actions from the Magistrates' Court to the High Court

Under Section 50 of the Magistrates' Courts Act No. 32 of 1944 (as amended by Section 3 of the Magistrates' Courts Amendment Act No. 9 of 1977), any action in which the amount of the claim exceeds N$5000, exclusive of interest and costs, may, upon application to the court by the defendant, or if there is more than one defendant, by any defendant, be removed to the High Court.

4.6.2.2 Criminal jurisdiction

All magistrates shall have criminal jurisdiction which is subject to certain limitations in respect of the seriousness of the offence, the nature of punishment, and territorial jurisdiction. As stated earlier Magistrates' Courts are the creation of a statute and therefore can only exercise powers and impose punishments provided for by the Act. Any exercise of jurisdiction outside the Act will be null and void. (Contrast this with the inherent jurisdiction of the superior courts.)

---

[244] Section 46 (1) of the Magistrates' Courts Act 32 of 1944.

[245] Section 46 (c) *ibid.* as amended by Section 2 of the Magistrates' Court Amendment Act No. 9 of 1997. Section 45 (1) provides as follows; Subject to the provisions of Section 46, the court shall have jurisdiction to determine any action or proceeding otherwise beyond the jurisdiction, if the parties consent in writing thereto; Provided that no court other than a court having jurisdiction under Section 28 shall, except where such consent is given specifically with reference to particular proceedings already instituted or about to be instituted in such court, have jurisdiction in any such matter.

4.6.2.2(a) Jurisdiction in respect of offences

The Regional Division of the Magistrates Court has jurisdiction over murder, culpable homicide and statutory offences under certain specific statutes and regulations such as the Combating of Rape Act, 8 of 2000, the Stock Theft Act, 12 of 1990 as amended by Act 19 of 2009, the Combating of Immoral Practices Act, 21 of 1980, as amended by Act 7 of 2000, the Abuse of Dependence-Producing Substances and Rehabilitation Centres Act 41 of 1971 and the Exchange Control Regulations No. 1112 of 1961[246].

4.6.2.2(b) Jurisdiction in respect of punishment

The jurisdiction of the court is limited with respect to the punishment it may impose. Under Section 92 of the principal Act as amended by the Section 6 of the Magistrates' Court Amendment Act No. 9 of 1997, the court may impose a sentence of imprisonment for a period not exceeding five years where the court is not the court of a regional division, or not exceeding twenty years, where the court is a court of a regional division. In the case of fines, the court may impose a fine not exceeding N$20 000.00 where the court is not a court of a regional division, or not exceeding N$100 000.00 where the court is the court of a regional division.

Apart from these general provisions relating to the jurisdiction of the court in respect of punishment, a magistrate's jurisdiction is sometimes increased or reduced by particular legislation. A particular statute that creates and prohibits a certain offence may also impose the sentence or the statutory offence. In this case, a magistrate may impose any fine or any sentence as it is prescribed so long as it is not beyond the prescribed penalty in the Act. As a general rule, certain enactments provide for a mandatory minimum sentence, in which case any convicted person must receive that minimum sentence irrespective of the peculiar circumstances of the case, including the mitigating circumstances.

4.6.2.2(c) Confirmation of punishment in excess of jurisdiction

The High Court has both express and inherent review jurisdiction over the proceedings of the Magistrates' Court. Consequently, if a magistrate in a certain matter is of the opinion that the peculiar circumstances of the case are such that a punishment beyond jurisdiction is warranted, the court may either impose such punishment and transfer to the High Court (as indicated above) or regional court, as the case may be, for confirmation or to the superior court for sentencing.

4.6.2.2(d) Territorial jurisdiction/local limits of jurisdiction

The local limits of jurisdiction or the territorial jurisdiction of the Magistrates' Court are provided for under the provisions of Section 90 of the principal Act as amended by The Magistrates' Courts Amendment Act No. 11 of 1985 as follows:

> **(1) Subject to the provision of section 89, any person charged with any offence committed within any district, district division or regional division may be tried by the court of that district, district division or regional division, as the case may be.**

[246] Section 89 of the Magistrates' Court Act 32 of 1944 as amended by the Magistrates' Court Amendment Act No.9 of 1997.

(2) When any person is charged with any offence-

(a) committed within the distance of four kilometres beyond the boundary of the district, district division or regional division; or

(b) committed in or upon any vehicle on a journey which or part whereof was performed in, or within the distance of four kilometres of, the district, district division or regional division; or

(c) committed on board any vessel on journey upon any river within the Republic or forming the boundary of any portion thereof, and such journey or part thereof was performed in, or within the distance or four kilometres of, the district, the district division or regional division; or

(d) committed on board any vessel on a voyage within the territorial waters of the Republic (including the territory of South West Africa), and the said territorial waters adjoin the district, district division or regional division; or

(e) begun or completed within the district, district division or regional division, such person may be tried by the court of the district, district division or regional division, as the case may be, as if he or she had been charged with an offence committed within the district, district division, or regional division, respectively.

(3) Where it is uncertain in which of several jurisdictions an offence has been committed, it may be tried in any of such jurisdictions.

(4) A person charged with an offence may be tried by the court of any district, district division or regional division, as the case may be where in any act or omission or event which is an element of the offence took place.

(5) A person charged with theft of property or with obtaining property by an offence or with an offence which involves the receiving of any property by him, may also be tried by the court of any district, district division or regional division, as the case may be, wherein he has or had part of the property in his possession.

(6) A person charged with kidnapping, child stealing or abduction may also be tried by the court of any district, district division or regional division, as the case may be, through or in which he conveyed or concealed or detained the person kidnapped, stolen or abducted.

(7) Where by any special provision of law a magistrates' court has jurisdiction in respect of an offence committed beyond the local limits of the district, district division or regional division, as the case may be, such court shall not be deprived of such jurisdiction by any of the provisions of this section.

(8) Where an accused is alleged to have committed various offences within different districts in the territory, the Attorney-General may in writing direct that criminal proceedings in respect of such various offences be commenced in the court of any particular district in the territory whereupon such court shall have jurisdiction to act with regard to any such offence as if such offence had been committed within the area of jurisdiction of that court, and the court of the district division or regional division within whose area of jurisdiction the court of such district is situated, shall likewise have jurisdiction in respect of any such offence if such offence is an offence which may be tried by the court of a district division or regional division.

4.6.2.3 Appellate jurisdiction

Magistrates' courts have the jurisdiction to hear and determine any appeal against any order or decision of a community court[247].

4.6.3 Community Courts

4.6.3.1 Establishment

Community courts are the creation of a statute, Community Courts Act No. 10 of 2003 which also provides detailed procedure and requirements for the establishment and recognition of community court in a particular traditional community. The Community Courts Act was promulgated, *inter alia,* to give legislative recognition to and formalise the jurisdiction of the traditional courts that have been rendering essential judicial services to members of the traditional communities who subject themselves to their jurisdiction and the application of customary law. The formal recognition will also bring the proceedings of the erstwhile traditional courts within the mainstream of the Judiciary in Namibia and subject their proceedings to formal evaluation and review by the superior courts.

Every community court shall be a court of record and the proceedings shall be recorded in writing by the clerk of the court[248]. This is an important provision not only in terms of review and appeals but also for purposes of precedents and authoritative ascertainment of customary law.

4.6.3.2 Composition

A community court shall be presided over by one or more justices appointed by the Minister (of Justice). A Justice of the community court must be conversant with the customary law of the area of his or her jurisdiction and must not be a member of Parliament, a regional council, or a local authority council. Furthermore, a person shall not be eligible for appointment as a Justice of a community court, if he or she is a leader of a political party, regardless of whether or not that political party is registered under Section 39 of the Electoral Act No. 24 of 1992[249]. The Minister has the power to remove any Justice of the community court from office if he or she becomes subject to any disqualification mentioned above but after consultation with the traditional authority concerned and after the Minister has afforded the Justice concerned the opportunity to be heard. This removal must be published in the *Gazette*[250].

A Justice of the community court may appoint one or more assessors to advise the court on any matter to be adjudicated upon by the court in the proceedings in question[251] but the opinion of the assessor(s) is not binding on the court, it is only advisory[252].

[247] See section 27 of the Community Courts Act No. 10 of 2003.

[248] Section 18 (1) and (2) *ibid.*

[249] Section 8 (1) (2) (a) (b) (c) *ibid.*

[250] Section 8 (3) *ibid.*

[251] Section 7 (2) *ibid.*

[252] Section 7 (6) *ibid.*

4.6.3.3 Jurisdiction in respect of cases and persons

The jurisdiction of the community courts is provided for under Section 12 as follows:

> **A community court shall have jurisdiction to hear and determine any matter relating to a claim for compensation, restitution or any other claim recognized by the customary law, but only if:**
>
> **(a) the cause of action of such matter or any element thereof arose within the area of jurisdiction of that community court; or**
>
> **(b) the person or persons to whom the matter relates are in the opinion of that community court closely connected with the customary law.**

The importance of this provision is that the jurisdiction of the community courts is not limited to only civil matters. They have both civil and criminal jurisdiction provided that they do not impose custodial sentences. Their jurisdiction therefore is limited to that extent.

4.6.3.4 Application and ascertainment of customary law

Since the community courts traditionally administered justice over persons and in jurisdictions where the operating and functional law was/is customary law, this practice was taken cognisance of when the Act was being promulgated and provisions were accordingly incorporated therein for the application of customary law by the community courts. Section 13 of the Community Courts Act No. 10 of 2003 provides as follows:

In any proceedings before it a community court shall apply the customary law of the traditional community residing in its area of jurisdiction: Provided that if the parties are connected with different systems of customary law, the community court shall apply the system of customary law which the court considers just and fair to apply in the determination of the matter.

The community court may rely on any submissions on customary law made to it and if it entertains any doubt thereafter, it is permissible and lawful for the court to consult decided cases, text books and other sources and may receive opinions, either orally or in writing to enable it to arrive at a decision in the matter, provided that such sources are made available to the other parties[253].

4.6.3.5 Representation

Under Section 16 of the Act, a party to any proceedings before a community court shall appear in person and may represent himself or herself or be represented by any person of his or her choice. It will appear from this provision that legal practitioners may be able to represent clients in the community courts. If this is the correct interpretation of the Act, then the Namibian situation is a departure from the positions obtaining in some jurisdictions where legal practitioners cannot represent clients in similar courts.

[253] Section 14 *ibid.*

4.6.3.6 Appeals against orders or decisions of community courts

A party to any proceedings in a community court, who is aggrieved by any order or decision of that community court, may appeal to the Magistrates' Court[254]. Furthermore, an appeal against an order or decision made or given by a Magistrates' Court shall lie to the High Court[255].

4.6.4

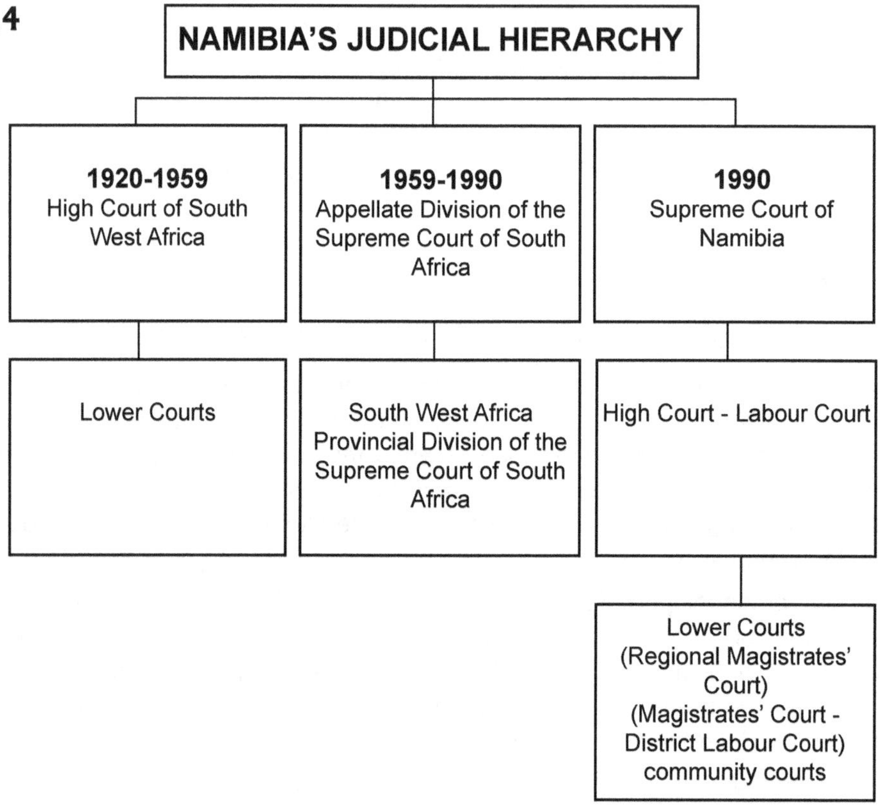

4.7 Review questions

1. Mr Clean and Mr Corn Man enter into a contract for the sale of the latter's Mercedes Benz antique motor car for N$20 000.00 (twenty thousand Namibian dollars). A term of the said agreement stipulates the payment of an initial deposit of the N$10 000.00 and the final payment to be made upon delivery of the motor car, which must be effected fourteen days after the payment of the deposit. Mr Clean paid the initial deposit four weeks ago but Mr Corn Man has as yet not delivered the car.

   Mr Clean wants to institute a legal action against Mr Corn Man.

   What court has jurisdiction over the case? Give reasons for your answer.

[254] Section 28 *ibid.*

[255] Section 29 (1) *ibid.*

2. You are consulted by Albert. He informs you that he was the plaintiff in a civil matter in which he claimed damages for the defendant for breach of contract. This matter was heard in the Magistrates' Court. Albert's claim was dismissed with costs and he is of the opinion that the Magistrate applied the law incorrectly to the facts of the case. Can Albert take any further steps in this matter? Advise him.

3. Write a note on the jurisdiction of the Superior Courts of Namibia in constitutional matters.

4. The Attorney-General wants an opinion on a matter which he or she thinks has constitutional implications. With case law authority advise him or her of the steps to be taken to obtain that opinion.

5. Discuss the original and appellate jurisdiction of the High Court.

6. What court will have jurisdiction in the following cases?
   (a) Angula and Sackey are married under Ovambo traditional customary law and have three children. Angula alleges that her husband has deserted her and lives with another woman with whom he has two children. She wants to institute an action for divorce and maintenance. What court has jurisdiction in the matter?
   (b) Elizabeth Frank wants to bring an action against the Ministry of Home Affairs for allegedly refusing to grant her a residence permit on ground of her sexual orientation.
   (c) Waterberg Big Game Hunting Lodge (PTY) Ltd is a registered company doing business as a hunting and safari lodge with its main place of business at Farm Otjahewita 291, Otjiwaranjo District. It enters into a contract with Kavango Fisheries (PTY) Ltd for the supply of tuna fish. Kavango Fisheries has its registered offices in Walvis Bay and the contact was entered into in Windhoek. Waterberg Big Game wants to bring an action against Kavango Fisheries for a breach of contract.
   (d) Peter is the registered owner of Erf 123 sub 3, Olympia Park, Windhoek and wants to institute an action against Joseph for unlawful occupation of Peter's property.

CHAPTER 5

INTRODUCTION TO CASES AND AUTHORITIES

5.1 Introduction

As stated in Chapter 2, Namibia belongs to the common law tradition and hence case law is one of the sources of law in Namibia. Article 66(1) of the Namibian Constitution provides that 'both the customary law and the common law of Namibia in force on the date of independence shall remain valid to the extent to which such customary law or common law does not conflict with this Constitution or any other law'.

This constitutional provision does therefore recognise common law as a source of law. The common law consists mainly of principles of law laid down in the decisions of judges. This is known as case law. The details of the nature of case law is discussed under judicial precedent and *stare decisis,* but for our present exercise, we shall devote our attention to the structure of a reported case in a law report. It normally consists of statement of facts, the legal issues raised by the facts, the court's exposition of the principles of law and judgment.

One method of case analysis is the case briefs method, which is simply a written summary of court opinion. One can devise one's own method of writing case briefs but for the purposes of our exercise we shall follow the method provided below.

5.2 The structure or anatomy of a reported case[256]

5.2.1 Citation of a case

By convention and common practice, the judgments and decisions of superior courts in both common law and civil law jurisdictions[257] are reported in law reports. These cases are identified by reference to the names of the parties involved and the particular law reports that are reported in, including references to the year, the volume and the pages. This method of identification is known as the *citation* of a

[256] See generally Van der Walt, A.J. 2002. *Law of Property: Casebook for Students/Sakereg: vonnisbundel vir studente*. 5th edition. Lansdowne: Juta & Co., Ltd.

[257] In the common law jurisdictions case law constitutes a source of law and therefore law reporting in law reports form an important and inextricable component of the doctrine of *stare decisis or judicial precedent.* In the civil law jurisdiction, however, more emphasis or weight is placed on the civil code rather than case law as a source law. But it must be added that because of the dynamics of the unification of Europe, there is a cross fertilisation of the two legal systems which is gradually affecting the nature of law reporting and the status of *stare decisis* in the civil law jurisdictions of Europe.

case. For example the Zambian case of *Chilufya* is cited or referred to as *Chilufya v City Council of Kitwe* 1967 ZR 115 and similarly, the Namibian case of *Kauesa* is cited or referred to as *Kauesa v Minister of Home Affairs and Others* 1994 NR 102 (HC); 1996 (4) SA 965 (NmS).

In the Zambian case of *Chilufya*, Chilufya and City Council of Kitwe refer to the names of the parties, the case name: 1967 stands for the year or/and volume of the law report; ZR stands for the title of the law report, in this case The Zambia Law Report. 115 stands for the page it appears on. The same explanation goes for the citation of the *Kauesa* case, except that in this case the letters in brackets (HC) are used to refer to the court that delivered the judgment or the decision, i.e. the High Court. In addition to the page references in the citation, it is the practice of the editors of some reports to number or identify the lines of the pages of a case with letters of the alphabet for purposes of quicker identification of specific areas of the case.

5.2.2 Headnotes or the flynotes of a case

The first part of a reported case normally consists of a headnote or the flynote of the case. In this part of the case the editors summarise the specific areas or branches of the law covered in the case, the findings of facts, the issues raised and the principles of law. For example in the *Nanditume* case, the reader will know from the headnote that the case deals with some aspects of labour law. The summary of the findings of facts and the court's decisions (including the principles of law) are always indicated by the word, "*Held*". Sometimes the words "*Quaere*" and "*Semble*" are also used. The former is used to denote that the matter was stated or that a question was posed but that no decision was taken. It simply means that the matter was left open. The latter means that although the court made a finding, it was not clearly or explicitly stated.

5.2.3 Counsel for the parties

The headnote or the flynote will be followed by the names of the advocates appearing for the parties. In the *Nanditume* case, for example, advocates D.F. Smuts and M.J. Figueira appeared for the applicant and T.J. Frank for the respondent.

At times, in some reports, this part of the case will contain a summary of the arguments by counsel, but these do not form part of the court's judgment since they are only submissions by counsel. This, however, does not mean that the arguments must be ignored as irrelevant and inconsequential. These arguments are important because they teach students or beginners the technique of presenting arguments and the sources and authorities of the areas of law discussed in the case.

5.2.4 Trial date and the date of judgment

The trial date is the date mentioned below the name(s) of the judge(s). In *Nanditume* one will discover that several dates are mentioned after J. Levy's name. This means that the case was postponed and that the actual judgment was handed down on the last date mentioned, 10 May 2000. In addition to the trial date, immediately after the headnote and the judgment, the words *"Cur ad vult"* (*curia advisari vult*) and "*Postea"* will be used to indicate that judgment was not handed down immediately but was given at a later date that follows the word "*Postea*". The phrase "*curia advisari vult*" means that the court wants to consider the matter and the word, "*postea*" simply means later or thereafter.

5.2.5 Structure of the judgment

5.2.5.1 Facts

The judgment itself starts with the name(s) of the judge(s) and then components such as: facts of the case; legal issues; the discussion of the relevant principles of law; application of the relevant principles of law to the facts and issues; the court's holdings; the court's reasoning; and the court order usually followed.

The facts of a reported case are the findings of facts arrived at by the court after scrutinising statements made by witnesses. If the court is satisfied with the veracity of the statement, it makes a statement to that effect and that finding of fact becomes part of the judgment or the ruling of the case, as the case may be. One exercise law students are required to do is the writing of case briefs or a legal opinion, as mentioned in Chapter 2. In writing the case brief, the student will be required to summarise the facts. In the recitation or restatement of the facts the student should be able to state the facts which are relevant to the legal issues that he or she intends to analyse in the brief. One will discover in this way that the facts are so connected with the legal issues that they cannot be separated and as it were, creating the relationship of a vicious cycle between the facts and the legal issues. The legal issues are the legal problems that are presented by the facts. The inclusion of any facts must be justified by relating them to the legal issues.

5.2.5.2 Legal issues

As stated earlier, the legal issues are the legal problems that are raised by the facts. The exposure of the legal issues present in a case is the key that unlocks the whole case to our understanding. However, the process of defining issues is complex and subtle. It is necessary to know where the points of stress are and where the legal collisions occur. It is not enough to identify a case as a mere civil case or a criminal case. If, for example, it is a civil case on contract and one party is alleging a breach of contract by the other contracting party, the issues may relate to whether or not there was a valid contract in the first place. If, for example, it is a homicide case, it is necessary to know, for instance, to what degree voluntarily induced drunkenness may mitigate a charge of murder, if it will at all, what degree of drunkenness is then required. In other words, the issue must be more refined and an accurate statement of the issues in a case nearly always demands an appreciation of the relationship of the competing legal principles involved. With time, patience and practice the skill of analysing cases can be mastered.

5.2.5.3 References to authorities

Courts usually employ the judicial methodology of references to authorities in the process of the resolution of the legal issues. This method involves identification, analysis and the application of the relevant law. In identifying the relevant authorities, the courts refer to the various sources of law as authorities, that is to say, the constitution, statutes, the common law, international conventions, juristic writings, etc. This process will be followed by the analysis of the authorities for the court to determine their relevance and applicability to the case and issues in question. This will include the techniques of distinguishing cases, identifying binding and persuasive precedents and the ratification and incorporation of international conventions in the municipal laws.

In the case of *Chilufya v City Council of Kitwe* 1967 ZR 115, for example, the authorities referred to are summarised and included in the headnote, under the subtitles cases are referred to and Statutes and notices are construed. One will notice, for example, that one of the issues to be determined by the court in that case was the legal nature of the plaintiff's right to trade in the market. In its resolution of the issue the court had to refer to the Markets Ordinance as its basic reference point and authority and thereafter consider such authorities as textbooks and cases in order to be able to make a final pronouncement on the nature of the plaintiff's right to trade in the market. To be more specific, the court referred to *Woodfall on Landlord and Tenant, Frank Warr & Co. Ltd v London County Council* [1904] 1 K.B. 713; *Wood v Leadbitter* (1845), 13 M. & W. 838; *Shelley v London County Council* [1949] A.C. 56; and *City of Salisbury v Mehta* 1961, R. & N. 1000.

5.2.5.4 The court's holdings

In most cases the holding of the court is the statement of the court relating to its position on the legal propositions at issue. It may be an affirmation or denial of the legal proposition at issue. If the court clearly states what its holding is in a particular case, all that needs to be done is to restate what the court has declared. Even if the court does not itself state what its holding is on a particular issue, this can be derived from the case as a whole. In some cases the court may make a declaration on a principle of law, which is based on hypothetical facts. Statements based on hypothetical facts are not classified as holdings; they are classified as *obiter dicta,* statements extraneous to a case.

The holdings of the court on legal propositions at issue are also at times referred to as the legal principles of law laid down by the court in a particular case, or the *ratio decidendi.*

5.2.5.5 Reasoning of a court

In addition to the holdings of the case, the court may also give its reasons for its decisions. At times both the principle of law and the reasoning are referred to as the *ratio decidendi.* If the court gives the reasoning behind a decision, this will be quite easy to identify. But in some cases the court may not record its reasoning for a certain decision. In such a case you may face two tasks: trying to establish what the unspoken reasons were and the degree to which these reasons are relevant to the rule of law, which purportedly is derived from the case.

5.2.5.6. The court order

The court's order is that part of the judgment that has direct bearing on the fate of the parties as it relates to their rights and obligations in the matter. It is binding *inter partes* and therefore must be distinguished from the *ratio decidendi* which is the binding element of the case as a precedent.

5.2.5.7 Concurring and dissenting judgments

When the court is composed of more than one judge, and in most cases of an uneven number of judges, it is important to find the judgment of the court, which is the majority judgment. The written judgments always indicate the names of the concurring and dissenting judges. In the judicial process it is discovered that at times, the dissenting judgments are treated as *obiter dicta*, which if affirmed and adopted later form part of binding precedents.

5.2.6 Criticism and evaluation

For most cases discussed in class, it will be expected of you to agree or disagree with the court's decision. You will be expected to be able to offer constructive criticism of the opinion and about the way in which it is reasoned. You will further be expected to suggest how you would decide the case as a judge and to demonstrate the persuasive legal reasoning you could bring to bear on the problem yourself. The reasoning you will be called upon to express should include an ability to show that your conclusions are at least permissible and preferably are the strongest within the range of possibilities available within the constraints of applicable statutes, previous cases and other legal principles. In addition you may want to persuade your class that your conclusions are the ones that should be reached in *public policy*, that will best serve the needs of Namibia.

5.3 Some hints on how to answer questions

5.3.1 Introduction

Most law, examination questions are problem questions. You are presented with a hypothetical situation and asked to use legal principles to advise or present an opinion, etc. You may use any format to answer the question, as long as the question is answered in a satisfactory manner. But one format you could consider using is what is provided below.

5.3.2 Identify the issues

If the question is presented in the form of a hypothetical situation, the first task is to identify the issues that are posed by the facts. The issues usually, emanate from conflicting legal principles.

5.3.3 State the relevant legal principles

After identifying the issues the next stage is to state and explain the relevant principles of law. This is probably the most important part of the answer. The exposition should be based on the law. It should not be a mere restatement of facts or opinions based on facts. Always support the law you are citing with authorities. If it is a statute, you must be prepared to give the details of the statute; if it is case law you must be able to give the citation, etc.

5.3.4 Application of the law to the facts

After the exposition of the relevant law posed by the facts, the next task is to apply the law to the facts and reconcile the issues.

5.3.5 Conclusion and advice

The final stage of the answer is the conclusion or advice, as the case may require. The conclusion or advice should be a logical sequel to the last two parts of the answer.

5.4 Examples of cases

5.4.1 Nanditume v Minister of Defence[258]

Labour Court

LEVY AJ

2000 April 17, 18, 19, 20; May 10

Labour law – Unfair discrimination in contravention of s 107 of Labour Act – What constitutes – Applicant applying to be enlisted in Namibian Defence Force – Applicant testing HIV positive and excluded on this ground – Court holding, in the light of medical and other evidence, such exclusion constituting unfair discrimination.

The applicant had applied to be enlisted in the Namibian Defence Force. A medical examination and blood test revealed that he was HIV positive. His application for enlistment was refused on this ground.

It appeared from the evidence that people who were HIV positive would most likely only contract AIDS after 8 to 12 years. Such persons would accordingly be fit for any kind of employment. Moreover, there were many other members of the Defence Force who were HIV positive or who had AIDS and they had not been tested nor excluded from enlistment. The Defence Force in fact practised a policy of non-discrimination. It also appeared that the applicant was in good health.

The Court held that the exclusion of the applicant from the Defence Force on the ground that he had tested HIV positive constituted unfair discrimination in contravention of s 107 of the Labour Act 6 of 1992, especially since the applicant was still in good health.

[258] 2000 NR 103.

Application for an order declaring that exclusion from employment on the ground that applicant was HIV positive constituted unfair discrimination in contravention of s 107 of the Labour Act. The facts appear from the reasons for judgment.

***D F Smuts* (with him *M J Figueira*) for the applicant.**

***T J Frank SC* for the respondent.**

Cur adv vult.

***Postea* (May 10).**

LEVY AJ: In this matter the applicant is represented by *Mr D F Smuts* assisted by *Ms M J Figueira* while respondent is represented by *Mr T J Frank SC*.

The issue raised in this application is whether the exclusion on the grounds of HIV status alone of a prospective applicant for enlistment to the Namibian Defence Force (hereafter NDF) constitutes unfair discrimination as contemplated in s 107 of the Labour Act (Act 6, 1992).

On 12 September 1997, by way of notice of motion supported by a solitary affidavit, applicant applied to Court for an order:

'(1) Directing that respondent discontinue discriminating against the applicant on the grounds of his being HIV positive in respect of his application for enlistment in the Namibian Defence Force (hereafter NDF);

(2) Directing respondent to process applicant's application for enlistment in the NDF, without having regard to the applicant's HIV status;

(3) Granting to the applicant such further and/or alternative relief as this Honourable Court deems fit.'

The solitary affidavit referred to above was attested by applicant himself and annexed to his affidavit were certain relevant documents to which I shall at a later stage refer.

Respondent opposed the application and filed an answering affidavit made by Mr Erastus Negonga, the Permanent Secretary in the Ministry of Defence. The defence also filed a solitary affidavit. Applicant replied to this and he annexed an affidavit by Dr Malcolm Steinberg MB ChB (Wits) MSc Epidemiology (London) and with extensive qualifications in the field of Human Immuno Deficiency (hereafter HIV) and Public Health.

When the case was called on 26 October 1998, the Court appreciating the magnitude of the issues involved, referred the matter for the hearing of oral evidence, such evidence to include the evidence of persons who had not made affidavits, provided written statements of the evidence which they intended to give, were served on the respective litigants. The Court also ordered discovery. It is necessary to refer specifically to paras (1) and (2) of the aforesaid order of Court. They are as follows:

'(1) The application is referred for the hearing of oral evidence on a date and time to be arranged with the Registrar of this Court, on the question whether the respondent's exclusion of the applicant from enlistment in the NDF on the grounds of his HIV status alone, is a reasonable criterion as contemplated by s 107(2) of the Labour Act 1992.

(2) The evidence shall be that of any witness that the parties or either of them may elect to call...'

It will be observed that para (1) of the order of Court of 26 October 1998, is not the same as claims (1) and (2) of the notice of motion. Notwithstanding, the explicit terms of the aforegoing sub-orders, both counsel informed this Court that the mutual intention was not to replace claims (1) and (2) of the original notice of motion. Those claims still remain for decision. The ambit of the inquiry, however, was substantially extended.

Furthermore, notwithstanding the wording of para (2) of that Court's order, this Court was still to take into account not only the oral evidence given in Court but also the affidavits already filed save and except that in respect of the written statement of one Alex van Heever, who did not testify, only pages 150-4, and pages 178-9 were to be considered.

In consequence of the aforegoing, this Court had to consider the evidence and affidavits of the following compassionate and learned persons:

On behalf of the applicant:

1. Dr Malcolm Steinberg MB ChB, MSc Epidemiology (London) Diploma Occupational Health, Managing Director of HIV Management Services (Pty) Ltd, Programme Leader of National AIDS

Research Programme, World Bank consultant on AIDS in South Africa, Medical Association of South Africa's HIV Clinical Guidelines Committee;

2. Abduraman Achmat Researcher in the Active AIDS Law Project in South Africa.
3. The applicant's affidavits. He did not testify orally.

On behalf of the respondent:

1. Dr Clive Evian MB ChB, MSc (Community Health) Director and Consultant of HIV/AIDS, Director of Aids Consulting Unit for Alexander Forbes, Director of City of Johannesburg AIDS Programme.
2. Mr Charles Murray Harebottle BSc Eng (Mech) MSc Eng (Ind), Henly Graduate Management Diploma, Corporate Management Consultant of Business and Practice Development. Involved in strategic response programmes to deal with HIV/AIDS.
3. Major Freddie Maiba, Namibian Defence Force, Operations Division and in charge of Policy and Planning. Formerly Military Engineer Instructor, Intelligence Physical Training Instructor, Intelligence Research Officer, Tactical Training Instructor. Has attended several courses in foreign countries.
4. Colonel Jakobus Johannes Crouse B Com LLB, SANDF Officer specializing in Medical Legal Sphere of SANDF, particularly HIV/AIDS epidemic in South Africa, active in programmes to combat HIV/AIDS epidemic.
5. Mr Erastus Negonga Permanent Secretary, Ministry of Defence who made the opposing affidavit did not testify orally.

Mr Alex van den Heever, a health economist, manager of Gauteng Health Department, MSc Econ (UCT) and experienced researcher in respect of HIV/AIDS economics, did not give oral evidence but relevant parts of his written and supplementary statements were referred to.

It is common cause between the litigating parties that Human Immuno Deficiency Virus (HIV) is a condition found in some human beings which predisposes a person with HIV to, and culminates in, Acquired Immuno Deficiency Syndrome, AIDS, within a period, on average of approximately 8 to 12 years. AIDS, however, is not a single disease but a collection of illnesses which affect people infected with HIV. Infection with HIV initiates a process which causes a slow, steady destruction of those cells known as CD4 T-Lymphocytes. These cells, according to the medical evidence, are an important component of the human immune system, which becomes progressively weaker, destroying the body's ability to fight infections and certain cancers. When the CD4 T-Lymphocytes cell count has been severely depleted, the immune system becomes so weak that the body succumbs to certain infections and cancers. Collectively these are called 'opportunistic diseases'. When this occurs the person is said to have AIDS.

If a person tests HIV positive that does not mean that such person has AIDS nor does it mean that such person is ill, nor does it mean that such person will become ill soon. It may take several years, on average 8 to 12 years, for the HIV to damage the immune system so much that the person can be said to be ill. Futhermore it may take one and a half to two months after being infected with HIV for there to be signs that an infected person has in fact become HIV positive. This is known as the 'window period'. Therefore a blood test which indicates that a person is HIV positive is not an indication of that person's health on that date, while a person who tests negative may nevertheless be HIV positive. Two other tests are necessary to determine whether an HIV positive person is ill. The first is to ascertain the infected person's CD4 count. This is measured as the number of cells per cubic millimetre of blood and indicates the degree of the damage to the immune system. The lower the CD4 count, the more damaged the immune system is. CD4 counts below 200 cm are associated with more rapid development of AIDS-related diseases. The second test necessary to ascertain the health of the person who is HIV positive, is known as the Viral Load test. It measures the amount of viruses multiplying in the blood at a given time.

A high viral load indicates high levels of viral infection and a shorter time to the inevitable development of the 'disease'. Obviously some people with HIV have low viral loads and some have high viral loads. A low viral load means a slower rate of disease progression. The experts agreed that a person with a CD4 count below 200 and a viral load in excess of 100 000 would not be fit for military duty.

There are drugs, that is, medicines and treatment which help to delay the onset and severity of the 'opportunistic infections', that is, AIDS proper. In the long run, however, it is at present, an incurable and fatal condition which for convenience is called the 'AIDS disease'.

In many countries of Africa it has reached epidemic proportions and these include Namibia and the Republic of South Africa as well as their neighbours. It poses an economic and financial threat to those African states with fragile economies.

It is a disease, which relatively, has only recently been identified. It is transmitted in only a few ways but largely by a mother who is infected with the disease transmitting it at birth to her unborn baby and predominantly in moments of sexual intimacy between two persons one of whom is infected. It is not transferred on toilet seats or in swimming pools or sharing food utensils or touching infected persons, nor is it transmitted in urine, faeces or sweat from the body or in saliva.

Because of the origins of the disease, the way it is transmitted, and its rampant magnitude, ignorance and prejudice have shrouded all aspects of the disease including its treatment and control.

Since time immemorial the world has had visitations of plagues and epidemics. But never before has the world been able to face a plague or giant-size epidemic, with the scientific technology which is available today. Never before have commerce and industry rallied to the side of medical research and never before has there been such a concentrated effort in the social and educational fields to control this plague and, if possible eliminate it. In the same vein, certain states have legislated or issued guidelines for implementation of policies to combat the disease or to ameliorate the suffering of those who have it. The United Nations have also made pronouncement in respect thereof.

In Namibia, the National Defence Force and the Police Force are not excluded from the operation of the Labour Act 1992, the State being regarded as the employer. On 3 April 1998 and in *Government Gazette* No 1835, Namibia issued 'Guidelines for the implementation of a National Code on HIV/AIDS in Employment'.

These guidelines are therefore applicable to the NDF but they are only guidelines, and do not have the force of law.

Clause 6.2.1. of the 'Guidelines' provides:

> *'Job access*
>
> There should be neither direct nor indirect pre-employment tests for HIV. Employees should be given the normal medical tests of current fitness for work and these tests should not include testing for HIV'.

Clause 6.5. provides:

> *'HIV testing or training*
>
> In general, there should be no compulsory HIV testing for training. HIV testing for training should be governed by the principle of nondiscrimination between individuals with HIV infection and those without and between HIV/AIDS and other comparable health/medical condition'.

Clause 6.6.2. provides:

> 'Employees with HIV related illness should have access to medical treatment and should be entitled, without discrimination, to agreed existing sick leave provisions'.

Clause 6.6.3. provides:

That HIV infected employees should work under normal conditions so long as they are fit to do so and if they can no longer do so, they should be offered alternative employment 'without prejudice to their benefits'.

While the aforegoing guidelines may well be implemented in certain instances, in others they could be economically impossible. As far as the military is concerned s 65(2) of the Defence Act (Act 44 of 1957) requires recruits to undergo a medical examination.

Mr Negonga lists some of the diseases for which recruits are examined. Any medical examination of a recruit must be fully carried out. In the light of what has

> been said above if the test is to ascertain whether a recruit is fit for military service, an HIV test only will not achieve this purpose. In addition to the HIV test, there must be a CD4 count test and a viral load test. If the military does not and will not do these latter two tests then the HIV test should also be abandoned. It will not achieve the purpose for which medical examinations are held.

In the supporting affidavit to his notice of motion applicant said that he had been a former Plan combatant, a member of SWAPO's National Liberation Struggle in exile from 1976 to 1989 and while in exile had undergone military training at Thobias Hainyeko Training Centre. In September 1996, he sought enlistment in the Namibian Defence Force. On 11 September 1996 applicant went to Oshakati State Hospital, where blood was taken for purposes of an HIV test. The results of the test were sent to the Okahandja base of the NDF. On 26 September 1996, at the Okahandja base, applicant was informed by Dr Shaenda, a medical officer in the NDF, that he had tested positive and that because of his HIV positive, he would not be accepted by the NDF. In his affidavit applicant asserted that except for being HIV positive, he was in sound health and in proof thereof, he annexed to his affidavit a medical report made and signed by a district surgeon or medical officer of the State, from which it appears that applicant was at that date in good and sound health. It is apparent from this comprehensive medical report that applicant had a thorough clinical examination. At the foot of this medical report, the following question is posed to the doctor:

> 'Do you consider that the applicant is in good health and free from any physical or mental defect, disease, or infirmity which should be likely to interfere with the proper performance of duty as a "Government Service Official in any part of South West Africa?" (For South West Africa read Namibia.)

To this question, the medical officer replied in the affirmative and signed and dated the Medical Report 31 October 1996, that is, approximately one month after the applicant to the knowledge of respondent, had tested positive for HIV.

It is therefore abundantly clear that the sole and only ground to refusing to enlist applicant as a member of the NDF, was because he was HIV positive and that he was nevertheless, at that time fit and able to perform the usual duties and functions in the NDF.

It is furthermore relevant to observe that it was respondent's doctor acting in the course and scope of his duties, who certified that applicant was in sound and good health and capable of performing his duties anywhere in Namibia.

Applicant avers in his supporting affidavit that the conduct of the NDF in refusing to enlist him solely on the basis of his HIV status constitutes discrimination in an unfair manner as contemplated by s 107 of the Labour Act, given his ability and capacity to do the duties as an NDF member. In the alternative, applicant says he was discriminated against on the impermissible ground of disability, by the respondent in conflict with s 107 of the Act.

At this stage, it is necessary to consider the provisions of s 107 of the Labour Act, as far as it is relevant hereto. Section 107(1) provides:

'107(1) Subject to the provisions of s 106 and s 2 of this section, if, upon an application made to the Labour Court in accordance with the provisions of Part IV by any person, the Labour Court is satisfied –

(a) that any person has discriminated or is about to discriminate in an unfair manner or is so discriminating against him on the ground of his ... disability, in relation to his employment ... the Labour Court may:

(b) issue an order in terms of which such person is ordered –

(*aa*) in the case of continuing acts of unfair discrimination ...to discontinue any such acts as may be specified ...

(*bb*) to perform or to refrain from performing any act specified

(*cc*) ...

(ii) make any such other order as the circumstances may require.'

The respondent originally only filed an affidavit made by Mr Erastus Negonga the Permanent Secretary for the Ministry of Defence.

Mr Negonga admits that applicant was rejected solely on the grounds that he tested positive for HIV, but he denies that this is discrimination in an 'unfair manner'.

It is common cause that there are military personnel in the NDF who are HIV positive.

When the NDF was established there was no testing for HIV and personnel who were HIV positive, may have been recruited. Furthermore, Mr Negonga says in his affidavit that 'military personnel are a population group notably at risk for developing and transmitting Sexually Transmitted Diseases (STD) including HIV'.

Consequently, certain personnel may well have acquired HIV subsequent to enlistment. Mr Negonga does not state how many HIV positive persons are in the NDF, but it appears from his own his own affidavit that the numbers are not small. Mr Negonga sets out in considerable detail the humane way persons who suffer from HIV and Aids are treated in the military. He says that when a member of the NDF is diagnosed as HIV positive or with Aids, the NDF accepts responsibility and follows a 'policy of non-discrimination as far as possible'. It disciplines persons who discriminate against HIV/AIDS personnel and where necessary deploys infected personnel to other positions 'where they run less risk of the process accelerating' but, this, he says, means 'rearranging personnel in the NDF. Such people are permitted to attend clinics and they receive "immune boosters" and hospitalization if necessary. They and their families receive counselling'. It is apparent therefore from the affidavit of Mr Negonga that the NDF has a large number of personnel who are infected with HIV/AIDS and that the NDF is geared to cope with these. The NDF is therefore complying with the clauses 6.6.2 and 6.6.3 of the 'Guidelines for the Implementation of a National Code for HIV/AIDS' and are to be commended for doing that.

The applicant annexed to his supporting affidavit a reference from the Secretary General of Swapo which relates and confirms that applicant was in the party's National Liberation Struggle from 1976 to 1989 and that he underwent military training at Thobias Hainyeko Training Centre. The Secretary recommends him as an 'employee'. If this is read with the medical report of 31 October 1996 that he is fit to do duty anywhere in Namibia, the refusal to enlist him, constitutes discrimination particularly as there are in the ranks of the NDF persons who are HIV positive and in some of these persons the disease had progressed to the extent that the persons concerned had been 'deployed to other positions where they run less risk of the process accelerating'.

Furthermore, the cost factor does not arise. The 'guidelines' enjoin employers to pay for medication and on Mr Negonga's showing if the necessity for medical treatment arises the machinery for doing so is already in place.

Apparently because of the large numbers of persons in the military who are HIV positive Dr Clive Evian who was called by respondent to testify, conceded that an HIV test, not followed by a CD4 and viral load test, before enlistment, cannot be justified on the basis of keeping 'the military an aids-free workplace'.

The case for applicant in this regard was considerably strengthened when Major Maiba testifying for respondent, said that personnel in the military, although this is a high risk environment, are not tested for HIV once they have enlisted. This applies even if they are selected to leave Namibia for peacekeeping operations in other countries in breach of a specific request made by the United Nations.

By reason of the aforegoing, I find that the exclusion of applicant from the military, solely because he was found to be HIV positive, constituted in September, 1996, discrimination in an unfair manner, in breach of s 107 of the Labour Act.

The act of unfair discrimination occurred in September 1996, that is approximately 4 years ago. I repeat what I have said previously. The medical experts who testified agreed that an HIV positive person can be as fit and as healthy as any other normal person in similar circumstances, but as that person's CD4 count decreases and the viral load increases such person's well-being progressively deteriorates. Clinically as soon as the CD4 drops below 200 such person is said to suffer from AIDS. A combination of these two indicators can serve as a prognosis as to the time period that will elapse before a person will suffer from AIDS proper. The two medical experts were in agreement that a person with a CD4 count below 200 and a viral load in excess of 100 000 would probably be incapable of participating in the strenuous and exacting work as required in the fighting units of the military. Common sense tells one that the different departments or divisions or categories or branches of the military have different degrees of stress, physical and mental, and this is confirmed by Mr Negonga in his affidavit where he says HIV positive personnel are transferred to such departments. Major Maiba says at present no-one is allocated to a particular department or activity when such person enlists. This only happens, he says, after everyone has done his or her basic training. The Major says this basic training is strenuous. Both medical experts were of the opinion that a person who contracts HIV is fit and healthy for several years and that the training routine would not be to his/her detriment. Dr Steinberg in fact said that regular exercise would be to such persons' benefit. This, however, depends on the progress of the 'disease' in later years. It is therefore essential that the date when HIV was contracted be established as accurately and as soon as possible. In this regard the co-operation and good faith of the recruit is essential. A comprehensive and proper test after basic training will enable the military authorities to place an HIV infected person in a suitable department of the NDF.

In the instant case, the applicant was not frank with the Court. He was diagnosed in September 1996 as being HIV positive but he did not inform the Court when he thought he may have contracted the condition. If he had contracted it four or five years prior to September 1996, to grant an order that respondent enlist him now, could be saddling the respondent with a recruit who could not do the basic training nor any of the duties which may arise in the military. Applicant must therefore be prepared to subject himself to the CD4 test and to the viral load test.

The order of the Court therefore is:

(1) Respondent shall enlist applicant in the NDF should applicant re-apply for enlistment, provided the applicant's CD4 count is not below 200 and his viral load is not above 100 000.

(2) The medical examination to which respondent is obliged to subject applicants, shall include an HIV test together with a CD4 count test and a viral load test and no person may be excluded from enlistment into the NDF solely on the basis of such person's HIV status where such person is otherwise fit and healthy unless such person's CD4 count is below 200 and his viral load is above 100 000.

Applicant's Legal Practitioners: *Legal Assistance Centre*. Respondent's Legal Practitioners: *Government Attorney.*

Review Questions – Nanditume v Minister of Defence

1. State the facts and the issues of the case.
2. What authorities were referred to by the Court?
3. Discuss the *ratio decidendi* of the case.
4. Do you think the judgment of the Court was based purely on legal principles or on other considerations?
5. What do you learn about HIV/AIDS and the law from this case?

****

5.4.2 Chilufya v City Council of Kitwe[259]

High Court

Mallon, AG. J.

22nd August, 1967

[1] *Landlord and tenant – Licence distinguished from lease – Effect of licence.*

The distinction between a lease and a licence is as follows:

(i) it is essential for the establishment of the relationship of landlord and tenant that there should be a demise, except where the relationship is created by statute;

(ii) a demise or lease is the grant of a right to the exclusive possession of land for a determinate term less than that which the grantor has himself in the land;

(iii) an exclusive right to do something on a property (as opposed to exclusive possession thereof) is merely a licence;

(iv) the effect of a licence is to give the licensee an authority to use the premises, without which he would be treated as a trespasser;

(v) a licence may be either gratuitous or for value. If the latter, the consideration may be given either once for all or by periodic payment.

[259] 1967 ZR 115.

[2] *Real property – Landlord and tenant – licence distinguished from lease – Effect of licence. See* [1] above.

[3] *Landlord and tenant – Licence – Granted for purpose of making profit – conveys no estate or interest in land.*

The fact that a licence is granted for the purpose of making a profit on land does not imply the grant of any estate or interest in that land.

[4] *Real property – Licence – Granted for purpose of making profit – conveys no estate or interest in land. See* [3] above.

[5] *Landlord and tenant – Termination of licence – Time to remove must be given.*

A licensee whose licence is terminated must be given a reasonable time to remove from the premises, whether his licence is revocable by notice or at will.

[6] *Landlord and tenant – Licence distinguished from lease – Marketeer paying a consideration – A licensee.*

A trader in a market having the written authority of the city council to occupy a space, for which he pays 1*s*. a day, and on which he has erected his own stall, is a licensee and not a tenant.

[7] *Local government – Control of markets – Markets Ordinance, section 3(a) – " Control and management" defined.*

The words "control and management" in section 3(*a*) of the Markets Ordinance give the city council power to grant and to determine licences to trade, and to do so by resolution.

[8] *Local government – Discretionary powers of local authority – Exercise must conform with general law and principles of natural justice.*

The power of local authorities to grant and to determine licences must be exercised subject to the general law and to the principles of natural justice.

[9] *Administrative law – Discretionary powers of local authority – Exercise must conform with general law and principles of natural justice.*

See [8] above.

[10] *Local government – Discretionary powers of public authority – Power of court to investigate exercise.*

Where a public authority has discretionary powers, the court is entitled to investigate its exercise of these powers in order to determine whether:

(a) it has taken into account matters which it ought not to have taken into account, and vice versa, and

(b) its decision was reasonable.

[11] *Administrative law – Discretionary powers of public authority – Power of court to investigate exercise.* See [10] above.

[12] *Local Government – Market licence – Termination by local authority – political considerations taken into account* – Ultra Vires.

A city council which terminates a trader's licence to occupy a market stall by resolution influenced by political considerations is acting unreasonably, unfairly and contrary to the principles of natural justice and, therefore, *ultra vires.*

[13] *Administrative law – Market licence – Termination by local authority – Political considerations taken into account* – Ultra Vires. *See* [12] above.

[14] *Local government – Market licence – Termination by local authority – Political considerations taken into account – Constitution of Zambia, section 25 – Whether "discriminatory".*

Such a termination of a licence is "discriminatory" within the meaning of the Constitution of Zambia, section 25(2) and 25(3).

[15] *Constitutional law – section 25 construed – meaning of "discriminatory" See* [14] above.

Cases referred to:

(1) *Byrne v Kamweka* **(1967) Z.R. 82**.

(2) *Frank Warr & Co., Ltd. v London County Council* **[1904] 1 K.B. 713**; *sub nom. Warr & Co. v London County Council*, **73 L.J. K.B. 362**.

(3) *Wood v Leadbitter* **(1845), 13 M. & W. 838; 153 E.R. 351**,

(4) *Kerrison v Smith*, **[1897] 2 Q.B.D. 445; [1895-9] All. E.R. Rep. 215**.

(5) *Shelley v London County Council* **[1949] A.C. 56**; *Shelley v London County Council* **[1948] 2 All E.R. 848**.

(6) *Metha v City of Salisbury*, **1961, R. & N. 911; on appeal** *sub nom. City of Salisbury v Metha*, **1961, R. & N. 1000**.

(7) *Re K. (H.) (an infant)*, **[1967] 1 All. E.R. 226**; *sub nom. In re H.K. (an infant)* **[1967] 2 Q.B. 617**.

(8) *Associated Provincial Picture Houses Ltd v Wednesbury Corp.*, **[1947] 2 All. E.R. 680; [1948] 1 K.B. 223**.

(9) *Fawcett Properties Ltd v Buckingham County Council* **[1960] 3 All E.R. 503; [1961] A.C. 636**.

(10) *Kruse v Johnson* **[1898] 2 Q.B. 91; [1895-9] All E.R. Rep. 105**.

Statutes and notices construed:

Markets Ordinance (Cap. 124), ss. 3(*a*) and 4(1), as amended.

The Kitwe Market By-Laws (Cap. 124 subsid.), By-Laws 5,6,7,13 and 16.

Constitution of Zambia (App.3), s. 25.

For the plaintiff: Ryan.

For the defendant: Millward.

Mallon, Ag. J.: By this originating summons the plaintiff, Adamson Chilufya, seeks a declaration against the defendants, the City Council of Kitwe, that a resolution of the health amenities and social services committee of the defendant council, passed on the 10th January, 1967, was *ultra vires* the powers of the defendant council and for the declaration that the removal from Chimwemwe Market, Kitwe, of the plaintiff's shop by the defendant council in pursuance of the said resolution was unlawful and unconstitutional; and for the determination of the following questions:

1. Whether a resolution of the health amenities and social services committee of the defendant council, passed on the 10th day of January, 1967, as follows: "That Adamson

Chilufya be no longer permitted to trade within the precincts of its markets", was *ultra vires* the powers of the defendant council?

2. Whether, if the said resolution was *intra vires* the powers of the defendant council, the said resolution and the removal of the plaintiff's shop from Chimwemwe Market, Kitwe, in pursuance of the said resolution, was an infringement of the plaintiff's Constitutional rights under sections 13 and 18 of the Constitution?

3. Whether pursuant to the provisions of the Markets Ordinance, or at all, the defendant council has the right to exclude a trader from trading in all of the markets under the defendant council's control, save for a breach on the part of the trader of the conditions or by-laws under the Markets Ordinance?

4. Whether the defendant council has got the power to exclude a trader from trading in markets under its control on the grounds that the trader is a member of a political party?

Under Order 7, rule 1(*b*) and Order 27, rule 11(3) of the High Court Rules, the hearing of such an originating summons would normally take place in chambers, but in view of the public importance of the issues involved I adjourned the hearing from chambers into open court, under the provisions of Order 27, rule 8 of the High Court Rules. Counsel for the plaintiff also relied upon the provisions of Order 15, rule 16 of the Rules of the Supreme Court and the notes thereon in support of the form of process which he had adopted. The evidence at the hearing consisted of an affidavit by the plaintiff dated 7th April, 1967, and an affidavit, in reply by Mr Chembe Harold-Hine Phiri, the Mayor of Kitwe, dated 18th June, 1967, I was informed by counsel that by agreement the latter affidavit contained certain legal arguments not strictly proper for inclusion in an affidavit, but that this course had been adopted by counsel in order that the issues involved could be put more fully before the court.

During the course of his argument, counsel for the plaintiff asked leave to amend his originating summons to include a reference to section 25 of the Constitution, which he submitted was particularly relevant to the subject matter of the originating summons and I allowed this amendment under Order 16, rule 1, of the High Court Rules in order that the real questions in issue between the parties would be determined. See *Byrne v Kamweka* [1].

From the affidavit evidence I make the following findings of fact.

1. The plaintiff, Adamson Chilufya, resides at No. 2281 Kamitodondo Suburb, Ktiwe, and is fifty-one years of age.

2. Between 1944 and 1967 the plaintiff carried on business as a trader at various municipal markets under the control of the defendants and their predecessors as follows:

   (a) From 1944 until 1953 at Kitwe Municipal Board Market.

   (b) From 1953 until 1955 at temporary Municipal Market at Buchi.

   (c) From 1955 until 1958 at the Municipal Market, Kamitondo.

   (d) From 1958 until 1961 at Kampemba Municipal Market.

   (e) From 1961 until 1967 at the Old Market, Chimwemwe.

3. During the whole of this period of approximately twenty-three years no complaint was charged or made against the plaintiff by the defendants or their predecessors for any breach of the defendant's market by-laws.

4. in 1964 the defendants permitted the plaintiff to erect a wooden stall, at a cost of £115, for the purpose of carrying on his trade.
5. There is not now in existence any document in the form of a licence or lease in respect of the plaintiff's occupation of a stall in the defendant's markets.
6. That the plaintiff paid a daily fee of 1*s*. to the defendants in respect of his right to trade in their markets.
7. That the plaintiff was nominated to stand as a candidate for the African National Congress in the Kitwe Municipal election which took place in September, 1966.
8. In August, 1966, during the election campaign his stall was badly damaged by a crowd of women.
9. The plaintiff repaired the damage to his stall and recommenced business, being provided with police protection through the defendants for a short period after the incident.
10. After the said incident the plaintiff continued to trade peacefully and successfully and his business increased.
11. At a meeting of the health amenities and social services committee of the defendants, held on 10th January, 1967, the following resolution was passed: "Resolved: that
    (i) Mr A. Chilufya be advised that he will no longer be permitted to trade within the precincts of any of Council's markets; and
    (ii) the Committee notes that no evidence has been adduced indicating the cause of the unrest in the Chimwemwe Market."

Part (ii) of the resolution referred to a report submitted to the committee by the Town Clerk, in which it was stated that the damage occasioned to the plaintiff's stall in August, 1966, was perpetrated by a group of alleged United National Independence Party supporters. This report was not accepted by the committee as proof of this contention.

12. The above resolution of the health amenities and social services committee was adopted as a resolution of the defendant and on 11th January, 1967, the Town Clerk addressed a letter to the plaintiff, a copy of which is produced with his affidavit, advising him that the defendant had resolved that he be no longer permitted to trade within the precincts of any of its markets, but, in order to enable him to run down his stocks, he was permitted to trade in the old market at Chimwemwe up to and including Wednesday, 11th January, 1967.
13. On 17th January, 1967, the plaintiff's stall was picketed by men who informed prospective customers not to trade with him, as a result of which no customers came to the shop, which the plaintiff then closed. The stall was subsequently dismantled by the defendant's servants and deposited at the plaintiff's house.
14. As a result of the defendant's action, the plaintiff has been deprived of the opportunity of earning his livelihood as a trader in any of the markets under the defendant's control.
15. The United National Independence Party has a majority in the defendant's council.

In paragraph 16 of his affidavit the plaintiff alleges that the real reason for the defendant's action in terminating his right to trade is the fact that he is a member of the African National Congress and that, in effect, the defendant is discriminating against him on the grounds of his political beliefs. This is strenuously denied by the defendant who claims that its action was *intra vires*, in that the resolution related to a market established in the City of Kitwe and under the control and management of the defendant by virtue of the provisions of section 3 of the Markets Ordinance. Paragraph 7(*a*) of the mayor's affidavit refers to section 3 (1) of the Markets Ordinance, but I would point out that a new section 3 was inserted in the Markets Ordinance by section 115 of the Local Government Act, 1965 (69 of 1965) and that the correct reference is now to section 3(*a*) of the Markets Ordinance. By its long title the Markets Ordinance is "An Ordinance to provide for the establishment and management of markets", and section 3(*a*) provides that:

"3. Every market established –

(a) in the area of a local authority, shall be under the control and management of that local authority;"

By sub-section (1) of section 4 a local authority is empowered to make by-laws for, *inter alia*, the following purposes –

"(a) regulating the use of markets and market buildings, and keeping order, preventing obstructions, and maintaining cleanliness therein or in the approaches thereto; ...

(e) enabling the local authority from time to time to determine by resolution stallages, rents or tolls and fees for inspection of produce and providing for the collection thereof;"

Section 5 is not relevant to the present case.

The Chimwemwe Market was established by Government Notice No. 165 of 1963 and the Kitwe Market By-laws were published in Government Notice No. 346 of 1963 and apply to all markets established by the then Municipal Council of Kitwe. By-law 6 provides that "All persons using any market shall obey the reasonable directions of the Market Master for the purpose of preserving cleanliness and order in the market". It is common ground that the plaintiff has never, at any time, been in breach of those by-laws.

I will now consider the legal position of the plaintiff in relation to the defendant. In paragraphs 7(d) and (e) of the mayor's affidavit, the plaintiff's right to trade is loosely described as "a daily tenancy or licence" and it is important first of all to decide, in law, which term is correct.

It will be noted that by-law 5 of the Kitwe Market By-laws refers to "stallages, rents or tolls and fees" and by-law 13 refers to a person "renting, holding or occupying a stall". Although it is not in evidence I was informed by counsel for the defendant that the usual practice is for the defendant to write to an applicant a letter granting him authority to occupy a stall on a day-to-day basis and drawing his attention to the by-laws and charges of 1*s.* per day.

[1][2] The legal distinction between a lease and a licence is fully discussed in *Woodfall on Landlord and Tenant*, 25th Ed., at pages 2 and 8, from which it is clear that it is essential for the establishment of the relationship of landlord and tenant that there should be a demise, except where the relationship is created by statute. A demise or lease is the grant of a right to the exclusive possession of land for a determinate term less than that which the grantor has himself in the land and a lease is therefore a species of conveyance. At page 9 the learned author points out that "the question is in all cases whether the arrangement made between the parties confers upon the tenant a right to the exclusive possession of any property. It is not sufficient that the agreement confers a right, even an exclusive right, of doing something on the premises, such as fixing and exhibiting thereon an advertisement;

the grant of such a right is the grant only of a licence. The effect of a licence is discussed at paragraph 17 on page 11, and it is clear that its effect is to give the licensee an authority to use the premises, which authority prevents his being treated as a trespasser. Such a licence may be a gratuitous licence or a licence for value. In the latter case the consideration may be given either once for all or may take the form of a periodic payment, as in this case. **[3] [4]** The nature of a licence was also fully considered by the Court of Appeal in England in the case of *Frank Warr & Co. Ltd v London County Council* [2], from which it is clear that the fact that a licence is granted for the purpose of making a profit on land does not imply any grant of any estate or interest in the land, and I would refer, in particular, to the judgment of Romer, L.J., at page 720. The law with regard to the revocation of a licence is set out in paragraph 18, on page 11, of *Woodfall* and it is clear that [5] a gratuitous licence is revocable by notice, but time must be given to the licensee to remove from the premises, and even where a licence to occupy is revocable at will, still a reasonable time must also be given to the licensee in which to quit.

[6] In the light of the above statement of the law, I have come to the conclusion that the true nature of the relationship between the plaintiff and the defendant in this case was that of licensor and licensee. There is not in existence any writing which could be termed a lease. Without the defendant's licence to trade in the market the plaintiff would be a trespasser and the daily fee of 1*s.* which he paid in respect of his stall was more in the nature of a licence fee than a payment of rent. I do not consider that the fact that the defendant allowed the plaintiff to erect a wooden stall in the market altered this situation.

[7] I must now consider what powers the defendant had, under the provisions of section 3(*a*) of the Markets Ordinance or otherwise, to grant a licence of the kind in question and to terminate it, and the decision on these points turns upon the interpretation to be placed upon the words "control and management" which appear in the said section. These words have been the subject of many judicial decisions in England, mainly in connection with their interpretation in the context of different English statutes, few of which are of real assistance in the present case. It is clear that at common law a licensor can terminate a licence at any time (*see Wood v Leadbitter* [3]), but such a termination can amount to a breach of contract resulting in damages (*see Kerrison and Smith* [4]). In my view, the section must confer upon the defendant power *inter alia* to grant licences or leases in respect of stalls in the markets under their control, and I would refer to the decision of the House of lords in the case of *Shelley v London County Council* [5], and in particular to the judgment of Lord Porter at page 65, where he discussed the effect of the words "general management, regulation and control of houses provided by a local authority", in section 83 of the Housing Act of 1936 (England). At the top of page 66 His Lordship sates:

[8][9] "'management' must in my view include a right to terminate the tenancy so far as the general law allows, i.e., after due notice. It is to my mind one of the important duties of management that the local body shall be able to pick and choose their tenants at their will. It is true that an ordinary private landlord cannot do so, but local authorities who have wider duties laid on them may well be expected to exercise their powers with discretion and in any case the wording of the Act seems to me to necessitate such a construction".

It was argued for the plaintiff that if the defendant had power to terminate the licence to trade it could only do so by by-law. I do not accept this argument, and I am satisfied that the defendant could properly terminate a licence or lease by resolution. It is clear from the by-laws that it was competent for the defendant to exercise many of its powers of control over its markets by resolution and I refer in particular to by-laws 5,7 and 16. **[7]** Section 3(*a*) of the Markets Ordinance, in my view, gives the defendant full authority to grant or terminate the licence or lease by resolution and it is not necessary in law for it to do so by by-law (*see City of Salisbury v Mehta* [6], in particular the judgment of Briggs, F.J., at letter H on page 1017). I will consider the full effects of the decision in this case later in this judgment.

[8][9] I am therefore satisfied in law that the defendant has power under section 3(*a*) of the Markets Ordinance to terminate a licence to trade in a proper case, e.g. if a licensee had failed to pay his stallage fee or to comply with the market by-laws, in my view the defendant would clearly be entitled to terminate his licence. The exercise of this power must, however, be carried out fairly and in accordance with the principles of natural justice. In other words, it is not an arbitrary power which a local authority could exercise regardless of the consequences and without due regard to the interests of the individual trader. I would refer to the case of *Re K. (H). (an infant)* [7], in which the Queen's Bench Division considered the question of the exercise of statutory powers by a public authority, in that case an immigration officer. In his judgment at page 233, letter B, Lord Justice Salmon said:

"What however is a quasi-judicial capacity has, so far as I know, never been exhaustively defined. It seems to me to cover at any rate a case where the circumstances in which a person who is called on to exercise a statutory power and make a decision affecting basic rights of others, are such that the law impliedly imposes on him a duty to act fairly".

Further down in the same paragraph, at letter D, His Lordship continued with reference to the powers of immigration officers:

"Their decisions are of vital importance to the immigrants since their whole future may be affected. In my judgment it is implicit in the statute that the authorities in exercising these powers and making decisions must act fairly in accordance with the principles of natural justice."

Lord Justice Salmond later discussed the effect of the court's decision in *Re K. (H.)* in an article in *The New Law Journal* of 13th July, 1967, at page 749, entitled "The Bench, The Last Bulwark of Individual Liberty". At page 750 he commented, "We laid down that whenever a statute such as the Immigration Act 1962 gave a minister or official or any body of persons power to make decisions concerning an individual's basic rights, it was implicit in the statute that in exercising those powers the principles of natural justice should be observed." Further down the same page His Lordship continued, "The importance of the case is that it reaffirmed the power and indeed the duty of the courts in certain circumstances to intervene in such cases in favour of the subject."

In *Judicial Review of Administrative Action*, by S.A. de Smith (2nd Ed.), on page 89, the learned author lays down the principle that, "Discretionary powers (vested in a public authority) must be exercised for the purposes for which they were granted; relevant considerations must be taken into account and irrelevant considerations disregarded; they must be exercised in good faith and not arbitrarily or capriciously. If the repository of the power fails to comply with these requirements it acts *ultra vires*."

[10] In *Associated Provincial Picture Houses Ltd v Wednesbury Corp.* [8], it was held that the court is entitled to investigate the action of the local authority, with a view to seeing whether it has taken into account matters which it ought not to have taken into account or, conversely, has refused to take into account matters which it ought to take into account. Once that question is answered in favour of the local authority it may still be possible to say that the local authority, nevertheless, has come to a conclusion so unreasonable that no reasonable authority could ever have come to it and, in such a case, the court can interfere. The power of a court, however, to interfere in any case is not that of an appellate authority to override a decision of the local authority but is that of a judicial authority which is concerned, and concerned only to see whether the local authority has contravened the law by acting in excess of the powers which Parliament has conferred upon it. In his judgment at page 682, letter D, Lord Greene, M.R., pointed out that:

"The courts can only interfere with an act of an executive authority if it be shown that the authority have contravened the law. It is for those who assert that the local authority have contravened the law to establish that proposition. On the face of it a condition of this kind is perfectly lawful. It is not to be assumed *prima facie* that responsible bodies like local authorities will exceed the powers and the court, whenever it is alleged that the local authority has contravened the law, must not substitute itself for the local authority. It is only concerned with seeing whether or not the proposition is made good. When an executive discretion is entrusted by Parliament to a local authority, what purports to be an exercise of that discretion can only be challenged in the courts in a very limited class of case. It must always be remembered that the court is not a court of appeal. The law recognizes certain principles on which the discretion must be exercised but within the four corners of those principles the discretion is an absolute one and cannot be questioned in any court of law."

Further down the same page, two lines below letter G, His Lordship continued:
'Expressions have been used in cases where the powers of local authorities came to be considered relating to the sort of thing that may give rise to interference by the court. Bad faith, dishonesty – those, of course, stand by themselves – unreasonableness, attention given to extraneous circumstances, disregard of public policy, and things like that have all been referred to as being matters which are relevant for consideration."

The above dicta of Lord Greene were applied by the House of Lords in *Fawcett Properties Limited v Buckingham County Council* [9], and I would refer in particular to the passage at the top of page 518 in the judgment of Lord Denning.

I have also considered the line of authority relating to the reasonableness or otherwise of by-laws made by a local authority as, in my view, the same principles which would apply in deciding whether or not a by-law is *ultra vires* should be applied in deciding whether or not a resolution of a council is also *ultra vires*, and I would refer to *Kruse v Johnson* [10], and in particular to the judgment of Lord Russell, C.J., at the bottom of page 99, where His Lordship held that the court would be entitled to find by-laws invalid as being unreasonable. "If for instance they were found to be partial and unequal in their operation as between different classes; if they were manifestly unjust; if they disclosed bad faith; if they involved such oppressive or gratuitous interference with the rights of those subject to them as could find no justification in the minds of reasonable men, the Court might well say,

'Parliament never intended to give authority to make such rules; they are unreasonable and *ultra vires*.'". The above dictum of Lord Russell has been applied in many cases since.

Counsel for the plaintiff relied heavily on the case of *Metha v City of Salisbury* [6], which was a decision of the High Court of Southern Rhodesia, which later came before the Federal Supreme Court. In this case the plaintiff, an Asian resident of Salisbury, sought a declaration that he was entitled to use a public bath in Salisbury, which the City Council had attempted by resolution to restrict for the use of Europeans. He was successful in obtaining such a declaration in the High Court and that decision was substantially upheld by the Federal Supreme Court on appeal. In essence the position in that case was that the plaintiff was clearly entitled, in terms of the city council's by-laws, to use the public bath in question and the city council without amending its by-laws had attempted to take away that right by resolution. It was held that the city council was bound by its own by-laws and could not remove the plaintiff's rights by resolution. The Kitwe Market by-laws do not provide specifically for the grant of licences to trade nor the machinery for applying for such licences, nor for their termination, and it could certainly be argued with some force that such by-laws could be made under the provisions of section 4(1)(*a*) of the Markets Ordinance in the light of the remarks by Clayden F.C.J., at letter H. on page 1007, on the meaning of the word "regulating". On balance, however, I very much doubt whether it would be desirable, or indeed possible, to govern by by-law the selection by a council of suitable stallholders, and I am certainly not prepared to hold that any council is bound to do so under the provisions of the Markets Ordinance. In my view, this is clearly a matter of individual application referred to by Briggs, F.J., at page 1017, in a passage to which I have already made reference.

In light of the legal principles which I have outlined above, I must now consider whether or not the plaintiff has succeeded in discharging the onus which rests upon him to establish, on a balance of probabilities, that the action of the defendant complained of was unreasonable, unfair and contrary to the principles of natural justice.

[12][13] The defendant gives its reasons for terminating the plaintiff's licence to trade in paragraph 7(*g*) of the mayor's affidavit, which is in the following terms:

"The plaintiff was so unpopular in the market that his presence therein constituted a security risk in relation to the efficient administration of the markets. The difficulties likely to have arisen if he had been permitted to continue to trade within the precincts of any of the defendant's markets would be such as to endanger the property of the defendant and also his own person.

The reason for his unpopularity at the time the decision was made was not considered by the Health, Amenities and Social Services Committee."

It is clear from the extract from the minutes of the meeting of the health, amenities and social services committee, which is produced with the mayor's affidavit, that the resolution to terminate the plaintiff's right to trade was taken after the committee had considered the Town Clerk's report on the cause of the unrest in the Chimwemwe Market in August, 1966 in which it was stated that the damage occasioned to the plaintiff's stall in August, 1966, was perpetrated by a group of alleged United National Independence Party supporters. The defendant admitted that the plaintiff's stall was badly damaged by a crowd of women during the election campaign, and after the plaintiff had been nominated to stand as a candidate for the African National Congress.

It is not unreasonable therefore to draw the inference from the evidence that the plaintiff's stall was damaged by political opponents, and it is clear that there had been no trouble in the market in connection with the plaintiff's stall prior to the announcement of his candidature. The defendant admits that, following upon the incident in August, the plaintiff recommenced business and was provided with police protection by the defendant for a short period after the incident, and I have found as a fact, which the defendants have not attempted to refute, that, after the said incident, the plaintiff continued to trade peacefully and successfully so that his business increased.

In paragraph 12 of his affidavit the plaintiff alleges that, for a short period prior to the passing of the resolution complained of, on many occasions youths shouted threats to the effect that all African National Congress supporters and Jehovah's Witnesses would no longer be allowed to trade in the market. This allegation is denied by the mayor in paragraph 9 of his affidavit, but in view of the background of unrest in the market which clearly existed after the August incident, I consider that on a balance of probabilities, the plaintiff's allegation is based upon fact, and some support for this conclusion is contained in paragraph 7(*g*) of the mayor's affidavit, when he refers to the plaintiff as being "so unpopular" in the market. In my view, the only possible inference from the evidence is that the plaintiff's "unpopularity" in the market only arose after he had announced his intention to exercise his Constitutional rights to stand as a candidate for the African National Congress in the municipal elections. The defendant has freely conceded that it has no complaints about his conduct of his business, which he has carried on for almost twenty-three years.

In addition, there is no evidence that he deliberately stirred up trouble in the market through his political activities and it is clear that, on the contrary, his efforts to continue peacefully trading have been interrupted by activities on the part of other people which were probably criminal and can only have been politically inspired.

It is significant that part (ii) of the defendant's resolution of 10th January, 1967, states that, "The Committee notes that no evidence has been adduced indicating the cause of the unrest in the Chimwemwe Market." I think it is a fair comment on this part of the resolution that it shows that there was no evidence indicating that the plaintiff was the cause of the unrest in the market, yet despite this fact the defendant proceeded to terminate his licence to trade.

In paragraph 7(*g*) of his affidavit, referred to above, the mayor states that the reason for the plaintiff's unpopularity at the time the decision was made was not considered by the committee, an assertion which I view with considerable reservations. If it was not considered it certainly should have been, as a material factor in deciding whether or not it would be reasonable to terminate the plaintiff's licence.

It is clearly the duty of a local authority, which is vested with wide statutory powers over the inhabitants within the areas of its jurisdiction, to exercise those powers fairly and impartially in the interests of all the inhabitants regardless of their political affiliations. If the plaintiff was being subjected to actual violence or threats of violence while peacefully carrying on his trade and through no fault of his own it was the defendant's duty to maintain law and order in the market either through their market master in terms of section 4(1)(9) of the Markets Ordinance and By-law 6, or by calling in the police as they did following upon the incident at the plaintiff's stall in August, 1966. Instead of taking this course, the defendant decided to terminate the plaintiff's licence to trade without making any attempt to protect his interests, or his livelihood, by maintaining law and order and, in my view, in so doing it acted unreasonably, unfairly and contrary to the principles of natural justice. From the evidence the conclusion is inescapable that the plaintiff became a "security risk" in the eyes of the defendant because of his political affiliations, and that its decision was materially influenced by political considerations and was therefore a decision taken in bad faith.

[**14**][**15**] There is one further aspect on the matter which is of considerable importance, and that is the plaintiff's rights under the Constitution of the Republic of Zambia. Counsel for the plaintiff submitted that the defendant's action constituted a breach of the plaintiff's fundamental rights under sections 13, 18 and 25 of the Constitution. Of these three sections, in my view, the one which is of particular relevance to the circumstances of this case is section 25, subsections (2) and (3), of which are in the following terms:

"(2) Subject to the provisions of subsections (6), (7) and (8) of this section, no person shall be treated in a discriminatory manner by any person acting by virtue of any written law or in the performance of the functions of any public office or authority, or any public authority;

(3) In this section, the expression 'discriminatory' means affording different treatment to different persons attributable wholly or mainly to their respective descriptions by race, tribe, place of origin, political opinions, colour or creed whereby persons of one such description are subjected to disabilities or restrictions to which persons of another such description are not made subject or are accorded privileges or advantages which are not accorded to persons of another such description".

Having carefully considered the evidence in this case, in the light of the above provisions, I am satisfied that the defendant, by terminating the plaintiff's licence to trade, treated him in a discriminatory manner because of his political opinions, in the performance of their functions as a public authority. I do not consider that section 18 of the Constitution is really relevant to the circumstances of this case.

I therefore find that, in law, the plaintiff has discharged the onus of proof upon him, and that the resolution of the defendant dated 10th January, 1967, terminating his licence to trade, was *ultra vires* its powers under the Markets Ordinance as being –

(a) unreasonable, unfair and contrary to the principles of natural justice; and

(b) a breach of the plaintiff's Constitutional rights under section 25 of the Constitution of Zambia.

As a consequence of the above, I also find that the plaintiff has established deprivation of property within the meaning of section 13 of the Constitution to the extent of the value of the wooden hut erected by him in the market with the defendant's permission, and removed therefrom by its servants. I find the value of the said hut to be £115.

In terms of the originating summons I therefore declare that the resolution of the health, amenities and social services committee of the defendant council, which was adopted as a resolution of the defendant itself, was *ultra vires* its powers and that the removal from Chimwemwe Market, Kitwe, of the plaintiff's wooden stall by the defendant in pursuance of the said resolution was unlawful and unconstitutional.

In view of the terms of the above declaration and my earlier findings in law, I do not consider it necessary formally to determine the question set out in the originating summons.

I award the costs of these proceedings to the plaintiff.

Judgment for the plaintiff

Note:

The Superior Courts of Namibia in their interpretation of Article 18 of the Namibian Constitution notably in the Elizabeth Frank and Sikunda cases (see Appendix) have held that Article 18 does not draw a distinction between *quasi* judicial and administrative acts and that an administrative body or official exercising any administrative discretion must comply with the principles of natural justice.

****

5.4.3 In the matter of the estate of Setrak Avakian

HIGH COURT

ADDIS ABABA

In the Matter of the Estate of; SETRAK AVAKIAN

Megabit 23,1955 E.C. (April 1, 1963 G.C.); Judges; Mr S. Stephenson, Captain Yassaou Gerbe Harwriat, Ato Guerra Work Agonaferi

Setrak Avakian, a resident of Addis Ababa, died on 2nd November 1962 (G.C.). His widow Chake Avakian, a resident of Addis Ababa, has petitioned the Court for probate of a will made by the deceased on the 16 of January 1961 (G.C.), appointing her, the petitioner, as his legatee by universal title.

The father of the deceased, Artin Avakian, has filed in Court his declaration of opposition to the will, in that he claims that it is of no effect by the reason of not fulfilling the requirements of law as to form. The opposition was filed in response to the citation published by order of Court in daily newspapers.

Since the will was made after the entry into force of the Civil Code the issue in respect to its validity is governed by the Code.

The will was made in English and in an Amharic version, both contained on a single sheet of paper. The contents of the will are in both original and typewritten versions. The date of their signing by the deceased are in both versions filled in handwriting. Both versions bear signatures to the will in witness of its signing in their presence by the deceased after its having been read over. One of the witnesses to the will was also given custody of originals; there is no dispute as to the fact.

The first question which arises is whether or not the will can have effect, as a public will according to Article 881 of the Civil Code. The answer must be that it cannot, because it was read prior to signing by the deceased in the presence of only three witnesses, while the law demands four witnesses. It results that there is no validly given will. This may seem a strange, and in the circumstances unsatisfactory result, since there can be no serious doubt about the deceased's intention to appoint his wife as his legatee by universal title, and that he may have died in the belief that she would succeed to all his properties. But the rules relating to the form of wills have been given in order to ensure that effect is given only to the indubitable intention of the testator to designate another or other successors to his estate than those who would otherwise have been his rightful heirs at law. Such rules must be strict, and the Court cannot, even in circumstances as the present ones, or in any circumstances, ignore them or allow any latitude in their observance.

SUPREME IMPERIAL COURT

MRS CHAKE AVAKIAN v MR ARTIN AVAKIAN

Tekemt 13, 1956 E.C. (OCTOBER 24, 1963 G.C.), Justices; Mr G. Debbas, Grazmatch Tessemma Negede, Ato Haile Aman;

This is an appeal against the judgment of the High Court whereby the appellant lost her petition for probate of the will of her husband appointing her as his sole heiress by universal title. The High Court declared the will invalid for lack of form only, although it commented and admitted that the husband wanted his wife, the present appellant to be his sole heiress.

The whole appeal interesting as it is, is about the validity of a will. When the widow petitioned the High Court for probate of the will of her late husband, the only opposer was her father in law, the present respondent. Certainly there was no opening for him, except to attack the form of the will. According to Article 881 of the Civil Code, four witnesses are necessary for a public will. In this very case, only three witnesses affixed their signature to witness the signing of the will by the testator and the reading out of it. The question that arises is whether or not those three witnesses are sufficient to validate will.

In order to decide on such very delicate cases, a court should not be blinded by the question of form; it should go a little further and find out the presumed intention of the testator, from surrounding circumstances, especially in cases of doubt or uncertainty. Not only one article of Code should bind a court, but the whole situation should be looked upon generally. It is more the intention of the testator than form of the will that is the real aim of the legislator.... Coming now to Article 881 of the Civil Code, which provides for four witnesses, and looking at the will, subject matter of this appeal, we have to go far beyond the articles referred to by both parties and try to find out the real intention of the testator, in view of the doubt that arises.

The real intention of the deceased testator is whether or not he died 'unwilling' to appoint his wife as his sole heiress. There is no argument that the testator died sincerely believing that his sole heiress would be his wife, i.e. the appellant ... it is already clear that the intention of the testator long before his death and before he wrote the will, was to assign the ownership of all his shares in that company to his wife; which fact clarifies his intention in the will that she shall be his sole heiress.

Our argument regarding the presumed intention of the deceased testator does not stop here but is reinforced by the comment in the judgment of the High Court.' It results that there is no validly given will ... the indubitable intention of the testator...'

From these words, and particularly the last sentence of the High Court's comment, the indubitable intention of the testator was to appoint his wife Chake Avakian as his sole heiress. The existence of the present will, coupled with the argument of the High Court regarding the intention of the testator ... lead us to believe that the indubitable intention of the testator was definitely to appoint his appellant widow as his sole legatee by universal title, to succeed to all his properties. It is consequently useless to continue discussing the intention of the testator. In such cases when the court of first instance knows that the presumed intention of the deceased is to let his wife succeed to all his properties, it should not blind itself with the question of form, especially when the form has all been complied with. An absence of one witness, when three are present and reliable, is of no importance.

Under the circumstances, and in view of the foregoing explanation, we hereby allow this appeal and quash the judgment of the High Court and declare the will of the late Strak Avakian appointing his wife Mrs Chake Avakian as his sole heiress, as valid.

Review Questions – Mrs Chake Avakian v Mr Artin Avakian

1. What are the issues and the *ratio decidendi* of the case?
2. Discuss the reasons for the decisions of the High Court and the Supreme Court.
3. In the light of the reasons given by the Supreme Court for its decision and in the context of the doctrine of separation of powers, is the decision of the Supreme Court inconsistent with the functions of the Judiciary?
4. What theories of law may be used to justify the decisions of both the High Court and the Supreme Court?
5. Do you agree with the decision of the Supreme Court? And why?

****

5.4.4 Deem v Millikin

The Statute

Rules of inheritance of property have sometimes been developed by custom. But today, in every American state, the process of descent and distribution of the property of a descendant who dies intestate is regulated by statute. The provisions of the Ohio statute which follow are unusually elaborate, telling who shall take the property in ten successively applicable contingencies. The dispositive part of the statute is as follows:

"§2105.06. Statute of descent and distribution. (GC §10503 - 4)

When a person dies intestate having title or right to any personal property or to any real estate or inheritance in this state, such personal property shall be distributed and such real estate or inheritance shall descend and pass in parcenary * * * in the following courses:

"(A) If there is no surviving spouse, to the children of such intestate or their lineal descendants, per stirpes; * * *

"(E) If there is no spouse and no children or their lineal descendants, to the parents of such interstate equally, or to the surviving parent; * * *."

A. The Decision in Deem v Millikin

In *Deem v Millikin*, 53 Ohio St. 668 (1895), the Supreme Court of Ohio simply wrote a memorandum order saying, "Judgment affirmed on reasoning of *Deem v Millikin et al.*, 60 C.C. Rep., 357". The opinion so approved, and the opinion in *Riggs v Palmer* which the lower court's opinion criticizes, are reproduced below. * * * * *

Deem v Millikin

Circuit Court of Preble County Ohio,

1892. 60. C.C. 357

Error to the Common Pleas Court of

Preble County

The defendants in error, by their answers and cross-petitions filed in the court of common pleas, allege that Caroline Sharkey died intestate, January 11, 1889, and seized in fee of certain real estate in said county, leaving her son Elmer L. Sharkey, her sole heir at law; that thereafter, said Elmer L. Sharkey executed to them several mortgages to secure the payment of certain promissory notes, their cross-petitions containing appropriate averments as to the execution of the notes and mortgages, and for the assertion of a lieu upon said real estate by virtue thereof.

Answering these cross-petitions, the plaintiffs in error, who are brothers and sisters of said Caroline Sharkey, deceased, admitting that said Elmer L. Sharkey was her son and only child, and that she died intestate, allege that on or about the 11th day of January, 1889, said Elmer L. Sharkey murdered her for the purpose of succeeding to the title to said real estate, and having by due process of law, been convicted of said crime, he was hanged therefor December 19, 1890; wherefore they allege that said real estate did not descend to him.

In the court of common pleas demurrers to these answers were sustained, and distribution was ordered in favour of said mortgages. The plaintiffs in error seek the reversal of that judgment.

SHAUCK, J.

The judgment under review is unquestionably right if the terms used in the statute of descents should, in all cases, receive their plain and natural meaning. Mrs Sharkey died intestate and seized in fee of the lands in controversy. There is neither condition nor exception in the statute which provides that they should descend to her son.

But recent decisions by courts of much respectability affirm that, in cases of this character, there should be judicially added to statutes such conditions or provisions as may be necessary to avert results believed to be inconsistent with the legislative conscience, and, therefore, foreign to the legislative intent. *Riggs v Palmer*, 115 N.Y. 506; *Shellenberger v Ransom*, 47 N.W. Rep. 700. In *Riggs v Palmer*, the court reached the conclusion that where a beneficiary under a will, in order to prevent a revocation of the provision in his favour, and to obtain speedy possession of the property, wilfully murders the testator, such beneficiary, by reason of his crime, takes no interest in the estate of his victim. The point held in *Shellenberger v Ransom*, is that if the owner of lands is murdered by one whom the statute designates as his successor in title, the crime intercepts the transmission of the property according to the terms of the statute. In neither case is a distinction attempted between devolution of title by devise and devolution by statute; but both disapprove *Owens v Owens*, 100 N.C. 240, where it was held that a widow convicted as accessory before the fact to her husband's murder was, nevertheless, entitled to dower in his lands according to the terms of the statute. The case of *Riggs v Palmer* was decided by a divided court, and contrary to the judgment of the Supreme Court; and *Shellenberger v Ransom* is believed to be now under re-consideration by the Supreme Court of Nebraska. We are without authoritative decision in our own state, and there is not found elsewhere such concurrence of opinion as would properly excuse us from a consideration of the principles upon which the rights of these parties should be determined.

It must be admitted that the most careful examination of *Riggs v Palmer* fails to discover any clearly stated and clearly applicable principle justifying the decision. The spirit of fearless inquiry was exorcised early in the opinion, when every one contemplating a conclusion different from that reached by the majority, was warned that if he should persevere, it would be disparagingly said of him "*qui haeret in litera haeret in cortice*". The conclusion derives no support from the rule quoted from Bacon's Abridgement: "By an equitable construction, a case not within the letter of the statute is sometimes holden to be within the mischief for which a remedy is provided."

The statute of descents neither recognizes a mischief nor provides a remedy. It is a legislative declaration of a rule of public policy. With respect to remedial statutes, the rule quoted has frequent and salutary operation. The mischief and the remedy indicate the intention of the legislature, and guide the court in giving it effect. But the rule affords no warrant for adding an important exception to a statute which, in clear language, defines a rule of public policy. Even in the consideration of remedial statutes, courts should be guided by the maxim "*iudex animi sermo*", and the interpretation should be consistent with the language employed. Knowledge of the settled maxims and principles of statutory interpretation is imputed to the legislature. To the end that there may be certainty and uniformity in legal administration, it must be assumed that statutes are enacted with a view to their interpretation according to such maxims and principles. When they are regarded, the legislative intent is ascertained. When they are ignored, interpretation becomes legislation in disguise. The well considered cases warrant the pertinent conclusion that when the legislature, not transcending the limits of its power, speaks in clear language upon a question of policy, it becomes the judicial tribunals to remain silent. *Hadden v The Collector*, 5 Wall 107; *Hyatt v Taylor* et al, 42 N.Y. 259; *In re Powers*, 25 Vt. 265; *State ex rel. v Liedtke*, 9 Neb. 468; *Plank road Co. v Woodhull*, 25 Mich. 99; *Jewell v Weed*, 18 Minn. 272; *Woodbury & Co. v Berry*, 18 Ohio St. 456; *Bruner v Briggs*, 39 Ohio St. 478; *Kent v Mahaffey*, 10 Ohio St. 204. The decision in *Riggs v Palmer* is the manifest assertion of a wisdom believed to be superior to that of the legislature upon a question of policy. Chief Justice REDFIELD, in *In re Powers*, observes: "It is scarcely necessary, we trust, at this late day, to say that the judicial tribunals of the state have no concern with the policy of legislation."

There should be no difficulty in distinguishing this case in which rights are vested by statute, from those cases in which the rights asserted have no foundation other than the fraudulent or unlawful conduct of a contracting party, nor from those in which attempts are made to use the process of courts for fraudulent purposes.

In a state where, by organic law, the powers of government are located, and the modes of their exercise defined, and the judicial is carefully distinguished from the legislative power, there should be no assumption of judicial infallibility.

No inference favourable to the plaintiffs in error can be drawn from the supposed familiarity of the law-makers with the principles of the civil law where, by an exception they who murder their ancestors are excluded from the inheritance. The natural inference is that when they incorporated the general rule into the statute, and omitted the exception, they intended that there should be no exception to the rule of inheritance prescribed.

If we felt at liberty to follow the example of the Court of Appeals of New York and to imagine the legislators who enacted this statute summoned to our presence, and answering as "upright and reasonable men" – that is, of course, such men as we are – "whether they intended to comprehend this case," we might receive an affirmative answer accompanied by suggestie reasons. The same rule which we are asked to apply to the slayer and his mortgages, if it be sound, should, out of respect for the logic of the law, in another case, be applied to the innocent claiming to inherit through him. One who cannot inherit cannot be a medium of inheritance.

The provisions of the 12th section of the Bill of Rights may have suggested the deliberate comprehension of this case within the provisions of the statute. "No conviction shall work corruption of blood or forfeiture of estate". Certainly, the construction claimed by counsel for the plaintiffs in error would not involve a forfeiture of estate, for their contention is that no estate vested in the slayer. But the law-makers may have entertained most serious doubt, if they contemplated the change in the statute which we are now asked to make, whether it would not contravene the Constitutional provision as to the corruption of blood. Corruption of blood and forfeiture of estates were, at common law, the consequences of attainder. Blackst. Com. 4, p.381. An attainted person can "neither inherit lands or other hereditaments from his ancestors, nor retain those he is already in possession of, nor transmit them by descent to any heir; but the same shall escheat to the lord of fee, subject to the king's superior right of forfeiture; and the person attainted shall also obstruct all descents to his posterity, whenever they are obliged to derive title through him to a remoter ancestor. Id.388. Since the Legislature did not undertake to create the supposed exception to the statute of descents, we are not required to determine whether it would have been repugnant to the Constitutional provision referred to. But in the field of speculation to which *Riggs v Palmer invites*, this provision suggests grave reasons why a legislative body, careful to respect both the letter and the spirit of the Constitution, should hesitate to attach to felonies any of the consequences of the corruption of blood.

The judgment is affirmed. * * * *

5.4.5 Riggs v Palmer

Court of Appeals of New York, 1889.

115 N.Y. 506

This action was brought to have the will of Francis B. Palmer, deceased, so far as it devises and bequeaths property to Elmer E. Palmer, cancelled and annulled.

EARL, J. On the 13th day of August 1880, Francis B. Palmer made his last will and testament, in which he gave small legacies to his two daughters, Mrs Riggs and Mrs Preston, the plaintiffs in this action, and the remainder of his estate to his grandson, the defendant, Elmer E. Palmer, subject to the support of Susan Palmer, his mother, with a gift over to the two daughters, subject to the support of Mrs Palmer, in case Elmer should survive him and die under age, unmarried and without any issue. The testator at the date of his will owned a farm and considerable personal property. He was a widower, and thereafter, in March 1882, he was married to Mrs Bressee, with whom before his marriage he entered into an ante-nuptial contract in which it was agreed that, in lieu of dower and all other claims upon his estate in case she survived him, she should have her support from his farm during her life, and such support was expressly charged upon the farm. At the date of the will, and, subsequently, to the death of the testator, Elmer lived with him as a member of his family, and at his death was sixteen years old. He knew of the provisions made in his favour in the will, and, that he might prevent his grandfather from revoking such provisions, which he had manifested some intention to do, and to obtain the speedy enjoyment and immediate possession of his property, he wilfully murdered him by poisoning him. He now claims property, and the sole question for our determination is, can he have it? The defendants say that the testator is dead; that his will was made in due form and has been admitted to probate, and that, therefore, it must have effect according to the letter of the law.

It is quite true that statutes regulating the making, proof and effect of wills, and the devolution of property, if literally construed, and if their force and effect can in no way and under no circumstances be controlled or modified, give this property to the murderer.

The purpose of those statutes was to enable testators to dispose of their estates to the objects of their bounty at death, and to carry into effect their final wishes legally expressed; and in considering and giving effect to them this purpose must be kept in view. It was the intention of the law-makers that the donees in a will should have the property given to them. But it never could have been their intention that a donee who murdered the testator to make the will operative should have any benefit under it. If such a case had been present to their minds, and it had been supposed necessary to make some provision of law to meet it, it cannot be doubted that they would have provided for it. It is a familiar canon of construction that a thing which is within the intention of the makers of a statute is as much within the statute as if it were within the letter; and a thing which is within the letter of the statute is not within the statute, unless it be within the intention of the makers. The writers of laws do not always express their intention perfectly, but either exceed it or fall short of it, so that judges are to collect it from probable or rational conjectures only, and this is called rational interpretation; and Rutherforth, in his Institutes (p.407), says: "When we make use of rational interpretation, sometimes we restrain the meaning of the writer so as to take in less, and sometimes we extend or enlarge his meaning so as to take in more than his words express".

Such a construction ought to be put upon a statute as will best answer the intention which the makers had in view, for *qui haeret in litera, haeret in cortice*. In Bacon's Abridgment (Statutes I., 5); Puffendorf (book 5, chapter 12), Rutherforth (pp.422, 427), and in Smith's commentaries (814), many cases are mentioned where it was held that matters embraced in the general words of statutes, nevertheless, were not within the statutes, because it could not have been the intention of the law-makers that they should be included. They were taken out of the statutes by an equitable construction, and it is said of Bacon: "By the equitable construction, a case not within the letter of the statute is sometimes holden to be within the meaning, because it is within the mischief for which a remedy is provided. The reason for such construction is that the law-makers could not set down every case in express terms. In order to form a right judgment whether a case be within the equity of a statute, it is a good way to suppose the law-maker present, and that you have asked him this question, did you intend to comprehend this case? Then you must give yourself such answer as you imagine he, being an upright and reasonable man, would have given. If this be that he did mean to comprehend it, you may safely hold the case to be within the equity of the statute; for while you do no more than he would have done, you do not act contrary to the statute, but in conformity thereto". In some cases the letter of a legislative act is restrained by an equitable construction; in others it is enlarged; in others the construction is contrary to the letter. The equitable construction which restrains the letter of a statute is defined by Aristotle, as frequently quoted, in this manner: *Aequitas est correctio legis generaliter latoe quo parti deficit.* If the law-makers could, as to this case, be consulted, would they say that they intended by their general language that the property of a testator or of an ancestor should pass to one who had taken his life for the express purpose of getting his property? In 1 Blackstone's Commentaries (91) the learned author, speaking of the construction of statutes, says: "If there arise out of them any absurd consequences manifestly contradictory to common reason, they are, with regard to those collateral consequences, void. * * * * When some collateral matter arises out of the general words, and happen to be unreasonable, then the judges are in decency to conclude that the consequence was not foreseen by the parliament, and, therefore, they are at liberty to expound the statute by equity and only *quoad hoc* disregard it; "and he gives as an illustration, if an act of parliament gives a man power to try all causes that arise within his manor of Dale, yet, if a cause should arise in which he himself is party, the act is construed not to extend to that because it is unreasonable that any man should determine his own quarrel.

There was a statute in Bologna that whoever drew blood in the streets should be severely punished, and yet it was held not to apply to the case of a barber who opened a vein in the street. It is commanded in the Decalogue that no work shall be done upon the Sabbath, and yet, giving the command a rational interpretation founded upon its design, the Infallible Judge held that it did not prohibit works of necessity, charity or benevolence on that day.

What could be more unreasonable than to suppose that it was the legislative intention in the general laws passed for the orderly, peaceable and just devolution of property, that they should have operation in favour of one who murdered his ancestor that he might speedily come into the possession of his estate? Such an intention is inconceivable. We need not, therefore, be much troubled by the general language contained in the laws.

Besides, all laws as well as all contracts may be controlled in their operation and effect by general, fundamental maxims of the common law. No one shall be permitted to profit by his own fraud, or to take advantage of his own wrong, or to found any claim upon his own iniquity, or to acquire property by his own crime. These maxims are dictated by public policy, have their foundation in universal law administered in all civilized countries, and have nowhere been superseded by statutes. They were applied in the decision of the case of the *New York Mutual Life Insurance Company v Armstrong,* (117 U.S. 591). There it was held that the person who procured a policy upon the life of another, payable at his death, and then murdered the assured to make the policy payable, could not recover thereon. Mr Justice Field, writing the opinion, said: "independently of any proof of the motives of Hunter in obtaining the policy, and even assuming that they were just and proper, he forfeited all rights under it when, to secure its immediate payment, he murdered the assured. It would be a reproach to the jurisprudence of the country if one could recover insurance money payable on the death of a party whose life he had feloniously taken. As well might he recover insurance money upon a building that he had wilfully fired."

These maxims, without any statute giving them force or operation, frequently control the effect and nullify the language of wills. A will procured by fraud and deception, like any other instrument, may be decreed void and set aside, and so a particular portion of a will may be excluded from probate or held inoperative if induced by the fraud or undue influence of the person in whose favour it is. (Allen v McPherson, 1 H.L. Cas. 191; Harrison's Appeal, 48 Conn. 202). So a will may contain provisions which are immoral, irreligious or against public policy, and they will be held void.

Here there was no certainty that this murderer would survive the testator, or that the testator would not change his will, and there was no certainty that he would get this property if nature was allowed to take its course. He, therefore, murdered the testator expressly to vest himself with an estate. Under such circumstances, what law, human or divine, will allow him to take the estate and enjoy the fruits of his crime? The will spoke and became operative at the death of the testator. He caused that death, and thus by his crime made it speak and have operation. Shall it speak and operate in his favour? If he had met the testator and taken his property by force, he would have had no title to it. Shall he acquire title by murdering him? If he has gone to the testator's house and by force compelled him, or by fraud or undue influence had induced him to will him his property, the law would not allow him to hold it. But can he give effect and operation to a will by murder, and yet take the property? To answer these questions in the affirmative, it seems to me, would be a reproach to the jurisprudence of our state, and an offence against public policy.

Under the civil law evolved from the general principles of natural law and justice by many generations of jurisconsults, philosophers and statesmen, one cannot take property by inheritance or will from an ancestor or benefactor whom he has murdered. (Domat, part 2, book 1, tit. 1, §3; Code Napoleon, §727; Mackeldy's Roman law, 530, 550). In the Civil Code or Lower Canada the provisions on the subject in the Code Napoleon have substantially copied. But, so far as I can find, in no country where the common law prevails has it been deemed important to enact a law to provide for such a case. Our revisers and law-makers were familiar with the civil law, and they did not deem it important to incorporate into our statutes its provisions upon this subject. This is not a *casus omissus*. It was evidently supposed that the maxims of the common law were sufficient to regulate such a case and that a specific enactment for the purpose was not needed.

For the same reasons the defendant Palmer cannot take any of this property as heir. Just before the murder he was not an heir, and it was not certain that he ever would be. He might have died before his grandfather, or might have been disinherited by him. He made himself an heir by the murder, and he seeks to take property as the fruit of his crime. What has before been said as to him as legatee applies to him with equal force as an heir. He cannot vest himself with title by crime.

My view of this case does not conflict upon Elmer any greater or other punishment for his crime than the law specifies. It takes from him no property, but simply holds that he shall not acquire property by his crime, and thus be rewarded for its commission.

Our attention is called to *Owens v Owens* (1000 N.C. 240), as a case quite like this. There a wife had been convicted of being an accessory before the fact to the murder of her husband, and it was held that she was, nevertheless entitled to dower. I am unwilling to assent to the doctrine of that case. The statutes provide dower for a wife who has the misfortune to survive her husband and thus lose his support and protection. It is clearly beyond their purpose to make provision for a wife who by her own crime makes herself a widow and wilfully and intentionally deprives herself of the support and protection of her husband. As she might have died before him, and thus never been his widow, she cannot be her crime vest herself with an estate. The principle which lies at the bottom of the maxim, *volenti non fit injuria*, should be applied to such a case, a widow should not, for the purpose of acquiring, as such, property rights, be permitted to allege a widowhood which she has wickedly and intentionally created.

The facts found entitled the plaintiffs to the relief they seek. The error of the referee was in his conclusion of law. Instead of granting a new trial, therefore, I think the proper judgment upon the facts found should be ordered here. The facts have been passed upon twice with the same result, first upon the trial of Palmer for murder, and then by the referee in this action. We are, therefore, of opinion that the ends of justice do not require that they should again come in question.

The judgment of the General Term and that entered upon the report of the referee should, therefore, be reversed and judgment should be entered as follows: That Elmer E. Palmer and the administrator be enjoined from using any of the personalty or real estate left by the testator for Elmer's benefit; that the devise and bequest in the will to Elmer be declared ineffective to pass the title to him; that by reason of the crime of murder committed upon the grandfather he is deprived of any interest in the estate left by him; that the plaintiffs are the true owners of the real and personal estate left by the testator, subject to the charge in favour of Elmer's mother and the widow of the testator, under the ante-nuptial agreement, and that the plaintiffs have costs in all the courts against Elmer.

Limitations of space compel the omission of a learned and earnest dissenting opinion by Judge Gray. The opinion is nevertheless worth reading.

All concur with EARL, J.; except GRAY, J.; who reads dissenting opinion, and DANFORTH, J.; concurring.

Judgment in accordance with the prevailing opinion. * * * *

B. The Later Ohio Decisions

Between 1895 and 1932, when the statute mentioned above at page 79 became effective, the specific question of the right of a felonious slayer to inherit under the statute of descent and distribution seems not to have been presented to the Supreme Court of Ohio. Since 1932, the only noninsurance case touching upon the problem and not governed by the statute has been *Oleff v Hodapp*, 129 Ohio St. 432 (1935).

The Oleff case concerned the right of one Tego to payment of the balance of a building and loan company account, amounting to $10,050, which he and one Apostol had established under a so-called joint and survivorship contract. It appeared that Apostol had since been killed in Yugoslavia. His killer had been found guilty of murder in the first degree, and Tego had been found guilty as "a moral author" of the crime.

Tego's claim to the balance of the account was contested by the heirs of Apostol. The statute authorizing such contracts of deposit provided that when, as here, a joint order had been given to the corporation that the deposit should be payable on the order of any one depositor notwithstanding the death or incapacity of another, the deposit should be so payable, and "no recovery shall be had against such corporation for amounts so paid and charged to such account".

Over the vigorous dissent of one judge, the Supreme Court of Ohio upheld Tego's claim. The majority said that the contract between Apostol and Tego carried "a present, vested interest to Tego, and that if the 1932 act had been in effect at that time, which it was not, it could not in no wise have affected his rights". It went on to say:

"* * * * Counsel insist that Tego's right should be denied him because to allow it would be in contravention of sound public policy and place a premium on murder. We are not subscribing to the righteousness of Tego's legal status; but this is a court of law and not a theological institution. We have no power to attaint Tego in any way, shape or form. Property cannot be taken form an individual who is legally entitled to it because he violates a public policy. Property rights are too sacred to be subjected to a danger of that character. We experience no satisfaction in holding that Tego is entitled to this account; but that is the law and we must so find".

In *Demos v Freemas*, 43 Ohio App. 426 (1931), a husband had shot and killed his wife, and later been committed to an insane asylum without any criminal proceedings having been brought. The wife's administrator thereafter brought a civil action for damages against the husband's guardian on behalf of the wife's brothers and sisters. The action was brought under the predecessor of the Ohio wrongful death statute reproduced at pp.180-81, above.

In the earlier version of the statute, the provision corresponding to the last clause of the first sentence of §2125.02 read as follows: "Such actions shall be for the exclusive benefit of the wife, or husband, and children, or if there be neither of them, then of the parents and next of kin of the person whose death was so caused".

The court affirmed a judgment for the defendant. It reasoned that the rights of the next of kin were secondary under the statute to those of the husband, and did not accrue unless he were in some way disqualified. It read *Deem v Milliken* as establishing that even murder would not disqualify him.

Notes and Review Questions

Note:

The courts in common law jurisdictions exercise the jurisdiction to interpret statutes. In cases where the provisions of the statute are not clear or are ambiguous, or what is known as the penumbral or the grey areas of the law, the courts employ a variety of rules of interpretation in arriving at an appropriate meaning of the law. The choice of a particular rule of interpretation will depend on variables to be considered by the court and in the process of resolving the issues the court will lay down principles of law; this is known as judicial activism.

1. The facts of the two cases, *Riggs v Palmer* and *Deem v Milliken* are quite similar. Can you distinguish the two cases?
2. What factors or variables, in your opinion, determined the choice of the rule of interpretation and consequently the different decisions of the two cases?

5.4.6 Re Sigsworth Bedford v Bedford[260]

[CHANCERY DIVISION (Clauson, J.), October 3, 1934]

[Reported [1935] Ch. 89; 104 L.J. Ch. 46; 152 L.T. 329; 51 T.L.R. 9; 78 Sol. Jo. 735]

Administration of Estates – Murder of owner of property – Intestacy as to property – Disqualification of murderer from benefiting under intestacy.

The principle grounded on public policy which precludes a sane murderer from benefiting under his victim's will precludes him from claiming a benefit conferred on by statute in the case of his victim dying intestate.

Notes. Considered: *Re Pollock, Pollock v Pollock,* [1941] 1 All E.R. 360; *Re Callaway* [1956] 2 All E.R. 451. Referred to: *Re Beresford v Royal Insurance Co.,* [1937] 2 All E.R. 243.

As to incapacity of a murderer to benefit from the estate of his victim, see I. HALSBURY'S LAWS (3rd Edn.) 10, para. 15, and for cases, see 44 DIGEST 226.

Cases referred to:

(1) *Cleaver v Mutual Reserve Fund Life Association*, [1892] 1 Q.B. 147; 61 L.J.Q.B. 128; 66 L.T. 220; 56 J.P. 180; 40 W.R. 230; 8 T.L.R. 139; 36 Sol. Jo. 106, C.A.; 12 Digest (Repl.) 271, 2082.

(2) *Re Pitts, Cox v Kilsby,* [1931] 1 Ch. 546; 100 L.J. Ch. 284; 145 L.T. 116; 47 T.L.R. 293; Digest Supp.

(3) *Re Houghton, Houghton v Houghton,* [1915] 2 Ch. 173; 84 L.J. Ch. 726; 113 L.T. 422; 31 T.L.R. 427; 59 Sol. Jo. 562; 18 Digest 18, 170.

Adjourned Summons

The testatrix, Mary Ann Sigsworth, by her will dated July 31, 1911, left all her property to her son, Thomas Bedford Sigsworth. The testatrix died some time between Sept. 17 and 21, 1933, and a coroner's jury on Sept. 23, 1933, found that she had been murdered by her son. The son died between Sept. 18 and 21, 1933, and the same coroner's jury found that he had committed suicide. The son had by his will left all his property to his father and mother. His father had predeceased him, and, therefore, as both of the only beneficiaries under his will had predeceased him, there was intestacy with reference to his property. The son left him surviving his maternal uncle and maternal aunt and his paternal uncle and paternal aunt. A summons was taken out by the maternal uncle, to whom letters of administration of the son's estate had been granted, and it asked whether (a) the son had become entitled to the estate of the testatrix under her will; or if not (b) had become entitled to her estate of which she had died intestate.

260 [1934] All. E.R. Rep. 113.

L.W. Byrne **for the plaintiff.**

Trevor Roberts **for the defendant, the maternal aunt of the son.**

Milner Holland **for the defendants, the paternal uncle and aunt of the son.**

CLAUSON, J. – In my opinion, the findings of fact by the coroner's jury at the inquests held with regard to the deaths of the testatrix and her son are not admissible in this court as evidence of those facts. In the absence of such evidence as I can accept in this court, and in the absence of some of the parties interested, I am not prepared to decide either that Thomas Bedford Sigsworth murdered his mother or that she died before him, but I am willing, for the guidance of the administrator, to decide the question of law which arises on the assumption that Thomas Bedford Sigsworth murdered his mother and that she died before him. The administrator, if he acts on my decision, will take the risk that the assumption of fact may conceivably hereafter turn out to be erroneous.

There can be no question, nor has it been disputed, that the claim of the plaintiff, as the personal representative of the son, to the estate of the mother under her will is bound to fail by reason of the well-settled principle that public policy precludes a sane murderer from taking a benefit under his victim's will. The result of that must be that the testatrix's estate which she left to her son was undisposed of at her death and passed, as upon her intestacy (subject to the question with which I proceed to deal), in accordance with the provisions of s 46 of the Administration of Estates Act, 1925.

The question, however, which I have to decide is whether the principle grounded on public policy which prevents a sane murderer from benefiting under the will of his victim applies with equal force to the case of the victim dying intestate so as to preclude the murderer (or his personal representative) from claiming, under the provisions of s 46 of the Act, the property in respect of which his victim died intestate.

In my judgment, the principle of public policy which precludes a murderer from claiming a benefit conferred on him by his victim's will precludes him from claiming a benefit conferred on him, in case of his victim's intestacy, by statute. The principle (to quote the language of FRY, L.J.) must be so far regarded in the construction of Acts of Parliament that general words which might include cases obnoxious to the principle must be read and construed as subject to it. This view of the law is adopted by FRY, L.J., in *Cleaver v Mutual Reserve Fund Life Association* (1) and by FARWELL, J. in *Re Pitts* (2), and must, in my judgment, prevail over the view taken by JOYCE, J., in *Re Houghton* (3); and, whether or not the opinions so expressed are binding on me, I agree with them and adopt them as my own.

The further question may arise whether the effect of my so deciding will be that the son should be treated as struck out of the Act, with the result of letting in the testatrix's brother and sister as the persons entitled to her estate under s. 46 (1)(v) of the Act, or whether her estate passed as bona vacantia to the Crown. In the absence of His Majesty's Attorney-General that question cannot now be decided; but I will order that the plaintiff be at liberty to add the Attorney-General as a defendant to the summons for the purpose of enabling him to claim the mother's estate on behalf of the Crown.

Solicitors: *C.V Young & Couper,* for *H.W. Faulkner,* Frome.

[*Reported by* J.H.G. Buller, Esq., *Barrister-at-Law*]

Review Questions

1. What is the *ratio decidendi* of this case? Is there a relevant theory of law that can be used to support the *ratio decidendi* of the judgment?
2. What was the justification for this judgment? Can you trace any relationship between the public policy mentioned in this case and the theory of law?
3. How was the judge able to incorporate a theory of law or public policy in this judgment?

5.4.7 R v Dudley and Stephens[261]

[QUEEN'S BENCH DIVISION (lord Coleridge, C.J., Grove and Denman, JJ., Pollock, B., and Huddleston, B.), December 4,9, 1884]

[Reported 14 Q.B.D., 273; 54 L.J.M.C. 32; 52 L.T. 107; 49 J.P. 69; 33 W.R. 347; 1 T.L.R. 118; 15 Cox., C.C. 624]

Criminal Law – Murder – Defence – Necessity to kill to preserve own life – No threat or violence against prisoner.

It is not lawful for any person, in order to save his own life, to kill another when that other is neither attempting or threatening his life nor is guilty of any illegal act of violence towards him. Anyone who kills an innocent and unoffending person to save his own life is guilty of murder.

The two prisoners were indicted for wilful murder, and on the trial the jury returned a special verdict, stating the facts, and referred the matter to the court. The facts stated in the special verdict were substantially as follows: the prisoners, able-bodied English seamen, and the deceased, an English boy between seventeen and eighteen years of age, the crew of an English yacht, were cast away in a storm on the high seas 1, 600 miles from land, and were compelled to put into an open boat. The food they took with them was consumed, and, they, having been for eight days without food and for six days without water, the prisoners killed the boy. The boy when killed was lying at the bottom of the boat, helpless, weak, and unable to make any resistance, and did not assent to his being killed. The prisoners and another man who was with them, fed upon the body and blood of the boy for four days, when they were picked up by a passing vessel. The verdict went on thus: "If the men had not fed upon the body of the boy, they would probably not have survived to be so picked up and rescued, but would within the four days have died of famine; the boy, being in a much weaker condition, was likely to have died before them; at the time of the act in question there was no sail in sight nor any reasonable prospect of relief; under the circumstances there appeared to the prisoners every probability that, unless they then fed, or very soon fed, upon the boy or one of themselves, they would die of starvation; there was no appreciable chance of saving life except by killing someone for the others to eat; assuming any necessity to kill anybody, there was no greater necessity for killing the boy than any of the three men."

Held: the facts as found afforded no justification for the killing of the boy, and the prisoners were guilty of wilful murder.

[261] *R v Dudley and Stephens* [1881-5] All. E.R. Rep.61.

Notes. Referred to: *R. v Steventon Parish* (1885), 1 T.L.R. 395; *R. v Staines Local Board* (1888), 4 T.L.R. 364; *R. v Brooke* (1894), 59 J.P. 6; *R. v Jameson* (1896), 60 J.P. 662.

As to the crime of murder, see 10 HALSBURY'S LAWS (3RD Edn.) 704-715; and for cases see 15 DIGEST (Repl.) 930 et seq.

Cases referred to:

(1) *Commonwealth v Holms,* 1 Wall Jr. 1.

(2) *R v Stratton* (1779), 1 Doug. K.B. 239; 99 E.R. 156; 21 State Tr. 1045; 14 Digest (Repl.) 75, 358.

Trial adjourned from Exeter Assizes for consideration of the special verdict returned by the jury.

The two prisoners, Thomas Dudley and Edwin Stephens, were indicted for the wilful murder of Richard Parker on July 25, 1884, on the high seas, within the jurisdiction of the Admiralty of England. They were tried at the winter assizes at Exeter on Nov 6, 1884, before HUDDLESTON, B., when, at the suggestion of the learned judge, the jury returned a special verdict, setting out the facts, and referred the matter to the Divisional Court for its decision.

The special verdict was as follows:

"The jurors, upon their oath, say and find that, on July 5, 1884, the prisoners, with one Brooks, all able-bodied English seamen, and the deceased, also an English boy, between seventeen and eighteen years of age, the crew of an English yacht, were cast away in a storm on the high seas, 1, 600 miles from the Cape of Good Hope, and were compelled to put into an open boat. That in this boat they had no supply of water and no supply of food, except two 1lb. tins of turnips, and for three days they had nothing else to subsist upon. That on the fourth day they caught a small turtle, upon which they subsisted for a few days, and this was the only food they had up to the twentieth day, when the act now in question was committed. That on the twelfth day the remains of the turtle were entirely consumed, and for the next eight days they had nothing to eat. That they had no fresh water, except such rain as they from time to time caught in their oilskin capes. That the boat was drifting on the ocean, and it was probably more than a thousand miles away from land. That on the eighteenth day, when they had been seven days without food and five without water, the prisoners spoke to Brooks as to what should be done if no succour came, and suggested that someone should be sacrificed to save the rest, but Brooks dissented, and the boy to whom they were understood to refer was not consulted. That on July 24, the day before the act now in question, the prisoner Dudley proposed to Stephens and to Brooks that lots should be cast who should be put to death to save the rest, but Brooks refused to consent, and it was not put to the boy, and in point of fact there was no drawing of lots. That on that day the prisoners spoke of their having families, and suggested that it would be better to kill the boy that their lives should be saved, and the prisoner Dudley proposed that if there was no vessel in sight by the morrow morning the boy should be killed. That next day, July 25, no vessel appearing, Dudley told Brooks that he had better go and have a sleep, and made signs to Stephens and Brooks that the boy had better be killed. The prisoner Stephens agreed to the act but Brooks dissented from it. That the boy was then lying at the bottom of the boat quite helpless, and extremely weakened by famine and by drinking sea water, and unable to make any resistance, nor did he ever assent to his being killed.

The prisoner, Captain Dudley, offered a prayer, asking forgiveness for them all if either of them should be tempted to commit a rash act, and that their souls might be saved. That the prisoner Dudley, with the assent of the prisoner Stephens, went to the boy, and telling him that his time was come, put a knife into his throat and killed him then and there. That the three men fed upon the body and blood of the boy for four days. That, on the fourth day after the act had been committed, the boat was picked up by a passing vessel, and the prisoners were rescued still alive, but in the lowest state of prostration. That they were carried to the port of Falmouth, and committed for trial at Exeter. That, if the men had not fed upon the body of the boy, they would probably not have survived to be so picked up and rescued, but would within the four days have died of famine. That the boy, being in a much weaker condition, was likely to have died before them. That at the time of the act in question there was no sail in sight, nor any reasonable prospect of relief. That under the circumstances there appeared to the prisoners every probability that, unless they then fed, or very soon fed, upon the boy or one of themselves, they would die of starvation. That there was no appreciable chance of saving life except by killing someone for the others to eat. That, assuming any necessity to kill anybody, there was no greater necessity for killing the boy than any of the three men.

"But whether upon the whole matter aforesaid by the said jurors in form aforesaid found the killing of the said Richard Parker by the said Thomas Dudley and Edwin Stephens done and committed in manner aforesaid felony and murder or not the said jurors so as aforesaid chosen, tried, and sworn, are ignorant, and pray the advice of the court thereupon. And if upon the whole matter aforesaid by the said jurors in form aforesaid found the court shall be of the opinion that the aforesaid killing of the said Richard Parker in manner aforesaid done and committed be felony and murder, then the said jurors on their oath say that the said Thomas Dudley and Edwin Stephens are each guilty of the felony and murder aforesaid in manner and form as in and by the indictment aforesaid above specified is against them alleged. And if upon the whole matter aforesaid by the said jurors in form aforesaid found the court shall be of the opinion that the aforesaid killing of the said Richard Parker in manner aforesaid done and committed be not felony and murder, then the jurors aforesaid on their oath aforesaid say that the said Thomas Dudley and Edwin Stephens are not guilty of the felony and murder aforesaid in manner and form as in and by the said indictment above specified is against them alleged. And if upon the whole matter aforesaid by the said jurors in form aforesaid found the court shall be of opinion that the killing of the said Richard Parker in manner aforesaid done and committed be felony and manslaughter, then the said jurors on their said oath say that the said Thomas Dudley and Edwin Stephens are each guilty of the felonious killing and slaying of the said Richard Parker. And if upon the whole matter aforesaid by the said jurors in form aforesaid found the court shall be of opinion that the aforesaid killing of the said Richard Parker be neither felony and murder nor felony and manslaughter, then the said jurors on their oath say that the said Thomas Dudley and Edwin Stephens are not guilty of the premises in the indictment specified and charged upon them.

Collins, Q.C., **H.** *Clark* **and** *L.E. Pyke* **for the prisoners.**

The Attorney-General (Sir Henry James, Q.C.), Charles, Q.C., C. Mathews **and** *Danckwerts* **for the Crown.**

Cur. adv vult.

Dec. 9, 1884. The following judgment of the court was delivered by

LORD COLERIDGE, C.J. – The two prisoners, Thomas Dudley and Edwin Stephens, were indicted for the murder of Richard Parker on the high seas on July 25 in the present year. They were tried before HUDDLESTON, B., at Exeter on Nov 6, and, under the direction of my learned brother, the jury returned a special verdict, the legal effect of which has been argued before us, and on which we are now to pronounce judgment. Form the facts, stated with the cold precision of a special verdict, it appears sufficiently that the prisoners were subject to terrible temptation and to sufferings which might break down the bodily power of the strongest man, and try the conscience of the best. Other details yet more harrowing, facts still more loathsome and appalling, were presented to the jury, and are to be found recorded in my learned brother's notes. But nevertheless this is clear, that the prisoners put to death a weak and unoffending boy upon the chance of preserving their own lives by feeding upon his flesh and blood after he was killed, and with a certainty of depriving him of any possible chance of survival. The verdicts find in terms that: "if the men had not fed upon the body of the boy, they would probably not have survived ..." and that "the boy, being in a much weaker condition, was likely to have died before them." They might possibly have been picked up next day by a passing ship; they might possibly not have been picked up at all, in either case it is obvious that the killing of the boy would have been an unnecessary and profitless act. It is found by the verdict that the boy was incapable of resistance, and, in fact, made none; and it is not even suggested that his death was due to any violence on his part attempted against, or even so much as feared by, them who killed him. Under these circumstances the jury say they are ignorant whether those who killed him were guilty of murder, and have referred it to this court to say what are the legal consequences which follow from the facts which they have found.

[His Lordship dealt with objections taken by counsel for the prisoners which do not call for report, and continued:] There remains to be considered the real question in the case – whether killing, under the circumstances set forth in the verdict, be or be not murder. The contention that it could be anything else was to the minds of us all both new and strange, and we stopped the Attorney-General in his negative argument that we might hear what could be said in support of a proposition which appeared to us to be at once dangerous, immoral, and opposed to all legal principle and analogy. All, no doubt, that can be said, has been urged before us, and we are now to consider and determine what it amounts to.

First, it is said that it follows from various definitions of murder in books of authority – which definitions imply, if they do not state, the doctrine – that, in order to save your own life you may lawfully take away the life of another, when that other is neither attempting nor threatening yours, nor is guilty of any illegal act whatever towards you or anyone else. But, if these definitions be looked at, they will not be found to sustain the contention. The earliest in point of date is the passage cited to us from BRACTON, who wrote in the reign of Henry III. It was at one time the fashion to discredit BRACTON because he was supposed to mingle too much of the canonist and civilian with the common lawyer. There is now no such feeling; but the passage upon homicide, on which reliance is placed, is a remarkable example of the kind of writing which may explain it. Sin and crime are spoken of as apparently equally illegal; and the crime of murder, it is expressly declared, may be committed lingua vel facto; so that a man, like Hero, "done to death by slanderous tongues", would, it seems, in the opinion of BRACTON, be a person in respect of whom might be grounded a legal indictment for murder. But in the very passage as to necessity, on which reliance has been placed, it is clear that BRACTON is speaking of necessity in the ordinary sense, the repelling by violence – violence justified so far as it was necessary for the object – any illegal violence used towards oneself. If, says BRACTON (Lib. iii, Art. De Corona, cap. 4, fol. 120), the necessity de "evitabilis et evadere posset absque occisione, tunc erit reus homicidii" – words which show clearly that he is thinking of physical danger, from which escape may be possible, and that "inevitabilis necessitas," of which he speaks as justifying homicide, is a necessity of the same nature.

It is, if possible, yet clearer that the doctrine contended for receives no support from the great authority of LORD HALE. It is plain that in his view the necessity which justifies homicide is that only which has always been, and is now, considered a justification. He says (1 Hale, P.C. 491):

"In all these cases of homicide by necessity, as in pursuit of a felon, in killing him that assaults to rob, or comes to burn or break a house, or the like, which are in themselves no felony".

Again, he says that the necessity which justifies homicide is of two kinds:

"(1) That necessity which is of a private nature; (2) That necessity which relates to the public justice and safety. The former is that necessity which obligeth a man to his own defence and safeguard; and this takes in these inquiries: 1. What may be done for the safeguard of a man's own life".

And then follow three other heads not necessary to pursue. LORD HALE proceeds (1 Hale, P.C. 478):

"1. As touching the first of these, viz., homicide in defence of a man's own life, which is usually styled se defendendo."

It is not possible to use words more clear to show that LORD HALE regarded the private necessity which justified, and alone justified, the taking the life of another for the safeguard of one's own to be what is commonly called self-defence. But if this could be even doubtful upon LORD HALE's words, LORD HALE himself has made it clear, for, in the chapter in which he deals with the exemption created by compulsion or necessity, he thus expresses himself (1 Hale, P.C. 51):

"If a man be desperately assaulted, and in peril of death, and cannot otherwise escape, unless to satisfy his assailant's fury he will kill an innocent person then present, the fear and actual force will not acquit him of the crime and punishment of murder if he commits the fact, for he ought rather to die himself than to kill an innocent; but if he cannot otherwise save his own life, the law permits him in his own defence to kill the assailant, for, by the violence of the assault and the offence committed upon him by the assailant himself, the law of nature and necessity hath made him his own protector cum debito moderamine inculpatae tutelae."

But, further still, LORD HALE, in the following chapter (1 Hale, P.C. 54), deals with the position asserted by the casuists, and sanctioned, as he says, by GROTIUS and PUFFENDORF, that in a case of extreme necessity, either of hunger or clothing,

> "theft is not theft, or at least not punishable as theft, and some even of our own lawyers have asserted the same; but I take it that here in England that rule, at least by the laws of England, is false, and, therefore, if a person, being under necessity for want of victuals or clothes, shall upon that account clandestinely and animo furandi steal another man's goods, it is a felony and a crime by the laws of England punishable with death."

If, therefore, LORD HALE is clear, as he is, that extreme necessity of hunger does not justify larceny, what would he have said to the doctrine that it justified murder?

It is satisfactory to find that another great authority, second probably only to LORD HALE, speaks with the same unhesitating clearness on this matter. SIR MICHAEL FOSTER, in chapter 3 of his DISCOURSE ON HOMICIDE, deals with the subject of "Homicide founded in Necessity," and the whole chapter implies, and is insensible unless it does imply, that, in the view of SIR MICHAEL FOSTER, necessity and self-defence (which in s. 1 he defines as "opposing force to force even to the death") are convertible terms. There is no hint. No trace of the doctrine now contended for; the whole reasoning of the chapter is entirely inconsistent with it. In EAST (1 East, P.C. 271), the whole chapter on "Homicide by Necessity" is taken up with an elaborate discussion of the limits within which necessity in SIR MICHAEL FOSTER's sense (given above) of self-defence is a justification of or excuse for homicide. There is a short section at the end (p.294), very generally and very doubtfully expressed, in which the only instance discussed is the well-known one of two shipwrecked men on a plank able to sustain only one of them, and the conclusion is left by SIR EDWARD EAST entirely undetermined. What is true of SIR EDWARD EAST is true also of MR SERJEANT HAWKINS. The whole of his chapter on "Justifiable Homicide" assumes that the only justifiable homicide of a private nature is in defence against force of a man's person, house, or goods. In s. 26 we find again the case of the two shipwrecked men and the single plank, with this significant expression from a careful writer: "It is said to be justifiable". So, too, DALTON, C. 150, clearly considers necessity and self-defence, in SIR MICHAEL FOSTER's sense of that expression, to be convertible terms, though he prints without comment LORD BACON's instance of the two men on one plank as a quotation from LORD BACON, adding nothing whatever to it of his own; and there is a remarkable passage at p.339, in which he says that even in the case of a murderous assault upon a man, yet before he may take the life of the man who assaults him, even in self-defence, "cuncta prius tentanda." The passage in STAUNDFORDE, on which almost the whole of the dicta we have been considering are built, when it comes to be examined, does not warrant the conclusion which has been derived from it. The necessity to justify homicide must be, he says, inevitable, and the example which he gives to illustrate his meaning is the very same which has just been cited from DALTON, showing that the necessity he was speaking of was a physical necessity, and the self-defence a defence against physical violence. RUSSELL merely repeats the language of the old textbooks, and adds no new authority nor any fresh considerations.

Is there, then, any authority for the proposition which has been presented to us? Decided cases there are none. The case of the seven English sailors referred to by the commentator on GROTIUS and by PUFFENDORF has been discovered by a gentleman of the Bar (Sir Sherston Baker), who communicated with HUDDLESTON, B., to convey the authority, if it conveys so much, of a single judge of the island of St. Kitts, when that island was possessed partly by France and partly by this country, somewhere about the year 1641. It is mentioned in a medical treatise published at Amsterdam (OBSERVATIONUM MEDICARUM by NICOLAUS TULPIUS), and is altogether, as authority in an English court, as unsatisfactory as possible. The American case (*Commonwealth v Holms* (1)) cited by STEPHEN, J., in his DIGEST from WHARTON ON HOMICIDE 237, in which it was decided, correctly indeed, that sailors had no right to throw passengers overboard to save themselves, but, on the somewhat strange ground that the proper mode of determining who was to be sacrificed was to vote upon the subject by ballot, can hardly, as STEPHEN, J., SAYS, be an authority satisfactory to a court in this country. The observations of LORD MANSFIELD in *R v Stratton* (2), striking and excellent as they are, were delivered in a political trial, where the question was, whether a political necessity had arisen for deposing a governor of Madras. But they have little application to the case before us, which must be decided on very different considerations.

The one real authority of former time is LORD BACON, who in his Commentary on the maxim, "Necessitas inducit privilegium quoad jura privata," lays down the law as follows:

"Necessity carrieth a privilege in itself. Necessity is of three sorts: Necessity of conservation of life, necessity of obedience, and necessity of the act of God or of a stranger. First, of conservation of life. If a man steals viands to satisfy his present hunger, this is no felony nor larceny. So if divers be in danger of drowning by the casting away of some boat or barge, and one of them get to some plank, or on the boat's side, to keep himself above water, and another to save his life thrusts him from it, whereby he is drowned, this is neither se defendendo nor by misadventure, but justifiable."

On this it is to be observed that LORD BACON's proposition that stealing to satisfy hunger is no larceny is hardly supported by STAUNDFORDE, whom he cites for it, and is expressly contradicted by LORD HALE in the passage already cited. As for the proposition regarding the plank or boat it is said to be derived from the canonists; at any rate, he cites no authority for it, and it must stand upon his own. LORD BACON was great even as a lawyer but it is permissible to much smaller men, relying upon principle and on the authority of others the equals and even the superiors of LORD BACON as lawyers, to question the soundness of his dictum. There are many conceivable states of things in which it might possibly be true, but, if LORD BACON meant to lay down the broad proposition that a man may save his life by killing, if necessary, an innocent and unoffending neighbour, it certainly is not law at the present day.

There remains the authority of STEPHEN, J., who both in his DIGEST (Art. 32) and in his HISTORY OF THE CRIMINAL LAW (Vol. 2, p.108) uses language perhaps wide enough to cover this case. The language is somewhat vague in both places, but it does not in either place cover this case of necessity, and we have the best authority for saying that it was not meant to cover it. If it had been necessary we must with true deference have differed from him; but it is satisfactory to know that we have, probably at least, arrived at no conclusion in which, if he had been a member of the court, he would have been unable to agree. Neither are we in conflict with any opinion expressed upon this subject by the learned persons who formed the commission for preparing the CRIMINAL CODE. They say on this subject:

> "We are not prepared to suggest that necessity should in every case be a justification; we are equally unprepared to suggest that necessity should in no case be a defence. We judge it better to leave such questions to be dealt with when, if ever, they arise in practice by applying the principles of law to the circumstances of the particular case.

It would have been satisfactory to us if these eminent persons could have told us whether the received definitions of legal necessity were, in their judgment, correct and exhaustive, and, if not, in what way they should be amended; but as it is we have, as they say, "to apply the principles of law to the circumstances of this particular case."

Except for the purpose of testing how far the conservation of a man's own life is in all cases and under all circumstance an absolute, unqualified, and paramount duty, we exclude from our consideration all the incidents of war. We are dealing with a case of private homicide, not one imposed upon men in the service of their Sovereign or in the defence of their country. It is admitted that the deliberate killing of this unoffending and unresisting boy was clearly murder, unless the killing can be justified by some well-recognised excuse admitted by law. It is further admitted that there was in this case no such excuse, unless the killing was justified by what has been called necessity. But the temptation to the act which existed here was not what the law has ever called necessity. Nor is this to be regretted. Though law and morality are not the same, and though many things may be immoral which are not necessarily illegal, yet the absolute divorce of law from morality would be of fatal consequence, and such divorce would follow if the temptation to murder in this case were to be held by law an absolute defence of it. It is not so.

To preserve one's life is generally speaking, a duty, but it may be the plainest and the highest duty to sacrifice it. War is full of instances in which it is a man's duty not to live, but to die. The duty, in case of shipwreck, of a captain to his crew, of the crew to the passengers, of soldiers to women and children, as in the noble case of *The Birkenhead* - these duties impose on men the moral necessity, not of the preservation, but of the sacrifice, of their lives for others, from which in no country – least of all it is to be hoped in England – will men ever shrink, as indeed they have not shrunk. It is not correct, therefore, to say that there is any absolute and unqualified necessity to preserve one's life. "Necesse est ut eam, non ut vivam," is a saying of a Roman officer quoted by LORD BACON himself with high eulogy in the very chapter on necessity, to which so much reference has been made. It would be a very easy and cheap display of common-place learning to quote from Greek and Latin authors – from HORACE, from JUVENAL, from CICERO, from EURIPIDES – passage after passage in which the duty of dying for others has been laid down in glowing and emphatic language as resulting from the principles of heathen ethics. It is enough in a Christian country to remind ourselves of the Great Example which we profess to follow.

It is not needful to point out the awful danger of admitting the principle which has been contended for. Who is to be the judge of this sort of necessity? By what measure is the comparative value of lives to be measured? Is it to be strength, or intellect, or what? It is plain that the principle leaves to him who is to profit by it to determine the necessity which will justify him in deliberately taking another's life to save his own. In this case the weakest, the youngest, the most unresisting was chosen. Was it more necessary to kill *him* than one of the grown men? The answer must be, No.

"So spake the Fiend; and with necessity, The tyrant's plea, excused his devilish deeds."

It is not suggested that in this particular case the "deeds" were "devilish"; but it is quite plain that such a principle, once admitted, might be made the legal cloke for unbridled passion and atrocious crime. There is no path safe for judges to tread but to ascertain the law to the best of their ability, and to declare it according to their judgment, and if in any case the law appears to be too severe on individuals, to leave it to the Sovereign to exercise that prerogative of mercy which the Constitution has entrusted to the hands fittest to dispense it. It must not be supposed that, in refusing to admit temptation to be an excuse for crime, it is forgotten how terrible the temptation was, how awful the suffering, how hard in such trials to keep the judgment straight and the conduct pure. We are often compelled to set up standards we cannot reach ourselves, and to lay down rules which we could not ourselves satisfy. But a man has no right to declare temptation to be an excuse, though he might himself have yielded to it, nor allow compassion for the criminal to change or weaken in any manner the legal definition of the crime. It is, therefore, our duty to declare that the prisoners' act in this case was wilful murder; that the facts as stated in the verdict are no legal justification of the homicide; and to say that, in our unanimous opinion, they are, upon this special verdict, guilty of murder.

The LORD CHIEF JUSTICE thereupon passed sentence of death in the usual form.

Judgment for the Crown

Review Questions

1. What was the issue that confronted the jury or the court?
2. Was there an existing rule to resolve the issue?
3. How did the court arrive at this rule or principle of law?
4. What theory of law, do you consider to be relevant and can be used as the jurisprudential basis for the judgment?

5.4.8 Holy Trinity Church v United States

Supreme Court of the United States, 1892

143 U.S. 457, 12 S. Ct. 511, 36 L.Ed. 226.

In error to the circuit court of the United States for the southern district of New York.

Mr Justice BREWER delivered the opinion of the court.

Plaintiff in error is a corporation duly organized and incorporated as a religious society under the laws of the state of New York. E. Walpole Warren was, prior to September, 1887, an alien residing in England. In that month the plaintiff in error made a contract with him, by which he was to remove to the city of New York, and enter into its service as rector and pastor; and in pursuance of such contract, Warren did so remove and enter upon such service. It is claimed by the United States that this contract on the part of the plaintiff in error was forbidden by chapter 164, 23 St. p.332; and an action was commenced to recover the penalty prescribed by that act. The circuit court held that the contract was within the prohibition of the statute, and rendered judgment accordingly, (36 Fed. Rep. 303,) and the single question presented for our determination is whether it erred in that conclusion.

The first section describes the act forbidden, and is in these words:

"*Be it enacted by the Senate and House of representatives of the United States of America, in Congress assembled*, that from and after the passage of this act it shall be unlawful for any person, company, partnership, or corporation, in any manner whatsoever, to prepay the transportation, or in any way assist or encourage the importation or migration, of any alien or aliens, any foreigner or foreigners, into the United States, its territories, or the District of Columbia, under contract or agreement, parol or special, express or implied, made previous to the importation or migration of such alien or aliens, foreigner or foreigners, to perform labour or service of any kind in the United States, its territories, or the District of Columbia."

It must be conceded that the act of the corporation is within the letter of this section, for the relation of rector to his church is one of service, and implies labour on the one side with compensation on the other. Not only are the general words "labour" and "service" both used, but also, as it were to guard against any narrow interpretation and emphasize a breadth of meaning, to them is added "of any kind;" and, further, as noticed by the circuit judge in his opinion, the fifth section, which makes specific exceptions, among them professional actors, artists, lecturers, singers, and domestic servants, strengthens the idea that every other kind of labour and service was intended to be reached by the first section. While there is great force to this reasoning, we cannot think congress intended to denounce with penalties a transaction like that in the present case. It is a familiar rule that a thing be within the letter of the statute and yet not within the statute, because not within its spirit nor within the intention of its makers. This has been often asserted, and the Reports are full of cases illustrating its application. This is not the substitution of the will of the judge for that of the legislator; for frequently words of general meaning are used in a statute, words broad enough to include an act in question, and yet a consideration of the whole legislation, or of the circumstances surrounding its enactment, or of the absurd results which follow from giving such broad meaning to the words, makes it unreasonable to believe that the legislator intended to include the particular act. * * *

* * * In *U.S. v Kirby*, 7 Wall. 482, 486, the defendants were indicted for the violation of an act of congress providing "that if any person shall knowingly and wilfully obstruct or retard the passage of the mail, or of any driver or carrier, or of any horse or carriage carrying the same, he shall, upon conviction, for every such offence, pay a fine not exceeding one hundred dollars". The specific charge was that the defendants knowingly and wilfully retarded the passage of one Farris, a carrier of the mail, while engaged in the performance of his duty, and also in like manner retarded the steam-boat Gen. Buell, at that time engaged in carrying the mail. To this indictment the defendants pleaded specially that Farris had been indicted for murder by a court of competent authority in Kentucky; that a bench-warrant had been issued and placed in the hands of the defendant Kirby, the sheriff of the county, commanding him to arrest Farris, and bring him before the court to answer to the indictment; and that, in obedience to this warrant, he and the other defendants, as his posse, entered upon the steam-boat Gen. Buell and arrested Farris, and used only such force as was necessary to accomplish that arrest. The question as to the sufficiency of this plea was certified to this court, and it was held that the arrest of Farris upon the warrant from the state court was not an obstruction of the mail, or the retarding of the

passage of a carrier of the mail within the meaning of the act. In its opinion the court says: "All laws should receive a sensible construction. General terms should be so limited in their application as not to lead to injustice, oppression, or an absurd consequence. It will always, therefore, be presumed that the legislature intended exceptions to its language which would avoid results of this character. The reason of the law in such cases should prevail over its letter. The common sense of man approves the judgment mentioned by Puffendorf, that the Bolognian law which enacted 'that whoever drew blood in the streets should be punished with the utmost severity', did not extend to the surgeon who opened the vein of a person that fell down in the street in a fit. The same common sense accepts the ruling, cited by Plowden, that the statute of 1 Edw. II., which enacts that a prisoner who breaks prison shall be guilty of felony, does not extend to a prisoner who breaks out when the prison is on fire, 'for he is not to be hanged because he would not stay to be burnt.' And we think that a like common sense will sanction the ruling we make, that the act of congress which punishes the obstruction or retarding of the passage of the mail, or of its carrier, does not apply to a case of temporary detention of the mail caused by the arrest of the carrier upon an indictment for murder." * * *

Among other things which may be considered in determining the intent of the legislature is the title of the act. We do not mean that it may be used to add to or take from the body of the statute, (*Hadden v Collector*, 5 Wall. 107,) but it may help to interpret its meaning. In the case of *U.S. v Fisher*, 2 Cranch, 358, 386, Chief Justice MARSHALL said: "On the influence which the title ought to have in construing the enacting clauses, much has been said, and yet it is not easy to discern the point of difference between the opposing counsel in this respect. Neither party contends that the title of an act can control plain words in the body of the statute; and neither denies that, taken with other parts, it may assist in removing ambiguities. Where the intent is plain, nothing is left to construction. Where the mind labours to discover the design of the legislature, it seizes everything from which aid can be derived; and in such case the title claims a degree of notice, and will have its due share of consideration." * * *

It will be seen that words as general as those used in the first section of this act were by that decision limited, and the intent of congress with respect to the act was gathered partially, at least, from its title. Now, the title of this act is, "An act to prohibit the importation and migration of foreigners and aliens under contract or agreement to perform labour in the United States, its territories, and the District of Columbia. Obviously the thought expressed in this reaches only to the work of the manual labourer, as distinguished from that of the professional man. No one reading such a title would suppose that congress had in its mind any purpose of staying the coming into this country of ministers of the gospel, or, indeed, of any class whose toil is that of the brain. The common understanding of the terms "labour" and "labourers" does not include preaching and preachers, and it is to be assumed that words and phrases are used in their ordinary meaning. So whatever of light is thrown upon the statute by the language of the title indicates an exclusion from its penal provisions of all contracts for the employment of ministers, rectors, and pastors.

Again, another guide to the meaning of a statute is found in the evil which it is designed to remedy; and for this the court properly looks at contemporaneous events, the situation as it existed, and as it was pressed upon the attention of the legislative body. *U.S. v Railroad*

Co., 91 U.S. 72, 79. The situation which called for this statute was briefly but fully stated by Mr Justice Brown when, as district judge, he decided the case of *U.S. v Craig*, 28 Fed. Rep. 795, 798: "The motives and history of the act are matters of common knowledge. It had become the practice for large capitalists in this country to contract with their agents abroad for the shipment of great numbers of an ignorant and servile class of foreign labourers, under contracts by which the employer agreed, upon the one hand, to prepay their passage, while, upon the other hand, the labourers agreed to work after their arrival for a certain time at a low rate of wages. The effect of this was to break down the labour market, and to reduce other labourers engaged in like occupations to the level of the assisted immigrant. The evil finally became so flagrant that an appeal was made to congress for relief by the passage of the act in question, the design of which was to raise the standard of foreign immigrants and to discountenance the migration of those who had not sufficient means in their own hands, or those of their friends, to pay their passage".

It appears, also, from the petitions, and in the testimony presented before the committees of congress, that it was this cheap, unskilled labour which was making the trouble, and the influx of which congress sought to prevent. It was never suggested that we had in this country a surplus of brain toilers, and, least of all, that the market for the services of Christian ministers was depressed by foreign competition. Those were matters to which the attention of congress, or of the people, was not directed. So far, then, as the evil which was sought to be remedied interprets the statute, it also guides to an exclusion of this contract from the penalties of the act.

A singular circumstance, throwing light upon the intent of the congress, is found in the extract from the report of the senate committee on education and labour, recommending the passage of the bill: "The general facts and considerations which induce the committee to recommend the passage of this bill are set forth in the report of the committee of the house. The committee report the bill back without amendment, although there are certain features thereof which might well be changed or modified, in the hope that the bill may not fail of passage during the present session. Especially would the committee have otherwise recommended amendments, substituting for the expression, 'labour and service', whenever it occurs in the body of the bill, the words 'manual labour' or 'manual service', as sufficiently broad to accomplish the purposes of the bill, and that such amendments would remove objections which a sharp and perhaps unfriendly criticism may urge to the proposed legislation. The committee, however, believing that the bill in its present form will be construed as including only those whose labour or service is manual in character, and being very desirous that the bill become a law before the adjournment, have reported the bill without change." Page 6059, Congressional Record, 48th Cong. And, referring back to the report of the committee of the house, there appears this language: "It seeks to restrain and prohibit the immigration or importation of labourers who would have never seen our shores but for the inducements and allurements of men whose only object is to obtain labour at the lowest possible rate, regardless of the social and material well-being of our own citizens, and regardless of the evil consequences which result to American labourers from such immigration. This class of immigrants care nothing about our institutions, and in many instances never even heard of them. They are men whose passage is paid by importers. They come here under contract to labour for a certain number of years. They are ignorant of our social condition, and, that they may remain so, they are isolated and prevented from coming into contact with Americans. They are generally from the lowest social stratum, and live upon the coarsest food, and in hovels of a character before unknown to American workmen. They, as a rule, do not become citizens, and are certainly not a desirable acquisition to the body politic. The inevitable tendency of their presence among us is to degrade American labour, and to reduce it to the level of the imported pauper labour." Page 5359, Congressional Record, 48th Cong.

We find, therefore, that the title of the act, the evil which was intended to be remedied, the circumstances surrounding the appeal to congress, the reports of the committee of each house, all concur in affirming that the intent of congress was simply to stay the influx of this cheap, unskilled labour. * * *

The judgment will be reversed, and the case remanded for further proceedings in accordance with this opinion.

Notes

1. In the construction of statutes the courts have adopted a favourable attitude toward the use of reports of standing committees, as in the principal case, and of special committees, as in *Pellet v Industrial Comm.*, 162 Wis. 596, 156 N.W. 956 (1916). See, generally, Chamberlain, The Courts and Committee Reports, 1 U. Chi. L. Rev 81 (1933); Jones, Extrinsic Aids in the Federal Courts, 25 Iowa L. Rev 737 (1940).

2. Should reports and materials of law revision commissions, or other commissions, or of other extra-legislative groups be treated differently? If so, how and why? See, e.g., In *re Tarlo's Estate*, 315 Pa. 321, 172 A. 139 (1934) (law revision commission) and *Sales v Stewart*, 134 Cal. App. 661, 20 P. 2d. 44 (1933). See, also, Note, Non-Legislative Intent as an Aid to Statutory Interpretation, 49 Col. L. Rev 676 (1949); Sutherland, Statutes and Statutory Construction §§ 48.09., 48.11 and 48.12 (4th ed. Sands 1973, Cumulative Supp. 1979).

3. On interpretation according to the "equity of the statute", see de Sloovere, Equity and Reason of a Statute, 21 Cornell L.Q. 591 (1936); Thorne, The Equity of a Statute and Heydon's Case, 21 Ill. L. Rev 202 (1936)

4. Contrast the nature of the problem posed for the Court in the principal case with that posed in *U.S. v Kirby* (discussed in the Holy Trinity Church case supra) and consider the result reached in the Kirby decision and the quoted justifications therefor. What other reasonable justifications, if any, might have been given? What are the implications of Kirby for the judicial function in interpretation? Compare Riggs v Palmer, 115 N.Y. 506, 22 N.E. 188 (1889). In that case, the beneficiary under a will had murdered the testator and then claimed the property pursuant to the will's provisions. The question was whether the beneficiary could have the property in such circumstances. It was acknowledged that the statutes regulating the making, proof and effect of wills and the devolution of property (which statutes did not in terms deal with "murdering heirs") would if literally construed give the property to the murderer. The Court however ruled that the murderer was not entitled to the property. *Inter alia*, the Court stated:

> "The purpose of [the statutes concerned] was to enable testators to dispose of their estates to the objects of their bounty at death, and to carry into effect their final wishes legally expressed; and in considering and giving effect to them this purpose must be kept in view. It was the intention of the law-makers that the donees in a will should have the property given to them. But it never could have been their intention that a donee who murdered the testator to make the will operative should have any benefit under it. * * *

"What could be more unreasonable than to suppose that it was the legislative intention in the general laws passed for the orderly, peaceable and just devolution of property, that they should have operation in favour of one who murdered his ancestor that he might speedily come into the possession of his estate? Such an intention is inconceivable. We need not, therefore, be much troubled by the general language contained in the laws.

"Besides, all laws as well as all contracts may be controlled in their operation and effect by general, fundamental maxims of the common law. No one shall be permitted to profit by his own fraud, or to take advantage of his own wrong, or to found any claim upon his own iniquity, or to acquire property by his own crime. These maxims are dictated by public policy, have their foundation in universal law administered in all civilized countries, and have nowhere been superseded by statutes. * * * "

Compare, in addition, *Glus v Brooklyn Eastern Dist. Terminal*, 359 U.S. 231, 79 S. Ct. 760, 3 L. Ed. 2d 770 (1959) , where, notwithstanding the existence of an express three-year statute of limitations, the Supreme Court held that an FELA action brought after more than three years was not barred where defendant misled the plaintiff into believing he had more than three years in which to sue. The court relied on the principle that no man may take advantage of his own wrong, noting that it had been shown nothing in the language or history of the Federal Employers' Liability Act to indicate a contrary result. Also illuminating on the issues here raised are No. 4 of the problems under the Comprehensive Drug Abuse Prevention and Control Act (infra p.593) and *Sorrells v United States*, 287 U.S. 435, 53 S.Ct. 210, 77 L.Ed. 413 (1932).

Francis Lieber: *Some Remarks on interpretation*[262]

* * * Let us take an instance of the simplest kind, to show in what degree we are continually obliged to resort to interpretation.

By and by we shall find that the same rules which common sense teaches every one to use, in order to understand his neighbour in the most trivial intercourse, are necessary likewise, although not sufficient, for the interpretation of documents or texts of the highest importance, Constitutions as well as treaties between the greatest nations.

Suppose a housekeeper says to a domestic: "fetch some soupmeat", accompanying the act with giving some money to the latter; he will be unable to execute the order without interpretation, however easy and, consequently, rapid the performance of the process may be. Common sense and good faith tell the domestic, that the housekeeper's meaning was this: 1. He should go immediately, or as soon as his other occupations are finished; or, if he be directed to do so in the evening, that he should go the next day at the *usual* hour; 2. that the money handed him by the housekeeper is intended to pay for the meat thus ordered, and not as a present to him; 3. that he should buy such meat and of such parts of the animal, as, to his knowledge, has commonly been used in the house he stays at, for making soups; 4. that

[262] Professor at Columbia's School of Law, 1860-1872. The quoted passage appears in Lieber's Legal and Political Hermeneutics, pp.17-20 (rev 3d ed. 1880). This work was originally published in *The American Jurist*, October 1837 and January 1838, and in a revised 2nd edition in book form in 1839.

he buy the best meat he can obtain, for a fair price; 5. that he go to that butcher who usually provides the family, with whom the domestic resides, with meat, or to some convenience stall, and not to any unnecessary distant place; 6. that he return the rest of the money; 7. that he bring home the meat in good faith, neither adding any thing disagreeable nor injurious; 8. that he fetch the meat for the use of the family and not for himself. Suppose, on the other hand, the housekeeper, afraid of being misunderstood, had mentioned these eight specifications, she would not have obtained her object, if it were to exclude all *possibility* of misunderstanding. For, the various specifications would have required new ones. Where would be the end? We are constrained then, always, to leave a considerable part of our meaning to be found out by interpretation, which, in many cases must necessarily cause greater or less obscurity with regard to the exact meaning, which our words were intended to convey.

Experience is a plant growing as slowly as confidence, which Chatham said increased so tardily. In fact, confidence grows slowly because it depends upon experience. The British spirit of civil liberty induced the English judges to adhere strictly to the law, to its exact expressions. This again induced the law-makers to be, in their phraseology, as explicit and minute and as possible, which causes such a tautology and endless repetition in the statutes of that country that even so eminent a statesman as Sir Robert Peel declared, in parliament, that he "contemplates no task with so much distaste as the reading through an ordinary act of parliament". Men have at length found out that little or nothing is gained by attempting to speak with absolute clearness and endless specifications, but that human speech is the clearer, the less we endeavour to supply by words and specifications that interpretation which common sense must give to human words. However minutely we may define, somewhere we needs must trust at last to common sense and good faith.

5.4.9 Temple v City of Petersburg

Supreme Court of Appeals of Virginia, 1944, 182 Va 418

29 S.E. 2d. 357.

Appeal from Hustings Court of City of Petersburg.

GREGORY, JUSTICE. The appellants, who were the complainants in the court below, filed their bill in equity against the city of Petersburg, praying that it be restrained and enjoined from using a tract of 1.01 acres of land acquired by it in 1942 for cemetery purposes. This plot of land adjoined Peoples Memorial Cemetery, which had been established and used as a cemetery for more than one hundred years.

The court below temporarily restrained the city from using the 1.01 acre tract as an addition to the cemetery. Later the city filed its answer to the bill and, by consent; the cause was set for the hearing upon the bill, the answer, and a stipulation of counsel. The court dissolved the injunction and refused the prayer for relief.

Code, sec. 56 (Michie 1942), provides in part as follows:

> "No cemetery shall be hereafter established within the corporate limits of any city or town, nor shall any cemetery be established within two hundred and fifty yards of any residence without the consent of the owner of the legal and equitable title of such residence; ..."

We are called upon to ascertain the proper meaning of the statute, and to decide whether or not it has been violated by the city. Specifically the controversy concerns the meaning to be given to the word 'established', used therein. The appellants maintain that under the statute the enlargement of an existing cemetery, such as is sought here, in reality is the establishment of a cemetery, while the appellee contends that to enlarge an existing cemetery is not the establishment of a cemetery and, therefore, constitutes no violation of the statute.

The appellants most strongly contend that the word, "established", as used in the statute, means 'located', and that the evil intended to be inhibited is the location of a cemetery in a city or town upon ground not previously dedicated for cemetery purposes, or the location of a cemetery within 250 yards of a residence, whether by enlargement or otherwise. They contend that the purpose of the statute is to protect residences and lands from the ill effects growing out of close proximity to a cemetery. They further contend that it is unreasonable to say that residences and lands are to be protected against the "establishment" of cemeteries, but are not to be protected against the encroachment or enlargement of existing cemeteries; that the evil created by one is equally as real as that created by the other.

The position of the appellee is that the word "established", has such a clear and precise meaning that no question of statutory construction arises. That the statute provides that no cemetery shall be hereinafter "established" in a city or town, and that this language does not mean that a cemetery already established shall not be hereafter enlarged. To hold otherwise would be not to construe the statute, but in effect, to amend it.

It is elementary that the ultimate aim of rules of interpretation is to ascertain the intention of the legislature in the enactment of a statute, and that intention, when discovered, must prevail. If, however, the intention of the legislature is perfectly clear from the language used, rules of construction are not to be applied. We are not allowed to construe that which has no need of construction.

If the language of a statute is plain and unambiguous, and its meaning perfectly clear and definite, effect must be given to it regardless of what courts think of its wisdom or policy. In such cases courts must find the meaning within the statute itself ...

In *Commonwealth v Sanderson*, 170 Va. 33, 195 S.E. 516, 519, we quoted with approval from *Saville v Virginia Ry. and Power Co.*, 114 Va. 444, 76, S.E. 954, 957, this statement of the rule: "it is contended that the construction insisted upon by the plaintiff in error is violative of the spirit or reason of the law. The argument would seem to concede that the contention is within the letter of the law. We hear a great deal about the spirit of the law, but the duty of this court is not to make law, but to construe it; not to wrest its letter from its plain meaning in order to conform to what is conceived to be its spirit, in order to subserve, and promote some principle of justice and equality which it is claimed the letter of the law has violated. It is our duty to take the words which the legislature has seen fit to employ and give to them their usual and ordinary signification, and, having thus ascertained the legislative intent, to give effect to it, unless it transcends the legislative power as limited by the Constitution' "...

The word "established" is defined in Webster's New International Dictionary 2d Ed. 1936, thus: "To originate and secure the permanent existence of; to found; to institute; to create and regulate; - said of a colony, a State or other institutions."

Just why the Legislature, in its wisdom, saw fit to prohibit the establishment of cemeteries in cities and towns, and did not see fit to prohibit enlargements or additions, is no concern of ours. Certain it is that language could not be plainer than that employed to express the legislative will. From it we can see with certainty that while a cemetery may not be established in a city or town, it may be added to or enlarged without running counter to the inhibition found in Section 56. We are not permitted to read into the statute an inhibition which the legislature, perhaps advisedly, omitted. Our duty is to construe the statute as written.

If construction of the statute were necessary and proper in this case, we would be forced to the same conclusion. Even if it be assumed that there is ambiguity in the language in section 56, the legislative history of its enactment and a consideration of Code, sec. 56, a related statute would remove all doubt as to what the legislature intended by its language in section 56.

Code, sec. 53, affords a complete answer to the question of legislative inent in the use of the word "established" in section 56, for the former section makes a distinction between "establish" and "enlarge" in these words: "If it be desired at any time to establish a cemetery, for the use of a city, town, county, or magisterial district, or to enlarge any such already established, and the title to land needed cannot be otherwise acquired, land sufficient for the purpose may be condemned ...".

The foregoing language, taken from section 53, completely demonstrates that the Legislature did not intend the words "establish" and "enlarge" to be used interchangeably, but that the use of one excluded any idea that it embraced or meant the other. As used, they are mutually exclusive. To enlarge or add to a cemetery is not to establish one within the meaning of section 56.

The language of the statute being so plain and unambiguous, and the intention and meaning of the Legislature so clear, we hold that the city of Petersburg has not violated Code, sec. 56, and the decree accordingly should be affirmed.

Affirmed.

Review Questions

1. Summarise the facts and issues of this case.
2. State the *ratio decidendi* of the case.
3. What rule of interpretation was used by the Court?
4. Write a legal opion in support of the Appellants.

5.4.10 The Attorney-General v Abdulla and Others (1960) E.A.C.A. 672.

MacDuff, J., read the following judgment of the court:

The respondents were charged as follows:

"Count 1 **Statement of Offence**

Besetting contrary to s. 91 of the Penal Code

Particulars of Offence

"Abdulla s/o Ibrahim, Maji s/o Nyawonga, Foyo s/o Mwavodo: on the 20th day of October, 1959, at Tudor Road, Mombasa, in the Coast Province, unlawfully beset the Tudor Road, Mobasa, with a view to preventing one Doney s/o Meheki from doing an act which the said Donye s/o Mechki was entitled to do, namely to ride a bicycle."

Section 91 B of the Penal Code provides as follows:

> "Any person who watches or besets any premises or the house or other place where any person resides or works or carries on business or happens to be, or the approaches to such premises, house or other place, with a view to preventing any person from doing, or compelling him to do, any act which person has a legal right to do or abstain from doing, is guilty of an offence and is liable to imprisonment for a term not exceeding six months or to a fine not exceeding five thousand shillings, or to both such imprisonment or fine."

The section then contains a provision which has no relevance to the present case.

The learned senior resident magistrate found the following facts to be admitted or provided:

"(1) Donye s/o Meheki is employed by M.M. Chadaria as Houseboy in the Old town, Mombasa.

(2) Donye lives in Tudor Estate, Mombasa.

(3) Donye goes to and from work by bicycle.

(4) On October 20 1959, Donye went to his employer's house in the morning but returned to his own house at about 9 a.m.

(5) Whilst returning from his house to his place of work Donye was stopped by three respondents in Tudor Road.

(6) The respondents asked Donye if he did not know that it was the 20th and that he should not cycle. The conversation continued about Jomo Kenyatta until the police arrived."

To support his decision the learned magistrate relied on certain authorities. The first of these is Stoud's Judicial Dictionary of which we have the 3rd edition. Under the title "place" there are numerous examples cited of the words "place" and "other place" being interpreted by the courts. We agree, however, that it is impossible to obtain from those examples any clear guidance as to the meaning to be given to the words "or other place" in an enactment not in pari material with one of the instances there quoted. The learned magistrate also refers to the title "other at para (6) (at p.2025 et. seq.), where he has apparently relied on the author's statement that;

> **"(6) "Where general words follow particular ones, the rule is to construe them as applicable to persons ejusdem generis" (per Tenterden, C.J. Sandiman v Breach, 7 B & C. 99). This rule has been 'acted upon in all times, but nowhere more clearly stated than by Lord Tenterden in Sandiman v Breach (per Denman, C.J. Kitchen v Shaw, 7 L.J.M.C. 16): and it is therefore sometimes called Lord Tenterden's Rule, which as regards the word 'other' may perhaps be more fully stated thus: where a statute, or other document,**

> **enumerates several classes of persons or thing, and immediately following and classed with such enumeration the clause embraces 'other' persons or things – the word 'other' will generally be read as "other such like", so that the persons or things therein comprised may be read as ejusdem generis with, and not of a quality superior to, or different from, those specifically enumerated. The principle of this rule as regards statutes was explained by Kenyon, C.J. in R. v Wallis, (5 T.R. 379), wherein he said that if the legislature had meant the general words to be applied without restriction it "would have used only one compendious word."**

This general statement is qualified in the same paragraph by the following statement:

> **"Yet, on the other hand, though 'it is very likely that in former days the doctrine was applied strictly, there are cases which show that the modern tendency is to reject a restricted construction' (Esher, M.R. Anderson v Anderson, (1895) 1 Q.B. 749), and very frequently the word receives its wide and larger interpretation of 'every other sort or thing'."**

And at para. (8), the author says:

> "(8) It is perhaps impossible to lay down any workable rule to determine which of these two interpretations the word should receive in any case not already covered by authority. Therefore, it would seem to be the most practically useful way to range, so far as possible, the cases into their two classes of interpretation.

A. Ejusdem generis

B. Unrestrictedly comprehensive."

He then goes on to give examples of both interpretations. In our view no assistance can be derived from this authority.

The learned magistrate next relied on Maxwell on the Interpretation of Statutes (7th Ed.), section V of Chapter XI at p.284 et seq. He does not refer to any passage in particular but it would appear from the generality with which he has treated this commentary as supporting the defence contention that he has taken it as an authority for the proposition that the words "or other place" must necessarily be construed under the ejusdem generis doctrine and to be restricted in application to the same genus as the words antecedent thereto. We do not think that the explanation given in Maxwell is properly capable of such an exlusive interpretation. We think the learned magistrate may have concentrated his attention on the following passage:

"But the general word which follows particular and specific words of the same nature as itself takes its meaning from them and is presumed to be restricted to the same genus as those words."

The sentence following, however, reads:

> "Of course the restricted meaning which primarily attaches to the general word in such circumstances is rejected when there are adequate grounds to show that it

> has not been used in the limited order of ideas to which its predecessors belong. If it can be seen from a wider inspection of the scope of the legislation that the general words, are nevertheless to be construed generally, effect must be given to the intention of the legislature as gathered from the larger survey."

It will be evident then that the question as to whether the words "or other place" are to be interpreted restrictively under the ejusdem generis doctrine or can be given a comprehensive interpretation falls to be considered in the light of the interpretation of legislation in pari material, if any, which has been the subject of judicial interpretation and in light of the intention of the legislature.

We were referred to the case of *Calley and others v Harrison* (2), (1956) 2 11 E.R. 254, where the words "house, room or other place" were used in s. 1 of the Sunder Observance Act, 1780, and Goddard, C.J., held that the meaning of the word "place" was not restricted by the words "house" or "room" which preceeded it and that part of a park used for a motor cycle competition was a "place" within the section. While we do not think that the decision is of sufficient authority to enable us to apply it in the present case since the evil aimed at was very different, it is at least illustrative of the application of the more comprehensive interpretation required to be given to those words to meet the intention of the legislature.

In *Charmock v Court* (3) (1899) 2 Ch. 35, however, this decision does not apply. This was a case which was decided on the meaning of s 7 of the Conspiracy and Protection of Property Act, 1875. The relevant parts of this section read:

"Penalty for intimidation or annoyance by violence or otherwise. Every person who with a view to compel any other person to abstain from doing or to do any act which such other person has a legal right to do or abstain from doing wrongfully and without legal authority: –

"4. Watches or besets the house or other place where such other person resides, or works, or carries on business, or happens to be, or the approach to such house or place. Shall on conviction thereof be liable..."

It was held that the words in the enactment covered a "landing-stage" and Stirling J., in his *ratio decidendi* stated:

> "The words 'place where he happens to be' seem to me to embrace any place where the workman is found, however casually."

We think it is clear that the wording of s. 91 B of the Penal Code was taken from the enactment under consideration in *Charmock's* case (3) and that in itself this decision constitutes strong persuasive reasoning for a like decision in the present case. Moreover, if we look, as we consider we must, to what we believe to have been the intention of the legislature in enacting s. 91 B. of the Penal Code, then we think this also provides a strong reason for not applying the ejusdem generis doctrine. Quite clearly the intention of the legislature in s. 91 B. of the Penal Code was to protect the unfettered liberty of the individual in going about his lawful occasions without let or hindrance and for that purpose to protect him in whatever "place he happened to be", We cannot conceive that the legislature could possibly have intended to protect the individual from being "beset" at his residence or workplace whilst leaving it open to wrongdoers to beset him on, for example, a public highway on his way to or from his home or workplace. We cannot see any reason to conclude that there was ever any intention, especially in view of the comprehensive nature of the words "happens to be", to restrict "other place" to a place of the genus of a "house".

The learned judge does not appear to have considered the meaning of the word "besetting", but in our view there was clear evidence of the complainant having been encircled by the respondents with the intent necessary to constitute the offence and that he was in fact "beset".

The answer to the question stated for our determination therefore is:

i. The learned trial magistrate was not correct in law in holding that the words "or other place" in sec. 91 B. of the Penal Code must be construed ejusdem generis with the words "any premises, or the house" in that section.

ii. The learned trial magistrate was not therefore correct in law in acquitting the respondents on the first count.

Notes and Review Questions

20th of October, was the day that Jomo Kenyatta, the first President of the Republic, who is also regarded as the founder of the nation, was arrested and detained by the colonial authorities in Kenya for subversion. This day has been officially recognised as the day that the Mau Mau and its leader Jomo Kenyatta launched the liberation struggle against colonialism that eventually led to the independence of Kenya.

1. What is the *ratio decidendi* of this case?
2. The principal issue of the case was the interpretation of the grey or penumbral areas of section 91 (B) of the Penal Code. This involved the choice or the application of two conflicting principles of interpretation of statutes. Both the Magistrates' Court and the Court of Appeal supported their choice of the relevant principle with authorities. Do you think that the judgment of the Court of Appeal was based purely on legal grounds or that it was motivated by extra-legal factors?
3. Is the concept of the inarticulate major premise of judges relevant in this case?
4. What theory of law, in your opinion, can be used to support the judgment?

5.4.11 S v Kola[263]

(APPELLATE DIVISION)

1966. *August* **19;** *September* **1. BEYERS, J.A., HOLMES, J.A., and TROLLIP, A.J.A.**

Criminal law. – Adoption of a disguise to conceal identity in contravention of sec. 1 of Law 2 of 1891 (T). – What constitutes. – Male deviate disguising himself as a woman. – Onus on State to prove that his intention was to conceal identity. – How discharged. – Statute. – Construction. – Use of preamble as an aid. -

Subject to section 2 of Law 1891 (T), any man who appears in a public road or place dressed as a woman in order to conceal his identity would contravene section 1 of the Law. The State must therefore prove that his intention was to conceal his identity and, in that regard, the effectiveness of the disguise would

[263] 1966 147 SA AD 322.

play an important part, for the more effective the disguise the easier the inference of that intention, and conversely. Thus where, having regard to the accused's disguise and its effectiveness, it is clear that the accused must have intended to conceal his sex and pass himself off as a woman, then, in the absence of any evidence from his explaining his conduct, it must further be presumed that he therefore intended to conceal his identity, for that would be a reasonable and probable consequence of concealing his sex. Moreover, even if it can be inferred that the only motive of the accused for disguising himself and concealing his sex was to satisfy some feminine instinct or urge, or perhaps to save himself from the embarrassment or inconvenience that his feminine characteristics, such as his voice, could cause him, the reasonable and probable consequence of that deliberate conduct, persisted in over an appreciable period with knowledge of its effect, was the concealment of his identity, which, in the absence of any evidence from him, must be presumed to have been his intention. His motive or reason must not be used to obscure or be confused with his legal intention.

Where a statutory provision is clear and unambiguous the preamble to the statute cannot be invoked as an aid to construing it.

Appeal by the Attorney-General from a decision in the Transvaal Provincial Division (VILJOEN, J., and DE VILLIERS J.), allowing an appeal from a conviction in a Magistrates' Court. The facts appear from the judgment of TROLLIP, A.J.A.

M. Imber, for the appellant: The provisions of sec. 1 of Law 2 of 1891 (T) admit of no doubt, are clear and unambiguous, and envisage an absolute prohibition against "the wearing or use of masks, false beards, or other means whereby disguises are effected". Assuming, however, for the purpose of argument, that the Court *a quo* was correct in its view that "...the section of the Act is by no means clear", then the intention of the Legislature must be gleaned from, *inter alia*, (*a*) the preamble of the law, which is couched in the past tense. See Steyn, *Die Uitleg van Wette*, 3rd ed. at pp.137-139 and (*b*) a comparison of the separate clauses or section of the Law. See *Die Uitleg van Wette*, *supra* at pp.130-132, and cf. the provisions of sec. 2 of Law 2 of 1891. In the result reading the Law as a whole, the Court *a quo* erred in holding that the section, under which the respondent was charged, placed an *onus* on the State to prove that the person who disguised himself did so with a view to either the one or the other of the matters referred to in the preamble.

H.C.J. Flemming, for the respondent: The respondent was charged not with effecting a disguise, but with the fact that he did "give out that he was a woman" by means of a disguise. That was not proven. The actual question must of necessity be, did the accused wear something whereby a disguise is effected. On the evidence, accused did not in any way conceal his identity. It was probably because of a preference due to physical and/or psychological difficulties. "Disguise" in its ordinary signification firstly means that the identity is concealed. Cf. *Concise Oxford Dictionary; s.v* "disguise", *Shorter Oxford English Dictionary; Funk & Wagnall*; van Dale, *Groot Woordeboek*; *Kritzinger, Labuschagne, Pienaar (1965), Verklarende Afrikaanse Woordeboek*; *Schoonees,* e.a.; Webster, *Third International Dictionary* (1961), p.649, *s.v* "disguise". Even if the said meaning is not the primary meaning of the word, it bears that meaning in the context as (*a*) the act is aimed at cases where identity would be concealed; (*b*) the word appears in the context of "middelen de vermommingen veroorzaken". In any event, the objection is against "perzonen" who are disguised and not against artificial means or clothes as such against the use of such means where it has the effect or is used with the intention of making the detection of the true formal sex more difficult. If either of the above meanings be correct, respondent's actions fell far short of a contravention. The point is perhaps well proven by the case of Dr. James Barry who always dressed and acted a male in Cape Town last century. If the truth is that he was a woman, there was nevertheless never any concealment of identity nor any disguise. The section clearly affects only artificial methods of creating disguise. The word "middelen" not only ordinarily implies such consciously applied outside agencies, but the enumerated items, viz. "mombakessen" and "valsche baarden", are of that class and in terms of the *eiusdem generis* principle, the "middelen" are confined to the same species. The respondent's hair, just as an own beard, could not be hit by the section in whatever fashion he wore it. As to the law, respondent will not rely on any moot point but on the ordinary principles of interpretation, viz. (1) in penal statutes a strict interpretation is to be used. See Steyn *Uitleg van Wette*, p.110; (2) the preamble is a permissible aid in interpretation. See Steyn *supra*, p.139; (3) words of general import used to encompass the field of specific enumerated instances are limited to further instances of the same type (*eiusdem generis*). See Steyn, *supra*, p.37; (4) the effect of the statute is limited to the underlying motive for the passing thereof. See *Steyn*, *supra*, pp.35, 31; (5) reference should be made to the circumstances which gave rise to the passing of the statute and the objects it sought to attain. See *Steyn*, *supra*, pp.22, 23. On statutes covering similar acts, the following decisions are known to respondent: *R v Ntokile Zulu*, 1947 (1) S.A. 241; *R. v Mapingwana Mkize*, 1940 (2) P.H. H. 107; *R. v Masikana*, 1950 (1) P.H. K. 43; *R. v Lesson*, 1906 E.D.C. 183. In any event, the imposition of the maximum sentence in this case was unwarranted.

Imber, **in reply.**

Cur. adv vult.

Postea **(September 1st)**

TROLLIP, A.J.A.: This appeal turns on the meaning of sec. 1 of Law 2 of 1891 of the Transvaal. The original statute was enacted in the Dutch language, but an English translation appears in the official, consolidated *Statute Law of the Transvaal*, compiled and edited by Jappe and van Pittius. That translation, in so far as it is relevant, reads as follows:

> "Whereas it has appeared that by the use of masks, false beards, or other disguises, fraud has more than once been committed by leading the public to believe that it has to deal with another person than is actually the case, and
>
> Whereas disguises are also made use of by fugitives, who thereby endeavour to escape prosecution:
>
> Be it hereby enacted and provided as follows:
>
> 1. The wearing or use of masks, false beards, or other means whereby disguises are effected, in public roads or other public places is forbidden.

2. Disguises at theatrical performances or other diversions, the holding of masked balls at places accessible to the public, shall not fall under this law. The masked or disguised persons may not, however, show themselves in the public roads unless in special cases such as processions and the like permission is granted by landdrost or any other official competent thereto in the district where such occurs.

3. Any contravention of this law shall be punished by a fine not exceeding £5, or in default of payment by imprisonment not exceeding fourteen days."

The accused, a 19-year-old Coloured male, was convicted by the magistrate of contravening sec. 1 or effecting a disguise by wearing female clothing on 26th May, 1965, in Bezuidenhoult Street, a public road, in Johannesburg. When he was arrested he was in the company of two other males, similarly dressed, he had make-up on his face, and he wore his hair long. The evidence of the district surgeon, adduced by the State, showed that, although his general physical configuration (e.g. his build and hips) and sexual organs were those of a male, the pitch and tone of his voice and the style of the hair on his head were feminine, that possibly he had a sexually inverted mind, which was congenital, and that he was in consequence a psychological misfit or deviate. The accused himself did not testify. In sentencing him to R10 or 14 days' imprisonment, the maximum laid down, the magistrate said that there was

> "no evidence on record that he was committing a crime or planning to commit a crime when he was arrested...he is perhaps a tragic case".

The Court *a quo* on appeal set aside his conviction and sentence. It held that, as the meaning of sec. 1 was not clear, the preamble could be invoked, which showed that the only disguises hit at by that section were those effected in order to defraud the public or to facilitate escaping from prosecution, and that the State had not proved that the accused had worn female clothing for either purposes. With the leave of that Court, the Attorney-General of the Transvaal has appealed to this Court. Because the precise meaning of sec. 105 of the Magistrates' Courts Act, 32 of 1944, under which this appeal is brought, is not quite clear, both counsel very properly conceded that the matter of law and the matter of issue mentioned in this section is whether or not the proved acts or conduct of the accused constituted a contravention of sec. 1 as correctly interpreted, and that it should not be confined to the correctness or otherwise of the Court *a quo*'s above view on its meaning.

Our first task is therefore to construe that section. It is clear that the lawgiver's fundamental concern was to prohibit persons from concealing their identity in public places. For example, in regard to masks and false beards, it could not have been the mere wearing or use of them that it was intended to prohibit; the intention must have been to prohibit their being worn or used on the face, which is what they are ordinarily designed for, in order to conceal identity. Similarly, "other means whereby disguises are effected" must also refer to other means effected in order to conceal identity. Moreover, the wording there used is wide enough and the context is such as to show that those "other means" are not, by being conjoined with "masks and false beards", to be confined to facial disguises; in conformity with the lawgiver's aforementioned object, they must include any disguise by which the personal appearance is changed in order to conceal the person's identity. That is confirmed too by the ordinary meaning of "disguise". As a verb it means

> "to change the guise, or dress and personal appearance, of (any one) so as to conceal identity; to conceal the identity of by dressing *as* some one or *in* a particular garb".

The *Oxford English Dictionary* says that that is now "the leading sense" of the word. As a noun it has the corresponding meaning of

> "altered fashion of dress and personal appearance intended to conceal the wearer's identity ... 'A dress contrived to conceal the person that wears it'; a garb assumed in order to deceive".

Some of the extracts that are given in that dictionary from English literature to illustrate those meanings are interesting and instructive in the present enquiry: of the verb – "The Shepherd's garb the woman shall disguise"; "She disguised him in woman's clothes"; and of the noun – "In 1648 (the Duke) was ... conveyed in a disguise or habit of a girl beyond sea".

Whether the English word, "disguise", or the Dutch word "vermommingen", is regarded, I have no doubt that it was used in the above sense in the Statute. The exception in sec. 2 relating to "disguises at theatrical performances or other diversions" indicates that. A disguise at such a performance or diversion often takes the form of a person dressing up as someone else or in a particular garb in order to conceal his identity, albeit for fun or entertainment, and, but for its exclusion by sec. 2, that would have been hit by sec. 1.

It is, therefore, clear that, subject to sec. 2, any man who appears in a public road or place dressed as a woman in order to conceal his identity would contravene sec. 1. The State must, of course, prove that his intention was to conceal his identity, in that regard, the effectiveness of the disguise would play an important part, for the more effective the disguise, the easier the inference of that intention, and conversely. The Court *a quo*, however, held that the State has to prove a different intention – one to defraud the public or to escape prosecution. It was that finding that really moved the Attorney-General to bring this appeal as, plainly, it drastically curtails the ambit of the statute. With respect I think that that finding was wrong. There is no hint in the wording of sec. 1 itself of such a qualification; and if it were to be so qualified, then the whole of sec. 2 would have been entirely unnecessary, for disguises at theatrical performances or other diversions are not usually effected in order to defraud the public or enable those disguised to escape prosecution. The Court *a quo* reached its conclusion, however, by invoking the preamble to the statute, but this was not one of those cases in which that is permissible. The general principle permitting such use was stated by INNES, C.J., in *Law Union and Rock Insurance Co. Ltd v Carmichael's Executor*, 1917 A.D. 593 at p.597, as follows:

> "A preamble has been described by an old English Judge as 'a key to open the minds of the makers of the Act and the mischiefs which they intended to redress'. But the key cannot be used if the meaning of the enacting clauses is clear and plain. In cases however where the wording is ambiguous, and in cases where the Court is satisfied that the Legislature must have intended to limit in some way the wide language used, then it is proper to have recourse to the preamble."

Here the wording of the enacted provisions of the statute is clear and unambiguous, and, because of sec. 2, there is every reason to believe that the lawgiver did not intend to limit the ambit of sec. 1. In my respectful view, therefore, the preamble could not be invoked as an aid in construing sec. 1.

I now turn to the facts. Mr *Flemming* contended in the course of an able argument for the accused that the State had failed to prove that he had effected the disguise to conceal his identity. It was proved that this youth of 19 years was psychologically aberrated, had a feminine voice, wore his hair in a feminine style, and was wearing female clothes and make-up when he was arrested. That combination of characteristics and conduct would ordinarily create effectively the impression that he was a woman and not a man. It is true that Detective Constable Bambridge, who arrested him, thought that he was a man, but his opinion is not decisive and there is other cogent evidence from which the effectiveness of his get-up can be inferred. Firstly, six months earlier, Detective Constable Heine saw him at Marshall Square, when presumably he was similarly dressed; the constable, probably because of the accused's voice and appearance, had his doubts about his sex, or he had him examined by the district surgeon to have it ascertained. Secondly, the magistrate, in his reasons for judgment, gave his impression thus:

> "On both occasions on which the appellant appeared in court he was dressed as, and had the appearance of, a woman."

Thirdly, his own attorney must have been impressed by his appearance because during the hearing he applied for a postponement "to have accused medically examined, he says that the sex of the accused is in dispute".

Ultimately, of course, it was proved and accepted by the defence that he was a male. For those impressions to have been created, the disguise must have been effective.

Having regard, therefore, to the accused's disguise and its effectiveness, it is clear that he must have intended to conceal his sex and pass himself off as a woman, and I think that, in the absence of any evidence from him explaining his conduct, it must further be presumed that he thereby intended to conceal his identity, for that would be a reasonable and probable consequence of concealing his sex. The failure of the accused to testify is of importance in that respect, because, as SCHREINER, J., observed in *R. v Mohr,* 1944 T.P.D. 105 at p.108, an observation that was approved of and applied in *R. v Deetlefs,* 1953 (1) S.A. 418 (A.D.) at p.422:

> "Where a question of the state of mind of an accused person is in issue, it is not easy for a Court to come to a conclusion favourable to the accused as to his state of mind unless he has himself given evidence on the subject"

It may be that, because of his psychological aberration, it can be inferred that his only motive or reason for distinguishing himself and concealing his sex was to satisfy some feminine instinct or urge, or perhaps to save himself from the embarrassment or inconvenience that his feminine characteristics, such as his voice, could cause him. But his motive or reason must not be used to obscure or be confused with his legal intention.

> "Intention is an operation of the will directing an overt act; motive is the feeling which prompts the operation of the will, the ulterior object of the person willing; e.g. if a person kills another, the intention directs the act which causes death, the motive is the object which the person had in view, e.g. the satisfaction of some desire, such as revenge"

(Halsbury, *Laws of England,* vol. 10, p.283, note (m)).

> "The consequences which a man contemplates or expects to result from his act are the consequences which he 'intends', but ... such consequences may not always be desired".

(*per* WATERMEYER, J.A. in *Rex v Peverett* 1940 A.D. 213 at p.219).

Thus, in *Rex v Kewelram*, 1922 A.D. 213, the accused's motive or reason in setting fire to his own goods store in the complainant's building was to defraud the insurer of the goods, but, as it was a reasonable and probable consequence of such a deliberate act that the building would also be burnt, it was inferred, in the absence of any rebutting evidence from the accused, that he must also have intended that consequence, which justified his conviction for arson, and in *Rex v Marshanga,* 1924 A.D. 11, the accused's motive or reason for cutting off the ears of his master's oxen was to vent his anger on them for having given him trouble, but, as the inevitable consequence of that deliberate act was to cause his master damage, it was inferred that he must have intended that consequence, so he was held rightly convicted of malicious damage to property. Similarly here, even if the accused had the above-mentioned motive or reason for concealing his sex, the reasonable and probable consequence of that deliberate conduct, persisted in over an appreciable period with knowledge of its effect, was the concealment of his identity, which, in the absence of any evidence from him, must be presumed to have been his intention.

I need only add in conclusion that that presumption is not rebutted by the accused's giving Detective Constable Bambridge his correct name when he was arrested. It was contended that that showed he harboured no intention of concealing his identity. But the constable asked him for his name after he had informed him he was a policeman; that he answered truthfully in those particular circumstances does not negative a general intention of concealing his identity from others in public places by his disguise.

In my view, therefore, the magistrate correctly found the accused guilty, the appeal must succeed and his conviction must be restored.

Mr Imber for the Attorney-General suggested that a sentence of a caution and discharge should be submitted for the sentence imposed by the magistrate, and without thereby implying any criticism of the magistrate, I agree that that should be done in the special circumstances of this case.

The appeal is upheld; the conviction of the accused of contravening sec. 1 of Law 2 of 1891 (T) is restored; but the sentence is altered to a caution and discharge.

BEYERS, J.A., and HOLMES, J.A., concurred.

Respondent's Attorneys: *Horwitz & Oosthuizen,* **Bloemfontein.**

16th May 2006

Review Questions

1. Discuss the facts and the issues of this case.
2. What is the *ratio decidendi* of the case?
3. Discuss the theory of law that may be used to justify the decision of the court and critically evaluate the decision of the court.

5.4.12 Port Elizabeth Municipality v Peoples Dialogue on Land and Shelter and Others

Southern Eastern Cape local division

Horn AJ

1999 October 28; November 17 **Case No 1808/99**

2000 (2) SA 1074 (SE)

Land – Unlawful occupation of – Eviction from – Prevention of Illegal Eviction from and Unlawful Occupation of Land Act 19 of 1998 – Two diametrically opposed fundamental interests in dealing with issue of eviction – On one hand traditional real right inherent in ownership reserving exclusive use and protection of property to landowner – On other hand genuine despair of people in dire need of adequate accommodation – Duty of Court in applying requirements of Act to balance opposing interests and bring out decision which was 'just and equitable' – Use of term 'just and equitable' relating to both interests, i.e, what is just and equitable not only to persons who occupied land illegally, but to landowner as well – Term also implying that court obliged to break away from purely legalistic approach and have regard to extraneous factors such as morality, fairness, social values, and implications and circumstances which would necessitate bringing out equitably principled judgment.

Land – Unlawful occupation of – Eviction from – Prevention of Illegal Eviction from and Unlawful Occupation of Land Act 19 of 1998 – Land owned by municipality unlawfully occupied – Municipality earmarking land for development for housing – Municipality bound to provide housing within recognised parameters – Such factors cannot be ignored when dealing with question of unlawful occupation – Section (1) of Act A specifically enjoining court to have regard to public interest when considering what is just and equitable – Public interest requiring legislative framework and general principles which govern process of housing development not to be undermined and frustrated by arbitrary and unlawful actions of small group of persons.

Land – Unlawful occupation of – Eviction from – South African Prevention of Illegal Eviction from and Unlawful Occupation of land Act 19 of 1998 – Manner in which occupiers obtained occupation of land is factor to be weighed against them.

Land – Unlawful occupation of – Eviction from – Prevention of Illegal Eviction from and Unlawful Occupation of Land Act 19 of 1998 – Act not specifying who has to supply information upon which court can make an informed decision as to whether alternative land available – Although applicant would be expected to make out case as to whether there is alternative land available, respondents should also deal with issue- Court having to decide whether there is sufficient information before it, irrespective whether information provided by applicant or respondents, that alternative accommodation existed.

The respondents had unlawfully occupied land owned by the applicant and earmarked by it for development for housing. The respondents had refused to vacate the land so that the applicant could proceed with its development. The applicant thereupon applied for their eviction from the land.

Held, that, in dealing with a matter such as the present one, one was dealing with two diametrically opposed fundamental interests. On the one hand there was the traditional real right inherent in ownership reserving exclusive use and protection of his property to the landowner. On the other hand there was the genuine despair of people in dire need of adequate accommodation. It was with regard to these two opposing interests that the Legislature had, by virtue of the provisions of the Prevention of Illegal Eviction from and Unlawful Occupation of Land Act 19 of 1998 (the Act), set about implementing a procedure which envisaged the orderly and controlled removal of informal settlements. It was the duty of the Court in applying the requirements of the Act to balance these opposing interests and bring out a decision which was 'just and equitable'. The use of the term 'just and equitable' related to both interests, that is what was just and equitable not only to the persons who had occupied the land illegally but to the landowner as well. The term also implied that a court, when having to decide a matter of this nature, would be obliged to break away from a purely legalistic approach and have regard to extraneous factors such as morality, fairness, social values and implications and circumstances which would necessitate bringing out an equitably principled judgment. (At 1081D-G.)

Held, further, that there were several requirements set out in various Acts of Parliament which bound the applicant to provide housing within recognised parameters. These were factors which simply could not be ignored when dealing with the situation which confronted applicant insofar as it concerned the respondents *in casu.* Section 6 (1) of the Act specifically enjoined the Court to have regard to the public interest when considering what was just and equitable in a particular case. The public interest required that the legislative framework and general principles which governed the process of housing development should not be undermined and frustrated by the arbitrary and unlawful actions of a relatively small group of persons. The well-structured housing policies of the applicant could not be allowed to be endangered by the unlawful intrusion of people at the expense of those inhabitants who may have had equal claims to be housed on the land earmarked for development by the applicant. The applicant had to organise and administer its affairs in accordance with the broader interests of all the inhabitants within its jurisdiction. In doing so the dictates of the public interest, including the safety, health and welfare of all the inhabitants, had to be uppermost in the applicant's order of responsibilities. There could have been no doubt that in principle the applicant had an inherent duty to enforce its housing policies in a fair and equitable manner. The failure by the applicants to have done so would have constituted a serious dereliction of its duty to act in the interests of the community to whom it was responsible. (At 1084E/F-H and 1085D-F/G.)

Held, further, that the manner in which the respondents had obtained occupation of the land was a factor which had to be weighed against them. It was clear from the papers before the Court that it had been a deliberate and premeditated act culminating in the unlawful invasion of a large tract of land. Notwithstanding negotiations with the applicant, the respondents had steadfastly refused to leave the land or make alternative arrangements. (At 1085H/I-I/J.)

Held, further, that the Act did not specify who had to supply the information upon which the Court could make an informed decision. Section 6 (3) of the Act seemed to imply that a removal could not take place unless there was alternative land available. However, in this regard it was not clear. One would have expected that in a matter such as the present the applicant would have made out a case as to whether there was alternative land available. However, the respondents should have also dealt with the availability or non-availability of land in their papers. What the Court had to do was to decide on the papers whether there was sufficient information before it, irrespective whether the information was provided by the applicant or the respondents, that the alternative accommodation existed. Without this information the Court was unable to satisfy itself that the requirement as to whether alternative land was available was met. Although the Court was hesitant to place an *onus* on either of the parties, they should both have dealt with this requirement in their papers. Accordingly, the Court was not in a position to ascertain whether there was alternative land available. (At 1086B/C-G.)

Held, further, that the application should not be dismissed out of hand merely because of the fact that the applicant had not dealt with the requirements as to whether there was alternative land available. Such a step would be detrimental to the applicant, the respondents, as well as the community in general, particularly those persons adversely affected by the unlawful occupation of the land by the further respondents. In any event, persons who purportedly did not have adequate accommodation could not simply move onto land unlawfully without any remedy being available to the owner of the land. The Act should not be interpreted in such a way which could give rise to the indirect expropriation of land by ignoring the rights of landowners. People could not be allowed to take the law into their own hands and, in principle, therefore, any unlawful occupation of land should be frowned upon. (At 1086G-1087N.)

Held, accordingly, that an order should be granted in favour of the applicant, but made subject to the availability of alternative land or accommodation as contemplated by s 6(3)(c) of the act. (At 1087D/E-E/F.)

Annotations:

Reported cases:

ABSA Bank Ltd v Amod 1999 (2) B All SA 423 (W): followed

Cape Killarney Property Investments (Pty) Ltd v Mahamba and Others 2000 (2) SA 67 (c): followed.

Statutes

The Prevention of Illegal Eviction from and Unlawful Occupation of Land Act 19 of 1998, s 6: see *Juta's Statutes of South Africa 1999 at 2-454.*

Application for eviction of persons unlawfully occupying land. The facts appear from the reasons for judgment.

R P van Rooyen SC (**with him** *G Goosen) for the applicants.*

A Beyleveld **for the respondents**.

Cur adv vult.

Postea (**November 17**).

Horn AJ: The applicant is the Port Elizabeth Municipality. The applicant launched these proceedings on an urgent basis; in which it claimed the eviction of the further respondents from the property described as Malabar Extension 6, Port Elizabeth. This is the return date of the rule *nisi*. It was common cause that the further respondents occupied the aforesaid property unlawfully.

The deponent to the founding affidavit of the applicant is John Graham Rischards, who is the town clerk of the applicant. By way of background he explained that Malabar Extension 6 was an open tract of land which bordered on the suburb known as Malabar. Malabar Extension 6 had a deeds office description with the name 'New Brighton' by reason of the fact that that portion of the land still formed part of a larger tract of land known as New Brighton. The surveying and opening of a township register was due to take place. The land was approximately 12 hectares in size and it consisted of mainly open veld, that is, it was undeveloped and the land was covered in bush and shrubbery. In view of the need for residential accommodation Malabar Extension 6 was earmarked some years ago by the applicant for development and it was envisaged that the land would be divided into approximately 300 erven which would be sold off to developers. The result would have been an area with a network of roads, services and approximately 300 houses.

When the applicant embarked on a project of this nature certain of the costs in relation to the development were incorporated into the selling price of the erven in order that these costs may be recovered from the purchasers. After conducting certain investigations it was determined that the costs of the project would result in the selling price of the various erven being beyond the means of that sector of the city's population who were identified as future occupants of Malabar Extension 6. This resulted in the project being put on hold in 1993. Since then the applicant had resolved to incorporate Malabar Extension 6 into the applicant's four-peg program. The four-peg program was a housing development program which was run on a predetermined format. This format took into account various factors, such as the nature of the land and the type of areas which were to be accommodated by certain members of the community. In view of the housing shortage in Port Elizabeth, the allocation of these sites and service erven was a matter which was handled with great circumspection. In order to ensure an orderly progression of the housing program and to avoid conflict as far as possible, a system had been devised in terms of which the erven were allocated in conjunction with the city councillors for each ward where there was a housing problem. The extent of the housing problem in each ward was identified and based on this information, each city councillor was allocated a specific number of erven where development was taking place within Port Elizabeth. The councillor, in consultation with the community in his ward, bearing in mind the guidelines concerning priorities, allocated the erven to individual families. The recipients of the erven were generally the poorest of the poor, with a maximum monthly *per capita* earning of R 1 500 but in many cases the recipients had little or no income. Initially a recipient would enter into an agreement with the applicant. At a later stage the recipient could purchase the property at a predetermined price and thereafter continue its development on his own. The ultimate aim of the program was to ensure that the recipient eventually became the owner of the erf which was developed by the recipient with the assistance of the applicant. The surveying, developing and servicing of the erven in the four-peg program for Malabar Extension 6 would be funded on a bridging finance basis by the applicant with funds obtained from the ratepayers of Port Elizabeth. Once a recipient received his housing subsidy, the applicant recovered the money expended by it in respect of the surveying, developing and servicing from the subsidy.

During February 1999 the applicant resolved to proceed with its four-peg program at the rate of 3000 erven per year, with Malabar Extension 6 being singled out for the development of approximately 680 erven. The aforementioned 3000 erven were situated in various areas of Port Elizabeth and it was envisaged that the program would be implemented in phases throughout the city. As servicing of the land included the construction of roadways, stormwater systems and water reticulation, it was not possible for the applicant to survey and service the land while it was occupied and for this reason it was necessary for the applicant to resolve the present situation which existed in Malabar Extension 6. In its papers the applicant stressed that it was aware of the need for accommodation in the suburb of Malabar and the surrounding areas and the applicant was furthermore aware of numerous families who lived in these areas under difficult conditions. This resulted in small groups of people erecting shacks on the land known as Malabar Extension 6 during the latter part of 1998. It was eventually agreed that 20 families could temporarily remain on the property. During April 1999 the applicant learned that many more families had moved onto the property and had erected shacks. Various discussions took place when the matter was discussed with the further respondents, who were represented during these discussions by the first and second respondents. However, an impasse had been reached and the upshot of all this was the litigation now before this Court, in which the applicant sought the removal of the further respondents from the land in question.

In order to come to grips with the problem which has arisen in this matter, regard should be had to the socio-economic and political changes which have occurred in recent years. The arrival on the South African scene of the informal settlement phenomenon brought with it significant social and economic implications which will no doubt have a profound effect on housing development in this country for many years to come. It will remain so at least until such time as the State and local authorities are able to provide accommodation for those of the inhabitants who were in desperate need of somewhere to stay. According to figures disclosed in the 1997 South African Yearbook it was estimated that, at that time, more than 8 million South Africans were living in informal settlements. Despite the provision of basic services and upgrading incentives, many of these communities lived in unhygienic conditions. Unlawful squatting has exacerbated the situation. Illegal squatting, which entails the wholesale invasion and taking over of unoccupied land, has added to the overall housing burden facing the State, exasperated farming communities and landowners, and has placed immense pressure on the country's resources. It is accepted that the urbanisation of vast numbers of black South Africans, particularly since the abolition of the structures placed on the free movement of blacks after the collapse of the apartheid government, was a major contributory factor to the burgeoning squatter problem. It is considered that by the year 2010 some 73% of the population will live in urban areas. Rapid urbanisation brings with it enormous social and economic problems. This trend is a fact of life which this country will have to come to terms with. It is a process which can only be reversed by the successful implementation of bold and enlightened building development schemes and housing projects. The 1992 issue of the Human Sciences Research Council's periodical In *Focus* vol 1 No 8, contains the following apt definition of the causes and effects of the squatting phenomenon:

> 'The squatters, shack dwellers, the informal settlers, have come to stay. They ironically convey an image of transitoriness, yet the very lifting of influx control measures implied a new acceptance of their permanence. Opening the gates is one thing; accommodating the incoming masses is another. When a flock of birds

is chased away from one place, they re-alight somewhere else. This is at the basis of the conflict that looms hugely and emotively over South African society; these people have nowhere to go.'

People squat because they have to, not because they want to. The squatters are this country's people of conscience. Whatever their status in society may be or might have been, they are people who had been caught up in the exuberance of a new political dispensation which brought about drastic changes and instilled in them an exaggerated sense of freedom and security. With the lifting of the racial restrictions as to where people could live and work, many of the unemployed in the former homelands migrated to the cities. They went in search of work, taking their families with them. The shortage of accommodation in the urban areas forced them to live in shack towns or squatter camps on open land. Their plight should be recognised and should be treated with awareness and understanding. Humane action is needed, not a sledge hammer. In the June 1997 issue of the *Local Government Digest* the following excerpt appears in an article dealing with the squatter problem.

'What must be remembered, when dealing with illegal squatting, is that we are dealing with people and their possessions. Whatever has to be done must be done in a humane manner. Resettling is extremely traumatic for the community involved. If not managed properly it could lead to serious problems, as many local authorities have experienced.'

(Quoting Eugene de Lange – consultant at Urbanisation Control Strategies.)

It may be fair to say that the acknowledgement of the reality of the squatter problem has understandably given rise to anxiety and frustration amongst landowners.

'The problem has evoked fierce reactions, mainly negative, from formal communities. Their property is threatened by devaluation as a result of illegal occupants living in unsightly shacks nearby. They are acutely aware of a security threat. Their sense of order is also endangered by what appears to be an imminent loss of control over standards should vast numbers of people arrive on a sight and set up their shacks without further ado.'

(In Focus supra)

It would seem therefore that we are dealing here with an almost inevitable social evil – one we cannot live without but one which needs to be controlled and regulated. The situation seems to cry out for efficient control and management systems, so that the resettling of these unfortunate people can take place on an organised, humane and fair basis. It is with this as background that one must look at the provisions of the Prevention of Illegal Eviction from and Unlawful Occupation of Land Act 19 of 1998 (hereinafter 'the Act').

'The Act is essentially socialistic. It is a piece of Welfare legislation formulated upon humanitarian lines. In the unreported decision of *Cape Killarney Property Investments (Pty) Ltd v Mahamba and Others** in the Cape of Good Hope Provincial Division, Hope DJP defined the purpose of the Act as follows:

'The Act is clearly intended to provide mechanisms for dealing equitably with a large number of people who have moved onto land without an owner's permission and established their homes thereon. All of this is clear from the introduction and preamble to the Act which can fairly be said to be a response by Parliament to one of the social phenomena of the post-apartheid era. In short, the object is clearly to bring about some form of control over informal settlements.'

(Compare *ABSA Bank Ltd v Amod* [1999] 2 B All SA 423 W) at 430d.) It is legislation which would in all probability not see the light of day in most democratic-capitalistic societies. At first glance the Act seems to encroach on the fundamental principles of ownership and to impinge upon the rights of owners of land to evict people who had moved onto their property illegally. However, what the Act does not do is to abolish the common-law right of an owner to the exclusive enjoyment of his property and the owner's inherent right to the legal protection of his property. The Act sets out to control in an orderly fashion those situations where it had become necessary to evict persons who had occupied land belonging to another unlawfully *(ABSA Bank Ltd v Amod supra at 4-8d).* The procedures prescribed by the Act which have to precede removals have made inroads into the rights of property owners to protect their property against unlawful occupation. The Act could very well give rise to serious abuse by homeless persons who deliberately invade an owner's land under the guise of the protection afforded by the Act. Once a group of people of the class referred to as homeless has identified a piece of land and decided to move onto the land, they would, in effect, set in motion a complex set of rules and, often, frustrating procedures which would have to be complied with by the landowner before he can evict them from his property. The provisions of the Act, particularly the negative implications they hold for rights of freehold in this country, are indeed worrisome. The deliberate invasion of an owner's land by people who would usually be those desperately in need of accommodation, could ultimately involve the landowner in a protracted legal battle which he could never have anticipated. One is dealing here with two diametrically opposed fundamental interests. On the one hand there is the traditional real right inherent in ownership reserving the exclusive use and protection of his property to the landowner. On the other hand there is the genuine despair of people in dire need of adequate accommodation. It is with regard to these two opposing interests that the Legislature had, by virtue of the provisions of the Act, set about implementing a procedure which envisages the orderly and controlled removal of informal settlements. It is the duty of the court in applying the requirements of the Act to, with the Wisdom of Solomon, balance these opposing interests and bring out a decision which is 'just and equitable.' The use of the term just and equitable relates to both interests, that is what is just and equitable not only to the persons who had occupied the land illegally, but to the landowner as well. The term also implies that a court, when having to decide a matter of this nature, would be obliged to break away from a purely legalistic approach and have regard to extraneous factors such as morality, fairness, social values and implications and any other circumstances which would necessitate bringing out an equitably principled judgment. The question arises whether the criticism levelled at the Act, that it reflects the unreasonable interference by the State with the rights of private ownership, is justified. State interference with land ownership rights is nothing new. The Roman-Dutch jurists recognised the principle that private ownership was subject to the overriding right of the State to expropriate land where the need arose. The overriding ownership concept was based on the notion that all land initially belonged to the State. Private ownership emanated from the State and the transfer thereof took place on the condition that the State could claim it back once the public interest and exigency demanded it. (De Groot *De Iure Belli ac Pacis* 1.1.10.4.)

'It should be here merely mentioned that the property of private persons is subject to the common good: so that the sovereign has power, for reasons of general necessity or the benefit of the citizens, to take away from persons the free control of the property... This right of the sovereign is called overriding ownership.' Huber *Heedendaegse Rechtsgeleertheyt* 2.8.27 (Gane's translation).

The inviolability of private ownership stems from the basic concepts of natural law which envisaged the universal acceptance of the doctrine of exclusivity, that is, that the right to the unhindered and exclusive possession and use of private property formed the cornerstone of a civilised society. However, as already pointed out, this inviolability of private property was always subject to the principle of the overriding ownership concept of the State. Viewed against the historical background of land occupation and land rights in this country, the Act, despite justified criticism levelled at it, definitely has a role to fulfil. The apartheid era saw the indiscriminate removal and resettlement of families and whole communities. People were relocated to areas where they had never been before and where development was completely stultified. They were far removed from schools, work places, transportation routes and cities. Until 1991 the land tenure system was based on race. A vast and intricate system of land and tenure control emerged which made drastic inroads on the common law and communal tenure rights. A person's rights of tenure or where he could own or occupy land were governed by legislation. (Compare the Group Areas Act 36 of 1966.) The rights of blacks to occupy and own land were stringently controlled by the Black Land Act 27 of 1913, the Development Trust and Land Act 18 of 1936, the Black (Urban Areas) Consolidation Act 25 of 1945 and the Black Communities Development Act 4 of 1984. (Silberberg and Schoeman *Law of Property* 3rd ed at 493.) These statutes brought endless misery and strife to the black population and virtually cast them as sojourners in their own country. Any form of illegal occupation or squatting on land was prohibited (cf the Prevention of Illegal Squatting Act 52 of 1951).

Historically, therefore, State control of land ownership and tenure rights was a fact of life in South Africa. One should, therefore, be slow to brand the Act as constituting unreasonable interference with the rights of ownership by the State. Indeed many of the morally repugnant laws which regulated land ownership rights, have been repealed to make way for a more acceptable laissez approach to the problems facing the State with regard to the provision of housing. There has been an awareness by government to come to grips with the realities of the situation. This gave rise to the introduction of the Abolition of Racially Based Land Measures Act 108 of 1991, the Upgrading of Land Tenure Rights Act 112 of 1991, and the Extension of Security of Tenure Act 62 of 1997. The Restitution of Land Rights Act 22 of 1994 was introduced in an endeavour to restore previous imbalances by means of a claims procedure in respect whereof the Land Claims Court has acquired judicial recognition. An equitable remedy was envisaged with the coming into operation of the Act. The plight of the homeless and the realisation that informal settlements were here to stay saw the introduction of legislation with a view to regulating in an orderly fashion the removal and resettlement of these people. The Act, therefore, must be seen as an attempt by the Legislature to come to terms with the right of property owners to enjoy their property to the exclusion of all others and the basic needs of shack dwellers and squatters who have, through circumstances beyond their control, been caught up in a type of nomadic existence.

Viewed in this light, the Act although essentially socialistic and although it does encroach on the rights of landowners, should be seen as a natural consequence of a more liberal and enlightened land reform policy. The preamble to the Act spells out what the Legislature sought to achieve. The Act seeks to protect the cardinal rights of inhabitants of so-called informal settlements to share in the Constitutional right to housing and accommodation. It does not want to see people evicted from their homes without the intervention of the court. This can only happen once certain prescribed requirements have been met by the landowner and all the relevant circumstances of the situation have been taken into account by the court. Central to this enquiry are the interests of the respective parties and the fusion of these interests. It is all good and well to say that the further respondents have an undeniable Constitutional right to adequate housing. The counter to this is that property owners also enjoy the protection of the Constitution *vis-à-vis* their ownership rights. In an attempt to find viable solutions, regard must be had to realities and practicalities. Preferably the Act should be seen as an instrument for the protection of human rights and the orderly removal of informal settlements. What must, however, be prevented is an abuse of that protection by the selfsame people whom the Act sets out to protect. A premeditated invasion of another's property is, by its very nature, counter-productive. Even more so where such unlawful occupation would have an undermining effect on housing development in urban areas. The applicant is in a singularly unenviable position. It is a democratically elected body representing the inhabitants of the city of Port Elizabeth. It carries with it, once so elected, the mark of approval of government and the electorate. The applicant is charged with a miscellany of duties and responsibilities so as to ensure, insofar as is possible, the enjoyment by its inhabitants of the amenities and privileges available to them within the city limits. To this end the applicant is empowered to raise taxes, to levy rates and to organise finances to create amenities, build roads and, most importantly, to provide housing. Its policies are discussed and formulated in committee and out of this arises a structured and organised pattern of services which includes the provision of housing. The applicant represents all the citizens of Port Elizabeth. It does not curry favour with individuals or communities. Its housing policy constitutes a considered and codified formula based on expertise and experience, taking into account the fundamental needs of all its citizens. The duty resting on the applicant to provide adequate housing is, however, limited by the means at its disposal. It would be futile to insist that the applicant provide housing when it has not the means to do so. Provision goes hand in hand with availability. If there is no land available the applicant's duty to provide housing is suspended until land becomes available. So, too, where land is available, the applicant's duty to provide adequate housing will only arise if it has sufficient funds available to finance housing projects, including the infrastructure which goes hand in hand with such projects, for example the provision of sewerage, water reticulation and electricity.

Extensive planning goes into housing projects. There is often an appreciable lapse of time from the time when the project is mooted to the time when it is eventually set in motion. The applicant has the responsibility to ensure that the provision of housing takes place in a methodical and fair manner. Time spans are frequently worked out for development of the different areas. Schemes are set in motion so as to provide housing to those people who most desperately require accommodation, hence the so-called four-peg program.

The provision of sub-economic housing is primarily the task of local authorities. In fact, both the Housing Act 107 of 1997 and the Development Facilitation Act 67 of 1995 define general principles which are applicable to housing development and which are binding on all tiers of government, including local authorities. These Acts instruct the State and local authorities to, in managing their respective housing policies, give priority to the needs of the poor, ensure housing development is based on integrated planning, uphold the practice of good governance, promote conditions in which everyone meets the obligations in respect of housing development, create socially and economically viable communities for the safe and healthy living environment of all inhabitants, and prevent slums and slum conditions. The authorities are bound to provide adequate housing on a progressive basis; they must set housing delivery goals, identify and designate land for housing development and ensure the prevention of conditions which could be conducive to health hazards and insecurity amongst city dwellers. There are many more requirements set out in these Acts which bind the applicant to provide housing within recognised parameters. These are factors which simply cannot be ignored when dealing with the situation which now confronts the applicant insofar as it concerns the further respondents in this matter. Section 6 (1) of the Act specifically enjoins the court to have regard to the public interest when considering what is just and equitable in a particular case. The public interest requires that the legislative framework and general principles which govern the process of housing development should not be undermined and frustrated by the arbitrary and unlawful actions of a relatively small group of persons. The well-structured housing policies of the applicant must not be allowed to be endangered by the unlawful intrusion of people at the expense of those inhabitants who may have equal claims to be housed on the land earmarked for development by the applicant. Such will be the case should a group of people be permitted to randomly move onto land destined for housing development.

It is common cause that the further respondents came from the so-called northern areas. They, on their own papers, had identified the land, that is Malabar Extension 6, and they thereafter deliberately occupied the land on which they erected shacks. Initially only 20 families occupied the property, but the number has since increased to over 300. The further respondents say that they occupied the land because they needed somewhere to stay. They previously lived in backyards and rooms. The land which they occupied had been lying dormant, notwithstanding the applicant's intimation that the land was earmarked for development. The further respondents say that they have nowhere else to go, whilst the applicant's attitude is that the further respondents should return to the places which they occupied prior to the unlawful occupation of the land.

Section 6 (1) of the Act reads as follows:

(1) 'An organ of State may institute proceedings for the eviction of an unlawful occupier from land which falls within its area of jurisdiction, except where the unlawful occupier is a mortgagor and the land in question is sold in a sale of execution pursuant to a mortgage, and a court may grant such an order if it is just and equitable to do so, after considering all the relevant circumstances, and if -

(a) the consent of that organ of State is required for the erection of a building or structure on that land or for the occupation of the land, and the unlawful occupier is occupying a building or structure on that land without such consent having been obtained; or

(b) it is in the public interest to grant such an order.

(2) For the purpose of this section "public interest" includes the interests of the health and safety of those occupying the land and the public in general.'

The Act lays down prescribed procedures and criteria which must be followed before squatters may be evicted from the land which they are occupying unlawfully. No evictions can take place without a court order. The Act, while recognising the plight of squatters in these circumstances, appreciates the dilemma in which a local authority or organ of State may find itself should the unlawful invasion of land by homeless persons be left unchecked. The applicant must organise and administer its affairs in accordance with the broader interests of all the inhabitants of Port Elizabeth. In doing so the dictates of the public interest, including the safety, health and welfare of all the inhabitants must be uppermost in the applicant's order of responsibilities. There can be no doubt that in principle the applicant has an inherent duty to enforce its housing policies in a fair and equitable manner. Indeed, failure by the applicant to do so would constitute a serious dereliction of its duty to act in the interest of the community to whom it is responsible. The factors which the Court must take into account when considering the eviction of people in these circumstances are contained in s 6 (3) which reads as follows:

(3) 'In deciding whether it is just and equitable to grant an order for eviction, the court must have regard to-

(a) the circumstances under which the unlawful occupier occupied the land and erected a building or structure;

(b) the period the unlawful occupier and his or her family have resided on the land in question; and

(c) the availability to the unlawful occupier of suitable alternative accommodation or land.'

The manner in which the further respondents had obtained occupation of the land is a factor which must weigh against them. It is clear from the papers that it was a deliberate and premeditated act culminating in the unlawful invasion of a large tract of land. It is furthermore evident that notwithstanding negotiations with the applicant the further respondents steadfastly refused to leave the land or make alternative arrangements. Insofar as it concerns the requirement that the Court must have regard to the period which the unlawful occupiers and their families have resided on the land in question, very little appears in the papers from which this information can be gleaned. The lists supplied by the respondents and attached to their opposing affidavit do not assist. The lists simply reveal that certain families had moved onto the land. The lists do not supply any particularity as to when this had occurred, which families arrive when, the ages of the people involved, and so on. It is impossible, on the available information, to establish what time periods are applicable. In so far as the Court must have regard to the availability of suitable alternative accommodation of land this requirement is likewise problematic. The Act does not specify who must supply the information upon which the Court can make an informed decision. The section seems to imply that a removal cannot take place unless there is alternative land available. However, in this regard the Act is not clear. The fact remains that I have no information before me dealing with the availability of alternative land. One would have expected that in a matter such as this the applicant, being the one bringing the application for eviction, should have made out a case as to whether there was alternative land available. However, in my view, the further respondents should also have dealt with the availability or non-availability of land in their papers. For example, the further respondents have not given any acceptable reasons for moving onto the land. There is no suggestion that they were compelled to move. What the Court has to do is to decide on the papers whether there is sufficient information before it, irrespective whether the information is provided by the applicant or the further respondents, that alternative accommodation exists. Without this information the Court would be unable to satisfy itself that the requirement whether alternative land or accommodation is available as contemplated by s 6 (3) (c) of the Act had been met. I would hesitate to go so far as to say that any of the parties bear an *onus* in this respect. I do believe, however, that it was incumbent upon the applicant and the further respondents to at least deal with this requirement in their papers. The applicant simply takes the view that the further respondent should return to where they came from, while the further respondents say that they have nowhere to go. I am, therefore, not in a position to ascertain, on the papers, whether in fact there is alternative land available.

I do not believe that the application, by reason of the fact that it does not deal with the requirement that there should be information placed before the Court regarding the provision of alternative land, should in this particular instance be dismissed out of hand. Such a step would be detrimental to both the applicant, the further respondents, as well as the Port Elizabeth community in general, particularly those persons who are being adversely affected by the unlawful occupation of the land by the further respondents. In any event I balk at the idea that persons who purportedly do not have adequate accommodation could simply move onto land unlawfully without any remedy being available to the owner of the land. This is particularly so where the applicant, a local authority, has the responsibility and duty to manage its housing policy in the interests of the community. It would wreak havoc with pre-determined procedures. It would wreak havoc with ownership and possessionary rights. Housing policies might as well be scrapped and any endeavour to create orderly housing standards would be futile. I do not believe that the Act should be interpreted in a way which could give rise to the indirect expropriation of land by ignoring the rights of landowners. The Constitution of South Africa Act 108 of 1996 provides that no one may arbitrarily be deprived of his property, certainly not without compensation. People must not be allowed to take the law into their own hands and, in principle; therefore, any unlawful occupation of land should be frowned upon. Obviously each case will have to be decided on its own facts, but eventually it would be up to the Courts to find a fine balance between the rights and the needs of the respective parties. The problem of illegal squatting arises because of the massive backlog which exists with regard to the provision of housing by the authorities. This is a problem which will no doubt remain for many years to come. Hopefully, once the housing shortage has been overcome, incidents of unlawful invasion of property by desperate communities in search of accommodation will disappear. In the interim the courts will, when considering applications of this nature, have to do the best they can and apply criteria which are just and equitable and acceptable to all concerned. What remains essential is that removals must be done in a fair and orderly manner and preferably with a specific plan of resettlement in mind.

The order which I propose making is one which I believe would be just and equitable and serve the interests of the applicant and the respondents. It will entail the granting of the order more or less in the form proposed by the applicant. I intend making the order subject to the availability of alternative land or accommodation as contemplated by s 6(3)(c) of the Act. Insofar as it concerns the costs, I am of the view that there is no reason to deviate from the general principle that the successful party should be entitled to his costs. The applicant has been substantially successful and is therefore entitled to his costs. Moreover, I am satisfied that the first and second respondents were parties to the litigation and they were correctly joined in the application. They should, therefore, be jointly liable together with the further respondents for the costs. The order which I make is the following:

1. The further respondents are hereby evicted from the property of the applicant, being the land known as Malabar Extension 6.
2. The order in terms of para 1 above is suspended pending the availability of suitable land or accommodation for the resettlement of the further respondents.
3. In terms of para 1, and subject to para 2 above, the further respondents are required to vacate the property known as Malabar Extension 6, failing which the Sheriff of this Court:
   (a) shall, in terms of s 4(10) and (11) of Act 19 of 1998, carry out the eviction order in para 1 above; and
   (b) shall, insofar as may be necessary, demolish and/or remove any buildings or structures erected and/or occupied by the further respondents upon the land known as Malabar Extension 6; and
   (c) shall be entitled to obtain the assistance of the South African police services in giving effect to this order.
4. The respondents shall pay the costs of the application jointly and severally, the one paying the other to be absolved, which costs shall include the costs of the two counsel.

Applicant's Attorneys: *McWilliams & Elliot Inc.* **Respondents' Attorneys:** *Pagdens Inc.*

Note

See also the decision of the appellate court of the Eastern Cape Division in Port Elizabeth Municipality v Peoples Dialogue on Land Shelter and Others 2001 (4) SA 759.

Review Questions

1. Discuss the facts and issues of the case.
2. What is the *ratio decidendi* of the case?
3. What theories of law may be used to justify the decision of the Court?
4. Discuss the extent to which this case helps you to understand the concept of public interest and its relevance in the judicial process.

CHAPTER 6

JUDICIAL PRECEDENT: LAW-MAKING THROUGH THE CASES

6.1 Introduction

6.1.1 Judicial law-making

As mentioned in Chapter 2, Namibia as a result of its judicial and legislative connections with South Africa, belongs to the common law tradition. We have also seen that Roman-Dutch common law became the common law of South West Africa/ Namibia by virtue of Proclamation 11 of 1921 and by adopting the common law tradition, Namibia has incorporated the doctrine of judicial precedent as part and parcel of its judicial system[264].

Article 44 of the Namibian Constitution vests legislative power in the National Assembly with the power to pass laws with the assent of the President subject to the powers and functions of the National Assembly. It is therefore quite clear that legislative functions in Namibia are meant to be the exclusive jurisdiction and preserve of Parliament. The functions and powers of the courts are in general the interpretation and application of the existing rules of law. This is the natural consequence of the application of the doctrine of separation of powers and the Judiciary accordingly does recognise the legislative functions of Parliament. As stated by Wessels J, in the case of *Seluka v Suskin & Salkow,* the function of the courts is "*ius dicere non dare*"[265] i.e. the function of the courts is to declare the law and not to make the law. In the eighteenth century Blackstone said "the decisions of courts of justice are the evidence of what is common law"[266] and as late as 1892 Lord Esher said in the case of *Willis v Baddeley*[267]:

> **'There is in fact no such thing as judge-made law, for the judges do not make the law though they frequently have to apply existing law to circumstances as to which it has not previously been authoritatively laid down that such law is applicable'.**

Therefore according to this view, there is little creativity to the judicial role: the judge merely has to look to the opinions of his predecessors for principles from which to deduce the proper rule for the case at hand. These views were re-echoed by the late

---

264 See also Article 66 of the Namibian Constitution.

265 *Seluka v Suskin & Salkow* 1912 TPD 285 at 270.

266 *Commentaries* (13th ed.) vol. I, p.88-89.

267 *Willis v Baddeley* (1892) 2 Q.B. 324 at p.2312.

Lord Jowitt, Lord Chancellor from 1945 to 1951 in his address at the Australian Law Convention of 1951 as follows:

> **It is quite possible that the law has produced a result which does not accord with the requirements of to-day. If so, put it right by legislation, but do not expect every lawyer, in addition to all other problems, to act as Lord Mansfield did, and decide what the law ought to be. He is better employed if he puts himself to the much simpler task of deciding what the law is ... please do not get yourself into the frame of mind of entrusting to the judges the working out of a whole new set of principles which does accord with the requirements of modern conditions. Leave that to the Legislature, and leave us to confine ourselves to trying to find out what the law is[268].**

This view has received the support of such eminent judges as Lords Porter, Simonds, Evershed and Asquith. In support of this view they point out that for example, the effect of overruling a precedent is that the decision overruled has never been law. In other words the effect of overruling is retrospective. The exponents of the declaratory theory maintain that even in cases of first impression a judge is at most a judicial Christopher Columbus discovering what was already existent, though previously unknown. As Judge Jerome Frank put it:

> **Judges are simply 'living oracles' of law. They are merely 'the speaking law'. Their function is purely passive. They are 'but the mouth which pronounces the law'. They no more make or invent new law than Columbus made or invented America.[269]**

However, in jurisdictions where case law is a source of law, the doctrine of judicial precedents is invariably, a *sine qua non* of the judicial methodology and system. Therefore, it can be seen that the view expressed above in its strictest sense or complete form, does not accord with reality. The doctrine of judicial precedent becomes an integral part of the judicial process and the legal system and therefore cracks are created into the pedestal foundations of the 'Blackstonian theory' or the Declaratory theory embedded in the doctrine of legislative sovereignty of Parliament by the recognition of the law-creating functions of judges, or judicial activism, in the legal system. The Declaratory Theory is based on a general principle but the realities of the methodology employed by the courts operating in the common law tradition allow for the exercise of the residual law-making powers of the courts as part of their inherent jurisdiction. Among the English Judges, Lord Denning stood out almost alone on the side of judicial law-making, and he stated his position in the following words in the context of interpretation of statutes and the doctrine of *stare decisis*:

> **The law is what the judges say it is. If the House of Lords were to give an Act of Parliament a meaning which no one else thought it could reasonably bear, it is their construction of the words used in preference to the words themselves that would become the law[270].**

[268] Friedman, W. 1967. *Legal Theory*. London: Stevens & Sons.

[269] Jerome, F. 1930. *Law and the Modern Mind*. New Torte Brentano's.

[270] Delvin, P. 1962. *Samples of Law-making*. London: Oxford University Press.

He, however, received judicial support from judges in America. In addition, the great weight of modern jurisprudential opinion from Bentham to Dias has rejected the strict Declaratory Theory. Bentham, for example writes:

> **With equal propriety again would the word law according to the definition be applicable to any *judicial* order, to any order which in the course of a cause of any kind of man might have occasion to issue in the capacity of a judge. Yet the business of a judicature is constantly looked upon as essentially distinct from the business of legislation and as constantly opposed to it: and the case is the same between the judicial and the legislative power. Even suppose the order to have been ever so general, suppose the persons to whom it is addressed to be ever so numerous and indeterminate, and the duration of it ever so indefinite, still if issued in the course of a forensic contestation, the act of issuing it would not be looked upon in general as coming under the notion of an act of legislation, or as an exercise of legislative power. The fate of a province may be determined by a judicial decree: but the pronouncing of the decree will not on that account be looked upon as being capable with any sort of propriety of being termed an act of legislation...**[271]

Dias describes judicial creativity in this way, "judges do administer laws as they find them, but there is a greater measure of discretion in the process than is popularly supposed."[272] He states elsewhere that "notwithstanding the fact that judges acknowledge the supremacy of the Crown in Parliament, what becomes "law" is their interpretation of statute through the operation of *stare decisis.* As Lord Devlin has put it:

> **The law is what the judges say it is. If the House of Lords were to give an Act of Parliament a meaning which no one else thought it could reasonably bear, it is their construction of the words used in preference to the words themselves that would become the law.**

In this way the judicial doctrine of *stare decisis* comes to be as it were, superimposed upon the doctrine of the supremacy of the Crown in Parliament."[273]

John Austin dismisses the Declaratory Theory as "the childish fiction employed by our judges that Judiciary or common law is not made by them, but is a miraculous something, made by nobody existing, I suppose, from eternity, and merely declared from time to time by judges".[274]

First and foremost among the reasons for judicial activism or creativity is perhaps the very nature of the doctrines of judicial precedent and *stare decisis.* The doctrine of judicial precedent is based on the principle that a previous judicial decision can be used as a guide or a binding rule of law for similar cases to be heard in future. The doctrine therefore simply means that a rule of law in a judicial decision becomes a rule of law for the future. This basic principle of judicial precedent is reflected in

[271] Bentham, J. 1970. *Of Laws in General.* London: Athlone Press.

[272] Dias, R.W.M. 1970. *op.cit.*

[273] *Op.cit.*

[274] *Jurisprudence* 5th ed. vol. II.

the Latin maxim, *stare decisis et non quieta movere,* which means to stand by the decisions, and not to disturb settled points. By the application of this principle judges consider themselves bound on a point of law in a previous judicial decision. This position logically confirms the inherent law-making powers of the Judiciary and the elements of legal growth; there can be no escaping this fact.

There is ample evidence that some branches of English law, as in the law of equity, the doctrine of consideration in the law of contract, are almost entirely, the product of case law. The position in the South African legal system has been stated by Hosten as follows:

> **Few judges in South Africa will deny that the judge – if not sitting in a court of first instance, then certainly sitting at full bench level in a provisional division and most definitely in the appellate division - does create law"[275].**

The exercise of the inherent law-making powers by judges can also be found where judges are confronted with cases of first impression. Cases of first impression involve a situation where, although there is ample evidence that the complainant's right has been violated by the conduct of another person, there is no existing standing rule regulating such conduct. This means that the existing law did not anticipate the possibilities of the occurrence or, otherwise, of such conduct. In principle, the law should anticipate the conducts which are capable or possible of happening or occurring but in practice, not every conduct is covered by the provisions of the law. If a court is confronted with such a situation, it will have to formulate a new principle of law to deal with the issues raised. Courts normally do this in accordance with well established principles of justice. As stated by Judge Tanaka:

> **We cannot deny the possibility of some degree of creative element in ... judicial activities. What is not permitted to judges, is to establish law independently of any existing legal system, institution or norm**[276].

Judicial creativity is incidental to the judge's main duty of dispute settlement. As was stated in the case of *Fellner v Minister of Interior* 1954 (4) SA 531, "In so far as the law is built up by judicial precedent, it is built up not deliberately in order to create a body of law, but as a result of the discharge by the Court of its function of settling the dispute between the parties".

In the context of interpretation of constitutions and legislative enactments and especially in cases involving interpretation of the penumbral areas of the law, a court's departure from the application of the literal rule of interpretation implies the creation of a new rule of law which, by virtue of the principle of *stare decisis,* becomes a precedent. Judicial decisions in this respect become sources of law. Judicial decisions in this context are quite often influenced by policy considerations and the inarticulate premise of a particular judge, dictated by predominant variables.

The above does indicate therefore that today the Blackstonian theory does not accord with reality and that judges do in fact exercise law-making functions.

[275] Hosten, W.J.; Edwards, A.B.; Bosman, F. & Church, J. 1997. *op.cit.*

[276] In the case of *South West Africa; Ethiopia v South Africa: Liberia v South Africa.* ICJ Reports.1966, p.6 at 277.

6.2 The doctrine of *stare decisis* and its application

As stated earlier, the doctrine of *stare decisis* is embodied in the doctrine of judicial precedent. This principle demands that like cases must be decided alike. As stated by Rupert Cross, "The rule of *stare decisis* causes the judges to reason by analogy because the principle that like cases must be decided alike involves the analogical extension of the decision in an earlier case"[277]. From the nature of the dynamics and the processes involved in judicial law-making, one may conclude that the method of inquiry employed by the Courts in arriving at a decision or a precedent is a combination of the deductive and inductive methods[278].

The doctrines of *stare decisis* and binding precedents operate within a hierarchy of courts whereby the decisions of the superior courts bind the inferior courts. The inferior courts do not have the jurisdiction, express or inherent, to lay down principles of law. As a general principle the decisions of the Supreme Court are binding on all other courts including the High Court. Until 1966, for example, the House of Lords, at the head of the English judicial hierarchy held itself bound by its own decisions. The position has, however, changed. The House of Lords refused to follow an earlier decision of its own in 1974[279]. The Supreme Court is not bound to follow its own decisions, but it generally does until it has good reasons to depart from its own decisions. The position is the same in Namibia. Article 81 of the Namibian Constitution stipulates that a decision of the Supreme Court is binding on all other Courts in Namibia and all persons in Namibia unless it is reversed by the Supreme Court itself or is contradicted by an Act of Parliament lawfully enacted.

With regard to the binding status of the decisions of the High Court, there are different situations to be considered. The decisions of the High Court are binding on all inferior courts but whether the High Court will regard itself bound by its decisions will depend on the ranking of the court and the number of judges that constitute the court. As a general principle, the High Court regards itself bound by the decisions of a 'superior court' but not by the decision of a 'lower court'. Decisions of inferior courts do not bind any other court. Decisions of superior courts from other jurisdictions are persuasive but not binding.

Other factors that courts take into consideration in determining the binding effect of a decision of a court include: the standing of the court in the judicial hierarchy, whether the court is a court of first instance or an appeal court; the eminence of the judge or judges who decided the case; whether there were dissenting judgments; whether any inconsistent cases were cited in argument.

---

[277] Cross, R. 1977. *op.cit.*

[278] The deductive method involves the process whereby conclusions are made from a basic legal position. The inductive method involves the process whereby conclusions are made after observation and consideration of legal principles.

[279] *Johanna Oldendorf* (1974) A.C. 479 overruling *The Aello* (1961) A.C. 135 on the test for determining when a ship becomes an "arrived ship".

6.3 The binding part of a case/the *ratio decidendi*

6.3.1 The *ratio decidendi*

It is not all of the decision of the court that is binding; it is the *ratio decidendi* that is binding. The *ratio decidendi* has been defined as 'the material facts of the case plus the decision thereon'[280]. As Glanville Williams puts it:

> **English Courts make a habit of following their previous decisions within more or less well-defined limits. This is called the doctrine of precedent. The part of a case that is said to possess authority is the *ratio decidendi*, that is to say, the rule of law upon which the decision is founded. Finding the *ratio decidendi* of a case is an important part of the training of a lawyer. It is not a mechanical process but is an art that one gradually acquires through practice and study. One can, however, give a general description of the technique involved.**
>
> **What the doctrine of precedent declares is that cases must be decided the same way when their material facts are the same. Obviously, it does not require that *all* the facts should be the same. We know that in the flux of life all the facts of a case will never recur; but the legally material facts may recur and it is with these that the doctrine is concerned[281].**

In order to understand the nature of the *ratio decidendi* it is important to understand the general structure of a judicial decision. A case when viewed as a decision will usually contain:

(a) the findings of fact – the facts which constitute or gave rise to the case.

(b) the order which the court makes i.e. the final pronouncement that, for example, the accused is guilty; or that the defendant must pay a sum of money or deliver a certain property. This is also referred to as the judgment or decree. For the parties to the dispute, it is this element in the decision that concerns them most because it determines their rights and liabilities in relation to the subject matter in dispute.

(c) the statements or the legal principle – these are the statements which set out the legal grounds for the order made by the court or the particular judge, also referred to as the *ratio decidendi* or the underlying principle or rule of law on which the decision of the case depends.

6.3.2 The *obiter dictum*

In a single decision there may be several statements of law but it is not all statements of law which a judge makes in the course of a decision that constitute the *ratio decidendi*. Only those statements of law which form part of the rule based on the material facts of the case and upon which the decision is based form the *ratio decidendi*. All other statements or rule of law are *obiter dicta* or *obiter dictum*

[280] Goodhart, A.L. 1931. "Determining the *Ratio Decidendi* of a Case." In Essays in *Jurisprudence and the Common Law*. New York: McMillan Co.

[281] Williams, G. 1982. *Learning the Law*. London: Stevens & Sons.

(singular). An *obiter dictum* may simply be defined as a statement contained in a judgment which is not necessary to the decision of the case and which is based on hypothetical facts. As a general rule, an *obiter dictum* is not binding but it may be accorded great weight and respect and consequently adopted as a binding principle of law in a future case depending on the status and eminence of the author. The reasons why *obiter dicta* are not binding are that they are either based on hypothetical facts or that the point may not have been properly argued, or not argued at all, and that their full implications may not have been considered.

6.3.3 Ascertainment of the *ratio decidendi*

As stated earlier, judicial precedents constitute a source of law in jurisdictions that follow the common law tradition. Therefore, when a judge is confronted with a case, one of the sources of law he or she can refer to for the relevant principle of law or the rule is the common law or a judicial precedent. With regard to the ascertainment of the *ratio decidendi* there are two aspects that need mentioning: extraction and application of the *ratio decidendi.*

6.3.3.1 Extraction

Theories have been propounded on how a principle of law or the *ratio decidendi* may be extracted from a case where one exists and also how the court creates one where none exists. None of these theories supplies a simple way of performing the task or supplies a rule of thumb. A lot of skill and experience is the answer.

However, one of the most canvassed theories is that by Professor Goodhart. He proposed that a *ratio decidendi* is formulated or extracted by reference not to all the facts but to the material facts of the case and the decision thereon. The material facts are the facts that the judge who heard the precedent case decided or regarded as material.

According to Dr Goodhart "the *ratio decidendi* of a case is determined by ascertaining the facts treated as material by the judge. It is the principle to be derived from the judge's decision on the basis of those facts. Any court bound by the case must come to a similar conclusion unless there is a further fact in the case before it which it is prepared to treat as material, or unless some other fact treated as material in the previous case is absent"[282].

The material facts according to Dr Goodhart are those facts treated by the judge as material and on which his decision is based. It is by his choice of the material facts that the judge creates law. If a court finds in a case before it a further fact that it decides to treat as material then the court will not find the previous decision binding because the two cases are distinguishable. Dr Goodhart's formula for extracting the *ratio decidendi* can be illustrated with two cases, the English case *Donoghue v Stevenson* (1932) A.C. 562; 147 L.T. 281 and the Zambian case *Chilufya v City Council of Kitwe* (1967) Zambia Law Reports p.115.

***Donoghue v Stevenson* (1932) A.C. 562; 147 L.T. 281**

[282] Cross, R. 1977. *op.cit.*

1. **Statement of the Facts**

By an action brought in the Court of Session the appellant sought to recover damages from the respondent, who was a manufacturer of aerated waters, for injuries she suffered as a result of consuming part of the contents of a bottle of ginger-beer which had been manufactured by the respondent, and which contained the decomposed remains of a snail. The appellant by her condescendence averred that the bottle of ginger-beer was purchased for the appellant by a friend in a café at Paisley, which was occupied by one Minchella; that the bottle was made of dark opaque glass and that the appellant had no reason to suspect that it contained anything but pure ginger-beer; that the said Minchella poured some of the ginger-beer out into a tumbler, and that the appellant drank some of the contents of the tumbler; that her friend was then proceeding to pour the remainder of the contents of the bottle into the tumbler when a snail which was in a state of decomposition, floated out of the bottle; that as a result of the nauseating sight of the snail in such circumstances, and in consequence of the impurities in the ginger-beer which she had already consumed, the appellant suffered from shock and severe gastro-enteritis. The appellant further averred that the ginger-beer was manufactured by the respondent to be sold as a drink to the public (including the appellant); that it was bottled by the respondent and labelled by him with a label bearing his name; and that the bottles were thereafter sealed with a metal cap by the respondent. She further averred that it was the duty of the respondent to provide a system of working his business which would not allow snails to get into his ginger-beer bottles, and that it was also his duty to provide an efficient system of inspection of the bottles before the ginger-beer was filled into them, and that he had failed in both these duties and had so caused the accident.

The Lord Ordinary rejected the respondent's plea-in-law that the appellant's averments were irrelevant and insufficient to support the conclusions of the summons and allowed a proof.

The Second Division, by a majority, recalled the interlocutor of the Lord Ordinary and dismissed the action.

The House of Lords, by a majority, allowed the Appeal, i.e. the House held that there was a valid cause of action.

2. **Material Facts and Levels of Abstraction (or generality)**

"A manufacturer of products which he sells in such a form as to show that he intends them to reach the ultimate consumer in the form in which they left him with no reasonable possibility of intermediate examination, and with the knowledge that the absence of reasonable care in the preparation or putting up of the products will result in an injury to the consumer's life or property owes a duty to the consumer to take reasonable care."

(a) a negligent manufacturer of ginger-beer is liable for <u>internal physical damage</u> to the ultimate consumer where there is no likelihood of an intermediate inspection.

(b) A negligent manufacturer of <u>bottled beverages</u> is liable for <u>physical damage</u>

to the ultimate consumer where there is no likelihood of an intermediate inspection.

(c) A negligent manufacturer of products is liable for any damage to the ultimate consumer where there is no likelihood of an intermediate inspection.

(d) Anyone who negligently damages another whom he ought reasonably to have contemplated as likely to be affected, is liable.

***Chilufya v City Council Of Kitwe* (1967) Zambia Law Reports 115**

1. **Statement of the Facts**

By an originating summons the plaintiff, Adamson Chilufya sought a declaration against the defendants, the City Council of Kitwe, that a resolution of the health amenities and social services committee of the defendant council passed on the 10th January, 1967, was *ultra vires* the powers of the defendant council and for the declaration that the removal from Chimwemwe Market, Kitwe, of the plaintiff's shop by the defendant council in pursuance of the said resolution was unlawful and unconstitutional. From his affidavit evidence, the plaintiff averred that between 1944 and 1967 he carried on business as a trader at various municipal markets under the control of the defendants and their predecessors; that during the whole of this period of approximately twenty-three years no complaint was charged or made against the plaintiff by the defendants or their predecessors for any breach of the defendant's market by-laws; that in 1964 the defendants permitted the plaintiff to erect a wooden stall, at a cost of 115 pounds, for the purpose of carrying on his trade; that the plaintiff paid a daily fee of 1*s.* to the defendants in respect of his right to trade in their markets; that the plaintiff was nominated to stand as a candidate for the African National Congress in the Kitwe Municipal election which took place in September, 1966; that in August 1966, during the election campaign his stall was badly damaged by a crowd of women; that at a meeting of the health amenities and social services committee of the defendants, held on 10th January, 1967, the committee passed a resolution that the plaintiff would no longer be permitted to trade within the precincts of any of the Council's markets.

2. **Material Facts and Levels of Abstraction (or generality)**

"The power of local authorities to grant and to determine licences must be exercised subject to the general law and the principles of natural justice."

(a) A trader in a market having the written authority of the city council to occupy a space, for which he pays a fee and on which he has erected a stall, is a licensee and not a tenant.

(b) Where a public authority has discretionary powers, the court is entitled to investigate its exercise of these powers in order to determine whether it has taken into account matters which it ought not to have taken into account, and vice versa, and whether its decision was reasonable.

(c) A city council which terminates a trader's license to occupy a market stall by resolution influenced by political considerations is acting unreasonably, unfairly and contrary to the principles of natural justice and, therefore, *ultra vires.*

(d) Such a termination of a licence is discriminatory.

6.3.4 Application of the *ratio decidendi*

After the Court has extracted the *ratio decidendi* it has to decide whether it is applicable to the instant case. The first factor to take into consideration is the levels of similarity of the material facts. If the material facts of the precedent and the instant case are the same, then the *ratio decidendi* is in point and applicable. This will be followed by the standing of the court where the precedent emanates from. If the precedent emanates from a higher court in the same hierarchy then the instant court is bound to apply the *ratio decidendi.* If it emanates from any other court, then it is persuasive.

There are other techniques employed by the courts in determining the application of the *ratio decidendi* of precedents.

6.3.4.1 Overruling

Higher courts can overrule the precedents of lower courts. The process of overruling a case affects the rule of law upon which the decision is based and this can be done by statute or by a higher court. A decision may be overruled by a higher court on grounds that it was arrived at *per incuriam.* Overruling a decision must be distinguished from reversing a decision. As stated earlier overruling involves a rule of law whereas reversal on appeal affects the decision in the case.

6.3.4.2 Distinguishing

Courts also take into consideration the differences or similarities in the material facts of the cases in order to decide whether the precedent is binding or not. If the material facts are not on all fours, the court will declare that the precedent or the *ratio* is not binding or does not apply to the instant case because of the differences in the material facts.

6.3.4.3 Obiter Dicta

As stated earlier, a statement of law classified as *obiter* is not binding.

6.3.4.4 Overruling by legislation

Judicial precedents can be overruled by legislation.

6.3.4.5 Precedents from foreign jurisdictions

These are persuasive and not binding. In any sovereign state, the highest court of the judicial hierarchy becomes the highest court of appeal of that sovereign state and therefore is not bound by the decisions of the court of another country. However, it is a common practice for judges, especially in cases of first impression, to refer to the precedents of other jurisdictions for guidance and the trend of the law. These are persuasive and it is the discretion of the court to determine the acceptability of the precedent in question.

6.4 Limitation of judicial legislation

Judicial creativity does not mean that the courts have a freehand like the Legislature. Unlike the Legislature that has the constitutional power to initiate any law, the law-making powers of the courts are limited in that regard. The courts can only lay down a principle of law in an actual case they are confronted with. They also have to give reasons for their judgments. As stated by Professor Geldart:

> **In the absence of clear precedents which might govern a question, we find judges relying on such considerations as the opinions of legal writers, the practice of conveyancers, the law of other modern countries, the Roman law, principles of 'natural justice', or public policy. The proper application of these may be a matter of dispute and difficulty but in any case the judge is applying a standard; he shows that he is not free, as a legislator would be, to decide as he pleases; he is bound to decide according to principle**[283].

Rupert Cross describes limitations of judicial legislation as follows:

> **It has been said to be 'merely misleading' to speak of judicial legislation, and it must be admitted that to do so is to use highly metaphorical language. There is no equivalent to the authoritative text of a statute, and even when they are bound by a statute or indistinguishable precedent, the judges' power to innovate is limited by what they cannot consider as well as by what they must consider. They cannot conduct those extensive examinations of empirical data and considerations of social policy which precede, or should precede, much legislation.**
>
> **The modern English judge is at a disadvantage as a law-maker when contrasted with the legislature because he cannot unmake law which has been effectively declared by statute, or, in spheres in which there is no statute, by decisions which are binding upon him. He is subject to the even greater restriction that he can only make law on such specific issues as happen to be litigated before him**[284].

Judges' law-making functions and discretion are limited by both the principle of constitutional supremacy and the judicial hierarchy and in the area of interpretation of statutes, the judicial discretion is limited within the parameters and boundaries of the purpose of the legislation[285].

6.5 Advantages and disadvantages of judicial precedents

6.5.1 Advantages

Given the eminence and the standing of the courts and the principles they apply in arriving at a decision, the principle of law in a judicial precedent, is the most universal in nature and scope. It transcends the political boundaries of a country in which it

[283] Geldart W.M. 1929. *Elements of English Law*. London: Thornton Butterworths.

[284] Cross, R. 1977. *op.cit.*

[285] *Zimnat Insurance Co Ltd v Chawanda* 1991 2 SA 825 (Z SC) 832 H-I.

was made and has the qualities of being applied in other jurisdictions regardless of the linguistic media in which it was made.

Whilst a precedent remains authoritative in the jurisdiction of its origin and creation, it remains persuasive in other jurisdictions but it may be used as a guiding principle or even adopted in such countries in situations where there is no authoritative precedent.

Precedent as a source of law is dynamic and not static because it can either be overruled or modified by the judges in subsequent cases. The judge in cases of first impression has the jurisdiction to establish new principles of law and thereby help with the growth of law in the judicial precedent.

As stated by Dias:

> **As long as one thinks only in terms of the present moment, there is a temptation to suppose that a case has some one fixed *ratio* which is "there" and discoverable once and for all. The very nature of case-law, however, indicates that *ratio* should always be considered in a time-continuum. For, in the first place, every decision refers to some past event, but the *ratio* of it seeks to control the future. No one can foresee the sort of situations that will arise, so that the *ratio* has to be capable of covering an indefinite range of broadly similar situations, i.e., it is a generalization from a specific happening. Secondly, it has to be pointed out that a condition of continued existence of *stare decisis* is its adaptability to the demands of justice and changing conditions. This requires that the *ratio* has to be malleable. Thirdly, no word has one proper meaning, nor can anyone seek to fix the meaning of words for other for the future, so the interpretation of the *ratio* is never finished, but remains open-ended and flexible. All this means that there is no fixed *ratio decidendi;* it is not only the ruling given by the deciding judge for his decision, but any one of a series of ruling as elucidated by subsequent interpretation[286].**

6.5.2 Disadvantages

There is a principle of justice against retroactivity together with its related principle of promulgation of laws so that the individual can regulate his conduct accordingly. One disadvantage of judicial precedent is that its application is potentially retroactive and the principle of law is not announced or pronounced before it is applied.

Precedent law is not as comprehensive and all embracing as other sources of law since by its nature and composition it is restricted and limited to the facts of the dispute in which it was made.

6.6 Review questions

1. "The finding of the *ratio decidendi* is not an automatic process; it calls for lawyerly skill and knowledge." (Glanville Williams)

   Discuss and illustrate.

[286] Dias, R.W.M. 1970. *op.cit.*

2. "Since the maintenance of stability is not the only goal of the legal order, judges should be given authority to set aside former decisions which are hopelessly obsolete and thoroughly ill-advised and contrary to social welfare." (Bodenheimer)

   Do you agree?

3. We cannot deny the possibility of some degree of creative element in ... judicial activities. What is not permitted to judges, is to establish law independently of any existing legal system, institution or norm." Per Judge Tanaka of Japan of the International Court of Justice, in the case of *South West Africa: Ethiopia v South Africa: Liberia v South Africa. ICJ* Reports 1966, p.6 at 277.

   In the light of the doctrine of *stare decisis,* discuss the reasons for and the limitations on judicial activism and the technique used by the courts to arrive at judicial precedents.

4. "The search for a *ratio decidendi* is a fruitless inquiry".

   To what extent does this statement reflect what happens in practice?

5. How has it been possible for the courts to develop the law within the framework of the doctrine of *stare decisis.*

6. "The *ratio decidendi* of a case consists of the material facts of the case found by the judge plus the decision thereon" (Goodhart). Is this an adequate account of the identification of the *ratio decidendi*?

7. "Judicial declaration unaccompanied by judicial application is not binding authority" (Salmond).

   Discuss.

8. Evaluate Goodhart's theory for the determination of the *ratio decidendi* of a case.

9. "Whatever the reasons for a decision may be, it is the principle to be extracted from the case, the *ratio decidendi,* which is binding, and not necessarily the reasons given for it". *Collet v Priest, (1931) AD 290* at 320.

   Discuss.

Reading List

G Williams:	Learning the Law (11th ed., 1982)
R Cross:	Precedent in English Law (3rd. ed. 1977)
Hosten, Edwards	Introduction to South African Law and Legal Theory. Nathan & Bosman (latest edition)
HR Hahlo & E Khan	The South African Legal System (latest edition).

CHAPTER 7
INTERPRETATION OF STATUTES

7.1 Introduction

Article 44 of the Namibian Constitution vests the legislative power of Namibia in the National Assembly which has the power to pass laws with the assent of the President as provided for in the Constitution subject, where applicable, to the powers and functions of the National Council. Legislative function therefore, resides primarily within the jurisdiction of Parliament. Legislative enactments are fashioned in the form of statutes the provisions of which are articulated in the words of the official language(s) of a jurisdiction. The actual words used are themselves part of the law; in fact, the words not only contain the law but in a sense constitute the law. Statute law therefore represents the deliberate formulation of the law by Parliament in such a way that the actual words used not only contain but also constitute the law. However, on account of linguistic inexactitude or elasticity, the language of the Act may not always convey the intended message with mathematical precision and with respect to the nature of the English language as succinctly stated by Lord Denning in the case of *Seaford Court Estates Ltd v Asher*[287], "(t)he English language is not an instrument of mathematical precision" and quite often courts have to grapple with the problem of determining the meaning of the words. Moreover, the use of the drafting device of ellipsis[288] by its very nature creates the demand for judicial interpretative intervention and therefore affords the Judiciary a creative role in the process of interpretation. Furthermore, statutes are intended to regulate factual situations which will occur in future, and it happens that Parliament has not considered every kind of case that has in fact occurred. As circumstances change in the course of time, problems arise as to the applicability of statutory provisions to new conditions. In all these situations, the role of the courts is not simply interpretive; it is also creative. Therefore, the courts, in the process of the performance of their constitutional function as the organ responsible for the interpretation and application of legislative enactments perform a responsibility which involves judicial intervention and activism. This phenomenon is described by Frank, J. as follows:

> **The enactment of many a statute thus, by implication, calls on the courts to engage in supplemental law-making. That activity should always, of course, be modest in scope. But the necessary generality in the wording of many statutes, and ineptness in drafting of others, frequently compels the courts, as best as they can, to fill in the gaps, an activity which, no matter how one may label it, is in part legislative**[289].

---

[287] (1949) 2 KB. 481 at 499.

[288] Ellipsis is a device whereby the draftsman leaves unsaid some portion of what he means to say.

[289] See *Guiseppi v Walling,* 144 F (2d) 608, at 620-2 (CCA 2d, 1944) 621.

The courts' primary task in this exercise is said to be the ascertainment of the intention of the Legislature as articulated in the words of the particular legislative enactment or statute. However, as has been pointed out in most literature on the topic, the intention of parliament is a fiction[290] and therefore in the judicial process, its ascertainment involves judicial creativity. As Dias puts it:

> **An Act is the product of compromise and the interplay of many factors, the result of all this being expressed in a set of words. Ascertaining the "intention of the legislature", therefore, boils down to finding the meaning of the words used – the "intent of the statute" rather than of Parliament**[291].

Similarly, Van den Heever in the case of *Sachs v Donges*[292] describes the creative role of courts during the process of legislative interpretation when he says that 'judges while purporting to expound and apply the law sometimes make law in the process'.

The ascertainment of the intention of Parliament and the meaning of the provisions of a statute require a great deal of skill, common sense and the application of rules of interpretation or construction developed by the courts. The process involves looking up the meaning of a word in the dictionary and if the dictionary meaning is not satisfactory, the judge may look for the meaning in the context of the whole statute and even at earlier legislation dealing with the same subjectmatter for it is assumed that when Parliament passed an Act, it probably had the earlier legislation in mind and probably intended to use words with the same meaning as before[293]. This latter rule that requires the meaning to be sought in the context of the whole statute is sometimes expressed in the Latin maxim *noscitur a sociis,* which means a word may be known by the company it keeps. The court may also refer to the definition section of a particular statute which assigns special meanings to some of the words in the statute to ascertain the meaning of certain words in the statute. In addition to the interpretation or definitions section of a particular statute, there is also the Interpretation of Laws Proclamation No. 37 of 1920, which serves as a standing legal dictionary of some of the most important words used in statutes.

7.2 The literal rule

The literal rule is derived from the text-centred approach which seeks to derive answers to litigated disputes from the words of the statute itself. It seeks to give effect to the plain meaning of the words even if the result would be absurd or contrary to the spirit of the legislation. The application of this rule simply involves the judge's reliance on the common understanding of the language of the text and the use of sources such as dictionaries to discern the meaning of the words of the statute.

---

[290] Williams, G. 1982. *op.cit.*

[291] Dias, R.W.M. 1970. *op.cit.*

[292] 1950 (2) SA 265.

[293] Maxwell. 1937. *Interpretation of Statutes.* London: Sweet & Maxwell.

In the case of *Venter v Rex*[294] the literal rule was defined by Innes, C.J. as follows:

> **"If the words of an Act are clear, you must follow them, even though they lead to an absurdity. The Court has nothing to do with the question whether the legislature has committed an absurdity". Hoexter JA in *R v Tebetha*[295] pronounced that *"jus dicere non dare* is the function of the court, and the language of an Act must neither be extended beyond its natural sense and proper limits in order to supply omissions or defects, nor strained to meet the justice of an individual case".**

Various reasons have been advanced for the application of the literal rule by the courts but one commonly advanced is that judges do not want to be seen as usurping the functions of the Legislature or be accused of making political judgments that are at variance with the purpose of Parliament when it passed the Act[296]. As stated by Ogilvie Thompson C.J., "unlike the system that obtains in the United States, where, in certain spheres, the Supreme Court in effect itself legislates by pronouncing its own constructions of the general precepts of the Constitution, in our country a judge must interpret the enactments of Parliament and the provincial councils and administer the law, not as he would like it to be, or as he might consider it ought to be, but as set out in the relevant statutory provisions as interpreted .... Once a judge has determined what he conceives to be the intention of the Legislature, he must perforce give effect to the intention so determined"[297].

There are two elements in the process of the ascertainment of the intention of Parliament alluded to in the above statement. The first part is the reference to the literal rule of interpretation together with its related concept of legislative supremacy and the second element is the inherent jurisdiction and discretion of the courts or judicial creativity. Prior to the promulgation of the new South African Constitution and the independence of Namibia, the South African courts, the decisions of which were binding on the South West African/Namibian courts, relied a great deal on the literal rule of interpretation as a consequence of the then prevailing doctrine of legislative supremacy[298]. This reliance on legislative supremacy and analytical positivism earned the South African Judiciary a great deal of criticism[299]. With the promulgation of the new Constitution in South Africa and Namibia's Independence Constitution, however, the doctrine of legislative supremacy has been replaced by that of constitutional supremacy. The courts in both jurisdictions therefore are bound by the higher principles

[294] *Venter v R* TS 910 at 913.

[295] *R v Tebetha* 1959 2 SA 337 (AD) at 346. See also Baron J in the case of *Hewlett v Minister of Finance & Another* 1982 (1) SA 490 (ZSC) at 509E, and *Seluka v Suskin & Salkow* 1912 TPD.

[296] Williams, G. 1982. *op.cit.*

[297] See 1972, 89 South African Law Journal.

[298] See *Harris and Others v Minister of the Interior and Another* (1952) 2 SA p. 428 where Centlivres CJ stated that 'Courts of law are not concerned with the question whether an Act of Parliament is reasonable, politic or impolitic'.

[299] See Dugard, J. 'The Judicial Process, Positivism and Civil Liberty'. 1971 88 *SALJ* 181-200 and Dugard, J. 'Some Realism About the Judicial Process and Positivism'. 1981 98 *SALJ* 372-387.

of the Constitution in their interpretive functions. The Namibian courts have adopted the purposive approach to the interpretation of the Constitution[300]. This approach is value-oriented and in this respect has a pedigree relationship with the hermeneutical theory which emphasises the role of the interpreter during the interpretation process and the fact that the science of understanding is not a mechanical exercise, but also involves value judgments.

7.3 The golden rule

The golden rule of legislative interpretation is different from the literal rule as it involves the consideration of other factors and variables other than the mere language of the Legislature. The application of the literal rule may be adequate and appropriate in cases where the word to be interpreted has a core meaning. This, however, may not necessarily be the case where the word has a penumbral quality, in which case the court may rely on the golden rule. De Villiers propounded the golden rule as follows:

> ***Prima facie*, the intention of the legislature is to be deduced from the words which it has used. It is true that, owing to the elasticity which is inherent in language, it is admissible for a court in construing a statute to have regard not only to the language of the legislature, but also to its object and policy as gathered from a comparison of its several parts, as well as from the history of the law and from the circumstances applicable to its subject matter. And if, on considerations of this nature, a court is satisfied that to accept the literal sense of the words would obviously defeat the intention of the legislature, it would be justified in not strictly adhering to that sense, but in putting upon the words such other signification as they are capable of bearing. The same principle is embodied in Lord Wensleydale's well-known 'Golden Rule'....**[301].

The golden rule justifies an interpretation which is a departure from the application of the literal rule, if the words of an Act admit of two interpretations and the primary meaning of the words of the Act after the application of the ordinary and grammatical construction of the words would lead to an absurdity such as the Legislature would never have contemplated, or which would be plainly contrary to the general scheme disclosed in the context of the statute[302]. The courts have not laid down any rule of thumb to determine what constitutes an absurdity. What constitutes an absurdity must be determined by the peculiar facts and circumstances of each case. The courts, however, as a general rule, may rule that an interpretation amounts to an absurdity: if it is inconsistent with the higher principles of the Constitution; if it deprives an individual of an existing right; if it is in conflict with an existing statute; or if it is inconsistent with public policy or principles of morality. In the case of *New*

[300] See for example *Government of the Republic of Namibia and Another v Cultura 2000* 1993 NR 328 (SC) at 340 B-D.

[301] De Villiers in *Principal Immigration Officer v Hawabu* 1936 AD 26 at 30-1.

[302] Innes CJ in *Venter v RR* TS 910.

Rietfontein Gold Mines Ltd v Mishum 1912[303], it was stated that an interpretation that would cripple the operation of an Act would constitute an absurdity.

The case of *R v Takawira and Others*[304] illustrates what may constitute an absurdity. In that case the statute concerned, without any qualification or exception, made it an offence to be in possession of subversive material. If interpreted literally this would mean that 'the policeman who took possession of the subversive statement, the public prosecutor who tendered it as evidence, the judicial officer who examined it at the trial would all be guilty of offences and, as a result, it would never be possible to secure a conviction under the statute at all, and as a result the intention of the Legislature would be completely frustrated. In these circumstances it would be permissible to qualify the literal meaning by reading into the clause the words such as "without lawful authority" so as to permit officials to be in possession of the statement in the exercise of their duties.

The court may also apply the golden rule by using an interpretation language couched in the context of the intention of Parliament so that as Hosten states "(i)n this way, judges do just what they steadfastly refuse to do under the 'golden rule', where the statute's language is clear and unambiguous; namely, they modify or cut down or vary the words used by the Legislature in order to achieve a reasonable result"[305]. In this sense Hosten[306] concludes that "both Innes CJ and Solomon J approved the 'golden rule' and applied it to the facts of *Venter's*[307] case. Seen in this light, the golden rule may be said to have been applied to the *Setra Avakian*[308] and *Holy Trinity Church* cases[309].

7.4 The mischief rule

The approach to interpretation of statutes that attaches a meaning to words in a statute by ascertaining the legislative intent with reference to the 'mischief' or the 'disease' that Parliament was intending to redress is known as the mischief rule. The nature of this mischief may have changed as a result of time, change of policies, etc. and therefore factors to be taken into consideration in deciding what constitutes the mischief may vary, which underscores the need for judicial interpretation. The mischief rule was laid down in *Heydon's Case*[310] as follows:

> **"four things are to be discussed and considered: 1st, What was the Common Law before making the Act; 2nd, What was the mischief and defect for which the Common Law did not provide; 3rd, What remedy hath the Parliament resolved**

[303] 1912 AD 704.

[304] 1965 R.L.R. 162 (R., A.D.).

[305] Hosten, W.J.; Edwards, A.B.; Bosman, F. & Church, J. 1997. *op.cit.*

[306] *Ibid.*

[307] *Supra.*

[308] Tekemt 13, Supreme Imperial Court of Ethiopia, 1956 E.C. (October 24,1963 G.C.).

[309] Supreme Court of the United States, 1892, 143 US. 457,12 S.Ct. 511, 36 L.Ed. 226.

[310] 3 Co. Rep.7a.

> **and appointed to cure the disease of the commonwealth; and 4th, The true reason of the remedy; and then the office of all judges is always to make such construction as shall suppress the mischief and advance the remedy, and to suppress subtle inventions and evasions for continuance of the mischief, and *pro privato commodo,* and to add force and life to the cure and remedy according to the true intent of the makers of the Act *pro bono publico."***

The application of the mischief rule "contemplates a wide inquiry into the policy and purpose behind the statute"[311]. In the case of Holy *Trinity Church v United States*[312], the plaintiff in error, the Holy Trinity Church, was a corporation duly organised and incorporated as a religious society under the laws of the State of New York. E. Walpole Warren was, prior to September 1887, an alien residing in England. In that month the plaintiff in error made a contract with him, by which he was to relocate to the city of New York, and enter into its service as rector and pastor; and, in pursuance of such contract, Warren did so relocate and enter upon such service. It was claimed by the United States that this contract on the part of the plaintiff was forbidden by chapter 164, 23 St. p.332; and an action was commenced to recover the penalty prescribed by that Act. The circuit court held that the contract was within the prohibition of the statute and rendered judgment accordingly. The single question presented for the determination of the Supreme Court was whether the circuit court erred in that conclusion.

The relevant section of the Act proscribing that type of act provided as follows:

> ***Be it enacted by the senate and house of representatives of the United States of America, in congress assembled,* that from and after the passage of this act it shall be unlawful for any person, company, partnership, or corporation, in any manner whatsoever, to prepay the transportation, or in any way assist or encourage the importation or migration, of any alien or aliens, any foreigner or foreigners, into the United States, its territories, or the District of Columbia, under contract or agreement, parol or special, express or implied, made previous to the importation or migration of such alien or aliens, foreigner or foreigners, to perform labour or service of any kind in the United States, its territories, or the District of British Columbia.**

The Supreme Court of the United States guided by the mischief rule reversed the judgment of the circuit court on the grounds that the intent of Congress in passing the act in question was the prohibition of the importation and immigration of unskilled labourers. In the words of Justice Brewer who delivered the opinion of the court, "the title of the act, the evil which was intended to be remedied, the circumstances surrounding the appeal to congress, the reports of the committee of each house, all concur in affirming that the intent of congress was simply to stay the influx of this cheap, unskilled labour."

In the American case of *U.S. v Kirby*[313] the defendants were indicted for the violation of an act of congress providing "that if any person shall knowingly and wilfully obstruct or retard the passage of the mail, or of any driver or carrier, or of

[311] Dias, R.W.M. 1970. *Jurisprudence*. London: Butterworths.

[312] *Ibid.*

[313] 7 Wall. 482, at 486.

any horse or carriage carrying the same, he shall upon conviction, for every such offence, pay a fine not exceeding one hundred dollars." The specific charge was that the defendants knowingly and wilfully retarded the passage of one Farris, a carrier of the mail, while engaged in the performance of his duty, and also in like manner retarded the steam-boat *Gen. Buell,* at that time engaged in carrying the mail. To this indictment the defendants pleaded that Farris had been indicted for murder by a court of competent authority in Kentucky; that a bench warrant had been issued and placed in the hands of the defendant Kirby, the sheriff of the county, commanding him to arrest Farris, and bring him before the court to answer to the indictment; and that in obedience to this warrant, he and the other defendants, as his posse, entered upon the steam-boat Gen. *Buell* and arrested Farris, and used such force as was necessary to accomplish the arrest. The question as to the sufficiency of this plea was certified to this court, and it was held that the arrest of Farris upon the warrant from the State court was not an obstruction of the mail, or the retarding of the passage of a carrier of the mail, within the meaning of the Act. In its opinion the court says: "All laws should receive a sensible construction. General terms should be so limited in their application as not to lead to injustice, oppression, or an absurd consequence. It will always, therefore, be presumed that the Legislature intended exceptions to its language which would avoid results of this character. The reason of the law in such cases should prevail over its letter. The common sense of man approves the judgment mentioned by Puffendorf, that the Bolognian law which enacted that 'whoever drew blood in the streets should be punished with the utmost severity', did not extend to the surgeon who opened the vein of a person that fell down in the street in a fit. The same common sense accepts the ruling, cited by Plowden, that the statute of 1 Edw. 2, which enacts that a prisoner who breaks prison shall be guilty of felony, does not extend to a prisoner who breaks out when the prison is on fire, 'for he is not to be hanged because he would not stay to be burnt'. And we think that a like common sense will sanction the ruling we make, that the act of congress which punishes the obstruction or retarding of the passage of the mail, or of its carrier, does not apply to a case of temporary detention of the mail caused by the arrest of the carrier upon an indictment for murder.

7.5 The purposive approach to the interpretation of the Constitution

After the attainment of independence and sovereignty Namibia adopted a constitution with an entrenched Bill of Rights and a provision that elevates the constitution as the supreme law of Namibia[314]. This effectively replaced the doctrine of legislative sovereignty (and the over-reliance of the South African and Namibian Judiciary on analytical positivism), which from the history of the legal systems of both South Africa and Namibia, equated legislative supremacy with that of constitutional supremacy. The new constitutional dispensation has provided the Namibian

[314] Article 1(6) of the Namibian Constitution provides that this Constitution shall be the Supreme Law of Namibia.

Judiciary with a constitutional leverage to promote the principles of the rule of law and constitutionalism and protect and advance the fundamental rights of the individual. This exercise has involved the interpretation of the Constitution and Namibian courts have adopted a value-oriented or purposive approach to the interpretation of the constitution since independence and have thereby developed a jurisprudence based on value judgments and an epistemological paradigm rooted in the values and norms of the Namibian people. Strydom, C.J. in his address to the judicial officers at the first Retreat of the Office of the Attorney-General at Swakopmund 20-22 November 2002, entitled "*Namibia's Constitutional Jurisprudence – the First Twelve Years*", stated that:

> **(I)t is trite that ordinary presumptions of interpretation will not independently suffice in interpreting such a document (Constitution) and that our Courts must develop guidelines to give full effect to the purport and aim of our Constitution. The Constitution remains the Supreme Law of Namibia from which all laws always flow and against which all laws can be tested ... in interpreting the Constitution, particularly Chapter 3, the Courts are often called upon to exercise a value judgment. It was this exercise that led the Court in the Corporal Punishment[315] decision to encompass both aspects of constitutional interpretation and judicial independence.**

Chapter 3 of the Namibian Constitution of Namibia provides for the fundamental human rights and freedoms, which are entrenched. The Constitution, however, draws a distinction between rights and freedoms and with regard to the latter, Article 21(2)[316] for example, provides that they "shall be exercised subject to the law of Namibia, in so far as such law imposes reasonable restrictions on the exercise of the rights and freedoms conferred by the said Sub-Article, which are necessary in a democratic society and are required in the interests of the sovereignty and integrity of Namibia, national security, public order, decency or morality, or in relation to contempt of court, defamation or incitement to an offence".

These limitations together with the general nature of the provisions of a constitution, *prima facie*, require the exercise of the constitutional jurisdiction of the courts in interpreting the grey or penumbral areas of the Constitution as to, for example, what constitutes decency or morality. The Namibian courts have, since independence, been called upon to interpret similar provisions of the Constitution and as mentioned earlier have adopted what may be termed, to borrow John Dugard's expression, a natural law–cum–realist or a purposive approach and have developed a particular jurisprudence based on the constitutionality of legislative provisions or practices relating to corporal punishment[317] the restraining of prisoners by chaining them to each other by means of metal chains[318], homosexual relationships[319], etc.

---

[315] 1991 (3) SA 76 (NmS).

[316] Article 21 provides for the freedom of speech and expression, thought, religion, association, etc.

[317] See *Ex Parte Attorney-General, Namibia: in re Corporal Punishment* 1991 (3) SA 76 (NmS).

[318] See *Namunjepo & Others v Commanding Officer, Windhoek Prison & Another*, 2000 (6) BCLR 671 (NmS).

[319] See *The Chairperson of the Immigration Selection Board v Erna Elizabeth Frank & Another,* Supreme Court of Namibia Case No. SA 8/99.

In the address mentioned above, Strydom, C.J. stated that:

> **in the two *Mwandingi* cases the High and Supreme Courts of Namibia accepted the principle that a Constitution, and more particularly one containing a Bill of Rights, calls for an interpretation different from that which courts traditionally apply to ordinary legislation. Dealing with instances where the courts were required to make value judgments the corporal punishment case authoritatively laid down that a court, in coming to its conclusion, should objectively articulate and identify the contemporary norms, aspirations and expectations of the Namibian people and should have regard to the emerging consensus of values in the civilized international community. These cases set the tone for Namibian Courts and the way it was required of them to interpret the Constitution.**
>
> **In the case of *Minister of Defence v Mwandinghi*[320] the Namibian Supreme Court approved the *dictum in S v Acheson*[321] that:**
>
> **(T)he Constitution of a nation is not simply a statute which mechanically defines the structures of government and the relations between the government and the governed. It is a mirror reflecting the national soul, the identification of the ideals and aspirations of a nation; the articulation of the values bonding its people and disciplining its government. The spirit and tenor of the Constitution must therefore preside over and permeate the processes of judicial interpretation and judicial discretion.**

In the case *Government of the Republic of Namibia & Another v Cultura 2000*[322], the late Mahomed, C.J., reiterated this approach to the interpretation of the Constitution by stating:

> **A Constitution is an organic instrument. Although it is enacted in the form of a statute, it is *sui generis*. It must broadly, liberally and purposively be interpreted so as to avoid the 'austerity of tabulated legalism' and so as to enable it to continue to play a creative and dynamic role in the expression and the achievement of the ideals and aspirations of the nation, in the articulation of the values bonding its people and disciplining its Government.**

7.6 Conclusion

Statute law represents the deliberate formulation of the law by Parliament in such a way that the actual words used not only contain the law but constitute the law. Under the doctrine of separation of powers, legislative function is vested in Parliament but every enacted law has to be interpreted in order to be applied and the courts,

[320] 1992 (2) SA 355 (NmSC).

[321] 1991 NR 1 (HC) at 10 AB.

[322] 1993 NR 328 (SC) at 340 B-D; 1994 (1) SA 407 NmSC, at 418 F-G. See also *Minister of Defence, Namibia v Mwandinghi*, 1993 NR 63 (SC) at 68-71 1992 (2) SA 355 (NmS) at 361-3); *S v Acheson* 1991 NR 1 (HC) at 10 A-C; *S v Acheson* 1991 (2) SA 805 (Nm) at 813 A-C).

representing another organ of State, are recognised as the interpreters to perform such function. Because language, which is one vehicle of communication, does not always convey the intended message with mathematical precision, quite often courts have to grapple with the problem of determining the meaning of words to ascertain the intention of Parliament, which as stated earlier, is a fiction. It is inevitable that doubts should arise regarding whether a particular provision covers a particular set of facts. In all this, the courts are not simply performing an interpretive function but a creative one. In performing such function the courts apply rules and aides of interpretation and construction, some of which have been discussed above.

7.7 Extracts

HINZ, M.O.; AMOO, S.K. & VAN WYK, D. (editors)

The Constitution at Work: 10 Years of Namibian Nationhood (2002)

Constitutionality of Legislation Relating to the Distribution of Governmental Powers in Namibia: A Comparative Approach *C Okpaluba*[323*]

4. APPROACH TO THE INTERPRETATION OF THE CONSTITUTION

One major factor, among others, distinguishing a statute from a constitution is the approach to the interpretation of both documents[324]. It was the Australian High Court that called attention to the fact that in interpreting a constitution one has to constantly bear in mind that one is dealing with a constitution, "the mechanism under which laws are to be made" and not an Act of Parliament which declares what the law is to be"[325]. Justice Stone of the United States Supreme Court once warned that "the revelation of the great purposes which were intended to be achieved by the constitution as a continuing instrument of government distinguishes it from 'legislative codes' "[326]. Even after initial hesitation[327] given its traditional background in statutory and not constitutional interpretation, the Privy Council came around to interpreting the Constitution as a document *sui generis*. In *Minister of Home Affairs (Bermuda) v Fisher*[328], Lord Diplock expounded the virtues of interpreting the

---

323 *Professor of Law, University of the North, South Africa.

324 *Swart v Minister of Home Affairs, Namibia* 1998 (3) SA 338 (NmHC) at 343I-J and 344A-C citing Dale Gibson. 1982. "Commnetary on the interpretation of the Canadian Charter of Rights and Freedoms" in Tarnapolsky & Beaudoin (eds) *The Canadian Charter of Rights and Freedoms: Commentary Toronto: The Carswell Company Limited* 26. See also Okpaluba. 1992. *Judicial approach to Constitutional interpretation in Nigeria* (1992) 8-17. Matt Madek & Co.

325 Higgins in *A-G of New South Wales v Brewery Employees Union of NSW* (1908) 6 CLR at 611-612. See generally, Latham "Interpretation of the Constitution." in *Else*-Mitchell (ed). 1970. *Essays on the Australian Constitution* ch-1; Wayne *Legislative, executive and judicial powers in Australia* ch II.

326 *U.S. v Classic* 313 US 299 (1941). A Constitution must not be interpreted like any regulatory statute and certainly not "like a last will and testament", lest indeed it becomes one – Freund "The Supreme Court of the United" (1951) 29 *Canadian Bar Review* 1080 at 1087.

327 *Edwards v A-G for Canada* [1930] AC 124 at 136; *British Coal Corporation and The King* [1935] AC 500 AT 518 (PC).

328 [1980] AC 319. See also the same Law Lord in *Hinds v The Queen* [1976] 1 All ER 353 at 359; per Lord Salmon in *A-G for St Christopher, Nevis & Anguilla v Reynolds* [1980] 2 WLR 171 at 182.

Constitution of Bermuda, especially its fundamental rights provisions in such a manner as to achieve the purpose it was designed to achieve. Accordingly, the courts in Nigeria[329], Namibia and South Africa[330] have since adopted this generous but purposive approach to the interpretation of their respective country's Constitution.

Soon after the Namibian Constitution came into force, the late Chief Justice of Namibia (later of South Africa) had made one of his great speeches on constitutional interpretation when in *S v Acheson*[331], he said:

> **The Constitution of a nation is not simply a statute which mechanically defines the structures of government and the relationship between the government and the governed. It is a "mirror reflecting the national soul", the identification of the ideals and aspirations of a nation; the articulation of the values bonding its people and disciplining its government. The spirit and the tenor of the Constitution must therefore preside and permeate the processes of judicial interpretation and judicial discretion.**

The Full Bench of the Supreme Court adopted a similar approach in *Minister of Defence, Namibia v Mwandinghi*[332] where, in terms similar to those of Lord Diplock in *Fisher*, it held that the "Namibian Constitution must therefore be broadly, liberally and purposively interpreted, to avoid the austerity of tabulated legalism[333]".

A number of deductions can be made from the Namibian judicial approach. The first is that a construction which is most "beneficial to the widest possible amplitude[334]" must be given to the provisions of the Constitution, so that in interpreting article 140(3) under which the new government had undertaken to shoulder certain obligations of the former regime, one cannot do so in such a narrow and pedantic manner as to limit the operation of the words "anything done" only to acts lawfully done[335]. Secondly, it means that a broad and liberal spirit must inspire the construction of the Constitution[336] in that, it is a document

[329] See *Nafiu Rabiu v The State* (1981) 2 NCLR 293 at 321, 326; *Archbishop Okogie v A-G of Lagos State* (1981) 2 NCLR 337 at 348, 353; *Bronik Motors Ltd v Wema Bank Ltd* (1983) 1 SNCLR 296 at 321; *Savannah Bank of Nigeria Ltd v Ajilo* (1989) 1 NWLR (97) 305 at 326. See generally, Okpaluba (n 52) 13-16, 159-165, 375-379, 529-556 respectively.

[330] See generally, Devenish. 1999. *A Commentary on the South African Bill of Rights.* Durban: Butterworths. ch 31 where the South African and Namibian cases and the relevant literature are discussed; in Chaskalson, Kentridge & Spitz. 1998. "Interpretation" in. *Constitutional Law of South Africa*. Cape Town: Lutta.

[331] 1991 (2) SA 805 (NmH) 813; 1991 NR 1 (HC) 10A *per* Mahomed AJ (as he then was).

[332] 1992 (2) SA 355 (NmS) 362.

[333] See also *Government of the Republic of Namibia v Cultura 2000* 1994 (1) SA 407 (NmS) 418; *S v Heidenreich* 1996 (2) SACR 171 (NmH) 176f-g; *Swart v President of the Republic of Namibia* 1998 (3) SA 338 (NmH).

[334] *James v The Commonwealth* [1936] AC 578 at 614 per Lord Wright; *British Coal Corporation v The King* [1935] AC 500 at 518.

[335] See also in *Cultura* (n 62) 418F-G.

[336] *Kauesa v Minister of Home Affairs* 1996 (4) SA 965 (NmH) 975.

that has the greatest claim to be construed *ut res magis quam pereat*[337]. And in doing so, a court cannot be selective and apply this approach only when dealing with limitations on freedom of speech. It must apply to the consideration of the limitations on fundamental rights, including a situation where a fundamental freedom is in conflict with a fundamental right[338]. Even so, the Court should approach the matter in a balanced and even-handed manner so that in interpreting the fundamental rights provisions such as article 12 which was being considered in *S v Van den Berg*[339] it must do so in the context of say, articles 6, 7, 8, 13 and 16, read with articles 5 and 25.

Thirdly, in interpreting the Constitution, sight must not be lost of the circumstances surrounding its coming into being, that is, the character and origin of the Constitution must be given full recognition[340]. In the case of Namibia and South Africa, such circumstances could easily be read in the preamble to the respective Constitutions[341]. Consequently, in interpreting the Constitution, those values and aspirations of the founders must be borne in mind[342]. Another instance is that the interpreter must not neglect the recognized norms of international law and the emerging consensus of values in the civilized international community of which Namibia is part. For example, when construing the fundamental rights and freedoms which in any case derive from the United Nations Conventions[343] and instruments of its various agencies, the Court must have regard to principles of international law. Closely associated with this point is the caveat that at all times when the constitutionality of legislation is under consideration, the Court must begin by looking at the provisions of the Namibian Constitution which is the supreme law of the Republic

[337] In the Nigerian case of *Nafiu Rabiu v State* (1981) 2 NCLR 293 at 326 Sir Udo Udoma JSC had said: "It is my view that the approach of this court to the construction of the Constitution should be, and so it has been, one of liberalism, probably a variation on the theme of the general maxim *ut res magis veleat quam pereat.* I do not so construe any of the provisions of the Constitution as to defeat the obvious ends the Constitution was designed to serve where another construction equally in accord and consistent with the words and sense of such provisions will serve to enforce and protect such ends". See to the same effect Idigbe JSC at 302-303. See also Seervai. *The Constitutional Law of India* (3ed) vol 1. Bombay: NM Tripathi Pty Ltd.

[338] *Kauesa v Minister of Home Affairs* supra at 56J-57C.

[339] 1995 (4) BCLR 479 (Nm) 495I-J.

[340] *Ex parte A-G, Namibia: In re Constitutional Relationship between the Attorney-General and the Prosecutor-General* 1995 (8) BCLR 1070 (NmS); *Cultura* (n 62) 418F-J.

[341] All these factors were applied by the Chief Justice in *Cultura 2000* (n 62), in determining whether the State Repudiation (Cultura 2000) Act 32 of 1991 whereby the Government sought to repudiate within the context of art. 140(3) of the Constitution certain generous gifts of money made by a retreating apartheid administration to an organisation whose main objective was to preserve the culture of "superiority" of the white race was unconstitutional. It was held that the interpretation of 140(3) as to limit its potential operation only to acts by merely giving power to Parliament to disown or turn its back upon acts perpetrated by the previous administration which were "uncompleted" would not give to the clear words of the article a construction which is "most beneficial to the widest possible amplitude".

[342] *Ex parte A-G of Namibia: In Re Corporal Punishment by Organs of State* 1991 (3) SA 76 (NmS) 78A per Mahomed AJA.

[343] Universal Declaration of Human Rights 1948; International Convenant on Economic, Social and Cultural Rights 1966; International Covenant on Civil & Political Rights 1966.

and not that of other countries with constitutions fundamentally different[344]. Above all, the court must interpret the Constitution in such a manner as to enable it to continue to play a creative and dynamic role in the expression and the achievement of the ideas and aspirations of the nation and, if need be, err on the side of the protection of the individual as against government and its agencies[345].

7.7.1 Interpretation of Laws Proclamation, No. 37 of 1920

September 1920

Interpretation of Laws

Whereas it is desirable to interpret and shorten the language of Laws now or hereafter in force in this Protectorate.

Now therefore under and by virtue of the powers vested in me I do hereby declare, proclaim and make known as follows:

1) In the interpretation of every law (as in this Proclamation defined) now or hereafter in force in the protectorate or in any portion thereof, and in the interpretation of all by-laws, rules, regulations, or orders made under the authority of any such law, the definitions or other provisions in this proclamation contained shall, unless there be something in the language or context of the law, by-law, rule, regulation or order, repugnant to such definitions or provisions or unless the contrary intention therein appear, be adopted and applied.

2) The following expressions shall, unless the context otherwise requires or unless in the case of any law it is otherwise provided therein, have the meanings hereby respectively assigned to them, namely:

   "christian name" shall mean any name prefixed to the surname, whether received at Christian baptism or not;

   "Gazette" shall mean the Official Gazette of the Protectorate;

   "district" shall mean the area subject to the jurisdiction of the court or any magistrate:

   "Governor-General" shall mean the officer for the time being administering the government of the union of South Africa acting by and with the office of the executive council thereof;

   The "Administration" or "this Administration" shall mean the Administration of the mandated territory of South West Africa;

   "Administrator", when used in relation to the administration of those matters in respect of which it is for the time being competent for the Legislative Assembly for the territory to make ordinances shall mean the Administrator of the Territory in Executive committee and when used in relation to the administration of any other matters shall mean the Administrator of the Territory,

   The "territory" or "This territory" shall mean the mandated territory of South West Africa;

---

[344] *Kauesa* (n 65) 56A per O'Linn J. See also *S v Minnies & Another* 1991 (1) SACR 355 (Nm) 370g-h; *Ex parte A-G of Namibia: In re Corporal Punishment by Organs of State* 1991 (3) SA 76 (NmS) 86I-J, 96H-97A; *S v Tcoeib* 1993 (1) SACR 274 (Nm) 281f-282a.

[345] Per du Toit AJ in *S v Minnies* 1991 (3) SA 364 (Nm) at 385B-C.

"law" shall mean and include any law, proclamation or any other enactment having the force of law;

"month" shall mean a calendar month;

"oath" and "affidavit" shall in the case of persons allowed by law to affirm or declare instead of swearing, include affirmation and declaration and the expression "swear" shall in the like case, include "affirm" and "declare".

"Parliament" shall mean the Parliament of the Union of South Africa;

"person" shall include –

a) municipal council, or like authority; or

b) any company incorporated or registered as such under any law; or

c) any body of persons corporate or unincorporated;

"Province" shall mean a Province in the Union of South Africa;

"The Protectorate" shall mean the territory of South West Africa lately under the Sovereignty of Germany and at present under the administration of the Government of the Union of South Africa;

"The Union" shall mean the territorial limits of the union of South Africa as constituted for the time being in accordance with the South Africa Act 1909, or any amendment thereof.

3) In every law, expressions relating to writing shall, unless the contrary intention appears, be construed as including also references to typewriting, lithography, photography, and all other modes of representing or reproducing words in a visible form.

4) When any particular number of days is prescribed for the doing of any act or for any other purpose, the same shall be reckoned exclusively of the first and inclusively of the last day, unless the last day shall happen to fall on a Sunday or on any other day appointed by or under the authority of a law as a public holiday, in which case the time shall be reckoned exclusively of the first day and exclusively also of every such Sunday or public holiday.

5) In the measurement of any distance for the purpose of any law that distance shall unless the contrary intention appears, be measured in a straight line on a horizontal plane.

6) In every law, unless the contrary intention appears,

a) words importing the masculine gender shall include females; and

b) words in the singular number shall include the plural and words in the plural number shall include the singular.

7) Where any law authorizes or requires any document to be served by post, whether the expression: "serve" or "give" or "send" or any other expression is used, then, unless the contrary intention appears, the service shall be deemed to be effected by properly addressing, prepaying and posting a registered letter containing the document, and unless the contrary is proven, to have been effected at the time at which the letter would have been delivered in the ordinary course of post.

8) In every other law unless the contrary intention appears, the expression "rules of the court" when used in relation to any court shall mean rules made by the authority having for the time being power to make rules or orders regulating the practice and procedure of that court. The powers of the said authority to make rules of the court,

as above defined, include a power to make rules of court for the purpose of any law directing or authorizing anything to be done by the rules of a court.

8*bis*. "Any criminal proceedings given as instituted in the name of the state shall for all purposes be deemed to have been instituted in the name of the Republic of South Africa."

9)(1) When a law confers a power or imposes a duty then, unless the contrary intention appears, the power may be exercised and the duty shall be performed from time to time as occasion requires.

(2) Where a law confers a power, jurisdiction or right or imposes a duty on the holder of an office as such, unless the contrary appears, the power, jurisdiction or right may be exercised and the duty shall be performed from time to time by the holder for the time being of the office, or by the person lawfully acting in the capacity of such holder.

(3) Where a law confers a power to make rules, regulations, or by-laws, the power shall, unless the contrary intention appears, be construed as including a power exercisable in like manner and subject to the like consent and conditions (*if any) to rescind, revoke, amend, or vary the rules, regulations, or by-laws.

10) Where an act or omission constitutes an offence under two or more statutes, or is an offence against a statute, and at common law, the offender shall, unless the contrary intention appears, be liable to be prosecuted either by statute or common law, but he shall not be liable to more than one punishment for the act or omission constituting the offence.

11)(1) Where a law repeals and re-enacts, with or without modifications, any provisions so repealed shall be construed as references to the provisions so re-enacted.

(2) Where a law repeals any other law, then, the repeal shall not -

(a) revive anything not in force or existing at the time at which the repeal takes effect; or

(b) affect the previous operation of any law so repealed or anything duly done or suffered under the law so repealed;

(c) affect any right, privilege, obligation or liability acquired, accrued, or incurred under any law so repealed; or

(d) affect any penalty, forfeiture or punishment incurred in respect of any offence committed against law so repealed; or

(e) affect any investigation, legal proceeding, or remedy in respect of any such right, privilege, obligation, liability, forfeiture, or punishment as is in this sub-section mentioned; and any such investigation, legal proceedings, or remedy may be instituted continued, or enforced, and any such penalty, forfeiture, or punishment may be imposed as if the law had not been passed.

(3) When a law repeals wholly or partially any former law and substitutes provisions for the law so repealed, the repealed law shall remain in force until substituted provisions come into operation.

12)(1) The expressions 'commencement' and 'taking effect' when used in any law in reference thereto, shall mean the day on which that law comes or came into operation, and that day shall, subject to the provisions of sub-section (2) of this section and unless some other day is fixed by or under the law for the coming into operation thereof, be the day when the law was first published in the *Gazette* as law.

(3) Where any law, or any order, warrant, scheme, rules, regulations, or by-laws made, granted, or issued, under the authority of a law, is expressed to come into operation

on a particular day, the same shall be construed as coming into operation immediately on the expiration of the previous day.

(4) Where a law confers a power -

(a) to make any appointment; or

(b) to make grant or issue any instrument, order, warrant, scheme, rule, regulations, or by laws; or

(c) to give notices; or

(d) to prescribe forms; or

(e) to do any other act or thing for the purpose of the law,

that power may, unless the contrary intention appears, be exercised at any time after the passing of the law so far as may be necessary for the purpose of bringing the law into operation at the commencement thereof, subject to this restriction that any instrument, order, warrant, scheme, rules, regulations, or by-laws, made, granted, or issued under the power shall not, unless the contrary intention appears in the law or the contrary is necessary for bringing the law into operation, come into operation until the law comes into operation.

13) When any act, matter or thing is by law directed or authorized to be done by the Governor-General or by the Administrator, or by any public officer, the notification that such act, matter, or thing has been done, may unless a specified instrument or method is by that law prescribed for the notification, be by notice in the *Gazette*.

14) When any by-law, regulation, rule or order is authorized by any law to be made by the Governor-General, the Administrator, or by any local authority, public body, or person, with the approval of the Governor-General or the Administrator, such by-law, regulation, rule, or order, shall, subject to the provisions relative to the force and effect thereof in any law, be published in the *Gazette* and production of a copy of the *Gazette* captaining a notice of the making or approval (as the case may be) of the by-law, regulation, rule, or order by the Governor-General or the Administrator shall be sufficient evidence of such making or approval.

This Proclamation may be cited for all purposes as the *'The Interpretation of Laws Proclamation, 1920'*.

7.8 Review Questions

1. "The enactment of many a statute thus, by implication, calls on the courts to engage in supplemental law-making. That activity should always, of course, be modest in scope. But the necessary generality in the wording of many statutes, and ineptness in drafting of others, frequently compels the courts as best as they can, to fill in the gaps, an activity, which no matter how one may label it, is in part legislative". Per Frank J. in *Guiseppi v Walling* 144 F (2d) 608, 620-2 (CCA 2d, 1944) 621.

   Discuss, using relevant constitutional provisions and case law authority, both the nature of the legislative function of the courts and the factors that necessitate the assumption of that creative role by the Courts.

2. "The principle of Parliamentary sovereignty means neither more or less than this, namely, that Parliament thus defined has, under the English Constitution, the

right to make or unmake any law whatever; and, further, that no person or body is recognized by the law of England as having a right to override or set aside the legislation of Parliament". A. V Dicey, *An Introduction to the Study of the Law of the Constitution* 10th ed. p.39-40.

To what extent does the above statement describe the role of the Courts in relation to Acts passed by the Parliament of Namibia?

3. "In my opinion the rule has always been this – if the words of an Act admit of two interpretations then they are not clear; and if one interpretation leads to an absurdity, and the other does not, the Court will conclude that the legislature did not intend to lead to an absurdity, and will adopt the other interpretation. It is quite possible that such a construction might become imperative; but in order to justify a departure from the primary meaning of the words of the legislature, it must be shown either that the ordinary and grammatical construction of the words would lead to some absurdity, such as the legislature would never have contemplated, or that it would be plainly contrary to the general scheme disclosed in the context of the statute." Per Innes CJ in *Venter v R* 1907 TS 910.

   Discuss, using relevant case law authority, how the Courts have determined what constitutes an absurdity.

4. "Courts of law are not concerned with the question whether an Act of Parliament is reasonable or unreasonable, politic or impolitic." Per Centlivres CJ in *Harris & Others v Minister of Interior 1952* (2) SA 428 (AD) at 456.

   In the light of the Namibian Constitution and rules of interpretation, discuss the extent to which the above statement reflects the function of the Courts with regard to statutory interpretation.

5. "*Prima facie,* the intention of the legislature is to be deduced from the words which it has used. It is true that, owing to the elasticity which is inherent in language, it is admissible for a court in construing a statute to have regard not only to the language of the legislature, but also to its object and policy as gathered from a comparison of its several parts, as well as from the history of the law and from the circumstances applicable to its subject matter. And if on considerations of this nature, a court is satisfied that to accept the literal sense of the words would obviously defeat the intention of the legislature, it would be justified in not strictly adhering to that sense, but in putting upon the words such other signification as they are capable of bearing. The same principle is embodied in Lord Wensleydale's well-known 'Golden Rule'." Per De Villiers JA in *Principal Immigration Officer v Hawabu* 1936 AD 26 at 30-1.

   Discuss the statement above in the light of the cases of *Venter v Rex* 1907 TS 910 and *S v Takaendesa* 1972 (4) SA 72 and any other case law authority indicating the Courts' attitude towards deviation from the application of the literal rule of interpretation.

6. "Unlike the system that obtains in the United States, where in certain spheres, the Supreme Court in effect itself legislates by pronouncing its own constructions of the general precepts of the Constitution, in our country a judge must interpret the enactments of Parliament and the provincial councils and administer the

law, not as he perhaps would like it to be, or as he might consider it ought to be, but as set out in the relevant statutory provisions as interpreted. Once a judge has determined what he conceives to be the intention of the legislature, he must perforce give effect to the intention so determined." Per Ogilvie Thompson CJ, 1972 89 SALJ 30 at 33-4.

Discuss the above statement in the light of the Namibian Constitution and relevant case law.

7. Discuss, using relevant case law authority, the circumstances under which the court may deviate from the clear and unambiguous provisions of an Act.

8. "The intention of Parliament is not to be judged by what is in its mind, but by its expression of that mind in the statute itself'. Per Lord Thankerton in *Wicks v DPP* (1947) A.C. 362.

   Discuss this statement with reference to the rules of interpretation. Credit will be given for citation and discussion of cases.

9. "The incompleteness of textualism is most conspicuous when Parliament has explicitly or implicitly delegated law-making power to the Courts or when Parliament or the legislature has simply left a gap. In cases of delegated power or gap filling, the problem is not that words are susceptible to more than one interpretation, but instead require courts to look outside of the text. The problem of delegation or gap-filling must be distinguished from a 'gap' that is best taken as a legislative decision not to prohibit conduct or not to change the status quo. Here is a situation of straight-forward absence of law." CR Sustain; "Interpreting Statutes in the Regulatory State', *Harvard Law Review* vol. 103 p.421.

   Discuss this statement in the light of the opinions of Chief Justice Innes and Solomon JA in *Venter v R* 1907 TS 911, and Chief Justice Beadle in *S v Takaendesa* 1972 (4) SA 72 (AD).

10. "*Jus dicere non dare* is the function of the court, and the language of an Act of Parliament must neither be extended beyond its natural sense and proper limits in order to supply omissions or defects, nor strained to meet justice of an individual case". Per Hoexter JA in *R v Tebetha* 1959 (2) SA 337 (AD) at 346.

    Discuss the extent to which the above statement reflects the function of the court.

11. By far the most important rule to guide courts in arriving at that intention is to take the language of the instrument, or of the relevant portion of the instrument, as a whole, and when the words are clear and unambiguous, to place upon them their grammatical construction and give them their ordinary effect". Per Innes CJ in the *Venter v R* 1907 TS 910 at 913.

    In light of the rules of interpretation of statutes, how far does the above statement reflect the function of the courts?

12. "If the words of an Act are clear, you must follow them, even though they lead to a manifest absurdity. The Court has nothing to do with the question whether the legislature has committed an absurdity. In my opinion, the rule has always been this – if the words of an Act admit of two interpretations, then they are not

clear; and if one interpretation leads to an absurdity and the other does not, the Court will conclude that the legislature did not intend to lead to an absurdity, and will adopt the other interpretation." Per Lord Esher in The *Queen v Judge of the City of London Court* (1892) 1 QBD 290.

Discuss the above statement with specific reference to the rules of interpretation of statutes and case law authority.

Reading List

(a) Legislation

Interpretation of Laws Proclamation 37 of 1920

Constitution of Namibia: Articles 25 (1), 81 & 131

(b) Books

CJ Botha: *Statutory Interpretation* (Cape Town: Juta, 1996)

G Cockram: *The Interpretation of Statutes* (Cape Town: Juta, 1993)

VCRA Crabbe: *Understanding Statutes* (London: Cavendish, 1994)

GE Devenish: *Interpretation of Statutes* (Cape Town: Juta, 1992)

LM du Plessis: *The Interpretation of Statutes* (Durban: Butterworths, 1986)

HR Hahlo & E Kahn: *The South Africa Legal System and its Background* (Cape Town: Juta, 1968); p.176-212 & Chapter 9, p.304-325

EA Kellaway Principles of Legal Interpretation of Statutes, Contracts & Wills (Durban: Butterworths, 1995)

JR de Ville: Constitutional & Statutory Interpretation (Interdoc Consultants 2000)

(c) Articles

C Balmford: 'Adding Value by Writing Clearly' 1994 111*SALJ* 514-41

D Cowen: 'The Interpretation of Statutes and the Concept of the Intention of the Legislature' 1980 43 *THRHR* 374-99

D Cowen: 'Prolegomenon to a Restatement of the Principles of Statutory Interpretation' 1976 *TSAR* 131-67

J de Ville: 'Meaning and Statutory Interpretation' 1999 62 *THRHR* 373-89

AM Dlamini: 'Is There a Literal Interpretation in Law?' 1991 6 *SAPR/PL* 16-30

J Duggard: 'Statutory Interpretation as an Exercise in Choice' 1978 SALJ 451

L du Plessis: 'Tentative Reflections on the Systemization of the Rules and Presumptions of Statutory Interpretation 1981 98 *SALJ* 211-17

C Forsyth: 'Interpreting a Bill of Rights: the Future Task of a Reformed Judiciary' (1991 7 *SAJHR* 1-23)

J Kentridge & D Spitz: 'Interpretation in M Chaskalson et al (eds) *Constitutional Law in South Africa* (Cape Town: Juta, 1996, loose-leaf edition), Chapter 11

AS Mathews: 'The South African Judiciary and the Security System' 1985 1 *SAJHR* 199-209

GJC Strydom: 'A Bill of Rights and Value Judgments versus Positivism: The Namibian Experience' in Kruger & B Currin (eds*) Interpreting a Bill of Rights* (Cape Town: Juta, 1994) pp 94-102

J Wills: 'Statutory Interpretation in a Nutshell' 1938 40 *SALJ* 187-94 & 322-36.

(d) Cases

(i) Sources of Interpretation of Statutes

De Villiers v The Cape Divisional Council 1875 Buch 50

Ex parte Hettish & Marine, In re Luderitz Verein 1923 SWA 39, 41

(ii) The role of the Judges

Sachs v Donges 1952 (2) SA 265

Seluka v Suskin and Salkow 1912 TPD 258.

R v Tebetha 1959 (2) SA 337

Union Government v Thompson 1919 AD 404,425

Ellis Stadium Ltd V Minister of Justice 1989 3 SA 898 (T), 903

J. Duggard, Human Rights and the South African Legal Order **(**Cape Town: Juta, 1978) Especially pages 370-81 and 303.

AS Mathews, 'The South African Judiciary and the Security System' (1985) 1 SAJHR 199-209.

(iii) The Intention of the Legislature

Farrar's Estate v CIR 1926 TPD 501-6

Holy Trinity Church v United States Supreme Court of the United States, 1892. 143 U.S. 457, 12 S.Ct. 511, 36 L. Ed. 226

In the Estate of Setrak Avakian Tekemt 13, 1956 E.C.

Engels v Allied Chemical Manufacturers 1992 NR 372 (HC)

Hannah v Government of Namibia 2000 4 SA 940 (NmLC)

Ngeve Raphael Sikunda v GRN (High Court)

(iv) The Literal Rule

Venter v R 1907 TS 910, 914-5

S v Takaendesa 1972 (4) SA 72

Volschenk v Volschenk 1946 TPD 486

Dadoo v Krugersdorp Municipality 1920 AD 530

R v Detody 1926 AD 198

Union Government v Mack 1917 AD 731 750

Seluka v Suskin & Salkow 1912 TPD 258,270

Sachs v Minister of Justice 1934 AD 1

Minster of Interior v Lockhat 1961 2 SA 587 (A)

Omar v Minister of Law & Order 1987 3 SA 859 (A)

Magor & St Mellons v Newport Corporation 1950 2 ALL ER 1226 (CA)

Hleka v Johannesburg City Council 1949 1 SA 842 (A), 852 (mischief rule)

S v Negongo 1992 NR 352 (HC)

(v) The Golden Rule

Venter v R TS 910

Elliot v C (a minor) 1983 2 All ER 1005 (QBD), 1010

Dadoo v Krugersdorp Municipal Council 1920 AD 530

Monnakale v Republic of Bophutatswana 1991 1 SA 589,615

J. Duggrad: 'The Opinion on SWA (Namibia): The Teleologists Triumph' (1971) 88 SALJ 460.

Holy Trinity Church v United States 143 U.S. 457, 12 S.Ct. 511, 36 L.Ed. 226

R v Takawira and Others 1965 RLR 162

In the Estate of Setra Avakian (the application of the teleological theory based on the principles of equity and fairness).

R v Detody 1926 AD 198, 229

R v Oakes 1959 2 All ER 92

Chandler and Others v DPP 1962 3 All ER 142

(vi) The Mischief Rule

The Rule in Heydon's case

Holy Trinity Church v United States

In the Estate of Setra Avakian

(vii) *Restrictiv*e or Unrestrictive Interpretation

(viii) The *iusdem generis* rule

The Attorney General v Abdullah and Others (1960) E.A.C.A. 672

S v Buthelezi 1979 (3) SA 1439

S v Sayed 1962 (2) SA 128

S v Van der Merwe 1977 (2) SA 774

S v Makandingoa 1981 (4) SA 439

CHAPTER 8

THE CONCEPT OF CONSTITUTIONALISM

8.1 Introduction

The writings of the 18th century philosophers, such as Montesquieu, on political and legal theories emphasised the need for checks and balances on the powers of the separate branches of government in order to avoid the concentration of power in one particular branch of government and to prevent dictatorship and arbitrariness in government. It has been recognised by constitutional lawyers that one way of achieving this objective is the subjection of the exercise of powers of government to predetermined rules rather than some extra-legal means of restraint. This concept of limited government by predetermined rules is the subject matter of constitutionalism. Nwabueze describes the subject matter of constitutionalism as follows:

> **Government is universally accepted to be a necessity, since man cannot fully realise himself – his creativity, his dignity and his whole personality – except within an ordered society. Yet the necessity for government creates its own problem for man, the problem of how to limit the arbitrariness inherent in government, and to ensure that its powers are to be used for the good of society. It is this limiting of arbitrariness of political power that is expressed in the concept of constitutionalism. Constitutionalism recognizes the necessity for government but insists upon a limitation being placed upon its powers. It connotes in essence therefore a limitation on government; it is the antithesis of arbitrary rule; its opposite is despotic government, the government of will instead of law. Arbitrary rule is government conducted not according to pre-determined rules, but according to the momentary whims and caprices of the rulers; and an arbitrary government is no less so because it happens to be benevolent, since all unfettered power is by its very nature autocratic. A dictatorship is thus clearly not a constitutional government, however benevolent it may be, and a totalitarian regime is even less so[346].**

Constitutionalism[347] as a concept that deals with the limitation on government and the checks on unfettered exercise of power by government is evidently an all-

---

[346] Nwabueze, B.O. 1973. *Constitutionalism in the Emergent States.* London: C. Hurst.

[347] See also Vile, M.J.C. 1967. *Constitutionalism and the Separation of Powers.* Indianapolis: Liberty Fund. p.1 who defines constitutionalism as follows: "Governments wield considerable power. Constitutions, while they may create the institutions of government and allocate power to these institutions, also generally seek to control or restrain the exercise of power. The principle of Constitutionalism rests on this idea of restraining the government in its exercise of power. Constitutionalism, therefore, is to be set in contradistinction to arbitrary power".

embracing concept encompassing areas of law and political science. In a nutshell, it concerns itself with the doctrines of separation of powers, legislative sovereignty and constitutional supremacy (including judicial review of legislation), the independence of the Judiciary, judicial review of administrative action and the rule of law. In this chapter, the concept will be dealt with under the areas mentioned with emphasis on the limitation that is placed on government in order to ensure that government is conducted according to law and not according to the momentary whims and caprices of the rulers. The general principles will be discussed in the context of the Namibian constitutional regime and practice.

8.2 Separation of powers

According to the general principles of Montesquieu's theory of the constitutional separation of powers, the three organs of State in the exercise of their constitutional functions are said to be independent of each other and in the exercise of the functions of government, as provided for under the constitution, one branch of government should not interfere with the functions of another organ of State. The doctrine recognises the existence of these organs of State, the Executive, the Legislature and the Judiciary, as provided for by Art. (1)(3) of the Namibian Constitution[348] but it also recognises the fact that in order to guarantee and protect the civil liberties of the individual, and to prevent dictatorship and absolutism, there should be established mechanisms that are capable of putting constitutional and legal restraints on the powers of government or the various organs of State. The doctrine of separation of powers therefore can be considered as a tool, or *sine qua non*, for the achievement of constitutionalism.

8.2.1 The Executive

Executive power of the Republic of Namibia vests in the President and the Cabinet[349]. The Namibian Constitution, like those in most African States, creates the system of executive presidency and therefore, the President as the head of the Executive chairs the meetings of the cabinet[350]. These responsibilities place him in a position to have considerable influence over policies and bills to be tabled before Parliament. He is also responsible for the appointments (and dismissals) of the Prime Minister, Ministers and Deputy Ministers, the Attorney-General, the Director General of Planning, and on the recommendation of the appropriate Service Commissions appoints the Chief Justice, the Judge President of the High Court, and other Judges of the Supreme Court and High Court, the Ombudsman, the Prosecutor-General, the Auditor-General, the Governor and Deputy-Governor of the Central Bank, the Chief of the Defence Force, the Inspector General of Police, and the Commissioner of Prisons[351]. He is

[348] Article (1) (3) of the Namibian Constitution. The main organs of State shall be the Executive, the Legislature and the Judiciary.

[349] Article (27) (2) ibid.

[350] Article (32) (3) ibid.

[351] See generally Article 32 ibid.

also vested with certain legislative functions[352] and has jurisdiction to appoint six persons as members of Parliament. In his capacity as the Executive President, he is the Commander in Chief of the Defence Forces. It is evident from these provisions, that the President is vested with a great deal of power and responsibilities, which, if not restrained, may potentially lead to the creation of a dictatorship.

Therefore, there is a general provision[353] that subjects the exercise of the presidential executive functions to the overriding terms of the Constitution, the laws of Namibia, the rule of law and obliges the president to uphold, protect and defend the Constitution as the supreme law. The constitutional and other legal restraints constitute the subject matter of constitutionalism which is discussed.

It must be mentioned, first and foremost, that although the President enjoys immunity from civil and criminal proceedings for any act done in his or her official capacity as President or during his or her tenure of office as President, under the provisions of Art. 31(3)(b), Parliament may by resolution subject the President to impeachment proceedings and have him or her removed from office as President. Such a measure will result in the deprivation of the immunity and subject the President to civil or criminal proceedings.

Under Art. 32(2) the President during the presentation and consideration of budget is obliged to attend Parliament and during such session the President shall address Parliament on the state of the nation and on the future policies of the previous year and be available to respond to questions. This practice serves as an effective restraint on the powers of the Executive by the Legislature in situations where there is an effective opposition and an independently minded Legislature. In certain democracies, the rejection of the official budget by Parliament will necessitate a resolution for a vote of no confidence.

The exercise of executive powers is also subject to judicial review, under the generality of the provisions of Articles 25 and 18 of the Constitution. Art. 25[354], *inter alia* empowers the Judiciary to declare invalid any executive action which abolishes or abridges the fundamental rights and freedoms conferred by Chapter 3 of the Constitution and Art. 18[355], which deals with administrative justice, empowers the courts to review administrative action.

8.2.2 The Legislature

Article 44 of the Namibian Constitution vests legislative functions in the National Assembly with the assent of the President, subject to the powers and functions of the National Council. It can therefore be said that the Namibian Legislature has two

[352] Article 32 (5) (a) (b) ibid.

[353] Article 32 (1) ibid.

[354] See *Ex Parte Attorney-General: In re Corporal Punishment by Organs of State* 1991 NR 178; *Kauesa v Minister of Home Affairs and Another* 1995 NR 175; *S v Sipula* 1994 NR 41.

[355] See pp.304-309 and also *Nanditume v Minister of Defence* 2000 NR 103 where it was held that the exclusion of the applicant from the Defence Force on the ground that he had tested HIV positive constituted unfair discrimination in contravention of s. 107 of the Labour Act 6 of 1992.

Houses and operates under the bicameral system. However, principal legislative authority is vested in the National Assembly[356] and the functions of the National Council in relation to those of the National Assembly are, in principle, advisory[357]. Legislative functions are collectively exercised by the President, National Assembly and National Council. This function is granted by the Constitution, *exclusively* to the legislative branch of government and therefore Parliament in Namibia is vested with legislative sovereignty.

The concept of legislative or parliamentary sovereignty is an important concept in constitutionalism as it describes and delimits the power relationships and dynamics between the various branches of government. The nature of a constitution of a particular jurisdiction will determine what constitutes parliamentary sovereignty and the nature of restraints imposed on Parliament. This will be determined by whether the constitution is a written or unwritten constitution. A.V. Dicey in his exposition of the English Constitution states that:

> **(t)he principle of Parliamentary sovereignty means neither more or less than this, namely, that parliament thus defined has, under the English Constitution, the right to make or unmake any law whatever; and further, that no person or body is recognized by the law of England as having the right to override or set aside the Legislation of Parliament.**[358]

The description of the nature of parliamentary sovereignty of the English Constitution given by Dicey, ousts the jurisdiction of the courts to review an act of Parliament. It must be pointed out, however, that the English Constitution is said to be unwritten and it is now a cardinal principle of constitutionalism that under a written constitution the concept of the sovereignty of the Legislature does not necessarily exclude the supremacy of the Constitution. It must also be added that even in England the principle of parliamentary supremacy does not completely oust the jurisdiction of the courts to review legislation.

Namibia operates under a written constitution which is the supreme law of the land[359]. Parliament derives its authority from the Constitution and the exercise of legislative functions of Parliament is subject to the constitution. Therefore, under the Namibian Constitution legislative sovereignty is limited by supremacy of the constitution. The inherent jurisdiction of the courts to interpret and review legislation and uphold the fundamental rights of the individual in jurisdictions where the concept of constitutional supremacy operates is a recognised concept in constitutional and

---

[356] Article (63) (1) of the Namibian Constitution.

[357] A case in point relates to the *modus operandi* adopted by National Council in the process of the promulgation of the Married Persons Equality Bill into law. It is common knowledge that the National Council had embarked on a national public opinion exercise to assist it in formulating its recommendations to National Assembly and that the National Assembly did not feel itself bound by these recommendations and therefore were not incorporated in the final Bill to the President.

[358] Dicey, A. V. 1982. *An introduction to the Study of the Constitution.* Indianapolis: Liberty Classics.

[359] Article (1) (6) of the Namibian Constitution provides that '[T]his Constitution shall be the Supreme Law of Namibia'.

human rights law. The common law precedent in the famous American case of *Marbury v Madison*[360], recognising the jurisdiction of the courts to review acts of Congress, has been given the constitutional fiat. As mentioned earlier, Art. 25(1)(a) of the Namibian Constitution gives a court of competent jurisdiction the power to declare an act of parliament, which is inconsistent with the provisions of Chapter 3 of the Constitution or the Bill of Rights, invalid. It must be added, however, that instead of declaring the act of parliament invalid, the court has the discretion to refer it to the National Assembly for the defect in the impugned law to be corrected. The Judiciary in Namibia has exercised this discretion to review legislation and in appropriate cases declared the unconstitutionality of the laws in question[361]. The process of judicial review involves an interpretive exercise and under the common law tradition of binding precedent and *stare decisis*, which are followed by the Namibian legal system, such decisions become binding precedents and form part of the laws of Namibia. This indicates the role of the Courts as the custodian of the Constitution and more especially the rights of the individual and it also goes to confirm the law creating functions of the courts.

The jurisdiction granted to the Courts by Art. 25 to review legislation and declare its constitutionality, it would appear, relates only to the substantive law. There is no express provision in the Constitution that grants the Courts the jurisdiction to review legislation and declare such legislation invalid, as the case may be, on grounds of procedural defect. In the English case of *Pickin v British Railways Board*[362], Lord Reid stated that "no court in England has the power to declare invalid any act of parliament on grounds of procedural defect." This view, however, is a consequence of the nature of the parliamentary sovereignty in England. In jurisdictions operating under written constitutions the view or the precedent in the case of the *Bribery Commissioners v Ranasinghe*[363] appears to be the correct view of the law. In that case the Judicial Committee of the Privy Council held that under a written constitution which prescribes a procedure for law-making, the courts are not only entitled to go outside the official copy of the act of Parliament in order to enquire into the question of procedure, but have a duty to declare the act invalid if in fact it was passed without due form.

Notwithstanding the control over legislation granted to the courts by the Namibian Constitution, there are other constitutional control mechanisms over legislative sovereignty These include the Executive's right of veto[364] and dissolution of Parliament[365], the subjection of the Legislature to the will of the Electorate, and the legislative element implicit in the concept of referendum.

[360] *Marbury v Madison*, 5 U.S. 137, 2L E. 60 (1803).

[361] See footnote 231 supra.

[362] *Pickin v British Railways Board* (1974) AC 765.

[363] *The Bribery Commissioner v Ranasinghe* (1965) A.C. 172.

[364] Article 64 of the Namibian Constitution.

[365] Article 32 (3) of the Namibian Constitution.

8.2.3 The Judiciary

An analysis of the jurisdiction given to the Courts over the exercise of the mandates of the other two organs of State will indicate that the Judiciary is entrusted with the important, and at times the unenviable task, of maintaining the checks and balances between the two organs of State to ensure that one organ does not usurp the functions of the other and more significantly to protect and defend the rights of the individual granted by the Bill of Rights. The exercise of this responsibility enjoins the courts to

> **safeguard the judicial branch from all forms of encroachment, either by way of legislation or executive conduct, into the exercise of public justice. This raises the crucial question of the independence of the Judiciary which is the bedrock of the doctrine of separation of powers and the foundation upon which the success or otherwise of constitutional democracy is based."[366]**

Article 78 of the Namibian Constitution that establishes the judicial branch of government does recognise and provide for the independence of the Judiciary but the maintenance of this independence depends on a multiplicity of factors not excluding the integrity and fortitude of the judges to resist the temptations of political patronage and interference, subtle or otherwise, from the other branches of government. This is not a disconcerting observation if cognisance is taken of the fact that judicial appointments and dismissals, and the administration of the Judiciary are vested in the Executive.

8.3 Judicial review of administrative action

8.3.1 Administrative justice

Under the common law principles of administrative law, the exercise of administrative discretion is subject to judicial review and extra-judicial adjudication. This principle enjoins administrative officials and bodies to comply with certain legal rules in the exercise of administrative discretion granted by law. Under the principles of judicial review of administrative action, an individual aggrieved by the exercise of administrative discretion or administrative action has the right to judicial redress. This makes the right justiciable under the common law: the courts have the jurisdiction to review that administrative decision or action and make an appropriate order. In Namibia, this common law right to judicial review and extra-judicial adjudication granted to the individual has been elevated to a fundamental human right protected by the Constitution.

Article 18 of the Namibian Constitution provides that administrative bodies and administrative officials shall act fairly and reasonably and comply with the requirements imposed upon such bodies and officials by common law and any relevant legislation.

[366] Okpaluba, C. "Constitutionality of legislation relating to the distribution of governmental powers in Namibia: A Comparative Approach". In: Hinz, M.O.; Amoo, S.K. & Van Wyk, D. (eds.) 2002. *The Constitution at Work: 10 years of Namibian Nationhood.* Windhoek: University of Namibia.

Persons aggrieved by the exercise of such acts and decisions shall have the right to seek redress before a competent court or tribunal. This article comes under the entrenched provisions of the Bill of Rights and therefore under the Namibian legal system, the jurisdiction of the courts to review administrative action and the justiciability of this right by any person aggrieved by the exercise of administrative discretion come under the regime and protection of the constitution. Judicial review of administrative action is therefore one of the constitutional mechanisms meant to protect the rights of the individual and prevent the potential abuse of discretionary power.

The nature of present day public administration is such that a certain degree of administrative discretion is indispensable for the effective and expeditious day to day running of government. It promotes flexibility by individualising the treatment of problems and permits the adjustment of public power to varying circumstances in order to avoid the undesirable restraints resulting from the rigid application of general standards and requirements of bureaucracy of public administration. An administrative body or official is said to have discretion in a matter when that official or body has the power or liberty to choose between alternative courses of action and the correctness or incorrectness of the decision cannot be demonstrated. J.M. Evans[367] defines the concept of discretion as:

> **power to make a choice between alternative courses of action. If only one course can lawfully be adopted, the decision taken is not the exercise of a discretion but the performance of a duty. To say that somebody has a discretion presupposes that there is no uniquely right answer to his problem.**

Discretion may be vested in an administrative authority either by the Constitution itself or a statute and in the case of the latter, the discretionary power must be within constitutionally permissible limits. There is no discretion vested by virtue of common law, but since it is the law courts that are the ultimate interpreters of statutes, the scope of discretionary powers is determined by the law courts.

It is evident from the very nature of administrative discretion that it is potentially susceptible to abuse. As a general principle, discretionary power is not susceptible to external control because once the legislature has vested the necessary discretionary powers in the administrator, it has little control over the misuse and abuse of the powers. Even judicial control, which is granted by Art. 18, is limited because, as it will be explained, to the extent that an administrator may act within his discretionary powers, judicial control is virtually non-existent. The exercise of a discretion may be impugned on grounds contemplated under Art. 18. In the case of *Chairperson of the Immigration Selection Board v Frank & Another*[368] C.J. Strydom, in his analysis of the nature of administrative discretion in the context of the powers given to the officials of the Ministry of Home Affairs to grant permanent residence permits, held that:

> **there is also authority for the principle that a foreign national cannot claim permanent residence as of right and that the State has an exclusive discretion as to**

[367] Evans, J.M. 1980. *De Smith's Judicial Review of Administrative Actions.* London: Stevens & Sons Ltd.

[368] *Chairperson of the Immigration Selection Board v Frank & Another* 2001 NR 107 (SC).

> **whether it would allow such nationals in its territory. However, as far as Namibia is concerned, this principle is subject to the provisions of Art. 18 of the Constitution and as long as the Board acts fairly and reasonably and in accordance with a fair procedure there is no basis for interference by a Court of Law.**

The application of the provisions of Art. 18 is limited to acts by administrative bodies and officials[369] who have been exhaustively defined to include the Executive, regional and local government, the public service, the parastatals and employees[370] thereof. The provisions of the article enjoin them, *inter alia,* to 'act fairly and reasonably and comply with requirements imposed upon such bodies and officials by common law…'. In the English case of *Board of Education v Rice*[371] the concept of fairness was interpreted to mean that the interpreter must comply with the principles of natural justice. In the Namibian case of *Chairperson of the Immigration Selection Board v Frank & Another*[372] it was held that the article does not draw a distinction between quasi judicial and administrative acts and administrative justice whether quasi judicial or administrative in nature requires not only reasonable and fair decisions, based on reasonable grounds, but inherent in that requirement are fair procedures which are transparent. The old common law rule that the requirements of the principle of natural justice are to be applied where an administrator acts in judicial or quasi judicial capacity has been replaced by this constitutional requirement which enjoins administrators in the exercise of their discretion to apply the principles of natural justice. Chief Justice Strydom also alluded in his judgment to the requirement that the principles of natural justice must be applied under the principle of legitimate expectation. It can be inferred from his judgment that the concept is part of the common law of Namibia. The concept of legitimate expectation, which was developed in order to mitigate the harsh effects of the categorisation of administrative acts, means that:

> **the rules of natural justice are extended to cases where the affected party has no vested right, but does have a potential right or legitimate expectation that his application will succeed, and has therefore gained a right to be heard by virtue of his expectation.**[373]

The common law principles of natural justice are the *audi alteram partem* rule and the *nemo iudex causa* rule. The *audi alteram partem* rule, which imposes on the administrator the duty to grant a fair hearing in the exercise of administrative discretion, was also discussed in the *Frank case*[374]. C.J. Strydom stated in that case that the rule embodies various principles, the application of which is flexible

[369] Parker, C. "The Administrative Justice Provision of the Constitution of the Republic of Namibia: a Constitutional Protection of Judicial Review and Tribunal Adjudication under Administrative Law", 24 *Comparative and International Law Journal of Southern Africa* 1991.

[370] C. Parker ibid.

[371] *Board of Education v Rice,* 1911 AC. 179.

[372] *Chairperson of the Immigration Selection Board v Frank & Another* 2001 NR 107 (SC).

[373] Hosten, W.J.; Edwards, A.B.; Bosman, F. & Church, J. 1997. *op.cit.* p.1062-3. See also *Administrator of Transvaal v Traub* 1989 4 SA 731.

[374] *Chairperson of Immigration Selection Board v Frank & Another* 2001 NR 107 (SC).

depending on the circumstances of each case and the statutory requirements for the exercise of a particular discretion. In Namibian jurisprudence, he laid down the following requirements as some of the demands of the rule.

> **(i) The board or the administrator need not in each instance give an applicant an oral hearing, but may give an applicant an opportunity to deal with matter in writing.**
>
> **(ii) If a board or administrator acts on information they are privy to or information given to them by the Chief of Immigration and if such information is potentially prejudicial to an applicant, it must be communicated to him or her in order to enable such person to deal therewith and to rebut it if possible. However, where an applicant should reasonably have foreseen that prejudicial information or facts would reach the appellant (board or administrative official), he or she is duty bound to disclose such information.**
>
> **(iii) It is implicit in the provisions of Art. 18 of the Constitution that an administrative organ exercising a discretion is obliged to give reasons for its decision. There can be little hope for transparency if an administrative organ is allowed to keep the reasons for its decision secret. The article requires administrative organs and officials to act fairly and reasonably. Whether these requirements were complied with can, more often than not, only be determined once reasons have been provided. This also bears relation to the specific right accorded by Art. 18 to persons to seek redress before a competent Court or Tribunal where they are aggrieved by the exercise of such acts or decisions.**

The other rule of natural justice is that a person should not be a judge in his own cause; this is known as *nemo judex in causa sua*. This is a rule against bias. This rule, however, has limited application in relation to the exercise of administrative power in the sense that:

> **in modern public administration there are many instances where the administrative body or administrative official may be both the decision-maker and the judge in the same matter. What the natural justice rule against bias seeks to prevent is personal bias and not, it would appear, ministerial or agency bias where the official is enforcing policies of his ministry, for instance.**[375]

For the Court to set aside the decision of an administrator on grounds of bias substantial or real bias must be established. Pecuniary interests and other interests in the result of the decision have been held to constitute bias that will justify the nullification of the decision of an administrator on grounds of bias[376].

Lack of compliance with the principles of natural justice will justify the intervention of the courts by nullifying and setting aside the decision but as stated by C.J. Strydom in the *Frank case*[377] as a general principle courts are not permitted to substitute their decisions for the decision of the administrator because the discretion is granted to

[375] Parker, C. (*op cit*).

[376] *Metropolitan Properties Co (FGC) Ltd v Lannon* 1969 1 QB 577.

[377] *Chairperson of Immigration Selection Board v Frank & Another* 2001 NR 109 (SC).

the administrator and to do otherwise will amount to usurpation of the power of the administrator and a breach of the principles of separation of powers. However, a court would exercise the discretion itself where there are exceptional circumstances present[378]. And examples of instances where the courts have exercised their jurisdiction not to refer a matter back include cases where there were long periods of delay, where the applicant would suffer prejudice or where it would be grossly unfair[379].

The Article also requires that administrative bodies and officials act 'reasonably'. As contrasted with the requirements of natural justice, this requirement deals with the substance of the decision itself. As C. Parker[380] explains:

> **natural justice and fairness are concerned with procedural constraints on administrative action. But the requirement that an administrative body or an administrative official should act reasonably, is concerned with the substance of the discretion or the act itself. That is to say, the courts reviewing an administrative action should go beyond procedural requirements and examine the nature of the decision or act even where the administrative authority purportedly acted in pursuance of a discretionary power.**

The purpose of this requirement is for the courts to be vested with jurisdiction to ascertain whether the exercise of the discretion was tainted with abuse of power. Areas of abuse of power may include bad faith, ulterior purpose, and failure on the part of the repository of the discretion to apply his mind to the question before him or to take into account extraneous considerations. In the Zambian case of *Chilufya v City Council of Kitwe*[381] it was held that a city council which terminates a trader's licence to occupy a market stall by resolution influenced by political considerations is acting unreasonably, unfairly and contrary to the principles of natural justice and therefore, *ultra vires.*

The other requirement of Art. 18 is that administrative bodies and administrative officials must comply with the requirements imposed by common law and any relevant legislation. The common law requirements referred to are the principles relating to application of the principles of natural justice in the exercise of discretion, which are discussed above. The demands of the latter requirement accord with the general objectives of the doctrine of constitutionalism. It has already been discussed under the nature of administrative discretion that the discretion is granted by either the Constitution or a statute and in the context of the demands of constitutionalism

---

378 See *W.C. Greyling & Erasmus (Pty) Ltd v Johannesburg Local Road Transportation Board and Others* 1982 (4) SA 427.

379 See *Greyling (*ibid), *Dawlaan Beleggings (Edms) BPK. v Johannesburg Stock Exchange (Edms) Bpk and Others* 1983 (3) SA 344 (WLD) at 369G-H and *Local Road Transportation Board and Another v Durban City Council and Another* 1965 (1) SA 586 (AD) at 598 d-599.

380 Parker, C. (*op cit*).

381 *Chilufya v City Council of Kitwe* 1967 ZR 115 at 116. See also the case of *Administrator, Transvaal, and Others v Traub and Others* 1989 (4) SA 731 at 750, where similar sentiments were raised with regard to the factors that motivated the Director 's decision.

that the powers of government must be controlled in order to prevent abuse and arbitrariness, and even more so in the exercise of administrative discretion on account of the very nature of discretion. It is therefore, the general practice for limitations to be imposed by the Constitution or a particular statute granting the discretion. The Constitution or the statute that grants the discretion will normally state the scope of discretion and the procedure to be followed in the exercise of the discretion. These constitute limitations in the sense that non-compliance will be a ground for judicial review and a possible declaration by the courts that the decision is *ultra vires* and therefore void. In the case of *Sikunda v Government of the Republic of Namibia*[382], the Court set aside the deportation order issued under the hand of the Minister of Home Affairs on the ground that the Security Commission was not properly constituted when it purported to consider the Minister's request and made its recommendation. A statutory precondition for a valid decision by the Minister was not fulfilled and consequently the Minister did not have the jurisdiction to make the deportation order in question. This was upheld on appeal by the Supreme Court. It must also be added that the act of parliament that grants the discretionary power must itself be consistent with the provisions of the Constitution, especially Chapter 3 thereof.

Under the provisions of the constitution and common law, any person aggrieved by the exercise of discretion can bring an action for the review of the decision or administrative action for any of the remedies, *certiorari*, prohibition or interdict, mandamus, habeas corpus and damages.

8.4 The rule of law, the Namibian Constitution and the Bill of Rights

The doctrines of the rule of law and constitutionalism are related concepts because they both deal with the limits on the exercise of the powers of government. Simply defined, the doctrine of rule of law deals with governance according to law, and not according to momentary whims and caprices of government, and the protection of the fundamental rights of the individual. It also underscores the need for a workable legal and political system that guarantees the achievement of the objectives of the doctrine. A.V. Dicey[383] attributes three meanings to the doctrine:

> **We mean, in the first place, that no man is punishable or can be lawfully made to suffer in body or goods except for a distinct breach of law established in the ordinary legal manner before the ordinary courts of the land. In this sense the rule of law is contrasted with every system of government based on the exercise by persons in authority of wide, arbitrary, or discretionary powers of constraint.**
>
> **We mean in the second place, when we speak of the 'rule of law' as a characteristic of our country, not only that with us no man is above the law, but (what is different is a different thing) that here every man, whatever be his rank or condition, is**

[382] *Sikunda v Government of the Republic of Namibia* 2001 (3) NR (HC) 181.

[383] Dicey, A.V. 1982. *op.cit.*

> **subject to the ordinary law of the realm and amenable to the jurisdiction of the ordinary tribunals.**
>
> **There remains yet a third and a different sense in which the "rule of law" or the predominance of the legal spirit may be described as a special attribute of English institutions. We may say that the Constitution is pervaded by the rule of law on the ground that the general principles of the Constitution (as for example the right to personal liberty, or the right of public meeting) are with us the result of judicial decisions determining the rights of private persons in particular cases brought before the courts; whereas under many foreign Constitutions the security (such as it is) given to the rights of individuals results, or appears to result, from the general principles of the Constitution.**

The obvious relationship between Dicey's definition of rule of law and the English system demands that its utility and application will be limited to reliance on general principles. In the context of the Namibian legal system, Dicey's exposition will serve as a point of departure. The definition will serve as a source of general principles. The general principles are the preconditions and prerequisites of fair trial and punishment, equality before the law and the provision and enforcement of human rights. An analysis of the Namibian constitutional and legal system indicates that the principles embodied in Dicey's exposition are accommodated in the Namibian system.

Namibia operates under the concept of constitutional supremacy. The civil and criminal laws of Namibia are interpreted and administered by competent courts duly established under the provisions of the constitution or relevant legislation. Kangaroo and *ad hoc* courts do not exist under the constitution. The constitution has a Bill of Rights which is entrenched and one of which is equality before the law. Dicey emphasises the rule of law as essential in ensuring the elimination of arbitrariness and dictatorship by government and in enforcing constitutionalism in government. In the Namibian context, this can be achieved if there is even the minimum adherence to constitutional governance. As stated earlier the Namibian Constitution has a Bill of Rights that is based on principles of various international conventions and standards that are meant to promote the rule of law and the maintenance and protection of the rights of the individual.

Under Chapter 3 of the Constitution these fundamental rights and freedoms are enshrined and entrenched and they include protection of life, protection of liberty, respect for human dignity, abolition of slavery or forced labour, equality and freedom from discrimination, arbitrary arrest or detention, access to fair trial, the guaranteeing of privacy and respect for family, the right to acquire property, the right to association, freedom of speech, etc. The Namibian Courts have handed down a number of cases upholding the rights of individuals under the Bill of Rights including the rights of persons with HIV/AIDS[384] and the right of accused persons to legal representation provided by the State[385].

---

[384] *Nanditume v Minister of Defence* 2000 NR 103.

[385] *Government of the Republic of Namibia & Others v Geofrey Kupuzo Mwilima & Others* Supreme Court Case No: SA 29/2001.

Under Art. 25 of the Constitution, the courts are given the power to declare any law or any action of the Executive and agencies of the government that is inconsistent with the provisions of Chapter 3, invalid. However, it may be added that the derogation from or the suspensions of some of these rights are permitted under Articles 24 and 26 where a state of emergency, a state of national defence and martial law, have been declared. But the exercise of the power granted to the Executive under Chapter 4 must comply with the provisions of Art. 24(2), so that if these provisions are not complied with the exercise of these powers can be challenged.

The short history of Namibia's existence as a sovereign State abounds with experiences and evidence that the desire for a constitutional order that did not only motivate the strong desire for the struggle for self-determination but also that the dictates and precepts of the doctrine of constitutionalism and rule of law have become the guiding principles and dictates behind the exercise of power by the three branches of government. The Namibian Judiciary has demonstrated its resolve to protect and maintain the rights of the individual through a number of cases which have even involved the nullification of Executive action and the declaration of the unconstitutionality of some legislation. There have been pronouncements on the part of the Executive not only to respect the decisions of courts but also to maintain its independence which is crucial if the rule of law and constitutionalism are to be maintained in Namibia.

8.5 Extracts

HINZ, M.O.; AMOO, S.K. & VAN WYK, D. (editors).

The Constitution at Work: 10 Years of Namibian Nationhood (2002)

'Constitutionality of Legislation relating to the Distribution of Governmental Powers in Namibia: A Comparative Approach'

C Okpaluba[386*]

1. INTRODUCTION

The coming of modern written constitutions has brought with them the dichotomy of constitutionality/unconstitutionality whereby both the acts of the executive and the legislature are tested having regard to the provisions of the constitution upon which governmental powers are exercised in the first instance. Judicial review under the Constitution does not therefore begin and end with the interpretation of statutory powers; it has more to do with the interpretation of the Constitution. For instance, the rules of natural justice, a veritable ground for review at common law[387], have been incorporated into many of the modern constitutions[388] such that any person who alleges that his or her right has been breached by a government department or public authority in disregard of these principles, in what

[386] *Professor of Law, University of the North, South Africa.

[387] The leading text, *De Smith's Judicial Review of Administrative Action*, now in its 6th edition by Woolf & Jowell 1995 is a monumental evidence of this type of system. See also Fordham (2ed 1997) *Judicial Review Handbook*.

[388] See s 33, Constitution of the Federal Republic of Nigeria 1979; s 33, Constitution of the Republic of South Africa 1996. See now the Promotion of Administrative Justice Act No 3 of 2000 (RSA).

is purely an administrative law situation, would also point to the relevant provisions of the constitution that protect the rights alleged to have been breached[389]. A study of judicial review in this context[390] is largely an exercise in constitutional interpretation[391].

Under these Constitutions where functions are clearly distributed among the three organs of state, the legislature, the executive and the judiciary, there becomes the need that one of these organs be entrusted with the power, whenever called upon, to constantly keep the other organs in check in the performance of their duties and to ensure the observance of the constitutional distribution of the powers by all the organs. That organ is the Judiciary. In effect, the doctrine of separation of powers needs to be enforced by the court under the current system, a form of judicial control, whereby the legislative and the executive arms account for their observance or non-observance of their respective constitutional mandates. In this state of affairs, the courts have the duty to adjudicate disputes between the legislature and the executive, and sometimes too, between any of these organs and the judiciary, so that neither usurps the functions of the other. Particularly, the court must safeguard the judicial branch from all forms of encroachment, either by way of legislation or executive conduct, into the exercise of public justice. This raises the crucial question of the independence of the judiciary which is the bedrock of the doctrine of separation of powers and the foundation upon which the success or otherwise of constitutional democracy is based.

The coming into effect of the Constitution of the Republic of Namibia in March 1990, brought the budding Republic face to face with modern democratic values such as constitutionalism and the rule of law within the framework adumbrated by the various agencies of the United

---

[389] See *Du Preez v Truth & Reconciliation Commission* 1997 (3) SA 204 (SCA); *Transvaal Agricultural Union v Minister of Land Affairs* 1997 (2) SA 621 (CC); *Farjas (Pty) Ltd v Regional LCC, Kwazulu-Natal* 1998 (2) SA 900 (LCC); *Premier, Eastern Cape v Cekeshe* 1999 (3) SA 56 (TkD); *Premier, Province of Mpumalanga v Executive Committee of the Association of Governing Bodies of State-Aided Schools* 1999 (2) SA 91 (CC).

[390] Take the case of a fair hearing, a direct derivative of the common law principles of natural justice in criminal trials and civil litigation, has been incorporated into the Constitution as a fundamental right to a fair trial in art 12 of the Constitution of the Republic of Namibia 1990. Thus in dealing with similar provisions in s 33 of the Constitution of the Republic of Nigeria 1979, one had to discuss fair hearing in both the administrative law setting as well as in criminal proceedings. See e.g. Chuks Okpaluba (2ed, 1990). *The right to a fair hearing in Nigeria*. There is another issue for mention. The inclusion of the right to administrative justice in art. 18 of the Namibian Constitution brings the rights therein listed within the province of judicial review under the Constitution such that a breach of any of these rights guaranteed in art. 18 is an unConstitutional act. Furthermore, ordinary legislation cannot derogate from (art. 24(3)) nor delete any of these entrenched fundamental rights (art. 113) from the Constitution not even the stringent requirements of two-thirds majority in the National Assembly and a national referendum for amending the Constitution could detract from the entrenched rights (132(5)(a)).

[391] The situation in Namibia is apt here since the Constitution has entrenched administrative justice as a fundamental right. A perusal of art 18 shows that it was intended to incorporate administrative law principles into the 1996 Constitution. The South African Parliament in compliance with the dictates of s 33 (3) of the Constitution has enacted the Promotion of Administrative Justice Act 3 of 2000, which now embodies the principles of just administrative action within the meaning of s 33(1).

Nations especially the International Commission of Jurists[392]. The Constitution became the supreme law of the land[393] and Parliament ceased to be the sovereign law giver. The Constitution made provisions for the division of functions of the executive, the legislature and the judiciary[394]. The limits of legislative law-making powers were defined[395] and the duty to declare whether in any given circumstance the legislature had exceeded its law-making powers was thrust upon the courts in Namibia[396]. In the process of discharging this onerous duty, hitherto unknown to the courts whose membership was bred in British and South African constitutional jurisprudence of parliamentary sovereignty, the new Namibian Courts had to promptly adapt and develop an approach to the interpretation of the new Constitution as well as to reconcile with its enormous power of review of the legislation of parliament – laws made by those popularly elected by the people (in the exercise of their constitutional sovereign right)[397] to make laws and direct the economic, social and political fortunes of the nation. The principles identified below accordingly provide the theoretical foundation for judicial review under the Constitution and need to be examined further in this context.

2. SUPREMACY OF THE CONSTITUTION

True to the pattern established by the emerging Westminster model Constitutions of the early sixties[398], the Namibian Constitution provides that: "This Constitution shall be the Supreme Law of Namibia"[399]. This is a total departure from Dicey's theory[400] and the British practice of parliamentary sovereignty – a principle so dear to the heart of the founders of the

[392] The various attempts by this agency to formulate the rule of law for the countries of the world were documented in: *The Act of Athens* (1956); *The Declaration of Delhi* (1959); *The Law of Lagos* (1961); the *ICJ Congress in Rio de Janeiro* (1962).

[393] Article 1(6) of the Namibian Constitution 1990.

[394] Article 1(3).

[395] The supremacy of the Constitution (art. 1(6)); the provisions guaranteeing fundamental rights (art. 5-24) and especially art. 25(1) on their enforcement; the entrenchment of the said fundamental rights (art. 131); the rigid procedure for amending the Constitution (art. 132) and the prohibition form interference with the entrenched rights (art. 132(5)(a)) are some of the visible fetters on the legislature's power to make laws.

[396] Article 78(1).

[397] In Namibia, all power belongs to the people who can exercise "their sovereignty through the democratic institutions of the State: art. 1(2).

[398] The Nigerian independence Constitution of 1960 was widely reputed to have established the pattern followed by the other independent Constitutions of Commonwealth African and West Indian nations. One simply needs to compare that Constitution (this country has had so many Constitutions since that time, some of which are only consigned to the archives of history) with, say, the 1962 Constitutions of Jamaica and Trinidad & Tobago, respectively or the 1964 Constitution of Zambia or the 1966 Constitution of Botswana. This pattern persisted to a large extent up to the time the Zimbabwe Constitution 1980 was written. It is correct to say that it was indeed the Namibian Constitution that charted a clear departure from Marlborough House fashioned Constitutions. Of course, the recent developments in South Africa and their 1993 and 1996 Constitutions have shown how much the Westminster Constitutions of the sixties were not totally autochthonous.

[399] Art. 1(6), Constitution of Namibia 1990; s. 2 and the preamble to the Constitution of South Africa 1996.

[400] Dicey, A.V. 1959. *The Law of the Constitution*. (10th ed by E.C.S. Wade) ch 1.

infamous apartheid system in South Africa and the then South West Africa and which the judges upheld without question[401]. By the theory[402] and practice of sovereignty of parliament, it is held that parliament in Great Britain can make or repeal any law whatsoever on any subject with no corresponding competence on the courts to question the validity of any law so made. This means that any other law-making organ under the British Constitution as well as the executive and the judiciary are subordinate to the Westminster Parliament. None, not even the courts can override or set aside the legislation of paliament[403].

The situation in South Africa was not different from that of Britain[404]. Unlike the British, however, the South African legislature made mince-meat of the parliamentary sovereignty principle by enacting all manners of unimaginable laws racially dividing the society and depriving one group of rights – individual, group, social, property, economic, political and social rights[405]. A valiant attempt by the Appellate Division to review one of those racially based segregation laws – the Separate Representation of Voters Act 46 of 1951 – in *Harris v Minister of Interior*[406] was repealed by subsequent legislation and promptly followed by the insertion of a strongly worded ouster clause in section 59(2) of the Republican Constitution of 1961.

Although the 1990 Constitution, unlike some Constitutions in Commonwealth Africa, did not contain the general provision that any law inconsistent with its provisions shall to that extent be invalid[407], it does provide however, with specific reference to enforcement of fundamental rights and freedoms that:

> **Save in so far as it may be authroized to do so by this Constitution, Parliament or any subordinate authority shall not make any law, and the Executive and the**

---

401 See *Collins v Minister of the Interior* 1957 (1) SA 552 (A); *S v Tuhadeleni* 1969 (1) SA 153 (A).

402 Dicey (1959): 39-40. op cit.

403 See Lords Reid and Morris in *Pickin v British Railways Board* [1974] AC 765 at 782 and 790 respectively; Lord Reid in *Madzimbamuto v Ladner-Burke* [1969] 1 AC 645 at 723B; Lord Campbell in *Edinburgh & Dalkeith Railway v Wauchope* (1842) 8 C1 & F 710 at 725; Willes J in *Lee v Bude & Torrington Railway Co* (1871) LR 6 CP 577 at 582.

404 The history and development of this subject in South Africa has been documented in Carpenter.1987. *Introduction to South African Constitutional law.* Butterworths ch 6; Boulle et al. 1989. *Constitutional and administrative law.* Futa Cape Town, 132.

405 For samples of the legal scenario created through legislative and government policies of the apartheid past, reference may be made of some judicial observations: per Mahomed DP (as he then was) in *Shabalala v A-G of Transvaal* 1996 (1) SA 725 (CC) para 26 speaking on the South African situation whose constitution is, like that of Namibia, a decisive break from the past and unto one constitutionally protected culture of openness and democracy and universal human rights for all persons of all ages, classes and colour; O'Regan J also spoke of the pernicious race discrimination and racial segregation of the past in *Brink v Kitshoff NO* 1996 (4) SA 197 (CC) para 40. and for another Constitutional Court Judge's remark, this time focusing particularly on land ownership and residential segregation, the cornerstone of the apartheid policy, see Ngcobo J in *Ex parte Western Cape Provincial Government: In Re DVB Beshuising (Pty) Ltd v North West Provincial Government* 2000 BCLR 347 (CC) para 41.

406 1952 (2) SA 428 (A), overruling *Ndlwana v Hofmeyr NO* 1937 AD 229.

407 Cf s 1(1) and (3), Constitution of the Federal Republic of Nigeria 1979. Unless otherwise stated, reference to the Nigerian Constitution is to the 1979 version of that country's many constitutions of the last 40 years.

> **agencies of Government shall not take any action which abolishes or abridges the fundamental rights and freedoms conferred by this Chapter, and any law or action in contravention thereof shall to the extent of the contravention be invalid...**[408]

It has been suggested that the principle of supremacy of the constitution need not be expressly stated in the constitution itself, for "essentially attached"[409] to the written constitution is the principle that laws inconsistent therewith are *pro tanto* void, unless the constitution otherwise provides. The implication of the supremacy clause is that any law enacted by the legislature or any action taken by the executive must comply with the dictates of the constitution since, within the hierarchy of laws, the constitution, the organic and basic law, is the apex norm, the *Grundnorm* in Kelsenian terms. By a combination of the supremacy clause and Art. 25(1) aforementioned, it is thus unconstitutional and invalid for the legislature in this scheme of things, to enact a law in excess of powers granted it by the constitution. It is thus a veritable ground for judicial review for the legislature, for example, to make a law which infringes any of the fundamental rights and freedoms[410] guaranteed the individual except within the limits authorized by the Constitution. After all, constitutions are written to safeguard the rights of the citizen against the state; to define the functions of the executive and essentially to set the limits of legislative powers and actions. The matter is better expressed in the words of the late Mahomed CJ while commenting on the 1996 Constitution of South Africa in *Speaker of the National Assembly v De Lille*[411] he observed:

> **This enquiry must critically rest on the Constitution of the Republic of South Africa Act 108 of 1996. It is supreme – not Parliament. It is the ultimate source of**

[408] Art. 25(1) of the Namibian Constitution 1990.

[409] De Smith. 1964. *The New Commonwealth and its Constitutions.* London Stevens & Sons [Toronto Casswell].

[410] Chapter 3 of the Namibian Constitution of 1990. Challenges of unconstitutionality of legislation occur more frequently on the ground that the law infringements a fundamental right or freedom. Several of the laws existing as at the time of independence, have been challenged for running counter to the cherished rights of the Constitution. Notable among such challenges are: *Kauesa v Minister of Home Affairs* 1996 (4) SA 965 (NmSC), reversing 1995 (1) SA 51 (NmHC) – where certain regulations were invalidated for breaching the applicant's freedom of speech (art 21(1)(a)); *Namunjepo v Commanding Officer, Windhoek Prison* 2000 BCLR 671 (NmS) where the practice of placing prisoners in leg irons or chains was declared an infringement of the right to human dignity and right not to be subjected to cruel, inhuman and degrading punishment (art 8(1) and (2)); to the same effect is the landmark judgment in *Ex parte Attorney-General of Namibia: In Re Corporal Punishment by Organs of State* 1991 (3) SA 76 (NmS); cf *S v Tcoeib* 1993 (1) SACR 274 (Nm) where this same art 8(1) and (2) was held not to have been violated by the imposition of life sentence; *S v Vries* 1996 (2) SACR 638 (Nm), minimum or mandatory sentences not per se unConstitutional. Far-reaching legislative cleansing has however been done in the area of fair trial where the court has found that several sections of the Criminal Procedure Act 51 of 1977 has in numerous instances infringed the accused person's rights to a fair trial in criminal matters guaranteed in art 12. Accordingly, the Constitutionality of certain provisions of that Act has been tested in the following reverse *onus* cases: *S v Pineiro* 1991 NR 424 (HC); *S v Mbatha; S v Prinsloo* 1996 (2) SA 464 (CC); *S v Coetzee & Others* 1997 (3) SA 527 (CC); *S v Mello & Another* 1998 (3) SA 712 (CC); *S v Manyonyo* 1999 (12) BCLR 1438 (CC); *S v Manamela* 2000 (5) BCLR 491 (CC). Cf. in *S v Baloyi* 2000 (2) SA 425 (CC).

[411] 1999 (4) SA 863 (SCA) para 14.

all lawful authority in the country. No Parliament, however *bona fide* or eminent its membership, no President, however formidable be his reputation or scholarship, and no official, however efficient and well-meaning, can make any law or perform any act which is not sanctioned by the Constitution. Section 2 of the Constituion expressly proves that law or conduct inconsistent with the Constitution is invalid and the obligations imposed by it must be fulfilled. It follows that any citizen adversely affected by any decree, order or action of any official or body, which is not properly authorized by the Constitution is entitled to the protection of the Courts. No Parliament, no official and no institution is immune from judicial scrutiny in such circumstances.

In view of the foregoing, the doctrine of separation of powers inherent in the distribution of the three distinct powers of government in the Constitution and the avowed and constitutionally entrenched duty of the legislative and executive organs to respect and maintain the independence of the judiciary[412]. The question that remains to be answered, is whether any legislation that seeks to infuse both legislative and executive powers where the Constitution has sought to separate them, is for that reason invalid, unconstitutional and accordingly reviewable in a court of law? In other words, can the legislature, in the absence of constitutional provisions to that effect, confer upon itself either executive or judicial powers? Can it delegate to the executive its plenary legislative powers? By the same token, can the executive exercise the plenary law-making powers of the legislature? It is also important to investigate the extent to which the courts can review legislative actions; for if there is a power on the part of the judiciary to review legislation, does that power extend to the review of the internal affairs of the legislature? This inevitably brings us face to face with the consideration of what constitutes the internal business of the legislature and its traditional, constitutional and sometimes statutory privilege of controlling matters within its domain.

Another broad ground of judicial review of legislation is that commonly found in a federal structure of government such as exists in Australia, Canada, India, Nigeria and the United States[413] or the co-operative-cum-federal model of South African[414] vintage with their inherent share-out of governmental powers among the federating or co-operating states/provinces and the central/federal/national government, peculiar responsibilities are imposed on the courts. Here, the courts are often called upon to determine whether the central or the provincial/state legislature has transgressed the boundaries of its legislative

[412] Okpaluba "Constitutionality of legislation relating to the exercise of judicial power: the Namibian experience in comparative perspective" forthcoming (2001) *TSAR* (*Journal of South African Law*).

[413] Much has been written on federal systems and their operations in the respective countries but for a cute summary of the underlying principles of federalism where the various models have been surveyed, see Nwabueze. 1983. *Federalism in Nigeria under the Presidential Constitution*. London: Sweet & Maxwell. pp.1-22.

[414] The framework of the co-operative government system is laid down in ch 3 of the Constitution of the Republic of South Africa Act 108 of 1996. Virtually every textbook on modern South African Constitutional Law has dealt with this topic: see eg Rautenbach IM & Malherbe E.F.J. 2000. *Constitutional Law* 3rd edition. Lexis Nexis Butterworths; Devenish G.E. (1998), *A commentary on the South African Constitution*. Durban: Butterworths; De Waal et al. (2000). *The Bill of Rights Handbook. Tutta & Co. Ltd.*

competence as clearly demarcated by the Constitution[415]. Since the Republic of Namibia is a unitary State[416], this aspect of judicial review of legislation would hardly arise and little is therefore said of it in this chapter. In any event, a discussion of the distribution of governmental powers focuses on how powers conferred on the three important organs of state: the law-making, the law-administering and the law-interpreting organs are to be exercised and by which organ. We are not concerned for the present moment with the arrangement whereby legislative or executive powers are shared within the country and between national, country-wide government and a number of regional or provincial autonomous or semi-autonomous legislative and executive entities. This paper essentially deals with judicial review on separation of powers grounds in so far as it pertains to the distribution of legislative and executive powers.

3. CONSTITUTIONALISM AND THE RULE OF LAW

Long before constitutionalism became the vogue in the modern democratic era, constitutional theorists had written about the rule of law[417]. In spite of the fact that the theories have generated so much controversy, it is generally accepted that in simple terms, the expression, *rule of law*, means no more than that government business must be conducted according to law[418]; not arbitrarily and not in accordance with the whims and caprices of those governing. Without necessarily dabbling into the life-long debate on what this rather intractable expression means[419], it stands to reason that when the Namibian Constitution states in its very opening sentence that it is founded upon the principles of democracy, the rule of law and justice for all, the founders must have had in their contemplation certain well established standards of good governance and democracy, including, but not exclusive to the following:

---

[415] For recent South African cases on the subject see *Western Cape Government: In Re DVB Behuising (Pty) Ltd* 2000 (4) BCLR 347 (CC); *Ex parte President of the RSA: In Re Constitutionality of the Liquor Bill* 2000 (1) SA 732 (CC); *Executive Council, Western Cape v Minister for Provincial Affairs & Constitutional Development; Executive Council, Kwazulu-Natal v President of the Republic of South Africa* 2000 (1) SA 661 (CC); 1999 (12) BCLR 1360 (CC); *Premier of the Province of the Western Cape v President of the RSA* 1999 (4) SA 382 (CC).

[416] Article 1(1), Constitution of the Republic of Namibia 1990. Apart from the Constitution expressly so stating, the Constitutional arrangement in Namibia is unitary in nature notwithstanding that the Constitution makes provision for regional councils and some form of devolution of power. One only needs to take a second look at Art. 108(b) to see that such regional bodies as are established "will perform such duties as may be assigned to them by Act of Parliament and as may be delegated to them by the President". In federal systems, functions and duties of federating units, indeed powers exercised by them which of essence must include executive and law-making powers, are donated primarily by the Constitution itself not an Act of Parliament and certainly not by a benevolent national executive.

[417] Aristotle *Politics* vol III 16; Bracton *De Legibus et consuetudinibus Angliae* f 5 b; Dicey.1885. *The law of the Constitution* 183; Holdsworth. *History of English law* vol II 441-442; vol X 647-649.

[418] See the definition of this concept by the European Court of Human Rights in *Sunday Times v UK* (1979) 2 EHRR 245 para 49; *Malone v UK* (1984) 7 EHRR 14; *Halford v UK* (1997) 24 EHRR 523.

[419] Jenning. *The law and the Constitution.* 1959. Heuston. 1964. *Essays on Constitutional law.* London: Stevens & Son; Beinart 1962. "The rule of law" *Acta juridical* 99; Allan "Legislative supremacy and the rule of law: Democracy and Constitutionalism" 1985 *CLJ* 111.

- that governmental powers can only be exercised in accordance with the law, not arbitrarily[420] or capriciously. This means that every act of government or its officials must have a valid foundation in the law and that in acting, the government or authority must not exceed his powers or act without constitutional or statutory authority[421];
- that the exercise of governmental acts must be subject to review by the courts of law, so that, it is not in the spirit of the rule of law for the legislature to enact laws that take away the ordinary jurisdiction of the courts; there must be access to the court for the ventilation of disputes and grievances[422];
- that each organ of state must treat the other with respect, especially, the executive must not only respect the due process of law but must also treat the judgments of courts of competent jurisdiction with uttermost respect. This entails the absence of resort to the use of brute force or self-help as against using the judicial process to settle disputes[423];

---

[420] Take the decision in *Pharmaceutical Manufacturers Association of South Africa: Ex parte President of the Republic of South Africa* 2000 (1) SA 674 (CC) para 85 where the Constitutional Court laid emphasis on the absence of arbitrariness as a fundamental requirement of the rule of law in the exercise of public power by the executive and other functionaries. The Court further observed that decisions of such bodies must be rationally related to the purpose for which the power was given, otherwise, they could be arbitrary and inconsistent with this requirement and the standards demanded by the Constitution.

[421] See *Fedsure Life Assurance Ltd v Greater Johannesburg Transitional Metropolitan Council* 1999 (1) SA 374 (CC) para 56-58; *President of the Republic of South Africa v Hugo* 1997 (4) SA 1 (CC) paras 6-8; *President of the Republic of South Africa v South African Rugby Football Union* 1999 (10) BCLR 1059 (CC) para 148.

[422] Arts 12(1)(a) and 25(2), Constitution of Namibia; s 34 and 35(3)(c), Constitution of South Africa and see *Chief Lesapo v North West Agricultural Bank* 2000 (1) SA 409 (CC). Cf the situation often encountered in military regimes who, through decrees, strain to take away the powers of judicial review of not only legislative but also of executive authority. The Nigerian statute books are replete with decrees such as Constitution (Suspension & Modification) Decree No 107 of 1993 and Federal Military Government (Supremacy & Enforcement of Powers) Decree No 12 of 1994 both of which contained hideous ouster clauses. An example of the struggle by the courts to keep the exercise of judicial power intact in the face of apparent military usurpation of judicial powers see the latest of the Nigerian cases: *Guardian Newspapers Ltd v Attorney-General of the Federation* (1995) 5 NWLR (398) 703 (CA). Cf *A-G of Anambra State v A-G of the Federal Republic of Nigeria* (1993) 6 NWLR (302) 692 (SCN) where the Supreme Court took a literalist view in its interpretation of the exclusive original jurisdiction vested in it by the 1979 Constitution as subsequently modified by Military Decrees between 1984 and 1994.

[423] The pronouncements of the Nigerian Supreme Court in this regard is eloquent testimony of the attempt by the courts even under the aberration called military rule to maintain rule of law at the least to the extent that disputes are referred to the courts and not settled through the threat of the barrel of the gun. See *Registered Trustees of the Apostolic Church of Nigeria v Olowoleni* (1990) NWLR (158) 514; *Obeya Memorial Specialist Hospital Ltd v A-G of the Federation* (1987) 3 NWLR (60) 325; *Governor of Lagos State v Ojukwu* (1986) 1 NWLR (18) 621 (SCN).

- that as a consequence of the foregoing, the constitutional state must ensure the independence and impartiality[424] of the judiciary, the organ of government upon which the settlement of disputes between the government and its citizens is entrusted[425];
- that the law should conform to certain minimum standards of justice[426], both substantively and procedurally[427];

[424] Although these two words appear often inseparable, the independence of the judiciary is traditionally addressed to the institution, while impartiality points to the state of mind of the judge as to whether he would maintain an open mind to the adjudication of the issue before him. The conduct and utterances of the judge during proceedings and his previous association with one of the parties in court are some of the factors leading to the apprehension of the judge's partiality. Allegations of lack of impartiality are not to be lightly made. See *President of the Republic of South Africa v SARFU* (2) 1999 (7) BCLR 725 (CC); *SACCAWU v Irvin & Johnson Ltd (Seafods Division Fish Processing)* 2000 (8) BCLR 886 (CC).

[425] The vital link between the doctrines of separation of powers and the independence of the judiciary was extensively deliberated upon recently by the Constitutional Court in *South African Association of Personal Injury Lawyers v Hendrik Willem Heath* 2001 (1) SA 883 (CC) especially at para 45 and 46. The Court was dealing with the Constitutionality of a law that established a Special Investigating Unit (SIU) vested with the power to investigate the criminal conduct, serious maladministration and a host of other forms of improprieties by government departments and public officials. The challenge was based on the fact that the Unit was headed by a judge of the High Court and, in terms of the Act, it was clearly under the control of the President who formulated what it had to investigate. It was to the President that the Judge, as head of the unit, must report from time to time. These statutory provisions raised the question of the apparent interference by the legislation of the independence of the judicial head of the unit and the consequent breach of the doctrine of separation of powers. In reversing the trial judge and holding that both principles were entrenched in the Constitution of South Africa and that they were both infringed in the circumstances by the Act, the Court held that: first, the functions of the SIU were far removed from "the central mission of the judiciary". The nature of the investigations which were determined by the President, the inextricable link between the unit as an investigator and litigator, the indefinite nature of the appointment which precluded the head of the unit from performing his judicial functions were all factors that rendered the appointment of the judge incompatible with the judicial office and contrary to the separation of powers required by the Constitution. Secondly, under the Constitution, the judiciary has a sensitive and crucial role to play in controlling the exercise of power and upholding the Bill of Rights. It is thus important that the judiciary be independent and be seen to be so. It is inimical to the principle of the independence of the judiciary for judges to be appointed for indefinite terms to executive posts or to perform other executive functions not appropriate to the "central mission of the judiciary". The contrary would undermine the separation of powers and the independence of the judiciary, crucial for the proper discharge of functions assigned to the judiciary by the Constitution and fundamental to the constitutional order. Section 3(1) of the contentious Special Investigating Units and Special Tribunals Act 74 of 1996 and the Proclamation appointing Judge Heath to what was clearly an executive trouble-shooting post were therefore unconstitutional and invalid.

[426] The entire ch 3 of the Namibian Constitution, like ch 2 of the Constitution of South Africa, among other provisions, represents what the people of these respective countries regard as minimum standards of justice.

[427] Article 12 of the Namibian Constitution prescribes the standards for the attainment of procedural justice in criminal trials whereas art. 18 not only guarantees standards of substantive governmental behaviour in relations between the administration and the citizen but of procedural justice as well in those regards.

- that every person including public functionaries and officials are equal before the law[428], so that public officials are as well subject to effective legal sanctions just as other citizens; and that government officials, except with the express authorization of the law, must not discriminate against citizens in respect of public privileges and rights;
- that the State is itself subject to law[429]. For instance, it is beyond the state to purport by way of policy decision to alter the right which a citizen has acquired by virtue of the Constitution, nor could the legislature give effect to such policy by way of legislation without following the due process of amending the Constitution[430].

The list is of course inexhaustible for the modern concept of constitutionalism and can conveniently be enveloped by the doctrine of the rule of law and *vice versa*. The independence of the judiciary aside, the requirement that judges themselves must be impartial in adjudicating disputes and must not condemn anyone of any offence which will deprive that person of his liberty, right to property or means of livelihood, without according that person the elementary but fundamental right to be heard, the opportunity to present his own side of the story without any inhibition whatsoever, are aspects of the fundamental principles contemplated by the rule of law, these are the values upon which the Namibian Constitution is founded, and in turn, they form an integral part of the entrenched fundamental rights and freedoms in the Constitution.

It is difficult to say wherein the principle of the rule of law ends and where that of constitutionalism begins. It is however probable that a discussion of one invariably represents a discussion of the other with a different label. They are both broad political doctrines. It is appropriate here to refer to the speech of Leon AJA of the Supreme Court of Namibia which captures the point for discussion when, in *Ex parte Attorney-General, Namibia: In Re: The Constitutional Relationship between the Attorney-General and the Prosecutor-General*[431], he said:

> **In a constitutional state the government is constrained by the Constitution and shall govern only according to its terms, subject to its limitations and only for agreed powers and agreed purposes. But it means much more. It is a wonderfully**

[428] Equality per se is a critical issue in any democratic state; it is, for obvious reasons, more so in Namibia and South Africa both countries having been infested in the past by the virus of inequality of inconceivable proportions and ingenious dimensions. From the preambles of these Constitutions, it is clear that they were written ostensibly to redress the malady of institutionalised, political, cultural, social and economic inequality created by the monster that was apartheid. For some of the South African jurisprudence on equality, see the various contributions (1998) 14 *SAJHR* 220-349 some of the Namibian cases on the subject include: *Mwellie v Ministry of Works, Transport & Communications* 1995 (9) BCLR 1118 (NmH); *Muller v President of the Republic of Namibia* 2000 (6) BCLR 655 (NmS); *S v K* 2000 (4) BCLR 405 (NmS). See generally the analysis by Cassidy "Art. 10 of the Namibian Constitution: A look at the first ten years of interpretation of the rights to equality and non-discrimination and predictions for the future", also published in this book.

[429] *Eleso v Government of Ogun State* (1990) 2 NWLR (133) 420 (SCN).

[430] See *Alberts v Government of Namibia* 1993 NR 85 (HC) 89I-J per Frank J.

[431] *Ex parte Attorney-General, Namibia: In Re: The Constitutional Relationship between the Attorney-General and the Prosecutor-General* 1995 (8) BCLR 1070 (NmS) 1078H.

> **complex and rich theory of political organization. It is a composite of different historical practices and philosophical traditions. There are structural limitations and procedural guarantees that limit the exercise of State power. It means in a single phrase immortalized in 1656 by James Harrington in the *Commonwealth of Oceana* "a government of laws and not of men[432]".**

Suffice it to say that by virtue of the concept of constitutionalism, both legislative and executive powers must be subject to judicial review and the testing powers of the courts. These powers must not be exercised in such a manner as to infringe the provisions of the Bill of Rights guaranteed the individual by the Constitution. The Constitutional Court of South Africa has emphasised that the exercise of presidential constitutional powers is subject to the principle of legality[433] and as is implicit in the Constitution the President must act in good faith and must not misconstrue his powers[434]. Again in *S v Makwanyane*[435] the Constitutional Court pointed to the past characterized by arbitrariness and unequal operation of the law, as against the present where arbitrariness is dissonant with the core concepts of the new constitutional order. Under the new order, the legislature cannot limit the rights entrenched in the Bill of Rights without showing the justifications laid down in the Constitution[436]. Such a legislature cannot, unlike its predecessor of the past known for perversive inequality, authoritarianism and repression, pass a law purporting to distinguish the citizens on grounds of race or ethnicity for the Constitution "articulates a jurisprudential

---

[432] Olivier. 1994. *Constitutionalism in the new South Africa.* South Africa's Crisis of Constitutional Democracy. The U.S. Constitution. Licht A. (ed. Cape Town. Tutta & Co. Washington D.C. The AEI Press.

[433] In *President of the RSA v SARFU (3)* 2000 (1) SA 1 (CC) para 148, the Constitutional Court spoke of the constraints on the exercise of the President of his Constitutional powers within section 84(2) of the 1996 Constitution in these words: "...the President is required to exercise the powers personally and any such exercise must not infringe any provision of the Bill of Rights; the exercise of the powers is also clearly constrained by the principle of legality and, as is implicit in the Constitution, the President must act in good faith and must not misconstrue the powers".

[434] *President of the Republic of South Africa v Hugo* 1997 (4) SA 1 (CC) paras 68-69.

[435] 1995 (3) SA 391 para 156.

[436] The Constitution carries with it a limitation or derogation clause. See s 36 of the SA Constitution. The fundamental rights and freedoms in the Namibian Constitution are accompanied by a derogation clause (Art. 24) as well as the power of the President to suspend their operation during the period covered by a declaration of a state of emergency (art. 26(5)(b)). Sometimes, too, individual guarantees contain their own limitations. Such is the case with the right to participate in peaceful political activity (Art. 17) intended to influence the composition and policies of government which carries in sub-art (3) limitations which Parliament in respect of specified categories of persons on such grounds of infirmity or on such grounds of public interest or morality as are necessary in a democratic society. Cf in *DTA of Namibia v Prime Minister of Namibia* 1996 (3) BCLR 310 (NmH), where the Judges of the High Court of Namibia were split on the issue of whether the impugned s 93(4) of the Electoral Act 24 of 1992, which prohibited the opening or inspection of contents of the packets described in subsection (2) without the order of the court meeting the requirements of what was necessary in a democratic society in relation to art. 17(3).

philosophy which, in ringing tones, repudiates legislative policies based on the criteria of race and ethnicity[437]".

7. DELEGATING LEGISLATIVE POWER TO THE EXECUTIVE

The question here is whether the doctrine of separation of powers inherent in written constitutions prohibits the delegation by the legislature of its plenary law-making powers to the executive and where such a delegation had taken place, whether a court, in the process of judicial review of legislation, can or should declare the law purporting to authorize such delegation unconstitutional and invalid?[438] This enquiry takes two approaches: first, there is the historical incidence of the British parliamentary system which denies the existence of any separation between legislative and executive powers of government which had been impressed upon by several judgments of Her Majesty's Privy Council and, secondly, the American approach whereby the principle of separation of powers renders unconstitutional for Congress to indulge in extensive delegation of its legislative powers to the executive branch.

7.1 The Westminster parliamentary model

The question which had arisen since the days of British imperialism has been whether the legislative councils of the colonies were agents of the Imperial Parliament in that having been mandated by the latter to make law for the order and good government of the colonies

---

[437] Per Mahomed CJ in *Government of the Republic of Namibia v Cultura 2000* 1994 (1) SA 407 at 411. and in *S v Van Wyk* 1992 (1) SACR 147 (NmS) 172-173, where the Supreme Court had applied the analogy of the Art. 23(1) mandate to Parliament to enact legislation in order to render punishable practices of racial discrimination and apartheid to sentencing in a criminal offence motivated by racial hatred. Mahomed AJA concurring stated: "Throughout the preamble and substantive structures of the Namibian Constitution there is one golden and unbroken thread – an abiding 'revulsion' of racism and apartheid. It articulates a vigorous consciousness of the suffering and the wounds which racism has inflicted on the Namibian people 'for so long' and a commitment to build a new nation 'to cherish and to protect the gains of our long struggle' against the pathology of apartheid. I know of no other Constitution in the world which seeks to identify a legal ethos against apartheid with greater vigour and intensity".

[438] It is to be noted that one is not concerned with that situation whereby the legislature directs the executive to bring an enactment into operation by virtue of a proclamation. This is not the delegation contemplated in this context for, in *S v Lofty-Eaton (1)* 1993 NR 370 (HC) 388, O'Linn J had held that when an Act of Parliament empowers the executive to promulgate the date of the operation of an Act, this may be regarded as an administrative act or a delegated legislation or a combination of both. On the other hand, the Constitutional Court of South Africa has held that such directive in an Act is neither administrative nor subordinate legislation although it is closer to the legislative process than to the administrative process: *Pharmaceutical Manufacturers Association of SA: In Re Ex parte President of the Republic of South Africa* 2000 (2) SA 674 (CC) para 79. Although neither the Namibian High Court nor the South African Constitutional Court decision is conclusive on the classification of the nature of the function of bringing an Act into operation, both were of the view that it is neither outright law-making nor was it law-making at all although both Courts were of the view that the act of the executive in that regard, be it resultant upon pure administrative bungling as the South African situation, was subject to judicial review. Viewed from either perspective, it does not fit into the category of delegation of plenary law-making powers of the legislature and therefore outside the scope of this discussion.

or dominions, it could not further delegate that power given to them by that Parliament to another body of persons or authority. This argument was based on the common law doctrine which forbids a delegate to further delegate the power vested in him since the maxim *delegates non potest delegare*, would apply to nullify such unauthorized delegation. The Privy Council – the Imperial Court of final appeal for the colonies – rejected this argument in a number of cases.

First, in the often cited Canadian case on this point[439], the Privy Council rejected an argument that where a legislature committed important regulations to agents or delegates as the Ontario Provincial Legislature had done to the local boards of licence commissioners, it had effaced itself. It was held that the argument was founded on a misconception of the true character and position of the provincial legislatures, which were "in no sense delegates of or acting under any mandate from the Imperial Parliament". In holding that the provincial legislature was entitled to entrust to a board of commissioners authority to enact regulations relating to tarverns, Sir Barnes Peacock stated on behalf of the Board:

> **When the British North America Act enacted that there should be a legislature for Ontario, and that its legislative assembly should have exclusive authority to make laws for the province and for provincial purposes in relation to the matters enumerated in section 92, it conferred powers not in any sense to be exercised by delegation or as agents of the Imperial Parliament, but an authority as plenary and as ample within the limits prescribed by section 92 as the Imperial Parliament in the plenitude of its power possessed and could bestow[440].**

Secondly, it was held in *R v Burah*[441] that the Indian legislature had powers expressly limited by the Act of the Imperial Parliament, when enacting within those limits set by the Act was intended to have the plenary powers of legislation, "as large, and of the same nature as those of Parliament itself'. As much as the Privy Council observed in *Hodge* that too much delegation might be invalid, it stated in *Burah* that "the Governor-General-in-Council could not by any form of enactment, create in India, and arm with general legislative authority a new legislative power, not created or authorized by the Council's Act" (i.e. the imperial Act which established the Indian Legislature in the first instance[442]). At the same time, their Lordships emphasised in *Hodge* that the provincial legislature retained its powers intact, and could, whenever it deemed it fit, "destroy the agency it has created and set up another, to take the matter directly into its own hand, how far it shall seek the aid of subordinate

[439] *Hodge v R* (1883) 9 App Cas 117.

[440] *Ibid* 131. While the Privy Council affirmed its opinion in *Hodge* when it observed in *Re Initiative & Referendum Act* [1919] AC 935 that a provincial legislature in Canada could, while preserving its won capacity intact, seek the assistance of subordinate agencies, but that it does not follow that it can create and endow with its own capacity a new legislative power not created by the Act to which it owes its existence, went on to hold that the Act sought to be impugned was invalid in that it rendered the Lieutenant-Governor who was part of the legislature powerless to prevent a proposed law from becoming an actual law if approved by a majority of the voters. So, since the Lieutenant-Governor was "wholly excluded from the new legislative authority", the Act was beyond the power of the Manitoba legislature.

[441] (1878) 3 App. Cas. 889.

[442] *Ibid* 904-905, per Lord Selborne.

agencies, and how long it shall continue them, are matters for each legislature, and not for courts of law, to decide[443]".

Thirdly, Lord Morris speaking for the Privy Council in *Cobb & Co Ltd v Kropp*[444] held that the power which the Australian State of Queensland had to make laws for peace, welfare and good government of that State denoted plenitude of "sovereign legislative power, even though that power be confined to certain subjects or within certain reservations[445]", it would seem surprising if the enactment of the various Transport Acts challenged in this case was not within such power. In approving its earlier decisions in *Hodge*; *Burah* and *Powell v Appollo Candle Co*[446] (the latter emanating from New South Wales), the Privy Council held that there was nothing comparable with "a new legislative power" armed with "general legislative authority" having been created by the passing by the Queensland legislature of the various Transport Acts. The circumstance that the commissioner for transport created by the Act was endowed with certain powers of decision and measures of discretion does not in any realistic sense support the contention that the state legislature of Queensland exceeded its plenary and ample powers. In effect, the State legislature were fully warranted in legislating in terms of the Transport Acts having preserved their own capacity and retained perfect control over the commissioner for transport inasmuch as they could at any time repeal the legislation and withdraw such authority and discretion as they had vested in the commissioner. It was further held that Parliament was entitled to set up an agency to deal with the "multitudinous matters and considerations" arising daily in "a vast transport system" and in using the commissioner for transport as their instrument to fix and recover the licence and permit fees. In so doing, the State legislature were not abrogating their powers to levy taxes nor were they transferring power to the commissioner. "In no sense did the Queensland legislature assign or transfer or abrogate their powers or renounce or abdicate their responsibilities. They did not give away or relinquish their taxing powers. All that was done was done under and by reason of their authority[447]".

While the foregoing cases imply that the courts would not readily accept the proposition that legislative organs as considered above cannot be limited in their power to delegate their legislative powers, since there were no requirements under these Constitutions that legislative and executive powers be exercised by separate and independent bodies[448], the Australians have made no bones about it for "in truth the full theory of 'separation of powers' cannot apply under our Constitution[449]" and, in the words of Dixon J: "...I have never understood how the theory which is applied to the United States, that the legislature could not [delegate] at all any authority considered to be legislative could have any place in our Constitution[450]". Thus, when Sir Owen Dixon was considering whether in the exercise

443 Note 132 131.

444 [1967] 1 AC 141 at 154.

445 See also *McCawley v R* [1920] AC 691; 36 TLR 387 (PC).

446 (1885) 10 App Cas 282 (PC).

447 [1967] 1 AC 141 at 157.

448 Hogg (n 128) 14-15.

449 Per Evatt J in *Victoria Stevedoring & General Contracting Co Pty Ltd v Dignan* (1931) 46 CLR 73 at 117.

450 *Wishart v Fraser* (1947) 64 CLR 470 at 484.

of its legislative power, Parliament is restrained from reposing any power essentially legislative in another organ or body in the *Digman* case[451], held: "I, therefore, retain the opinion I expressed in the earlier case[452] that *Roche v Kronheimer*[453] did decide that a statute conferring upon the executive a power to legislate upon some matter contained within one of the subjects of the legislative power of the Parliament is a law with respect to that subject, and that the distribution of legislative, executive and judicial powers in the Constitution does not operate to restrain the power of the Parliament to make such a law". Evatt J held that the only known limitation on such delegation is in respect of trade and commerce with other countries or among States. Evatt J however held that: "...the Parliament of the Commonwealth is not competent to 'abdicate' its powers of legislation. This is not because Parliament is bound to perform any or all of its legislative powers or functions, for it may elect not to do so, and not because the doctrine of separation of powers prevents Parliament from granting authority to other bodies to make laws or by-laws and thereby exercise legislative power, for it does so in almost every statute; but each and every one of the laws passed by Parliament must answer the description of a law upon one or more of the subject matters stated in the Constitution. A law by which Parliament gave all its law-making authority to another body would be bad merely because it would fail to pass the test last mentioned[454]".

7.2 The American approach

The principle of non-delegability of legislative powers is well-known in American constitutional law since the United States Supreme Court decisions in *Panama Refining Co v Ryan*[455] and *Schechter Poultry Corporation v United States*[456] where legislative powers delegated to the President by Congress under the National Recovery 1933 were held to be in excess of the powers of Congress and unauthorized delegation of congressional powers. Chief Justice Hughes stated the underlying rationale for the court's reasoning in these cases as follows:

> **The Constitution provides that "all legislative powers herein granted shall be vested in a Congress of the United States which shall consist of a Senate and a House of Representatives ... And Congress is empowered" to make all laws which shall be necessary and proper for carrying into execution its general powers ... The Congress manifestly is not permitted to abdicate, or to transfer to others, the essential legislative functions with which it is thus vested. Undoubtedly legislation must often be adapted to complex conditions involving a host of details with which the national Legislature cannot deal directly. The Constitution has never been regarded as denying to Congress the necessary resources of flexibility and practicality, which will enable it to perform its function in laying down policies and establishing standards, while leaving to selected instruments the making of subordinate rules within**

[451] *Victoria Stevedoring & General Contractors Co. Pty Ltd v Digman* (1931) 46 CLR 73 at 100.

[452] Referring to *Huddart Parker Ltd v Commonwealth* (1931) 44 CLR 492.

[453] (1921) 29 CLR 329.

[454] (1931) 46 CLR 73 at 121.

[455] 293 US 388 (1935).

[456] 295 US 495 (1935).

> **prescribed limits and the determination of facts to which the policy as declared by the legislature is to apply. Without the capacity to give authorisations of that sort we should have the anomaly of a legislative power which in many circumstances calling for its exertion would be but a futility: But the constant recognition of the necessity and validity of such provisions and the wide range of administrative authority which has been developed by means of them cannot be allowed to obscure the limitations of the authority to delegate if our constitutional system is to be maintained[457].**

Implicit in this approach is that although some delegation may be permissible, such delegation must not be so broad or vague that the authority to whom the power is delegated is thereby empowered to make law rather than act within the framework of law made by Congress. Taft CJ offered an explanation for this seeming inconsistency in the following words: "The true distinction, therefore, is, between the delegation of power to make the law, which necessarily involves a discretion as to what it shall be, and conferring an authority or discretion as to the execution, to be exercised under and pursuance to the law. The first cannot be done; to the latter no valid objection can be made[458]".

The American approach apparently based on the theories of Montesquieu[459] and Locke[460] was distinguished in the *Dignan*[461] case in Australia. While Dixon J rested his decision on the British tradition of responsible government, Evatt J made it clear that the close relationship between the legislature and the executive in Australia does not exist as in the United States and that this must be borne in mind when dealing with the doctrine of separation of powers. However, Evatt J pointed out that a wholesale delegation of the federal legislative power would amount to abdication by the Commonwealth Parliament. This line of distinction appeared to have attracted the High Court in *Giris Pty Ltd v Commissioner of Taxation*[462] where, although some members of the Court recognised that this case was very close to requiring the consideration of the constitutional validity of the delegation of responsibility from parliament may delegate legislative power it may not abdicate it". It is however ironical that the attitude of the Australian High Court in this regard is totally different from their approach whenever they consider legislative infringement of judicial power for in that respect they had harped on the similarity between the Australian Constitution and that of the United States and have stated in countless occasions that the Australian Constitution is based on the American doctrine of separation of powers[463]. In the United States itself,

[457] *Panama Refining Co. v Ryan* 293 US 388 (1935). See also *U.S. v Curtis-Wright* 299 US 304 (1936); *U.S. v Rock Royal Corporation* 307 US 533 (1939); *Arizona v California* 373 U.S. 546 (1963); *Opp Cotton Mill v Administrator* 312 US 121 (1941).

[458] *Hampton & Co. v US* 276 US 394 (1928) at 407. See also *per* Ranney J in *Wilmington & Zanesville Railroad Co. v Commissioners* 1 Ohio St 77 (1852).

[459] Montesquieu *L'Esprit des Lois* bk XI 3-6.

[460] Locke. 1690. *Second Treatise of Civil Government.* ch 12-13.

[461] Note *supra*.

[462] (1969) 119 CLR 365, 373-4, 381 and 385.

[463] See *New South Wales v The Commonwealth* (1915) 20 CLR 54; *Waterside Workers Federation of Australia v JW Alexander Ltd* (1918) 25 CLR 434; *A-G of the Commonwealth v The Queen*; *Ex parte Boilermakers Society of Australia* (1957) 95 CLR 529 at 537; (1957) AC 288 (PC) 311-312; (1956) 94 CLR 254 (Aust. HC).

the non-delegability doctrine has been said to be "almost a complete failure". For one thing, it has not prevented delegation of legislative power nor has it accomplished the purpose of assuring that delegated power will be guided by meaningful standards and further, "a modern regulatory agency would probably be an impossibility if power could not be delegated with vague standards"[464].

Another criticism of this approach is that the US Supreme Court has had to construe narrowly statutes which sought to delegate rule-making power so as to avoid the task of invalidating them for undue delegation[465].

7.3 Nigeria

Yet the American approach has its adherents. In adopting this approach, the Irish Courts have drawn a distinction between delegating parliamentary law-making powers to the executive as against regulatory law-making by the executive under a law made by Parliament[466]. Arguments similar to those raised in Australian and Canadian Courts have been rejected by the post independence Supreme Court in Nigeria in *Williams v Majekodumni*[467] while similar arguments succeeded during Nigeria's Second Republic. Following the British tradition, it was held in *Williams* that in so far as primary law as are passed by the legislature itself, subsidiary legislation by a person or body authorized by the legislature to supplement its enactments, does not constitute abdication on its part of power to legislate. But there are two judgments, one of the High Court and the other, of Court of Appeal both of which adopting the line of reasoning embedded in the American approach, arrived at contrary conclusions on this issue, although the Court of Appeal case concerned delegation of legislative power to the Judiciary.

The question before Balogun J in *Sule Balogun v Attorney-General of Lagos State*[468] was whether the Lagos State Legislature could delegate its power to legislative over local government councils to the executive and the ancillary question of the applicability of the American non-delegability of legislative functions to the executive to the Nigerian situation. The trial judge held that this doctrine applied to Nigeria under the 1979 Constitution so that the legislature could not delegate its legislative powers except under a limitation of a prescribed standard in appropriate cases. And since the State House of Assembly did not follow the standards stipulated in the Constitution, it overstepped its legislative authority by delegating its powers to the Governor of the State contrary to the doctrine of separation of powers embedded in the 1979 Constitution. Accordingly, the Lagos State Local Government Law 1980 was unconstitutional and invalid.

The circumstances of the *Williams* and *Balogun* cases arose in Nigeria during what may be described as democratic lucid intervals for it is obvious that whenever the military takes over the reigns of political power, the first thing they do is usurp both legislative and executive powers by suspending the Constitution. Whenever this happens, the line dividing legislative

[464] Davis, KC (1969). "A New Approach to Delegation" 36 *University of Chicago LR* 713 at 720.

[465] *Kent v Dulles* 357 US 116 (1958). See also *INS v Chada* 462 US 919 (1983).

[466] *Cityview Press Ltd v An Chomhairle Oiliuna* (1980) IR 381.

[467] (1962) 1 All NLR 413 at 420 per Bairamian FJ.

[468] (1981) 2 NCLR 589 at 654.

and executive functions evaporates into thin air. Fusion, rather separation of powers, dominates the command structure of government during the military interregnum[469]. Yet the Court of Appeal was able to find improper delegation of legislative authority in a military governmental arrangement in *Okhae v Governor of Bendel State*[470]. The court entertained the case because it did not question the essential structure of the military government nor its authority to make law. The challenge concerned a State Governor's Edict which had sought to establish a Customary Court of Appeal of the State which was undoubtedly within the powers of the State to legislate but the litigation particularly questioned the composition and jurisdiction of such a court as regulated by the Edict as against the provisions of the Constitution regarding the composition of appellate courts in Nigeria. It is not this aspect of jurisdiction that is our concern here, rather, it is that part of the State Law whereby the President of the Customary Court of Appeal was conferred with the discretion to direct two or more judges to sit and determine a substantial point of law or custom or both. This type of question may not ordinarily raise a separation of powers issue, but in the 1979 Constitution[471], the discernible pattern was that appellate courts were established as multi-member courts so that a Customary Court of Appeal of a State, being an appellate court, could not by that same standard, be properly constituted by a single judge of that court. The next question was: who was to determine that matter – the legislature, the executive or the judiciary? The Court of Appeal held that by enacting that it was the President of the Court who should decide that issue in his own discretion, the State law-maker had delegated to the President of the Court legislative power vested in the State by the Constitution, that is, of determining the Constitution of the court for the purpose of exercising the jurisdiction conferred on it by the Constitution. It was held that it was improper for the Governor to do so by way of the enactment in the face of the maxim: *delegates non potest delegare*[472].

In coming to that conclusion, the Court of Appeal applied the full effect of an earlier case where the Supreme Court expressed an opinion on the question of delegation of legislative powers though not to the executive or the Judiciary but to some other body of persons within the law making organ. The Supreme Court had stated in that case that where legislative power has been vested in a legislative organ, there could be no question of delegating that deliberative legislative power, nor could such power be usurped by another body or authority[473]. It was held in the *Bendel State* case that as much as the legislature, under the doctrine of separation of powers, is master of its own household, its sovereignty is subject to the restrictions contained in the Constitution under which it operates. Accordingly, legislative powers cannot be exercised in such a manner as to contravene or convert a clearly expressed provision of the Constitution. Eso JSC had specifically held that the

[469] Quite often the military authorities strain to annex the judicial function to their already acquired legislative and executive powers. This they do either by garnishing their edicts and decrees with hideous ouster clauses or by establishing military tribunals to try civilians for perceived political offences.

[470] (1990) 4 NWLR (144) 327.

[471] See s 214 relating to the composition of the Supreme Court; s 226 on the Court of Appeal and s 243 for the Sharia Court of Appeal of a State.

[472] (1990) 4 NWLR (144) 327 at 367G per Ogundare concurred in by the full Court of the Court of Appeal.

[473] *A-G, Bendel v A-G, Federation* (1982) 3 NCLR 1.

power to legislative was vested in the National Assembly made up of the Senate and the House of Representatives, so there was no question of delegation such legislative power to a Joint Committee of both Houses, certainly, "that power can never be usurped by a Committee of the Assembly[474]".

7.4 South Africa

One fundamental difference between the Constitutions of the United States of America (the US) and the Federal Republic of Nigeria on the one hand and that of the Republic of South Africa on the other, is that the former Constitutions are based on the presidential system of government whereby the President, elected on a separate ticket from that of the members of Congress or the National Assembly as the case may be, is not a member of the legislative organ nor are the Ministers. In the case of South Africa, although the President must first be elected into the National Assembly through the system of proportional representation like all other members, he or she ceases to be such a member upon his or her election by that august body to the office of President. Unlike in the US or Nigerian situations, the Ministers in South Africa retain their seats in Parliament upon appointment. This arrangement obviously tilts the South African governmental structure towards the parliamentary system. However, the question for the purposes of this discussion is: whether this arrangement of essence would dictate the adoption of the parliamentary system approach so that the South African Constitutional Court would uphold the constitutionality of the delegation by the National Assembly of its plenary legislative powers to the executive or, whether there is anything in the Constitution of South Africa that would enable that Court to adopt a different approach?

The opportunity to resolve the problem posed above presented itself in *Executive Council, Western Cape Legislature v President of the Republic of South Africa*[475] and the Constitutional Court took the opportunity to lay down the South African approach to the issue by considering the implications of the separation of powers under the 1993 Constitution; the "manner and form" provisions of sections 59, 60 and 61; the implications of the supremacy clause in section 4 and the requirement of section 37 that Parliament shall make laws in accordance with the Constitution. Section 16A of the Local Government Transition Act 209 of 1993 had empowered the President, acting with the approval of the Select Committee on Constitutional Affairs of the National Assembly and the Senate, to amend the Act and its Schedules by proclamation. Accordingly, the President effected certain amendments to the Act by Proclamations R58 of 7 June 1995 and R59 of 8 June 1995. Proclamation R58 amended section 3(5) of the Act by transferring the power to appoint and dismiss committee members from the Executive Councils of the provinces to the national government. Appointments of members of a committee made by the Executive Council of a province after 30 April 1995 were terminated, effectively nullifying the appointment of the fourth and fifth applicants as members of the committee. Proclamation R59 amended section 10 of the Act and made the exercise of an administrator's powers to make proclamations relating *inter alia* to the demarcation of local government structures and the division of such structures into wards subject to the provisions of a new subsection, section 10(4) of the Act.

[474] *Ibid.* 109.

[475] 1995 (4) SA 877 (CC) (the first *Western Cape* case).

In a majority opinion read by Chaskalson P, it was held, *inter alia*, that:

- there was nothing in section 37 or any other part of the Constitution which prohibits Parliament from delegating subordinate regulatory authority to other bodies. This is implicit in the power to make laws and necessary for effective law-making. However, there is a difference between delegating authority to make subordinate legislation within the framework of a statute under which the delegation is made, and assigning plenary legislative power to another body such as here, the power to amend legislation made by Parliament is quite different[476];
- the Constitution of the Republic of South Africa shows a clear break away from the British legacy of parliamentary supremacy hence to delegate to the Executive the power to amend or repeal Acts of Parliament could be subversive of the "manner and form" provisions of sections 59, 60 and 61 of the Constitution which prescribe how laws are to be made and changed and are part of a scheme which guarantees the participation of both Houses of Parliament in the exercise of legislative authority vested in Parliament by the Constitution. There may be exceptional circumstances such as war or emergencies in which there will be necessary implication that laws can be made without following the forms and procedures prescribed by sections 59, 60 and 61. The conditions under which the impugned section 16A was enacted fell short of such an emergency nor could an unrestricted power to amend the Transition Act be justified on the grounds of necessity[477];
- the authorisation of legislation such as section 16A allows control over legislation to pass from Parliament to the Executive. It would also render ineffective the special procedures prescribed by sections 60 and 61[478]. Once it is found that Parliament does not have the power to vest in the President the power to amend an Act with far-reaching implications, the reasonableness of the delegation or the absence of objection is irrelevant. There is no other way Parliament could effect such delegation without amending the Constitution, and having not amended the Constitution, the general power vested in the President to amend the Transition Act was unconstitutional[479].

The question whether there is constitutional authority in any given case for the legislature to delegate its power is a matter of constitutional interpretation depending ultimately on the language used in the Constitution and the context in which the provisions being construed occur. This was the unanimous view of the Constitutional Court in the second *Western Cape* case[480] where it was called upon to determine the constitutionality of another Local

[476] Chaskalson, P. at para 51. Cf. the approach of Sachs, J. at para 205.

[477] Para 62. See also the concurring judgment of Langa, J. at para 192.

[478] Para 63.

[479] Mahomed DP held that notwithstanding the argument that a case can be made for the delegation of special legislative powers to the President to make the amendments, s 16A, from any approach, "goes too far and effectively constitutes an abdication of Parliament's legislative function in terms of s 37 of the Constitution, leaving the President absolutely free to change the entire structure and policy of the Act in his or her absolute discretion as long as the approval of the relevant committees is obtained" (para 141).

[480] *Executive Council of the Western Cape v Minister for Provincial Affairs & Constitutional Development of the Republic of South Africa; Executive Council of KwaZulu-Natal v President of the Republic of South Africa* 1999 (12) BCLR 1360 (CC) para 124. Although O'Reagan J (Mokgoro J and Cameron AJ concurring) at paras 140 and 174 dissented on the question of the Constitutionality of s 4, 5 and 6(2) of the Act, she concurred on this aspect of Ngcobo J's majority opinion on the unconstitutionality of s 24(1) of the Act.

Government legislation, this time around, the Local Government: Municipal Structures Act 1998[481]. Several provisions of this Act which was one in a series of legislation designed to usher in a new system of local governance thereby dismantling the transitional arrangements contrived by virtue of the Local Government Transition Act 1993. One of the challenges related to section 24(1) of the Municipal Structures Act which purported to empower the Minister responsible for Local Government to fix the term of office of municipal councils. It was argued that this constituted an impermissible assignment of plenary legislative power to the Minister and it was not the power to make subordinate legislation within the meaning of section 239 of the 1996 Constitution.

In its unanimous decision on the invalidity of section 24(1) of the Municipal Structures Act 1998, the Court held that by virtue of section 159(1) of the Constitution, Parliament was required to fix the term of office of municipal councils itself. Thus, this section also stipulates that the councils would have a uniform term of office subject to a maximum of five years. This was a matter which Parliament could not delegate; it required its determination by itself. The delegation was, therefore, impermissible and section 24(1) was inconsistent with section 159(1) of the Constitution. The Court affirmed the views it expressed in the first *Western Cape* case[482] on the competence of Parliament to delegate its law-making function as a principle of "universal application...recognised in many countries" but that such authority was subject to the Constitution[483]. And since section 159(1) does not permit of such delegation, section 24(1) of the Act which purported to do so was unconstitutional and invalid.

8.6 Review Questions

1. It is this limiting of the arbitrariness of political power that is expressed in the concept of constitutionalism. Constitutionalism recognises the necessity of government but it insists upon a limitation being placed upon its powers. It connotes in essence therefore a government limitation on government; it is the antithesis of arbitrary rule; its opposite is despotic government, the government of will instead of law." Ben Nwabueze, *Constitutionalism in the Emergent States p.1.*

With specific reference to the Namibian Constitution and any other relevant authorities, discuss how this limitation on arbitrariness of political power is achieved through the concept of separation of powers.

2. Mr Gaoseb has been operating a stall at the Katutura Soweto market since 1991. At the end of last month he applied for a renewal of his licence and he received a reply from the Soweto Market Council that his application for renewal was unsuccessful. The Soweto Market Council has the statutory power to consider applications for licences to operate business at the market.

   Mr Gaoseb strongly feels that his application was refused purely on tribal grounds. He wants to institute a legal action before the High Court for an order that his licence should be renewed.

481 117 of 1998.

482 1995 (4) SA 877 (CC) para 51.

483 1999 (12) BCLR 1360 (CC) para 124.

Advise Mr Gaoseb of his rights explaining the circumstances under which the court may review the decision of the Council and grant the order that he is asking for. Your answer should include, *inter alia,* the discussion of the *Chilufya* and *Erna Elizabeth Frank* cases.

3. 'For us an Act of Parliament duly passed by Lords and Commons and assented to by the King, is supreme, and we are bound to give effect to its terms..." Per the Lord Chief Justice General in the case of *Mortensen v Peters* (1906 14 STL 227)

With reference to relevant case law authority and Constitution of Namibia, discuss the accuracy of the above statement.

4. "The great theme of the advocates of constitutionalism, in contrast either to the theorists of utopianism, or of absolutism of the right or of the left, has been the frank acknowledgement of the role of government in society, linked with the determination to bring that government under control and to place limits on the exercise of its power". MJC Vile, *Constitutionalism and the Separation of Powers* (1967) p.1.

Discuss the above statement with specific reference to the Namibian Constitution.

5. To what extent does the doctrine of the rule of law protect the individual against the excesses and abuse of administrative or executive power?

6. Discuss the significance of Art. 18 of the Namibian Constitution.

7. "The principle of Parliamentary sovereignty means neither more or less than this, namely, that Parliament thus defined has, under the English Constitution, the right to make or unmake any law whatever, and, further, that no person or body is recognised by the law of England as having a right to override or set aside the legislation of Parliament.... The principle then of Parliamentary sovereignty may, looked at from its positive side, be thus described: Any Act of Parliament, or any part of Parliament, which makes a new law, or repeals or modifies an existing law, will be obeyed by the courts". A.V Dicey, *An Introduction to the Study of the Law of the Constitution.* 10th ed. 39-40.

Discuss the extent to which the above statement describes the nature of the legislative powers of the Parliament of Namibia.

8. Discuss Dicey's exposition of the rule of law and the contribution of other writers to the concept of the rule of law. Credit will be given for references to the Namibian Constitution and the judicial system.

9. Discuss the nature of administrative discretion and the circumstances under which the decisions and acts of administrative bodies and officials can be reviewed by the Courts.

BIBLIOGRAPHY

1. Austin, J. 1965. *The Province of Jurisprudence Determined*. Lecture VI. London: Love & Brydone Printers Ltd.
2. Balmford, C. 1994. 'Adding Value by Writing Clearly' Vol. 111. *South African Law Journal*. pp.514-541.
3. Botha, C.J. 1996. *Statutory interpretation*. Cape Town: Juta.
4. Cockram, G. 1993. *The Interpretation of Statutes*. Cape Town: Juta.
5. Cowen, D. 1976. 'Prolegomenon to a Restatement of the Principles of Statutory Interpretation'. *TSAR*. pp.131-167.
6. Cowen, D. 1980. 'The Interpretation of Statutes and the Concept of the Intention of the Legislature' 43 *THRHR*.
7. Crabbe, VC.R.A. 1994. *Understanding Statutes*. London: Cavendish.
8. Cross, R. 1977. *Precedent in English Law*. 3rd edition. Oxford: Clarendon Law Series.
9. Curzon, L.B. 1979. *Jurisprudence*. Macdonald & Evans Ltd.
10. De Ville, J. 1999. 'Meaning and Statutory Interpretation'. 62 *THRHR* pp.373-389.
11. Devenish, G.E. 1992. *Interpretation of Statutes*. Cape Town: Juta.
12. Dias, R.W.M. 1970. *Jurisprudence*. London: Butterworths.
13. Dicey, A.V *An Introduction to the Study of the Law of the Constitution* 10th edition.
14. Dlamini, A.M. 1991. 'Is There a Literal Intepretation in Law?" 6 *SAPR/PL* pp.16-30.
15. Dugard, J. 1978. *Human Rights and the South African Legal Order*. Cape Town: Juta.
16. Dugard, J. 1981. 'Some Realism About the Judicial Process and Positivism'. *South African Law Journal*. Vol. 98 pp.372-387.
17. Dugard, J. 1978. 'Statutory Interpretation as an Exercise in Choice' *SALJ* p.451.
18. Dugard, J. 1971. "The Judicial Process, Positivism and Civil Liberty" Vol. 88, *South African Law Journal* pp.181-200.
19. Du Plessis, L.M. 1992. *An Introduction to Law*. Cape Town: Juta & Co.
20. Du Plessis, L. 1981. 'Tentative Reflections on the Systemization of the Rules and Presumptions of Statutory Interpretation'. *South African Law Journal*. Vol. 98 pp.211-217.
21. Evans, J.M. *de Smith's Judicial Review of Administrative Action*. 4th edition.
22. Goodhart, A.L. 1931. "Determining the *Ratio Decidendi* of a Case." In *Essays in Jurisprudence and the Common Law*.
23. Forsyth, C. 1991. 'Interpreting a Bill of Rights: The Future Task of a Reformed Judiciary' *South African Journal of Human Rights* 7 pp.1-23.
24. Freeman, M.D.A. 2001. *Lloyd's Introduction to Jurisprudence*. 7th Edition. London: Sweet & Maxwell.
25. Friedman, W. 1967. *Legal Theory*. 5th edition. London: Stevens & Sons.

26. Fuller L. 1940. *The Law in Quest of Itself.* Beacon Press.
27. Fuller, L. 1969. 'The Morality of Law'. Revised Edition: *Yale University Press.*
28. Geldart. *Elements of English Law.* 1st edition.
29. Hahlo, H.R. & Khan, E. 1973. *The South African Legal System and its Background.* Cape Town: Juta.
30. Hart, (ed.). Bentham, J. 1970. *Of Laws in General.*
31. Hosten, W.J.; Edwards, A.B.; Bosman, F. & Church, J. 1997. *Introduction to South African Law and Legal Theory.* 2nd edition. Durban: Butterworths.
32. Kellaway, E.A. 1995. Principles of Legal Interpretation of Statutes, Contracts & Wills. Durban: Butterworths.
33. Kelsen, H. 1945. *General Theory of Law and State.*
34. Kentridge, J. & Spitz, D. 'Interpretation' in Chaskalson, M. *et al.* (eds.). 1996. *Constitutional Law in South Africa.* Cape Town: Juta.
35. Legal Assitance Centre 1997. *NAMLEX: Index to the Laws of Namibia.* Windhoek: Legal Assistance Centre.
36. Mathews, A.S. 1985. 'The South African Judiciary and the Security System'. *South African Journal of Human Rights* 1 pp.199-209.
37. Maxwell. *Interpretation of Statutes.* 12th edition.
38. Nwabueze, B.O. 1973. *Constitutionalism in the Emergent States.*
39. Okpaluba, C. 'Constitutionality of legislation relating to the distribution of governmental powers in Namibia: A comparative Approach' in M.O. Hinz; Amoo, S.K. & van Wyk, D. (eds.) 2002. *The Constitution at Work: 10 Years of Namibian Nationhood.*
40. Parker, C. 1991. 'The Administrative Justice Provision of the Constitution of the Republic of Namibia: A Constitutional Protection of Judicial Review and Tribunal Adjudication under Administrative Law' 24 *Comparative and International Law Journal of Southern Africa* pp.90-92.
41. Pound, R. 1959. *Interpretations of Legal History.* New York: The MacMillan Co.
42. Stone, J. 1965. *Human Law and Human Justice.* London: Stevens & Sons Ltd
43. Strydom, G.J.C. 'A Bill of Rights and Value Judgments versus Positivism: The Namibian Experience' in Kruger & Currin, B. (eds.). 1994. *Interpreting a Bill of Rights.* Cape Town: Juta.
44. Vile, M.J.C. 1967. *Constitutionalism and Separation of Powers.*
45. Williams, G. 1982. *Learning the Law.* 11th edition. London: Stevens and Sons.
46. Wills, J. 1938. 'Statutory Interpretation in a Nutshell'. *South African Law Journal* 40 pp.187-94 & pp.322-36.

ANNEXURE I
THE RULE OF LAW

Address by Justice Mtambanengwe to the Society of Law Teachers of Southern Africa (SLTA) Congress 2003.07.02

The topic of my address to you tonight is the Rule of Law in context.

When I was asked if I could address this gathering I was advised I could choose any legal topic. That at first appeared to make the task easy for me: but I soon realized it was not that easy seeing that I would be addressing an audience composed of people well versed in the law and whose occupation is to teach law, and seeing that teachers, unlike Judges and practising lawyers generally have far more time to devote to research and will generally have a wider knowledge of any area of the law that they teach than those of us restricted by pressure of work to a case by case research on many and varied aspects of the law as is the lot of judges and practitioners in small jurisdictions where specialization is practically impossible.

It behoved me then to choose a topic that I could discuss with you without appearing to waste your time by repeating what would be quite familiar to all of you. In line with the theme the law in context, I eventually decided on this topic for various reasons, the most important of which being that while everybody talks about the Rule of Law and has some pretty good idea of what it entails, in practice for many people the concept of the Rule of Law seems very difficult to live by and to implement. That goes for even the most sophisticated individuals and governments. My address therefore will be limited to an attempt to illustrate what I mean by this statement.

Many, if not all of us in Namibia will have read in The Namibian a few months ago of two traditional leaders who were murdered in the Ohangwena Region by mobs who believed that the two leaders were witches. One can put those two incidents in historical context and recall the era in England when trial by ordeal was the rule of the day. One might reflect that the fundamental principle that no one is allowed to take the law into his own hands is unknown in the communities involved in the two murders but those incidents, which are not peculiar to Namibia, are but an example of what some people might want to describe as the primitive extreme. But to digress a bit I invite you to reflect on the many genocidal events of recent occurrence in Africa, which would have left us as Africans extremely exposed to the derision of the rest of the world that would have been quick to point to our primitiveness, but for Kosovo and other similar and contemporary events in Eastern Europe.

Any student of legal history will know that while ancient Rome developed a legal system that today remains the foundation of common law in Roman-Dutch Law jurisdictions, to be firmly established in Europe the concept of the Rule of Law took many a twists and turns over, many a centuries to culminate in the concept as it is known, and practised today.

It may sound ironic to state that the Ohangwena incidents are replicated and exemplified in the international field by the recent invasion of Iraq by America and Britain brushing aside the United Nations and ignoring the dictates of international law. Saddam Hussein in their view, like the two traditional leaders in the Ohangwena Region, was a witch to be got rid of under any pretext, and damn what anybody says.

Both on the individual or community level as well as at Government level one might talk of a syndrome besetting or militating against a practical appreciation or implementation of the Rule of Law. What the Rule of Law is, is easy enough to define. One finds the concept embodied in the doctrine of the separation of powers with the Judiciary being the custodian and ultimate upholder of the Rule of Law. To the extent that this relates to Governmental action or Governments' interaction with its citizenry someone recently described Judicial Review as the Rule of Law in practice or in action.

The syndrome I referred to above persists and influences attitudes of Governments and Civil servants to the extent that this supervising jurisdiction of the courts embodied in Acts of Parliament, in Constitutions and official codes, is hardly favourably looked upon by officialdom. Was it Henry the 8th who told the Lord Chancellor in England some days gone by "You have made your decision, now enforce it."

In *Traub and Other v Administrator, Transvaal and Others* 1989 (4) SA 731 at 761 Corbett JA (as he then was) discussing the concept of legitimate expectation as a ground for review in administrative law cautioned that legitimate expectation like public policy was an unruly horse unless curbed and a fair balance must be kept between the need to protect the individual from decisions unfairly arrived at by public authority and the desirability of avoiding undue judicial interference in their administration. In proper context that admonition could apply to the attitude, which I have observed on the bench, of many civil servants, particularly Permanent Secretaries namely that "We are The Government and therefore we are the Law". The idea that their decision or Government's decisions can be challenged and in many cases nullified by the courts is for some difficult to swallow let alone to digest.

The Rule of Law concept is vulnerable to other considerations in the realm of Government. I have referred to the Iraq invasion above. That example illustrates how vulnerable the concept is in the face of a Government determined to trample under foot or ride rough shod over the rights of its citizens or other people to achieve certain perceived national objectives. Gwynne Dyer in an article in The Namibian said of the Americans vis-à-vis their invasion of Iraq:

> **"Their purpose, after all was to scare all America's rivals and enemies into submission by demonstrating its military power and making it clear that no consideration of international law would stand in Washington's way."**

He was of course referring to the so-called neo-conservatives in Bush's Administration like one Paul Wolfowitz who recently revealed what many would have known or guessed anyhow that it was for oil that the Americans went into Iraq and that the so called W.M.D were only used and as core reason. On Wednesday 25 June 2003 this article appeared in *The Namibian*:

"Former General Wesley Clark told anchor Tim Russert that Bush administration officials had engaged in a campaign to implicate Saddam Hussein in the September 11 attacks – starting that day.

Clark said that he'd been called on September 11 and urged to look at Baghdad to the terror attacks, but declined to do so because of a lack of evidence.

Clark's assertion corroborates a little-noted CBS Evening News story that aired on September 4 2002. According to CBS, a Pentagon aide's notes from that day quote Rumsfeld asking for the "best info fast" to "judge whether good enough to hit SH at the same time, not only OBL". (The initials SH and OBL stand for Saddam Hussein and Osama bin Laden.) The notes then quote Rumsfeld as demanding, ominously, that the administration's response "go massive…sweep it all up, things related and not". – Fair, June 20 2003. The truth's coming out in snippets!!

To come nearer home, one often hears of or reads statements like the following:

> **"It is sad when we are forced as a Government to use teargas against our own youth who are being misled, but we have to do it in the interest of peace and security. We don't want to make our people suffer. We want our people to be free to express their free views."**

This would sound hallow, in the face of events unfolding in many countries with shocking records of human rights abuses within the region.

Having said what I have tried to illustrate above, one must give credit to Namibia for its practically demonstrated adherence to the Rule of Law. First one recalls that a few years ago the Judiciary came under heavy political criticism in connection with a case where the High Courts issued an interim order restraining the Minister of Home Affairs from deporting some people from Namibia. Then the Government issued a statement through the Minister of Justice affirming its commitment to the Rule of Law. The statement *inter alia* emphasized the supremacy of the Constitution and the independence of the Judiciary and reminded all that judges should not be interfered with.

I quote only parts of the statement.

> **"The Independence of the Judiciary**
>
> **The outside world has hailed the Namibian Constitution as a 'model constitution', that is a progressive democratic instrument guaranteeing among other things justice and freedom to the citizens and those who find themselves in the country. All Cabinet Ministers take oath before the President of Namibia in which they swear or affirm to defend and protect the Namibian Constitution. One of the provisions which has earned our Constitution the title of a 'model constitution' is Art. 78 which provides, among other things, as follows:**

(3) No member of the Cabinet or the Legislature or any other person shall interfere with Judges or judicial officers in the exercise of their judicial functions and all organs of the State shall accord such assistance as the Courts may require to protect their independence, dignity and effectiveness, subject to the terms of this Constitution or any other law.

The Government of the Republic of Namibia undoubtedly upholds the letter and spirit of this provision. It is acknowledged that Ministers and Ministries are tasked to administer numerous laws, regulations and legal directives. But all these are subject to the Constitution, which is the supreme law.

The Constitution guarantees, among other freedoms, the freedom of speech, which should be enjoyed and exercised within the perimeters of the law of Namibia, which may impose reasonable restrictions on its enjoyment.

It is important to inform the public that the independence of the Judiciary means a number of things. Among these is the requirement that judges should not be interfered with in the performance of their judicial functions. It also means that judges should not be threatened, ridiculed, abused, derided. Persons exercising their freedom of speech, which touches on the Judiciary, are subject to the restrictions set by the Constitution and any other law. Persons who utter words that may be construed to be in contempt of court, shall, therefore, be personally responsible to justify their utterances if charged with contempt of court.

Minister of Home Affairs' statement about the Judiciary

A meeting was held at the Supreme Court on Tuesday 5th September 2000 attended by the Chief Justice (Justice Strydom), the Judge President (Judge Teek) the Minister of Home Affairs (Honourable Ekandjo) and myself, convened at the request of the Honourable Minister of Home Affairs to clarify his statement on the role of the Judiciary in general and the so-called "foreign judges" in particular.

The Minister of Home Affairs informed the judges on how he came to make the statement. He said he was misled by the information he received regarding the meaning and implication of the High Court interim order. He therefore wanted to meet the judges in order to –

a) apologise to the Judiciary on the statement he made regarding so called "foreign judges" in Namibia being "reactionary";

b) assure the judges in particular and public in general that he upholds the Namibian Constitution as the supreme law of the land;

c) reaffirm as one of the authors of that Constitution, his commitment to all that the Constitution provides and stands for; ensure the judges that their decisions, orders, judgments shall be enforced in accordance with the law and by and through the machinery provided by that law;...

If any one makes himself or herself guilty of contempt of court he or she should face the charges.

Government Assurance on the Observance of the Rule of Law

The government would like to assure the Namibian people, the Judiciary, the SADC States and the international community that it has not been, it is not and it shall not be the policy or practice of the Government to interfere with the independence of the Judiciary or orders or judgments of courts of law. The lower courts, the High Court and the Supreme Court shall continue to operate in accordance with the provisions of the Constitution and relevant laws and the Rule of Law. The Law enforcement agencies of the State shall continue to carry out their functions in accordance with the law of Namibia.

Namibia has acceded to a number of important international conventions among these are notably, the African Charter on Human and Peoples' Rights, the International Conventions on Refugees (1951) and the Organization of African Unity Convention on the Status of Refugees. Namibia is aware of its international obligations under these Conventions. In this connection the international community should be assured that Namibia is committed to honour, respect and carry out its international obligations under such Conventions without fail. This undertaking includes, of course, the treatment of the applicants in the Osire Stars case of Alfonso Ngoma and the Minister of Home Affairs.

I am sure this explanation cleared the misunderstanding and the issue raised by Honourable Ekandjo are now put to rest once, and for all.

We should now look forward, march forward and work in peace and harmony in our beloved country.

"LONG LIVE DEMOCRATIC NAMIBIA"

I think it is on occasions like this that the Judiciary must respond in Unison:

"LONG LIVE THE DEMOCRATIC REPUBLIC OF NAMIBIA"

On the international arena Namibia adopts the dualistic approach to international law and conventions. Dualism unlike monoism sees international law and domestic law as operating on separate planes – it stipulates norms governing the relationship between individuals within the State or between individuals and the State, in the dualistic conception international law plays no role in the domestic legal order except in so far as domestic law adopts an international rule. The Supreme law of Namibia i.e. the Constitution adopts international law in terms of Art. 144:

> **"Unless otherwise provided in this Constitution, the general rules of public international law and international agreements binding upon Namibia under this Constitution shall form part of the law of Namibia."**

This must be read with Art. 32(3)(e) and Art. 63(2)(d)(e). The former provides for the function, powers and duties of the President and in subsection 3(e) says one of these powers is

> **"to: negotiate and sign international agreements and to delegate such power."**

The latter defines the functions and powers of the National Assembly *inter alia*, as

> **(2)(d) "to consider and decide whether or not to succeed to such international agreements as may have been entered into prior to independence by administrations within Namibia in which the majority Namibian people have historically not enjoyed democratic representation and participation.**
>
> **(2)(e) to agree to the ratification of or accession to international agreements which have been negotiated and signed in terms of Art. 32(3)(e) hereof.**

Time constrains me to mention but one illustration in this area post the ministerial statement, I have just quoted.

The pending Caprivi Treason Trial has resulted in a constitutional case that ended with the Supreme Court of Namibia sitting for the first time as a full bench of 5 judges in an appeal from a full bench of the High Court on 25-28 March 2002.

One hundred and twenty nine (129) of the trial awaiting prisoners brought an application whose main purpose was to obtain legal aid. The High Court ordered the Legal Aid Directorate which was cited as second respondent with the Government of the Republic of Namibia and the Prosecutor General as 1st and 3rd respondents respectively. The appeal was against the order of the High Court directing Second Respondent – to provide such legal aid to Applicants as assessed by him so as to enable them to have legal representation for the defence of all the charges brought against them.

I need not got into the various constitutional issues raised and debated in the matter both on appeal and in the High Court, the judgment is available. Suffice it to say for present purposes the Court made the following order:

> **"(a) First Respondent is directed to provide such legal aid to those of the applicants who are indigent as assessed by it so as to enable them to have legal representation for the defence of all the charges brought against them in the trial referred to as the Caprivi Treason Trial.**
>
> **(b) First Respondent shall pay the costs in the Court** *a quo* **and the costs of appeal in this Court limited to disbursements and to include therein the costs of two instructed Counsel provided that provision is made therefore in the Deed of Trust of the Legal Assistance Centre".**

In part of the reasoning the Chief Justice, who wrote the judgment in which all the other judges of appeal concurred, remarked:

> **'there would be instances where the legal aid scheme falls short but where the dictates of a fair trial require that an accused should be legally represented. See** *R v Rowbotham, supra.*

For the same reasons, set out above, I cannot agree with Ms. Ereinstein Ya Toivo that the provisions of Art. 14(3)(d) of the International Covenant on Civil and Political Rights are in conflict with the Namibian Constitution and can therefore be ignored. The Namibian Parliament acceded to this Covenant on 28 November 1994. It also, on the same date, acceded to the First and Second Optional Protocols. This Article is as follows:

> **"14(3) In the determination of any criminal charge against them, everyone shall be entitled to the following minimum guarantees in full equality:**
>
> **(a).........**
>
> **(b).........**
>
> **(c).........**
>
> **(d) to be tried in his presence, and to defend himself in person or through legal assistance of his own choosing; to be informed, if he does not have legal assistance, of this right; and to have legal assistance assigned to him, in cases where the interests of justice so require, and without payment by him in any such case if he does not have sufficient means to pay for it."**
>
> **(My emphasis)**
>
> **According to Art. 63(2)(e) read with Art. 144 "...international agreements binding upon Namibia under this Constitution shall form part of the law of Namibia." From this it does not follow that the said Article is now part of the Namibian Constitution but being part of the law of Namibia, it must be given effect to. As such it lays down the parameters within legal representation on an indigent accused is required namely, in cases where the interest of justice so requires. Although no law is permitted to limit the rights set out under Chapter 3 of the Constitution, except (a) is provided for under the Chapter itself, the interests of justice lies at the root of a fair trial and the provisions of the Covenant is therefore clearly compatible with the tenets of a fair trial. As was pointed out by Mr Smuts the State not only has an obligation to foster respect for international law and treaties as laid down by Art. 96(d) of the Constitution but it is also clear that the International Covenant on Civil and Political Rights is binding upon the State and forms part of the law of Namibia by virtue of Art. 144 of the Constitution.**

The Government of Namibia has, to its credit, implemented the Supreme Court order and provided legal aid to the accused in the coming Caprivi Treason Trial.

ANNEXURE II
SELECTED CASES

CASE NO.: SA 8/99

IN THE SUPREME COURT OF NAMIBIA
2001 NR 107 (SC)

In the matter between

THE CHAIRPERSON OF THE IMMIGRATION SELECTION BOARD	**APPELLANT**
And	
ERNA ELIZABETH FRANK	**FIRST RESPONDENT**
ELIZABETH KHAXAS	**SECOND RESPONDENT**

CORAM: Strydom, C.J.; Teek, A.J.A. et O'Linn, A.J.A.

HEARD ON: 09 - 10/10/2000

DELIVERED ON: 05/03/2001

APPEAL JUDGMENT

STRYDOM, C.J.: This is an appeal against orders made by a Judge of the High Court of Namibia whereby –

"(a) The decision of the Immigration Selection Board of 29th July 1997 refusing a permanent residence permit to Erna Elizabeth Frank is reviewed and set aside.

(b) The Immigration Selection Board is directed to authorise the issue to Erna Elizabeth Frank of a permanent residence permit within thirty days of date of the order of this Honourable Court.

(c) There is no order as to costs."

By agreement between the parties the appeal was brought directly to this Court in terms of section 18(2)(a)(ii)(aa) of the High Court Act, Act No. 16 of 1990.

Before setting out the background history and facts of the case mention must be made of the fact that the appellant did not file the record of appeal timeously with the result that in terms of Supreme Court Rule 5(5) the appeal is deemed to have lapsed. Application for condonation of this failure was made by the appellant which is opposed by the respondents.

Mr Oosthuizen, instructed by the Government Attorney, appeared for the appellant and Ms Conradie, for the Legal Assistance Centre, appeared for the respondents. Neither Counsel appeared for the parties in the Court *a quo*. Because the merits of the appeal are also of importance for the application of condonation and re-instatement of the appeal, Counsels were allowed to address us simultaneously on both issues.

The background history of this matter is as follows. In the Court below the respondents were the first and second applicants who launched a review application against the appellant, then the respondent, for the relief set out herein before, as well as some alternative relief which is not relevant to the present proceedings. For the sake of convenience I shall refer to the parties as they appeared before us, namely as the appellant and the first and second respondents.

In her founding affidavit the first respondent stated that she was a German national. During 1982, and whilst still a student at the University of Bremen, the first respondent joined the Anti-Apartheid Movement and assisted members of SWAPO as a translator and interpreter at political meetings and rallies. She obtained a Bachelor of Arts degree and a Diploma of Education at the La Trobe University, Melbourne, Australia, during 1976 and 1977 respectively.

Thereafter first respondent moved to Bonn, Germany, where she taught English to development workers and German to Turkish immigrants. In 1982 she started a four year course known as the Erstes Staatsexamen für Lehramt at the Bremen University. This she completed in 1990. First respondent started working for the Centre for African Studies/Namibia Project during March 1988 at the University of Bremen.

During 1990 first respondent visited Namibia. During 1991 she applied for the first time for a temporary work permit. Since then these employment permits have been renewed regularly. In October 1995 first respondent applied for the first time for a permanent residence permit. During June 1996 she was informed by the Ministry of Home Affairs that this application was unsuccessful.

First respondent re-applied for a permanent residence permit during June 1997. Together with this application a letter was sent by her legal representatives. In this letter the appellant Board was requested to allow first respondent to appear before the Board to answer any queries they may have or to deal with any information which may adversely affect the application or to supplement further information if required by the Board. Attached to this letter were various communications supporting the application of the first respondent. In this regard there were letters *inter alia* from the Minister of Finance and permanent secretaries of the two Ministries.

By letter dated 30 July 1997, the first respondent was again informed that her application for a permanent residence permit had been unsuccessful. No reasons for this decision were given by the appellant.

During the period of her stay in Namibia, first respondent worked as a senior researcher and later as Deputy Director of the Centre for Applied Social Sciences (CASS). Since October 1997, she has worked for CASS as a consultant.

In the letter by her legal representative, which accompanied the 1997 application for permanent residence, the relationship between the first and second respondents was set out. In her founding affidavit first respondent stated that she has had a relationship with the second respondent, Elizabeth Khaxas, since 1990. She pointed out that her sexual orientation was lesbian and that if it was legally possible to marry she and second respondent would have done so. First respondent furthermore set out the extent of her relationship with the second respondent and the latter's son Ricky Martin. Because of certain statements by, *inter alia*, the President and other members of Government, the first respondent has expressed the fear that her lesbian relationship with the second respondent may have been the reason why her application for a permanent residence permit has been rejected.

First respondent further pointed out that if her relationship with a Namibian citizen was a heterosexual one, she could have married and would have been able to reside in Namibia or apply for citizenship in terms of Art. 4(3)(a) of the Namibian Constitution. She said that the appellant did not take this factor into account and therefore violated her right to equality and freedom from discrimination guaranteed by Art. 10, her right to privacy guaranteed by Art. 13(1) and protection of the family guaranteed by Art. 14 of the Constitution.

In conclusion the Court *a quo* was asked to review the decision of the appellant in terms of the common law and Art. 18 of the Constitution on the following grounds:

1. That there was no evidence, alternatively no reasonable evidence to justify the decision;
2. That she, in all the circumstances, had a legitimate expectation that she would be informed of all information in possession of the appellant, particularly adverse information, and also that she would be given an opportunity to deal with such information;
3. That the appellant failed to apply the principles of natural justice, particularly that of *audi alteram partem*;
4. That the appellant failed to take into account relevant factors and considerations, such as her long period of residence in Namibia, her long-term relationship with a Namibian citizen and her qualifications, skills and work experience; and
5. That the appellant failed to give any reasons for its decision.

At this stage mention must be made of the application whereby the second respondent was joined in the proceedings. In her founding affidavit second respondent confirmed the relationship between herself and first respondent. She further stated that the decision by the appellant infringed her constitutional rights guaranteed by Articles 10, 13(1), 14(1) and (3), 21(1)(g) and 21(1)(i).

One Simwanza Simenda acted as chairperson of the appellant Board when the application for a permanent residence permit by the first respondent was considered and rejected.

Regarding the requests made by first respondent through her legal representative to appear in person before the appellant, it was stated by appellant that first respondent's application was complete and fully motivated and that there was therefore no necessity for the appellant to call upon her to appear. The members of appellant also had no specific queries for the first respondent. There was further no specific information before the appellant which adversely affected the application and neither was it necessary to supplement the application with further information.

Regarding the qualifications, skills and experience of the first respondent, the appellant stated that it took these into consideration and came to the conclusion that the University of Namibia had graduates qualified in first respondent's field of expertise and that employment must be found for them. This process is continuing, and more and more Namibians who can perform the work first respondent is involved in are being trained. Moreover, numerous volunteers who serve as in-service trainers and research officers at different levels are coming into Namibia on temporary permits.

Furthermore even if there is at this stage a shortage of persons with the qualifications, skills and experience of the first respondent, the appellant cannot ignore the fact that the labour market is limited and that employment must be found for Namibian citizens who will obtain similar qualifications, skills and experience over the next few years.

Regarding the fact that the first respondent is a lesbian, the appellant denied that this played any role in the decision taken by it. It is stated that the first respondent's sexual preference was considered to be a private matter having no bearing on her application for a permanent residence permit.

The appellant furthermore denied that the first respondent could have a legitimate expectation as alleged by her and further denied that it failed to apply the principles of natural justice and stated that it took into account all information relevant to the first respondent's application. The appellant admitted its failure to give reasons for its decision but denied that it was in law obliged to do so.

Appellant also agreed as to the effect of Art. 4(3)(a) of the Constitution and stated that the present relationship of the first respondent with the second respondent was not recognised in law and was also not covered by sec. 26(3)(g) of the Immigration Control Act.

In her reply, first respondent denied that there were sufficient persons with her qualifications, skills and experience in Namibia and pointed out that the record clearly showed that appellant did not rely on any facts or data which could justify such a finding. First respondent also pointed out that the appellant misdirected itself by equating graduates with persons with experience such as herself and stated that a university graduate cannot start training teachers, developing syllabi and textbooks without first gaining practical teaching experience.

This then was the background history and facts put before the Court *a quo* on basis of which that Court set aside decision of the appellant and ordered it to grant to first respondent a permanent residence permit.

In regard to the application for condonation and re-instatement of the appeal, affidavits were filed by Mr Taapopi for the appellant and Mr Asino of the Government Attorney's Office. Mr Taapopi stated that he was informed that an appeal was duly noted on 22 July 1999. He was waiting to be informed of the date of appeal but was under the impression that the Court roll was full and did not expect the appeal to be argued in the near future. He was then informed that the record of appeal was not filed in terms of the Rules of Court. He said he did not know the procedures required to prosecute an appeal and was unaware that the legal practitioner had not complied therewith.

Mr Taapopi referred to the complicated constitutional issues involved in the case and the necessity to have an authoritative judgment on the issues which will also serve as a guideline to the appellant in future. He further stated that the appellant recognised the fact that the respondents have a right to prompt adjudication of the matter and stated that the appellant had no intention of delaying the matter for the purpose of frustrating the administration of justice. In order to obviate the potential personal harm occasioned by the late filing of the record, the Immigration Selection Board had renewed first respondent's employment permit for a period of 1 year so that she might earn a living while the Court decided this matter.

Mr Asino stated that after the appeal was noted he neglected to lodge the record within the period required by the Rules. He humbly apologised and stated that he could offer no excuse for his neglect. He said that he knew that it was his responsibility to assure that all the procedures were followed and all documents were filed timeously and that he had failed to do so. He added however that his dereliction was not intentional.

Mr Asino further explained that he was alerted to the fact that he failed to lodge a record by the legal practitioner of the respondents. This was by letter dated 9 February 2000. He then met with the respondents' legal practitioner in order to obtain the latter's consent to the late filing. This was refused and he was informed that he should apply for condonation. The legal practitioner however indicated that he would consult first respondent to find out whether she would object to the late filing of the record. Finally, on the 7th March 2000, he was informed by first respondent's legal practitioner that she was not willing to give such consent. He thereupon prepared the record and the application for condonation which were then filed.

In her answering affidavit to the application for condonation by appellant, first respondent informed the Court that no employment permit was issued to her notwithstanding the allegation made in this regard by Mr Taapopi. She further informed the Court that her employment permit expired at the end of September 1999. Although she had applied for a renewal during September 1999, no employment permit was issued to her. Repeated enquiries addressed to the Ministry of Home Affairs met with no success. During February 2000 she was informed by an employee of the Ministry that her application was now in the hands of the Government-Attorney. Since then she has heard nothing further.

Mr Light, who then represented the respondents, also filed an affidavit in opposition to the application for condonation. He said that when it became apparent that appellant did not take any further steps to prosecute the appeal, he addressed a facsimile dated 9 February 2000 to appellant's legal practitioners. This was sent on 10 February 2000. A copy of the facsimile and confirmation are annexed to the affidavit. Therein reference is made to the relevant Rule of Court and the fact that the appeal was deemed to have been withdrawn. The appellant was called upon to comply with the High Court order and to issue a permanent residence permit within 30 days. Counsel said nothing further happened and on 17 February 2000 he phoned Mr Asino. The latter confirmed that he had received the fax and wanted to know whether the respondent's would be prepared to not oppose the application for condonation, if they gave the first respondent an employment permit. Light said that he refused and told Mr Asino that they would have to bring an application and that respondents would then have to consider their position. Mr Light said that he made a note of this telephone conversation contemporaneously or shortly thereafter. The note is annexed to the affidavit. Mr Light denied the impression created by Mr Asino that the latter contacted him or met with him after he had received the facsimile.

Mr Light further stated that prior to the telephone conversation; he had already discussed the issue with first respondent, who instructed him not to consent to the late filing of the record or to the application for condonation but to hold this over to see whether there was any merit in the application.

On the 7th March 2000 Mr Light sent a further facsimile to Mr Asino reiterating his previous request to issue a permanent residence permit to the first respondent. On this occasion there was reaction from Mr Asino who again wanted them to agree, Mr Light was not quite sure to what, but Asino was again informed that they would not agree not to oppose the application for condonation.

Mr Light categorically denied what he termed "(the) extremely vague assertion in paragraph 7 of his affidavit that he met me at some unidentified place on some unspecified date". Mr Light consequently denied that he indicated to Mr Asino that he would consult first respondent to see if she would object to the late filing of the record and he denied the allegation by Mr Asino that he was only informed on 7 March 2000 that first respondent would not consent to such an agreement.

No replying affidavits were filed by the appellant.

The chronological sequence of events concerning the prosecution of this appeal is the following: A written judgment was handed down by the Court *a quo* on 24 June 1999. Notice of appeal, together with an agreement in terms of section 18(2)(a)(ii)(aa) of Act No. 16 of 1990 to appeal directly to this Court, was filed on 22 July 1999. The record of proceedings was lodged, according to first respondent, on 9 March 2000 and an application for condonation for the late filing of the record and re-instatement of the appeal was filed on 14 March 2000. The appeal was heard on 9 October 2000. The requirement for the lodging of the record is set out in Rule 5(5) of the Rules of this Court, which provides as follows:

> **"5(5) After an appeal has been noted in a civil case the appellant shall subject to any special directions issued by the Chief Justice -**
>
> **(a) .....**
> **(b) in all other cases within three months of the date of the judgment or order appealed against or, in cases where leave to appeal is required, within three months after an order granting such leave;**
> **(c) within such further period as may be agreed to in writing by the respondent,**
>
> **lodge with the registrar four copies of the record of the proceedings in the court appealed from, and deliver such number of copies to the respondent as may be considered necessary ..."**

Discussing the effect of the non-compliance with AD Rule 5(4) of South Africa, which is in all material respects similar to our rule 5(5), Vivier, J.A., in the case of *Court v Standard Bank of S.A. Ltd; Court v Bester NO and Others,* 1995(3) SA 123 (AD) at 139 F - I, came to the conclusion that such failure results in the appeal lapsing and that it was necessary to apply for condonation to revive it. This in my opinion is also the effect of a failure to comply with Supreme Court Rule 5(5).

At the latest the record of the proceedings in this matter should have been lodged by 24 September 1999. Instead it was lodged some five and a half months later and that only after the legal representative of the appellant was alerted to the non-compliance with the Rule by the representative of the respondents.

Both counsels referred the Court to the case of *Federated Employers Fire and General Insurance Co. Ltd and Another v McKenzie*, 1969(3) SA 360 (A) where the following was said by Holmes, J.A. at p.362G - 363 A, namely:

> **"In considering petitions for condonation under Rule 13, the factors usually weighed by the Court include the degree of non-compliance, the explanation therefore, the importance of the case, the prospects of success, the respondents interest in the finality of his judgment, the convenience of the Court and the avoidance of unnecessary delay in the administration of justice; see** *Meintjies v H.D. Combrinck (Edms.) Bpk.,* **1961(1) SA 262 (AD) at p.264 A - B;** *Melane v Santam Ins. Co. Ltd,* **1962(4) SA 531 (AD); and** *Kgobane's* **case,** *supra.* **The cogency of any such factor will vary according to the circumstances, including the particular Rule infringed. Thus, a badly prepared record - Rule 5(7) to (10) - involves both the convenience of the Court and the standard of its proceedings in the administration of justice. A belated appeal against a criminal conviction Rule 5(5) - may keenly affect the public interest in the matter of the law's delays. On the other hand the late filing of the record in a civil case more closely concerns the respondent, who is allowed to extend the time under Rule 5(4)(c)."**

Mr Oosthuizen relied strongly on the importance of the case in his bid to get condonation. In this regard he referred to the necessity to have an authoritative interpretation of the Aliens Control Act and more particularly sec. 26 thereof. Counsel also dealt with various Articles of the Constitution although in his reply Mr Oosthuizen submitted that because of a concession made by Mr Light in the Court *a quo* the Court could not deal with this issue.

Ms Conradie, although she conceded that the case was important, submitted that a reading of cases in the Supreme Court of Appeal in South Africa shows a tendency to refuse condonation where there has been a flagrant non-observance of the Rules. She further submitted that no explanation was given by Mr Asino for his failure to file the record on time. Counsel further referred to the respondents' interest in a final judgment and urged the Court to refuse condonation.

A reading of the cases of the Supreme Court of Appeal shows in my opinion more than a tendency to follow a hard line. These cases show that a flagrant non-observance of the Rules of Court coupled with an unsatisfactory explanation for the non-observance of the Rules and delays more often than not ended in a refusal of condonation. In certain instances the Court declined to consider the merits of a particular case even though it was of the opinion that there was substance in the appeal. (See, *inter alia*, *Moraliswani v Mamili*, 1989(4) SA (AD); *Rennie v Kamby Farms (Pty) Ltd,* 1989(2) SA 124 (A); *Ferreira v Ntshingila*, 1990(4) SA 271 (AD); *Southern Cape Car Rentals cc t/a Budget Rent a Car v Braun*, 1998(4) SA 1192 (SCA); *Darries v Sheriff, Magistrates' Court, Wynberg, and Another*, 1998 (3) SA 34 (SCA) and *Blumenthal and Another v Thomson NO and Another*, 1994(2) SA 118 (AD).

A reading of cases of the High Court of Namibia shows that the situation is not different from that in South Africa and the Court has refused condonation or relief in similar circumstances or issued warnings where there was non-compliance with the Rules. (See *S v Wellington*, 1991(1) SACR 144; *Maia v Total Namibia (Pty) Ltd,* 1992 (2) SA 352, 1998 NR 303; *Swanepoel v Marais and Others*, 1992 NR 1; *S v Gey van Pittius and Another*, 1990 NR 35; *Adriaans v McNamara*, 1993 NR 188; *Xoagub v Shipena*, 1993 NR 215; *S v Nakapela and Another*, 1997 NR 184; *Johnston v Indigo Sky Gems (Pty) Ltd,* 1997 NR 239; *Mutjavikua v Mutual Federal Insurance Co. Ltd,* 1998 NR 57 and *Meridien Financial Service Pty Ltd v Ark Trading*, 1998 NR 74.)

Although the above Namibian cases deal with the rules of the High Court there was no reason to accept that this Court would apply different principles or would be more accommodating.

Many of the above cases also show that "there is a limit beyond which a litigant cannot escape the results of his attorney's lack of diligence or the insufficiency of the explanation tendered. To hold otherwise might have a disastrous effect upon the observance of the rules of this Court". (*Saloojee & Another v Minister of Community Development*, 1965(2) 135 (AD) at 141 C - D.) See further *P.E. Bosman Transport Works Committee and Others v Piet Bosman Transport (Pty) Ltd,* 1980(4) SA 794 (AD).

A legal practitioner who fails to comply with the Rules of Court must give a full and satisfactory explanation for the non-observance of the Rules and any delays that might have occurred. Furthermore a legal practitioner should also as soon as he or she realises that a breach of the Rules has occurred, prepare and file an application for condonation. This presupposes that the legal practitioner knows the rules and would know when non-observance thereof occurred. Lack of knowledge due to ignorance of the Rules and failure to inform him or herself of the provisions of the Rules can hardly serve as an explanation for failure to apply timeously.

In the present instance, I must agree with Ms Conradie that no explanation was placed before the Court concerning the non-observance of Rule 5. All that the affidavit contains is an admission that the legal practitioner was negligent. This was no news to the Court. In the absence of any explanation it followed that the cause for the failure was neglect on the part of the legal practitioner. But that still did not explain why the legal practitioner neglected to comply with the Rules of Court. In the absence of even an attempt to explain such neglect the only conclusion to which this Court can come, is that after the notice of appeal was filed, the whole matter was allowed to sink into oblivion. Why this was allowed to happen is unknown. There is further no indication in the affidavit as to when the instruction was given for the preparation of the record. In fact the legal practitioner's affidavit does not even inform the Court when the record was lodged. This information only emerged from the first respondent's answering affidavit to the application. What we do know is that the legal practitioner said that after, according to him, he was informed, on 7 March, that the first respondent was not willing to give her consent, the record was prepared and lodged, and only then an application was prepared for condonation. From this the only conclusion that can be drawn is that this only happened after the legal practitioner was alerted to this problem by Mr Light on 10 February.

There is also no explanation what the cause was of the delay after 10 February and until the record was lodged. Seemingly nothing happened until Mr Light contacted Mr Asino telephonically on the 17th. An attempt was then made to get the respondents not to oppose an application for condonation. Again nothing happened thereafter until a second fax was sent by Mr Light on the 6th of March, whereafter a second attempt was made to get respondents to agree to not oppose an application for condonation. Mr Taapopi's statement in his affidavit that he was away on an official trip from 7 to 11 March and could therefore not depose of his founding affidavit shows that the legal practitioner was only now jolted into action.

One asks oneself how it is possible that such a situation can arise. I would think that it is elementary that when one appeals that it has now become necessary to prepare and lodge the record of the proceedings. How else will the Court of appeal be able to deal with the matter? Rule of Court 5(5) is very clear and explicit as to what the duties of an appellant are concerning the lodging of the record and if the legal practitioner was unsure as to what to do, a mere glance at the Rule would have told him all what he needed to know. This, evidently, did not happen and the matter was left to take care of itself.

A further aspect which is relevant to the application for condonation is Mr Taapopi's statement in par. 10 of his founding affidavit namely: "...the Immigration Selection Board has renewed her (first respondent's) employment permit for a period of 1 year so that she may earn a living while this Honourable Court decides the matter". This statement was obviously made to convince the Court that the delay which occurred by the late lodging of the record was not done to frustrate the administration of justice and to counter any potential harm for the first respondent which may have been occasioned thereby. This is said in so many words by Mr Taapopi.

However, shortly before the appeal was due to be heard, an affidavit was filed by the first respondent in which she stated that notwithstanding the assurance by Mr Taapopi she was not issued with an employment permit. She also set out in the affidavit her attempts and that of her legal representative to follow up the statement made by Mr Taapopi. To this extent they also called upon the assistance of Mr Asino. By now the first respondent's own attempts to secure an employment permit had grinded to a halt. It seems that the statement by Mr Taapopi blew new life into the attempts of the first respondent and her legal practitioner to get the permit issued. They were unsuccessful.

When the matter was argued we asked Mr Oosthuizen what the position was and we were informed that an employment permit was not granted to the first respondent. As the statement by Mr Taapopi was obviously made to support the application for condonation and to convince the Court that any potential harm caused to the first respondent by the delay was countered by the issue of a further employment permit for a year, we asked for an explanation and allowed the parties to file further affidavits on this aspect. These have been done.

In his affidavit Mr Taapopi stated that the Immigration Selection Board, against his advice, refused to grant a work permit to first respondent and that he as an individual was therefore not able to make good his undertaking. The reasons given for the refusal were that first respondent had stopped working for CASS and now wanted to be self-employed.

The deponent further submitted that the failure to issue a permit did not prejudice her as she continued to work and also understood that she could not be interfered with as long as her case was still pending in this Court. Finally it was submitted that the first respondent was not prejudiced by the failure of the Board to issue a permit as was undertaken by Mr Taapopi in his affidavit. First respondent admitted that she worked but said that it was on an *ad hoc* basis as she was afraid to take a full time work without having a permit. She also admitted that she was not hindered by the appellant and said that she also assisted at the offices of Sister Namibia but this was mostly voluntary work. During this period, and when it was necessary, she was financially supported by her parents and the second respondent.

However, the issue is not whether, objectively speaking, the reasons for the refusal of an employment permit were good or not good. What concerns me in this application is the obvious conflict between what was stated by Mr Taapopi in par. 10 of his application for condonation and what has now come to light in the supplementary affidavit and, as he put it, prevented him from honouring his undertaking given in his application for condonation. However what was set out in par. 10 of the application for condonation was not an undertaking to arrange for an employment permit but was a statement of fact that a permit was indeed granted, and this allegation was made with a specific purpose to assist the appellant in its application. Nothing can be clearer than the words "...the Immigration Selection Board has renewed her employment permit for a period of 1 year so that she may earn a living while this Honourable Court decides the matter". What is more, no attempt was ever made to put the correct facts before the Court until the Court insisted on an explanation. Not even after the first respondent had joined issue thereon. Also in regard to the short affidavit of Mr Asino, the impressions created changed substantially and notwithstanding the fact that Mr Light's affidavit was in direct conflict with that of Mr Asino on various issues it was thought, so it seems, advisable not to reply thereto.

So far I have dealt only with the non-compliance with the Rules of Court and as I have tried to do, show that there was no explanation whatsoever put forward justifying or attempting to justify such non-compliance. I have also tried to show that the explanation, as far as it goes, did not set out fully what the circumstances were and that the appellant and its legal practitioner were not always frank with the Court.

Nevertheless I am of the opinion that this is not an instance where the Court should decide the application without having regard also to the merits of the appeal in relation to the other factors which were mentioned.

Two further factors, mentioned by Holmes, J.A., in *Federated Employers Fire & General Insurance Co. Ltd*-case, *supra*, are the importance of the case and the interest of the respondents in the finality of the judgment. As was pointed out by Vivier, J.A., in *Court v Standard Bank of SA Ltd; Court v Bester, NO and Others*, 1995(3) SA 123 (AD) the latter factor militates against the granting of the indulgence (p.127C). See also *Mbutuma v Xhosa Development Corporation Ltd,* 1978(1) SA 681(A) at 686F - 687A. In this case the Court approved of what was stated by Solomon, J.A., in *Cairns Executors v Gaarn*, 1912 AD 181 at 193, namely:

> **"When a party has obtained a judgment in his favour and the time by law for appealing has lapsed, he is in a very strong position, and he should not be disturbed except under very special circumstances".**

In the present instance, although the appeal was timeously noted, it lapsed due to the fact that no record was lodged and that up to the 17th of February 2000, a period of almost five months, there was no indication whatsoever that appellant intended to continue with the appeal.

Concerning the constitutional issues raised by the respondents in their founding affidavits, regard must be had to the following excerpt from the judgment of the Court *a quo*.

Dealing with the issue of the respondents' lesbian relationship Levy, A.J., stated as follows at p.322 of his judgment:

> **"In the opposing affidavit concerning the applicants' lesbian relationship, Mr Simenda says:**
>
> > **'...the fact that the applicant is a lesbian played no role whatsoever in the decision taken by the Board, I also deny the unfounded and unsubstantiated allegation that the Board might have been influenced in the manner suggested herein. The Applicants' sexual preference was considered to be a private matter having no bearing on the Applicants' application.'**
> >
> > **When Mr Light on behalf of applicants addressed this Court, he said that in the light of this categorical statement the applicant's sexual orientation was no longer an issue in these proceedings."**

This statement by Mr Light is difficult to reconcile with an intention to raise the constitutional issues. One would have thought that this statement by Mr Simenda would have strengthened Mr Light's argument that in terms of the Constitution it was wrong for appellant to regard the lesbian relationship as neutral. What is more, after referring to what was said in this regard by Mr Light the Court *a quo* did not rely for its judgment in respondents' favour on any of the constitutional issues raised in the application concerning the lesbian relationship. The Court *a quo* referred to certain articles of the Constitution, namely Articles 10, 16 and 21(1)(e), but this referred to the forming of a universal partnership and the protection of property and freedom of association.

There is also no indication that because the Court *a quo* came to its conclusion on different grounds it did not find it necessary to deal with the constitutional issues. In my opinion it would have said so if that was the case.

This situation creates an uncertainty as to whether the constitutional issue was before the Court *a quo* and whether Mr Light, when he made his statement in that Court, did not abandon that issue. Because also of the conclusion to which I have come, and certain concessions made by Mr Oosthuizen, it is wise not to deal with this issue at this stage.

As far as the prospects of success on appeal are concerned, these are greatly influenced by two concessions made by Counsel for the appellant, namely that Art. 18 of the Constitution applied to the proceedings whereby appellant refused to grant to first respondent a permanent residence permit. Secondly that from the reasons supplied by appellant, it is clear that the Board came to their conclusion on an issue which was not canvassed by the first respondent and in regard of which she should have been informed by the Board and given an opportunity to deal with. Counsel's concession amounts thereto that the order of the Court *a quo* whereby it set aside the decision of the appellant in refusing to grant to the first respondent a permanent residence permit was correct albeit for other reasons than those stated by that Court. Counsel however submitted that the Court *a quo* was nevertheless wrong in directing the appellant to issue such permit and should have referred the matter back to the Board. Counsel therefore submitted that this Court should set aside paragraph (b) of the order of the Court *a quo* and refer the matter back to the appellant Board.

Concerning the first concession made by Mr Oosthuizen I am of the opinion that there cannot be any doubt that Art. 18 of the Constitution applies. This was also the finding of the Court *a quo*. This Article provides as follows:

> **"18 <u>Administrative Justice</u>**
>
> **Administrative bodies and administrative officials shall act fairly and reasonably and comply with the requirements imposed upon such bodies and officials by common law and any relevant legislation, and persons aggrieved by the exercise of such acts and decisions shall have the right to seek redress before a competent Court or Tribunal."**

Article 18 is part of Chapter 3 of the Constitution deals with Fundamental human rights and freedoms. The provisions of the Chapter clearly distinguishes which of these provisions apply to citizens only (e.g. Art. 17), and which to non-citizens (e.g. Art. 11(4) and (5)). Where such distinction is not drawn, e.g. where the Article refers to persons or all persons, it includes in my opinion citizens as well as non-citizens. The Article draws no distinction between *quasi* judicial and administrative acts and administrative justice whether *quasi* judicial or administrative in nature "requires not only reasonable and fair decisions, based on reasonable grounds, but inherent in that requirement fair procedures which are transparent" (*Aonin Fishing v Minister of Fisheries and Marine Resources*, 1998 NR 147 (HC)). Art. 18 further entrenches the common law pertaining to administrative justice and in so far as it is not in conflict with the Constitution.

Concerning fair procedure, I am of the opinion that it is not now the time to determine *numerus clausus* of rules and that this part of the law should be allowed to develop as the present case is to my knowledge the first one where Art. 18 has pertinently required the attention of the Supreme Court. For purposes of this case it is enough to say that at the very least the rules of natural justice apply such as the *audi alteram partem* rule and not to be the judge in your own cause, etc.

For the above reasons I am satisfied that the concession made by Mr Oosthuizen, namely that Art. 18 of the Constitution applied to the proceedings whereby the appellant refused to issue to first respondent a permanent residence permit, was correct. The right of the first respondent to be treated fairly and reasonably is therefore not based on a legitimate expectation but on the Constitution itself.

In order to determine the cogency of the second concession made by counsel for the appellant, it is necessary to consider the relevant provisions of the Immigration Control Act to determine *inter alia*, what requirements were imposed by any relevant legislation on the appellant Board in the exercise of their discretion (Art. 18).

The appellant is constituted in terms of sec. 25 of the Act and is required to consider applications for permanent residence permits subject to the provisions of section 26 of the Act.

Sec. 26 of the Immigration Control Act, Act No. 7 of 1993 (the Act), provides as follows:

"(1) (a) An application for a permanent residence permit shall be made on a prescribed form and shall be submitted to the Chief of Immigration.

(b) Different forms may, for the purpose of paragraph (a), be prescribed for different categories of persons.

(2) Subject to the provisions of subsection (7), the Chief of Immigration shall submit every application received by him or her to the Board together with such information relating to the applicant as he or she may have obtained and shall furnish such further information to the Board as it may require in connection with such applicant.

(3) The Board may authorize the issue of a permit to enter and to be in Namibia for the purpose of permanent residence therein to the applicant and make the authorization subject to any condition the Board may deem appropriate: Provided that the Board shall not authorize the issue of such a permit unless the applicant satisfies the Board that -

(a) he or she is of good character; and

(b) he or she will within a reasonable time after entry into Namibia assimilate with the inhabitants of Namibia and be a desirable inhabitant of Namibia; and

(c) he or she is not likely to be harmful to the welfare of Namibia; and

(d) he or she has sufficient means or is likely to earn sufficient means to maintain himself or herself and his or her spouse and dependent children (if any), or he or she has such qualifications, education and training or experience as are likely to render him or her efficient in the employment, business, profession or occupation he or she intends to pursue in Namibia, and

(e) he or she does not and is not likely to pursue any employment, business, profession or occupation in which a sufficient number of persons are already engaged in Namibia to meet the requirements of the inhabitants of Namibia; and

(f) the issue to him or her of a permanent residence permit would not be in conflict with the other provisions of this Act or any other law; or

(g) he or she is the spouse or dependent child, or a destitute, aged or infirm parent of a person permanently resident in Namibia who is able and undertakes in writing to maintain him or her.

(4) When the Board has authorized the issue of a permanent residence permit, the Chief of Immigration shall issue such permit in the prescribed form to the applicant."

Sub-sec. (5) of sec. 26 deals with the lapsing of a permanent residence permit and sub-sec. (6) allows a person who is in Namibia on an employment permit, student's permit or visitor's entry permit to be issued with a permanent residence permit whilst such persons are in Namibia. Sub-sec. (7) regulates the period or other circumstances after which re-application can be made after the Board had rejected an application for a permanent residence permit.

Section 26 makes it clear that the appellant does not have an absolute discretion. Sub-sec. (3)(a), (b), (c), (d), (e) and (f) contain certain requirements which an applicant for a permanent residence permit must satisfy the appellant before a permit may be issued. If the Board is not so satisfied it has no choice but to refuse the application.

In dealing with sec. 26 the Court *a quo* went one step further. It concluded that where an applicant for a permanent residence permit satisfies the Board as aforesaid the Board is obliged to grant the permit. At p.326 of the judgment the Court *a quo,* referring to the affidavit of Mr Simenda, found as follows:

> **"I firstly draw attention to paragraph 9.2 of his affidavit where he says:**
>
> > **'9.2 There was also no specific information before the Board that adversely affected the Applicant's application.'**
>
> **From this it is apparent that there were no grounds whatsoever for refusing the applicant. This statement of Mr Simenda is sufficient to justify this court setting aside the Board's decision without any further ado."**

The Court *a quo* then dealt with the reasons given by the appellant for refusing to grant the permit set out in par. 10.1, and 10.2 of Simenda's affidavit. In par. 10.2 the appellant stated that even if there was at present a shortage of persons with the qualifications, skills and experience of the first respondent the appellant took into account that more and more Namibian citizens will in the years to come acquire the necessary qualifications etc. and that these citizens will have to be accommodated in the limited labour market of Namibia.

Dealing with this statement the learned Judge *a quo* found that the appellant, in refusing the application for a permanent residence permit believed that it was acting in terms of section 26(3)(e) of the Act whereas sec. 26(3)(e) only refers to persons already engaged in Namibia in any employment, business, profession or occupation. Therefore the appellant could not take into consideration what the position may be in the future.

I find myself unable to agree with this interpretation of sec. 26. There is in my opinion no indication in the section itself which would limit the exercise of a discretion by the appellant to the absence of the requirements set out in sub-section (3)(a) - (f). In such an instance the appellant would normally exercise no discretion at all. All that would be required of it, is to determine in each instance whether the requirements set out in sub-section (3)(a) - (f) were complied with or not. If they were complied with, the Board is obliged to issue a permit. If they were not complied with, the Board is obliged to refuse a permit.

Furthermore the fact that sub-section (3) begins with the words "the Board may authorize the issue of a permit ..." (my emphasis) is clear indication that the appellant has a wide discretion once the circumscribed part, set out in sub-section (3)(a) to (f), has been satisfied. This interpretation also conforms with the other provisions of the Act. See in this regard sec. 24 of the Act which prohibits the entry or residence in Namibia of non-citizens, with a view to permanent residence unless such person is in possession of a permanent residence permit. Also in regard to temporary residence no person is allowed to enter or reside in Namibia without being in possession of an employment permit, issued in terms of section 27, or a student's permit, issued in terms of section 28, or a visitor's entry permit, issued in terms of section 29. See further in general sections 6, 7, 8, 9, 10, 11 and 12 of the Act. There is also authority for the principle that a foreign national cannot claim permanent residence as of right and that the State has an exclusive discretion as to whether it would allow such nationals in its territory. See *Everett v Minister of Interior*, 1981(2) SA 453 at 456 D - 457 E; *Naiderov v Minister of Home Affairs and Others*, 1995(7) BCLR 891 (T) at 901; *Xu v Minister van Binnelandse Sake*, 1995(1) SA 185 (TPA) at 187 G - 188 E. See also *Foulds v Minister of Home Affairs and Others*, 1996 (4) SA 137 (WLD). However, as far as Namibia is concerned, this principle is subject to the provisions of Art. 18 of the Constitution and as long as the Board acts fairly and reasonably and in accordance with a fair procedure there is no basis for interference by a Court of Law. I therefore agree with the submissions made by Mr Oosthuizen that the appellant, once satisfied that the requirements set out in section 26(3)(a) - (f) were complied with, could consider other relevant factors provided of course, that they have done so where necessary, in compliance with Art. 18 of the Constitution.

However, this is not the end of the matter. In her argument Ms Conradie submitted that the appellant did not comply with the *audi alteram partem* rule and did not give the first respondent an opportunity to address the issue of qualified and experienced staff who could provide the services which first respondent was able and willing to render. Counsel further pointed out that it was clear from the record filed by the appellant as well as the affidavits filed by it that there was not a scrap of evidence concerning these issues before the appellant Board.

At one stage Mr Oosthuizen submitted that the respondents should have cross-appealed if they now want to rely on non-compliance by appellant with the *audi alteram partem* rule. This seems to me to be incorrect as the respondents would be entitled to argue that the appeal could also not succeed because of such non-compliance. See *Mufamadi and Others v Dorbyl Finance (Pty) Ltd,* 1996 (1) SA 799 (AD) at 803 G - H.

The first respondent's right to be treated fairly and in accordance with a fair procedure, placed the appellant under a duty to apply the *audi alteram partem* rule. This rule embodies various principles, the application of which is flexible depending on the circumstances of each case and the statutory requirements for the exercise of a particular discretion. (See *Baxter: Administrative Law* p.535 ff and *Wiechers: Administrative Law* p.208 ff.)

In the context of the Act, the process for the application of a permit was set in motion by the submission of a written application by the first respondent. If on such information before it, the application is not granted, and provided the Board acted reasonably, that would be the end of the matter. However, there may well be instances where the

Board acts on information they are privy to or information given to them by the Chief of Immigration (see sec. 26(2)). If such information is potentially prejudicial to an applicant, it must be communicated to him or her in order to enable such person to deal therewith and to rebut it if possible. (See *Loxton v Kendhardt Liquor Licensing Board*, 1942 AD 275 and *Administrator SWA v Jooste Lithicum Myne (Edms) Bpk,* 1955 (1) SA 557 (A). However, where an applicant should reasonably have foreseen that prejudicial information or facts would reach the appellant, he or she is duty bound to disclose such information. (See Wiechers *op. cit.* p.212.)

In the absence of any prescription by the Act, the appellant is at liberty to determine its own procedure, provided of course that it is fair and does not defeat the purpose of the Act. (Baxter, *op. cit.* p.545). Consequently the Board need not in each instance give an applicant an oral hearing, but may give an applicant an opportunity to deal with the matter in writing.

Furthermore, it seems to me that it is implicit in the provisions of Art. 18 of the Constitution that an administrative organ exercising a discretion is obliged to give reasons for its decision. There can be little hope for transparency if an administrative organ is allowed to keep the reasons for its decision secret. The Article requires administrative bodies and officials to act fairly and reasonably. Whether these requirements were complied with can, more often than not, only be determined once reasons have been provided. This also bears relation to the specific right accorded by Art. 18 to persons to seek redress before a competent Court or Tribunal where they are aggrieved by the exercise of such acts or decisions. Art. 18 is part of the Constitution's Chapter on fundamental rights and freedoms and should be interpreted "... broadly, liberally and purposively..." to give to the article a construction which is "... most beneficial to the widest possible amplitude". (*Government of the Republic of Namibia v Cultura 2000,* 1993 NR 328 at 340 B - D.) There is therefore no basis to interpret the Article in such a way that those who want to redress administrative unfairness and unreasonableness should start off on an unfair basis because the administrative organ refuses to divulge reasons for its decision. Where there is a legitimate reason for refusing, such as State security, that option would still be open.

Although appellant initially refused to give reasons for its decision, such reasons were later set out in the affidavit of Mr Simenda. These were that many Namibians graduated and will continue to graduate with the same qualifications and expertise as that of the first respondent and that employment must be found for them. Also many volunteers on temporary permits are in Namibia as in-service trainers and research officers. Secondly, it is stated that even if it can be said that at present there is a shortage of persons with the qualifications, skills and experience of the first respondent then the Board took into account that more and more Namibians will qualify for such employment in the next few years and they must be accommodated.

The second reason given very much qualifies the veracity of the first one. It is clear that the Board's considerations were based on assumptions made by it rather than factual evidence and that it was expressing what policies it was applying under the circumstances. There can be no doubt that the application of the first respondent was prejudicially affected by a policy that was operating against her based on assumptions, both of which she was unaware of. (See *Lukral Investments v Rent Control Board, Pretoria*, 1969(1) SA 496 (T) at 509 - 510 and *Moleko v Bantu Affairs Administration Board (Vaal Triangle Area),* 1975 (4) SA 918(T) at 925 - 926.) It may have been perfectly in order for the appellant to have a policy in regard to the granting of permanent residence permits and that it was fair and reasonable to apply it in the present instance. However, before it could do so, it had to inform the first respondent what it considered doing in this regard and to give her an opportunity to deal with such issues. First respondent denied in her replying affidavit these assumptions made by the appellant. When the application was submitted first respondent, through her legal practitioner, offered to appear before the Board to deal with any information which may adversely reflect upon her application. This was in all probability anticipated because her 1996 application was turned down. (See annexure "EF6".) A perusal of the application form, prescribed for permanent residence, also showed that it contained nothing which would have alerted an applicant to the fact that the appellant would apply these policy considerations.

For the reasons set out above, I agree that the second concession made by Counsel for the appellant was also correctly made. It follows therefore that the Court *a quo* was correct in setting aside the decision taken by the appellant on the 29th July 1997 and that in this regard the appeal before us cannot succeed. All that remains is Mr Oosthuizen's submission that the Court should nevertheless set aside the direction given by the Court *a quo* and refer the matter back to the appellant so that they can reconsider the first respondent's application after complying with the *audi alteram partem* rule.

The Court *a quo* had a discretion whether to refer the matter back to appellant or to order the appellant to issue the permit. (See *W.C. Greyling & Erasmus (Pty) Ltd v Johannesburg Local Road Transportation Board and Others*, 1982 (4) SA 427 (AD) at 449 F- H.) (The reference to authority in South Africa in this regard is also apposite as in terms of Art. 78(4) of our Constitution the Supreme and High Courts of Namibia retained inherent jurisdiction which vested in the Supreme Court of South West Africa immediately before independence.) Generally a Court would only exercise the discretion itself where there are exceptional circumstances present. (See the *W.C. Greyling*-case, *supra.*) Examples of instances where the Courts have exercised their jurisdiction not to refer a matter back include cases where there were long periods of delay, where the applicant would suffer prejudice or where it would be grossly unfair. (See the *Greyling*-case, *supra; Dawnlaan Beleggings (Edms) Bpk. v Johannesburg Stock Exchange (Edms) Bpk and Others*, 1983 (3) SA 344 (WLD) at 369 G - H and *Local Road Transportation Board and another v Durban City Council and Another*, 1965(1) SA 586 (AD) at 598 D - 599.)

Although there may be some substance in Mr Oosthuizen's submission that the Court *a quo* should have referred the matter back to the appellant Board for reconsideration, also because one of the factors on which the Court based the exercise of its discretion was its interpretation of sec. 26 of the Act, I am not convinced that this is sufficient to tip the scales in favour of the appellant and that this Court should therefore grant the appellant condonation. As was pointed out by the Court *a quo* there was no legal impediment against the granting of the permit as the appellant was seemingly satisfied that the first respondent has complied with the provisions of sec. 26(3)(a) - (f) and that strong support from notable persons was expressed in favour of the granting of the permit. That this was so is also clear from the fact that at no stage did appellant rely on non-compliance by first respondent of the qualifications set out in sec. 26(3).

For a period of more than three years the respondent's residence in Namibia was in the balance and was clothed in a veil of uncertainty. To the extension of this period and to the uncertainty the legal representative of the appellant contributed significantly. The result of the delay, which is completely unexplained, had the effect that this appeal which could have been heard during the October 1999 session, was only heard a year later. This was rightly conceded by Mr Oosthuizen. This was a review application where no other evidence necessitated time in the typing and preparing of a record for the Supreme Court. All that was necessary to be added to the already prepared record, which was before the Court *a quo*, was that Court's judgment, the grounds of appeal and the consent to appeal directly to this Court. This is further confirmed by the fact that when the legal representative of the appellant realised what was required of him he was able to prepare the record and file it within a period of two days, namely from the 7th to 9th of March. Because of the delay the matter could also not be heard during the April 2000 session of this Court. Also the assurance which this Court was initially given that the appellant tried to alleviate the situation by issuing to the first respondent a temporary employment permit, in order to counter any possible prejudice to the first respondent, was later found not to have materialised.

Especially in a case such as the present, which involves the continued residence of the respondents, the possibility of a complete uprooting was always present, and there can be little doubt that this uncertainty must have caused anguish and hardship to the respondents which was further prolonged by the unwarranted delay caused by the failure to comply with the Rules of the Court. Such possibility was after all foreseen by the appellant.

In the present instance this Court is dealing with this issue in the context of an application for condonation where further considerations such as the interest of the respondents in the finality of the proceedings, is a most relevant factor. To require of the respondents, after a period of more than three years, to have to go through the same uncertainty and anguish and to face the risk of again making the same tiresome way through the Courts will constitute an injustice which this Court is not prepared to sanction. Although the delays which occurred were not always caused by the appellant the fact of the matter is that the non-compliance of the appellant's with their constitutional duties necessitated the institution of these proceedings.

Since September 1998 the first respondent was without an employer's permit which renders her stay in Namibia illegal and also affects her ability to do any work. Any further delay will only prejudice her further. For the above reasons it seems to me that the importance of the case must give way to the interest of the respondents in the finality of the case and the prejudice which a referral back to the Board will cause. All this coupled with the fact that the non-compliance with the Rules was flagrant and was not at all explained have convinced me that this is a case where the Court should refuse the appellant's application for condonation.

In the result the appellant's application for condonation is dismissed and the order of the Court *a quo* must be complied with within 30 days of delivery of this judgment.

(signed) STRYDOM, C.J.

O'LINN, A.J.A.: I have read the judgment of my brother Chief Justice Strydom. Although I agree in substance with many of the facts and findings of law set out in the judgment, I am unable to concur in the result.

In the circumstances it is not necessary for me to traverse all the facts relating to the history of the proceeding, the relevant facts relating to the application for condonation and the merits of the appeal.

I find it convenient to first summarise the main points of agreement and will as far as appropriate, quote the relevant passages or parts thereof as it appears in the aforesaid judgment.

SECTION A: POINTS OF AGREEMENT WITH THE JUDGMENT OF THE CHIEF JUSTICE

1. In applications by a litigant for condonation for non-compliance with rules of Court, "the factors usually weighed by the Court include the degree of non-compliance, the explanation for it, the importance of the case, the prospects of success, the respondent interest in the finality of the judgment, the convenience of the Court and the avoidance of unnecessary delay in the administration of justice. The cogency of any such factor will vary according to the circumstances, including the particular rule infringed[484].

   Furthermore, where the failure to comply with the rules is due to the negligence and/or incompetence of the litigant's legal representative, there is a limit beyond which a litigant cannot escape the result of his attorney's lack of diligence or the insufficiency of the explanation tendered. To hold otherwise might have a disastrous effect upon the observance of the rules of this Court."

2. Notwithstanding the unsatisfactory features of the explanation for the non-compliance by appellant's attorney, "this is not an instance where the Court should decide the application without having regard also to the merits of the appeal in relation to the other factors which were mentioned".

3. Article 18 of the Namibian Constitution relating to "administrative justice" is applicable to the case of the respondents. "At the very least the rules of natural justice apply such as the *audi alteram partem* rule".

[484] *Federated Employers Fire and General Insurance Co. Ltd & An. v McKenzie,* 1969(3) SA 360 (A) at 362G - 363A.

3.1 In the context of the Immigration Control Act No. 7 of 1993, "the process for the application of a permit was set in motion by the submission of a written application ...

If on such information before it, the application is not granted, and provided the board acted reasonably, that would be the end of the matter. However, there may well be instances where the Board acts on information they are privy to or information given to them by the Chief of Immigration... If such information is potentially prejudicial to an applicant, it must be communicated to him or her in order to enable such person to deal therewith and to rebut it if possible... However, where an applicant should reasonably have foreseen that prejudicial information or facts would reach the appellant, he or she is duty bound to disclose such information...

In the absence of any prescription by the Act, the appellant is at liberty to determine its own procedure, provided of course that it is fair and does not defeat the purpose of the Act... Consequently the board need not in each instance give applicant an oral hearing, but may give an applicant an opportunity to deal with the matter in writing."

3.2 It is implicit in Art. 18 that "an administrative organ exercising a discretion is obliged to give reasons for its decision." Where however, "there is a legitimate reason for refusing such as State Security that option would still be open". It should be noted however, that such reasons, if not given prior to an application to a Court for a review of the administrative decision, must at least be given in the course of a review application.

4. "Section 26 (of the Immigration Control Act) makes it clear that the appellant does not have an absolute discretion. Sub-sections (3)(a), (b), (c), (d), (e) and (f) contain certain requirements on which an applicant for a permanent residence permit must satisfy the appellant before a permit may be issued. If the Board is not so satisfied, it has no choice but to refuse the application.

   In dealing with section 26 the Court *a quo* went one step further. It concluded that where an applicant for a permanent residence permit satisfies the board as aforesaid, the board is obliged to grant the permit. I find myself unable to agree with this interpretation of section 26."

SECTION B: FURTHER ANALYSIS OF THE JUDGMENT OF THE COURT *A QUO*

It is convenient to pause here to deal further with the approach and findings of the Court *a quo* because that approach and those findings must of necessity weigh heavily in deciding whether or not the appellant has reasonable prospects of success on appeal.

As is evident from point 4, *supra,* the learned Judge *a quo* misinterpreted section 26 and as a consequence the whole basis of his decision fell away.

The following further misdirections need be mentioned:

(i) It is stated in the judgment: "During the period of her stay in Namibia, first respondent worked as a senior researcher and later as Deputy-Director of the Centre for Applied Social Sciences (CASS). Since October 1997, she has worked for CASS as a consultant."

It appears from affidavits filed by the parties at the request of the Court, that the contract of the 1st respondent with CASS "had expired in March 1997" and that after that date, she had only "provided a short-term research consultancy, which was also no longer in existence by 10th May 2000, according to a letter from CASS attached to an affidavit by Niilo Taapopi, the permanent secretary of appellant. The content of this letter was divulged by the first respondent herself in an undated letter to appellant after 10th May 2000. There is presently no dispute about the situation. It also appears from a letter from CASS contained in appellant's record disclosed under Rule 53 dated 22/9/97, that first respondent was at that stage no longer an employee and the intention was to make use of her services on a consultancy basis, only "as the need arises in future". When first respondent applied for the second time for a permanent residence permit in June 1997, she was no longer an employee of CASS and not the Deputy-Director of CASS.

In first respondent's aforesaid application for permanent residence during June 1997, she quoted from a letter dated 25 March 1997 addressed to the Ministry of Home Affairs wherein she had referred to her employment with CASS, first as a senior researcher and then as "Deputy-Director of CASS". Nowhere did she say that the employment as Deputy-Director had already terminated in March 1997. No wonder that Levy, A.J., who considered respondent's review application, assumed that the first applicant, the respondent herein, was at the time of her second application for a permanent residence permit, employed as the Deputy-Director of CASS and was so employed at all relevant times up to the date of that judgment. The learned Judge put it as follows: "She is the Deputy-Director of CASS and is responsible for staff training and office management".

The Court *a quo* consequently laboured under a misapprehension, caused primarily by the vague and misleading particulars provided by the first respondent in her application for a permanent residence permit which was reproduced in her application to Court for the review of the decision of first respondent.

The Review Court built further on this faulty base:

"To suppose that volunteers with temporary permits or recent graduates from the University could rise to the position which first appellant has in a foreign sponsored organisation namely Deputy-Director or that students who have recently qualified from the University could do the work which first applicant as Deputy-Director is doing, is fatuous particularly in the light of the fact that there is no evidence whatsoever to support such an allegation. For the sake of completeness I repeat briefly what I have already said about the work first applicant is doing. As a Deputy-Director of CASS, she is responsible for staff training and office management."

The truth of the matter is that she was not holding the job of Deputy-Director since March 1997, more than two years before the hearing of the review application before Levy A.J. The question may be asked: How did CASS manage to function without first respondent?

The Court seems to make a third point in regard to CASS where it states: "This organization sponsored by foreign sources was certainly not the type of employment or occupation which section 26(3)(e) had in mind and in terms whereof respondent believed it was acting..."

It is a misdirection to suggest that because an organisation such as CASS is "sponsored by foreign sources", it will not employ Namibian graduates. There is no such evidence and no grounds whatever for such an assumption. It is common knowledge that donor organisations implement the Government's affirmative action policies.

(ii) The Court criticized the Board for allegedly having taken into consideration employment opportunities for Namibians. The judgment reads:

"Further Mr Simenda says in respect of these students who continue to graduate from the University, we have to find employment for them'.

(See too the affidavit of Mr Taapopi.) Finding employment for people is not one of the functions of respondent. Respondent is not a labour bureau. There is no such provision in the Act."

The Court in my respectful view, also erred in this regard. Although the Immigration Selection Board is not a labour bureau, it can certainly in the exercise of its general discretion, consider the interests of Namibian entrants into the labour market and not only those already qualified, but those in the process of qualifying. One must keep in mind that one of the functions of the Board in terms of sections 27 of the Immigration Control Act is to consider applications for employment permits and in the course of exercising that function, it must consider whether there is a sufficient number of persons, already engaged in that particular labour field. If in its opinion there is, then it is obliged to refuse the application. But over and above this duty, it may in the exercise of its discretion, as already indicated in regard to section 26, consider also the interest of those Namibians in the process of graduating and entering the labour field in the immediate or near future.

In the course of the Board's aforesaid function it of necessity and as part and parcel of its function, considers employment opportunities for Namibians at the time when it considers an application for an employment or residence permit by an alien, as well as such opportunities in the immediate or near future. Obviously the consideration of the latter type of opportunities are not in the same category as the consideration of whether or not there are "a sufficient number of persons already engaged in Namibia to meet the requirements of Namibians". (My emphasis added.)

It is also necessary to emphasise that the function exercised by the Board under section 26(3)(e) as well as under section 27(2)(b), is tied to the objective of serving the inhabitants of Namibia and whether or not the application of an alien is granted is consequently measured not against the interest and requirements of an alien or immigrant, but against the requirements and interests of the inhabitants of Namibia.

(iii) The Court stated:

"In his affidavit Mr Taapopi referring to the lesbian relationship between the applicants, said that 'applicant's long term relationship was not one recognized in a Court of Law and was therefore not able to assist the first applicant's application.

This too is an incorrect statement of the law. In *Isaacs v Isaacs*, 1949 (1) SA 952(C) the learned Judge dealt with the position in common law where parties agree to put in common all their property both present and any they may acquire in future. From the common pool they pay their expenses incurred by either or both of them. They can enter into this type of agreement by a specific undertaking verbal or in writing or they can do so tacitly. Such an agreement is known as a universal partnership.

A universal partnership concluded tacitly has frequently been recognised in our courts of law between a man and a woman living together as husband and wife but who have not been married by a marriage officer.

(See *Isaacs, supra,* and *Ally v Dinath,* 1984(2) SA 451 (TPD)).

Article 10 of the Namibian Constitution provides:

'(1) All persons shall be equal before the law.

(2) No person may be discriminated against on the grounds of sex, race, colour, ethnic origin, religion, creed or social or economic status.'

If therefore a man and a woman can tacitly conclude such a partnership because of the aforesaid equality provision in the Constitution and the provision against discrimination on the grounds of sex I have no hesitation in saying that the long term relationship between applicants in so far as it is a universal partnership, is recognised by law. Should it be dissolved the court will divide the assets of the parties according to the laws of partnership.

Furthermore in terms of Art. 16:

'(1) All persons shall have the right in any part of Namibia to acquire, own and dispose of all forms of immovable or movable property individually or in association with others and to bequeath their property to their heirs or legatees.' (My emphasis.)

This is exactly what applicants have done.

Finally Art. 21(1)(e) provides *inter alia* that all persons have the right to freedom of association.

In the circumstances the Chairperson was wrong when he said the long-term relationship of applicants is not recognised in the law.

Not only is this relationship recognised but respondents should have taken it into account when considering first applicant's application for permanent residence and this respondent admits it did not do."

It is necessary to make the following comments:

(a) As correctly pointed out by appellant in its application and by its counsel Mr Oosthuizen in argument, the concept of "universal partnership" was never relied on by respondents and never raised in argument - not by counsel for the parties and not even *mero motu* by the Court. What the respondents relied on was their alleged "lesbian relationship".

The Court however, did not deal with the impact the lesbian relationship should have had on the decision of the Board, because the Court understood respondent's counsel to have conceded that the issue became irrelevant when Mr Taapopi on behalf of the Immigration Board averred that the fact that the respondents were lesbians, was regarded as a private matter and a neutral factor in regard to the application.

(b) It seems to me that if the respondents wished to rely on a so-called "universal partnership", it was for them to raise it before the Board in the first place and at the latest in their review application. If they raised it, they would have had to prove its existence and its relevance to the application for a permanent residence permit. In my respectful view, it was a misdirection for the Judge to raise it *mero motu* for the first time in his judgment.

Furthermore even if such a partnership was proved and relied upon by respondents the failure to regard it as a factor relevant to the application and to give it any weight in favour of respondent's application, would have been a matter falling within the discretion of the appellant Board.

(c) The Court's criticism that Taapopi made "a wrong statement of the law" when he said in his affidavit that "applicants' long term relationship was not one recognised in a Court of Law and was therefore not able to assist the respondents", was not wrong in the sense that the Courts in Namibia had never in the past recognised a lesbian relationship as a factor in favour of a lesbian alien applying for permanent residence in Namibia *inter alia* on the ground of her lesbian relationship with a Namibian citizen. Taapopi obviously also had in mind that the Immigration Control Act under which his Board exercised its jurisdiction gave a special status and exemption to a spouse of a Namibian citizen recognised by virtue of a marriage according to Namibian law - but did not recognise a "partner" in a lesbian relationship as a "spouse" for the purpose of that law. And in that regard, no Court in Namibia had up to now declared any provision of the Immigration Act unconstitutional.

The Court's attitude that the lesbian relationship which was placed before the Court became irrelevant because counsel for applicants allegedly conceded that, is difficult to reconcile with the attitude that a universal partnership not even mentioned by any of the parties, is relevant.

(d) I find it difficult to see the relevance of Art. 10, 16(1) and 21(1)(e) of the Namibian Constitution, dealing respectively with equality before the law, the right to acquire property in any part of Namibia and the right to freedom of association, applied to the argument based on a "universal partnership".

Art. 10 is certainly relevant to any argument as to whether or not a lesbian relationship should be treated on an equal basis with marriages sanctioned by statute law, but the Court was not dealing with that problem. As far as Art. 16 and 21(1)(e) are concerned, these rights do not assist in deciding whether or not either a "lesbian relationship" or "a universal partnership" should be recognised by the Immigration Selection Board as a relevant factor in considering an application for permanent residence.

(e) The Court concluded:

"Not only is this relationship recognized but respondents should have taken this into account when considering the application for permanent residence and this respondent admits it did not do."

The Board did not admit that it did not consider a "universal partnership". It also did not admit that it did not consider the alleged lesbian relationship. What it admitted was that it regarded the "lesbian relationship" as a private matter and regarded it as "neutral".

For the above reasons, the Court has in my respectful view, misdirected itself when it held that the Immigration Selection Board "should have taken it into account when considering first applicant's application for permanent residence."

(iv) The Court in its judgment refers to the letter of commendation by Mr Wakolele, the then Permanent Secretary of the Ministry of Information and Broadcasting wherein Wakolele said that: "...Namibia has a serious shortfall of trained researchers and writers..." The Court then comments that: "This is a statement of fact from someone who can speak with authority on the subject of research. Respondent's reply constitutes generalities and is obvious hearsay. An affidavit from the University may have been of assistance to respondent and respondent does not say why there is no affidavit. In any event the tenor of both paragraphs 10.1 and 10.2 is in respect of student researchers who will qualify in future whereas section 26(3)(e) specifically refers to people already engaged in the alleged activity."

The following points must be made:

(a) The Court thus required the Board to produce an affidavit from the University of Namibia to substantiate its viewpoints contained in an affidavit before Court, but accepted a mere letter by the Permanent Secretary of the Ministry of Information as "a statement of fact". Why? What Mr Simenda said in this regard in his opposing affidavit is the following:

"10.1 The Board did in fact take into account that the Applicant's qualifications, skills and experience are no longer in short supply in this country. The University of Namibia has put out graduates in Applicant's field of expertise and we have to find employment for them. Even more the said University and other institutions of higher learning continued to produce qualified people to perform the work that the Applicant is involved in. Moreover, numerous volunteers are coming into Namibia as in-service trainers and research officers at different levels. They are here on temporary permits. There is thus, at this point in time, no demand to attract immigrants with the Applicant's qualifications, skills or experience.

10.2 Even if it can be said that there is at present a shortage of persons with the qualifications, skills and experience of the Applicant the Board has also to take into the account that more and more Namibian citizens will obtain similar qualifications, expertise, skills and experience in the next few years and that these citizens will have to be accommodated in the limited labour market of the Republic of Namibia..."

"12. I deny the allegations contained herein and repeat that the Applicant's application was rejected because the Board was of the considered opinion that Namibian citizens must be given preference in the employment market and that there was no demand to attract immigrants with the qualifications, skills and experience of the Applicant. The Board was furthermore of the opinion that any short-term demand for such services could sufficiently be met by issuing work permits to persons duly qualified to do the work. For this very reason the Board recommended that the Applicant's work permit be extended for a further period of 12 months."

Whether the Court meant that the Board had to obtain an affidavit from the University in order to properly evaluate the respondents' application or whether it meant that it had to supplement its affidavit of opposition with such an affidavit in the review proceedings, is not entirely clear.

There was however no justification for the Court on review to assume that Wakolele spoke with authority and that his letter of recommendation was a "statement of fact" on the issue.

If the Board's statement is hearsay, on what basis can the statement of Mr Wakolele be regarded as fact?

As far as the Mbumba letter of commendation is concerned there is nothing in that letter controverting the contents of par. 10 and 12 of the affidavit of Simenda. He did not say as Mr Wakolele did, that: "Namibia has a serious shortfall of trainer researchers and writers" and he did not say that there is "not a sufficient number of persons already engaged in Namibia to meet the requirements of Namibians". Furthermore, none of Messrs Wakolele and Mbumba controverted the second leg or alternative leg of the Board's case, i.e. the factor set out in par. 10.2 of the said affidavit namely that "the Board has also to take into account that more and more Namibian citizens will obtain similar qualifications, expertise and skills in the next few years and that these citizens will have to be accommodated in the limited labour market of the Republic of Namibia.

The Court itself in its above-quoted *dicta* did not controvert anything said in the aforesaid par. 10.2 but relied on its assumption that what was said in the said paragraph was irrelevant, because section 26(3)(e) dealt with the present and did not allow the Board to go outside its parameters.

The Court's statement that the tenor of both par. 10.1 and 10.2 is in respect of student researchers who will qualify in future is also wrong. Par. 10.1 deals with graduates <u>already</u> put out and the continuing process. In addition it deals with volunteers "<u>coming</u>" into the Country. It then alleges that: "There is thus, at <u>this point in time</u>, no demand to attract <u>immigrants</u> with the applicant's qualifications, skills and experience".

(My emphasis added.)

The Board, by the very nature of its duties and responsibilities, acquire in the course of time certain knowledge, e.g. regarding the number of volunteers coming into Namibia through organisations rendering development aid to Namibia, and requiring temporary work permits for that purpose. It is also a notorious fact that there is a University of Namibia and various Technicons turning out people who acquire degrees and certificates. It is also not inconceivable that individual members of the Board have acquired certain knowledge through their own training and/or experience. Furthermore, the Board is not a Court. The Board may certainly make use of hearsay, even hearsay in the form of a letter or statement by Mr Wakolele or Mr Mbumba. There is no doubt that the Board also had to consider the information and recommendations contained in such letters. It could not arbitrarily ignore it or reject it.

Administrative authorities are entitled to rely upon their own expertise and local knowledge in reaching decisions[485].

It must also be obvious that such bodies can take notice of facts which are notorious. So e.g. the Board and a considerable percentage of the public, will know that Namibia has a university which has for years, prior to independence as well as thereafter, turned out graduates with BA degrees. Similarly it is general knowledge that there have been teachers training colleges before Namibian independence as well as thereafter, turning out qualified teachers; and technical colleges, turning out academically qualified persons in many fields. And as far as the allegations of Simenda in par. 10.2 of his affidavit is concerned, the assumption made about the "next few years" is certainly a reasonable assumption based on well-known and even notorious facts.

Furthermore administrative tribunals can rely on hearsay, to a much greater extent than Courts of law. But, in a case where such knowledge or hearsay could not reasonably be expected to be known to an applicant, the dictates of administrative justice may make it necessary to apprize the applicant for a work and/or residence permit of such knowledge or information to enable such applicant to controvert it[486].

On the other hand it is trite law that administrative bodies, irrespective of whether their powers are "*quasi-judicial*" or "purely administrative", need not notify an applicant beforehand of every possible reason for coming to a particular conclusion[487].

In regard to the letter of Mr Mbumba, the Minister of Finance, in support of the application for permanent residence, the Court held that the Board "did not apply its collective mind to this information furnished by the Minister of Finance".

There was no allegation in the respondent's founding affidavit nor in the replying affidavit in the review application that the Board "had not applied

---

[485] *Loxton v Kenhardt Liquor Licensing Board*, 1942 (AD) 275 at 291 *Clairwood Motor Transport Co. Ltd V Pillai & Ors*, 1958 (1) SA 245 NPD at 253G - 254A

[486] *Foulds v Minister of Home Affairs & Ors*, 1996(4) SA 137 WLD at 147 B - 149 F.

[487] *Minister of the Interior & An. v Sundaree Investments*, 1960 (3) SA 348 at 3.

its collective mind" to the supporting letter by Minister Mbumba. It may very well be that the Board did not apply its mind to the supporting letters of Messrs Wakolele and Mbumba. But the applicants did not make such an allegation and did not prove such an allegation. It may be that the Board merely did not agree with Messrs Wakolele and Mbumba and did not regard them as experts.

The onus to prove such allegations if made, is clearly on the applicant in review proceedings[488].

(v) The Court was clearly impressed by the assistance the applicant gave to "comrades from SWAPO" in the pre-independence period and as a member of the anti-apartheid movement. The Court further stated:

"Despite a life-long dedication to the democratic cause of Namibia, its trials and tribulations, its struggles and its successes, the respondent repeatedly refused to grant first respondent permanent residence and refused to provide her with reasons for their decision."

It seems that the Court expected the Board to give the applicant more favourable or preferential treatment on account of the aforesaid patriotic credentials.

If the Board did so, it may have been accused by others of breaching the fundamental right to non-discrimination and equality before the law provided for in Art. 10 of the Namibian Constitution, so strongly relied on by applicant and her legal representatives in other respects – such as e.g. the fact of applicants' lesbian relationship.

But even if the aforesaid patriotic past was a relevant consideration for the Board, it would have been in the Boards discretion how to evaluate it and what weight to be given to it.

The question may also be asked whether it was a proper consideration for the Board in view of Art. 4(6) of the Namibian Constitution, section 6 of Namibian Citizenship Act 14 of 1990 and 35 of the Immigration Control Act.

Sub-Art. 6 of Art. 4 of the Constitution provides that:

> "Nothing contained herein shall preclude Parliament from authorizing by law the conferment of Namibian citizenship upon any fit and proper person by virtue of any special skill or experience or commitment to or services rendered to the Namibian Nation either before or at any time after the date of independence."

Section 6(1) of Act No. 14 of 1990 provides: "When, in the opinion of the President, any person who is not a Namibian citizen has rendered any distinguished service to Namibia, the President may grant such person honorary citizenship of Namibia..." Section 35 of the Immigration Control Act, empowers the Minister to exempt any person or category of persons from the provisions of this part of the Act.

---

488 Rose-Innes. *Judicial Review of Administrative Tribunals in South Africa. p.*30; Herbstein & Van Winsen. *The Civil Practice of the Supreme Court of South Africa.* 4th ed., p.944; *Rajah & Rajah (Pty) Ltd v Ventersdorp Municipality,*1961(4) SA 402 (AD), 407 D - 408 A. *Barnes v Port Elizabeth Liquor Licensing Board,* 1948 (1) SA 149 AD; *Jockey Club of SA & Ors v Feldman,* 1942 (AD) 340.

The respondent Frank may have, but has not, applied to the President for honorary citizenship and may still do so. Respondent may apply to the Minister for exemption but has not done so and may still do so.

The applicants have also failed to join the Minister as a party to the proceedings.

Although Art. 4(6) of the Namibian Constitution, read with section 6 of the Citizenship Act and section 35 of the Immigration Control Act, provide for some relief or remedy to the respondents, the fact that these courses are open to them, militate to some extent against an argument that the respondent Board had a duty to consider such a factor in favour of the applicant Frank.

(vi) The Court did not argue that the Board had failed to apply the *audi alteram partem* rule in regard to adverse information or own knowledge or policy considerations of which the applicants may not have been aware. If it did, it would have been on solid ground.

Unfortunately it held:

"The decision to refuse first applicant permanent residence was for reasons set out above motivated by several factors which should not have been taken into account while some relevant factors were not taken into account at all.

For all these reasons the decision of the 29th July refusing first applicant permanent residence is reviewed and set aside."

I have shown above that the Court had erred in most of its findings regarding what had to be taken into account and what had not to be taken into account. The decision of the Board could therefore not be set aside on those grounds.

The Court also refused to refer the matter back to the Board for reconsideration because the Court had held that section 26(3) of the Immigration Control Act prevented the consideration by the Board of any factors other than those specified in paragraphs (a) - (e) of subsection 3 of section 26 and in regard to those paragraphs there was no evidence or information on which the Board could rely for refusing the permanent residence permit.

The first reason, as I have shown, was based on the wrong interpretation by the Court of section 26(3). The second reason was based on the assumption that the Board had no facts, information or knowledge which could justify refusal because Mr Simenda, chairperson of the Board, had stated in his replying affidavit. "There was also no specific information before the Board that adversely affected the applicant's application." (My emphasis added.) This was a wrong inference drawn from the quoted paragraph.

The above-quoted sentence from par. 9 of Mr Simenda's statement appears in a paragraph in reply to paragraph 13 of respondent Frank's founding affidavit wherein she had stated:

"The Board failed to respond in any way to my requests conveyed in the letter from my legal practitioners dated 3 June 1997 (Annexure EF6) ..."

The letter Annexure EF6 stated *inter alia*:

> **"Our client is in particular prepared to appear personally before the Immigration Control Board to respond to any specific queries that members of the Board may have regarding her application. Our client would in any event wish to deal with any information that is in your possession that reflects adversely on her application, as well as supplement her application with any further information that may be required by the Immigration Selection Board..."**
> **(My emphasis added.)**

Mr Simenda's affidavit in the immediately following par. 10 and 12 sets out the alleged facts on which the Board relied and the reasons for its decision.

Paragraphs 10 and 12 can be reconciled with the sentence above-quoted relied on by the Court, by assuming that the Board made use of its own expertise and knowledge of relevant facts and followed policy principles and guidelines which it believed it was entitled to do in the proper exercise of its duties and responsibilities. This, the Board was entitled to do as shown above.

What the Board was not entitled to do was to fail to apply the principles of administrative justice, in particular, the *audi alteram partem* rule.

The principles of administrative justice require that in circumstances such as the present, the Board should have disclosed such facts, principles and policies to the applicants for the resident permit and allowed an opportunity, to respond thereto by letter or personal appearance before the Board or both. This, the Board had failed to do.

It must be kept in mind that Namibia only became a sovereign independent country in March 1990 and the Immigration Control Act was enacted only in 1993. The result is that the whole of Namibia is undergoing a learning process. How the Namibian Constitution and the multiplicity of old and new laws must be interpreted and applied, remains a mystery to many and at best a difficult problem, not only to most people in Government and officials in the Administration, but even to legal representatives and presiding judicial officers in Courts of law.

This is even borne out by the difference between the approach of the Board, the Court *a quo* and the Supreme Court.

The Court *a quo* misdirected itself in regard to the interpretation and application of the law and applicable procedure. That Court should have set aside the decision of the Board, but for the reason that the Board had failed to apply the *audi alteram partem* rule properly. In the premises, the application should have been remitted to the Board for a rehearing, where the applicants are given the opportunity to respond to the contents of the aforesaid paragraphs 10 and 12 of the Board's replying affidavit.

This was not a case where exceptional circumstances existed, e.g. where there were long periods of delay, where applicant would suffer grave prejudice or where it would otherwise be grossly unfair[489].

By not referring the matter back to the Board for compliance with the *audi alteram partem* rule, the Court has prevented the Board from considering and imposing, if deemed appropriate, conditions to the residence permit, should it decide to grant the permit. In that sense it has usurped the function of the Board created by Parliament for that purpose.

The aforesaid power, is part of the Board's wide powers in considering applications for permits. It provides that the Board may make authorisation for a permit "subject to any condition the Board may deem appropriate".

The Court *a quo* did not comment on the merits of the arguments in regard to the applicant's lesbian relationship because it assumed that the legal representative of the applicants had abandoned the issue.

Apart from this issue with which I will deal in greater detail in due course, it follows from my analysis of the judgment of the Court *a quo*, that there is at least "reasonable prospects" of success on appeal to this Court.

SECTION C: MAIN POINTS OF DISAGREEMENT WITH THE JUDGMENT OF MY BROTHER STRYDOM, C.J.:

It is in this latter regard that my view begins to differ substantially from that of my brother Strydom, C.J.

In the latter judgment it is stated:

> **"Although there may be substance in Mr Oosthuizen's submission that the Court *a quo* should have referred the matter back to the appellant Board for reconsideration, also because one of the factors on which the Court based the exercise of its discretion was its interpretation of section 26 of the Act, I am not convinced that this is sufficient to tip the scales in favour of the appellant and that this Court should therefore grant the appellant condonation. As was pointed out by the Court *a quo* there was no legal impediment against the granting of the permit as the appellant was satisfied that the first appellant has complied with the provisions of section 26(3)(a) - (f) and that strong support from notable persons was expressed in favour of the granting of the permit."**

I must make the following comment:

(i) Although not altogether clear, it seems that my brother found that there were reasonable prospects of success on appeal in that there was "some substance in Mr Oosthuizen's submission that the Court *a quo* should have referred the matter back to the appellant Board for reconsideration". However, if it was

[489] *W.C. Greyling & Erasmus (Pty) Ltd v Johannesburg Local Road Transport Board & Ors,* 1982 (4) SA 427 (AD) 449 F - H; *Daconlaan Beleggings (Edms) Bpk v Johannesburg Stock Exchange (Edms) Bpk & Others,* 1983 (3) SA 344 (WLD) at 369 E - H; *Local Road Transportation Board & An v Durban City Council & An,* 1965(1) SA 586 (AD) 598 D - 599.

meant that there are no reasonable prospects of success on appeal, then I differ profoundly.

(ii) The remark that "I am not convinced that this is sufficient to tip the scales in favour of the appellant...", I understand to refer to the tipping of scales against the gross-negligence of the appellant Board in not filing the record for the appeal within the three months allocated by the rules but only eight months after the judgment appealed against, causing the appeal to be heard a year later. In addition the position was aggravated by a wrong statement in the affidavit by the Board's attorney wherein the latter affirmed under oath that a work permit had been granted to applicant Frank to mitigate some of her inconvenience due to the delay caused by the said attorney's negligence.

(iii) The statement "as was pointed out by the Court *a quo* there was no legal impediment against the granting of the permit as the appellant was satisfied that the first respondent has complied with the provisions of section 26(3)(a) - (f) and that strong support from notable persons was expressed in favour of the granting of the permit". (My emphasis added.)

Neither Mr Simenda on behalf of the appellant, nor his counsel in argument before us has ever admitted that section 26(3)(a) - (f) had been complied with. Nor did they admit that there was therefore "no legal impediment against the granting of the permit".

Even the Court *a quo* did not say or suggest that the Board "was satisfied that the first respondent has complied with the provisions of section 26(3)(a) - (f).

The Court *a quo* came to the conclusion that there was no "impediment", but as I have tried to show, that conclusion was itself based on a wrong interpretation of the section and wrong reasons.

As far as the "strong support from notable persons" is concerned, the undated letter of recommendation of Minister Mbumba, does not allege that there are not "a sufficient number of persons already engaged in Namibia to meet the requirements of the inhabitants of Namibia...". Consequently that letter does not controvert the allegations made by Mr Simenda in paragraphs 10.1, 10.2 and 12 of his affidavit on behalf of the Board.

(iv) It seems to me that as far as the Chief Justice is concerned, even if there were reasonable prospects of success on appeal, such factor is overshadowed by the grossness of the negligence of appellant's attorney in not having prepared and submitted the appeal record within the three months provided for such action in the Rules of the Supreme Court. Instead appellant attorney only submitted the appeal record on 9th March 2000 whereas the deadline for its submission was 24th September 1999. This according to my brother's judgment, meant that the appeal was heard one year later than it could have been heard.

I agree that the attorney for appellant, Mr Asino, was grossly negligent, but do not agree that this negligence justifies penalising the appellant Board to the extent that condonation for the late filing of the record is refused, notwithstanding reasonable prospects of success on appeal and the importance of the case, particularly the importance to all the parties of an authoritative decision on the issues raised.

I wish to stress the following points:

(a) The appellant Board did take the necessary steps to note an appeal and to attempt to get an authoritative decision by negotiating with respondents on agreeing to have the appeal decided by this Court, without first appealing to the full Bench of the High Court.

The appeal was duly noted on 22 July 1999.

(b) No case can be made out of negligence on the part of the appellant Board, but only on the part of the government attorney. Although the negligence of a legal representative can be imputed to his principal, this should only be done in exceptional cases where some blame can fairly be attributed to the principal e.g. where such principal did not take reasonable steps to keep abreast of developments regarding the progress of the appeal.

The Courts are reluctant to penalise a litigant for the conduct of a legal practitioner[490].

(c) I do not agree with respect to the statement that the default was "completely unexplained" or "was not explained at all".

Mr Taapopi, the chairperson of the Board, stated in his supporting affidavit:

"After consultations with the appellant's legal practitioners and the Honourable Attorney-General, I instructed that the judgment of the High Court be appealed against. ...

I am informed that a notice of appeal, a copy of which is annexed hereto and marked Annexure 'C' was duly filed herein on 22 July 1999. ...

Having been informed that the said notice of appeal had been filed, I was waiting to be informed of the date on which the appeal would be argued. I did not expect the appeal to be argued in the near future, since I was under the impression that the Court rolls are quite full. ...

However, I have now been informed that the appellant's legal practitioner, Mr Asino, did not file the record of appeal within the period required by the rules of this Honourable Court and that in terms of the said rules, the appeal is deemed to have lapsed. I refer in this regard to Mr Asino's affidavit annexed hereto marked 'B'. Since I am not familiar with the procedures required to prosecute an appeal, I was previously unaware that my legal practitioner had not complied with them....

I humbly request the Honourable Court to condone the late filing of the record of appeal. I submit that the subject matter of this appeal involves complicated constitutional issues and that it is of the utmost importance for the appellant and also in the interest of justice that an authoritative judgment on those issues be obtained which will also serve as a guideline to the appellant in future...."

It is clear from the above that the appellant at all relevant times intended to appeal and instructed the Government-Attorney to take the necessary steps. The Board certainly had reason to assume that the Government-Attorney would have the necessary expertise to take the necessary procedural steps.

[490] *Regal v African Superslate (Pty) Ltd,* 1962(3) SA 18 (AD) at 23C - D.

There can therefore be no doubt that the appellant at no stage wished the appeal to lapse. Even the attorney, Mr Asino, did provide an explanation, even though the explanation put his competence and dedication in a very bad light. He stated in his affidavit:

> **"Despite the appellant's desire to shorten the appeal process, I regrettably neglected to file the record within the three-months time period required by the Rules of this Honourable Court...**
>
> **I hereby humbly apologize to the Honourable Court for failure to file the record within the stipulated period and can offer no excuse for my neglect. I know that is my responsibility to assure that all procedures are followed and all the documents are filed timeously and I have failed to do so. I can only add that my dereliction was unintentional.**
>
> **I wish to inform the Court that I had informed the appellant that a notice of appeal had been filed and that I had given him no reason to believe that the requisite appeal procedures were not being followed. The responsibility for the failure to file the record timeously lies with me alone. For this reason, and for the reasons set forth in the founding affidavit, I humbly pray that this Court do not penalize appellant for my failure not to comply with the rules, but instead in the interest of justice to permit the appeal to proceed."**

What more could this attorney say. He says that he was negligent and takes the blame without trying to make all sorts of excuses.

I have previously in this judgment explained the adjustments required after Namibian independence in 1990. The Courts have to live with these new realities. We all have to share in the new learning process and have to be patient and understanding in order to ensure that justice is done.

In the circumstances it is wrong, in my respectful view, to say that there is no explanation at all for the default and to use that together with the admitted gross negligence of an attorney, against a litigant, as justification for refusing to decide important issues of public interest on the merits.

(v) Much has been made of time lapse of more than three (3) years between the refusal of the permanent residence permit on 29th July 1997 and the hearing of the Board's application for condonation and appeal at the October 2000 session of this Court and the prejudice to the respondent because of that. It is said that "to the extension of this period the legal representative of the appellant contributed significantly". It is also stated that because of the negligence of the said representative "this appeal which could have been heard during the October 1999 session, was only heard a year later". I disagree with this apportionment of blame and must point out:

(a) It is common cause that the appellant had until 24 September 1999 to submit the appeal record.

If the appellant did so on or shortly before 24th September 1999, it would have been too late to place the matter on the roll of the Supreme Court for the session of the Court from 1 October - 5 October 1999. The earliest date for the hearing of the application for condonation was therefore during the April 2000 session.

If the parties cooperated, the application for condonation may still have been heard during the April 1999 session, particularly if the Court's indulgence was sought by the parties on the basis that the matter was urgent.

But even if the only practical date for a hearing was during the October 2000 session, the appellant's attorney could only be held responsible for a 6 months delay and not a year.

(b) During the period between judgment of the Court *a quo* on 24 June 1999 and 24 September 1999, the parties agreed, on the initiative of the appellant, to proceed directly to the Supreme Court.

(c) The attorney for the respondents, Mr Light, did not at any stage alert appellant's attorney that he had not submitted the record as required by the Rules except on 10th February 2000, approximately seven months after the judgment and five months after the deadline for the submission of the record, when Light sent a facsimile to appellant's legal practitioners, claiming the issue of the permanent residence permit in accordance with the order of the High Court of 24th June 1999.

Negotiations then followed wherein appellant's attorney attempted to obtain the cooperation of respondents and their attorneys not to oppose an application for condonation.

The attorneys for appellant and respondents are not completely *ad idem* in regard to the details of the negotiation but suffice to say, there were negotiations and these negotiations failed. When it became evident to appellant's attorney that respondents' consent to an unopposed application for condonation could not be obtained, he filed the record on 9th March 2000 and the application for condonation and the reinstatement of the appeal on 14th March 2000.

(d) The decision of the appellant Board was given already on 29th July 1997. But the first respondent Frank, only filed a review application in the High Court for the review of that decision on 13th February 1998, more than six (6) months after the date of the Board's decision.

No explanation has been offered for this delay on the side of the respondent.

(e) Then on 3rd April 1998, a default judgment was wrongly granted on the application of first respondent.

Application then had to be made for the setting aside of the default judgment. Application for the setting aside was launched on 30th April 1998. The application for setting aside was not opposed by respondent. The default judgment was then set aside on 3 July 1998.

(f) Respondents only completed their review application by applying on 7 May 1999 for the joinder of Elizabeth Khaxas as 2nd applicant – approximately one (1) year and three (3) months after launching the review proceedings.

(g) The more than "three (3) years of uncertainty" is mainly due to the fact that respondent took the decision of appellant Board on review and this led to a decision in their favour in the High Court and an appeal and application for condonation to the Supreme Court.

The appellant Board has no control over the fact that the Supreme Court has only three sessions a year.

Consequently in my respectful view, only (six) 6 months of the whole period can be attributed to the negligence of the appellant's attorney.

(vi) I agree with the critical remarks by the Honourable Chief Justice regarding Mr Taapopi's statement in his affidavit dated 14 March 2000 in support of the application for condonation that "the Immigration Selection Board has renewed her (first respondent's) employment permit for a period of one (1) year so that she may earn a living while this Honourable Court decides the matter". This statement was denied by first respondent in her replying affidavit. As a consequence, this Court asked appellant's counsel for an explanation during oral argument and when it was confirmed that the permit was never issued, this Court requested an explanation on affidavit. In response another affidavit was filed by Mr Taapopi where the failure to issue the permit was explained and justified. Part of the explanation was that the Board, unfortunately "did not follow my undertaking in my founding affidavit in the application for condonation". Mr Taapopi is also Chairperson of the appellant board.

Mr Taapopi missed the point altogether. In his supporting affidavit he did not "undertake" to have the permit issued, but represented to the Court that it had been issued.

He had thus misrepresented the position to this Court in his aforesaid supporting affidavit and for this misrepresentation there is no explanation.

If this misrepresentation was deliberate, it would have amounted to contempt of court and/or perjury. Unfortunately, this Court only viewed the complete set of affidavits relating to this issue after the oral hearing and did not give the parties and Mr Oosthuizen on behalf of the appellant Board the opportunity to deal with the Court's concern relating to this apparent misrepresentation.

As there was no prejudice to the respondents, the Court did not think it necessary to reconvene the Court to pursue the matter.

It may be that the aforesaid representation was negligently made in the belief at the time that it will be honoured. I cannot believe that Mr Taapopi could think that this misrepresentation will not be discovered in view of the known participation of the first respondent and her legal representatives in the proceedings. Nothing could therefore be achieved by a deliberate misrepresentation.

In the circumstances I do not think it justified to regard the said misrepresentation as deliberate or intentional but nevertheless it is justified to regard it as a serious blemish on the manner in which the chairman of the Board, its members and the Government-Attorney on their behalf, conduct their official business.

I also take into consideration that the respondents were not prejudiced by this particular misrepresentation.

It is necessary to point out in this regard that the first respondent also made a serious misrepresentation to the Board and also to the Court *a quo*, by failing to disclose that she was at the time of her application to the Board and her review application to the Court, no longer employed as a Deputy Director of CASS. This clearly misled the review Judge, who continuously relied on first respondent's position with CASS.

In the circumstances I do not regard this incident as a reason or even as one of the reasons for refusing to return the respondent's application to the appellant Board for reconsideration with the specific instruction to apply the *audi alteram partem* rule in regard to the aforesaid paragraphs 10.1, 10.2 and 12 of the replying affidavit of Mr Simenda, a member of the appellant Board.

(vii) I have already pointed out *supra* that by not referring the matter back to the Board, the Court will in effect nullify the provision that even where the Board grants an application, it can impose any condition "the Board may deem appropriate".

(viii) The Chief Justice accepts in his judgment that the Board would have been entitled to refuse the application on the grounds stated in the above-stated paragraph 10.2 of Mr Simenda's affidavit provided it has complied with the *audi alteram partem* rule. By allowing the order of the Court *a quo* to stand however, this Court will prevent the Board from giving effect to that consideration after applying the *audi alteram partem* rule. If this Court now substitutes its opinion for that of the Board, it would do so regardless of whether the points made by the Board in paragraph 10.1, 10.2 and 12 are in fact well-founded or not. Furthermore, the Court will take the summary course without being in possession of the information which the Board may have available and without being in a position to consider whether or not conditions should be attached to the granting of the permit.

(ix) It is true that the respondents have lived in a state of uncertainty for three (3) years or more, but this is inherent in a situation where the one party is a citizen of another country and wishes to acquire permanent residence status, *inter alia* because she wants to legitimise and pursue a relationship, in this case a lesbian relationship, which up to the present has not been legitimised as such by the laws of Namibia and consequently not recognised by the authorities.

An issue such as the "lesbian relationship" relied on by respondents, is a very controversial issue in Namibia as in all or most of Africa and whether it should be recognised and if so to what extent, is a grave and complicated humanitarian, cultural, moral and most important, constitutional issue which must of necessity take time to resolve.

It would seem in all fairness that <u>most</u> of respondents' "uncertainty" and agony is caused by the non-recognition of their lesbian relationship.

In this respect it is necessary to keep in mind that none of the respondents are refugees fleeing from persecution or oppression. <u>First respondent</u> is a citizen of Germany, which country is generally regarded as democratic and civilized and probably tolerant to lesbians. That remains her home country available as such until she changes her citizenship by her own choice. <u>Second appellant</u> is

> a Namibian citizen, born and bred in Namibia where her child was born from a heterogeneous relationship. This home remains available to her and her child until she changes her citizenship by her own choice.
>
> The Court *a quo* did not deal with the issue of the "lesbian relationship" and its impact on the application for permanent residence. The Chief Justice does not deal with this issue either. How then will the uncertainty and the anguish of the respondents be removed by following the course suggested?

Although this Court, as well as the High Court, undoubtedly has wide powers to set aside the decisions of administrative tribunals and even to substitute its own decision on the merits for that of such a tribunal in appropriate circumstances, the present case is not one where the substitution of our decision for that of the Board is justified. In my respectful view, that would amount to usurping the function of the Board, entrusted to it by the Legislature of a sovereign country.

For the reasons set out above, I am of the view that there is considerable merit in the appellant's appeal. That being so, the negligence of the legal representative of the appellants should not prevent the order of the Court *a quo* to be amended by returning the application of applicants/respondents to the Board for reconsideration, unless the issue of the lesbian relationship justifies a different order[491].

What remains therefore, is to deal with the issue of the respondents' lesbian relationship and its impact on the applicant's application for a permanent residence permit and the appropriate order to be made by this Court.

SECTION D: THE ISSUE OF RESPONDENTS' LESBIAN RELATIONSHIP AND ALLEGED BREACH OF THEIR FUNDAMENTAL RIGHTS

The Court *a quo* as indicated *supra* did not directly deal with the issue raised by respondents because it understood the respondents' counsel to have conceded that the issue of the lesbian relationship became irrelevant when Mr Taapopi on behalf of the Board stated that the "lesbian relationship" was regarded as neutral and played no role in its decision.

In argument before this Court, Ms Conradie, who appeared before us for respondents, submitted that the Court *a quo* misunderstood the attitude of Mr Light, who appeared for respondents in the Court *a quo*. Ms Conradie proceeded to argue that the issue of the "lesbian relationship" had to be considered and decided upon by this Court, unless the appellant's application for condonation is rejected on other grounds, making it unnecessary to consider and decide the issue of the lesbian relationship and particularly its impact on the application by first respondent for a permanent residence permit.

In the first respondent's first application to the Board for permanent residence in 1996 there was no mention of the lesbian relationship.

[491] *Civil Practice of the Supreme Court of South Africa* by Van Wyk *et al*, 4th ed. at 901.

In the second application of 25th March 1997, first respondent stated:

> **"Since 1990 I have lived together in Windhoek with my life partner, Elizabeth Khaxas, and her son Ricky Khaxab. We are living together as a family and I have taken on parental responsibilities for Ricky. Although Ms. Khaxas and I cannot officially marry we have committed ourselves to each other and wish to share the rest of our lives together in Namibia ..."**

A letter of support from Elizabeth Khaxas broadly affirming and supporting the application was attached.

When the application was refused, the following allegations were made in the application to the Court for the review of the Board's decision in regard to the respondents' lesbian relationship:

> **"17. I will be severely prejudiced should I be required to leave Namibia. I have made my life in Namibia. I reside here with my life partner and her son who are both Namibian citizens. My present residence in Namibia is uncertain, because I could be refused an employment permit at any time in the future. In that event, Elizabeth and her son would then have to try and live with me in another country. This would mean that I would have to leave my home and Elizabeth and Ricky would have to leave the country of their birth and nationality. I do not know where we would go or which country would admit us as a family. I respectfully submit that the Immigration Selection Board failed to take this relevant factor into account.**
>
> **18. If I was involved in a heterosexual relationship with a Namibian citizen we would have been able to marry and I would have been able to reside in Namibia and apply for Namibian citizenship in terms of Art. 4(3)(aa) of the Constitution. This is not possible because of our sexual orientation. I therefore respectfully submit that the Immigration Selection Board has failed to take this relevant factor into account, or to give it sufficient weight. I respectfully submit that its decision for these reasons has violated my rights to equality and freedom from discrimination guaranteed in Art. 10, privacy guaranteed in Art. 13(1) and the protection of the family guaranteed in Art. 14 of the Constitution."**

It must be noted that neither first respondent in her 1977 application to the Board, nor 2nd respondent in her letter of support, had alleged that they rely on any fundamental right in support of first respondent's application.

The Board consequently was not alerted to any specific fundamental rights on which first respondent and Khaxas relied and no issue was made at the time of fundamental human rights. It was also not then or even in the review application claimed that the applicant Frank was the spouse of Khaxas in terms of section 26(3)(g) and therefore entitled to be granted a permanent residence permit.

Had the first respondent then claimed that they relied on the fundamental right to equality, non-discrimination, family, dignity and privacy, the Board may have given these matters more attention and at least taken a stand on these issues.

I must emphasise at the outset that the argument before us on behalf of respondents was not that the Board had infringed their fundamental rights as individuals in that it had e.g. failed to deal with them on a basis equal to other unmarried heterosexual individuals. The argument was that the Board had failed to accord their lesbian relationship equal status and privilege with that accorded men and women who are legally married and by this failure, the Board had violated their fundamental right to equality and non-discrimination and their fundamental rights to live as a family and to privacy and freedom of movement.

Before I deal with the specific submissions on behalf of respondents in regard to the alleged infringement of their fundamental rights and freedoms, it is apposite to first deal with the general approach of the Court in regard to claims that a litigant's fundamental human rights have been infringed.

1. THE NECESSARY PARTIES

A litigant approaching the Court claiming a remedy for an alleged infringement of a fundamental right or freedom, must ensure that the necessary parties are before Court.

The joinder of all the necessary parties is a principle of procedure in the Courts of law which can rightly be described as trite law[492].

But this principle has added significance where, as in the instant case an applicant relies on Art. 5 of the Namibian Constitution, read with Art. 25(1)(a) and (b) and where the remedy or part thereof may be that the Court would order Parliament, or any subordinate legislative authority or the Executive and agencies of Government, to remedy the particular defect within a specified period.

So e.g. a Court will decline to make an order against the Minister of Home Affairs, if such Minister is not a party to the proceedings. Similarly, the Court should not declare a law of parliament unconstitutional and/or to be amended, unless at least the State or the Government is represented in Court, at least by a Minister, whose Ministry is directly affected[493].

2. THE BURDEN OF PROOF WHEN A PERSON ALLEGES AN INFRINGEMENT OF A FUNDAMENTAL RIGHT OR FREEDOM

I proceed from the position that there is an important resemblance between the burden of proof in the case of fundamental rights compared with fundamental freedoms, but also an important difference.

The Namibian Constitution makes a distinction between the fundamental rights contained in Articles 6 - 20 and the freedoms (or rights to freedoms) enumerated in Art. 21(1).

---

492 *The Civil Practice of the Supreme Court of South Africa* by Van Winson *et al*, 4th ed, at 170, 176 *Collin v Toffie*, 1944 AD 45; *Fourie v Lombard*, 1966 (3) SA 155 (O).

493 Compare the cases of: *National Coalition for Gay & Lesbian Equality & Ors. v Minister of Home Affairs & Ors.*, 1999 (3) SA 173 (CPD). *National Coalition for Gay and Lesbian Equality v Minister of Justice & Others,* 1999(1) SA 6 (CC).

In regard to the aforesaid freedoms there is a general qualification contained in sub-article (2) of Art. 21 which provides that the freedoms must be exercised subject to the laws of Namibia, but places limitations on the laws to which the freedoms are subject.

The South African Constitution, both the interim Constitution of 1993 and the final Constitution of 1996 contained in the Constitution of the Republic of South Africa Act No. 108 of 1996, makes no distinction between fundamental rights and freedoms as is the position in Namibia. The general qualification clause in the South African Act applies to both fundamental rights and freedoms.

The resemblance in regard to fundamental rights and freedoms in terms of the Namibian Constitution is this:

> **In both cases, whether we are dealing with a fundamental right or freedom, the applicant will have the burden to allege and prove that a specific fundamental right or freedom has been infringed. This will necessitate that the applicant must also satisfy the Court in regard to the meaning, content and ambit of the particular right or freedom.**[494]
>
> **In regard to fundamental rights, the burden of proof remains throughout on the applicant to prove that a fundamental right has been infringed at least in regard to all those fundamental rights where no express qualification or exception is provided for in the wording of the fundamental rights such as in Articles 6 - 12, 14 and 18. Where an express qualification or exception is provided for as in Articles 13, 17(1), 20(3) and 20(4), the burden of proof may shift as in the case of the fundamental freedoms. But this question has not been argued and need not be decided in this case.**

The position in regard to the burden of proof in cases of alleged infringements of fundamental human rights is the same in Zimbabwe where the Chief Justice said:

> **"I consider that the burden of proof that a fundamental right of whatever nature has been breached is on him who asserts it."**[495]

In the case of the fundamental freedoms provided for in Art. 21(1) of the Namibian Constitution, the initial burden is on the person alleging an infringement to prove the infringement and as part thereof, satisfy the Court in regard to the meaning, content and ambit of the fundamental freedom.

This initial onus corresponds to the "initial onus" referred to by Chaskalson, P, in the decision of the South African Constitutional Court in *State v Makwanyane and Another* [496].

[494] *Namunjepo & Ors v Commanding Officer, Windhoek Prison & A*, 2000 (6) BCLR 671 (NmS) 671 at 677 J - 678 C and 678 I - J and the decisions referred to therein. *S v Namundjebo, NmHC, May 1998, unreported, p 47 - 49. S v Vries,* 1996 (2) SACR 638 (Nm) at 663d - 667i *Kauesa v Minister of Home Affairs & Ors,* 1996 (4) SA 965 (NmS) at 979J - 980C.

[495] *Catholic Commission for Justice and Peace v Attorney-General, Zimbabwe*, 1993(2) SACR432 (ZS) at 440 I. *S v Van den Berg,* 1995(4) BCLR 479 (Nm) at 497 B.

[496] *State v Makwanyane and Another,* 1995 (3) SA 391 (CC) at 410 B - 435 D - 436 A.

Once the initial burden is discharged, the burden then shifts to the party contending that the law, regulation, or act in question, providing the exception or qualification, falls within the reasonable restrictions on the freedom provided for in Sub-article (2) of Art. 21.

3. THE MEANING, CONTENT AND AMBIT OF A FUNDAMENTAL RIGHT OR FREEDOM

3.1 The significance of the wording

In my respectful view, the starting point in interpreting and applying a constitution, and establishing the meaning, content and ambit of a particular fundamental right, or freedom, must be sought in the words used and their plain meaning. This principle is endorsed by *Seervai* in his authoritative work "*Constitutional Law of India*" where he quotes with approval from the "*Central Provinces case* (1939) FCR 18 at 38:

> **"...for in the last analysis the decision must depend upon the words of the Constitution which the Court is interpreting and since no two constitutions are in identical terms, it is extremely unsafe to assume that a decision on one of them can be applied without qualification to another. This may be so even when the words or expressions are the same in both cases, for a word or phrase may take a colour from its content and bear different senses altogether."**[497]

But I am mindful of the dictum of this Court in the *Namunjepo*-decision where the learned Chief Justice Strydom said:

> **"A court interpreting a Constitution will give such words, especially the words expressing fundamental rights and freedoms, the widest possible meaning so as to protect the greatest number of rights..."**

The "widest possible meaning" however, means no more than what Kentridge, J.A. said in the case of *Attorney-General v Moagi*[498].

He declared: "... a Constitution such as the Constitution of Botswana, embodying fundamental rights, should as far as its language permits be given a broad construction...".

And as Friedman, J. comments in *Nyamkazi v President of Bophuthatswana*, "this is in my view the golden mean between the two approaches" meaning the approaches of the "positivist" and "libertarian" schools. (My emphasis added.)

I am also mindful of the many Namibian decisions where the basic approach in interpreting a constitution has been expressed in poetic and stirring language. So e.g. it was said in *Government of the Republic of Namibia v Cultura 2000*,[499]:

[497] Seervai. *Constitutional Law of India*, 3rd ed. at 104 *S v Van den Berg*, 1995 (4) BCLR 479 Nm at 496 B - D.

[498] *Attorney-General v Moagi*, 1982 (2) Botswana LR 124 at 184 - 5 *Attorney-General v Moagi* 1992 (4) SA 540 BGD at 566 J - 567 A.

[499] *Government of the Republic of Namibia v Cultura 2000* 1994 (1) SA 407 (NmSC) at 418 F - G.

> **"It must be broadly, liberally and purposively interpreted so as to avoid the 'austerity of tabulated legalism' and so as to enable it to continue to play a creative and dynamic role in the expression and the achievement of the ideals and aspirations of the nation, in the articulation of the values bonding its people and in disciplining its Government."**
> **(My emphasis added.)**

But as pointed out by Seervai, citing what was said by Gwyer, C.J.,

> **"... a broad and liberal spirit should inspire those whose duty it is to interpret the constitution, but I do not imply by this that they are free to stretch and pervert the language of the enactment in the interests of any legal or constitutional theory, or even for the purposes of supplying omissions or correcting supposed errors. A Federal Court may rightly reflect that a Constitution of Government is a living and organic thing, which of all instruments has the greatest claim to be construed** *ut res magis valeat quam pereat.*"
> **(My emphasis added.)**

This dictum was quoted by this Court, apparently with approval, in the decision of *Minister of Defence, Namibia v Mwandingi*[500].

In the aforesaid decision, this Court also relied *inter alia* on a dictum by Lord Wilberforce in *Minister of Home Affairs & An. v Fisher & An.*, wherein the learned Law Lord had said:

> **"A constitution is a legal instrument giving rise, amongst other things, to individual rights capable of enforcement in a Court of Law. Respect must be paid to the language which has been used and to the traditions and usages which have given meaning to that language. It is quite consistent with this, and with the recognition of the character and origin of the instrument, and to be guided by giving full recognition and effect to those fundamental rights and freedoms with a statement of which the constitution commences..."**
> **(My emphasis added.)**

Kentridge, A.J., who wrote the unanimous judgment of the South African Constitutional Court in the *State v Zuma*, quoted with approval the following passage from a judgment of Dickson, J., (later Chief Justice of Canada) in the decision *R v Big M. Drug Mart Ltd:*

> **"The meaning of a right of freedom guaranteed by the Charter was to be ascertained by an analysis of the purpose of such a guarantee; it was to be understood, in other words, in the light of the interests it was meant to protect. In my view this analysis is to be undertaken, and the purpose of the rights or freedom in question is to be sought by reference to the character and larger objects of the Charter itself, to the language chosen to articulate the specific right or freedom, to the historical origins of the concept enshrined, and where applicable, to the meaning and purpose of the other specific rights and freedoms with which it is associated within the text of**

[500] *Minister of Defence, Namibia v Mwandingi* 1992 (2) SA 355 (NmS) at 362 E.

the Charter. The interpretation should be ... a generous rather than legalistic one, aimed at fulfilling the purpose of a guarantee and the securing for individuals the full benefit of the Charter's protection."[501]

Kentridge, A.J., also pointed out in *S v Zuma & Ors* that "it cannot be too strongly stressed that the Constitution does not mean whatever we might wish it to mean..."[502]

In the same decision, Kentridge said:

> **"Both Lord Wilberforce and Dickson, J., later Chief Justice, of Canada, had emphasised that regard must be had to the legal history, traditions and usages of the country concerned, if the purposes of its constitution must be fully understood. This must be right."**[503]
> **(My emphasis added.)**

The dictum was again approved by the Constitutional Court in *State v Makwanyane and Another* although Chaskalson, P., in his judgment added:

> **"Without seeking in any way to qualify anything that was said in the *Zuma*'s case, I need say no more in this judgment than that s 11(2) of the Constitution must not be construed in isolation, but in its context, which includes the history and background to the adoption of the Constitution, other provision of the Constitution itself and, in particular, the provisions of chap. 3 of which it is part. It must also be construed in a way which secures for 'individuals the full measure' of its protection**[504]**.**

It was also pointed out in the latter decision that background material, such as the reports of technical committees which advised the Multi-party negotiating process, could provide a context for the interpretation of the Constitution[505].

In my respectful view, in Namibia, the 1982 Constitutional Principles validated by international agreement and resolutions of the Security Council will qualify as such background material as well as the deliberations of the technical committees and the elected Constitutional Assembly itself[506].

It follows from the above that when a Court interprets and applies a constitution and adheres to the principles and guidelines above-stated, a "purposive" interpretation also requires that a Court has regard to "the legal history, traditions and usages of the country concerned, if the purposes of its constitution must be fully understood".

To sum up: The guideline that a constitution must be interpreted "broadly, liberally and purposively", is no license for constitutional flights of fancy. It is anchored in the provisions of the Namibian Constitution, the language of its provisions, the reality of

---

501 *R v Zuma & Ors,* 1995 (2) SA 642 CC, at 651 F - G.

502 IBID, at 363 F - I.

503 *R v Zuma & Ors,* 1995 (2) SA 642 CC, at 651 F - G.

504 *State v Makwanyane,* 1995 (3) SA 391 at 403G - 404A.

505 IBID, 404F - 407E. *Constitutional Law of South Africa*, Chaskelson *et al*, 11 - 18 and 11 - 17.

506 *State v Heita & An,* 1992 NR 403 HC, *at 405H - 406G.*

its legal history, and the traditions, usages norms, values and ideals of the Namibian people. The Namibian reality is that these traditions, usages, norms, values and ideals are not always "liberal" and may be "conservative" or a mixture of the two. But whether or not they are "liberal", "conservative" or a "mixture of the two", does not detract from the need to bring this reality into the equation when interpreting and applying the Namibian Constitution.

3.2 The value judgment

This Court has recently, after a comprehensive review of decisions in Namibian Courts since independence, held that the "general consensus of these judgments is that in order to determine whether there is an infringement of Art. 8(2)(b) involves a value judgment based on the current values of the Namibian people".

The Court went on to say:

> **"... That, in my opinion, presupposes that such exercise is undertaken to give content and meaning to the words used in the Article. Once this is done there is no basis on which the legislation which is in conflict therewith can be found to be constitutional and in that sense all agreed that the Article is absolute. Lastly it was accepted in all these cases that the people of Namibia share basic values with all civilized countries and for that reason it is useful and important to look at interpretations of other jurisdictions although the determining factor remains the values expressed by the Namibian people as reflected,** *inter alia,* **in its various institutions."**[507]

I must make the following comments:

(i) Although this Court in *Namunjepo* did not expressly state that it accepts the aforesaid "consensus" as the binding case law in Namibia in a matter of this nature, I assume that it did.

(ii) I understand the explanation regarding the "absolute" character of the article to be that the article is only "absolute" in the sense that there is no clause of general qualification or exception applicable to it as is the position in the case of the "freedoms" and also no specific qualification or exception contained in the article itself or in any other part of the Namibian Constitution. The terminology in Art. 8 does not define the fundamental right precisely. For that reason the true meaning, content and ambit must thus be ascertained *inter alia* by reference to the current values of Namibians as found in the Namibian Constitution as well as Namibian institutions[508]. Whether or not an act or omission constitutionally violates the provision, is mostly a question of degree and proportionality.

(iii) This Court also referred in this regard to the summary of the law regarding such value judgment as contained in *State v Tcoeib* and I assume that summary of the law to have been acceptable to this Court.

[507] *Namunjepo & Ors v Commanding Officer, Windhoek Prison & An.,* 2000 (6) BCLR, 671 NmS, 678 F - I.

[508] *Ex Parte Attorney-General: In re Corporal Punishment,* 1991 (3) SA 76 (NmS).

The summary contains the principles and guidelines which I believe are applicable whenever the Court must make a value judgment in regard to fundamental rights and/or freedoms which are not clearly defined as is the case in Articles 7, 8, 10, 13 and 14.

It reads as follows:

> **"(a) When the Court must decide whether or not a law providing for a particular punishment is cruel, inhuman or degrading and thus in conflict with Art. 8 of the Namibian Constitution and whether such law and such punishment is therefore unconstitutional and forbidden, the Court must have regard to the 'contemporary norms, aspirations, expectations, sensitivities, moral standards, relevant established beliefs, social conditions, experiences and perceptions of the Namibian people as expressed in their national institutions and Constitution', as well as the consensus of values or 'emerging consensus of values' in the 'civilised international community'.**
>
> **(b) The resultant value judgment which the Court must make, must be objectively articulated and identified, regard being had to the aforesaid norms, etc., of the Namibian people and the aforesaid consensus of values in the international community.**
>
> **(c) Whilst it is extremely instructive and useful to refer to, and analyse, decisions by other Courts such as the International Court of Human Rights, or the Supreme Court of Zimbabwe or the United States of America, the one major and basic consideration in arriving at a decision involves an enquiry into the contemporary norms, aspirations, expectations, sensitivities, moral standards, relevant established beliefs, social conditions, experiences and perceptions of the Namibian people.**
>
> **(d) In order to make an objective value judgment, an enquiry of some sort is required, which must at least comply with the mandatory provisions of the Supreme Court Act and the High Court Act as well as with the elementary requirements for a judicial tribunal in deciding issues of fact and law in any proceeding" (at 286j - 287d)."**[509]
>
> **(e) An example of a provision for a fundamental right which is indeed "absolute" and where no value judgment is brought into the equation is that part of Art. 6 which reads as follows:**
>
> > **"... No law may prescribe death as a competent sentence. No Court or Tribunal shall have the power to impose a sentence of death upon any person. No execution shall take place in Namibia."**

(iv) The "institutions" referred to were also described in the decision of the High Court in *State v Tcoeib, supra.* The *Shorter Oxford English Dictionary* was referred to wherein the following definition appears:

> **"an established law, custom, usage, practice, organization or other element in the political and social life of the people; a well-established or familiar practice or object; an establishment, organization or association, instituted for the**

[509] *Namunjepo case, supra,* at p.676E - I.

> **promotion of some object, especially one of public utility, religion, charitable, educational, etc."**

The Namibian Parliament, courts, tribal authorities, common law, statute law and tribal law, political parties, news media, trade unions, established Namibian churches and other relevant community-based organisations can be regarded as institutions for the purposes hereof[510].

In this Court's judgment in *S v Namunjepo*, it was also accepted that "Parliament, being the chosen representatives of the people of Namibia, is one of the most important institutions to express the current day values of the people."

(v) The value judgment, as stated in *S v Vries*, "can vary from time to time but which is one not arbitrarily arrived at but which must be judicially arrived at by way of an attempt to give content to the value judgment by referral to the prevailing norms which may or may not coincide with the norms of any particular judge. As was pointed out in *Coker v Georgia* 433 US 584 (1977) at 592 these judgments:

> **'should not be, or appear to be, merely the subjective views of individual justices; judgment should be informed by objective factors to the maximum possible extent.'"**[511]

(vi) The objective factors can be derived from sources which include, but are not limited to: the Namibian Constitution; all the "institutions" of Namibia as defined, *supra,* including: debates in Parliament and in regional statutory bodies and legislation passed by Parliament; judicial or other commissions; public opinion as established in properly conducted opinion polls; evidence placed before Courts of law and judgments of Court; referenda; publications by experts.

The relevance and importance of public opinion in establishing the current or contemporary values of Namibians when the Court makes its value judgment, has been discussed in various decisions, including the decision in *State v Vries*, referred to *supra*. To avoid any misunderstanding, I reiterate what I said in *State v Vries* in this regard:

> **"In my respectful view the value of public opinion will differ from case to case, from fundamental right to fundamental right and from issue to issue. In some cases public opinion should receive very little weight; in others it should receive considerable weight. It is not a question of substituting public opinion for that of the Court. It is the Courts that will always evaluate the public opinion. The Court will decide whether the purported public opinion is an informed opinion based on reason and true facts; whether it is artificially induced or instigated by agitators seeking a political power base; whether it constitutes a mere 'amorphous ebb and flow of public opinion' or whether it points to a permanent trend, a change in the structure and culture of society... The Court therefore is not deprived of its role to take the final decision whether or not public opinion, as in the case of other sources, constitutes objective evidence of community values..."**[512]

[510] Compare: *S v Tcoeib,* 1993 (1) SACR 274 Nm at 284 d - e.

[511] S v Vries, 1996(2) SACR 638 (Nm) at 641 c - d.

[512] *State v Vries,* IBID, 658.

The methods of which a Court can avail itself to obtain the necessary facts for the purpose of the enquiry, includes, but is not limited to: taking judicial notice of notorious facts; testimony in *viva voce* form before the Court deciding the issue; facts placed before the Court by the interested parties as common cause; the compilation of special dossiers compiled by a referee in accordance with the provisions of Art. 87(c) read with Art. 79(2) of the Namibian Constitution and sections 15 and 20 of the Supreme Court Act and Rule 6(5)(b) of the Rules of the Supreme Court and Rule 33 of the High Court Rules[513].

(vii) The footnote by the Supreme Court in *State v Tcoeib* to the effect "that no evidential enquiry is necessary", does not deny that an enquiry by the Court is necessary. Furthermore, it does not necessarily mean that an "evidential" enquiry will not be appropriate or useful on occasion[514].

At any event, the opinion voiced in the said footnote appears to be an obiter opinion and consequently need not be followed by this Court.

In my respectful view, it should not be followed if it is construed to mean that an "evidential" enquiry is impermissible. I say this for the following reasons: no reasons whatsoever were given for the remark; it is not clear what was meant by the remark; the point was not raised at the hearing of the appeal and no argument was addressed to the Court on this point.

If an evidential enquiry is held to be impermissible, such finding will make nonsense of the principle that consideration must be given to the "contemporary norms, aspirations, expectations, sensitivities, moral standards, relevant established beliefs, social conditions, experiences and perceptions of the Namibian people as expressed in their national institutions and constitution".

Berker, C.J., in his separate but concurring judgment in *Ex Parte Attorney General, Namibia: In re: Corporal Punishment by Organs of State,* 1991 (3) SA 76 Nm, stated that

> **"the one major and basic consideration in arriving at a decision involves an enquiry into the generally held norms, approaches, moral standards, aspirations and a host of other established beliefs of the people of Namibia".**[515]

I cannot imagine that Berker ever meant that an evidential enquiry is excluded.

One wonders how the dynamic nature of the values and the changes inherent therein, underlined by both Mahomed, A.J., as he then was, and Berker, C.J., can be established, if an evidential enquiry is not permissible at all[516].

---

[513] See *Namunjepo & Ors v Commanding Officer, Windhoek Prison & An,* Nm, May 1998, unreported, p.43 - 44. See also the Supreme Court judgment, *supra*, 678 H.

[514] *S v Tcoeib*, the Supreme Court judgment, *supra*, at 398 I, footnote 11. *Namunjepo & Ors v Commanding Officer, Windhoek Prison & An,* the Supreme Court Case, *supra,* at 680 G.

[515] 1991(3) SA 76, quoted in *S v Vries*, 1996 (2) SACR, 638 (Nm) at 651g - 652a.

[516] *S v Vries,* 1996(2) SACR, 638 (Nm) at 652d - 653a, 655b - 659I *Namunjepo & Ors v Commanding Officer Windhoek Prison & An.* the Supreme Court decision referred to, *supra*, at p.680 G - J.

In most cases the sources and means enumerated herein *supra*, other than an "evidential enquiry" may suffice, but in some instances an "evidential enquiry" may be the only appropriate way to achieve the purpose of establishing the contemporary norms and values, etc.

If the Court then refuses or fails to launch an evidential enquiry, it will fall into the trap of substituting its own subjective views for an objective standard and method. The requirement to consider the Namibian norms and values will then become a mere cliché to which mere lip service is paid.

This will be a travesty of justice, particularly if at the same time, the Courts refer to and rely primarily on the alleged contemporary norms in the USA and Europe.

(viii) It follows from the above that what was said in the decisions regarding the interpretation and application of Art. 8 of the Namibian Constitution applies *mutatis mutandis* to the interpretation of all those articles which are not clearly defined and which are relative and not "absolute" in that sense. In the result the question to be answered in each case where the Court has to make a value judgment, is whether or not the alleged infringement "constitutionally" violates the fundamental right or freedom and is therefore "constitutionally impermissible".

3.3 The important difference between the provisions in the South African Constitution and the Namibian Constitution relating to the role of the Courts and other tribunals or forums in interpreting and giving effect to the Constitution

Art. 39(1) and (2) of the South African Constitution states:

(1) When interpreting the Bill of Rights, a Court, tribunal or forum -

(a) must promote the values that underlie an open and democratic society based on human dignity, equality and freedom;

(b) must consider international law; and

(c) may consider foreign law.

(2) When interpreting any legislation, and when developing the common law or customary law or legislation, every court, tribunal or forum must promote the spirit, purport and objects of the Bill of Rights…"

(My emphasis added.)

It must be noted that the duty is not only placed on Courts but also on tribunals or forums.

And it is envisaged, so it seems, that all of these institutions will engage in interpreting the Bill of Rights and develop the common law or customary law and legislation. When they interpret the Bill of Rights, they must all "promote the values which underlie an open and democratic society based on human dignity, equality and freedom".

The provision in the South African Constitution leaves no room for the positivist school of thinking in the interpretation and application of the Constitution and not even room for a "golden mean" between the "positivist" and "libertarian" schools as expressed by Friedman, J. in *Nyamkazi v President of Bophuthatswana*, referred to *supra*.

It seems to me that in Namibia, the "golden mean" should not be crossed.

In South Africa, the judicial authority is stated in Art. 165 to vest exclusively in the Courts but as I have pointed out Art. 39 vests wide powers, not only in the Courts, but in "tribunals" or "forums" which appear to have "judicial" powers when "interpreting" the "Bill of Rights".

In regard to the judicial authority, the Namibian Constitution is ambiguous. The judicial authority is vested in the Namibian Courts by Art. 78(1). But 78(2) makes their independence subject to the Constitution and the law. Although Art. 78(2) provides that the Cabinet or Legislature or any other person may not interfere with the Courts in the exercise of their judicial functions, Art. 81 provides that a decision of the Supreme Court is no longer binding if reversed by its own later decision or if contradicted by an Act of Parliament. This means, so it would appear, that Parliament is not only the directly elected representative of the people of Namibia, but also some sort of High Court of Parliament which in an exceptional case, may contradict the Supreme Court, provided of course that it acts in terms of the letter and spirit of the Namibian Constitution, including all the provisions of Chapter 3 relating to fundamental human rights.

Although there can be no doubt of the power of the Namibian High Court and Supreme Court to declare any statute, or part thereof, unconstitutional in terms of Art. 5, it seems that Parliament has the last say[517]. Furthermore, as acknowledged in this Court's decision in *Namunjepo and Others,* Parliament is one of the most important institutions to express the present day values of the Namibian people.

Much has been said in the decisions referred to regarding democratic values, but it should not be forgotten that perhaps one of the most important democratic values enshrined in the Namibian Constitution is that contained in Art. 1(2) which reads:

> **"All power shall vest in the people of Namibia who shall exercise their sovereignty through the democratic institutions of the State."**[518]

It follows from the above that the Namibian Courts are in a much weaker position than their counterparts in South Africa particularly in regard to "developing the common law or customary law or legislation".

It is also significant that Art. 39 of the South African Constitution provides for the Courts, tribunals or forums to consider international law and foreign law, but nothing is said about its own contemporary values, norms, aspirations, expectations and sensitivities as embodied in its institutions, other than the constitution.

[517] See the decision of the Full Bench of the High Court in *Namunjepo & Ors v The State,* June 1998, unreported.

[518] The High Court decision in the *Namunjepo* case, unreported, July 1998, points 8.

At least the Namibian courts have from the very beginning determined that in interpreting and applying the fundamental rights in Namibia, the value judgment that it has to make must take cognisance in the first place of the traditions, values, aspirations, expectations and sensitivities of the people of Namibia.

There can be no doubt about the need to apply this principle of interpretation in Namibia. A refusal or failure to do so, would strengthen the perception that the Courts are imposing foreign values on the Namibian people. This will bring the Courts as well as the Constitution into disrepute and undermine the positive role it has played in the past and must continue to play in the future in regard to the maintenance and development of democratic values and fundamental human rights.

One of the problems in Namibia to date has been to apply this principle in practice.

I conclude this part by quoting from a comment by Justice White in the American case of *Bowers, Attorney-General of Georgia v Hardwich et al* referred to in the recent majority decision of the Zimbabwe Supreme Court in *S v Banana:*

> **"The court is most vulnerable and come nearest to illegitimacy when it deals with Judge-made constitutional law having little or no cognisable roots in the language or design of the constitution."[519]**

4. THE CASE MADE BY THE RESPONDENTS ON THE ALLEGED INFRINGEMENT OF THEIR BASIC HUMAN RIGHTS AND FREEDOMS

4.1 Infringement of rights to family life

Although the respondents alleged that they are lesbians in that "they are emotionally and sexually attracted to women", they did not allege that they are "spouses" and that the board should have acted in terms of section 26(1)(g) to grant a permit to first respondent. This subsection of the Immigration Control Act provides that the board may grant a permanent residence permit on the ground that "he or she is the spouse ... of a person permanently resident in Namibia..."

They admit that they are not married and that they cannot marry in terms of the law although they would have married if the law provided for such marriage.

They also do not ask for any particular law or part of such law to be declared unconstitutional. In any case they have not joined the State or Government as a party by e.g. joining the Minister of Home Affairs as a party.

What we have then is a complaint that the Immigration Selection Board should have given them equivalent status to that of spouses in a lawful marriage and as members of a family.

[519] *S v Banana,* 2000 (2) SACR 1 (ZSC) at 49H.

However, it must be pointed out at the outset that this Court has declared in the recent judgment in *Myburg v The Commercial Bank of Namibia* that pre-independence statutes remain in force until declared unconstitutional by a Court of Law. As far as the common law is concerned, any provision of the common law in conflict with the Namibian Constitution, is *ipso jure* invalid as from the date of entering into force of the Namibian Constitution and any declaration by the Court to this effect, merely confirms this position. However in regard to post-independence statutes or government actions which "abolishes or abridges the fundamental rights or freedoms" conferred by Chapter 3, the position is slightly more complicated for the following reason: the first part of Art. 25 provides that although any such law or action is invalid to the extent of the contravention, "a competent Court may, instead of declaring such law or action invalid, shall have the power and the discretion in an appropriate case to allow Parliament or any subordinate legislative authority, and the Executive and agencies of Government as the case may be, to correct any defect in the impugned law or action within a specified period, subject to such conditions that may be specified by it. In such event and until such correction or until the expiry of the time limit set by the Court, whichever is the shorter, such impugned law or action shall be deemed to be valid."

The pre-independence statutes regarding the legislation and recognition of marriage such as the Marriage Act 25 of 1961 will consequently remain the law in force until a declaration of unconstitutionality[520].

The Board would consequently have been within its legal rights to regard marriages as those recognised in the aforesaid pre-independence laws.

As far as the Namibian Constitution itself is concerned, the marriages which in terms of Art. 4(3) qualify a spouse of a citizen for citizenship, is clearly a marriage between a man and woman, that is a heterosexual marriage, not a homosexual marriage or relationship.

For this purpose a marriage under customary law is deemed to be a marriage, provided that Parliament may enact legislation to "define the requirements that need to be satisfied".

Although homosexual relationships must have been known to the representatives of the Namibian nation and their legal representatives when they agreed on the terms of the Namibian Constitution, no provision was made for the recognition of such a relationship as equivalent to marriage or at all. It follows that it was never contemplated or intended to place a homosexual relationship on an equal basis with a heterosexual marital relationship.

The reference to "spouse" in sub-article (3)(a)(bb) of Art. 4 also clearly refers to the spouse in a heterosexual marriage.

The concession was thus correctly made by counsel for respondents to the effect that not only can they not legally marry, but that first respondent cannot claim citizenship under Art. 4(3) of the Namibian Constitution.

---

[520] *Myburgh v The Commercial Bank of Namibia*, NmS, 28/12/2000, not reported.

It follows then that when Namibia's Parliament enacted the Immigration Control Act in 1993, it used the word "spouse" in subsection 3(g) of section 26, in the same sense as it is used in the Namibian Constitution.

In South Africa a similar expression in the Aliens Control Act was regarded as connoting a married person, not partners in same-sex relations[521].

In regard to Art. 14, Counsel for respondents conceded that while Art. 14(1) of the Namibian Constitution only refers to heterosexual marriages, sub-article (3) is not limited to such a family. I do not agree.

In regard to the protection of the "family", the Namibian Constitution in sub-article (3) of Art. 14 of the said Constitution, provides for the protection of the family as a fundamental right in regard to which the duty to protect is laid upon Society and the State. But the "family" is described as the "natural" and "fundamental" group unit of society. It was clearly not contemplated that a homosexual relationship could be regarded as "the natural group unit" and/or the "fundamental group unit".

Sub-article (1) and (2) of Art. 14 make it even clearer what is meant by "family". It says: "Men and women of full age, without any limitation as to race, colour, ethnic origin, nationality, religion, creed or social or economic status, shall have the right to marry and found a family. They shall be entitled to equal rights as to marriage, during marriage and at its dissolution".

The marriage is between men and women – not men and men and women and women.

> **"(2)Marriage shall be entered into only with the free and full consent of the intending spouses."**

The word "spouses" are clearly used in the same sense and context as in 4(3)(a)(bb) of the Constitution.

In the recent decision of this Court in *Myburgh v Commercial Bank,* the Court also dealt with Art. 14. It was assumed that the Article dealt with marriage between men and women. Art. 14 clearly does not create a new type of family. The protection extended is to the "natural and fundamental group unit of society as known at the time as an institution of Namibian society.

The homosexual relationship, whether between men and men and women and women, clearly falls outside the scope and intent of Art. 14.

The African Charter on Human and Peoples' Rights which was adopted by the African Heads of State and Government in Nairobi, Kenya, on 27th June 1981 and which entered into force on 21st October 1986 in accordance with Art. 63 of the Charter, provides in Art. 17.3 that:

> **"the promotion and protection of morals and traditional values recognized by the community shall be the duty of the State."**

[521] *Natural Coalition for Gay and Lesbian Equality & Ors v Minister of Home Affairs and Ors,* 2000 (2) SA 1 (CC) at 20 E - 21 C.

Art. 18 provides:

> "18. 1. The family shall be the natural unit and basis of society. It shall be protected by the State which shall take care of its physical health and morals.
>
> 2. The State shall have the duty to assist the family, which is the custodian of morals and traditional values recognized by the community..."
>
> (My emphasis added.)

It must be noticed that the wording in Art. 18.1 is almost identical to that used in Art. 14.3 of the Namibian Constitution.

Our Art. 14 is also similar to Art. 16 of the United Nations Universal Declaration of Human Rights. And as the writer Heinze concedes in his book – Art. 16 "clearly refers to the heterosexual paradigm"[522].

The International Covenant on Civil and Political rights also relied on by respondents' counsel, has almost identical provisions in its Art. 23 in regard to the "family" than the Namibian Constitution in its Art. 14. The only difference is that the sequence of the sub-paragraphs have been changed in the Namibian Constitution.

As pointed out in this Court's decision in *Namunjepo & Others v Commanding Officer, Windhoek Prison & Others,* the Namibian Parliament on 28 November 1994 acceded to this Covenant[523].

It should be noted in passing that this Covenant in its Articles dealing with the prohibition on discrimination, specifies "sex" as one of the grounds on which discrimination is prohibited but not "sexual orientation".

Article 14.3 of the Namibian Constitution apparently gave effect to or was influenced by Art. 16 of the said Charter, Art. 18.1 of the African Charter and Art. 23 of the International Covenant on Civil and Political Rights.

Counsel for respondents referred us to some decisions in American and European Courts.

The majority decision in *Braschi v Stahl Associates Company,* (1989) 74 NY 2d 201, relied on, was not a decision interpreting the American Constitution but New York City Rent and Eviction Regulations. It dealt with American society, not African or Namibian society and stressed repeatedly that the Court dealt with the item "in the context of eviction".

The Court cannot interpret the Articles of the Namibian Constitution by comparing it with Regulations for rent and eviction purposes in the U.S.A.

The House of Lords decision in *Fitzpatric v Sterling Housing Association Ltd* 1999 (4) All ER 705 (HL) relied on by counsel, again dealt with the term "family" as used in the Rents Act.

---

[522] Heinze. *Sexual Orientation: A Human Right.* Chapter 2, p.34, 39 last par.

[523] The *Namunjepo* decision, *supra,* 682.

For the same reason as stated in regard to the *Braschi's* decision it is not very helpful to decide what was meant by the term "family" in the Namibian Constitution.

Counsel further contended that respondents and second respondent's minor son constitutes a family for the purposes of Art. 14(3).

The minor son, is not born of a marriage between respondents. He has not even been adopted by first respondent. The claimed benefits to the son of second respondent may even be diminished by the confusion created by a son, born from a heterosexual relationship, forced to adapt to and grow up in a homosexual "family" where he would possibly not be certain who takes the role of father and who of mother; who is the "spouse" and how do the "spouses" give effect to their sexual relationship in regard to sexual satisfaction. No evidence has been produced by respondents as to the emotional and psychological effect on the child nor has any material benefit to the child been indicated by having first respondent as his appointed guardian. In so far as it is suggested that to grant a permanent residence permit to the first respondent is in the interests also of the child of second respondent, the following remarks may be apposite. The Namibian Constitution in its Art. 15, the African Charter in its Art. 18(3), the International Covenant on Civil and Political Rights in its Art. 24, all require measures by the State for the protection of the child. Whether or not the interest of the minor child of Khaxas is protected by being raised within this lesbian partnership, is a debatable and controversial issue which was not debated before this Court and need not be decided in this case. What is clear however, is that the "family" unit relied on by respondents, is not the "natural and fundamental group unit" referred to in Art. 14(3) of the Namibian Constitution. Furthermore, a lesbian relationship has never been recognised as a Namibian "institution" in the sense that the word has been used in judgments of the Courts relating to value judgments which the Courts must make. It is altogether a different concept than the marriage institution with its laws, rules, objectives and traditions.

The "family institution" of the African Charter, the United Nations Universal Declaration of Human Rights, the International Covenant on Civil and Political Rights and the Namibian Constitution, envisages a formal relationship between male and female, where sexual intercourse between them in the family context is the method to procreate offspring and thus ensure the perpetuation and survival of the nation and the human race.

In my respectful view the respondents claim that their rights to family life has been infringed, must be rejected.

4.2 The respondent's right to privacy

Respondents rely on Art. 13.1 of the Namibian Constitution which reads:

> **"No persons shall be subject to interference with the privacy of their homes, correspondence or communications save as in accordance with law and as is necessary in a democratic society in the interests of national security, public safety or the economic well-being of the country, for the protection of health or**

morals, for the prevention of disorder or crime or for the protection of the rights or freedoms of others."

How the fact that the appellant Board refused first respondent's application for a permit, considering that first respondent is an alien with no existing right to residence, can amount to interference with both respondents' right to "the privacy of their homes, correspondence and communications" is difficult to imagine.

Next counsel for respondents' claim a breach of Art. 17 of the International Covenant on Civil and Political Rights which provides:

"1. No one shall be subjected to arbitrary or unlawful interference with his privacy, family, home or correspondence, nor to unlawful attacks on his honour and reputation.

2. Everyone has the right to the protection of the law against such interference or attacks."

Again, I fail to see the relevance of this provision.

After all, the Namibian Constitution is the Supreme Law, in terms of the Namibian Constitution and there is nothing in the Constitution or even in the said covenant justifying the claim of respondents of the infringement of either Art. 13(1) of the Namibian Constitution or Art. 17 of the said covenant. There seems to be no causal connection or rational connection between the refusal of an alien's residence permit and the said Articles.

4.3 The second respondent's right to reside and settle in any part of Namibia and to leave and return to Namibia

Respondents rely on the fundamental freedom contained in Art. 21(1)(h) and Art. 21(1)(i) of the Constitution.

Art. 21(1)(h) and (i) provide as follows:

"All persons shall have the right to:

(h) reside and settle in any part of Namibia;

(i) leave and return to Namibia."

First respondent, as an alien, does not have such a right. Even though the introduction to (h) and (i) appear to grant such a right, it must be clear that the said right is subject to the law of Namibia, which does not allow such a right. And as far as second respondent is concerned, her right is not infringed.

Counsel submitted:

"She is in effect given the Hobson's choice – remain in Namibia, without your life partner or leave Namibia with your life partner, for an uncertain future, not knowing which country will admit you and your son, as residents."

Nobody ordered second respondent to leave Namibia. If she leaves, she may return. But of course, if she renounces or waives her right by becoming a citizen of another country, she is the cause of her own harm if any and not the Namibian authorities.

I have already indicated earlier in this judgment that the agony and anxiety claimed by respondents is exaggerated. Surely, if all the claims regarding the countries that do not discriminate on the basis of sexual orientation are true, then second respondent will at least have no difficulty to qualify in Germany, the home country of first respondent, for residence and even citizenship as of right.

Counsel for respondents again referred to several decisions beginning with the Zimbabwean Courts. She says that these cases laid down the right of the citizen to reside permanently in Zimbabwe, but to do so with one's spouse, even if the latter is a foreigner. The problem for counsel for respondents is that the right which extends to the spouse, is the spouse in a recognised marital relationship not a "partner in a homosexual relationship".

The South African case relied on namely *Patel and Another v Minister of Home Affairs and Another,* 2000 (2) SA 343 which allegedly followed the Zimbabwean decisions, again dealt with the case where the spouse was a South African citizen married to an alien.

The same principle does indeed apply under the Namibian Constitution where Art. 4(3) provides for the right to citizenship of such a spouse and section 26(3)(g) which provide that permanent residence may be granted to such a spouse.

Counsel then referred to the South African decision in *National Coalition for Gay and Lesbian Equality and Others v Minister of Home Affairs and Others,* 2000 (2) SA 1 (CC) where Ackermann, J. referred to the Zimbabwean decision in regard to freedom of movement of the resident spouse as affected by the refusal to grant a foreign spouse residence rights.

Although the Court referred obiter also to the decisions of the Zimbabwean Courts regarding foreign spouses, it did not decide the case before it on that ground.

In my respectful view the alleged infringement of the freedom of movement of respondents is farfetched and a grasping at straws.

4.4 The infringement of the fundamental rights to equality and non-discrimination

In this regard respondents' counsel has again leaned heavily on decisions of South African Courts, particularly the Constitutional Court.

The South African Constitutional Court in its above-mentioned decision found that the South African Aliens Act did not extend its protection of spouses to same-sex life partnerships and as such it infringed on the fundamental right to equality and the right to dignity of permanent residents in the Republic being in permanent same-sex life partnerships with foreign nationals. The Court found *inter alia* that the omission in section 25(2) of the Aliens Control Act, after the word "spouse", of the words "or partner in a permanent same-sex life partnership" is unconstitutional, because it was in conflict with provisions of the Constitution relating to non-discrimination on the basis of "sexual orientation" in section 9 of the Constitution and the protection of dignity in Art. 10 of the South African Constitution. The Court accordingly ordered that the said section 25(5), is to be read as though the following words appear therein after the word "spouse": "or partner in a permanent same-sex life partnership".

It was further ordered that this order "comes into effect from the moment of the making of this order".

Although the Minister of Home Affairs was joined as a party to the proceedings, the said Minister failed to file opposing affidavits in accordance with the rules and the application for leave for the late filing of such affidavits was dismissed in the Court *a quo* and the dismissal was confirmed on appeal to the Constitutional Court.

Notwithstanding the fact that the Minister was not allowed to file opposing affidavits late, the Court did not refer the matter back to the Ministry or to Parliament. It took a short cut and summary course and in fact legislated for Parliament by not only telling Parliament what should have been in its law, but putting the alleged missing part into the law without further ado.

This decision followed on a prior decision by the South African Constitutional Court in which the law providing that sodomy is a crime, was declared unconstitutional on the ground that it infringed the fundamental rights prohibiting discrimination on the ground of "sexual orientation" and the infringement of a person's dignity.

Article 9(3) of the South African Constitution provides that: "The State may not unfairly discriminate directly or indirectly against anyone on one or more grounds, including race, sex, pregnancy, marital status, ethnic or social origin, colour, sexual orientation, age, disability, religion, conscience, belief, culture language and birth".

Whereas the word "sex" can be defined as "being male or female", or "males or females as a group", "sexual orientation" could encompass in theory "any sexual attraction of anyone towards anyone or anything"[524].

The prohibition against discrimination on the grounds of sexual orientation is so wide, that a case may even be made out for decriminalizing the crime of bestiality, particularly, when done in private.

Article 10 of the Namibian Constitution reads:

> "(1) All persons shall be equal before the law.
>
> (2) No persons may be discriminated against on the grounds of sex, race, colour, ethnic origin, religion, creed, or social or economic status."

In Namibia, as in Zimbabwe, the Constitution does not expressly prohibit discrimination on the grounds of "sexual orientation".

[524] *Oxford Advanced Learners Dictionary.* Heinze: *Sexual Orientation: A Human Right,* p.46 and 60 et seq.

If Namibia had the same provision in the Constitution relating to sexual orientation and no provisions such as Art. 14 relating to the duty to protect the natural and fundamental group unit of society and also no provision equivalent to Art. 4(3), the result would probably have been the same as in South Africa.

Ackermann, J., pointed out in the South African decision that in recent years there has been a notable and significant development in the statute law of South Africa in the extent to which the Legislature had given express or implied recognition to same-sex partnerships. He says:

> **"A range of statutory provisions have included such unions within their ambit. While this legislative trend is significant in evincing Parliament's commitment to equality on the ground of sexual orientation, there is still no appropriate recognition in our law of the same-sex life partnership to meet the legal and other needs of its partners."**
> **(My emphasis added.)**

It is significant that the aforesaid "legislative trend" flows from the provision in the South African Constitution prohibiting discrimination on the ground of "sexual orientation".

In Namibia as well as Zimbabwe, not only is there no such provision, but no such "legislative trend". In contrast, as alleged by the respondents, the President of Namibia as well as the Minister of Home Affairs, have expressed themselves repeatedly in public against the recognition and encouragement of homosexual relationships. As far as they are concerned, homosexual relationships should not be encouraged because that would be against the traditions and values of the Namibian people and would undermine those traditions and values. It is a notorious fact of which this Court can take judicial notice that when the issue was brought up in Parliament, nobody on the Government benches, which represent 77 percent of the Namibian electorate, made any comment to the contrary.

It is clear from the above that far from a "legislative trend" in Namibia, Namibian trends, contemporary opinions, norms and values tend in the opposite direction.

In Zimbabwe, the Zimbabwean Supreme Court has recently, in the case of *State v Banana*, refused to follow the South African decisions in this regard and has refused to decriminalise sodomy.

The opposition against the decriminalising of sodomy in Namibia, is part and parcel of the Government resistance to promoting homosexuality. In Namibia, this Court had to date not considered the constitutionality of the crime of sodomy and there is consequently no decision decriminalising the crime. The reason for the Courts not having considered the issue in Namibia is because unlike South Africa, the issue has not been pertinently and properly raised by litigants before Namibian Courts.

The Namibian Constitution corresponds to that of Zimbabwe in regard to the provision for equality and non-discrimination. The "social norms and values" in regard to sexual behaviour of Namibians appear to correspond more to that of Zimbabweans than to that in South Africa as reflected in judgments of the Constitutional Court of South Africa. Although the *Banana* decision dealt with the issue of whether or not it is unconstitutional to criminalise the crime of sodomy, many of the remarks by McNally, J.A., who wrote the majority judgment, are applicable, *mutatis mutandis*, to the issues to be decided in this case. He motivated the judgment as follows:

> **"I do not agree that the provisions of the Constitution of Zimbabwe have the effect of decriminalizing consensual sexual intercourse per annum between adult males in private. For the sake of brevity I will use the phrase 'consensual sodomy' in this sense.**
>
> **Let me begin by making certain general observations.**
>
> **There seem to be three ways in which consensual sodomy has moved away from being regarded as criminal. In some countries, such as England and Wales, there was a gradual development of a more tolerant and understanding popular attitude towards such conduct. After widespread national debate, legislation was passed for the precise purpose of decriminalizing the conduct. This was the Sexual Offences Act of 1967.**
>
> **In other countries, such as South Africa, a new Constitution made provision specifically outlawing discrimination on the grounds of sexual orientation. That Constitution was widely and publicly debated and accepted. The legislation and common-law provisions criminalizing consensual sodomy clearly fall away in the face of such explicit provision.**
>
> **The third situation arose in jurisdictions such as Ireland and Northern Ireland, where the majority of the people and the Courts, were disinclined to decriminalize the offence, but were overruled by a supra-national judicial authority - in their cases the European Court of Human Rights. Thus, for example, the Irish Supreme Court (by a majority) held in** *Norris v The Attorney-General* **1984 IR 36 that the laws against consensual sodomy were not inconsistent with the Irish Constitution, and in particular were not invidiously discriminatory nor an invasion of privacy. Then the European Court overturned that decision. And in** *Dudgeon v United Kingdom* **1982 (4) EHRR 149 it is apparent that such acts were regarded in Northern Ireland as criminal (though not in recent times prosecuted) until the European Court intervened.**
>
> **In the United States of America the position of the individual states is not uniform. In** *Bowers, Attorney General of Georgia v Hardwick* **478 US 186, 106 S Ct 2841, the Federal Supreme Court, by a 5-4 majority, declined to invalidate the State of Georgia's sodomy statute on the ground, among others, that 'the Constitution does not confer a fundamental right upon homosexuals to engage in sodomy'. It appears from the judgment that in 1986 there were 25 states in which consensual sodomy was a crime.**

> **I am aware that the judgment has been criticised. I appreciate the intellectual force of that criticism. It does not follow that the judgment is wrong. There are always two points of view upon such basic issues. The fact remains that the present stand of perhaps the most senior court in the western world is that it is not unconstitutional to criminalise consensual sodomy. That stance remains in force, despite the ruling in** *Romer v Evans* **517 US 620 (1996), which did not overrule the earlier decision.**
>
> **Historically, consensual sodomy, along with a number of other sexual activities which were regarded as immoral, were dealt with by the Ecclesiastical Courts. Such immoral activities included adultery and fornication, i.e. sex outside marriage. In 1533 the offences of sodomy and bestiality (collectively called buggery) were brought within the jurisdiction of the secular courts by King Henry VIII. Since then, and in very general terms, there has been a tendency in the western world to reverse that process. Adultery and fornication became sins rather than crimes. For those who drifted away from the churches the concept of sinfulness became less and less meaningful. Consensual sodomy has, in many but not all parts of the western world, joined that drift from crime to sin to acceptable conduct.**
>
> **It is of some interest to note, courtesy of Milton's** *SA Criminal Law and Procedure* **vol. 2 3rd Ed at 250-1 that in pre - Christian Rome (and I would add, Greece) such conduct carried no social or moral opprobrium, whereas Hebraic and Germanic laws were strongly disapproving. See also footnote 6 to Justice Blackmun's dissenting judgment in** *Bowers v Hardwick* **(*supra*).**

What then of Zimbabwe?

I would remark first that this case has not, from its very beginning, been treated as a constitutional test case. No evidence was led in the court *a quo* from psychiatrists, psychologists or other experts. No evidence was led to suggest that the customary laws of Zimbabwe are more akin to those of the Romans and Athenians than to the Germanic or Hebraic customs. I cannot therefore speak with authority on the customary law in this respect. I note, however, that Goldin and Gelfand's well-known book on Customary Law says, at 264, the following:

> **'*Kurara nemumwe murume* (homosexuality) is called *huroyi*. This is considered extremely wicked but is rare.'**

It seems to me that this is a relevant consideration, from two points of view. From the point of view of law reform, it cannot be said that public opinion has so changed and developed in Zimbabwe that the courts must yield to that new perception and declare the old law obsolete. Mr Andersen expressly disavowed any such argument. The Chief Justice does not dispute this. His view, if I may presume to paraphrase it, is that the provisions of the Constitution, properly interpreted, compel one to the conclusion that the criminalisation of consensual sodomy is actually contrary to those provisions.

From the point of view of constitutional interpretation, I think we must also be guided by Zimbabwe's conservatism in sexual matters. I have always agreed with the Chief Justice's view of constitutional interpretation, expressed for example in *Smyth v Ushewokunze* 1997 (2) ZLR 544 (S) at 553B - C, 1998 (2) BCLR 170 (ZS) at 177I - J that:

> **'what is to be accorded is a generous and purposive interpretation with an eye to the spirit as well as to the letter of the provision; one that takes full account of changing conditions, social norms and values, so that the provision remains flexible enough to keep pace with and meet the newly emerging problems and challenges. The aim must be to be move away from formalism and make human rights provisions a practical reality for the people.'**

In the particular circumstances of this case, I do not believe that the 'social norms and values' of Zimbabwe are pushing us to decriminalize consensual sodomy. Zimbabwe is, broadly speaking, a conservative society in matters of sexual behaviour. More conservative, say, than France or Sweden; less conservative than, say, Saudi Arabia. But, generally, more conservative than liberal.

I take that to be a relevant consideration in interpreting the Constitution in relation to matters of sexual freedom. Put differently, I do not believe that this Court, lacking the democratic credentials of a properly elected Parliament, should strain to place a sexually liberal interpretation on the Constitution of a country whose social norms and values in such matters tend to be conservative.

Against that background I turn to consider those provisions of the Declaration of Rights, namely ss 11 and 23, which might be thought to make it necessary for the Court to decriminalise consensual sodomy.

(a) Section 11 of the Constitution: the right to privacy

This section was quite significantly altered by the provisions of Act 14 of 1996, which came into effect on 6 December 1996. The section became in effect a preamble, and now says nothing at all about privacy.

Prior to 6 December 1996 the section did contain a passing reference to the fundamental right of every person in Zimbabwe to 'protection for the privacy of his home'. But, in the context, this provision is clearly a reference to the right, elaborated later in s 17, to protection from arbitrary search or entry. It has nothing whatsoever to do with whether or not consensual sodomy is a crime.

Count 1, which is the only count relating to consensual sodomy, relates to activities between 11 August 1995 and 31 December 1996. It extends over the currency of both versions of s 11. Neither version is relevant. I note that the privacy question was only faintly argued by Mr Andersen. Nor did the Chief Justice rely on s 11 in coming to his conclusion. I will not therefore dwell further upon it.

(b) Section 23 of the Constitution: protection from discrimination

This is the section upon which the Chief Justice relied in coming to the conclusion that the criminalisation of consensual sodomy was:

(a) discriminatory on the ground of gender;

(b) not reasonably justifiable in a democratic society.

I will not set out s 23 in full because it appears in the judgment of the Chief Justice.

I make first the obvious point, which was made by the Judge *a quo*, that the framers of the South African Constitution found it necessary to include 'sexual orientation' as well as 'gender' in the list of grounds on the basis of which discrimination is not permitted. Had our Constitution contained those words, there would have been no argument. But it does not.

Discrimination on the basis of gender means simply that women and men must be treated in such a way that neither is prejudiced on the grounds of his or her gender by being subjected to a condition, restriction or disability to which persons of the other gender are not made subject.

It is important to bear in mind that what is forbidden by s 23 is discrimination between men and women. Not between heterosexual men and homosexual men. That latter discrimination is prohibited only by a Constitution which proscribes discrimination on the grounds of sexual orientation, as does the South African Constitution...."

After dealing with some other points not particularly relevant to the issues in this case the learned judge in conclusion remarked:

> **"Are we to say that 25 American states are not democratic societies? And, in any event, democratic states are in various stages of development. Some might say, in various stages of decadence. (I do not propose to become involved in that argument.)**
>
> **I do not believe that it is the function or right of this Court, undemocratically appointed as it is, to seek to modernise the social mores of the State or of society at large. As Justice White said in** *Bowers v Hardwick (supra):*
>
> **'The Court is most vulnerable and comes nearest to illegitimacy when it deals with judge-made constitutional law having little or no cognizable roots in the language or design of the Constitution.'"**

It must be pointed out that although the sexual act between males has been criminalised in our common law as the crime of sodomy, the sexual act between lesbian females has never been criminalized in South African and Namibian common law. The reason may have been that the lesbian relationship and the sexual act performed in such relationship never became so clearly defined and notorious as in the case of the homosexual relationship between men. However, the matter was not raised or argued before us. There is therefore no justification for dealing with this issue in great detail.

Article 10 of the Namibian Constitution has recently been discussed and considered in the decision in *Müller v President of the Republic of Namibia and An*[525] and in the decision mentioned *supra* of *Myburgh v the Commercial Bank of Namibia*[526].

[525] *Müller v President of the Republic of Namibia and An,* 2000 (6) BCLR 655 (NmS).

[526] *Myburgh v the Commercial Bank of Namibia*, unreported, dated 8/12/2000.

In the *Müller* decision the decision in *Mwellie v Minister of Works, Transport and Communication & Another*[527] was referred to wherein the Court held:

> **"Art. 10(1) ... is not absolute ... but it permits reasonable classifications which are rationally connected to a legitimate object and that the content of the right to equal protection take cognisance of 'intelligible differential and allows provision therefore ..."**

The Court held that as far as Art. 10(2) is concerned, it prohibits discrimination on the grounds of sex, race, colour, ethnic origin, religion, creed or social or economic status. Apart from the provisions of Art. 23, any classification made on the grounds enumerated by the sub-article will either be prohibited or subject to strict scrutiny.

This Court in *Müller's* case also emphasised the need to take cognisance of the differences in the constitutions when considering the relevance of and the weight to be given to decisions and rulings in other jurisdictions. The Court accepted that Art. 10.1 requires the Court to give content to the words "equal before the law" so as to give effect to the general acceptance that

> **"... in order to govern a modern country efficiently and to harmonise the interests of all its people for the common good, it is essential to regulate the affairs of its inhabitants extensively. It is impossible to do so without classification which treat people which abound in everyday life in all democracies based on equality and freedom... In regard to mere differentiation the Constitutional State is expected to act in a rational manner. It should not regulate in an arbitrary manner or manifest 'naked preferences' that serve no legitimate governmental purpose for that would be inconsistent with the rule of law and the fundamental premises of the Constitutional State ... Accordingly, before it can be said that mere differentiation infringes s 10 it must be established that there is no rational relationship between the differentiation in question and the governmental purpose which is proffered to validate it (see *Prinsloo's* case (*supra*) at 1024)."**

The Court then concluded:

"The approach of our courts towards Art. 10 of the Constitution should then be as follows -

(a) Article 10(1)
The questioned legislation would be unconstitutional if it allows for differentiation between people or categories of people and that differentiation is not based on a rational connection to a legitimate purpose (see *Mwellie's* case *(supra)* at 1132 E - H and *Harksen's* case (*supra*) page 54).

(b) Article 10(2)
The steps to be taken in regard to this sub-article are to determine-

(i) whether there exists a differentiation between people or categories of people;

---

[527] *Mwellie v Minister of Works, Transport and Communication & Another,* 1995 (9) BCLR 1118 (NmH) at 1132 E - I.

(ii) whether such differentiation is based on one of the enumerated grounds set out in the sub-article;

(iii) whether such differentiation amounts to discrimination against such people or categories of people; and

(iv) once it is determined that the differentiation amounts to discrimination, it is unconstitutional unless it is covered by the provisions of Art. 23 of the Constitution."

This Court further said:

> **"Although the Namibian Constitution does not refer to unfair discrimination, I have no doubt that that is also the meaning that should be given to it."**

The words of the writer and jurist Ramcharan in regard to the right to equality as dealt with in "The International Bill of Rights: The Covenant of Civil and Political Rights", are apposite. He says:

> **"Equality it has sometimes been said, means equality for those equally situated and indeed, equal treatment for unequals, is itself a form of inequality."**

Equality before the law for each person, does not mean equality before the law for each person's sexual relationships.

To put it another way: It is only unfair discrimination which is constitutionally impermissible, and which will infringe Art. 10 of the Namibian Constitution.

It follows that in considering whether or not the refusal of a permanent residence permit to the lesbian partner of a Namibian citizen infringes Art. 8 or 10 of the Namibian Constitution, such consideration must be done with due reference to the express provisions of Art. 4(3) and 14 of the Namibian Constitution.

4.5 The violation of the respondents' fundamental right to dignity

The respondents have not alleged in their review application to the High Court that the Board's decision had violated their fundamental right to dignity. It is therefore not necessary to deal with the issue in this judgment.

Suffice to say that most of the argument put forward in this judgment will apply *mutatis mutandis* to any contention that the respondents' dignity has been violated.

The Namibian Parliament has, in the letter and spirit of Art. 5 of the Namibian Constitution read with the said express provisions of Art. 4 and 14 of the Constitution enacted a law for the admission of aliens and applications for permanent residence. In this law, Parliament provided for a spouse, in a recognised marital relationship, to obtain permanent residence without having to comply with all the requirements which another applicant will have to satisfy.

In my view the failure to include in section 26(3)(g) of the Namibian Immigration Control Act an undefined, informal and unrecognised lesbian relationship with obligations different from that of marriage, may amount to "differentiation", but do not amount to "discrimination" at all.

In providing for a special dispensation for partners in recognized marriage institutions and or the protection of those institutions, Parliament has clearly given effect to Art. 14 of the Namibian Constitution and to similar provisions in the African Charter relating to the protection of the family, being the "natural and fundamental unit" of society. In this regard Parliament has also given effect to this court's repeated admonitions that the Namibian Constitution must be interpreted and applied "purposively".

A Court requiring a "homosexual relationship" to be read into the provisions of the Constitution and or the Immigration Act would itself amount to a breach of the tenet of construction that a constitution must be interpreted "purposively".

In the light of the provisions of the Namibian Constitution and decisions of the Courts, I do not regard it as justified for a Namibian Court to effectively take over Parliament's function in this respect, by ordering a law of Parliament to be regarded as amended, by adding to the word "spouse" in section 26(3)(g) of the Namibian Immigration Control Act - the words : "or partner in a permanent same sex life partnership".

Counsel for the respondents has also referred to various other decisions and practices in other countries. I do not find it necessary, in the light of this already extensive judgment, to deal with all those decisions and practices. I must however point out, that even if I came to a different conclusion, it would nevertheless not have been justified to make an order as in the South African decision in *National Coalition for Lesbian Equality & An. v Minister of Justice and An.*, because no minister has been cited in the case before us. This is a typical case of non-joinder, where a necessary party has not been joined.

I must emphasize in conclusion: Nothing in this judgment justifies discrimination against homosexuals as individuals, or deprives them of the protection of other provisions of the Namibian Constitution. What I dealt with in this judgment is the alleged infringements of the Namibian Constitution in that section 26(3)(g) of the Namibian Immigration Control Act does not provide for homosexual partners on a basis equal to that of the spouses in recognised heterosexual marital relationships and the alleged failure of the Board to regard the applicants' lesbian relationship as a factor strengthening the first applicant's application for permanent residence.

In view of the fact that appellant Board denied that it had discriminated against the respondents on moral grounds and the respondents had failed to make out a case that they had been discriminated against on moral grounds, applicant Frank's application should continue to be considered on its own merits, and as the application of an unmarried alien who is not a spouse for the purpose of section 26(3)(g) of the Namibian Immigration Control. However, the appellant Board may, in the exercise of its wide discretion consider the special relationship between respondents and decide whether or not to regard it as a factor in favour of granting the application for permanent residence.

Whether or not an amendment shall be made to section 26(3)(g) to add the words "or partner in a permanent same-sex life partnership", is in my view a matter best left to the Namibian Parliament.

I believe that Parliament has the right to decide, in accordance with the letter and spirit of the Namibian Constitution, on the legislation required for the admission of aliens to citizenship and/or residence and or employment in Namibia.

It is also the right and responsibility of Parliament to provide in legislation which classes or categories of persons should be given special dispensation and which not. In this function Parliament is entitled *inter alia,* to consider and give effect to the traditions, norms, values and expectations of the Namibian people, provided it does so in accordance with the letter and spirit of the Namibian Constitution.

For the foregoing reasons, the issue of the respondents' lesbian relationship, does not alter my view that the order of the Court *a quo* should be set aside.

I must reiterate in conclusion that, in my respectful view, this Court should not allow a judgment or order of a lower Court to stand when it is patently wrong, even if the gross negligence of the appellant's attorney, caused substantial delay in reaching finality.

In the result the following order should be made:

1. Appellant's application for condonation for the late submission of the appeal record, is granted.
2. The appeal is upheld and the order of the High Court dated 24 June 1999 is set aside.
3. The decision of the Immigration Control Board to refuse a permanent residence permit to first respondent Frank, is set aside and the issue is referred back to the Board to reconsider and decide after complying with the *audi alteram partem* rule.
   3.1 The first respondent is allowed 30 days from the issue of this order to make written representations to the Board in regard to the issues raised by the Board in paragraphs 10 and 12 of the opposing affidavit of Mr Simenda.
   3.2 The said Board must thereafter within 30 days reconsider the aforesaid representations if any, apply the guidelines set out in this judgment and decide afresh whether or not to grant the permanent residence permit to applicant Frank.
4. As a mark of disapproval of the extremely negligent conduct of the attorney of the appellant Board, and the misrepresentation made to the Court by the chairman of the appellant Board, the Court makes no order as to costs.

(signed) O'LINN, A.J.A.

I agree.

(signed) TEEK, A.J.A.

ANNEXURE III

SELECTED CASES

CASE NO.: SA 5/2001

IN THE SUPREME COURT OF NAMIBIA

In the matter between:

THE GOVERNMENT OF THE **APPELLANT**

REPUBLIC OF NAMIBIA

And

NGEVE RAPHAEL SIKUNDA **RESPONDENT**

CORAM: Strydom, C.J.; O'Linn, A.J.A. ***et*** **Chomba, A.J.A.**

HEARD ON: 03/10/2001

DELIVERED ON: 21/02/2002

APPEAL JUDGMENT

O'LINN, A.J.A.:

SECTION A:

INTRODUCTION

This is an appeal by the Government of the Republic of Namibia against the whole of a judgment by a full bench of the High Court of Namibia (Mainga and Hoff, J.J.) in which the said High Court made the following order on an application by one Ngeve Raphael Sikunda:

"1. The decision of the Minister of Home Affairs dated 16 October 2000 ordering the removal of José Domingo Sikunda from Namibia and declaring the aforementioned person *persona non grata* is set aside.

2. The Respondent's Minister of Home Affairs and/or his officials are restrained from unlawfully detaining and harassing José Domingo Sikunda.

3. The Minister of Home Affairs is ordered to pay costs of this application on an attorney and own client scale.

4. The release of José Domingo Sikunda has been complied with and that part of the *rule nisi* is discharged."

The applicant in the Court *a quo* is now the respondent in this appeal and the respondent in the Court *a quo* is now the appellant in this appeal. This is confusing. I will consequently hereinafter refer to the parties as they were referred to in the Court *a quo.* The applicant's father will be referred to as "Sikunda Snr". Adv Smuts, assisted by Adv Cohrssen, appeared for the applicant in the Court *a quo* in arguing the main application as well as the application in the Contempt of Court proceedings whereas Frank, S.C., argued the case for the Government.

In this appeal, Smuts, assisted by Cohrssen, continued to appear for the applicant, whilst Adv Maleka, appeared for the Government.

The applicant, Ngeve Raphael Sikunda, the son of José Domingo Sikunda, brought an urgent application on motion before Manyarara, A.J., on 24TH October 2000 for the release of Sikunda Snr, from detention, the setting aside of the Minister's order for his removal from Namibia and certain ancillary relief.

The Minister's order for detention and removal from Namibia of Sikunda Snr, was purportedly made in terms of section 49(1) of the Immigration Control Act No. 7 of 1993.

After hearing argument from Mr Cohrssen for applicant and Mr Asino for the respondent, Manyarara, A.J., issued the following order:

"It is ordered

1. That applicant's non-compliance with the provisions of rule 6(12) of the rules of this Honourable Court is condoned and leave is granted to the applicant to bring this application on an urgent basis.
2. That a *rule nisi* do hereby issue calling upon the Respondent to show cause, if any, to this Court of Friday 10 November 2000 at 10h00 why:
   2.1 The decision of the Minister of Home Affairs dated 16 October 2000 ordering the removal of José Domingo Sikunda from Namibia and declaring the aforementioned person *persona non grata* should not be set aside.
   2.2 The person of José Domingo Sikunda shall not be immediately released from custody pending the final determination of this application.
   2.3 The respondent Minister of Home Affairs and or his officials should not be restrained from unlawfully detaining and harassing José Domingo Sikunda further.
   2.4 The Minister of Home Affairs, the Honourable Mr Jerry Ekandjo, shall not be ordered to pay the costs of this application *de bonis propriis*, alternatively pays the costs of this application on an attorney and own client scale.
3. That prayers 2.1 to 2.3 above shall operate as an interim interdict."

The interim interdict consisted of three parts, being firstly the setting aside of the order of removal of Sikunda, Snr, from Namibia, and declaring him *persona non grata*, secondly that Sikunda, Snr, be immediately released from custody and thirdly that the Minister of Home Affairs and his officials are restrained from unlawfully detaining and harassing Sikunda further.

The first and third parts of the interim interdict were prohibitory or restrictive in nature in that it ordered the respondent to refrain from doing something, whereas the second part constituted a mandatory injunction, in that it ordered the respondent to do something.

Although, Mr Asino from the Office of the Government Attorney appeared in Court when the interim order was heard and granted and addressed the Court, he appeared in response to a written notice of set down and a telephone message from applicant's attorneys of the intended application to the Court later that afternoon. When Mr Asino appeared in Court, the written application had not yet been served on the respondent. The application in writing was only served on the office of the Minister of Home Affairs, together with the interim order on the 25th of October at 13h50, the day after the application was already heard and the aforesaid order issued during the evening of the previous day, i.e. on the 24th of October 2000.

The record of the proceedings relating to the granting of the *rule nisi* and that relating to the respondent's attempt to anticipate the return date of the *rule nisi*, was however placed before this Court by consent.

It appears from the record of the granting of the *rule nisi,* that the respondent had no reasonable opportunity to be heard before the granting of the *rule nisi*. That in itself creates no problem when a *rule nisi* is applied for in an urgent application, but may become problematical when an interim interdict is granted in the nature of a mandamus (i.e. an order or writ issued by a Court commanding that an act be performed), without a reasonable opportunity for a respondent to put his or her or its case. This caution should receive even greater attention when security interests of the country is a relevant issue in the case.

Particularly worrying is the fact that when the learned presiding judge asked Mr Asino whether he had any objection to the Court hearing the argument of Mr Cohrssen, Mr Asino replied "Yes, indeed."

This was apparently misunderstood by the presiding judge or alternatively brushed aside. The Court then forthwith allowed Mr Cohrssen to argue his case. Mr Cohrssen presumed that this meant that the Court had now condoned the applicant's non-compliance with the rules. He proceeded with his argument on the merits. When he had concluded his argument, Mr Asino told the Court that he first wanted to address the Court on the question of urgency. Mr Asino indicated that he first wished to see the "papers" and "see why they say that the matter is so urgent". Mr Asino was then asked whether he "would like five, ten or fifteen minutes" and Mr Asino said: "Fifteen minutes would be safe". After the adjournment Asino said: "Your Lordship, I have just managed to peruse at the document or the affidavit of the applicant although it is very difficult for me to just jump in and to, I will try my best".

Mr Asino then dealt with the question of urgency as well as the merits as best he could.

In the course of the argument Mr Asino also agreed to an interim interdict incorporating an undertaking by the Minister, that the detainee would not be removed to Angola pending the return date of the *rule nisi.* Mr Asino however, argued that the Court should not order the detainee's release in the interim.

Mr Cohrssen however, refused to consent to such an order and insisted on an interim interdict including an order for the immediate release of the detainee. Mr Asino in turn, was unable to agree to this.

The Court then confirmed to the respondent in the clearest terms that the Government has the remedy to anticipate the return date on 24 hours notice.

Mr Asino once again stated that he has no objection to an interim interdict interdicting the respondent from removing the detainee in the interim.

The Court nevertheless granted the order as drafted by the legal representatives of the applicant. It is clear that when the Court granted the order as prayed, it did so assuming that the respondent would have the right to anticipate the return date on 24 hours notice and granted the order after having given the assurance to respondent's attorney in Court, without any indication by Mr Cohrssen that respondent would not be so entitled.

It can consequently be reliably inferred that the learned presiding judge would probably not have issued the mandatory injunction, if he did not proceed on the aforesaid assumption and assurance to respondent.

As will be seen later, however, when the respondent attempted to anticipate the return day, Mr Smuts who now strengthened the applicant's legal team, argued before Levy, A.J., that respondent was not entitled to do so, because Mr Asino on its behalf had appeared in Court for respondent when the applicant's application for a *rule nisi* and certain interim relief was heard. The crisp point argued by Mr Smuts was that the respondent could not anticipate the return date, because the rule only allows such a proceeding when the original relief was granted *ex parte* and the appearance of Mr Asino for the Government in Court, meant that the order granted was not granted *"ex parte"*.

I do not think that this is the correct approach. The rule aforesaid regarding anticipation of the return date was intended to avoid and/or mitigate the prejudice to a litigant who is faced with an interim order, which may be in the form of an interim interdict, even in the form of a mandatory injunction as in this case, without having had a reasonable hearing. To give the attorney for such litigant telephonic advance notice of an urgent application an hour or two later, without the application being properly served on the respondent and then expecting the respondent and/or his attorney to make a proper and sufficient response, is an abrogation of the *audi alteram partem* principle, which in my view, underlies Rule 6(8) of the Rules of the High Court and which principle has been described by the Appellate Division of the South African Supreme Court as "sacred"[528].

[528] See: The Law & Practice of Interdicts by Prest 223 and the cases there quoted. See also: Von Moltke v Costa Areaso Pty Ltd, 1975 (1) SA 255 (c) at 257A.

The applicant's counsel indicated that applicant's application was in essence a "*habeas corpus*" application. But even in such an application, the respondent is called upon not only to produce the person detained, but to show cause why he or she should not be released. (My emphasis added.)

This is an important remedy for persons illegally deprived of their freedom. But part of it is the opportunity for the person called upon, to show cause. The problem the Minister and the Chief of Police had in releasing the detainee without a proper opportunity to state their case, was that the released detainee could abscond or flee and so irreparably frustrate the proper finalization of the proceedings and even prejudice State security as seen by the respondent.

Although no fault can be found with the *rule nisi* and the interim interdict prohibiting the removal of the detainee to Angola, the granting of the mandatory injunction for the immediate release of Sikunda, should in the circumstances, not have been granted without first having given the respondent a fair opportunity to reply. This could have been done by allowing the respondent 1 – 3 days to prepare a replying affidavit and proper argument after service of the application on it, before deciding on the aforesaid mandatory injunction.

In this manner, the interests of justice would have been better served by balancing the fundamental rights and freedoms of Sikunda, Snr, with the security interests of the State as represented by the Minister of Home Affairs and Chief of Police.

I mention this because the conduct of the respondent, as will be seen later, is used by the applicant to justify a punitive cost order against the Government not only in the Court *a quo*, but also in regard to the appeal proceedings. That being so, the Minister's conduct must be seen in context and perspective.

Furthermore it is opportune and even necessary to emphasize that the granting of an interdict in the form of a mandatory injunction without a fair hearing to the party against whom it is issued, is not a proper judicial practice and may cause unnecessary tension between the Courts and those institutions and members of the public who find themselves at the receiving end of such orders in a particular case. Courts should approach such applications with greater circumspection, particularly in those cases where the respondent government claims that the security interests of the State are at stake.

The application for committal of the Minister for Contempt of Court was decided prior to argument and decision on whether or not the *rule nisi* in the main application should be confirmed. The Minister was convicted of Contempt of Court at the hearing of the Contempt of Court proceedings and reprimanded. The Contempt of Court proceedings were not placed before this Court and have only been referred to in regard to the application for a special costs order in this appeal. It is however, not necessary to refer to the Contempt proceedings in any detail because the order in that proceeding is not on appeal and only the fact of the conviction and the reason for it is of some relevance.

The Government Attorney gave notice already on 26th October, i.e. the day after the granting of the aforesaid *rule nisi*, interdict and mandamus, of an application to anticipate the return day of the *rule nisi* from 10th November to the 31st of October.

However, by the time respondent's legal representatives appeared in Court on 31st October, the applicant's counsel applied for the setting aside of respondent's notice to anticipate. By then the applicant's legal representatives had also launched an application for the committal of the Minister and/or the Inspector-General of the Namibian Police for Contempt of Court for not having released the detainee Sikunda to date.

During argument, before Levy, A.J., Mr Smuts contended that the notice was irregular in that the original application was not "*ex parte*" because Mr Asino was in Court. Mr Frank, for respondent, did not agree with this argument but agreed that the matter should be heard on the original return date of the *rule nisi*. Levy, A.J., indicated that he also had difficulty with the argument of Smuts. The learned Judge also raised the issue of the release of a detained person in the position of Sikunda without having given the Minister an opportunity to be heard in the matter.

Levy, A.J., eventually ordered the respondent's notice for the anticipation of the return date to be set aside, but on the basis that both parties had now agreed in Court that the original return date of the 10th November should remain the return date of the *rule nisi*.

Levy, however, also ordered that "respondent permits access to José Domingo Sikunda by his legal representatives and if necessary to transport him to Windhoek for the purpose of preparing and filing affidavits". This part of the order appears to be inconsistent with the mandamus granted on 24th October by Manyarara, A.J., that Sikunda should be immediately released from detention. It is difficult to reconcile the order of the 31st with the order of the 24th in this regard. It could even be argued that the order of the 31st by implication set aside the order of the 24th in so far as the order of the 24th ordered the immediate release of Sikunda Snr. Levy, A.J., however confirmed another part of the order of the 24th October, by ordering that the respondent "refrains from deporting the said José Domingo Sikunda to any place whatsoever until this matter is finally adjudicated upon, which shall include final adjudication on appeal".

The Minister of Home Affairs only released Sikunda Snr, on 9th February 2001. The matter was not heard on the return date on 10th November but after several postponements and extensions of the return date, only heard on 16 February 2001.

Mainga, J., who wrote the judgment in the Court *a quo*, on the main application, first set out the background facts before dealing with the merits. It is convenient to repeat those facts for the purpose of this appeal as contained in the aforesaid judgment:

> **"The background.**
>
> **On 19 September 2000, the Minister of Home Affairs addressed a letter, bearing the Minister's date stamp of 20 September 2000 to the chairperson of the Security**

Commission, Mr Ithana and apparently another letter on 14 September 2000 which letter was not filed with the documents before us. The letter of the 19th September 2000 reads as follows:

'Dear Mr Ithana

SUBJECT REMOVAL OF FOREIGN NATIONAL CONSIDERED SECURITY THREAT TO THE REPUBLIC OF NAMIBIA

1. I have the pleasure of bringing to your attention the above stated subject matter.
2. Our security forces have identified a number of UNITA activists, sympathisers and soldiers as well as foreign nationals from Rwanda and Burundi who are considered to be a security threat to the Republic of Namibia. These foreign nationals are involved in terrorist activities in Namibia, furthering the interests of UNITA and that of their respective countries to the detriment of Namibia. According to our records, none of them hold refugee status but have different status to stay in Namibia. There are also those recorded to be illegally in Namibia.
3. As their presence endangers the security of the State, I implore the Security Commission to recommend to me to declare them *persona non grata* and their removal from the Republic of Namibia.
4. This is to be carried out in terms of Section 49(1) of the Immigration Control Act of 1993, Act No. 7 of 1993 which states:

"Notwithstanding anything to the contrary in this Act or any other law contained, the Minister may, on the recommendation of the Security Commission established under Articles 114 of the Namibian Constitution, forthwith remove or cause to be removed from Namibia by warrant issued under his or her hand any person who enters or has entered or is found in Namibia and whose activities endanger or are calculated to endanger the security of the State, whether or not such person is a prohibited immigrant in respect of Namibia.

(2) An immigration officer may:
(a) if a person referred to in subsection (1) is not in custody, arrest such person or cause him or her to be arrested without a warrant, and
(b) pending his or her removal from Namibia under that subsection, detain such person in the manner and at the place determined by the Minister.
(3) No appeal shall lie against any decision of the Minister under subsection (1)."

5. Furthermore, Namibia being a member state of the UN Security Council and committed to making sure that the UN Security Council Resolutions 1127 (1997) 1135 (1997) imposing sanctions on UNITA are observed, should not be seen to be accommodating elements who are furthering the cause of UNITA and other clandestine organizations in violation of UN Security Council Resolutions as mentioned above. The UN Security Council further requests Member States to take action on the said resolution.
6. In addition the Government of the Republic of Angola has circulated information on 21 October 1997 at the United Nations providing the names of countries hosting UNITA representatives, Namibia included.

7. It is against this background that I am requesting you to call a meeting of the Security Commission to recommend the removal of persons as listed in Annexure "A".
8. I wish to take this opportunity to thank you in anticipation for your usual co-operation and prompt response.

Yours sincerely

Jerry Ekandjo, MP

Minister.'

The four-member Security Commission in its letter titled 'secret' dated 3 October 2000 responded positively in the following terms:

'SECRET

DECISION OF THE SECURITY COMMISSION

ORIGIN: THE HON. MINISTER OF HOME AFFAIRS

SUBJECT: REMOVAL OF FOREIGN NATIONALS CONSIDERED SECURITY THREAT TO THE REPUBLIC OF NAMIBIA

DECISION: The Security Commission at its Second Meeting held on October 3, 2000, deliberated on the two correspondence from the Honourable Minister of Home Affairs dated 14th and 19th September 2000, in which the Hon. Minister requested the Security Commission to recommend the removal of 98 foreign nationals who are considered security threat to the Republic of Namibia.

The Security Commission recommends in terms of Section 49(1) of the Immigration Control Act, 1993 (Act No. 7 of 1993), that these foreign nationals be removed from Namibia on the grounds that they are considered security threat to the Republic of Namibia.

The initialized list containing names of the implicated foreign nationals are attached.'

On 10 October 2000, the Minister of Home Affairs addressed a letter, bearing the Minister's date stamp of 16 October 2000, to the father of the applicant, José Domingo Sikunda, which reads as follows:

> **'10 October 2000**
>
> **Mr Josef Domingos Sikunda**
>
> **Rundu**
>
> **Dear Mr Josef**
>
> **RE: REMOVAL FROM THE REPUBLIC OF NAMIBIA: YOURSELF**
>
> 1. **It has been established that your activities and presence in the Republic of Namibia endanger the security of the State.**
> 2. **Therefore, in terms of powers vested in me under Part VI; Section 49(1) of the Immigration Control Act (Act 7 of 1993) and on the recommendation of the Security Commission established in terms of Art. 114 of the Namibian**

Constitution, I order your removal from the Republic of Namibia and henceforth declare you a prohibited immigrant (*Persona Non-Grata*) in respect of the Republic of Namibia.

3. **Your attention is further drawn to section 49(2) and (b) of the same Act.**
4. **I count on your co-operation.'**

On 16 October 2000 a warrant of detention bearing the head letter of the Minister of Home Affairs and the date stamp of 24 October 2000 of the Inspector General was issued.

'WARRANT OF DETENTION

(SECTION 42)

TO:	The Officer in Charge	The Chief of
	(1) Police	Immigration

Whereas the person named hereunder

SURNAME : SIKUNDA

FIRST NAMES : JOE DOMINGO

AGE : 62 YEARS

has been found in Namibia and is suspected on reasonable grounds to be a prohibited/illegal immigrant in terms of this Act:

> **NOW THEREFORE, you are under the provisions of Section 42(1)(a)(b) requested to receive and detain such person in the prison cell/police cell [pending investigations] [for the period of 14 days] for which this shall be your warrant.'**

I should mention from the documents filed, the applicant states that his father was removed on 17 October 2000 from his home in Rundu. That assertion should be correct as it is not disputed. That will mean the applicant's father was arrested and detained before a warrant of detention was issued as it bears the dates of 18 October 2000 of the issuing officer and that of the Inspector-General dated 24 October 2000. Nevertheless Sikunda Snr was detained until his release on 9 February 2001.

On 7 October 2000, the Minister of Home Affairs addressed a letter, carrying a date stamp of 24 October 2000, to the Snr Liaison Officer at the United Nations High Commission for Refugees in Windhoek requesting that office to settle elsewhere, other than Namibia persons declared *persona non grata* by the Government of the Republic of Namibia. In this letter he categorised such persons in two groups. The first group on the list marked "A" were eighty (80) foreign nationals arrested as soldiers of UNITA involved in subversive and terrorist activities in Namibia and that these eighty (80) persons have so confessed.

The second group, in which José Domingo Sikunda is listed as number 11 the Minister in his own words described that group as follows:

'The second category, Annexure "B", is UNITA activists, sympathizers and soldiers as well as foreign nationals from Angola, Rwanda and Burundi who are considered to be a security threat to the Republic of Namibia. These foreign nationals are involved in terrorist activities in Namibia, furthering the interests of UNITA and that of their respective countries to the detriment of Namibia. According to our records, none of them hold a refugee status but have different status to stay in Namibia. There are also those recorded to be illegally in Namibia.'

He quoted the provisions of Section 49(1) of the Immigration Control Act, 1993 (Act 7 of 1993) in its entirety and continued in paragraph 4 and 5 of his letter to state as follows:

'Furthermore, Namibia being a Member State of the UN Security Council and committed to making sure that the UN Security Council resolutions 1127 (1997) 1135 (1997) imposing sanctions on UNITA are observed, should not be seen to be accommodating elements who are furthering the cause of UNITA and other clandestine organizations in violation of UN Security Council Resolutions as mentioned above. The UN Security Council further requests Member States to take action on the said resolution.

In addition the Government of the Republic of Angola has circulated information on the 21 October 1997 at the United Nations providing the names of countries hosting UNITA representatives, Namibia included.'"

SECTION B: THE MERITS

The Court *a quo* identified the following three issues in its judgment namely:

"1. Whether José Domingo Sikunda is a citizen and/or domiciled in Namibia;

2. Whether the decision of the Minister to declare Sikunda *persona non grata* without affording him an opportunity to make representation, is valid;

3. Whether the four member Security Commission was properly constituted."

The Court pointed out that if the Court finds that Sikunda Snr was a citizen of, or domiciled in Namibia, the Minister could not act in terms of section 49(1) of the Immigration Control Act of 1993 (Act 7 of 1993).

The Court furthermore stated that the parties are *ad idem* on this point. On appeal before us, Mr Maleka could not and did not deny that counsel for the respondent had made that concession when the matter was argued in the Court *a quo* but now tried to withdraw that concession made by Frank, S.C., on behalf of respondent.

Notwithstanding the view that a finding that Sikunda Snr was either a citizen of or domiciled in Namibia, would make the Minister's order invalid, and obviously be fatal to the Government's case, the Court chose not to decide the issue of citizenship and/or domicile.

The Court explained its approach as follows:

"The rule can be confirmed or discharged on the single question of whether the decision taken by the respondent pursuant to section 49 is consistent with the

> **principle of natural justice and in particular of the respondent's failure and/or the Security Commission to afford the applicant's father the right to be heard as it is embodied in the** *maxim audi alteram partem***."**

This approach notwithstanding, the Court went on to also decide the issue whether or not the Security Commission was properly constituted when it made its recommendation to remove from Namibia 89 alleged foreign nationals, including Sikunda Snr and following from this, whether its recommendation was nevertheless valid and met the requirements of section 49(1) for a valid decision by the Minister.

All three of the aforesaid issues were fully argued by counsel in the Court *a quo* as well as in this Court on appeal.

The first issue, namely domicile and/or citizenship and the legal implications thereof on the Minister's power to issue an order as he had done purportedly in terms of section 49(1), would not only be decisive of the question whether or not the Minister's present order is invalid and a nullity, but whether or not the Minister would be empowered in future to make a similar order against Sikunda Snr

In the case of the second and third issues however, a decision in favour of the applicant and against the respondent would result in the setting aside of the Minister's order in the present case, but would not prevent the Minister from making a similar order in future, if a constitutionally fair procedure is followed and if the Security Commission is properly constituted.

1. THE ISSUE WHETHER OR NOT JOSé DOMINGO SIKUNDA IS A CITIZEN OF AND/OR DOMICILED IN NAMIBIA AND IF SO, WHETHER THE MINISTER IS EMPOWERED AGAINST HIM IN TERMS OF SECTION 49(1) OF THE IMMIGRATION CONTROL ACT

    1.1 The first leg of the enquiry is whether or not the Minister is legally empowered to act against a person in terms of section 49(1), if that person is either a Namibian citizen, or domiciled in Namibia.

    As I have already indicated *supra*, counsel for both parties in the Court *a quo* agreed that the powers given to the Minister under section 49(1) could not legally be used against a Namibian citizen or a person legally domiciled in Namibia.

    Mr Maleka on appeal, sought to distance himself from the concession made by his predecessor Frank, S.C., in the Court *a quo*. Mr Smuts and Mr Cohrssen, for applicant, persisted in their original argument in the Court *a quo*.

    Mr Maleka now argued that the issue of citizenship and/or domicile is misconceived, because "the provisions of section 49(1) of the Act override anything to the contrary contained in the Act or any other law, for that matter, the overriding effect of the provisions of section 49(1) is fortified by the opening words of that section".

    It seems that this was also the approach of the Honourable Minister as well as that of the Security Commission. I have no doubt whatsoever that Mr

Maleka's argument in this regard is without any substance whatsoever. It is best to begin by quoting section 49(1) in full:

> "**Notwithstanding anything to the contrary in this Act or any other law contained, the Minister may, on the recommendation of the Security Commission established under Art. 114 of the Namibian Constitution, forthwith remove or cause to be removed from Namibia by warrant issued under his or her hand any person who enters or has entered or is found in Namibia and whose activities endanger or are calculated to endanger the security of the State, whether or not such person is a prohibited immigrant in respect of Namibia."**
> **(My emphasis added.)**

Section 2 of the said Act deals with the applicability of certain parts of the Act to certain persons and situations. In the margin opposite section 2 the following words appear: "Application of Act".

The relevant part of section 2(1) then reads:

"Subject to the provisions of subsection (2), the provisions of PART V, except sections 30, 31 and 32 thereof, and Part VI of this Act shall not apply to –

(a) a Namibian citizen;

(b) any person domiciled in Namibia who is not a person referred to in para (a) or (f) of section 39(2) ..."

(My emphasis added.)

Section 49(1) is contained in PART VI of the Act which contains sections 39 – 52 under the heading:

"PROHIBITED IMMIGRANTS – ARREST DETENTION AND REMOVAL OF PROHIBITED IMMIGRANTS"

No provision of Chapter VI is consequently applicable to the persons dealt with in subsection (1) which include citizens and persons domiciled in Namibia, except as provided in subsection (2) of section 2.

Subsection (2) applies to "any person appearing before an immigration officer at any port of entry with the intention to enter and remain in Namibia unless such person satisfied such immigration officer that he or she is a person referred to in that subsection."

Sikunda Snr is not a person as described in subsection (2). Consequently it does not affect the provisions of subsection (1) in so far as it related to Sikunda Snr.

Section 49(1) vests draconian powers in the Minister. It is obvious that it was never intended to apply to a citizen of Namibia because it would remove with a stroke of the pen all the rights and freedoms to which any person, is entitled to in terms of the Namibian Constitution. To remove a citizen in accordance with section 49(1) would also be an absurdity because such citizen would not be entitled to stay in any other country except if he is granted political asylum. If the Legislature really intended by enacting section 49(1) to grant such powers to a Minister in regard to citizens, such provision would certainly be unconstitutional and null and void.

Although a person domiciled in Namibia is not for all purposes in Namibian law in as strong a position as a citizen, no distinction is made between citizen and a person so domiciled in subsection (1) of section 2 of the Immigration Control Act.

I consequently find that the Minister is not empowered to act in terms of subsection (1) of section 49 of the Immigration Control Act against a Namibian citizen or a person domiciled in Namibia. Any such purported action is null and void *ab initio.*

1.2 The second leg of the enquiry is whether or not Sikunda Snr is either a citizen or a person domiciled in Namibia.

It is not necessary for the purposes of this appeal to decide whether or not Sikunda Snr is a citizen of Namibia. It seems to me however, that when an office bearer wishes to exercise a statutory jurisdiction bestowed upon him or her, the onus, or burden of proof would be on such office bearer to prove the jurisdictional fact entitling him or her to act against a particular person. In other words the office bearer must, in the case of a dispute, prove that the person against whom he acts falls within the ambit of his or her powers. Such proof need only be on a balance of probabilities. The respondent in this case tried to prove that Sikunda Snr was neither citizen nor legally domiciled in Namibia. Respondent succeeded in my view to prove on a balance of probabilities that Sikunda Snr was not a citizen of Namibia at the relevant time, i.e. when the Minister made his order, but failed to prove that he was not domiciled in Namibia at all relevant times.

Even if I am wrong in holding that there is an onus on the Minister, it seems to me that the applicant has proved on a balance of probabilities that his father was legally domiciled in Namibia at the relevant time. I say this *inter alia* for the following reasons:

(i) Domicile for the purposes of the issue before us, is the domicile as defined for the purposes of the Immigration Control Act, in the said Act itself.

It is defined in section 1 of the Act as follows:

"'Domicile' subject to the provisions of Part IV, means the place where a person has his home or permanent residence or to which such person returns as his or her permanent abode, and not merely for a special or temporary purpose."

As it stands domicile can consist of either or:

(a) the place where a person has his home; or

(b) permanent residence; or

(c) the place to which such person returns as his or her permanent abode, and not merely for a special or temporary purpose.

The above requirements are qualified in PART IV of the Act, which provides that

"(1) No person shall have a domicile in Namibia unless such person-

(a) is a Namibian citizen;

(b) is entitled to reside in Namibia and so resides therein, whether before or after the commencement of this Act, in terms of the provisions of section 7(2)(a) of the Namibian Citizenship Act, 1990 (Act 14 of 1990);

(c) is ordinarily resident in Namibia, whether before or after the commencement of this Act, by virtue of a marriage entered into with a person referred to in paragraph (a) in good faith as contemplated in Art. 4(3) of the Namibian Constitution;

(d) in the case of any other person, he or she is lawfully resident in Namibia, whether before or after the commencement of this Act, and is so resident in Namibia, for a continuous period of two years.

(2) For the purposes of the computation of any period of residence referred to in subsection (1)(d), no period during which any person -

(a) is or was confined in a prison, reformatory or mental institution or other place of detention established by or under any law;

(b) resided in Namibia only by virtue of a right obtained in terms of a provisional permit issued under section 11 or an employment permit issued under section 27 or a student's permit issued under section 28 or a visitor's entry permit issued under section 29;

(c) involuntarily resided or remained in Namibia;

(d) has entered or resided in Namibia through error, oversight, misrepresentation or in contravention of the provisions of this Act or any other law; or

(e) resided in Namibia in accordance with the provisions of paragraph (d), (e), (f) or (g) of section 2(1), shall be regarded as a period of residence in Namibia."

In view of the exclusion of citizenship for the purposes of argument, the only requirement in subsection (1) of section 22 under which Sikunda Snr can qualify is the provisions of subparagraph (d) of subsection (1), read with the definition of "domicile" in section 1.

Sikunda Snr was thus not prevented from acquiring a domicile in Namibia as defined in section 1 of the Act quoted *supra,* if "he ... is lawfully resident in Namibia, whether before or after the commencement of this Act, and is so resident in Namibia, for a continuous period of two years".

None of the qualifications for such period of residence stated in subsection (2) of section 22 is applicable to Sikunda Snr.

(ii) It is common cause between the parties, also conceded by respondent's counsel on appeal, that Sikunda Snr was at the relevant time legally resident in Namibia for a continuous period of at least two years before or after the Immigration Act entering into force.

(iii) That being so, all that remains is to enquire whether or not he was domiciled in Namibia in accordance with the elements of the definition of domicile set out *supra*, i.e. whether or not he had his home or permanent residence in Namibia or whether that is the place to which he returns as his or her permanent abode and not merely for a special or temporary purpose.

In this regard the following facts listed by applicant's counsel in the heads of argument as common cause or not in dispute, supports the above conclusion:

(a) Sikunda Snr is not a prohibited immigrant and was not a prohibited immigrant at the time of the Minister's order or thereafter in terms of section 39(2)(a) and (f) of the Immigration Control Act.

(b) He has been continuously resident in Namibia since 1976 and has the fixed intention to remain permanently in Namibia in future.

(c) He has family roots in Namibia, as is evident by the fact that three of his children were born in Namibia.

(d) He occupies property on a long-term basis and has business interests in Rundu.

(e) Upon arrival of his family and himself in Namibia in 1976, he requested and applied for citizenship, whereafter the South West Africa Identity document was issued to him.

(f) In 1986 he was issued with an exemption certificate, exempting him from other provisions relating to permanent residence.

Mr Maleka however, argued that this "exemption permit was issued in terms of section 7 *bis* of the Aliens Act and was thus deemed to be a temporary permit in terms of section 5 of the Act.".

This cannot be correct. It is common cause that the said certificate issued in 1986 clearly states in its heading that it exempts its holder from the provisions of section 2 of the Aliens Act No. 1 of 1937.

The said section 2 placed a number of restrictions on aliens: The exemption clearly meant that these restrictions do not apply to the holder.

Counsel for the applicant contends that it must have been issued under sections 12(1) of the Aliens Act which exempted a person who has lawfully acquired domicile in South West Africa from the restrictions of section 2. It also purports to recognise that the holder has lawfully acquired domicile in South West Africa. It could however also have been issued under section 7 *bis* which also provides for the granting of "Exemptions from the provisions of the Act".

Be that as it may, the exemption certificate proves at least legal residence and is also a strong indicator of the recognition by the authorities that Sikunda Snr was regarded as being lawfully domiciled in South West Africa at the time.

The said exemption did not lose its meaning and effect when the new Immigration Control Act was enacted in 1993.

Section 60(3) of the 1993 Act provides *inter alia* that any exemption under a law repealed, "shall be deemed to have been made, granted, issued, given or done under the corresponding or allied provision of this Act".

Section 35 of the Immigration Control Act in turn provides for exemptions to any person or category of persons from provisions of the Act.

> The exemption given to Sikunda in 1986 consequently remains valid in accordance with section 35 of the present Act, read with section 60(3).

In conclusion on this issue I hold that the Government had failed to prove that Sikunda Snr was not legally domiciled in Namibia. Alternatively, that the applicant has proved that Sikunda Snr was legally domiciled in Namibia at all relevant times and that as a consequence, the Honourable Minister of Home Affairs had no legal jurisdiction to act against Sikunda Snr in terms of section 49(2). As a further consequence, the order for the detention and removal of Sikunda Snr was void *ab initio*.

It follows that the appeal by the Government must fail on this ground alone.

There are however, at least two reasons why the remaining issues should be dealt with however, briefly. These are: Counsel for applicant have asked not only for confirmation on appeal of the special cost order granted by the Court *a quo*, but also for a further special cost order in regard to the appeal proceedings. In support of this submission, counsel has argued that "the Procedures were extensively and fundamentally tainted by illegality and manifold irregularities, compounded by the flagrant Contempt of Court for failing to release respondent's father after the High Court of Namibia had ordered his release". The second reason is that the issue in question will probably arise frequently in future and some guidance by the Supreme Court on the main issues argued before it as well as in the Court *a quo*, is appropriate and justified in the circumstances.

2. <u>THE ISSUE WHETHER OR NOT THE SECURITY COMMISSION WAS PROPERLY CONSTITUTED WHEN IT MADE ITS RECOMMENDATION AND IF NOT – HOW DOES THAT AFFECT THE LEGALITY OF THE MINISTER'S DECISION</u>

The Minister's power to "forthwith remove or cause to be removed from Namibia by warrant under his hand any person, who enters or has entered or is found in Namibia and whose activities endanger or are calculated to endanger the Security of the State, whether or not such person is a prohibited immigrant in respect of Namibia", is subject to the recommendation of the Security Commission. Without a positive recommendation of the Security Commission in the particular instance, the Minister's purported exercise of his power would be invalid and null and void. To put it another way: The aforesaid positive recommendation is a jurisdictional requirement, without which, the Minister has no jurisdiction to act and the purported exercise of his power would be null and void, *ab initio*, i.e. without any legal force and effect from the beginning.

It is obvious that the onus, i.e. the burden of proof will, in the case of dispute, be on the Minister to establish that he in fact acted on such a valid recommendation by the Security Commission.

The Court *a quo*, in its well-reasoned judgment, found that the Security Commission was not properly constituted at the time, because there were only 4 (four) members instead of six when it took the decision to make the recommendation and when it in fact made the recommendation. Consequently it found that the decision of the Minister was also invalid on this ground.

This finding was attacked by Mr Maleka on appeal on several grounds, being:

(i) At issue was whether or not the Security Commission which made the decision was properly constituted. However, the Court below found that "There was no Security Commission in existence at the time ... the Commission made the recommendation".

What the Court *a quo* probably meant was that at the time of the decision to recommend, the Commission was not properly constituted. Whether or not that means that the Commission "was not in existence" at the time does not take the matter any further and is not necessary to decide.

I must point out however: This is not a case where the Tribunal was properly composed, but some members were merely absent. The present case is worse. The Commission was no longer properly constituted, and this situation continued for a considerable period.

It is obvious that the Commission could not come into existence, unless (six) 6 members were appointed, because in such a case the tribunal lacked the essentials for its coming into existence. Similarly, if for a considerable period, there are only four (4) members instead of six (6) because vacancies were never filled, the Commission lost the essentials for its continued legal existence.

But as I have already pointed out, it is not necessary for the purpose of this decision to decide whether or not the Commission, as contemplated by Art. 114 of the Constitution, was no longer in existence. It suffices for present purposes to decide the validity of the decision to recommend, on the ground that the Commission was not properly constituted at the time for the taking of a valid decision.

The general rule was stated by Innes, C.J., in Schierhout v Union Government[529] already in 1919. The learned Chief Justice stated:

> **"We were referred to a number of authorities in support of a principle which is clear and undisputed. When several persons are appointed to exercise judicial powers, then in the absence of provision to the contrary, they must all act together, there can only be one adjudication, and that must be the adjudication of the entire body (Billings v Prinn, 2 W. Bl., p.1017). And the same rule would apply whenever a number of individuals were empowered by Statute to deal with any matter as one body; the action taken would have to be the joint action of all of them (see Cook v Ward, 2 C.P.D. 255; Darcy v Tamar Railway Co., L.R. 3 Exch., p.158, etc.) for otherwise they would not be acting in accordance with the provisions of the Statute. It is those provisions which in each instance must be regarded; and the question here turns upon the construction of section 2(6) of Act 29, 1912."**

As the Court *a quo* correctly points out, the case of S v Naude[530], relied on by Frank, S.C., in the Court *a quo*, can clearly be distinguished from a case such as the present.

[529] 1919, AD, 33 at 44.

[530] S v Naude 1975 (1) SA 681 A.

Article 114 of the Namibian Constitution provides for the establishment of a Security Commission. The section reads:

(1) There shall be a Security Commission which shall have the function of making recommendations to the President on the appointment of the Chief of the Defence Force, the Inspector-General of Police and the Commissioner of Prisons and such other functions as may be assigned to it by Act of Parliament.

(2)(i) The Security Commission shall consist of the Chairperson of the Public Service Commission, the Chief of the Defence Force, the Inspector-General of Police, the Commissioner of Prisons and two (2) members of the National Assembly, appointed by the President on the recommendation of the National Assembly."

(ii) Mr Maleka contends that the effect of the finding is that "the provisions of section 49(1) may not be invoked or applied by the Minister against any person, because the legitimate constitutional organ established to make recommendations to the Minister was found not to exist. The whole statutory scheme of section 49(1) of the Act which is intended to protect or promote the security of the State is effectively dislocated".

This argument is indeed tenuous. The Court was only doing its duty as laid down by the constitution. If there is a "dislocation" – the blame must certainly be sought elsewhere. Mr Maleka, when questioned by the Court was unable to say why the two vacancies to be filled from members of the National Assembly, appointed by the President on the recommendation of the National Assembly, was not in fact filled after a long period of time.

(iii) Mr Maleka also took the point that the finding of the Court affected the Security Commission and that the Commission had a direct and substantial interest and thus had to be joined as a party in the proceedings before the Court *a quo*.

This point also has no substance in the circumstances of this case. The Government has been cited as the respondent. The chairman of the Commission is a witness for respondent in the proceedings. Respondent had to prove that its Minister had the necessary authority to act and that necessitated proof that the Security Commission had recommended the Minister's action.

(iv) The main contention put forward by Mr Maleka was that the Security Commission remained a Security Commission as envisaged by Art. 114 of the Constitution, even if it consisted of only four members instead of the six (6) prescribed by the Namibian Constitution. Furthermore, it was sufficient for the proper functioning of the Commission if, when it took decisions required by section 49(1) of the Immigration Control Act, it consisted of only four members or if only four members participated in the consideration and making of the recommendation. He submitted that the four members "all fall within the designated categories specified in subsection (2) of Art. 114, namely Chairperson of the Public Service Commission, the Chief of the Defence Force, the Inspector-General of the

> Police and the two members of the National Assembly, who did not fall within the designated categories. They did not therefore possess the kind of expertise or experience ordinarily expected from members falling within the designated categories. Their absence from the meeting of the Security Commission which considered and made the relevant recommendation did not deprive it of the expertise such as that falling within the designated categories".

This is a spurious argument.

I say so for the following reasons:

(a) Art. 114(2) is peremptory in so far as it prescribes the composition of the Security Commission. That it shall consist of six members as defined, is beyond any doubt.

The said article contains no exceptions or qualifications whatsoever.

(b) It takes little imagination to understand why the representatives of the Namibian people in the Constituent Assembly regarded it as necessary to include two members selected from the National Assembly, and appointed by the President on the recommendation of the National Assembly.

It is obvious that the said Constituent Assembly wanted to make the Security Commission as representative as possible and to make a wider expertise available to the Commission in executing its very onerous functions. One of the members of the Security Commission who had vacated his office was the Attorney General, whose legal expertise and independent state of mind could be of great assistance when matters of legal procedure and the protection of fundamental human rights and freedoms had to be considered. The other member was the then leader of the opposition in the National Assembly.

In view of the letter and spirit of the Namibian Constitution, security concerns have to be addressed with due regard for fundamental rights, and freedoms. The two members drawn from the National Assembly would probably also possess common sense and this would be helpful to the representatives from so-called "designated categories".

I make bold to say that if the Security Commission was composed as provided for by the Constitution, then the recommendation in question may never have been made and the Minister may never have taken the decision he took.

(c) Article 114 does not allow any Minister or other official to decide on a composition of the Security Commission as they deem fit.

(d) The Legislature enacting the Immigration Control Act did also not attempt to supplement Art. 114 of the Namibian Constitution by providing for a different composition for certain purposes. There was also no attempt to provide for a quorum of less than six in certain circumstances. There was also no need to provide for or attempt to provide for such a quorum because the so-called "members from designated categories" would always be available – because those posts would or could always be filled in due course or alternatively, may probably be substituted by their deputies, acting for them, or temporary appointments. As far as vacancies in the case of the two members of parliament are concerned – those could also always be filled without delay, provided those responsible to ensure that any vacancies are filled, do their job.

(e) The Immigration Control Act itself provides an example of the nature of the necessary provisions when the Legislature deems a quorum of less than the full complement of members, desirable or necessary. Section 43(6)(a) deals with Immigration Tribunals and provides:

"The decision of the majority of the members of the Tribunal, and in the event of an equality of votes, the Chairman shall have a casting vote in addition to his or her deliberative vote."

(f) If section 49(1) of the Immigration Control Act, read with Art. 114 of the Constitution, created some obstacles to summary and arbitrary decisions relating to the Government's security concerns, it must be kept in mind that if there really are reasonable grounds for believing that any person, even a citizen, is engaged in murder, assault, robbery, theft, terrorist activity or conspiring with the enemy to commit such act, then charges can be laid against such person or persons and the matter be resolved in Court.

I conclude therefore that the Security Commission was not properly constituted when it purported to consider the Minister's request and made its recommendation. It consequently could not make a valid decision for the purpose of section 49(1) of the Immigration Control Act. A precondition for a valid decision by the Minister was not fulfilled. The Minister consequently did not have the jurisdiction to make the order in question.

In the result the Minister's aforesaid order is void *ab initio*, i.e. of no force and effect from the beginning.

This finding is in itself fatal to the respondent's appeal.

3. THE ISSUE WHETHER THE DECISION OF THE MINISTER TO DECLARE SIKUNDA SNR, *PERSONA NON GRATA* IS VALID, NOTWITHSTANDING THE FACT THAT NEITHER THE SECURITY COMMISSION NOR THE MINISTER, HAD APPLIED THE *AUDI ALTERAM PARTEM* RULE, (I.E. THE RIGHT OF AND OPPORTUNITY TO SIKUNDA TO BE HEARD)

The Court *a quo* based its decision on this point. It found that this principle was not complied with and that the decision of the Minister must therefore be set aside.

It was common cause that neither the Commission nor the Minister had afforded Sikunda the opportunity to be heard before the decision was taken. Mr Maleka on appeal did not dispute that Sikunda Snr had the right to be heard but he made the following two basic submissions:

(i) The Security Commission need not apply the *audi alteram partem* rule because its recommendation is not a decision which has a final effect in that the Minister can accept or reject it. The decision of the Commission is therefore not reviewable.

(ii) Although the Minister is required to observe the *audi alteram partem* maxim, "the application of this maxim in the context of the provisions of section 49(1) is not absolute. This is so because the latter provisions deal with the protection or promotion of the security of the State, particularly where the removal of the targeted individual is on the ground that his activities endanger or are calculated to endanger the security of the State. In this connection it has been recognized in early and recent times that the repository of power, (the Minister *in casu*) can act on confidential information and would be entitled not to disclose such information to the affected person".

I will now deal briefly with these contentions.

Ad(i) Mr Maleka's submission that the Security Commission need not apply the maxim

I do not agree with this contention *inter alia* for the following reasons:

(a) The recommendation of the Commission is at the same time also a "decision". It is a "decision" to recommend or not to recommend. Before the Commission can make a recommendation as envisaged by section 49(1) or refuse to make such a recommendation – it in essence has to decide whether or not to make a recommendation. If I understand Mr Maleka's argument correctly, he does not contend that the Commission does not make or take a decision.

(b) Although the Minister cannot make an order against a person in terms of section 49(1) without a positive recommendation by the Commission to this effect, the Minister may decline to issue an order, against a person, notwithstanding a positive recommendation from the Commission, recommending that he acts.

In such a case, the person who was targeted by the Commission will have no right of review of the Commission's decision. However, when the Minister decides to make an order in terms of section 49(1), he can only do so if he has the prior recommendation/decision of the Security Commission. If the Minister acts on this recommendation/decision the party who is targeted by his or her decision is prejudiced, not only by the decision of the Minister, but by the preceding decision of the Commission.

In such a case the Minister's decision as well as the Commission's decision can be reviewed in one composite review as was done in the instant case.

Mr Maleka relies on the Australian decision in Australian Broadcasting Tribunal v Bank and Others,[531] where the Mason, C.J. *inter alia* said:

> **"...That answer is that a reviewable 'decision' is one for which provision is made by or under a statute. That will generally, but not always, entail a decision which is final or operative and determinative, at least in a practical sense, of the issue of fact falling for consideration. A conclusion reached as a step along the way in a course of reasoning leading to ultimate decision would not ordinarily lead to a reviewable decision, unless the statute providing for the making of a finding or ruling on that point so that the decision, though an intermediate decision, might accurately be described as a decision under enactment. Another essential quality of a reviewable decision is that it be a substantive determination..."**

[531] Australian Law Reports, 11(HCA) at 23.

How this decision can be of assistance to the Government's case, is difficult to fathom, because:

There is no separate and independent review of the Commission's decision, but only a composite review, where the Commission's decision-making and decision is attacked because it was an integral and essential part of the Minister's decision. Furthermore it was a "decision", and "one for which provision is made for or under a statute"; "the statute provided for the making of a finding or ruling on that point so that the decision, though an intermediate decision, might accurately be described as a decision under an enactment"; it is also "a substantive determination".

(c) The Security Commission is so structured that it is in an ideal position to apply the *audi alteram partem maxim*.

(d) The Security Commission has a heavy responsibility. It is inconceivable that it can reach a fair decision without hearing the person or persons targeted. Even if its decisions cannot be taken on review separately and independently, that does not mean that it has no duty to apply the *audi alteram partem* rule.

(e) The Commission is certainly an "administrative body" and its members "administrative officials" as contemplated by section 18 of the Namibian Constitution and consequently has to act fairly and reasonably.

The impact and requirements of this article was set out in the recent judgment of Strydom, C.J., in the case of Chairperson of the Immigrating Selection Board v Frank and Another[532].

> **"18 Administrative Justice**
>
> **Administrative bodies and administrative officials shall act fairly and reasonably and comply with the requirements imposed upon such bodies and officials by common law and any relevant legislation, and persons aggrieved by the exercise of such acts and decisions shall have the right to seek redress before a competent Court or Tribunal.'**
>
> **Article 18 is part of Chapter 3 of the Constitution which deals with Fundamental human rights and freedoms. The provisions of the Chapter clearly distinguishes which of these provisions apply to citizens only (e.g. Art. 17), and which to non-citizens (e.g. Art. 11(4) and (5)). Where such distinction is not drawn, e.g. where the Article refers to persons or all persons, it includes in my opinion citizens as well as non-citizens. The Article draws no distinction between *quasi* judicial and administrative acts and administrative justice whether *quasi* judicial or administrative in nature "requires not only reasonable and fair decisions, based on reasonable grounds, but inherent in that requirement fair procedures which are transparent" (*Aonin Fishing v Minister of Fisheries and Marine Resources*, 1998 NR 147 (HC).) Art. 18 further entrenches the common law pertaining to administrative justice and in so far as it is not in conflict with the Constitution."**

[532] SA 8/1999 of 5 March 2001 (NmS) at 22 of the minority judgment.

The following further dicta from the same judgment are also applicable to the present case, *mutatis mutandis*:

> **"This rule embodies various principles, the application of which is flexible depending on the circumstances of each case and the statutory requirements for the exercise of a particular discretion. (See** *Baxter: Administrative Law* **p.535 ff and** *Wiechers: Administrative Law* **p.208 ff.)**
>
> **In the context of the Act, the process for the application of a permit was set in motion by the submission of a written application by the first respondent. If on such information before it, the application is not granted, and provided the Board acted reasonably, that would be the end of the matter. However, there may well be instances where the Board acts on information they are privy to or information given to them by the Chief of Immigration (see sec. 26(2)). If such information is potentially prejudicial to an applicant, it must be communicated to him or her in order to enable such person to deal therewith and to rebut it if possible. (See** *Loxton v Kendhardt Liquor Licensing Board*, **1942 AD 275 and** *Administrator SWA v Jooste Lithicum Myne (Edms) Bpk*, **1955 (1) SA 557(A)"...**[533].
>
> **"In the absence of any prescription by the Act, the appellant is at liberty to determine its own procedure, provided of course that it is fair and does not defeat the purpose of the Act. (Baxter,** *op. cit.* **p.545). Consequently the Board need not in each instance give an applicant an oral hearing, but may give an applicant an opportunity to deal with the matter in writing.**
>
> **Furthermore, it seems to me that it is implicit in the provisions of Art. 18 of the Constitution that an administrative organ exercising a discretion is obliged to give reasons for its decision. There can be little hope for transparency if an administrative organ is allowed to keep the reasons for its decision secret. The Article requires administrative bodies and officials to act fairly and reasonably. Whether these requirements were complied with can, more often than not, only be determined once reasons have been provided. This also bears relation to the specific right accorded by Articles 18 to persons to seek redress before a competent Court or Tribunal where they are aggrieved by the exercise of such acts or decisions. Art. 18 is part of the Constitution's Chapter on fundamental rights and freedoms and should be interpreted "... broadly, liberally and purposively..." to give to the article a construction which is "... most beneficial to the widest possible amplitude". (***Government of the Republic of Namibia v Cultura 2000,* **1993 NR 328 at 340 B - D.) There is therefore no basis to interpret the Article in such a way that those who want to redress administrative unfairness and unreasonableness should start off on an unfair basis because the administrative organ refuses to divulge reasons for its decision. Where there is a legitimate reason for refusing, such as State security, that option would still be open"**[534].

[533] Ibid, pp.8-30 of the minority judgment.

[534] Ibid, pp.29-30 of the majority judgment.

I must point out that although the aforesaid approach was set out in the judgment of Strydom, C.J., in his dissenting judgment, the majority of O'Linn, A.J.A. and Teek, A.J.A. agreed with the approach as set out by Strydom C.J.

I must also draw attention to the last sentence in the above quotation which reads: "Where there is a legitimate reason for refusing, such as State Security, that option would still be open".

To this remark the majority added the following rider:

> **"It should be noted however, that such reasons, if not given prior to an application to a Court for a review of the administrative decision, must at least be given in the course of a review application"[535].**
>
> **It follows that an administrative tribunal, which deals with and decides on a matter affecting the fundamental rights of a person as well as state security and refuses to provide the reasons for its decision to the person targeted on the grounds of "State Security", must give explicit reasons for its refusal. Nevertheless, the administrative tribunal cannot avoid to give reasons for its decision altogether and in my respectful view, such a principle was not intended by the Chief Justice in the sentence from his judgment abovementioned relating to "State Security". Reasons for the decision must be given, not necessarily in great detail but at least in substance.**
>
> **The Tribunal may delay giving the reasons to the targeted person, but cannot avoid providing the reasons, at least in substance, in the course of a judicial review.**
>
> **The withholding of reasons for the decision must be distinguished from withholding information of a confidential nature, such as information given by informers, although the decision is often based on the information. Information, the disclosure of which may jeopardise State Security, may be withheld more readily than reasons for the decision, but again, there would seldom be sufficient justification for withholding the substance of the information on which the decision is based. If this is not so, the fundamental rights of the targeted person to be heard and to put his or her case, would be prejudiced to such an extent that his right would become ephemeral[536].**

(f) Article 12 of the Namibian Constitution is more explicit and goes much further than Art. 18.

Sub-article (1)(a) provides:

> "In the determination of their civil rights and obligations or any criminal charges against them, all persons shall be entitled to a fair and public hearing by an independent, impartial and competent Court or Tribunal established by law: provided that such Court

[535] Ibid, p.3 of the majority judgment. Compare also: *Du Preez & An v Truth and Reconciliation Commission*, 1997(3) SA 204 (SCA) 231a – 232d.

[536] *Administrator, Transvaal & Others v Traub and Others*, 1989 (4) SA 731(A) *Du Preez & An v Truth and Reconciliation Commission*, 1997(3) SA 204 (SCA) at 231G – 232D.

or Tribunal may exclude the press and/or the public from all or any part of the trial for reasons of morals, the public order or national security, as is necessary in a democratic society."

The right to remain domiciled in Namibia and not to be removed arbitrarily to another country, can be regarded as a person's "civil right". A good case can probably be made out for saying that the Security Commission, being a Tribunal, must also act in accordance with Art. 12(1)(a) when it decides whether or not to make a recommendation for the removal of a person from Namibia.

But this issue need not be decided finally at this juncture. Suffice to say that even if the letter of Art. 12(1)(a) is not applicable, at least the spirit thereof underlines and is supportive of what has been said above about the effect of Art. 18 and the application of the rules of natural justice – including the *audi alteram partem* rule and the requirement that the decision will be considered and made by an independent, impartial and competent Court or Tribunal.

Lastly it must be emphasised that even if there is justification for not disclosing to the targeted person confidential information, such as the identity of the informer or for not disclosing the details of the reasons for the decision or even the substance thereof at the initial stage, the right of the targeted person to be heard in a meaningful and fair manner before the decision is taken, alternatively, and only in exceptional cases, after the decision is taken, cannot be doubted.

(g) At the initial stage of the action against Sikunda Snr, the Minister even purported to declare Sikunda a "prohibited immigrant". This is a further indication of how the Honourable Minister either misconceived his function under section 49(1) or for some other unknown reason, misapplied his powers under the provisions of the Immigration Control Act.

Mr Nilo Taapopi, the Permanent Secretary in the employ of the Ministry of Home Affairs even protested in reply to the affidavit of applicant that the Minister "did not 'purportedly' declare the detainee a prohibited immigrant in terms of Part VI of the Immigration Control Act. He in fact did declare him as such".

Nevertheless it was neither argued in the Court *a quo* nor in the appeal before us that Sikunda Snr, was a prohibited immigrant in terms of section 39(2) of the Act or properly declared as such at any stage.

At any event sections 43 – 48 of the Act, provides for elaborate procedure for the establishment and functioning of Tribunals "for the hearing and determination of applications for the removal of persons from Namibia in terms of this Act or any other law." Application for such removal in terms of section 43 – 48 must be made to such a Tribunal. The procedure in such Tribunal provides extensively for application of the *audi alteram partem* principle and it seems, complies not only with the requirements of Art. 18 of the Namibian Constitution, but even Art. 12(1)(a).

Such a procedure was never applied to Sikunda Snr. Section 49(1) does not provide expressly for such a procedure, but on the other hand provided for a decision by the Security Commission, as a precondition for the Minister's decision to remove a person from Namibia.

(h) If the Legislature in section 49(1) of the Immigration Control Act or for that matter in any other law, purported to abolish or diminish from the provision of Art. 18 and 12 of the Namibian Constitution, such provision would be unconstitutional and invalid.

(ii) The failure by the Commission to apply the *audi alteram partem* rule is compounded by the failure of the Minister to apply the rule.

Whether or not the Minister's decision could have been saved if he at least applied the rule is debatable. Because of the importance of the Commission's decision, as a precondition for the Minister's order, it can strongly be argued that the Commission's failure to apply the rule cannot be remedied even if the Minister applied the rule before making the order against Sikunda Snr.

It can even be argued that if the Commission had applied the rule properly and there is a proper record of its proceedings, the Minister can have regard to such proceedings and may not be required to again apply the *audi alteram partem*. But this is not necessary to decide, because in this case, both the Commission and the Minister had failed to apply the rule.

I must however, point out at this junction the shocking fact that the Commission, according to the respondent's reply to a Rule 35(12) notice, apparently kept no record of its proceedings. And as far as the Minister is concerned, he apparently did not care. What he was interested in, was to receive the "recommendation" which he had "implored" the Commission to make. In this regard I need only refer to the Rule 35(12) notice by applicant requesting *inter alia* the record of the meeting of the Security Commission and the respondent's reply to this notice which read:

> **"The annexures to the said documents and the record of the Security Commission, if one exists, are privileged and will not be disclosed, on grounds of national security and public interest."**
> **(My emphasis added.)**

Ad(iii) Mr Maleka's submission that the right to be heard could be exercised after the decision was taken and that there was in fact such an opportunity given to Sikunda Snr.

(a) It is correct that the opportunity for the right to be heard can be given after the decision is taken, but such a course would only be justified in exceptional circumstances. This position is adequately set out in the following two decisions referred to by counsel for the applicant:

In the decision of the Appellate Division of the Supreme Court of South Africa in Administrator Transvaal & Ors v Traub and Ors., Corbett, C.J., stated:

> **"Generally speaking, in my view, the *audi alteram partem* principle requires the hearing to be given before the decision is taken by the official or body concerned, that is, while he or it still has an open mind on the matter. In this way one avoids the natural human inclination to adhere to a decision once taken (see Blom's case,**

supra, **at 668C – E, Omar's case,** ***supra*** **at 906F; Momoniat v Minister of Law and Order and Others; Naidoo and Others v Minister of Law and Order and Others, 1986(2) SA 264(W) at 274B – D). Exceptionally, however, the dictates of natural justice may be satisfied by affording the individual concerned a hearing after the prejudicial decision had been taken (see Omar's case,** ***supra*****, at 906F – H; Chikane's case,** ***supra*** **at 379G; Momoniat's case,** ***supra*****, at 274E – 275C). This may be so, for instance, in cases where the party making the decision is necessarily required to act with expedition, or where for some other reason it is not feasible to give a hearing before the decision is taken. But the present is, in my opinion, not such a case. There is no suggestion that the decision whether or not to appoint the respondents to the posts applied for by them had to be taken in a hurry: in fact all the indications are to the contrary. Nor is there any basis for concluding that for some other reason a hearing prior to the decision was not feasible."**

Corbett, C.J., further stressed that this right to be heard would also presuppose being apprised of adverse material to the person exercising that right[537].

In Mamabolo v Rustenburg Regional Local Council, the test was reaffirmed in the following terms:

"The importance to be accorded to the ***audi*** **principle in the present context is compounded by the far reaching import of the decision itself and the deprivation of further remedies to an affected person by section 49[538].**

Mr Smuts, on behalf of applicant, made the following points:

"It is submitted that the exceptional circumstances referred to in the authorities do not apply to the circumstances of this matter given the fact that Mr Sikunda's name appeared in the list some three years prior to the purported decision. There was ample opportunity to provide him with the right to be heard. There was also absolutely no attempt to afford him the right to be heard immediately upon his seizure and detention – even in the most attenuated form. Even after the respondent was alerted to the ***audi*** **principle on 8 November 2000, there was still then no attempt to provide the applicant's father with the right to be heard until nearly 3 months later and at a time when the applicant's father had been detained without trial for more than 3 months – despite a court order directing his release. We also point out that the Minister's decision taken in terms of section 49 under review was not in any sense of a provisional nature. It was distinctly final. Steps were also in fact taken by the Minister to implement it – by causing the arrest of Mr Sikunda and addressing a letter to the UNHCR to give effect to the removal of Mr Sikunda from the Republic of Namibia.**

It is submitted that this offer so belatedly made in the Minister's affidavit on 1 February 2001 is thus not in good faith in the strict legal sense and in any event would and does not comply with the dictates of the ***audi*** **principle in the circumstances of**

537 1989(4) SA 731(A) at 750C-F and 750I.

538 2001(1) SA 135(SCA) at 144 C – D.

the present matter. Had there been any genuine attempt to entertain representation, this would have occurred at a far earlier stage and not some 4 months after the purported decision was taken and more than 3 months after Mr Sikunda's detention – and after more than 3 months of contempt of court on the part of the Minister.

Furthermore, it is submitted that there would be no prospects of the Minister having an open mind in the matter, having "implored" the Security Commission to make the recommendation he desired and after he had deposed to two affidavits spanning some considerable time in which he was insistent upon the correctness of his decision. This is further compounded by the Minister's persistence for more than 3 months in acting in contempt of the Court order (for which he has been convicted) in refusing to release the detainee. The Minister's subsequent conviction for contempt yet further compounds the matter.

Clearly the Minister would not be capable of making a decision – nor could this decision be made – without bias or at least a reasonable suspicion of bias in those circumstances. The Minister's own predilection to persisting in his decision was in fact demonstrated already in his earlier correspondence and his letter of 19 September 2000 in which he "implored" the Security Commission to make their recommendation. The Minister's subsequent persistence to sticking to his decision is further demonstrated by his 2 affidavits and his flagrant contempt. This aspect is further referred to below where the relevant authorities are also cited in relation to impermissible bias, predetermination and the failure to have the required "open mind" to make a decision, stressed by Corbett, C.J., in the Traub-matter. The much belated attempt to cure the failure to comply with the *audi* principle must fail."

I must point out that the offer made by the Honourable Minister was made on 1st February 2001, included in an additional affidavit filed on behalf of the respondent. It seems to me that there is considerable substance in the above submissions by counsel for applicant.

In view of the fact that the Minister now had the whole case of Sikunda Snr, on affidavit before him, he had a golden opportunity, to demonstrate his *bona fides* and bring an end to the matter, by indicating that he was now willing to agree to the setting aside of his previous order. What confidence can one have in the Minister's objectivity and *bona fides,* if he at this late stage merely offered to receive representations by or on behalf of Sikunda Snr?

It is also necessary to stress that quite apart from the three basic points dealt with in this judgment, the procedure followed by the Commission and the Minister, as well as their decisions on the merits, were severely criticized on many other points by the Counsel for applicants as well as by the Court *a quo* and much of this criticism appears to be well-founded. It would however, prolong this judgment unnecessarily, to deal with all these points and I therefore decline to do so.

What should be mentioned however, is that there is no indication whatever that either the Minister or the Security Commission considered whether or not

Sikunda Snr was a citizen of or domiciled in Namibia. The reason for this was possibly that they had not realized that the power under section 49(1) could not be exercised against a person who is either a citizen of or domiciled in Namibia. That would mean that both decisions should also be set aside on the ground that the Minister as well as the Commission had also misconceived its power to act in this regard. The decisions taken are also null and void for this reason.

No wonder that the applicant and Sikunda Snr, declined the belated offer of the Minister to consider further representations from the applicant and Sikunda Snr. In the circumstances the said offer by the Honourable Minister cannot be regarded as a proper and sufficient compliance with the rules of fairness, including the *audi alteram partem* rule.

For the same reason there is no justification for setting aside the orders made by the Court *a quo* in its well-reasoned judgment and substitute it with an order – setting aside the Minister's order as it stands and referring it back to him for reconsideration and decision, after complying with the *audi alteram partem* rule.

In any event, even if this Court was inclined to refer the matter back to the Minister as suggested, that course would be an exercise in futility because of the finding of this Court that Sikunda Snr, was legally domiciled in Namibia and that the Minister had no jurisdiction whatever to act against him under section 49(1). Furthermore, the finding that the Security Commission was not properly composed at the time when it made the recommendation aforesaid, would remain a fatal impediment to such a course for as long as it was not properly composed.

There is also no reason for interfering on appeal with the special order of costs granted against the respondent in the Court *a quo*.

What remains, is whether or not a special order of costs should be made on appeal in regard to the appeal proceedings.

There is considerable merit in the argument for an order of costs against the Government on an attorney and own client basis. On the other hand, the following factors must also be considered by this Court:

The Government has already been penalized for the conduct on which the applicant relies by a punitive costs order in the Court *a quo* and a humiliating order against the Minister for Contempt of Court, against which he has not appealed. Furthermore I am not convinced that the rule *nisi* granted initially by Manyarara, A.J., should have included an interim interdict against the Minister and Chief of Police in the form of a mandatory injunction, ordering the release of Sikunda Snr, without a proper hearing first being afforded the Minister. As I have indicated earlier in this judgment, an interim interdict prohibiting the Minister from removing Sikunda Snr, was necessary, but the order for the immediate release of Sikunda Snr, without a proper opportunity for the said Minister and Chief of Police to put their case was not justified, particularly not when the legal representative of the Minister at the outset offered to consent to an interim order to the effect that Sikunda Snr, may not be removed from the country and the applicant rejected this offer.

This part of the interim order probably caused some frustration on the side of the Government, leading to the refusal and/or failure of the Minister to comply with the Court order until after the conviction for Contempt of Court. The Government attempted to get finality in the legal proceedings at the earliest possible date. First it attempted to anticipate the return date from the 10th November to the 26th October but it was frustrated in that attempt by the legal representatives of the applicant. The long delay which ensued before the matter could be argued on 16th February 2001, was caused by an unforeseeable course when the Judge who had to hear the matter, first postponed it and when the postponed date arrived, he recused himself from the hearing, causing another postponement. Neither the Minister nor the Chief of Police was to blame for this long delay. The Minister's conduct in this regard was not justified, but it was to some extent mitigated.

The decisive factor however, is that the procedures used by the appellant to detain and continue to detain Sikunda Snr were indeed tainted to such an extent by irregularity and illegality and was such a grave infringement of his fundamental rights, that the applicant must not only succeed, but should not be out of pocket by granting an ordinary order of costs.

There is also an application before us for the condonation of Respondent's non-compliance with the Rules of Court relating to the preparation of the record of appeal. Respondent's counsel did not object to the granting of condonation. There is also no good reason why condonation should be withheld.

In the result the following order is made:

1. Condonation is granted for Respondent's failure to prepare the appeal record properly.
2. The appeal is dismissed.
3. The appellant is ordered to pay the costs of the appeal on the basis of attorney and own client.

(signed) O'LINN, A.J.A.

I agree.

(signed) STRYDOM, C.J.

I agree.

(signed) CHOMBA, A.J.A.

/mv

COUNSEL ON BEHALF OF THE APPELLANT:	Adv I.V Maleka
ASSISTED BY:	Adv V Erenstein ya Toivo
ON BEHALF OF:	Government Attorney
COUNSEL ON BEHALF OF THE RESPONDENT:	Adv D.F. Smuts
ASSISTED BY :	Adv R.D. Cohrssen
ON BEHALF OF :	Theunissen, Louw and Partners

/mv

COUNSEL ON BEHALF OF THE APPELLANT:	Adv G.H. Oosthuizen
	Government Attorney
COUNSEL ON BEHALF OF THE RESPONDENT:	Ms L. Conradie
	(Legal Assistant Centre)

BOOKS

Allen, C.K. 1964. *Law in the Making*. Oxford: Oxford University Press 31, 67

Amos, M. & Walton, F. 1967. *Introduction to French Law*. Oxford: Clarendon Press.............................62

Aquinas, T. 1915. *Summa theologica*. Literally translated by Fathers of the English Dominican Province.London: Burn Oates and Washborune Ltd Publishers of the Holy See 3, 13

Aristotle. 1962. *The Politics*. Translated by T.A. Sinclair. Harmondsworth, Middlesex: Penguin 331

Austin, J. 1869. *Lectures on Jurisprudence*. London: John Murray 25

Austin, J. 1995. *The Province of Jurisprudence Determined*. Lecture VI Cambridge: Cambridge Unversity Press. 21

Bentham, J. 1970. *Of laws in general*. London: Athlone Press.. 279

Boulle, L.; Harris, B. & Hoexter, C. 1989. *Constitutional and administrative law: Basic principles*. Cape Town: Juta. 328

Cardozo, B.N. 1921. *The Nature of Judicial Process*. Yale: New Haven 69

Carpenter, G. 1987. *Introduction to South African constitutional law*. Durban: Butterworths. 328

Cross, R. 1977. *Precedent in English law*. Oxford: Clarendon Press. 62, 281, 283, 287

Daniëls, E. 1964. *Common Law in West Africa*. London: Butterworths..69

De Smith, S.A. 1964. *The new Commonwealth and its constitutions*. London: Stevens & Sons.........329

De Waal, J. & Currie, I. 2000. *Bill of rights handbook*. 3rd edition. Kenwyn: Juta. 330

De Wet. 1988. *Die Ou Skrywers in Perpektief*. Durban: Butterworths..82

Del Vecchio, G. 1914. *The Formal Bases of Law*. Boston: Boston Book Co...6

Devenish, G.E. 1999. *A commentary on the South African bill of rights*. Durban: Butterworths...312, 341

Devlin, P. 1962. *Samples of Law-making*. London: Oxford University Press 278

Devlin, P. 1965. *The Enforcement of Morals*. London: Oxford University Press. 7

Dias, R.W.M. 1970. *Jurisprudence*. London: Butterworths.. passim

Dicey, A.V. 1982. *An Introduction to the Study of the Law of the Constitution*. Indianapolis: Liberty Classics. 28, 316, 323

Du Plessis, L.M. 1992. *An Introduction to law*. Kenwyn: Juta & Co.. 113

Dugard, J. 1971. "*The Judicial Process, Positivism and Civil Liberty*". South African Law Journal........21

Duggal, N.K. (ed.). 1981. *Toward a New Legal System for Independent Namibia*. Lusaka: United Nations Institute for Namibia...104

Evans, J.M. *De Smith's Judicial Review of Administrative Actions*. London: Stevens & Sons.........319

Finch, J.D. 1974. *Intoduction to Legal Theory*. 2nd edition. London: Sweet & Maxwell 3

Frank, J. 1959. *Courts of Trial*. Princeton: Princeton Press..62, 74

Freeman, M.D.A. 2001. *Lloyd's Introduction to Jurisprudence*. 7th edition. London: Sweet & Maxwell Ltd .3

Friedman, W. 1967. *Legal theory*. London: Stevens & Sons...278

Friedmann, W. 1953. *Legal Theory*. 3rd edition. London: Stevens & Sons.. 10

Friedrich, C.J. 1963. *The Philosophy of law in historical perspective*. Chicago: University of Chicago Press. 38

Fuller, L.L. 1940. *The Law in Quest of Itself.* Beacon Press........4

Fuller, L.L. 1969. *The morality of law*. New Haven: Yale University Press 4

Fuller, L.L. 1976. *Anatomy of the Law*. Greenwood Pub. Group........24, 43

Gibson, Dale 'Commentary on the interpretation of the Canadian Charter of Rights and Freedoms'. In: Tarnapolsky, W.S. & Beaudoin, G.A. (eds). 1982. *The Canadian Charter of Rights and Freedoms: Commentary*. Ontario: Carswell. 300

Gluckman, M. 1967. Judicial process among the Barotse. In: Bohannan, P. (ed.). *Law and warfare: Studies in the anthropology of conflict*. New York: The Natural History Press. 102

Grotius, H. 1652. *De jure belli pacis*. Oxford: Clarendon Press 16

Hahn, C.H.L., Vedder, H. and Fourie, L. 1928. *The native tribes of South West Africa*. New York: Barnes and Noble. 104

Hart, H.L. 1963. *Law, Liberty and Morality*. London: Oxford University Press........7

Hart, H.L. 1961. *Definition and Theory in Jurisprudence*. Oxford: Clarendon Press. 22

Hinz, M.O. 2003. *Customary law in Namibia: Development and perspective*. Windhoek: CASS. 104

Hobbes, T. 1651. *Leviathan*. Oxford: Blackwell 17

Holdsworth, W.S. [s.a.]. *A history of English law*. [S.l.: s.n.]. 331

Hosten, W.J.; Edwards, A.B.; Bosman, F. & Church, J. 1997. *Introduction to South African law and legal theory*. 2nd edition. Durban: Butterworths........ passim

Jerome, F. 1930. *Law and the Modern Mind*. New Torte Brentano's........278

Kant, I. 1999. *The Metaphysical Elements of Justice*. 2nd edition. Indianapolis: Hackett Publishing Company, Inc........6

Kelsen, H. 1957. *What is justice? Justice, law and Politics in the mirror of science*. Berkeley: University of California Press. 37

Kelsen, H. 1945. *General theory of Law and State*. Cambridge: Harvard University Press........34

Kleyn, D. & Viljoen, F. 2002. *Beginner's guide for law students*. 3rd edition. Landsdowne: Juta Law...121

Kocourek, A. 1930. *An Introduction to the Science of Law*. Baston: Little, Brown & Company. 31

Laski, H.J. 1941. *A grammar of politics*. London: George Allen & Unwin. 38

Latham "Interpretation of the Constitution". In: Else-Mitchell, Rae (ed.) 1961. *Essays on the Australian Constitution*. Sydney: Law Book Company........300

Llewellyn K.N. 1960. *The common law tradition: Deciding appeals*. Boston: Little, Brown & Company. ...50

Llewellyn, K.N. 1930. *The bramble bush*. New York: Oceana. 49

Lloyd, D. 1964. *The Idea of law*. London: Penguin........38

Locke, J. 1690. *Treatise on Civil Government in Two Treatises on Government*. London: Cambridge University Press........18, 340

Maine, H.S. 1996. *Ancient Law*. Bristol: Thoemmes Press. 30

Maxwell. 1937. *Interpretation of Statutes*. London: Sweet & Maxwell........292

Montesquieu, C. 1750. *Spirit of the Laws*. Cambridge: University Press 20

Nwabueze, B.O. 1973. *Constitutionalism in the emergent States*. 313, 345

Nwabueze, B.O. 1983. *Federalism in Nigeria under the Presidential Constitution*. London: Sweet & Maxwell. 330

Okpaluba, C. 'Constitutionality of legislation relating to the distribution of governmental powers in Namibia: A Comparative Approach'. In: Hinz, M.O.; Amoo, S.K. & Van Wyk, D. (eds.) 2002. *The constitution at work: 10 years of Namibian nationhood*. Windhoek: University of Namibia. 318, 330

Olivecrona, K. 1971. *Law as Fact*. London: Stevens & Sons 6

Pollock, F. 1890. *Oxford lectures and other lectures*. London: Macmillan Company 110

Pound, R. 1922. *Introduction to the philosophy of the law*. Yale University Press. 46

Pound, R. 1959. Interpretation of Legal History. New York: Macmillan 39, 44

Pound, R. 1959. *Jurisprudence*. vol. 111. West Publishing Co. 44, 45

Radbruch, G. 1946. *The Philosophy of Law in the Philosophical Review Vol. 53* 9

Rousseau, J.J. 1762. *The Social Contract*. London: Penguin 20

Schultz, F. 1946. *History of Roman Legal Science*. New York: Oxford University Press 11

Shearer, I.A. 1994. *Starke's international law*. 11th edition. London: Butterworths. 110

Stone, J. *Human Law and Human Justice*. London: Stevens & Sons 39

Twining, E. 1973. *Llewellyn and the realist movement*. London: Weidenfeld and Nicolson. 49

Van der Walt, A.J. 2002. *Law of property: Casebook for students/Sakereg: vonnisbundel vir studente*. 5th edition. Landsdowne: Juta & Co., Ltd 199

Van Zyl and Van der Vyver. 1982. *Inleiding tot die Regswetenskap*. 2nd edition. Durban: Butterworths. 78

Van Zyl. 1979. *Geskiedenis van die Romeins-Hollandse Reg*. Durban: Butterworths 78

Vile, M.J.C. 1967. *Constitutionalism and the separation of powers. Indianapolis*: Liberty Fund. 313

Wasserstrom, R.A. 1961. *The Judicial Decision*. Stanford: Stanford University Press 67

Williams, G. 1982. *Learning the law*. London: Stevens & Sons 282, 292, 293

Wolff, C. 1740. *Jus Naturae*. Dordrecht: Kluwer Academic Publishers 19

Wortley, B.A. 1967. *Jurisprudence*. New York. Oceana Publications. 9

ARTICLES, PAMPHLETS AND MIMEOGRAPHS

TABLE OF CASES

TABLE OF ENACTMENTS

INDEX

A

B

C

D

E

F

G

H

I

J

K

L

M

N

O

P

R

S

T

U

V

W

Z

www.ingramcontent.com/pod-product-compliance
Lightning Source LLC
LaVergne TN
LVHW060016210926
848481LV00013B/3723